Theories of Perception
——and the——
Concept of Structure

Theories of Perception
and the
Concept of Structure

A REVIEW AND CRITICAL ANALYSIS WITH AN
INTRODUCTION TO A DYNAMIC-STRUCTURAL
THEORY OF BEHAVIOR

FLOYD II. ALLPORT

Professor of Social and Political Psychology,
Maxwell Graduate School of Citizenship
and Public Affairs, Syracuse University

JOHN WILEY & SONS, INC., NEW YORK

London · Sydney

Library of Congress Catalog Card Number: 55–6130

To Helene Willey Hartley

Preface

If three years ago some amiable forecaster had predicted that my name would now be appearing on a volume on perception, I would have been much surprised and perhaps a little alarmed. The surprise, not to say the alarm, might have been shared by students, colleagues, and friends who had happened to know something of my earlier work. "What business," they might have asked, "has a behavioristic social psychologist to write upon such a topic? Is it because, nowadays, social psychology to be considered sound must be based upon perception? Has he given up his 'objective' leanings and decided that the final answers, after all, must come through phenomenology?" No, neither of these explanations fit the case; for I subscribe to neither of these views. Let me try to explain.

Although over the years I have been pursuing with my graduate students an active program of research, my interests have also tended strongly toward methodology and theory. In the latter role, through no one's fault but my own, I have been somewhat of a lone worker so far as the main current of psychological thinking is concerned. The course I have taken, both in theory and experiment, has been directed toward an extensive and exacting enterprise; and for some time I have been immersed in a sea of "theoretical troubles." As I began finally to come up to the surface grasping the outlines of an apparently reasonable solution, I decided that it was high time to avoid the dangers of autistic thinking by becoming better acquainted with other psychological theories. This decision, as it worked out in practice, led me to the fascinating subject of the modern theories of perception. To these I turned, at first, as a means of appraising my own endeavors. Did the existing formulations in this field support my position, or did they give other and better answers? Had what I wanted to say already been said? Or, on the other hand, were other theorists caught in the same dilemmas from which I had started? And could my present labors be of help to those who were struggling in waters still too deep?

As the study of the theories progressed it became increasingly clear to me that the modern systems of perception sum up a great body of careful research and constitute a rich contribution to psychological thinking. My own horizon, through perusing them, had been greatly extended. In them, if they are taken all together, lie the essentials of our present knowledge of one of the most important activities of living beings. Quite aside from my own project, but without in any way relinquishing that objective, it seemed to me that if these theories, now scattered and uncoördinated, were brought together in connected form and subjected to a systematic overall study, a useful purpose for students and teachers of psychology might be served. The recognition of this need and the desire to present such a review have constituted an additional reason for my interest in the topic, an interest of which this book is, in part, the result.

The book has thus had a devious history. It has a serious purpose, in fact, a dual purpose—first, to review and examine the trend of psychological thinking about perception and, second, to tell the reader something about the solution I have found for my own problem and the possible relation of that solution to the problems which perceptual experiment and theory must solve. The Foreword will explain these objectives more fully.

If the reader should not be interested primarily in analysis, but should desire only an account of existing theories and a summary of what is known or believed concerning the processes underlying perception, the following chapters will provide such a view. For the benefit of those who are impressed by the need of still better conceptualizations and are trying, like the writer, to arrive at more basic understandings in psychology as a whole, the review has been projected in a somewhat broader setting. Since the analysis of many problems is developed in a consecutive fashion, it is recommended that the chapters be read in sequence. One task that had to be faced was that of adapting the work to readers at different levels of psychological training and experience. For this purpose I have from time to time included materials that may be already familiar to some readers. New points of view, however, are presented; and it is hoped that advanced students as well as professional psychologists will find something that is fresh and stimulating.

I wish to express my thanks and appreciation to Dean Eric H. Faigle of the College of Liberal Arts, to Dean Carl R. Bye of the Graduate School, and to other administrative officers of Syracuse University for the generous grant of time and other aids that were necessary both for the writing of this book and for the continuation of the project

into the future. In this connection I desire especially to thank Dean
Paul H. Appleby of the Maxwell School, not only for allowance of
time and material assistance but also for his appreciation and close
understanding of my work and his unfailing loyalty as a counsellor
and friend. Whatever success the entire enterprise, of which this
volume is the first installment, may attain will be in no small measure
due to his continued encouragement and support.

My treatment of the theories of perception has been much facilitated
by the excellent historical and general surveys that have been prepared by a number of writers in this and related fields. Though these
aids have been acknowledged in specific cases I wish to thank these
authors generally for the help their work has given me. My thanks
are due to Professors Walter Pitts and Warren S. McCulloch, and to
the editor and publishers of the *Bulletin of Mathematical Biophysics,*
for permission to reproduce the figure from the article, "How We
Know Universals"; and to Professor Edwin G. Boring and Appleton-
Century-Crofts, Inc., for permission to reprint, from Dr. Boring's
Sensation and Perception in the History of Experimental Psychology,
the arrangement of the Hering and Wundt figures shown on page 39.
I wish also to thank the many secretarial assistants who have had a
part in the preparation of the manuscript. Among these should be
mentioned Mrs. Anne James, Mrs. Thelma Flynn, Mrs. Susan Clark,
Mrs. Jean Gilman, Mrs. Lenora Reaves, Mrs. Shirley Alvord, Mrs.
Arline Stephany, and Mrs. Ruth Rehme.

Both in the present work and in laying the basis, over the years, for
a later volume in which the theory of structure will be more fully
developed, continual inspiration and unfailing help have been given
me by my wife and colleague whose professional name appears upon
the dedication page. The dedicating of these works to her has
seemed an inevitability. However inadequate such a token may be,
it is a symbol of a profound and abiding sentiment which words fail
altogether to express.

Syracuse   F. H. A.
November, 1954

Contents

xi

Contents

Contents

Contents

of the Inside-Outside Problem; Structure of Collectivities or "Groups" (660). Event-Structure Theory as a Methodological Reorientation (663). Conclusion (665).

Foreword

This book represents an effort to survey carefully the contributions that modern psychologists have made to the theory of perception and to canvass the state of our knowledge of the important process by which organisms gain an understanding of, and a basis for reacting to, the world in which they live. It is hoped that it may help to bring some clarification into this confused field and that possibly, to some extent, it may be of aid in the present complex and uncertain state of psychological theory in general. But, as intimated in the Preface, there was another purpose, at least equally impelling, for which the book was written. It is the first installment in the carrying out of a more comprehensive plan, of whose nature the reader should be informed.

As a psychologist serving on the staff of a well-known school of social science, the writer has had considerable freedom to indulge his curiosities about human relationships and the social scene, and more particularly about the nature of behavior. Realizing that there was something lacking in his own earlier approach, he began, about fifteen years ago, to take a different direction. It occurred to him, as it probably has to many, that, in spite of its so largely unpredictable nature, its flux so changing that we are hard pressed to find its laws, there must be in human behavior, both individual and collective, some kind of orderly and dynamic pattern. The reason why so many attempts to find such a pattern have failed or have only moderately succeeded seemed to the writer to be twofold. First, the approach was not made wholeheartedly, with a willingness to break from tradition and envisage the pattern as a law or paradigm in its own right. Second, such attempts have been forced by the complexity and often by the vagueness of the subject matter to compromise with the rigorous requirements of objectivity and to introduce, at the social and often at the individual behavioral level, explanatory concepts of a rather philosophical, telic, and untestable character. What was needed, it seemed to the writer, was neither the familiar and easy functionalism nor the intangible notion of a "whole," a "configuration," or a "field"—but an overall, explicit concept of *structure*.

This concept, however, must envisage a structure of a peculiar sort. Others, of course, have used the term in attempting to explain both behavior and society. One besetting difficulty, however, has been that structure has usually connoted something fairly architectonic and static, or at least constrained to definite motions such as those familiar to us in machines. A forced and probably misleading distinction arose between structure or mechanism on the one hand and function on the other. Such a rigid view does not comport with the highly varied and changeable character of life and behavior. The flow of an ever-changing and adapting function does not come out of a machine-like system. But if, on the other hand, structure were to be more flexibly conceived, there then seemed to be no possibility of the explicit denotation of its elements and their relationships. A flowing and changing function does not permit itself to be reduced to such constant, identifiable elements as the idea of structure would seem to require. Structure, as applied to behavior or social action, thus had to remain a nebulous and metaphorical concept. Structure as contrasted with function seemed clear enough in the machine, or perhaps even in anatomy and physiology; but the distinction and the relationship were not at all clear in human behavior or society. Those who eschewed teleological formulations and preferred to remain mechanistic could not describe behavior adequately; those who clung to teleology and renounced mechanism had little besides an intangible and unrewarding vitalism to offer.

Another difficulty was that quantification in the psychological and social sciences, even if it were to achieve a requisite level of precision, did not seem to be on the way toward providing any clear conception, other than purely numerical, of the occurrences whose relationships were being quantified. We have been able increasingly to measure individual and social stimulus-conditions on the one hand, and their outcomes, on the other, and to combine these measures into fairly dependable covariation laws and equations. We have plotted curves that show what quantities covary with what, and in what way, as learning, behavior, and social action take place. But though useful predictions are thus made possible, we are scarcely any nearer than before to an understanding of the processes or interactions in which the quantities whose relations we are predicting are involved. Again, we can describe functions, both mathematically and telically, but we cannot relate them in clear detail to the pattern of what is happening in the organism or society. Opportunistic devices such as "intervening variables" or a vague concept of the "social field" or situation have had to suffice for filling in the gaps. The actual structures that might be said to "perform" the behavioral functions are nowhere observed.

Bearing in mind these difficulties the writer has endeavored to work toward a conceptualization and a method by which they could be surmounted, one that would reveal and preserve the "structural format" of behavior and collective action and yet give the degree of freedom that life, behavior, and collective activity require—in other words toward the concept of a structure that would itself be, *as* a structure, so mobile, flexible, and dynamic that the distinction between structure and function would not be needed, and toward a conception in which quantitative laws would take their proper places as variable dimensions within the total dynamic design.

This effort soon convinced the writer that, if such a notion of structure were at all sound, it would have to hold in other levels of nature besides those of behavior and society. To find its foundations we would have to go down to simpler orders in the organic and even in the inorganic realm. One cannot make a structure out of simpler elements unless those elements also are structured, at least to the extent of being self-closed and bounded in space or time or motion. One cannot build order out of chaos, but must work with the elementary bits of order that are already present in nature. Any other view would force us back upon the necessity of explaining how structure comes into being only at particular levels, such as those of organisms or societies; and there would probably be no answer except to invoke some unenlightening theory such as the doctrine of "emergence," which confers "vital" structure by some mysterious process that is peculiar to the level at which it appears and neglects the role of structuring that is concurrent in the lower or component orders. Structure should probably be presumed to be pervasive and to be lawfully connected everywhere if it is to exist at all. It should be a law as broad and as deep as the physical world in which its foundations probably lie. Since it is hard to relinquish the belief that there must be some prevailing unity in nature, we might even imagine that there is some one basic structural paradigm that is universal, that characterizes and unites the orders from the meson, proton, or electron up to organized society. We might, indeed, postulate that there are two types of natural law, not one. There is quantitative law, on the one hand, and non-quantitative, or structural, law, on the other. Our failure to find the latter directly in the behavioral sciences, or perhaps anywhere, might explain why purely quantitative statements, however precise and thorough, have not sufficed for complete explanation. If such a structural law exists, would it not of necessity be operative also between aggregates within the same order, and would its understanding not therefore contribute basically to our knowledge of all phenomena and their interrelationships, whether they be within inorganic nature, within the organism, or in social and technological systems? To define structure as we have tried to define it, denotably, yet dynamically and flexibly, and without binding it to specified quantities, might be a necessary first step toward the formulation of such a universal structural concept.

The writer, who evidently has a predilection for formidable undertakings, has been working upon such a theory. He calls his effort a theory of the structuring of events; and he has tried within the limits of his competence to shape its outlines in the physical, biological, behavioral, and social realms. Though there are, of course, defects (and probably no theoretical system will ever be perfect), the conception has now matured to the point where he wishes to give it wider expression. Because of the unfamiliar nature of its concepts it has seemed advisable, however, not to present it directly or in its most general and rigorous form, but, as a first step, to bring out its possible implications in some well-known field of inquiry where they might be better understood and more readily examined. In order to disclose such need as there might be for the theory and to try its worth as an explanatory system, it was deemed desirable to develop its concepts and objectives against a background of the current psychological theories and the empirical laws upon which they are based. The original plan was to survey all the leading psychological theories for this purpose. That project, however, was soon found to be too vast; the writer has had to curb his ambition and take a more limited course. In short, he has settled for the theories of perception.

The immediate plan, then, is to present an exposition and critical analysis of the major theories of perception, bringing out as clearly as possible their respective achievements, their limitations, and their relationship to the theme discussed above. Throughout the review an effort will be made to show the structural implications of the various systems, how they dealt with the problem, where they succeeded or failed, and the possible bearing of their successes or failures upon their explanatory achievements or their limitations. Tentative quasistructural interpretations will be introduced along the way, and in the last two chapters the discussion will draw these together and will suggest what they, together with the contributions from the various theories, can offer toward the formulation of a general structural point of view. In the final chapter the writer will give a preliminary statement of his own theory of structure; and an effort will be made to apply this formulation to the data and problems of perception as they have come to light throughout the book. In a later volume he hopes to state the theory more rigorously and to develop its further implications for the various fields of science.

The preceding explanation tells a part of the story of this book—but only a part. No one who is interested in acquiring an understanding of behavior can read the stimulating work that has been done in perceptual experimentation and theory without becoming aware not only of its engrossing interest but also of its profound importance both for the science of psychology and for the practical business of living. Whatever theoretical presuppositions or preferences one may bring to it, the field of perception stands out, in its own right, as one of the most significant areas for human study. The aim has been to bring to the reader as much of the wealth and variety of the theories in this field as possible, to sift the theories, and to present them in the light of a thoughtful analysis and interpretation. That they need sifting and analysis will soon be apparent, for with all its richness and intensity the area of perceptual theory, as indeed of psychological theory as a whole, presents, today, a turbulent and perplexing scene.

Notwithstanding the more general purpose and directional tendency earlier described, the reader will therefore find this book to be primarily a work on the theories of perception. Though it may digress at times, the interest will center in, and ever return to, this focal point. The writer has tried to the best of his ability to make the accounts of the theories and their criticism objective, accurate, and lucid, and at the same time as full and representative as limitations of space would permit. The rest of the story of this book, then, lies in the intrinsic fascination of the theories themselves, in the enjoyment the writer has had in studying and trying to present them, and in the interesting task of attempting to sum up what is now known about perception and of stating the problems that lie ahead. The writer hopes that he may be able to communicate some of this exciting interest to the reader as a recompense for the somewhat exacting experience he must ask him to undergo. He will explain more in the first chapter concerning the weighty aspects of the theories; but for the moment one may say that their unfolding is not unlike that of an absorbing drama. Vicissitudes, conflicts, crises, and denouement are all present as one proceeds from one theory to the next on the trail of ever-illusive themes. Mysteries arise, and some of them are cleared up. Humor and pathos are both found. Conceptions extend from

the twilight zone of manikins to Olympian heights of intellectual
clarity and rigor.   In the *dramatis personae* the experimental subjects
are ever prominent.   They range from direct introspectors of high
and noble forms, the "good figures" or symmetries of nature, through
steady and patient lifters of weights, through "wicked" introspectors
who insist on ringing in their cognitive interpretations, or irresponsible
self-deceivers whose introspection shows the deforming influence of
their own emotions, down to lowly rats and chicks that cannot introspect at all, and finally to machines, which cannot even perceive.   And
always, behind the scenes, there are at work the real promethean
heroes, the experimenters and theorists who are in search of the
truth which is always stranger and more wonderful than any drama
conceived by men.   For those to whom such a search appeals—and
to whom does it not—no further reason is needed for the study of
perception and of the theories of those who are trying to understand
it.   If in the end we shall be able to link up their insights and contributions with a general conception of structure in nature, the account may have a doubly happy ending.   But whether this objective
is reached or not, the theories of perception stand by themselves, even
though they may disagree and fall short of the ideal, as achievements
of lasting interest and worth.   With these two purposes of the book
in mind—its objective of reviewing and examining the theories of
perception and its use as a prelude to a more systematic approach to
structure—the reader will be properly prepared for the task that
follows.

An Orientation to
Psychological Theories

If that much-exploited observer from Mars could visit our halls of learning, he would witness within their psychological precincts a scene of flourishing, not to say exciting, activity. Fields of research are being rapidly extended. Human and animal laboratories are yielding new and interesting facts. The journals are filled with significant articles with a large backlog awaiting publication. Advanced craftsmanship, in apparatus, in recording, in controls, in experimental design, is continually rendering experimentation not only more resourceful but more flexible and precise. As for practical applications, there is scarcely any broad aspect of the humane side of living that has not been affected, and often improved, by the steady march of the science. Though cosmic standards are somewhat out of our line we might have good reason to expect that a Martian visitor viewing all this progress would give our planetary psychology a most complimentary rating.

Let us imagine then that such an appraiser from another planet is going the rounds accompanied by a group of able guides. As he is taken to visit one experiment after another he can scarcely conceal his admiration of the industry and versatility that he sees displayed. In every laboratory it seems that somebody is testing some hypothesis, either his own or someone else's. Thinking back over the progress of earth's science as he has observed it on previous occasions our visitor recalls how great epochs of theory and periods of flourishing experimentation were ever wont to go together. Accumulation of findings has led to broader conceptions, and these in turn have stimulated further research. Impressed by all this experimental fervor he concludes that some great synthesis or awakening in psychological understanding must have taken place on earth, like the formulation

1

of the cell theory in biology or the electromagnetic field theory in physics. Turning at length to his guides he exclaims:

"I think I have seen enough of your laboratories. What you have shown me seems first-rate. Now, if you don't mind, I would like you to take me to the places where your systematic psychology is being developed. I want to see what your *theory* looks like."

At this the guides appear a little hesitant. Their spokesman, however, speaks reassuringly: "Of course!" he says. "Only we'll have to take you to a good many places. Many of our experimentalists are able theoreticians as well. We have many theories—a *great* many; and some of them are very brilliant. To be sure, we are a little unsettled as yet—each working along his own line. You see, in our psychology we have a number of quite different schools and I'm sure . . . " Here the guide's words trail off, for he notices that the visitor is looking at him intently with lifted brows.

"So *many* theories?" The visitor's voice has a touch of plaintive consternation. "But as I look back over the years I seem to see in the progress of most sciences that the fundamental theories are becoming *less* numerous; at least there are a few theories that become more stable and widely accepted. And the fewer there are the more ground each seems to cover. We have seen that the whole range of facts of mechanics were brought into order through a few formulations of Galileo and Sir Isaac Newton."

The faces of the guides now become slightly red. One of them says something about the extreme youth of psychology as an experimental science, Wundt's laboratory, its starting point, having been founded only in 1879. A second guide follows with the explanation that the field of psychology is more complex and difficult than that of the older sciences. Disregarding the fact that the visitor's brows are still lifted, this guide continues: "We might have come to more agreement if we had been content to give up the peculiar problem of psychology and become merely physiologists or physicists. But we refused to do so.[1] Naturally it has taken us a longer time to define the area peculiar to psychology. That's why, for one thing, we have so many schools."

"But what if we do?" exclaims a third guide. "Nobody nowadays takes the schools very seriously. It's all friendly give-and-take among the different camps.[2] Schools are likely to indicate the immaturity of a science, and there are signs that they are passing in psychology."

[1] See Tolman, 1932. (References will be found listed by author and year in the Bibliography.)

[2] See Woodworth, 1948, Chapter 8.

"I'm not so sure of that," interposes the main guide who, in view of his responsibility, is disposed to be more reserved. "And if they *are* passing, that doesn't mean the issues they started from have been cleared up. Perhaps our friend here is right in doubting that we have been making basic theoretical progress."

"Come now," interrupts the former guide, "theoretical differences are to be expected in the earlier development of any science. We can't have too many theories at this stage. Out of it all come common understandings that take us that much further in the end."

At this point one of the guides who has been silent breaks in with considerable energy: "Haven't you all been making too much of this? I don't see why our guest should be so concerned about the present theoretical situation in psychology, or why we should have to defend it. The first job of any science is to get the facts. We're not ready for the job of major theory construction yet.[3] Why go out on a limb? Some of us are tired of all these 'hypothetical constructs' that you can't really test. We ought to experiment and get lots of data. Then we can simply plot curves that show relationships. No need for elaborate theories. There are some who question whether we need theories at all—at least in some fields."[4]

Here another guide speaks up: "I don't agree with you there. Theories are very useful if you know how to handle them. We need more caution in theory building. If you are willing to set up some intervening variable and are careful to define it *only in terms of what you can actually observe,* you can then deduce some useful relationships without going off the deep end. We've got some promising theories of that sort. When our friend has seen these he will have seen the best of what we have to offer; we can spare him the rest."[5]

The main guide evidently feels ill at ease at this disagreement within the family circle; but being a forthright soul he now thinks that some more positive stand should be taken to put the planetary psychology and the visitor's opinion of it upon a firmer basis. He therefore launches forth as follows:

"I don't agree with all this belittling and hamstringing of theory. Of course an accumulation of facts is necessary. But experimentation is never so fruitful when it's hit-and-miss as when it's guided by some intelligent hypothesis. A theory has to take a chance and tell us

[3] See Koch, 1951.
[4] See Skinner, 1950.
[5] See Hull, 1943a; Spence, 1944, 1948; and MacCorquodale and Meehl, 1948. See Tolman, 1936 and 1938; but see also Tolman in Bruner and Krech (eds.), 1950.

something. I agree that caution is necessary—but aren't you getting it in the wrong place? The place for caution is in the experimentation, controls, and conclusions from the results. Before we *start getting* our results we should set up theories that have some *ingenuity* and *imagination*. If you go on defining intervening constructs only as what you have observed and are afraid to come out with some kind of a model, you'll stay just about where you started. I don't call such theories promising.[6] A theory that's logically put together and testable by experiment often serves a purpose even if it's proved wrong. Why shouldn't we just remember that we are not infallible and feel free to set up hypotheses and to change them whenever we need to? It's better to keep striking out than to get a base on balls and die on first base.[7] And what's more, let's not hedge by letting our visitor see only our safe bets—the intervening variables. If he's to get any clear idea, he ought to see the strike outs as well as the bases on balls."

THE SIGNIFICANCE OF THEORIES AND THE TASK AHEAD

By this time our Martian visitor's task of evaluation seems to be getting out of hand. Where guides disagree in advance it is hard to be certain of what one is about to see. Let us pause and take stock of the situation. Can we not, as a starting point, accept the opinion, voiced or implied by most of the participants, that theory *is* important? We are not here using the term in the sense of explaining some relatively small fact seen in isolation. What we mean by theory is some broader statement intended as a generalization to cover the many aspects of a whole class of phenomena, or perhaps the subject matter of an entire science or even nature as a whole. A theory in this sense is a well-coördinated conceptual system. It attempts to give rational coherence to a body of known empirical laws; and from it can be deduced theorems whose predictive value can be tested, thereby appraising, in part, the validity of the theory. At the very least such conceptual systems, if not too tenaciously adhered to, have a value in stimulating research. At their best they serve not only in this capacity, but as the openers of wider horizons.

Good theories give us deeper understandings. They can suddenly change our entire outlook not merely upon this law or that, but upon a whole range of facts or laws. All the great insights or turning

---

[6] See Tolman, 1948, 1949; Köhler, 1940; Hebb, 1949; and certain other brave souls who have taken to model-building.

[7] See practically no one. This is an unpopular view.

points of science started as theories; and many still bear that appellation. For the most part they grew out of deep intellectual perplexities or "theoretical crises," and they often provided solutions that seemed to resolve apparent contradictions in nature. Though a background of observation lay behind them, they were the results of the attempt without further experiment at the moment, merely by *thinking about* what was already known, to put together the pieces of a puzzle that might reveal an order in nature never before envisaged. Any discipline in which theory in this sense is neglected, or in which theoretical obscurities never haunt us, is a poor science indeed. And, by the same token, any new theory that is born out of a crisis in human understanding and is thoughtfully conceived may have potentialities that cannot be ignored.

At first sight it might seem that the Martian visitor had been somewhat captious and his guides unduly on the defensive. Granting the importance of theory in science, do the present tremendous range and flourishing program of psychology *need* any apology upon the side of theory? Do they not presuppose in themselves an atmosphere in which theory must be shaping itself around to some pretty adequate understandings? This view seems plausible on the surface. It is nevertheless true that a large number of psychologists are viewing the matter of theory with growing concern. Many believe that parsimonious and truly general theories constitute a value in science for which there is no substitute, and that, notwithstanding our mounting wealth of data and our zeal in testing hypotheses, neither the facts we are discovering nor the hypotheses we are testing are fulfilling this need. It is not that the critics believe we have failed to appreciate the need of a deeper understanding or have been slothful in trying to attain it. They are, in fact, disturbed that there are *so many* theories on almost every topic and that by and large these theories are quite divergent. The theories do not become broader and coalesce; they merely multiply. There is, of course, no virtue in agreement for mere agreement's sake. The point is that, since all of these theories within any given area are, in one respect or another, in disagreement, not more than one of them at best can be wholly right. Their multiplicity therefore demonstrates not so much the advancement of understanding as the variety of ways in which we have managed to be wrong. It seems to some as though in the great complexity of the organism nature has set up some insuperable obstacle upon which the hope of achieving a unified explanation is doomed forever to be wrecked.

It would be unwise to prejudge any of these issues. This is a time not only of active theory-building in psychology, but it is also a period of earnest discussion and criticism, of contradictory opinions, and of groping for wider generalizations. Though the discord of voices is becoming more noticeable this fact may be, as one of the guides remarked, a good sign. Out of it may come new insights upon which, because they fulfill a deeper theoretical need, a more general agreement can be reached. But in order that such an outcome may be more than a vague hope theories must not be merely championed by their proponents, they must be studied sympathetically but critically by those who hold divergent views. All carefully devised theories should be heard and examined; none should be ignored. It is a task in which both eclectics and ardent theory-supporters should participate.

In this volume the writer is inviting the reader to join him in reviewing some of the major present-day theories of perception. It is an old field, one whose phenomena have perplexed scientists and philosophers for generations; and it is one of the first to have been subjected in psychology to scientific method and laboratory procedures. It is still a very active field, filled with interest for investigators, and is now becoming allied in important ways with personality-study, clinical and social psychology, and numerous other areas. Fresh and novel viewpoints have recently emerged from perceptual experiments; new phenomena are being discovered in what was thought to be a staid and settled discipline. Together with the closely related and to some extent rivalling field of learning, perception holds the center of the stage in present-day efforts to investigate behavior. The facts that have been disclosed will interest us here not so much from the experimentalist's standpoint as for their bearing upon attempts to understand the perceptual process in a broad and systematic way. We shall submit some of those attempts to a careful examination with the hope of disclosing their stronger and their weaker aspects and of discerning not only their differences but their common ground, the basic features that practically all observers have been compelled to recognize. It is our hope that through such a synoptic view major unsolved problems will reveal themselves and that by finding *common* problems we shall also discover such affinities as may exist between perception and other areas of psychology. Though we are holding out no promise, it is conceivable that such a review might help to point the way toward some solution of these problems.

As a guide in such an enterprise the writer claims no outstanding qualifications. Though not a perceptionist in the laboratory sense, he can say that he has given considerable thought to the problem of theory-construction and method in psychology. He would be less than candid, however, if he did not advise the reader, as he has already done in the Foreword, that he too has joined the ranks of theory-builders. It is inevitable, in analyzing issues and appraising contributions, that his own theory will enter and give some shape to the overall picture. The examination of the theories of perception will, in other words, be conducted from "a point of view." In his own defense the writer might say that a critique written from a definite standpoint is likely at least to prove more stimulating than a mere recital of views under the arbitration of a formal logic. So long as the reader is forewarned and is on the alert to separate factual and purely logical materials from the theoretical slanting of the writer— and this, we hope, can readily be done—no particular harm should result. And after all, what theoretician *can* approach a fascinating field like perception wholly free from prepossessions? It should be said, however, that this presentation of the theories will be as thoroughgoing and accurate as the writer's limitations will permit; and before starting, some criteria for theory evaluation will be adopted in an effort to enhance objectivity.

ATTITUDES TOWARD THEORY APPRAISAL

But if we are to embark upon such a venture, what attitude toward theories and theory-construction shall we assume? There are two possibilities. First, we could consider that psychology is now becoming a mature science and that as the result of a vast amount of experimenting theory development, even though somewhat compartmentalized, has reached a fairly settled state. Though no theory is perfect there have crystallized some definite systematic positions that will not be likely to change much in the future. If they are not the last word, at least they are an approximation to it and can be usefully employed in further experimentation and in standard treatises. We would also, in this case, accept the existing theories on the basis of whether or not they accomplish merely what their authors intended them to accomplish; we would often have to be content with limited generalizations applying only to specific areas. The main task would be that of minor revisions, checking, and attempted synthesis. This course would be a comfortable line of action; and the one who undertook it would not appear overbold.

Our attitude, on the other hand, might be quite different. We could begin with the assumption that psychology has not yet matured and that probably no science will ever be so well established that the door will not have to be held open to changes that may be far-reaching. We could question whether any theory has yet attained so close an approximation to the truth that it can be regarded as authoritative. We could also place upon the theory requirements more binding than those the author intended and lying outside the restricted area for which it was developed, on the ground that the most valuable scientific formulations are those that turn out to have the greatest generalizing and explanatory power. We would, in this instance, examine the theory critically, separating the strong points from the weak, and would exhibit the former not as finished products but as suggestions for the future. The aim would not be merely to reconcile existing systems, but, if occasion demanded, to set forth what had been accomplished in such a way that an entirely new theory might eventually appear, one that might use the insights of the past without being either an integration or a compromise. Such a program would be not merely a weighing of past accomplishments but also an appraisal and stressing of the present theoretical need. This course is a bolder one; it places a greater responsibility upon the reviewer. Yet in view of the large number of psychological theories and the apparently irreconcilable differences of many of them it is, perhaps, the method that might be more profitable in the end. Because of the values that lie in this second approach we shall try to adopt it as our mode of procedure.

CRITERIA FOR THE EVALUATION OF THEORIES

How then can we examine psychological theories in general, or the theories of perception in particular, in such a way that their relation to present theoretical needs will be most clearly shown? The writer suggests the six following criteria all of which are familiar and are for the most part commonly accepted.

1. *Agreement with the facts.* Are there facts which can be called upon to support the theory; and do the facts that *are* called upon really support it? The theory should also be consistent, or at least not inconsistent, with other known facts.

2. *Generality.* How many facts or laws does the theory "accomodate" in the sense not merely of not being inconsistent with them but of actively providing for them a place within its framework? If the theory is true, i.e., in agreement with the facts, how *widely* is its truth exemplified? For this criterion we suggest two levels of application. (*a*) Generality for the particular class or area of phenomena

with which the theory is concerned. That is to say, how many different aspects or specific phenomena of the class does it succeed in incorporating? We shall speak of this phase of generality as the *degree of completeness* of the theory. (*b*) Generality which transcends the phenomenon-class and covers the phenomena of a number of classes, approaching a basic conception for the science as a whole or perhaps for all the sciences. This aspect might be called the *systematic potentiality* of the theory. Since we shall be dealing mainly with theories of perception rather than with psychology as a whole the first of these levels will be used somewhat more than the second.

3. *Parsimony.* Generality should not be gained at the expense of an ad hoc multiplication of postulates to meet the need of special cases. The fewer the postulates, other things being equal, the better the theory.

4. *Immediate experimental availability.* The theory should be sufficiently operational in its statement to make it possible for it to be tested. Other things being equal, a theory is valuable in proportion as its concepts have clear, unambiguous, and manipulable referents.[8]

5. *Logical consistency.* The theory should be free from internal contradictions.

6. *Explanatory value.* The theory should help us to understand the phenomenon. It should provide more in the nature of an accounting than a mere analogy. There should be a feeling of inevitability about its explanations once its postulates are accepted and its rationale understood and the explanations given should be sufficiently clear and detailed to be convincing.

It is necessary to develop the meaning of this last criterion more fully. As the writer sees it, the essential task of science is always one of generalized description, that is, the description of phenomena by means of general statements or laws through which predictions about them can be successfully made. The term *explanation* will here be used to mean a description in terms that are more general than those with which we started. For example, if one were to "describe" the action of falling bodies crudely as "movement toward the earth," an "explanation" of this phenomenon would consist of stating some general principle embodying the conditions under which this phenomenon occurs and the quantitative or geometric relationships it involves, as, for example, in the Newtonian (or the relativity) laws of gravitation.

---

[8] In its *full* sense, therefore, this criterion is stricter than the familiar procedure of "intervening variable," a logical device that is now permitted so long as the construct used intervenes between items that can be operationally defined and measured.

The second statement is both more precise and more general than the first. It is still, however, a description. It is given in terms of what *universally* occurs or in what relative amounts something that happens will always be found to occur. Explanations by cause and effect are also generalized descriptions of happenings. In this case the descriptive formula takes a form somewhat like the following: A member of a certain class of occurrences, *B*, is always preceded by a member of a certain other class of occurrences, *A*; and an *A* is always followed by a *B*.

We frequently think of explanation as involving a statement of the "how" or the "why" of phenomena. Questions of "how" something happens in nature, or "why" something happens, are also answerable in the last analysis only through generalized description. For example, if one were asked *how* an organism assimilates its food, the answer might be that it is done through "osmosis." If pressed further for an explanation of *osmosis,* one could only give a lawful description of what happens, including a statement of what amounts of something are involved as osmosis is said to occur. That is, one might allude to the movement of dissolved food particles through membranes and to the quantitative variations and direction of this movement in relation to degrees of solvent and solute concentrations. All these statements would again be descriptions, but at the level of a more general law. If asked how *these* effects come about, one might then go into a description of cells and membranes, or laws of pressures or forces, and so on—always proceeding from the more particular to the more universal. If one were asked *why* an animal runs a maze, one might refer to some "motive" or "drive" which "activates" the animal. When asked for a fuller explanation of the "why," one again could only resort to a further description of what happens. One could refer to the quantities of energy the drive represents and to whatever distributions these energies are known to assume in the acting organism. No matter how such questions are asked, we always come back to a mere description of occurrences. For convenience we use the word explanation to apply more specifically to descriptions of a definitely stated and more widely generalized sort.

A further word, however, must be added to complete the meaning of the term explanation. Though explanation is description in the broader sense, we cannot say that a phenomenon is explained unless the connection between the generalization and the concrete case is made clear; that is, unless we can see how the general principle applies to the specific facts. To see that the laws of osmosis "explain" the assimilation of food we must also be shown that the organism possesses cells and cell membranes through which such action can take place. To explain drive through a generalization based upon the energy concept we must refer to the fact that the organism has receptors upon which stimulus energies act. We must deal also with energetic changes as shown in *neurons* and *muscle fibers*, and with glands and hormones as "distributors" of energy. These matters, of course, are also generalized descriptions, but they constitute *a special class* of general descriptions that are necessary in order to give the purely quantitative laws their frame of reference. Such features are frequently spoken of as the "mechanism" through which the law or process operates. This term is somewhat unfortunate in that it is too limited and suggests that the "law" represents something apart from, or over and above, the happenings themselves. But whatever this aspect may be called, it is clear that some reasonable and informative statement about it must be included if the theory is to rise to the status of an explanation. We have here a very crucial and necessary test of a theory, one that we shall repeatedly have occasion to employ.

The manner in which we shall use the term "understanding" follows from what has just been said. Understanding is what one gets as a result of adequate explanation. To understand some phenomenon means, first, to have available and to apprehend a generalized description of it and, second, to see that the generalization makes sense in terms of the specific arrangements that are characteristic of the phenomenon. In applying our sixth criterion the above-stated meanings of explanation and understanding, and of "how" and "why," will be consistently followed.

With reference to the full list of criteria it may be noted that they are not independent. Experimental availability, explanatory value, and generality, for example, are often interwoven. But in spite of this fact the criteria are sufficiently distinct to be employed in many instances as separate tests. For the purpose of applying the test of generality or completeness it will be necessary to define clearly the class of phenomena with which we are dealing, that is, perception, and to illustrate its various aspects, in order to see what the task is that must be accomplished by a perceptual theory before it can be regarded as complete.

Let us recall again the general objective. The aim is not the criticism of any theory as a means merely of rating the accomplishment of its author. We would not play the role of awarding prizes even if we were competent to do so. The purpose is merely to ascertain where psychology now stands in the development and progress of its perceptual theory. We need to canvass the present difficulties and to assess the present theoretical needs. This point of view will affect our employment of the criteria. They have been called criteria of evaluation. If they *are* standards for evaluating theories they should be so considered only in the light of this broader objective. How strictly, then, should they be applied? How fully should we require the particular theories to satisfy them? At first sight a "counsel of perfection" would seem unreasonable: it would imply that we ought to be already at the end of our quest. If we had a theory that met perfectly the tests of agreement with facts, explanatory value, generality, and all the rest, it might mean that we had solved all the relevant problems and that there would be nothing more to do. But looking at the matter in another way it is clear that there is actually little danger that so complete a coinciding of theory and fact will be achieved in any area of psychology for a long time; and in proportion as we more fully realize the ideal of the requirements, the more rapidly we shall advance toward that goal. From this standpoint the *complete* fulfillment of the criteria becomes the standard against which it is most helpful to measure the success of any present theory and, as such, will be used in our appraisal of the theories of perception.

One word more. Theory-construction and theory-sifting, though always dependent for their validity upon experimental evidence, are no less a part of the scientific work-process than the experiments themselves. The task here, however, is somewhat different; and it is equally arduous though in a different way. In the usual textbook the practice is to concentrate upon empirical findings, the known, hard, factual data, and to add the theories as a short appendix or perhaps a running commentary. In approaching the theory of a subject in its own right another method must be followed. Here we do not expect clear-cut answers, systematically arranged; and we must be prepared to sift through large masses of postulates, facts, and logical inferences, testing every item to see whether it is wheat or chaff, and being careful not to take seriously the chaff nor to miss any of the wheat. We must be persistent and patient, yet at the same time alert and imaginative; and we must be content with having some questions left unanswered. One must be satisfied that one's understanding is a little deeper, one's view slightly more general, than it was before.

Particular theories get finished either by being all tidied up in neat but limited enclosures or else, in the more grim sense, by receiving their last rites at the hands of new discoveries of facts. Theories therefore come and go. But the work of theory is never finished.

The task to which we have set ourselves is therefore not like factual textbook study.   Nor should one suppose that since no one knows the final answers, theories should not be taken too seriously, and that their perusal may be regarded as light but interesting reading for a hammock on a summer afternoon.   We have far more serious business on our hands.   For theory is the stage upon which experiments are conducted.   It is the logical groundwork for our hope that our findings may reward us with further knowledge.   The principal actor in the drama is no less imposing a figure than law itself; and the solution of the mystery, if we are so lucky as ever to reach it, may give us some glimpse into the constitution of the natural world.

In order to make our work worth while and not to miss the possible thrill of the denouement, it seems clear, therefore, that we must do it as well as we possibly can.   Otherwise it were perhaps better not to undertake it.   In carrying out this intention we shall have to go into many bypaths and sometimes into extended digressions.   Controversial issues and examples given in support of arguments must be examined from many points of view.   It is hoped that the reader will not be too much dismayed by these discussions, wanting to get on more quickly to the point and to the conclusions.   Let him remember that in most cases there are as yet no conclusions to come to.   We are working together in a common enterprise—the enterprise of groping! In part, such excursions into the "pro" and "con" will be necessary in order to find out where a theory stands and to get at its final kernel of truth.   In part they will be attempts to open new vistas of the subject, aspects not yet presented by any of the theories, and thus to give a look ahead.   Because of this feature the reader must be prepared to have the review interrupted at times to follow a line of thinking that may seem at first quite foreign to the topic under consideration. For these aspects we ask his indulgence and express the hope that they may afford some interest and enlightenment.   True to these forewarnings we shall begin our study with an extended examination of the problem of perception and the methodological perplexities it involves.[9]

[9] For other discussions of topics mentioned in this chapter, such as the role of theories, theory construction and evaluation, scientific explanation, and the use of models, see Klein and Krech, 1951; Hebb, 1951; Bertalanffy, 1951, Marx (ed.), 1951; Feigl, in Dennis (ed.) 1951, and Dallenbach, 1953.   Compendia of psychological theories and schools can be found in Helson (ed.), 1951; Marx (ed.), 1951; Woodworth, 1948; and Heidbreder, 1933.   Much material on certain theoretical viewpoints in perception, though not a complete or systematic account, will be found in Blake and Ramsey (eds.), 1951, and Bruner and Krech (eds.), 1950.   See also the brief but interesting account of the scope of perceptual theories by Gibson in Dennis (ed.) 1951.

2————————

The Problem of Perception
Its Place in the Methodology
of Science

How should perception be defined? What are its essential characteristics? As a first approximation let us say that it has something to do with our awareness of the objects or conditions about us. It is dependent to a large extent upon the impressions these objects make upon our senses. It is the way things look to us, or the way they sound, feel, taste, or smell. But perception also involves, to some degree, an understanding awareness, a "meaning" or a "recognition" of these objects. Koffka[1] stated the problem of visual perception by asking: "Why do things look as they do?" In order to include the full scope of our topic we need to broaden this question by asking why things or happenings appear or seem as they do. Thus we can include all the senses and can interpret perception as covering the awareness of complex environmental situations as well as of single objects. Though some psychologists tend to assign this last consideration to cognition rather than to perception the two processes are so closely intertwined that it would scarcely be feasible, especially from the standpoint of theory, to consider one of them in isolation from the other.

Though Koffka's question, "Why do things look as they do?" seems straightforward and simple it raises some challenging issues. As Koffka suggested, a person naïve in matters psychological might answer it, half-facetiously, by asking: "How else could things look, being what they are?" It would thus be assumed that there is no problem here for psychology; we are dealing merely with a matter of "reality." But things can and do look differently from the way they "are"; and when we realize this fact and begin to explore the reasons

[1] 1935, Chapter III.

14

for it we shall have gained light upon the meaning of perception and the problem it presents. In order to arrive at such understandings we must leave for a while the realm of familiar assumptions, taking a devious route into questions of objectivity and scientific method. For a while it may seem that we are forgetting perception or belittling its importance; but we shall return later to a full vindication and clarification of our topic.

SCIENCE AND EXPERIENCE: PHENOMENA

If, for some perverse reason, someone wanted to make a list of the most futile of occupations, one might reasonably recommend for early inclusion the following task: Try to imagine what the world or the universe would be like if there were no sentient beings to observe it. Whether an acorn falling in a forest with no one around to hear it makes a sound is an old philosophical riddle. But let us go further: suppose there were no observers *anywhere* to be aware of *anything*. We would then have to question not only whether there would be any "sound," but whether there would be such a thing as an "acorn," an "oak tree," or a "forest." Are we saying, then, that there would be nothing there at all? No. The scientist is not a solipsist; he believes there would probably be *something* there to which our present concepts of "acorn," "forest," and "sound" would correspond. The trouble would be that, since no one would be present to make any observations, no one (if we could imagine that someone existed in an entirely separate realm) would be able to do more than merely have this belief; he would be unable to say anything about what these "existences" were like. Concepts exemplified by "sound," "acorn," and "forest," are what we human beings must inevitably use; but they are so saturated with our own auditory and visual experiences and our own meanings that if these were stripped away, we could scarcely form any idea of the natural world. Even if we were to substitute for these familiar impressions the more exact descriptions of scientists such as quantities and magnitudes, we should find that these too depend in part upon the observer. They require the use of humanly devised measuring instruments as well as definitions and equations which, though highly general, still represent in part the observer's way of studying his world.

What we have been saying must seem to the reader old and trite. We have merely asserted what has been known for ages, namely, that all knowledge must come from experience. Nature, as the subject-matter of all scientific study, is experience; or at least it is given to us by experience. But if experience provides the content of scientific observation, we should then ask whether *all* of our experience is the proper ground for such study, or whether some parts are more acceptable for this purpose while others should be rejected? The reply to this question is not so immediately obvious. Upon reflection, however, we see that the first statement rather than the second is the logical answer. All parts or aspects of experience, as experience, are equally "real" or "valid" as content for observation. To decide differently would require us to have some standard in addition to experience by which we could distinguish the acceptable from the unacceptable. Such a standard we do not have. Some experience-contents may seem more *practicable to study* than others. As we shall see, there is within experience itself a differentiation that is significant and that slants inquiry in a certain direction. Yet since we do not wish to set up barriers marking limits within which scientific inquiry must be kept, we have to concede that everything that is experienced can, in principle at least, become the proper object of study and description.[2]

It is useful here to consider the terms "objective" and "objectivity." Sometimes this word is used to signify an object or a state of affairs that is "real" or "true" in the sense that it would exist in complete independence of any observer or his method of observing. Such a state of "objective existence" as this could never be determined. The term, if used in this sense would refer to something for which no possible operations could be found and would therefore be, by Bridgman's test, without meaning.[3] In order to have an operational meaning the word objective must refer not to nature as some object or condition of affairs believed to be "absolutely" existential, the philosopher's "thing in itself," but to something else. A more feasible usage is to employ

---

[2] Illusions, for example, and even hallucinations, are still experiences, and as such are as valid for investigation as the facts we call our "true" experiences of the physical world. They would be misleading if taken as some state of affairs in the world "outside" or independent of the subject. But if observed as an index of something that is happening within the subject, that it, as psychological phenomena, there is no reason why they are not as valid as any other experience-content. Whether they can be experienced by others or are only the private concerns of the subject, they are at least the *subject's* experiences. A great many illusions, moreover, are matters of common agreement as to the appearances involved. Inadequacies of technique or a lack of knowledge of neural events might discourage our attempt to investigate these phenomena. But difficulties of method of study should not be confused with the question of what it is legitimate to study.

[3] Cf. Bridgman, 1949.

the term to signify something upon whose description different observers agree. We shall later propose still another definition.

We have now arrived at a position that we can maintain: All experience is the legitimate ground or provider of content-matter for scientific observation and study. We have no reason, so far as its validity is concerned, for picking any favorites among experiences. Let us refer to this position as our "content-postulate." It will also be noted that we seldom if ever experience everything about us all at once. Certain portions of the total possible field, having a certain self-containedness and unity, are selected for attention or seem to force themselves upon us. We shall call whatever is thus selected for observation, whatever definite content is experienced at a given moment, a *phenomenon*. The term phenomenon thus defined covers not only objects or conditions such as rocks, trees, animal organisms, and electric discharges, but also such experience-content as sensory qualities, afterimages, illusions, and affective states. A phenomenon is merely some relatively self-delimited and unified item or aggregate of experience-content, something which, as we have said, is the legitimate ground for observation and report. Phenomena are the subject-matter of science.

THE MEANING AND CRITERIA OF OBJECTIVITY

The scientific procedure not only requires that we have some phenomenon to study, but that we emerge from our study with a careful description of it and, if possible, with generalizations suitable for its explanation or prediction. On the basis of past evidence we realize that we are prone to error. Later attempts or attempts of others to describe the phenomenon often contradict our earlier efforts. We have also learned that a very large source of the error either lies in ourselves or is a result of the very activities by which our observing and experimenting are carried on. Suppose then we change our original meaningless question that had to do with the elimination of all that was human from the scene of observation. Instead of asking how the world would appear if there were no one to observe and study it, let us inquire what the world would seem like if, in the act of observing and studying, all the manipulations, activities, presuppositions, meanings, feelings, and values of the observer were prevented insofar as humanly possible from disturbing that part of the experienced world that is under observation or from influencing the record of the observations or the conclusions drawn therefrom. It is admitted that such a prevention can never be complete; but let us suppose that the *amount* of disturbance of the object by the observer's state or activities and the *amount* of their coloring of the report is made as small as it can be under human limitations. How, then, would the world appear under *such* conditions?

We have now a question that is far from meaningless. It is so very meaningful that it constitutes the very basis of all scientific work. The continual *effort* to reduce the error due to the particular activity of the investigator as near to its absolute minimum as possible (even though one cannot even be certain that such a minimum is reached) is an inflexible requirement of all research. We shall refer to it as the "methodological rule." We need to reduce the possible influences of the observer or his method as much as possible because the more we do so, the greater will be the degree in which we can expect the account to represent nature as it is. We can never know that it does completely and accurately represent nature because our own act merely of experiencing the phenomenon is a possible disturbing factor we can never entirely eradicate. But we can make a probable *reduction* of the sources of error by noting occasions in which we can detect, or might infer, that some of our own activities *could* be entering. In these places it may be possible to eliminate or control such activities without eliminating the experience to be observed. The more we do this, the more we can conclude that our attempt at description is free from (at least this) distorting bias. The more fully the distortion due to the observer and his methods can be removed, the more certain we can feel that another observer, using the same or different but equally accurate methods, will get corresponding results. For natural phenomena, in themselves, are assumed to be respecters neither of the individuals who study them nor of particular methods used in their study. It is true that this is an assumption; but without it one could have neither the "faith of the scientist" in the independent existence of nature nor the postulate of a possible order in the universe which it is the objective of the scientist to discover.

Though the word objectivity has been employed with many meanings, the preceding discussion will give us a particularly useful way of defining it. We shall consider objectivity to be this effort to reduce to a minimum the influence of the observer's own activity upon the description of what is observed. Under this definition the term does not apply to the object to be described or to a fact of nature in itself; it designates a working method for describing the object or stating the fact. Furthermore, objectivity represents not a fully accomplished state, but only a sustained attempt to follow a methodological rule. And such an effort is probably seldom completely successful; it is, rather, a matter of degree. Though *facts* are not "objective," one set of theoretical concepts about the facts, or one experiment through which they are observed and studied, may be said to be more (or less) objective than another. Maximum attainable objectivity is always the aim. If the methodological rule were to be disregarded, the entire program of science would be undermined.

But in order to apply the rule of objectivity successfully we need criteria that will help us judge whether we are meeting it or falling short. Three rigorous standards can be mentioned that have stood the test of time. The first of these may be called the *degree of observer-involvement*. It is merely a restatement of what has already been said. The question to be asked here is whether that part of his experience-world which the observer is describing is so closely bound up with his own observing activities that it can scarcely be separated for succinct observation. And if so, can the methods of observing or describing be so changed that the observer will be freer from such involvement, or, more exactly, so that what is being described will be freer from involvement with him? The smaller the amount of observer-involvement, the more objective is the procedure.

The second criterion is the test of *contact* or *encounterability*. The question here is whether, in connection with the method that is being employed, the part of the experience-world under observation is actually being encountered. For this criterion the writer asks the privilege of employing, as a special name, a term usually used in a somewhat different context. Let us call it *denotation* or *denotability*. In order to use this word, which usually means "pointing out" or "demonstrating," we shall need to alter its sense for our present purpose. We shall mean by it not merely "pointing out" or "demonstrating" an object, but actually, physically *contacting* or *encountering* it. It is requested that the reader bear in mind this usage of "denotation" for future reference. To the extent that the observation and record can be controlled by, or restricted to, data from such a denotable (encounterable) source we have the most satisfactory assurance that what is being studied is probably independent of the observer and his methods, and that its description will be as objective and free from observer-influence as possible.

Our third criterion is a rule that we shall borrow from operationism in its stricter form. It stipulates that all concepts referring to what is being observed should be definable in terms of operations, and that these operations *should be capable of being "publicly" performed* so that other observers can reproduce them. The application of this precept secures the support of *observer-agreement*. The greater the proportion of "public" operations that can be applied to illustrate the concepts used in any investigation or theory the more objective is the method employed.

These three standards of objectivity are by no means distinct. They are merely different ways in which the same basic requirement can be met. As fundamental statements they are probably not of equal significance. The second, that of denotation or encounterability, is, in the writer's opinion, the fundamental operation upon which the other two depend and is, therefore, the basic criterion of objectivity in science. It is the principle that lies behind operationism, though the operationists themselves have not clearly recognized it. "Public" operations are not more trustworthy than "private" because they are *public*. They are *both* trustworthy *and* public because they are denotative. All three standards however are useful. Together they provide the experience-basis of a postulate of the physical world. They are our best evidence not merely that some portion of experience is before us which, like all experience, is valid ground for investigation, but that the portion concerned is experience that is derived from something that may exist independently of the observer, to be studied with the least possible intrusion of his methods into the result. They therefore not only help us to appraise the objectivity of our methods; they also single out for us a realm to which these methods can be most properly applied—the world, in short, of natural science.

PHENOMENOLOGICAL VERSUS PHYSICALISTIC EXPERIENCE AND METHOD: PERCEPT; DENOTATION

These criteria of objectivity are stock in trade in the physical sciences and in biology as well. The phenomena studied in these sciences present to the observer a basis for contact and manipulation either in a direct or an indirect fashion. The operations are all capable of public performance and duplication, and the results, in general, depend to as small an extent as possible upon the behavior of the investigator or the particular methods used. In both experiment and theory the frame of reference of the concepts employed is one which is set by the standards of observer-detachment, denotability, and the possibility of sharing the empirical procedure with others. The physical and biological sciences are natural areas for the development and use of objective methods.[4]

[4] Even in the case of such concepts as forces and the field, an encounter at the point of application of the forces must be employed in order to give oper-

When we come to psychology a different situation presents itself. In certain parts of its subject-matter, denotational standards and the test of observer-detachment do not seem readily applicable—some would even say they do not apply. With the realization of this difference of content and viewpoint psychologists are faced by a "methodological crisis," one that has immediate bearing upon the problem of perception. For the student of perception has a responsibility for a special assignment not given to the physicist or physiologist. His task is not merely to observe the character of objects or events considered to belong to a physical world unaltered by the observations of the observer, a world such as that of mechanical action, thermal changes, electrochemical occurrences, neural impulses, and muscle-contractions. The perceptionist is supposed, in addition, to include in his investigation the question of how the world *looks to the perceiver*. He must account not merely for how things "are," but for how they "appear." He must report not the character of the things that are perceived but the character of the perception, not the world that is experienced but the experience of that world as dependent upon the experiencing organism. He does not merely observe; he observes observation.

Given a subject who is observing and a student of perception who is observing this subject's observation (including the use of the indirect verbal-report method), is there any fundamental difference between the type of description here employed and that which would be used by physicists or physiologists in observing the materials of their respective fields? Is there, as between these two cases, any difference in the degree or manner in which the criteria of objectivity can be, or should be, applied? We are going to ask the reader to answer some questions by making certain observations; and the experiences he acquires in so doing should throw some light upon the matter.

Let us turn to Figure 1. If the reader is willing to act as a subject-observer, he will see that he can be led to adopt either of two quite different methods of observation, and that each of these methods is dictated more or less by what we stipulate as the experience-content he is to observe. As the *first* task, we shall ask the reader to observe and describe the experience which answers the question "How do

---

ational physical meaning to the field. Waves transmitted through media are demonstrable only through the displacement of something that encounters something else, either another particle or the recording instrument of the investigator. Waves that travel in "empty space" have their particle-aspect, and hence their possibility of impact, as well as their form and frequency.

these two lines look to you?" As the *second* assignment, we shall ask him to observe and report the experience that is relevant to the question "What are the facts concerning the two lines?" We shall begin with the first question—how do the lines look? The report will probably be that the lines look *straight and parallel*. In this procedure, which is the so-called "direct experience" method, the report is a description of the immediate experience of how the lines appear.

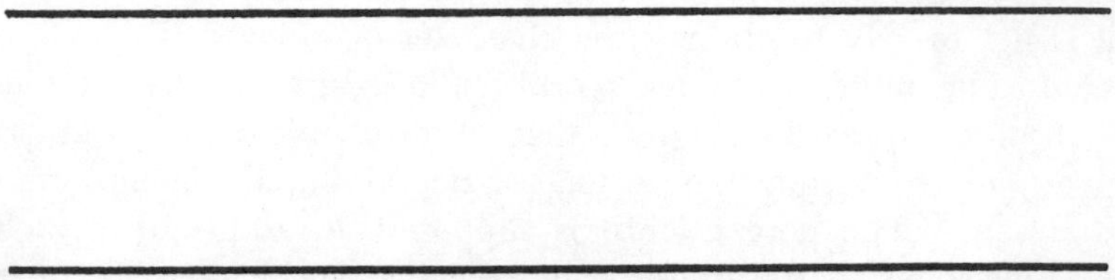

FIGURE 1.

Let us now apply to this method our three criteria of objectivity. It will be noted, first, that the reader as an observer was himself considerably involved in making this judgment. The experience and report entailed to a large extent his own unaided activity. No contact or encounter was made with the lines beyond the fact that light rays were reflected from the figure to his eyes. What evidence or authority does he have for reporting the experience of straightness or parallelness of the lines? One would promptly reply that no outside authority was needed under the conditions set. The experience carried its own validation, its own earmarks of reality; and the subject himself must be the judge. But does this not mean that there must have been some process of experiencing and describing going on inside the subject, some "inner" activity that coöperated with the stimulus pattern but did not demand any further evidence, in the way of checking, to lead to the judgment of "parallel and straight?" Such a conclusion is inescapable; and this situation is exactly what we mean by observer-involvement.

We note further that what the report refers to under the term "looks," namely, the experience-content, is, as such, not denotable. One cannot encounter the straight or parallel "looks" of the lines. And so our second criterion, denotability, is not met.

Regarding the third criterion, it is found that the inner operations that go on as the subject experiences "straightness" and "parallelness" are not, at least with present techniques, accessible to the experimenter. The operations are not public, but private. Though the experimenter may "understand," through the associations of a common language, what the subject means when he says that the lines "look" parallel and straight, he cannot be *sure* that his own experience-content is just like that of the subject. This point is overlooked in everyday life because we feel that we can tell from the subject's linguistic behavior whether his "perception" of the lines we are both looking at is what *we* would call straight and parallel. We trust our common language as a symbolic substitute for the experience. In order to put this assumption to a test we would need to institute behavioral operations other than language or other communications about the subject's "experience"; and such operations would of necessity be *public*.

Perhaps the reader will agree, then, that the method of observing employed in response to the question "How do the lines look?" has fallen considerably short of the methodological rule. It has been found wanting on all three of the criteria. But an immediate protest might be forthcoming. What else could you expect when the task set was made *subjective* by its very conditions? The protest is quite in order. There seems to be something inappropriate and "unnatural" in trying to employ the standards of objectivity for appraising an individual's "consciousness" of the lines. As soon as we ask how the lines "look" we are subtly steering attention away from the realm of "physical" facts and toward an order of experience in which the subject, by himself, must be regarded as supreme. When he says that the lines look to him straight and parallel, who is in a position to question his statement? Hence there seems to be here a special sort of experience to which objectivity tests cannot properly be applied; or at least any attempt to apply them will result in failure. Any experience reported as an answer to the question of how things "appear" as distinguished from how they "are," that is, as descriptions of "pure awareness" without further checking by the external stimulus-object, will be similarly lacking in amenability to the criteria of objectivity. Such forms or aspects of awareness we shall call *phenomenological* experiences. We shall refer to the procedure of observing and reporting them as the "phenomenological method." Another, historically important, term used in this connection is *introspection*. In the example used the introspection is very direct—simply a report of immediate phenomenological experience. In Chapter 4 a less direct method of introspection will be discussed. A phenomenological experience of an object, that is to say, the way some object or situation appears to the subject as dependent upon his own organism, as observer-involved, non-denotive, and "private," is called a *percept*.

A number of questions will now arise. Does not our entire experience of the world come to us as percepts? Are not all experiences phenomenological? Our whole conscious life, insofar as it is out-wardly oriented, is made up of the way in which objects and environ-mental circumstances "appear." Even the scientist must depend upon the way the scale-readings or positions of index-pointers look to him. The answer to these questions will come in a moment. Let us merely say here that phenomenology *as we have defined it,* however omnipresent it may be, and notwithstanding its presence even in the work of scientists, does not cover the *whole* of experience. There *is* another type of experience that comes to us when we are not looking inwardly at the "appearance" of things to us, but are answering the question of how things "are." One *could* call it a different "depart-ment" of phenomenology, or a different "class" of percepts if one wished; but the awareness involved is so different from the cases we have been considering that it seems best to classify it as a different experience-form. We shall presently show what is meant.

Whether one grants such distinctions or not, one cannot help but be amazed at the wealth and variety of experience that comes to us without benefit of the methodological rule. Our lives are lived, insofar as we deal with the "appearances" of things, in an aura of ob-server-involvements, private significances, and lack of clear, explicit denotation. And great is the burden placed upon language in trying to communicate these experiences to others. How can we adapt succesfully to our surroundings when so many of our daily observa-tions are so lacking in objective controls, so prone to a biasing by the involvement or activities of the observer? How can we be sure that the study of perception itself, the observation of observation, is suf-ficiently free from such influences to be worthwhile? These questions give point to what we have called the methodological crisis that must be faced by students of perception; and in discussing the theories of perception we shall see that it has played no small part in the dif-ficulties they have encountered. On the practical side, the lack of susceptibility of percepts to the criteria of objectivity does not have such altogether maladaptive consequences as one might expect. There are some remarkable compensating features that will be con-sidered later. But it is time to turn from phenomenology to see what more can be learned from the lines of Figure 1.

We shall now ask the reader the second question: "What are the *facts* about the two lines and their relationship?" Here we are in-quiring not how the lines "look," but, in effect, how they "are." We are *not* really asking how they are, or would be, *apart from any possibility of human observation,* for we have seen that that is a meaningless question. What we are asking is that the reader tell us something about the lines while using as his manner of observing them a method in which any influence that his activity of observing or his own prepossessions might exert upon their description *is reduced to a minimum*. Since the reader might not care to trust his unaided eye in meeting so exacting a requirement, he might wish to use a straight-edge (ruler or edge of a card). We urge him to do so. Having first applied the straight-edge to the lines and then having measured the distance between them at certain points, the reader will now probably report that the lines are straight and are everywhere equidistant, that is, they are "straight" and "parallel."[5] This report happens to agree with his earlier phenomenological description of his experience of the lines. It is, however, a report essentially of how the lines *are*, not of his experience of "how they look."

Though the descriptive adjectives used in the report are the same as before we must note that in arriving at them a different method of observation has been used. Let us apply our tests of objectivity to this second method. We see, first, that the second method was based upon detonation or encounter. The subject's hands encountered (denoted) the straight edge or ruler, and the straight-edge encountered (denoted) the ink of the lines. This was true both in testing for straightness and in measuring the distance between the lines. The denotation of the lines was somewhat indirect in that an instrument intervened between the subject's hand and the lines: two steps of contact or denotations were involved and one of them included a somewhat dubious auxiliary, the aid of light rays and vision. Contacts, however, were clearly present. Second, we find that the observer's activities were less significantly involved in the observation and report than was the case in the earlier, phenomenological, procedure. This fact might not be apparent at first. It might seem that even more was required of the subject in the nature of movements, adjustments, and the like. Though this is true, there is a difference in the *way* the observer was involved. There was outer activity or movement, to be sure, but the movements were directly and continuously related to the stimulus object. In applying a straight edge the observer is constrained at every application he makes by the lines themselves. He must put the straight-edge or ruler exactly along the lines and he must measure by it the exact distance between them. So engrossed is he in this operation that he has neither the inclination

---

[5] For determining whether the ruler or the edge of the card itself is straight one could look along its edge and employ operations involving rays of light reflected from points along the edge and producing alignment (or displacement) upon the eye.

nor the opportunity to observe how the lines "look." He probably does not even take notice of them as a whole by a single unaided glance. This new testing experience therefore supersedes and reduces, if indeed it does not eliminate, the earlier phenomenological description of the "looks" of the lines. Though the two methods might occur in rapid alternation they are, in practice, neither simultaneous nor similar.

A moment ago we said that in the second method the stimulus-object exerted a continual "constraint" upon the movements by the aid of which it was observed. This constraint is not only external but also internal. If at any point at which there happened to be some activity (bias) going on inside the observer that would tend toward inducing him to experience and report the lines in a way not exactly in accord with the experience provided by the straight-edge, the obligation of placing the straight-edge exactly at or along the line would, under ordinary circumstances, immediately cancel the effect of such a biasing activity. (This result would be *fully* assured, of course, only by making many spatially continuous applications of the instrument.) The procedure employed thus brings about an "object-control" of the experiences from the object and a corresponding effect upon the description of the object. The determination of the observation and report comes maximally from the object observed and less, or minimally, from the observing subject. The involvement of the observer's own activity as a *biasing* influence upon the report is thus materially reduced.

Can we say that it is eliminated? Hardly, for the observer still has to apply the straight-edge himself; and he has to "see" that the straight-edge and line are touching and that the same distance-marking applies at different points between the lines. It will probably be admitted, however, that the magnitude of the distortion due to these influences would probably be *comparatively* small. Rays of light must "mediate" between stimulus-object and experiencing subject as they did in the phenomenological observation; but there is this important difference. The "optical" appearance of straightness and parallelness can be continually checked, as it could not in the phenomenological procedure, by the use of the denoting or encountering instrument; and the more numerous the points of denoting along the lines, the less is the extent to which the observer's own irrelevant activities or prepossessions can construe the optical impression in such a way as to affect the result. Then too, we must regard our present straight-edge experiment as only a rough approximation to what could be attained under ideal conditions.

Let us consider this matter more fully in order to see what is really involved in the criterion of denotation. In careful physical investigations contacts much more precisely ascertainable than a straight-edge laid along a line are employed. Mechanical or electrical devices are used, and recording is made automatic. Denotation can be made so explicit and fine that encounters even at minute atomic and subatomic levels can be registered. The necessary mediating contacts of intervening devices can be carefully controlled and the action of the devices interpreted according to known natural laws. Though there is always left *some* phenomenological experience, some percept of how *these recordings* look to the scientist, the degree of observer-involvement is greatly reduced. The method is based essentially upon the principle of denotation and the operations are "publicly" performable.

In the physical and physiological sciences investigations are often conducted by having a *chain* of encounters (denotations) extending between the "x" that is to be described and the observer, a procedure that makes it possible to study the more minute levels. For example, a fog track left from the condensation of vapor particles as an electron passes is illuminated by an electric spark and photographed (contacts of photons reflected from the fog track to the plate); and the picture can then be handled and viewed by the observer who interprets what he sees as the "track of the electron." Cosmic ray particles strike the Geiger counter and amplified sound waves originating at these encounters strike the ear of the investigator. Denotable columns of mercury record "thermal changes" resulting from the kinetic energies and impacts of molecules or atoms. Denotable materials of compounds that can be experimentally contacted reveal chemical interactions interpreted at a finer level as the coming together or separation of submolecular elements. In many of these methods there is not only a chain of (probable) encounters, but an amplification of the results or a giving of the evidence of encounter *en masse,* so that the comparatively gross texture of the scientist's sensory receptors can pick it up. These procedures, though less direct and immediate than personal contact of the scientist with his "x," are still based upon the "principle" of encounter or denotation in the sense that the assumption that such minute encounters are occurring is the most plausible explanation, according to our present knowledge of natural laws, of the effects observed at the macroscopic level. We shall call this procedure the method of "quasi-denotation."

The expression "quasi," or "as if," is not used in any disparaging sense. For this methodology, though not logically perfect, has vindicated itself by an almost endless series of vital discoveries upon the basis of which predictive laws have been formulated. Another useful term, one that has been implied in the preceding account of denotation, is "grain" or "texture." If one were to touch a small pile of very small shot with one's finger, an onlooker might think that one was referring to the whole pile, or else the reference might be ambiguous. If, however, one were to use as a denoting instrument the point of a needle and were to touch only one shot, the reference would be somewhat clearer. In the first case, also, a thrust of the finger might upset the whole pile, while in the second, the disturbance would be of finer texture. What is true for the denoting observer's action is thus true also for the events of nature, which, as collisions, partake of that same "denotational" characteristic. That is one reason why denotation, as we have defined it, is so fundamental in scientific method. Both coarse and fine grains of denotation are needed for different purposes, according to the magnitude or spread of the structures to be studied. The quasidenotational procedures of science provide finer grains of denotation that enable the scientist to describe what is present or happening in the microcosm.

But let us look again at the two methods in our experiment with Figure 1. We have seen that the second method, in which the lines were encountered and their distances measured, gave both greater freedom from observer-involvement and a greater employment of denotation. There is still another difference. The operations employed in the second demonstration are readily capable of being duplicated by another person. Any one who was standing by could act as observer and apply the straight-edge. In doing so he will be likely to go through essentially the same procedures as the other observer. The operations, at least so far as the movements and manipulations are concerned, are "public." With respect to all three of the criteria of objectivity, therefore, we find a considerable difference between the two methods. In the terms we are using we would say that the second method is the more objective. Since it entails less observer-involvement it is to be preferred over the first as a means of answering the question: "What are the facts regarding the lines?" It so happens that the adjectives ("straight" and "parallel") used in the reports resulting from the two methods were the same; but if there *had* been a difference, we would have done better to have accepted, as an answer to the present question, the report given by the second method.

It is important to notice, further, that as soon as the principle of denotation was introduced it not only brought in a methodology that differed from that of phenomenological reporting, but it also gave rise to something new in the experience-content of the observer. The experience gone through in encountering and measuring in response to the question "What are the facts about the lines?" is a different sort of experience from that evoked by the question "How do the lines look?" Let the reader repeat the tests if he wishes to assure himself on this point.

It will now be understood why we narrowed our definition of percept as we did earlier, or else insisted that, if percept was to be used as a universal term, striking differences between certain classes of percepts must be recognized. Since experience-content affords a way of mapping out our experience into what we may roughly call "parts" or "regions" we can say that with the use of the objectivity-criteria, particularly with denotation, we are exploring a region of experience which is different from that described by the phenomenological procedure. The tasks with respect to these two areas of experience are also different. In the phenomenological method the intent is to describe the experience of the thing; in the objectively oriented method the intent is to describe the thing experienced. For denotational experience, as we shall see, gives us both an evidence of, and a means of describing, the "thing."

Speaking more generally, the three criteria of objectivity seem to lead us, when they are followed, to an order of experience having a uniqueness that sets it apart from purely phenomenological experiences which answer the question merely of how things "appear" but forego the question of how they "are" and make no appeal to criteria for reducing the influence of the observer upon his description. Objectively acquired experiences, in which denotive operations play the leading role, usually display a remarkable dependability and consistency from observation to observation and among the reports of different observers of the same phenomenon. So convincing is the stability of such experience that the criterion of denotation or encounter by which it is evoked is usually taken as the most reliable indication we have that there exists an order we call nature, and that the objects, conditions, and events that we study under this criterion exist independently of the activities of the observer and may be found to occur in certain universal, lawful ways. There are further reasons, also, for considering denotation or encounterability to be an indication of an independent order of nature. These will be presently discussed.[6]

---

[6] There is no proof, of course, that phenomenological experience (the percept) is not also a part of what we call nature. It may also follow certain laws. We have earlier stressed the point that, being an experience-field, it is as legitimate for study as any other part of experience. Such experience, however, from the

This order of experience is the subject-matter of the sciences of physics, chemistry, and physiology, and in fact all those disciplines which rest their case upon objective procedures. We shall call it *physicalistic* experience, in contradistinction to phenomenological, using the term physicalistic broadly to cover various fields of science. The method of observing, studying, and describing with the aid of data from this region of experience we shall call the *physicalistic method*. An approximation to it was used in the second observation of the lines in Figure 1.[7]

FURTHER ASPECTS OF DENOTATION

Our problem of defining perception may seem to have been unreasonably deferred by this long excursion into contrasting methodologies. The discussion, however, has been essential. We soon shall come to our objective more directly. But first we must tarry still longer to consider three points upon which exceptions might be taken or upon which misunderstandings might arise.

As a first point, it might be contended that in the phenomenological observation the subject was really using quasidenotation. Light rays reflected from the object made contact with his eyes, and further contacts, through neural impulses, were mediated to his brain. In reporting how the lines "look" was he not, therefore, following the usual objective procedure of science? So far, the argument sounds reasonable. There is, however, a difference between the phenomenological and the physicalistic description that is reflected in the two questions the subject is set to answer, namely, "How do the lines *look?*" and "What are the facts about the lines?" In the first case the subject is set, if the instruction is correctly understood, to describe his *experience* of the lines; in the second case he is set to describe *the lines themselves*. To do the latter he uses his experience, of course, but this time he relies more systematically upon his *denotive* experience. It might be said that the subject in the first, or phenomenological, description is "quasidenoting" the lines; but the lines are not what he is supposed to describe. It is, rather, his *experience* of the lines. In

---

standpoint of methodology, is clearly differentiated from the type we are here discussing. It does not possess those earmarks of objectivity which give us the assurance that our description of it has acquired the greatest validity possible through being separated from the disturbing influence of the observing process.

  [7] For another discussion of the experience-content of science see Reichenbach (1938).

order completely to follow objective procedure with respect to the first description (how the lines "look") one would have to trace denotively the neural paths and brain connections whose activity accompanies the "looks" of the lines; since it is the organism-dependent, perceiving process that is here concerned. This the subject cannot do; nor does he try. He limits himself to the phenomenological report. In order to deal objectively in the second description it is not necessary to treat denotively these neurological facts, even though they are involved in giving the description; it is only necessary to denote the lines. For the lines are what is being described. The distinction would have been clearer had the phenomenological report been in disagreement with that given by the physicalistic method. Such a case will presently be examined.

As a second consideration, it would be very natural, considering our usual habits of thinking, to infer that what really made the difference between the two methods was "measurement." Quantification and measurement are frequently regarded as the very essence of scientific (i.e., objective) method. It is felt that whenever we can measure we can be certain we are dealing with something clear and definite and that we know just what we are talking about. When we cannot measure we do not have this assurance. The whole story of the difference between the phenomenological and physicalistic methods can therefore be told simply by the "actual measurements taken."

Notwithstanding the fact that the writer is one of the firmest believers in the value of quantitative methods, and indeed in their *necessity*, in science and notwithstanding the fact that measurement *was* used to arrive at part of the physicalistic description, the writer believes that the analysis of the difference between the two methods as just stated does not reveal the essential distinction and is very misleading. Before we could even *begin* to measure in any accurate sense something else had to happen. *Contact had to be made between the measuring instrument and the lines.* Contact is not the same as measurement. It consists of an event, an event of denotation (literally, a collision). *Distances between* events can be measured and *numbers* of events can be counted; but the distances, numbers, and counts would, in themselves, be mere empty abstractions if it were not for the "framework of events," or contacts, that locate their beginnings and endings or their successions. Events in themselves are non-quantitative and non-continuous. They either happen or they do not happen. Quantities are *associated* with them, to be sure, but in order to state or describe them fully some terms *other than* quantitative must be used. The failure fully to grasp this subtle fact and its implications has resulted in many difficulties and will confront us repeatedly in the theories we are to review.

Another reason why measurement is not the true differential between phenomenological and physicalistic methods is that it is used frequently and successfully in the former as well as in the latter—witness measurements in psychophysics along a scale of "just noticeable differences" or "equal appearing" intervals. We come back therefore to our point that it is *denotation*, not measurement, that is the differentiating criterion between the phenomenological and physicalistic performances. By the same token non-quantitative denotational formulations are quite as essential as quantitative in the *theories* to which the descriptions of the phenomena lead. Structure can never be described wholly in terms of quantities, no matter how many quantities are taken or how carefully they are measured.

A third possible source of misunderstanding might arise from the reluctance to admit methodological differences within experience and from the thought that we build the world rationally out of whatever stuff our sensory impressions give us. Experience is experience, so why try to draw lines within it? The differences asserted may be merely matters of sensory mode or quality. Visual and auditory experience figure prominently in what has been called "phenomenology." Touch and kinaesthesis, giving us qualities of pressure and resistance, establish for us the "physicalistic" order. Each of the senses is at times right and at times wrong; but the *tangibility* of an object is usually a pretty good sort of evidence, and so we trust it. The writer, however, insists that the distinction with which we are concerned is one of methodology. It is not a distinction of sensory quality or modality.

Suppose that a man is spending the night in a camp and needs to find a flashlight which he believes to be on the table near his bed. His hand may strike a number of objects, and he may not be aware of what he has struck but only of the fact that he has had experiences of encounter. Both touch and kinaesthesis may, of course, be involved. Now if we use the term phenomenology in the sense of "how things appear," it must be said that there is here scarcely any phenomenological content at all. The things do not "appear" in much of any fashion or to be of any particular sort. There is only a bare experience of denotation. But in addition to such experiences, the man may also realize that he has "knocked over his cigarette lighter" or "upset the bottle of mosquito-lotion." Here we have more than a mere sense of encounter; there are meaningful phenomenological experiences, percepts. No doubt audition has played a part, but *might* the subject not also have obtained these experiences if he were deaf, that is, with the use *only* of touch and kinaesthesis? If, finally, the subject's hand encounters something that he believes to be the flashlight, he may still need a further test to reassure him. Is this not equivalent to saying that the realization that "there is something there" and the awareness of its character and meaning, i.e., how it "appears" or would appear with fuller sensory evidence, are two different experiences.

How does the subject attain this later "phenomenological" assurance? It can be done *with the same senses* that operated in the first bare denotational awareness. There is present in the individual through his past behavior and experience some imagery not only of what a flashlight "looks like" but also of what it "feels like." By applying the test of encounter more finely (i.e., at more points) he makes contact with the "crystal" at one end where it should be, or with the "barrel," or with the switch-button in its proper place, and so on. He does something of the same sort as the reader did in his second observation of the lines when he tested them by a straightedge. As in that observation, further points of contact with the "parts" are attained by which the percept tentatively aroused by the earlier phenomenological procedure can be checked as to its agreement with physicalistic experience. But a part of this confirmation of the "flashlight" percept (not of some object's bare existence) comes from the usual sensory qualities—textures, touch and kinaesthetic blends, and so on—that are aroused by the exploration of such a stimulus object. The same senses, therefore, are used as in the original act of denotation; but there is now evoked, in addition to the experience of encounter, a new experience, the phenomenological percept, that was not there before. As shown above, these two experiences are not identical.

In the second of his experiences it is to be noted that the subject seeking the flashlight may have used denotations of a finer grain (not the hand as a whole) in order to obtain descriptions that were more detailed and complete. He may have used, for example, the tip of his finger. If circumstances in life, speaking more generally, should make it necessary for him to employ a still finer grain, using perhaps a small instrument as encountering object and using quasi rather than direct denotation, he could readily do so. In this way he could experience the object, physicalistically, as fully and minutely as circumstances might require. He could virtually delineate the object by a closely packed series, or "shell," of encounters with its surface. Thus denotational description could become more precise and he could have a purely physicalistic experience of a "thing."

From what has been said we might infer that the blind live closer to the world of objective experience than the seeing. Even here, phenomenological and physicalistic features are clearly distinguishable; the experiences associated with tactual excitation are not one but two. In feeling an object given him a blind person might conclude at first that it is a "bottle" (percept arising through the senses of touch and kinaesthesis). Through using denotation further (i.e., encountering the object at other points) and also through gaining new touch qualities of various sorts, the percept might be made to change. The subject might now "see" the object as a bowling pin or a vase. And again, by carrying the process further, something still different might be perceived. *But in the case of every such change of percept* denotational encounter, so long as it is kept up, gives the subject continually the physicalistic experience that "there is *something* there." This experience, in itself, is quite independent of whatever phenomenological shifts may occur. It continues to exist even *between* percepts and during those instants when the subject may be having difficulty in conjuring up any phenomenology at all. Since the physicalistic does not *depend* on the phenomenological can we not conclude again that these two, though both may involve the same sensory mechanisms, are really separate experiential facts?[8]

In our daily lives we seldom analyze our experience closely enough to bring the two types separately to attention. In the ordinary use of vision we do not bring in direct encounter at all, since we do not usually suspect that we are the victims of hallucinations. We are content to accept the pattern given by light stimulation upon the retina, and to *infer* that an object would be there if we employed the denotational test. The infant combines sight with denotational experience. By encounter, which is a primary experience, and by vision accompanying encounter, he learns to attribute *both* his touch and his visual sensations to some source that is independent of himself (faith of the scientist). To emulate John Stuart Mills' famous dictum, we could say that the reality of the external world becomes to the child, and also to the adult, the "permanent possibility of denotation."

A further reason why the distinction we are making is so often overlooked is that *discrimination among* our experiences is usually a matter of greater practical concern. This is true, of course, only when and because our percepts are in pretty close accord with physicalistic data. Since we do not usually suffer from hallucinations, we do not ordinarily feel that we need to denote. It is enough, and more to the point, merely to discriminate. So important does this latter process

---

[8] The phenomenological may also occur without the physicalistic, as in the case of hallucinations.

seem in the life-adjustment of organisms that at least one psychologist has called it the fundamental operation not only of psychology but of all science.[9] This conclusion seems open to doubt. Behind phenomenology and discrimination, even behind the discriminatory response, there is always the question of objectivity and the methodological rule. If it were not for denotation, the occasion for discriminating the objects on the table in the dark would not be afforded.[10] If the physicist did not believe that the things he is studying are susceptible of some sort of denotation, he would see no point in discriminating among them.

Again we assert our belief that denotation, the experience of encounter, is the *basic* criterion of objective method. Because we here wish to recognize the need also of considering phenomenological experience in the study of perception we have not stressed this point as much as it deserves. A proponent of a phenomenological or idealistic philosophy might contend that the distinction we are making is not fundamental. He might say that in any case all we have is our "experience," and that this is elaborated on the basis of sensory impressions. Reality consists of that which is real to the subject. If he chooses to weight his tactual and kinaesthetic experiences more than his others in arriving at what he considers to be "the real," that is his affair. In any case it is only the weighting that produces the reality for the subject. Our answer must by this time be clear. It will not do to base the belief in reality upon such (allegedly) uncontrolled sensory choices of the subject. We must have a surer criterion; and experience as a whole provides a differential if we will only use it. The differential does not depend merely upon the weighting of certain sensory modalities. It is a methodological as well as a sensory ex-

---

[9] Stevens, 1935a, 1935b. These papers give a concise statement of the strict operational view in psychology. Stevens, however, does not treat discrimination phenomenologically, but as a "discriminatory response" that can be outwardly observed.

[10] In a suggestive article Boring (1937) depicts the activity of perception and overt response as that of an open systemic series, involving, for example, in audition, the stimulus source, air waves, bones of the middle ear, cochlea and its response, auditory nerve, cortical sensory system, motor area, efferent neurons, end-plates, muscular response, and environmental result. Instead of saying that the organism as a whole discriminates among various sounds this author speaks of the cochlea as "discriminating" among events in the middle ear, the eighth nerve as "discriminating" as to what goes on in the organ of Corti, and so on. He recognizes, however, that "discrimination" is not a good term to use in a physicalistic description and suggests that we employ instead a concept of "successive differentiations and the relations between them." One wonders if this concept does not lie pretty close to denotation.

perience. It would be fatal to ignore this differential. If we should disregard it consistently, death, nature's argument *ad hominem,* would ultimately resolve the issue against the phenomenologist. Any system of philosophy which, in postulating experience as the basis of reality, ignores so vital a difference within experience itself as that between the denotational and the non-denotational has failed to take account of the very experiential materials with which it is the business of the philosopher to deal.[11]

We recall the experiment performed by Stratton (1897) and Ewert (1930). Subjects who wore glasses that inverted the visual field were able after a few weeks' practice to make definite improvement in their adjustment to their visually altered surroundings. This improvement was due to the fact that the actual positions of environmental objects were unchanged and it was thus possible to readjust behavior in spite of the altered phenomenological arrangement. Whenever the subject made a wrong movement he was sure to be checked by an unanticipated contact with some object. The contact field itself, however, could hardly be inverted. Non-visual awareness of up and down is ordinarily dependent, through the experience of pressures exerted against our bodies, upon the law of gravitation. Let us suppose that the principle of encounter *could* be made physically deceptive. The only way this could be conceived would be by imagining that wherever the subject had an experience of encounter there was "nothing there," and that wherever he did *not* have such an experience something would be sure to bob up in his path. Could any organism adjust to so chaotic an experience-world as this? To deceive the organism in regard to denotation would be to deceive it about the conditions of life itself.

PHENOMENOLOGY VERSUS OBJECTIVITY: RESULTS OF THE TWO METHODS; VERIDICALITY

The ground is now cleared. We can go on without confusion to the more direct consideration of the nature and meaning of perception. And it is high time that we do so. For in stressing the difference between physicalistic and phenomenological experiences, and in

---

[11] It is for this reason that we have departed from the common practice of using the terms phenomenal and phenomenological as equivalent. We have classified phenomenological experience merely as one type under the broader heading of "phenomena," a generic term which includes physicalistic experience as its other component. Though the word phenomenological is cumbersome we shall use it consistently to convey the distinctive meaning here given it.

stating that the former is always the court of last appeal concerning the physical world, we seem almost to have lost the subject of perception by default. Though physicalistic experience and the criteria of objectivity give the best answer to questions about objects as parts of the physical world, they are *not* good ways of answering the question of how objects appear as dependent upon the perceiving organism. In fact they do not give any answer to that question at all. Yet that is the very question with which the study of perception begins. In checking and measuring the distance between the lines, the subject does not concern himself with "how the lines look." And if he is giving his attention to the latter question, he is then probably not contacting the lines. The setting in the two methods is so different that, if they are rigorously followed, they tend to exclude each other. If we are to stick to our original question, which concerns "how things appear," we must therefore include within our study of perception a set of observations in the attaining of which the objective method is laid aside and the subject gives himself unreservedly to phenomenological reporting.

It might be argued that if the objective method and physicalistic aspects of experience do not give us any answer to the question of why things appear as they do, because they do not permit us to describe their "appearance," then they ought not to be required in studying that aspect in which appearance *can* be described. If phenomenological observation can give us the answer concerning appearance, why not trust it completely for the purpose in hand? Why worry about objectivity in matters that are so clearly non-objective? Gestalt psychologists have made much of the method of direct, unanalyzed introspection, regarding it as a proper method for psychology and as needing no special safeguards against the involvement of the observer. Without a fairly high degree of observer-involvement there would *be* no phenomenological experience or percept.

In the writer's opinion the inability to apply objective standards to the reporting of a percept does not automatically absolve that description from possible errors due to the observer's accompanying activity of observing and reporting. The conditions might be so complex or the subject under such "internal pressure" that he might not be clear as to just how the object does appear. Later chapters will reveal instances where such a difficulty has arisen for perceptual theories. If we are to employ phenomenology (and in the traditional perceptual approach we can scarcely avoid employing it) we must do so not because we feel that the observer who has the experience can describe it accurately, but because no one else can describe it at all.

These caveats should neither discourage nor deter us, for there is much that is interesting and valuable in perceptual theory in spite of the methodological difficulties. And there is much more to be seen concerning the nature of perception that grows out of the two contrasting methods and modes of experience. To return for a moment to the earlier demonstrations, it will be recalled that the reader first made a report about the lines that was based merely upon their appearance to him. He was really describing his experience of the lines, not *facts about* the lines. Later he made another report on the basis of physicalistic methods of observation, reporting this time about the *lines themselves*. Here he contacted, or denoted, and measured. Though we have gone far in elaborating the differences between these two methods, one fact has been largely overlooked. *The reports made by using the two methods were exactly the same.* If the demonstrations were to end at this point, it might seem that great ado had been made over practically nothing. What have we gained by dividing experiences into these two realms and distinguishing their methods with such care? Is a distinction without a difference of result a matter of any real consequence? Why bother to apply the tests of objectivity? The subject can either conceive his task as being in the realm of "physicalistic experience" and object-description, or he can give himself over to phenomenology and statements about the percept —it makes no difference. Things look as they do because they are what they are and could not look any other way.

This judgment, however, is too hasty. Not all perceptual reports agree in their descriptive content with the corresponding physicalistic descriptions in the way in which they were found to agree in this example. We realize this fact immediately by looking at Figure 2. Here we see lines like those of Figure 1, but in a different setting. If the reader will now repeat his two observations exactly as before, the point can be readily made; and in making it we shall come at last to a true understanding of the problem of perception. First we ask, as before, the phenomenological question: "How do the lines appear?" The reply will probably be, for both the upper and the lower figure, that they look *curved*. For the upper figure the report will probably be that they look closest together at the extremes and furthest apart at the center, while for the lower figure they look closest together at the center and divergent at the extremes. Now we ask for the observation corresponding to the physicalistic question: "What are the facts regarding the lines?" If the reader will again use the straight-edge or ruler for testing both the upper and lower figures, thus again bringing in denotation, he will probably report that the lines in both cases are *straight and parallel*. Clearly then, phenomenological and physicalistic procedures may differ not only methodologically *but in their reported results*. The two methods of observing give answers that disagree. It cannot be altogether true that things look as they do because they are what they are.

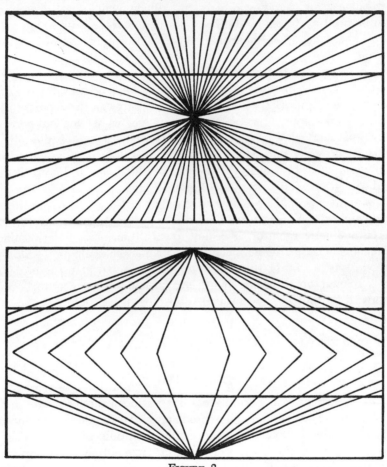

FIGURE 2.

Moreover, if a large number of observers went through the same two procedures for Figure 2 we would doubtless find this same difference of outcome in all the observations. Each type of description is in this case general for a population of observers and follows its own laws. It is evident that pursuing the objective method and satisfying the criteria of denotation, relative observer-freedom, and publicly performable operations may lead to an experience-content that is different from that produced by the phenomenological method with its failure to satisfy these criteria. The question of whether objectivity-criteria are to be used or not therefore becomes significant. One of these methods cannot be substituted for the other without running the risk not only of eliminating the type of experience pertaining to first, but also of changing the report. Phenomenological description must be used to state how the lines "look"; but if we want to know the "facts" about them, we must place our reliance upon the physicalistic account.

It has been seen from our experiments, however, that this hazard in interchanging the methods will not always become an actuality. In dealing with Figure 1 there was *agreement* between the reports in the two methods. For referring to the agreement between a percept-description and the related physicalistic experience of the object, where such agreement exists, perception psychologists have used the term *veridical*. The reader's percept of the lines in Figure 1 was veridical; his percepts of those lines in Figure 2 were non-veridical. But perhaps it would be better to say that in Figure 2 they were *less veridical* than in Figure 1; for the lines in Figure 2 appear only *slightly* curved and convergent or divergent toward their ends. Veridicalness in phenomenological experience is thus a matter of degree. Most of our percepts are fairly veridical, probably more so than those of Figure 2. Some, on the other hand, are so non-veridical as to become serious distortions of the physicalistic experience-content.

THE PERCEPTUAL PROCESS AS AN ORGANISMIC FUNCTION AND
PATTERN: EXAMPLES OF VERIDICAL AND NON-VERIDICAL
PERCEIVING

That the situation in Figure 2 can be generalized over a large range of phenomena is clear to all who have had extended acquaintance with the dramatic field of illusions, those not only of an optical sort, but also in virtually all the senses. Perceptions under excitement or emotional stress are also likely to be non-veridical, though there is at present a question as to what sensory attributes the distortion can affect. The delusions of psychopathic individuals seem to be supported by percepts of a highly non-veridical character. But there may also be some lack of veridicalness in most of our daily perceptions, though for the most part it is so small that it does not need to be compensated for by checking with the physicalistic experience.

The unmistakable cases of the non-veridical that do occur force the problem upon our attention and make us realize that perception, far from being an "epistemology" or a direct representation of truth, is a somewhat variable activity like breathing, digestion, or learning, a process by which organisms succeed in adapting themselves, within the limits of a "tolerable error," to the world in which they live. And like the processes named, it can, from a functional standpoint, occasionally go wrong. But just as a knowledge of physiology or tenable theories about it gives us generalizations for understanding the upsets of digestion as well as its normal course, so the knowledge and theory of the perceptual process should assist us in the explanation of the non-veridical as well as the veridical in perceptions. Acquaintance with the exceptional or illusory thus leads to a deeper realization of the important place of perception in psychological science. The fact that its study by the usual methods involves practices that are lacking in objectivity in no way detracts from its vital significance in behavior. In fact the very conditions that raise these methodological issues are directly related to its significance. Instead of taking it for granted that we see things "as they are" and then being startled, amused, or frightened when our seeing "goes wrong," we are led to wonder that through this process we can come as close as we do to the appraisal of our physical world and to marvel at the mechanism, if that is the proper word for it, that produces within the organism, or between the organism and its surroundings, so "reasonable a facsimile" of the physicalistically experienced order.

We do not have here merely the internal setting up of a photographic plate which we look at and then act accordingly. Such oversimplified explanations belong to the earlier faculty and manikin stages of psychology. There is somehow built up in the organism a dynamic pattern of events that we can say, for want of a better way of expressing it, is *approximately* "in tune" with the world about us. The facsimile of the perceived object or situation is usually not exact, but only "reasonable." It does not come automatically from sensory impressions, but is formed by being integrated or structured, just as the food taken into the body undergoes a structurization in the process of assimilation. Veridical and non-veridical do not constitute distinct categories having peculiar significance in themselves. They are merely particular stages or special cases in the structuring process.

Accompanying this structuring in the organism, which can itself be investigated only physicalistically, is the fact of "consciousness," the realm we have called the phenomenological. Closely related to the physiological, it is not experienced in the same way, in that, as an object of description, it lacks the denotive component. We do not yet know, either empirically or logically, how it is related to our physicalistically described being. Some think it is hopeless to consider it at all, and regard it as a mere "epiphenomenon." All we can truly say is that it seems to "run parallel" with the physical—but not parallel in the full sense, since there are gaps in it when we are asleep or unconscious. It also "checks," as we have seen, in a fairly, but not completely, veridical way, with our *physicalistic* experience of the things which, as stimuli, have given rise to it. And it probably checks to just the degree that the physiological structure of the perceiving process checks. The correspondence, however, is sufficient to build up a consistent phenomenological representation of the "outer world"; and the physiological structuring suffices for an adequate adjustment to that world in the field of overt behavior.

If this account of the perceiving process is in general correct, if there is no *exact* connection between the objects as physicalistically experienced and the physiological structure and its attendant phenomenology, and if the process is, so to speak, "built up" in the organism in its relation to outer objects, then it ought to be possible by some artificial means to produce the perceptual activity and experience by providing certain special features or "essentials" of the environmental situation, even though the situation we create is as a whole different from the one that normally leads to the percept. In other words we should be able to arouse a perceptual activity that is veridical under usual circumstances but non-veridical in the experimental instance in which it occurs.

This outcome is exactly what we find, and the phenomena concerned bring home to us the meaning of this amazing process. The experience of depth in space, usually fairly veridical, can be produced in a situation in which it is highly non-veridical. In looking at two flat pictures in a stereoscope the third dimension appears; but it is observer-involved and phenomenological. It seems to be constructed by our own private, or inner, operations. How non-veridical it is in this instance is realized by our ludicrous attempts to apply the physicalistic test of encounter to objects seen at various distances in the stereoscopic view. The phi-phenomenon (experience of apparent movement) or an evening at the motion-pictures illustrate a similar misplacement with respect to veridicality. A series of slightly varying static pictures shown rapidly at a certain rate is not perceived veridically as separate "stills," but as a single object in motion. The perceptual structuring and experience are there; but the complete environmental conditions that would make the percept veridical are absent, only certain essentials of the stimulus pattern being presented. What we see therefore comports only with a world of make-believe.

This activity seems to consist of a "fill-in," as it were, in perceptual structure and phenomenology of a stimulus-pattern consisting only of certain points. These points, deriving by stimulation from the stimulus object, as in the case of the flashlight for which we are groping, represent environmental items that are capable of producing a denotive, physicalistic experience. But not all the points in the environment, as usually present, are represented in the stimulation and the physiological pattern in the brain; hence there is not a complete correspondence with the physicalistic experience. It is the "fill-in" between these points, as they are neurologically projected on the cortex, together with the related phenomenological experience, that completes the perceptual process and determines, by its degree of correspondence with the stimulus pattern, the degree of veridicalness of the percept. If this conjecture is correct, it is evident that perceptions are not directly or entirely given by the stimulus-objects they represent but are partly works of construction in the organism. And the "facsimiles" that are structured by whatever processes, and that connect or fill in the point-representation of the denotable landmarks, will sometimes be close approximations of the physical objects, but sometimes only "reasonable" likenesses, and occasionally very poor.

Still another example is the non-veridical experience, when blindfolded, of hearing two exactly similar sounds from stimuli, coming from equal distances lateral to the two ears, as if they were one sound coming from somewhere in the median plane. These two air-wave disturbances lead to approximately the same physiological events as would normally be produced by air waves from a single vibrating object in the median plane and veridically perceived in that plane. The percept that is attained, to use Brunswik's conception (Chapter 11), seems to follow some "probability function" of the organism and its *usual* environment.

Perceptual constancies are a class of phenomena that bring the percept of the object into good accord with the physicalistic facts in spite of variations in the stimulus pattern that would tend otherwise to produce a misrepresentation. A table-top viewed at an angle with perspective produces on the retinal surface an irregular quadrilateral figure; but phenomenologically the table-top is experienced as a rectangle. Colors of objects characterizing their surface when seen amid normally experienced surroundings are seen in approximately their proper hues even though they are illuminated by light of a different hue. In these phenomena, instead of our percept being deceptive with regard to physicalistic experience, we find that most of the veridicalness that is "lost at the retina," or lost because of complications in the outer situation, is later restored in the central perceptual process. Physiological structuring and phenomenology can thus at times "fill in" for better rather than for worse.

How this can happen psychologists have never ceased to wonder. But as though to make the problem still more difficult, the percept does not become *completely* veridical. It is a compromise between the receptor image and the physicalistic experience, though leaning toward the side of the latter. To use Brunswik's apt expression it represents, phenomenologically, a "between-object." The key to the riddle seems to lie in our taking fuller account of the whole stimulus manifold, for when attendant features such as light sources, interposed objects, perspective, and the like are experimentally ruled out the percept conforms more nearly to the receptor stimulation-pattern than to the object. When, on the other hand, we take the whole situation into account the physiological structuring also becomes more inclusive. There are represented on the cortex projections from more denotable points in the surroundings, elements not only of the object but of other objects in relation to it. The "filling in" processes and the continuances that connect the mediated points are therefore more numerous and probably assume a more definite relation to one another. The structuring process thus has "more to work on." To state the matter in terms of our methodological principles, we could say that the increase in the number of denotable points, or rather in the mediated effects of such denotable points, takes us further along in the scale of veridicalness, just as a more systematic denotation of the flashlight we are groping for in the dark gives a more detailed objectivity to the physicalistic description and brings the phenomenological percept into closer accord with whatever is actually there.

The physiological basis for this, as for all our previous interpretations, is obscure in the present state of our knowledge. How it actually takes place in the organism is one of the great problems that perceptual theories are seeking to answer. One fact, however, stands out. Even if the popular notion were true that things appear as they do because they are what they are, explaining how we could perceive them as they are, in view of all the vagaries of the stimulus-pattern, would still be a major undertaking. The veridical in perception is as difficult to explain as the non-veridical.

From the functionalistic standpoint the tendency in perception would be expected to be toward the veridical. The physical world is ever present and is so pressing that an organism whose percepts and their physiological bases were not fairly well in keeping with it could not long survive. Functionalism thus becomes a strong note in perceptual theory. There are, however, definite limits to the knowledge which this interest can supply. We can know a good deal about functions without understanding much about the actual processes. We do actually find a wide range of degrees of veridicality in perception. A functional interpretation can usually be found for the various phases of the perceptual act; but it does not tell the whole story. Both the veridical and the non-veridical present their problems. An adequate theory must include both; and in the end it will probably provide a single set of answers by which both can be explained.

In order to realize the full scope of the difference between phenomenological experiences and their physicalistic counterparts let us consider a few more illustrations. The field is much broader than the stock of standard illusions. Estimates of time intervals, based on bodily tensions or on what has happened in the interval, may depart, according to the circumstances, from physicalistically recorded time. Experiences of accentuation or rhythm are usually present in listening to regular, non-accented beats such as those of a metronome. There is also the whole field of sensory qualities and intensities such as those which characterize colors, tones, noises, textures, pressures, smells, and tastes. These, to be sure, are correlated in a rather complex manner with the physicalistic aspects of the stimulus; yet we look in vain for them in the stimulus itself, or even in the physiology of the sensory and cortical systems.

At a more complex level we come to meaning. Phenomenological experiences almost always have a meaning; and we must assume that, in the physiological structuring we have earlier postulated, this aspect also must be represented. The meaning seems to derive from the fact that experience-elements do not come as single unrelated items; there is a complex or aggregate of elements having a certain interrelationship and unity. Unless we were to forego the criteria of objectivity we would not attribute the meaning to the stimulus object or situation itself. As in the case of subjective rhythm and sensory qualities we would consider that it is a contribution made by the perceiving organism.[12] It is not implied that the term meaning refers to

[12] Gestalt psychologists do seem to ascribe meaning to the external situation, as, for example, when one says that a waterfall is "majestic" or the rumbling of thunder "ominous." But it must be remembered that the environment here considered is one that is wholly private to the perceiver and a part of his phenomenology. Though Koffka calls it the "behavioral" environment, that term is very misleading from the standpoint of American objective psychology. Koffka is here referring only to how the environment "appears" to the individual, how he "sees" or "apprehends" it, without check or control by any criteria of denotation or objectivity. This is not the environment at all in the usual sense of that

something that is merely phenomenological. Far from it. Some day we hope to be able to denote its actual physiological process in the organism. We are here merely listing it among the features of perception that are contributed by the organism in their phenomenological or their physiological character.

These examples will suffice to show the lack of identity that exists between what is perceived and what is physicalistically observable in the stimulus-object. The demonstrations with the lines in Figure 2 under the two methods of observing have opened a vast field of inquiry and have shown us some of the phenomena with which theories of perception must deal.

EXPERIMENTATION IN PERCEPTION; THE PHYSIOLOGICAL ASPECT

In our analysis thus far we have repeatedly found it necessary to align upon the side of phenomenology or the percept the physiological basis in the organism that must be considered as its necessary condition. We have contrasted these two, on the one hand, with the physicalistically described stimulus situation on the other. It goes without saying that the *physiological* aggregate, like the stimulus object, is describable only in physicalistic terms. It requires an act of observing wholly separate from the phenomenological reporting—indeed it requires a separate observer. We have in both, however, some contributions that the organism itself is making to the process of perception. Neither the physiological facts nor the phenomenological experience conforms *exactly* to the stimulus-pattern that initiates the process; and in that respect the percept and its physiological basis are alike. We must keep in mind, nonetheless, that these two aspects, though intimately associated, are essentially different. One, the phenomenological, constitutes the non-objective observer-involved experience, the awareness of how things appear. The other, the physiological, is an activity going on in the perceiver's organism that is not observable by the perceiver, that belongs, from the standpoint of another observer, in the denotative realm familiar to the natural sciences. If it is to be observed, it must be done by objective, physicalistic methods, and by an observer who is not involved in the perceptual experience or activity.

---

term.   Objectivity-criteria would not reveal such meanings as resident in actual environmental objects; and indeed the *phenomenology* of *another perceiver* might not reveal them.

The account thus far has been rather one-sided, for we have not paid sufficient attention to this second, physiological, aspect. After all, perceiving is an activity of the organism and as such should be studied more broadly and also more directly than by merely describing its phenomenology or noting how the latter tallies or fails to tally with the stimulus object. It has been noted that perceiving is a process of adjustment like breathing, digestion, or circulation, or, on the behavioral side, like reasoning and learning. The implications of this statement for method and theory must now be indicated. From this standpoint our main attention is upon the description which an experimenter gives when he observes an individual who is perceiving, just as the study of learning, at least in part, is the observation of another individual while he is learning. The procedure always requires, at least in principle, the presence of another observer beside the individual whose perceptual process is being studied. This means that we have one individual, the "subject," who introspects and reports upon his experience or else does something overtly with the objects or apparatus at hand, and a second individual, the experimentalist-observer, who observes the observing activity of the first and records any report or other overt indications which the latter may give.

What should this report or these indications be like? Here opinions differ. We have, first, the possibility that it may be a phenomenological description, a statement of how the stimulus-pattern "appears" to the subject. In this case the theory to be developed would incorporate phenomenological considerations and would undertake some obligation as to their linkage with the physiological facts being gathered by the experimentalist-observer. This procedure has been more or less traditional and is still followed. Another possibility, now coming into practice, would be to consider what the subject says as merely a "verbal response," or to have him perform some manipulative discriminatory act with respect to the stimulus. Here phenomenology (the percept) would be completely ignored. The method would be entirely objective, or as nearly so as possible. The theoretical explanation would be in terms only of the behavior and, in some cases, if possible, the hypothesized neurological linkage between stimulus and response. No further responsibility would be undertaken, even though the phenomenological aspect was left hanging. An intermediate type of approach has also been employed. The subject can attempt to "externalize" or "depict" some aspect of his percept by physicalistic means. He cannot *really* do this, of course, for phenomenological data cannot be denoted. But he can, for example, arrange some expansible or contractible apparatus so that it appears to him to be the "same size" as the stimulus-object. Physicalistic determinations "as if" of the percept could thus be obtained from the setting of the apparatus and linked up for purposes of theory with some behavioral or neurophysiological considerations. One can thus use phenomenology as a starting point without giving it too much systematic importance or assuming an obligation to incorporate it, *qua* phenomenology, in a theoretical system.

Since, however, we have already canvassed the subject's report and its relation to the stimulus-object, our main interest now centers upon the perceptual process itself as it is studied by the experimentalist-observer in a purely physicalistic manner. The methodological rule of objectivity with all three of its criteria now comes fully into play. The stimulus-object will, of course, be brought into the picture since it is germane to the total process. But here the experimenter or theorist treats it merely for the part it plays as related to the physiological system of the perceiver; and he follows through with the operation of that system by the aid of hypotheses based on what he already knows about it, and, insofar as possible, by direct investigation to obtain new physiological facts.

The train of facts to be considered is as follows: There is, first, the object or the pattern of events to be perceived. This is sometimes called the "distal" stimulus object, since in the senses of vision and hearing, for example, it lies at a distance from the perceiver. Next there are, in such cases, the intervening light or sound waves or other conditions that lead to a pattern of energic change in a sense organ, that is, at a receptor surface. This pattern of peripheral excitation is called the "proximal" stimulus or stimulus proper. Following this phase there is a conduction of impulses toward the brain along afferent neurons, the impulses arriving at lower brain centers and also at the sensory projection areas of the cortex. There occurs then some pattern of events in the central nervous system, probably, though not exclusively, in the cortex. Such a pattern involves synaptic connections and excitations of other neurons in the area and extending into adjacent or remote "association" areas. To these steps there should be added, in order to include all the factors that might influence perceptual activity, the presence of organic states, correlates of need conditions, hunger, emotional excitement, fatigue, and the like. The autonomic system is thus brought into play. Both the blood stream and afferent impulses to the spinal cord and brain from visceral receptors are involved. But still another important set of processes must be considered. In many cases, at least, there is a discharge of efferent neural impulses from either cortical or lower motor centers, leading to some muscular or glandular reaction. The muscular contractions, in full or as changes of tonicity, in turn stimulate receptors in the muscles, tendons, and joints (proprioceptive or kinaesthetic stimulation) as the effectors act either by postural changes or by overt movements with reference to the stimulus-object. This phase is the "overt response" to the perceived object. As a result of such proprioceptive stimulation afferent impulses are "fed back" to the lower brain parts and the cortical sensory areas. A kind of circular arrangement, or circuit, of physiological ongoings and events is thus completed. Since these responses and their returning impulses play a part in perceptions and are therefore considered in a number of perceptual theories we need to include them in the total physiological equipment of the perceptual act.

The full physiological basis of perceiving is thus practically the same as that of any act of behavior; only we are now considering it not so much from the standpoint of what the organismic system overtly does, learns, or remembers as from the standpoint of how it physiologically "recognizes" or "differentiates" the objects and situations of its environment. From the phenomenological, in contrast with the behavioral, viewpoint we are also considering it for what it can contribute in answering the question, "Why do things appear to the perceiver as they do?"

The preceding account seems to have implied that the relevant details of the receptor processes, neurons, central nervous system, and musculature are readily accessible, at the most minute levels of denotation, to the experimenter. This, of course, is not true. Though considerable is known about these matters, neurophysiological techniques have not advanced sufficiently to permit such minute observation of all phases of the perceptual process. We therefore find that the "descriptions" attempted are often presented in conceptual rather than empirical terms. That is, denotation and quasidenotation are frequently employed only "in principle," rather than in actuality. Explanations are proffered in terms of denotable elements, though it may not yet have been entirely proved that such elements are present or that they operate in the manner required by the theory.

A way out of these difficulties is taken by some behaviorists who not only discount phenomenology but make a virtue out of an empirical necessity and say that the business of the psychologist is to "stay out" of the interior of the organism and develop his theory in terms of the behavior of the organism *as a whole*. This method is called the "molar" approach. By neglecting both phenomenology and neurology the problem not only remains entirely objective but at the same time is greatly simplified. It requires only macroscopic denotation of a very crude sort. As for what goes on in the organism when perception takes place, a "hypothetical construct" of some sort, mediating between the stimulus and the (perceptual) response, will take care of that. More will be told about this method presently, and in later chapters we shall discuss some of its successes and limitations. Some perceptionists remain "molar" without discarding the phenomenological percept; while some try to use a finer grain of denotation ("molecular") without worrying too much about phenomenology.

EXPLANATION AS LYING ON THE PHYSIOLOGICAL SIDE

We must now bring together the various strands of procedure, appraise them more fully, and try to see if they can be combined into one consistent program. From what angle can we best approach the task? Explanation is surely a primary objective of all theories and hence a good criterion for the evaluation of methods. Let us then begin by recalling the statement made about that criterion in Chapter 1. Explanation was defined as the providing of a more generalized description, combined with the demonstration that the instance before us is a case to which the generalization applies. In order to attain this more widely generalized description the study of perception, as we have shown, may well be pursued in both its phenomenological and its physicalistic aspects. For showing how the generalization fits the given case both methods, from a logical standpoint, could also be used.

It has been found in practice, however, that a theory based upon phenomenology is not highly rewarding for this purpose. Its method of ordering a specific phenomenon to a general principle is likely to be little more than obvious classifying of percept-characteristics. It tells us little we have not already received from the subject's report.[13] The non-denotive character of phenomenological description prevents the direct experimental availability of its explanatory concepts and makes it difficult to discern any fundamental connection between one of its parts and another. The physiological scene affords better explanatory opportunities. Even though our knowledge here is limited,

---

[13] For example, in the purely phenomenological part of gestalt theory, all we have is the demonstration that a certain figure illustrates "closure," another "prägnanz," another "requiredness," and the like. As an attempt to *explain*, this procedure would amount practically to tautology.

the very fact that receptors, neurons, and muscle fibers are denotable and that their processes are often capable of experimental detection and study helps us to see that, in a particular instance of perceiving, some broad physiologically or physically expressed principle underlying the phenomenology may be illustrated. For this reason a satisfactory theory of perception must carry on a large part of its work of explanation in the physiological rather than the phenomenological realm. It should convey some notion of an appropriate conceptual model described in denotational or quasidenotational terms; and most theories do include such a feature.

But at the same time we must recognize a limitation. For reasons of logic the conduct of explanation at the physiological level cannot be regarded as "crossing the gap" between our two orders of experience. In the last analysis explanation must remain in some respects incomplete. Phenomenological and physicalistic descriptions cannot be mingled as causes and effects in one explanatory account without a violation of basic physical principles. More will be said on this subject in Chapter 4. All we can say, at present, is that phenomenological experience (the percept) and the neurophysiology of the organism are conceived as "running parallel" to each other. Psychological theorists have never been able to get behind this postulate of psychophysical parallelism, though some have ignored it. Nevertheless, within the limits of a parallelistic assumption, it is generally agreed that an objectively conceived, physicalistic account of what is happening in the organism holds out better possibilities for explanation than do phenomenological concepts. A nexus of events can be traced at least upon the physiological side. This side affords a "mechanism" through which the operation of principles can be elucidated, while phenomenology does not. There is a tendency, therefore, for practical purposes, to assume that events of physiology and neural action are sufficient and satisfactory explanations of phenomenological experience. Especially is this so where an attempt is made to link the two in some formal or figural way (isomorphism). In discussing the various theories we shall proceed, though with the above stated reservation, upon this basis.

OPERATIONISM VERSUS PHENOMENOLOGY; INTROSPECTION VERSUS DISCRIMINATORY RESPONSE; ATTEMPTS TO RESOLVE THE DILEMMA

At this point the ground upon which perceptual theory is formulated is likely to seem a bit slippery. If the above considerations were to be pressed a little further, the whole question of perception and its method of study might come up for reappraisal. We have seen that the phenomenological method is lacking from the standpoint of objectivity. If now we see, further, that the responsibility for explanation is thrown over to the physiological side and that phenomenology cannot readily be integrated into a scheme of complete explanation, of what use then is phenomenology?

Before trying to answer this question let us review the situation and some of the consequences to which it has led. Thus far we have shown that there must be two observers in the investigation. On the one hand there is the subject, that is, the perceiver, whose task it is to tell us how things in his environment are appearing to him. His report (that is, the report of the phenomenology or "appearance") is relatively unsatisfactory in relation to the criterion of objectivity. It fails to provide anything that will satisfy the need for observer-detachment, encounterability, and public operations. But still it is a part of the total picture. Have we a right to ignore it? On the other hand there is the experimentalist-observer who can neither observe nor report the subject's experience, but whose duty it is to observe the subject as the latter is perceiving. In this task a relatively high degree of objectivity on all three criteria can be attained; and the report consists of all physicalistically describable matters, internal or external to the organism of the perceiver, as they are involved in the perceptual activity. This method, though its data cannot be ideally integrated in a single explanatory system with the phenomenological, affords the best available avenue to explanation. There is also the question of the degree of veridicalness of the subject's report, conceived merely as a descriptive response or discriminatory adjustment to the stimulus. For the determination of this feature the physicalistic method is again necessary, this time as applied to the description of the stimulus-object. The degree of veridicalness not only points up the fact that phenomenological and physicalistic experiences may be different, but constitutes in itself a finding that must be incorporated into perceptual theory whether that theory be wholly objective or otherwise.

This complex and various-sided program has not been satisfactory to a considerable number of psychologists. It seems to require an epistemological dualism that is disturbing in the consistently monistic scheme of science. In particular, the lack of objectivity of the phenomenological method has been challenged. Operations for defining the concepts with which we work, some say, should not be the purely private property of the observer. They should always be *publicly* performable and free from observer involvement. When the perceiver says that the lines in Figure 2 have the "appearance" of being curved we do not really know what he is talking about. But what, we may ask, are the consequences of this highly critical attitude? To apply rigidly the standard of the criteria of objectivity would, of course, rule out introspection altogether. One would not ask the perceiver how the world "appears" to him. The only legitimate procedure would be to study his behavior, and, if possible, his internal, physiological processes. We would thus abolish the phenomenological report, or else ignore it, and pin our whole faith upon objectively observable data.[14]

But would not such a procedure be equivalent to abolishing the whole problem of perception? Can we tell what the subject is perceiving, or that he is perceiving anything, if we do not have his report of how things appear to him? The critics would promptly reply that we can still tell whether the subject "has a perception"; though of course we must define perception differently and must answer the question by sound operational procedures.

For example, suppose that a subject who is unfamiliar with the English language, or at least with its color-names, has been trained through the conditioning of his speech mechanisms to react to a reflected light of a certain range of wave-lengths by speaking the word "blue" and to react to a light of a different wave-length range by speaking the word "red." It will be noted that the terms blue and red are not used here to describe any phenomenological appearance, but only as differentiating responses to different stimuli. Suppose now we take a number of objects that reflect light of the former wave-length range and mix them up with a number reflecting the latter wave-length range. We now ask the subject, on the basis of his training, to select all the objects for which he would speak the word blue and place them in one pile, and to place all those for which he would say "red" in a different pile. If he does this task correctly, we can say that he is "perceiving" blue and red. That is all there is to it. What the subject might be said to be inwardly experiencing in the nature of "color quality" or "hue" is of no consequence. The reaction made to one set of stimulus-objects that correctly separates it from another set is all we need. That reaction *is* the perception. It might even be possible to demonstrate illusions or perceptual constancy in a similar way.

This method can be summed up by saying that a perception can be regarded as nothing more nor less than a *discriminatory response*.

14 Cf. Stevens, 1935*a* and *b*.

The subject has behaviorally "discriminated" light of different wavelengths; or, as Boring would say, his nervous system has "differentiated" these two classes of stimuli. By such a procedure it is maintained that we can define and study perception, and we can do it in a manner in keeping with the objective methods of science. Psychology does not need to be an exception to the methodological rule.

To such an ignoring or dodging of the percept, psychologists of a different persuasion have taken vigorous exception. Without denying certain values of the behavioral approach or the need of the experimenter for objectivity, they contend that the report of the subject's own experience, that is, the way the world appears to him, is an essential part of the record and that theory should always proceed by taking this into account. Such experiences, even though personal to the subject, are too significant to be laid aside. The many sensory qualities, intensities, and experiences of magnitude, the many sights, sounds, feels, odors, and tastes, to say nothing of perceived spaces, times, shapes, and the multitudinous aesthetic and cultural meanings that we enjoy in daily life, constitute a manifold too rich and pervasive for psychologists to ignore. Reducing everything to a set of discriminatory responses is a ridiculous oversimplification. To sacrifice all this experience-content for a methodological canon, though such a rule may be highly useful in other connections, is to throw out the baby with the operational bath. Any rule that precludes the experimental and theoretical consideration of such phenomena is too narrow and should be reconstrued.[15]

And so the issue is joined. That it is a true dilemma can be readily seen. One thing, perhaps, that the stricter operationists have overlooked is that phenomenological experience is still *experience* and as such belongs in the domain of science as legitimate content for study. Though it is true that one can often tell whether a person is undergoing an illusion by the way he outwardly behaves, it is also true that he experiences that illusion and can tell you what it looks like. The word illusion can be defined in either way, and in either case some experience is involved. The percept-illusion is a phenomenon to the man who has it, and, in the case of many illusions, to nearly everyone else who reacts in the same situation. Since a characteristic of useful theories is their completeness of coverage of the phenomena in the area concerned, we have a plausible reason why phenomenological findings should not be ignored. Though one method of investigation may well be preferred over another, the question of *what* is to be

[15] For this general viewpoint see Pratt, 1939.

studied should not be confused with the question of the *method* by which it is to be studied.

The dilemma as it now presents itself is as follows: If we *incorporate* phenomenological description in the investigation and theory of perception, we must do so in clear violation of the rule of objectivity. We are dealing with something to which criteria of objectivity cannot be satisfactorily applied. We are also dealing with something which, *in itself*, is relatively poor in explanatory clues. If we *exclude* phenomenological description, we are excluding a portion of experience which is, per se, as valid a content for description and explanation as any other. We do not want to reject arbitrarily, or even on the grounds of reputable methodology, a whole realm of experiential facts. On the other hand our knowledge of the world of physicalistic experience is much more continuous, consistent, and dependable; and the criteria of denotability and observer-detachment are so important for giving us confidence in our findings that they have become universal and practically mandatory in science. And so we are forced to ask ourselves this question: Which is more important to us: to canvass in *some* way every class of phenomena that comes within our experience, whether the method available for its study be satisfactory or not, or to limit our investigations, and therefore our knowledge, within the bounds of an ideal method?

Physics, chemistry, and physiology are not beset by this dilemma. They can press objectivity to the limit without sacrificing any part of their subject-matter. The difficulty is peculiar to psychology; for psychology is the only discipline in which the question of why things *appear* as they do is asked. The problem, moreover, does not trouble us in many phases of psychological work; it is only in the traditional field of perception that it becomes acute. In the other sciences mentioned the scientist is simply and directly observing nature. The perception psychologist is also observing nature; but the aspect or part of nature that *he* is observing is not so direct and simple. For the part of nature that he is observing is the process of observing nature!

How can the dilemma be resolved? Perhaps we can do no better than to take the traditional course laid down by investigators of the past. Notwithstanding the importance of employing the rule of objectivity in every area where it can be employed, and fully recognizing this necessity, perhaps we can make an exception in the study of perception because we must. This decision is, of course, in no way an excuse. It must leave us with considerable doubt as to our findings and their significance; but we could say, at least, that we had not left any aspect of experience out. Phenomenology, after all, *is* experience. Why then do we not accept this fact and include the phenomenological observation and description provided by the perceiver? In so doing we simply do the best we can from the standpoint of methodology. When difficulties or doubts arise (and, as we shall see later, they will arise) we can then make liberal allowances for possible errors, always remembering the limitations and uncertainties of the method. We must of course use phenomenological description *in conjunction with* as full and careful a study as possible of the physiological aspects and a record of the subject's outwardly observable behavior. Such an objectively oriented part of the investigation is basic to any attempt to construct a sound and general theory. The study of these two realms combined, and the effort toward their conceptual integration within the total pattern of the organism's behavior, thus constitute a workable basis for the theory of perception.

Sometimes, perhaps, the report of the phenomenological experience can serve as a convenient guide to the physicalistic approach. It may help in bringing to light phenomena that should be explained or in suggesting regions for physicalistic observation, in much the same way that a pain reported at a certain location may be a diagnostic guide to the physician. In obtaining phenomenological descriptions, procedures having greater precision than uncontrolled estimates or language symbols can be employed. For example, in reporting how weights or sizes appear to the subject, comparisons with other weights or sizes, or perhaps the "production" method, in which the subject regulates some movable apparatus, can be used. Experiments can be so arranged that introspective reports will not interfere with the securing and accurate recording of physicalistic findings, and vice versa; and there are many devices by which phenomenological and physiological elements of a sort that are not germane to the hypothesis can be controlled. On the side of theory, the investigator can be careful that his explanations involve no "interaction" between phenomenologically and physicalistically described elements. The postulate of psychophysical parallelism and the avoidance of animistic explanations can be maintained.

Using this dual or combined method of study, but with many precautions of this sort, researches in perception and perceptual theory have made great strides. They have advanced our knowledge even though their methods have fallen short of perfection. Though workers will naturally follow the procedures that seem to them most adequate, there seems no good reason to relinquish all these gains and to leave suspended the large array of phenomenological data already gathered, without hope of coördinating them with objective description or incorporating them into any workable system. The road we have indicated above is the one that has been mainly travelled; and for our appraisal of the theories it would be best, for the present at least, to go along.

3

The Phenomena of Perception

But we are not yet through with Koffka's question. Before we begin our review of theories explaining why things appear as they do it would seem pertinent to inquire "How do they appear?" Though we have canvassed this question in Chapter 2 our treatment there was largely in terms of the agreement between the phenomenological appearance and the stimulus-object as objectively described. There are other phases of the appearance of things that are not well covered by that comparison; and some of these were also touched upon in the earlier discussion, but, again, from a somewhat specialized standpoint. We need now to bring these "aspects of appearance" together and look at them more directly as features of content that are characteristic of percepts in general and that should be related through investigation and theory to the study of the perceiving organism. Are there in all the endless variety of our perceptions a few broad categories into which the essentials of the phenomenology, and therefore of the associated physiological processes, will be found to fall, headings which, though distinct, are yet not isolated, but are parts of a total, integrated perceptual content and act? To set up any such primary classification requires a certain temerity, and different classifiers might disagree. Nevertheless it behooves us to make the attempt, since the listing of the major phenomena that must be explained by perceptual theories is a necessary starting point if we are to examine those theories intelligently, and particularly if we are to appraise their generality or completeness.

Most of the categories of phenomena we shall describe as making up the phenomenon-class of perception will be seen to be of a phenomenological character. They are statements of different but characteristic ways in which things appear to the perceiver. To some extent this emphasis is the result of the manner in which perceptual experiments and theory-building have been traditionally approached.

The viewpoint is a natural one. It leads to a method that is productive of interest and challenges our explanatory efforts from the start. Without it, as we have said, the experimental study of perception would seem rather barren. It should be remembered, however, that perception is also an activity of the organism. It involves receptors, neural impulses, cortical patterns, and motor elements, to say nothing of the possible influence of sets or of bodily states such as need, motivation, emotion, and the like. Some of these elements will be mentioned in the phenomenal categories we are to define. It should be assumed that the only reason why these physicalistic aspects are not *always* mentioned, along with the phenomenological, as phenomena of perception is because they are not yet clearly known or their roles are not yet clearly differentiated. It is upon our later knowledge of them that an explanation of the perceptual process must ultimately be based. In a very real sense, then, these physiological aspects, earlier summarized in Chapter 2, should also be considered as belonging among the phenomena of perception. Quite apart from the question of why things appear as they do, or even of how they appear, we have seen that the problem of the physiological perceptual aggregate and how it is structured in the organism into a similitude with objects in the environment, thus making possible an integration of the organism's entire behavior, goes to the very heart of the perceptual process.

SIX BROAD CLASSES OF PERCEPTUAL PHENOMENA

The phenomena of perception can be classified for our present purpose under six headings. These classes and their illustrations may seem quite elementary to the reader, taking him over ground with which he may be already familiar. The review of what may seem obvious, however, is essential in order to get the task confronting perceptual theorists clearly before us. We shall take our start by imagining that we are looking at various discs, circles, or other simple objects under a variety of conditions. Though for convenience our main examples will be visual, all the phenomena we shall consider could be readily illustrated in other sensory fields.

1. First, a small paper disc is shown on a white background. We notice that it appears red. Another disc is shown which looks blue, and so on. A certain experienced "quality"—in vision we call it hue or color—is one of the most obvious aspects of the way things appear. The tone we hear, the smell of a rose, a taste, a pain, an experience

of pressure, warmth, or cold are other familiar examples. We also observe that the quality has associated with it certain quantities or dimensions. In vision, at least, the quality is "spread out" or extended; it seems to occupy space. Related to quality we have also the experience of "intensity," or of "strength." One gray disc looks brighter or darker than another; one red is stronger (more "saturated") than another; one tone may be louder or softer than another; and so on. Qualitative experiences also endure through time. *Sensory qualities and dimensions,* therefore, constitute one general aspect of the way things appear to us.[1] It is true that these qualities and dimensions are often modified by the conditions or surroundings under which they are observed, such, for example, as background and illumination.   They may interact with one another in many ways, but the existence of qualities can never be fully accounted for by this interaction.   Though our perceptions as wholes are far more complex than the simple qualities and sensory dimensions, these latter are nevertheless present.

There has been some difficulty with classification and terminology in this field.   Looking at the matter from the standpoint of pure conscious awareness Titchener regarded sensations as elements of consciousness, and quality, intensity, extensity, duration, and clearness as attributes (or dimensions) of sensation.   This scheme proved unsatisfactory because there was nothing for the term sensation to mean *except* these five attributes.   Aside from these it was a pure abstraction.   The practice of making such fictitious "sensations" into elements or building blocks of consciousness represented the piecemeal, mosaic theory of experience which the gestalt psychologists so vigorously challenged.   It seems better, perhaps, to regard not sensation but the experience of "quality" as a basic fact in our awareness of our world, a fact contributed by the processes of the organism itself to the energies received from the stimulus.   Quality, as we have seen, is something that is unique.   It is different experimentally from the dimensions with which it is nevertheless always associated.   It "comes" in the dimensions of extensity, intensity, duration, and the like; but it can never be reduced wholly to these or any other dimensions.   It is true that it would disappear if intensity, extensity, or duration were reduced to zero.   But this fact makes sense because the same would be true of any objects, even those of the physically experienced world.

But is there a dimension in quality per se? Are qualities them-

[1] Helson has listed no less than eighteen possible dimensions of color experiences.   (See Helson (ed.), 1951, Chapter 8.)

selves distributed along an unbroken continuum of small steps? It has seemed to some psychologists as though this were true. The hues of the general modality of color, for example, have been described as arranging themselves in a continuous series along the base of a color pyramid. Discriminable tones, such as those of the musical scale, are a successive series of fairly small steps. This conception is probably what led the earlier introspectionists to call quality an attribute or dimension of an abstract construct, sensation. It would seem that there is a confusion here. The *primary* hues do not really form a continuum. Each is unique and at quite a distance from all the others as indicated by the corners of the color model. What lies between these regions might be called a continuum of intermediate qualities (blue-greens, oranges, purples, etc.) which resemble the primary components in varying degrees, but which terminate sharply at the primary quality itself. There are many intermediate series, blends, or fusions of qualities in different degrees of intensities or strengths. Each of these blends, it is true, is usually perceived as an unanalyzed, unique "whole." It is often possible, however, to attend to its primary components separately. Both the totality and its constituents are there, though the percept may not give us both with equal clearness in consciousness at the same time. To ignore or slight the elementary or primary qualities because of commitment to a particular theory or a method of introspection is to close one's eyes to facts that are matters of everyday experience.

2. Our second class of perceptual phenomena contrasts sharply with the first. Though like those in the first they are experiences arising from things in the environment, they seem even less determined by the stimulus and more determined by processes inside the organism. They exhibit strongly the effect of one thing upon another in the perceptual manifold, an effect which frequently produces optical or other illusions. They are concerned mainly with the formal properties of the things we perceive, such as shape, outline, grouping, and the like. Looking at a circle drawn with ink on a white card, we note that the appearance of its size is altered if it is placed between parallel lines, or enclosed in an angle. It can be made to appear distorted into part of a spiral by a twisting line along its course and by special features in the background. A square turned up on one of its corners looks quite different (diamond-shaped) from the way it appears when its upper and lower edges are in a horizontal position. Looking at the drawing of the circle again, but without accompanying lines or angles, we see that it encloses an area that is "segregated"

from the surroundings, and that the line of the circle itself is a "contour" that seems to belong to the circle as its edge and not to be the edge of a circular hole in the background. We see that the circle appears as a definite "figure," standing forward clearly, and that the rest of the card seems to extend beneath it as a less vivid "ground." Figure and ground are ubiquitous aspects of perceptions. In every sense-modality our world consists of figures appearing against grounds, and where other aspects are not in control there are a number of rules that determine which part shall be figure and which ground. In drawings in which either portion may serve as figure or ground there is usually a shift of the percept back and forth from one figure-ground experience to the opposite.

Figural units, dots, and the like appear to "go together" or to separate themselves into clusters according to conditions. If two figures are joined, they may seem to constitute a single larger figure or to separate into two figures according to certain arrangements they possess. A figure which is by itself simple and clear will often be very difficult to perceive when it is embedded as a part of a larger, closely knit whole. Parts, in joining, form uniquely perceived wholes. A part embedded in the context of a whole appears different from its appearance when it is experienced separately. Similar organizing and unifying effects occur in auditory experience. If we hear a series of regular taps, all equal in intensity, a rhythm possessing strong and weak beats subjectively imposes itself on them. Two spots of light shown near each other with a certain time interval between will appear as the continuous movement of a single spot. If the circle we are looking at is broken or is composed of a ring of dots, it will still be perceived, in effect, as a completed circular figure. A relationship between the parts in the unified "wholeness" of a percept can be shown to have some kind of existence which transcends the particular parts related, so that if the latter are changed, with due respect to their proportionalities, the relationship (wholeness) still remains recognizable. This fact is shown in the transposition of melodies from one key to another (form-quality). It is also demonstrated in experiments in which chicks trained by food-reward to respond to the darker of a pair of grays will, when the gray reacted to is paired with a new and still darker gray, be likely to choose the latter instead of the former, that is, instead of the specific gray to which they have been trained to respond.

The above facts show that perception proceeds by interrelationships within definite wholes, one part affecting other parts. Nothing ever occurs by itself; and a "whole-character" is formed by the ensemble that cannot be experienced in the parts when they are perceived separately. This then is our second large class of the aspects of perception. It will be seen that they are somewhat abstract, in that in order to experience them we must ignore much of the more obvious content of our experience of things. They relate to the form of the perceptual experience rather than to its content. Phenomena of this class are commonly known as the *figural* or *configurational* aspects of perception.

3. Suppose now there is presented a circular disc, first directly before us in the frontal plane where it is of course seen as circular, and then in a position tilted away from us so that the image it produces on our retinas is elliptical in shape. We *still* tend under the latter conditions to see the disc as circular, not as elliptical. We do not, however, see it as perfectly circular, but as a compromise that favors the circular more than the elliptical form. This is the phenomenon of *perceptual constancy.* It preserves for us a constancy of appearance and thus the means of recognizing and identifying objects when they are seen at different angles or in different positions. It is to be found also in the perception of sizes at different distances and of colors and brightnesses under differing conditions of illumination. Cues given by the object and surroundings enter intimately into perceptual constancies. These cues seem to be "utilized" in agreement with past experience; and for the most part they give us fairly veridical perceptions.

4. A fourth class of aspects appears when we are faced by the problem of giving absolute dimensional judgments concerning the members of a series of stimuli. This feature is not to be confused with sensory dimensionality as it was discussed in our first category where, for example, brightness or loudness were estimated with reference to some objective standard. The aspect we are now considering refers, rather, to the question of what we *call* "bright" or "dull," "light" or "heavy," "loud" or "faint," and the like with respect to stimuli that we experience. Suppose, for example, that we are presented with a lot of circular discs of the same size, one after the other. Let the discs, however, be in the form of spots of light thrown on a screen and differing over a fairly large range in brightness. We are to judge for each disc whether we consider it to be "bright" or "dim" or "medium." Though no standard of reference is *given,* there will probably be determined, after a series of stimuli has been pre-

sented, a degree of brightness that looks to the observer as "neutral," that is, a degree above which the discs appear to be "bright" and below which they appear to be "dim." The individual, in other words, forms his own subjective scale of judgment. We shall call this phenomenon the *dimensional frame-of-reference* of perception.

5. We come now to a universal aspect of perception that will seem almost too obvious to mention. It is quite distinct from any of the aspects we have described, though it is related to them. Though it is not necessary to do so, let us approach the matter by beginning with subthreshold conditions. Suppose we are looking at some object, with a view to identifying it, under very brief exposure or under an illumination insufficient for its recognition. The exposures in a series of trials are then gradually lengthened or the illumination is gradually increased. We see at first a kind of reddish blur having a roundish form, but identification of the object does not come. Exposure or illumination are further increased and we try again. A number of trials without success, or with "misperceptions," may occur. Then, all at once, we recognize it. *It is an apple.* It is not a red circular disc, it is not a beet or a round red ball—but an apple. There is no mistaking it, for it has many telltale features. We cannot say it is just a color experience. It is not adequately characterized by its configurational or "wholeness" properties alone. Though it has a certain texture, organization of parts, continuity of contour, and is seen as a figure against a ground, it is something more than any of these properties. It will obey the law of size or color constancy, and one can readily establish a frame of reference for "apples" stating whether this object appears, *as an apple*, to be large or small; but obviously neither of these aspects adequately describes it.

This aspect of perception is so universal and characteristic that it would be hard to find anything regarding the appearances of things that is more significant. Things and events appear to us not as mere qualities, dimensions, or forms, but as things and events. *Concrete object character*, as we shall call it (using the term object very broadly), is a fundamental property of practically all our perceptions. Perhaps the most salient feature of this phenomenon is that it represents "meaning." The meaning that it represents, however, is not that of mere configuration or wholeness of the object, not how large or bright the object is, but the experience of *what* the object is. Since events also are included in our broad definition of "object" we can extend this aspect to include the concrete character or meaning of actions and situations.

6. In the first three of the categories, sensory qualities and dimensions and the configurational and constancy features, we were describing aspects of perception that would be likely to hold true for all individuals at all times. In the fourth and fifth categories we have also noted features that would probably be largely the same for all individuals having a common background of experience. We come now to an aspect of perception in which individual differences, as well as differences in the state of an individual at different times, play an important role.

It has long been known that particular sets of the individual, or attitudes, either long standing or momentary, affect the selection of the objects that will be perceived and to some extent the readiness with which they are perceived. Phenomenologically they also result in a greater attentive clearness or vividness of those objects. To this aspect of perception the concrete-object character of the stimulus is especially relevant, for when we take the character and meaning of the object into account we can often see a relation between it and the state the individual is in. The phenomenon is most clearly shown with respect to objects that we are looking for or meanings that we are seeking to realize from stimulus-situations that are undetermined or vague. If, for example, we are not looking at relatively meaningless outline-circles or colored discs, but are in search of a valued brooch we have lost, our state of having a felt need, combined with our set to find that particular object (which includes our keeping in mind "how it looks"), greatly facilitates our search and may shorten its time. Perceptual sets or readinesses induced by needs are both common and important. Emotional states may also determine perceptual readiness or the manner in which we perceive certain objects or relationships. An illusion in which, on a dark night, one sees a tombstone in a cemetery as a ghost is a timeworn example. The way in which indefinite or ambiguous things are perceived may to some extent be influenced by the individual characteristics of the perceiver, a fact implied by the use of the Rorschach test for personality diagnosis. To complete our list we must therefore add a sixth phenomenal aspect of perception which we shall call *the effect of the prevailing set or state*. We should not, however, overlook the fact that the "set to perceive" may often be based not upon any strong motivating, emotional, or personality condition, but upon nothing more dramatic than the *frequency* and *familiarity* of the object in the observer's experience. The effects we have mentioned are usually matters of selective emphasis, determining what objects we are to perceive in our environment and what objects we are to ignore.

The foregoing account of the major phenomena of perception, though highly condensed and slighting the physiological aspect, is complete enough for our present purpose. The six aspects brought to light by the question "How do things appear?" are sensory quality and dimension, configuration, constancy, frame of reference, concrete-object character, and the effect of prevailing set or state. Together these aspects comprise the facts that any complete theory of perception will be expected to incorporate.

4

The Classical Theories
and Their Legacy
Core-Context Theory

Though the account of perceptual theories to follow will not be chronological, we shall do well at the start to gain some historical perspective. This chapter will deal with what may be called the classical views of perception, since these conceptions set the pace for much that followed and some of them laid down postulates or made other contributions that still stand. Naturally enough, the problems to which they were addressed were seldom completely solved and the theories were not well systematized. Issues were left standing that reappeared through later decades for other workers to resolve. As might be expected the six broad classes of phenomena of perception, as outlined in Chapter 3, were the primary curiosities of the earlier theorists. For the present account seven related stands of the earlier theoretical endeavor have been selected. They are as follows: (1) the correlation of the phenomenological and the physical (mind-body problem); (2) analytical introspection, sensationalism, and elementarism; (3) associationism and context theory; (4) functionalism and psychological agency; (5) determining tendencies and attitudes; (6) the nativism-empiricism controversy; and (7) phenomenological philosophy and formal configurational ideas.[1]

THE MIND-BODY PROBLEM: SPECIFIC ENERGIES; PARALLELISM; PSYCHOPHYSICS

Let us begin then with the old problem of the relation of the mental to the physical, the problem with which we dealt in more modern

[1] References to the authors cited, where not given, will be found in Boring (1942) or in Helson (1951). The writer is much indebted to these works, especially to Boring's excellent treatise upon which he has drawn extensively in preparing this historical account.

terms in Chapter 2. One of the most naïve but natural early views of "mind" was the conception of an inner being or agent that receives some form of communication from the outside and "acts accordingly." Anthropomorphic or manikin ideas have, in fact, shown some tendency to persist to the present day. In the earlier days the inner recipient of information from the outer world was called the Sensorium. It was thought that objects give off direct copies or images of themselves which, being carried to the Sensorium by the nerves, inform the Sensorium of the world outside. Psychologists soon became dissatisfied with this simple picture. Stimulation, afferent nerve conduction, and cortical processes must have characteristics of their own that enter into the process. It was considered unlikely that an exact and realistic image of the object was conveyed to the inner perceiving agent. In 1826 and 1838 Johannes Müller published his famous doctrine of the specific energies of nerves, maintaining that the Sensorium is aware only of the states of sensory nerves, not of the external objects themselves, and that each of the senses has nerves that possess their own "specific energies" or qualities. The same stimulus acting on different nerves gives rise to different qualitative experiences, and different stimuli acting on the same nerve give rise to the same sensory quality. The seat of the specificity lies in the nerve or in its termination in the brain, not in the receptor organ. Müller's theory has had great influence. Minus the concept of a sensorium and with certain other modifications, it remains even today as a working postulate.

But because each type of receptor organ has its "homologous" or "proper" stimulus, even though it may be excited by other forms of energy, theories of the special senses have been elaborated, such, for example, as the Helmholtz theories of audition and vision and the color-vision theory of Hering. Helmholtz accepted specific energies and, for audition, assumed, rather unparsimoniously, thousands of specific energies to account for all the discriminable pitches of tones. On the side of physics the relation between the stimulus and the receptor has been studied; but, though something has been learned, not too much success has attended these efforts, particularly as to the correlates of stimulus-dimensions and of the dimensionalities as perceived. While it is recognized that the receptors must be in some way selective as to qualities and dimensions these latter do not ultimately *depend* upon such receptor specificity. And so we are pushed back into the afferent neural processes and the brain for our locus of specific energies. In the former the search has not been very fruitful. Coming to the nerve-terminations in the projection areas of the cortex, we have the familiar facts of brain localization; but even here it seems doubtful that there are many qualitative differences at work; and so we must pursue the search further and examine the *connections* that the nerve endings make with adjacent fibers in the cortex. Here we become lost in a complex integrative pattern. How specificity of quality can result from a vast network of interrelated events remains a mystery. And behind this is an even deeper mystery. Assuming that we *could* find differentiating neural features for the sensory modes and qualities, what gives a particular quality the character it has? Why does red "look like" what it does? Here we not only have no answer, but apparently no possible method for finding an answer. We would have to get behind the nature of experience itself to solve this problem.

For the modern positivistic behaviorists the whole matter is simplified by a *tour de force*. Sensation means to them merely the route taken by the impulses in leading to a response of discriminating the stimulus employed or its magnitude. Anything "experienced" as quality or dimension by the subject is irrelevant. In this view the notion of specific energies would not have been needed; it is only the specific stimulus-response connections that would be significant.

Perhaps because of the failure to find a definite law of specificity or a suitable referent to explain it little is left of the specific energies doctrine. Furthermore it was not general, since it postulated a relationship only for quality and not for sensory magnitudes or intensities. Nevertheless it was better than the earlier "images" theory; and it is still adhered to as a working basis because it "sounds logical" and also for want of a better conception. At the very outset we find that classical theory, though it has clarified some matters, has also left some fundamental questions unanswered.

Another classical postulate, in much the same status, was that of "psychophysical parallelism." Do the mental and physical interact? Those who held the easygoing view that they do had to change their opinion when, about the middle of the nineteenth century, the laws of thermodynamics and conservation of energy were formulated. To believe that the physical interacts with the phenomenological, which to all our knowledge must be treated as an "incorporeal substance" subject to no known physical laws, is to run the risk of assuming the creating or abolishing of energy. The principle of "parallelism" by which interactionism was supplanted was formulated in a set of "psychophysical axioms" by G. E. Müller in 1896. The mere assumption that consciousness and the nervous system run in parallel fashion, though, like specific energies, a necessary doctrine, is neither very explicit nor very explanatory. The gestalt psychologists later tried to make it more definite by postulating a "topological correspondence" between the brain-pattern and the percept. Like specific energies, psychophysical parallelism has remained as a postulate underlying theories of perception not because it explained much, but because it seemed the only assumption that was logically tenable.

If one is willing to leave unanswered all questions as to the process mediating between the stimulus and its central effect or conscious accompaniment, one can still attempt to correlate the physical stimulus energies and receptor process, on the one hand, with the experience as reported by the subject on the other. Here we would have simply a parallelism between the stimulus-process and the resulting phenomenology. Such efforts have stressed the dimensional attributes of sensory experience, such as heaviness, size, brightness, and the like, and have been directed toward finding a lawful quantitative relationship between these experienced magnitudes and the corresponding property (weight, physical size, luminosity, etc.) of the stimulus. This field of study, which is known as *psychophysics,* has had a long and impressive history. Many ingenious methods have been developed for determining the psychophysical relation. There is involved the notion of *differential threshold or limen,* which is the amount of the stimulus-dimension that must be added to a stimulus already given in order that a "just noticeable difference" will be experienced. There is also the "absolute" threshold or limen below which amounts of stimulation are too small to give *any* experience of the attribute concern. Weber's famous law, which was formulated as early as 1834, may be stated as follows: $\Delta I/I = a$ constant, where ΔI is the increment of stimulation necessary to be added in order that a just noticeable difference will be experienced, and I is the stimulus-magnitude to which the increment is added. Fechner, whose main work was published in 1860, went further and tried to measure the amount of the sensory experience present in any given case. Assuming that all just noticeable differences are subjectively equal, he derived by their integration the formula: $S = k \log I$, where S is the magnitude of the sensation in appropriate units, I is the stimulus magnitude measured in terms of the absolute threshold as a unit, and k is a constant for the particular type of stimulus and the particular observer.

Fechner's law has met objections on the ground that the magnitude of every sensation is experienced as something unique and not as a compound made up by the addition of smaller sensory increments. Both Weber's and Fechner's laws have been still more drastically criticized because at the extremes of the psychophysical continuum they do not agree with the facts. Fechner considered that he was asserting a lawful relation between the realm of "mind" and the "physical world"; but later investigators have interpreted the psychophysical function as a relationship between stimulus properties and the sensory physiological mechanism. In spite of its shortcomings the so-called psychophysical law has had great influence, and the methods developed for its study have become bases for measurement not only in perceptual work but in other fields. The concept of threshold, especially the absolute limen, has been fundamental for the testing of hypotheses which perceptual theories have inspired and upon which they have depended. As for the law itself we shall note that it later became a contested point in an important theoretical controversy involving the nature of perception. Though it touched upon the problems of perception at many points the psychophysical movement in itself was scarcely broad enough to constitute the basis of a theoretical system.

INTROSPECTIONISM; MENTAL ELEMENTS AND ATTRIBUTES; SENSATIONALISM

Our *second* strand of the historical background again deals with the sensory qualities and dimensional attributes. In this case, however, interest focuses upon them as the stuff of which consciousness is made. Before the rise of behaviorism and before psychology was clearly separated from philosophy the "mind" was conceived in psychic or phenomenological terms. *Awareness* was considered to be the proper subject-matter of psychology—all else was secondary. Consciousness was conceived (to use Titchener's term) as something that is "existential." It was the given material or context to be examined and described. Since it was "given" it scarcely needed an explanation other than the statement that it runs parallel, with certain occasional gaps, to the happenings of the physiological realm. Psychologists always had to assume such a physiological "basis"; but what that basis really was, was the concern of physiologists.

But how could existential awareness be observed and described? Obviously by the only possible method: the observer, who in this method is also the subject, is plied with stimuli and with instructions for directing his mental activity toward them; and after the mental process has occurred, or perhaps at intervening stages, he sits back and introspects upon the course of the experience that has just taken place. The report of such observations was usually in verbal terms; hence the procedure was subject not only to the hazards of phenomenological observation discussed in Chapter 2, but also to the pitfalls of language.[2]   The subject was not to be passive in the situation.   He was to examine his experience closely and analyze it; for it was usually possible to recognize that it had components.   Analysis of the awareness into its *elements* was both suggested and supported by the work of chemists and biologists, who had long used analysis successfully.   Analysis, in fact, has always seemed a natural procedure for scientific investigation.   After analysis the components could then be aggregated or synthesized again (at least so it was thought), though the introspective method gave no information whatever about the actual process.   The whole system, though it was for certain reasons called "structuralism," fell far short of providing any account of how the perceptual synthesis, which is really the heart of the psychological problem, takes place.

In any event, the "elements" thus observed, analyzed, and reported, were regarded as the basic constituents of mind; and the laws of attention and association were the forces that selected them and joined them together.   Through such a joining of elements all the processes of psychology—perception, imagination, memory, association of ideas, thinking, and so on—were to be explained.   Such was the tradition of Wundt and Titchener which held sway for a long time before gestalt psychology, with its different method of introspecting, and behaviorism with its rejection of introspection altogether, came along and undermined it.

By about 1910 Titchener had recognized three types of elements: sensations, images, and feelings.   An attempt was made by the Würzburg School to add another called "imageless thought"; but

---

[2] The term phenomenological, in past usage, has been applied only to the gestaltist's type of introspection and not to that of the Wundt-Titchener school. The former school of psychologists employed only "direct and immediate experience," while the latter introspected further on the immediate experience in order to discover parts or aspects within it.   The word phenomenological, however, as defined in Chapter 2, has been used by us to include both these introspective approaches and the contents they described.   Since both were reports of pure awareness, of the experience as dependent on the perceiver, they were both observer-involved and private to the subject.   The *differences* between the two methods were of course important and will be later discussed.   The reader is cautioned that our use of the term phenomenological has been adopted in order to make a basic methodological distinction and to hold it clearly in mind. It is not strictly in accord with historical usage.   For an interesting account of the history of introspection and its present status see Boring, 1953.   This article also contains a developmental account of the backgrounds of psychological theory as related to the strand of introspective method.

Titchener and his colleagues failed to find any introspective evidence for it. They maintained that cognitive processes and perception always involve, in their earlier stages, some imagery. It was recognized, however, that images are but "faint copies" of sensations aroused by central processes, and that feelings consist, insofar as we are aware of them, of kinaesthetic or visceral sensory components. Existential consciousness thus came to be regarded as composed wholly of sensory experiences. Sensations were the stuff of which the mental life was composed. This conclusion made it all the more necessary to concentrate upon the attributes of sensation, later called dimensions, as the strategic items for the building of a system. Wundt employed only quality and intensity. Külpe increased the list; and Titchener came out, finally, with five: quality, intensity, duration (protensity), extensity, and clearness (attensity).

But, unfortunately, after the attribute doctrine was established the notion that sensations, the substratum of the attributes, were the elementary constituents of awareness suffered a logical extermination. When we look at a line we do not see it as a series of points (sensations) each with its own amount of extensity; we see the line as one continuous whole. It was also pointed out that no sensation exists in consciousness without its attributes. If we reduce all its dimensions to zero, nothing is left. The attributes, not the sensations, must be the elements. But there have been difficulties also with the doctrine of attributes. Without going into details we can note that one of the most troublesome features of attributes was the fact that they fail to vary independently as they should if they are to have a truly elementary status. A given attribute may be a joint function of several others. The loudness of a sound, for example, varies with pitch, and so does its volume. On the physiological side Helson has noted that afferent nerve fibers differ only in rate, frequency, amplitude of impulses, and number involved in an instance of stimulation. These differences are too few to account for the many perceived dimensions such as those listed, for example, in his table for color. Helson has dealt with sensory dimensions rather successfully from the field standpoint (op. cit).

The whole topic of sensation has come to be treated in many textbooks as separate from perception, and more attention has been paid to its physical and physiological aspects. As far as the analytical elementarists are concerned, though they believed they had discovered in the attributes the basic stuff of awareness, they could not straighten them out in consistent or logical terms. But certainly sensory quality and dimension are a genuine part of the phenomenology of perception—of the way the world appears to us. Again the classical theories opened an area for exploration but left their work unfinished. This strand of the classical legacy by no means ended with the bankruptcy of elementarism. In addition to the steady march of psychophysics, at least three dimensionally oriented theories of perception have later appeared, and other theories have employed such concepts as an indispensable means of proving their contentions.

ASSOCIATIONISM AND CORE-CONTEXT THEORY; THE PROBLEM OF MEANING

In the preceding account of mental elements we have omitted the consideration of a "linking" process that was believed to hold together the elements of the mind. Such a conception had been formulated even before the analytical-introspective program had gotten started and it continued thereafter. This linkage was supplied by the doc-- trine of association. It was supplemented, at least as early as the writings of Hume (cir. 1740), by the notion of "ideas." These were "faint copies" of sensory impressions that arise in memory and as images. The ideas were synthesized by association, which Hume called a "gentle force" of attraction between them. We shall not trace the long course of associationism. Let us recall merely that its main principle was the connection of ideas by their previous contiguity in space or time and, for some writers, by their similarity. There were also the conditions of frequency, recency, vividness, and so on, by which such connections were strengthened. Perceptions for Titchener were aggregations of sensations joined together by the special laws of sensory connection and the laws of attention. For him one of the outstanding features of perceptions was meaning. But ideas also have meanings, acquired by the same sort of process as in perception; and ideas are distinguished from perceptions in that they do not require a direct sensation from some outer object to arouse them. The association of *ideas* works not with simple sensory materials, as in the formation of percepts, but with larger complexes that are already formed, that already "mean." Titchener was careful to insist that neither those bits of conscious experience that make up a percept nor those that make up a pattern of associated ideas link onto each other actively in the associative process. They simply "occur." Their connection is provided by the underlying physiological mechanism that explains association. Since for Titchener there was a common associative process at work in perception as well as in ideas we shall include his main contribution, the context theory of perceptual meaning, along with associationism, as the *third* strand of the classical influence.

The preceding sections in which sensory elements and dimensions were discussed were rather atomistic in outlook. If we went no further, a false idea of both the earlier and the later views of perception would result. As we shall have many occasions to note, the perceptual process is not a single item but an aggregation of interacting parts. And it is not simply a lumping together of such parts, but a true integration into a kind of unity. It is closely knit; and in some way it transcends the bare sensory components of which it is composed. This integrative, and to some extent more-than-sensory, character of perception was recognized from fairly early times. It was implied in Chapter 2 where we spoke of a "structuring process" in the organism by which the external world was represented with a fidelity consistent with coördinated adaptive behavior. If we keep this thought in mind we shall be aided in understanding both the earlier and the later contributions to perceptual theory. In more specific terms this problem poses two questions: (1) What are the elements that are combined to form the perceptual activity of the organism with its accompanying phenomenological percept; and (2) how shall the process that combines those elements be described and explained? We have seen that sensationalism, culminating in Wundt and Titchener, was the classical answer to the first question. But it was not a simple sensationalism. Images or ideas, left as traces from past experience, must be combined with the sensations directly aroused by the object. The fact that perception is not fully explained by its sensory components because the latter do not possess meaning while perception does was central in Titchener's system. It belongs on the side of the combining process (our second question) rather than on the side of what is combined.

How was the combining process, either for percepts or for ideas, conceived throughout the period we are considering? We have already noted Hume's mechanistic but "gentle" force of attraction. But the problem was entangled somewhat with the earlier discussed question of objectivity. Thus Reid brought in the wisdom of the Deity to provide to all mankind, regardless of training or experience, the necessary sense of the *reality* of perceived objects. Divinity, rather than denotation, was Reid's "physicalistic" criterion. The laws of association became the explanation of the integrative process for many. Berkeley pointed to the fact that the idea of a particular object can arise from the evidence of different senses. There is thus conveyed the notion of the object as something in itself.

James Mill treated ideas by logical analysis, saying that the idea of a house comprises the ideas of boards, bricks, beams, nails, and so on, combined with ideas of quantity and position. This view was criticized on the ground that the idea of house *in consciousness* contains no such detailed components as this. The whole is in some respects *less* than the sum of its parts. John Stuart Mill in 1865 corrected his father's building-block notion, asserting that the mind has a more creative function and possesses a capacity for "expectation." He also introduced "mental chemistry." Certain parts or aspects of the elements are lost in the compound that comprises the total idea; but the compound has some properties that were not in the parts. Wundt described compounds of elements by such terms as *Vorstellungen,* which included perceptions and the ideas of memory and imagination. He also used such terms as fusions, assimilations, contrasts, and complications. Though his system leaned heavily upon association-theory he also recognized a gestalt-like "creative resultant." The combining process was changed radically in gestalt doctrine, a "supersummative whole" or prior "form-quality" replacing the integrating or fusing of elements.

It has seemed to the writer that the rejection of James Mill's building-block conception of ideas has been too cavalier. If we are looking at the "contents of consciousness," of course we do not find bricks, boards, and nails succinctly represented in the total idea of a house. The idea is usually schematic; and, as J. S. Mill has said, it is both less and more than the component parts. A synthetic process of some sort is added to the elements. But suppose we are considering the physiological basis of the idea or percept, rather than its phenomenological content, and are looking for some theory that will deal adequately with that basis. The writer has found that an excellent test of whether some item belongs in an aggregate is to omit that item and then see whether the aggregate will be essentially the same and will "operate," dynamically speaking, without it. We might call this method the "negative-causation test" of the aggregate. If a part is taken away, or if conditions are established under which it cannot operate, and if the whole aggregate then breaks down, would we not have to assume that that part is an essential item of the aggregate and that under normal conditions it is actually present and operating? This would certainly be a logical supposition in physiology; and it would be no less true if the part concerned were not clearly recognized in consciousness or were subordinated to the experience of the whole. Now if we were to apply this test, for example, in the perception of a brick house, and were thinking of the perceptual meaning of the house, we would set ourselves to suppose an instance of perception in which the elements representing "bricks," "roof," "window frames," and the like were either in part or totally taken away from the percept's physiological basis and thus from the percept, or else were so modified that they no longer had a representative relation to bricks, roof, or windows. Would we then have a perceptual meaning of "house"? It seems highly doubtful.

Of course, in perceiving a brick house as a whole, or in imagining one, we do not have a distinct perception or image of every brick or window that would be observable upon closer inspection. It is also conceded that the *ensemble* "house" is something more than a pile of so many discrete bricks or window frames. But does the negative-causation test not show that in order to have a perception of anything the *parts* of that thing, in their proper space (or time) positions, must have at least a certain minimal amount of representation in the physiological pattern that is set in operation by the simulus-object. And could not a similar case be made at a less intensive level for "ideas," Hume's "faint copies" of perceived situations? When the matter is looked at in this way a structural character is seen in perceptual meaning and the physiological aggregate that is not unlike the structure of the object or situation we are perceiving. The "perceptual" structure is more sketchy, to be sure, and it may be fleeting; nevertheless some structural replication of the perceived world, providing the minimum essentials necessary for the total structure of behavior, is still there.

We turn now to Titchener who was omitted from the discussion just preceding. It will be evident that the class of perceptual phenomena with which the various combining theories attempted, though none too successfully, to deal was concrete object-character or meaning. The important context (or core-context) theory of Titchener (1909, 1914, 1915) was addressed to the same topic. Though he did not solve the problem of meaning Titchener had some clear and decided views about it. His theory, extended and clarified by Boring (1946), stands as one of the most systematic of the earlier attempts to describe the perceptual process. A perception, said Titchener, consists, in its earlier stage, of the three following items: (1) a number of sensations consolidated and incorporated into a group under the laws of attention and the special principles of sensory connection; (2) images from past experience that supplement the sensations; and (3) meaning. The sensations are integrated and fused with the images so that the two are often indistinguishable. What then is meaning? Meaning is something that the sensations or images provide for one another. That is to say, meaning is *context*. One group of sensations is usually focal—this is spoken of as the "core." Other sensations or images that accompany the focal group provide, as its context, the *logical meaning* of the focal group. In the case of new perceptions it thus takes at least two sensations to make a meaning. One mental process is the meaning of another if it is that other's context. As to the question of what provides these contextual processes that accompany the focal experiences, the answer is that they are aroused through the total situation in which the organism finds itself and to which it reacts.

Examples of meaning through context can be readily given. The significance of a gesture or facial expression is often conveyed by accompanying aspects of the situation. The experience of auditory rhythm comes from kinaesthetic sensations resulting from movements of stress upon the accentuated beat, such muscularly aroused sensations providing a context for the focal auditory group. In learning to read a foreign language we are often painfully aware of contextual clues that we are summoning in order to find the meaning of a particular word. Word-imagery of equivalents in our mother-tongue are also present as context in these early stages.

Titchener used the notion of context to explain individual differences in perceiving. The sensory core would be the same for different individuals, but the imagery supplied as context (and hence the meaning) would be different for different persons according to their past experience. Boring (op. cit.) treated the context more broadly as something that modifies or corrects the data of the core as the perception is being formed. For example, the size of the retinal image of an object decreases with the distance of the object, a fact which would produce a false shrinkage in the object's perceived size if we had to depend on the size of the retinal image alone. The data from this image, however, becomes altered by other visual clues (context) that are associated with apparent distance, with the result that the object appears approximately in its actual (physical) size.[3] It will thus be seen that the core-context theory can be applied to the perceptual constancies.

In Titchener's view there is one special type of sensation that is paramount as a contextual, meaning-providing process, namely, kinaesthesis. As the organism faces the situation it adopts an attitude toward it, and the kinaesthetic sensations resulting from this attitude

---

[3] Such accompanying data have also been spoken of as "cues" that fuse automatically and rapidly into the total meaning and are therefore scarcely observable in themselves. (Woodworth, 1938.)

(assuming it to be a muscular tension or reaction) give the context and meaning of the object to which the organism is reacting. Here we have the beginnings of a motor theory of perception. Kinaesthetic images may come to replace these bodily sensations in later perceptions of the object, so that the meaning may depend upon a context purely of imagery. Word responses are also important as providers of meaningful contexts. The process of recognition, in its earlier but not its later stages, is likely to be one in which the *name* of an object or a person is associated with the core of visual experience.

Thus far we have spoken mainly of "new" perceptions, perceptual activities in the earlier stages of their formation. With repeated perceptions of the same object or situation there is a decay of the imagery. The context of sensations or images supplementing the core becomes less and less necessary. Images may reduce to some common denominator or a symbolic kind of shorthand. Thus when we greet a familiar acquaintance we no longer need to recall his name or other context in order to have a meaningful experience of his identity. The trained musician is not aware in sensory or imaginal terms of the key-signature of the piece of music he is reading. One glance at the signature at the beginning was enough to render the key-meaning automatic and to guide his fingers accordingly. Words of our mother-tongue do not require supporting context; we perceive their meaning immediately. The fact that context has thus faded out does not, of course, indicate that meaning has ceased to exist. It is now carried, said Titchener, in purely physiological terms. It lies in the physiological organization of the brain processes and can be immediately recalled in the form of context if required. The musician can always tell, if asked, the key in which he is playing. We can paraphrase, if asked to do so, the meaning of what we have just read. One might add here that if the stimulus situation had contained other contextual material not compatible with the meaning that was afoot, it would at once have been noted. An incongruous word in the text stands out like a sore thumb. These cases clearly signalize that meaning is present, that it represents an ongoing process in the nervous system even though it be totally outside of consciousness. But once meaning had reached this stage Titchener had little use for it, for it was no longer attached to the content of awareness and was related to nothing that could be introspectively described. In fact, since meaning in general was not substantive or "existential," but only contextual, it was considered to be essentially a physiological rather than a psychological matter.

Whatever the shortcomings of associationism and context theory might have been, and in spite of later gestalt strictures against building perceptions by cementing together a mosaic of elements, this strand of classical theory attained some important insights. First, its exponents realized that a perception is always an integrative process of some kind; it goes beyond mere detached sensations. Second, perception was seen to have a motor aspect: kinaesthetic sensations and images were involved and their contextual aspect was stressed. Third, being aware that perception had to do with the experience of concrete objects, Titchener took note of the problem of meaning and tried to deal with it. His contribution was influential and challenging. Some of the later theories of perception and meaning are "context-like," and the tradition of associationism still carries on.

In the core-context theory, however, Titchener developed a theory of meaning that took it right out of psychology. He "explained" it in such a way that psychologists washed their hands of its further explanation. To have seen that the process of combining or integrating sensory components to constitute an act of perception is essentially a process of *meaning* was indeed an achievement. But the bias toward analytical introspection and mental elements was such that it denied fundamental importance to anything but existential conscious facts. Contrary to the claims of the Würzburg school (*vide infra*) Titchener held that there was no such thing as an imageless element of pure thought or meaning. There were only sensations, images, and feelings—all probably sensory in their ultimate composition. Though it was evident that when meaning occurs there is some process at work, some physiological basis of association among the elements, meaning as such was not found to qualify as an introspectively established element. It was therefore considered as a logical rather than a psychological entity and was relegated to the logicians, on the one hand, as context, and to the physiologists, on the other hand, for its clarification in terms of associative brain-processes. The physiologists were too busy with their own affairs to give to the important clue of perceptual organization as the elaboration of meaning the attention it deserved. A promising insight was thus brought to an early demise, and classical theory again bequeathed to posterity an unsolved problem.

Core-context theory, however, will repay more careful examination, not only because it was one of the more fully elaborated of the earlier theories, but because there emerges from it an important problem that reappears in various guises in later theories of perception. In order not to interrupt the historical review we shall leave it at this point and return to it for a more detailed analysis at the end of the chapter.

FUNCTIONALISM, AGENCY, AND UNCONSCIOUS INFERENCE

To introduce the *fourth* strand of classical influence it will be well to say a little about the general character of the viewpoint known as functionalism. Men's interest in biological and psychological phenomena from the standpoint of their contribution to the organism's adjustment is probably very old. When one undertakes to describe phenomena from this standpoint one inevitably thinks first of purposes and results, and only second of the processes concerned. When processes *are* considered they are likely to be dealt with as serving smaller functions contributory to the main, or total purpose. One can descend into fairly minute levels and still talk in functional terms. Such a view leads naturally to treating the matter in terms of agency: One process or organ, in serving its function, does this, another does that, in the service of the overall adjustment. So interested are we in the "function" which the structure serves that we fail to see clearly what the structure *is*. But since we are not especially interested in what it is, in and for itself, anyway, we simply pass over the ignorance of its details and come to think of it merely as an "agency" for performing such and such a function. The rationale of functionalism therefore is both a practical convenience and a theoretical liability. Whenever we try to denote the agent closely and finely it disappears; we find that we are denoting merely some part of an aggregate of interrelated parts. We then have to give up the concept of a functioning agent or else refer it to the parts by treating *them* as smaller, subsidiary agents. This regressive line of thinking seems rather useless. The moral, therefore, is to keep away from denotation. But when we do that we are relinquishing one of the primary supports of objectivity in theory-construction.

Perhaps the earlier functionalistic contribution we are now to mention was too slight to be called a definite strand in the history of perceptual theory. Nevertheless it set the pace for later interpretations and its theme has reappeared in the development of a number of modern theories. Addressed to the old familiar question of how the elements of a perception get combined, it gives its answer not in connectionistic principles, but in terms of a perceiving agent. The theory to which we are referring is Helmholtz' much quoted notion of *unconscious inference*. In 1866 Helmholtz, recognizing that past experience contributes to perception and that that process resembles in its outcome a correct judgment as to what past experience would lead the perceiver to expect, gave forth the statement that perception is an instantaneous, unconscious inference, made upon the basis of whatever sensory data are received from the object and its surroundings. Many stimuli are received in the situation; many impressions are made on our sense organs. Perception is a process in which such an object is inferred to be present before us as would need to be there in order to produce just this pattern of stimulation upon our sensory receptors. What would the size of an object need to be, for example, that would give us a certain size of retinal image at the time when we were also bombarded by certain sensory data of perspective, parallax, atmospheric haziness, and so on? We make our judgment instantly, and without being aware of the process. When we see a man nearby in a fog the haziness makes him seem further away than he is; hence, with the size of the retinal image being, as it is, fairly large, the man looks abnormally large. Unconscious inference can thus sometimes be wrong. But such an admission fits in well with the theory by helping to explain sensory illusions.

The unconscious inference doctrine has been assailed on the ground that an "inference" usually means something that is conscious; and it needs more time to develop than our immediate spatial and size perceptions require. Neither of these objections, however, seem very forceful in the light of our present knowledge of the speed and complexity of neurophysiological processes. The gestalt psychologists were the most effective opponents of unconscious inference. They relied upon phenomenology, and phenomenological reports gave no evidence in ordinary perceptions of a process of "inferring." The gestaltists were vigorous in their attacks upon all supposed higher processes that imply an "interpretation" of data received through the senses.[4] Perceived size and other phenomenological properties, they held, are directly given at the start as *Gestalten*. Their physiological basis is some dynamic pattern in the brain that is isomorphic to the percept. Results of experiments with infant human and animal subjects, who, though very young, have constancies in their perception, also militate against the theory of complex unconscious judgments.

One of the strongest arguments against the theory lies in the· fact that it is either futile or illogical according to the way we look at it. If we "stand outside" the perceiving individual, taking the outside view of the aggregate, we *could* say that "he" is inferring from all the sensory data he receives from the situation. This, however, is a fairly

---

[4] Cf. Koffka, 1935, Chapter III, and Köhler, 1929.

obvious statement. We are willing, from this outside point of view, to let the entire organism of the perceiver act as an agent, as a being who perceives and then reports his perception. We can concede also that he is not usually conscious of the basis of his estimates or of the estimating process. The only drawback is that by this procedure we have not gained much knowledge of the perceiving process. We are not much wiser than before.

Let us now take the *inside* view of the aggregate. We now find that the notion of unconscious inference is troublesome because there is no one to make the inference. Can a neuron or a group of synapses in the brain make an inference? Scientific parsimony would suggest that we consider the perception more directly as merely the interacting of these internal elements. No "inferring agent" is to be found; so why complicate matters by setting one up? But the activity called inferring seems to require an "inferrer." To say that an inference is not made by anybody, but just goes on like the weather is to do some violence to the language. Can the brain, as the cybernetists believe, be a sort of "inferring machine"? Perhaps so, but then who would set it into operation in the situation, who would take the report, and to what end? Answers to all these questions can be given whenever we talk about the work of machines; for machines are controlled by human beings. Shall we then go back to the outside view and say that the perceiver, i.e., his body or organism as a whole, directs his brain-mechanism to begin inferring? This would sound rather foolish. If we say the organism is the agent that wants the inference made and the brain is the instrument or subagent by which it makes it, then the organism is using a part of itself as a tool, or is enlisting the service of a smaller agent within itself. Is not this, also, illogical? And we still do not know how perception operates. Such unanswerable questions, stated in terms that require agency concepts, unfortunately lead to the easygoing tendency to postulate an inner anthropomorphic replica of the perceiving organism. The manikin may be disguised by scientific terminology; but it is still a manikin.

It is one of the riddles of the history of psychology that a doctrine so unsatisfactory as unconscious inference should keep reappearing through successive generations. The answer probably lies in the fact that this sort of thinking is not readily escapable for those perceptionists who lean toward functionalism. Helmholtz was merely the classical example of this tendency. The theme appears again in the constancy theory of Brunswik, though it is there worked out in much greater detail, and with new concepts and experimental interpretations. Something resembling unconscious inference, in the sense of assumptions, purposive selection, and appraisal, is seen in the work of such men as Ittelson and Cantril and in the writings of Ames.[5] From another angle manikin tautology crept into the work of theorists who tried to show that *motivation* influences the perceptual process. In the course of these endeavors a "preperceiver" reared its head and had to be promptly exorcized. When the system was revised as an "hypothesis-theory" it was found that until the matter could be restated in more physiological terms it still had a resurrected odor of unconscious-inference. Cybernetics, the latest word in "teleological mechanisms," is unable fully to harmonize purpose with objective description (Chapter 18). The legacy bequeathed by Helmholtz is still on our hands.

ATTITUDE, SET, AND DETERMINING TENDENCY

The *fifth* thread of the earlier thinking had to do with the set or prevailing state of the perceiver. Near the beginning of the present century it was recognized that there was something else, hitherto unnoticed, that lay behind association and behind the conscious contents or the overt reaction. We do not always have perception, then will, then action; there may be a pre-established attitude that determines what is to be perceived and how one shall react. The volitional part of the experience may occur before the stimulus-object appears. When the stimulus does appear and the perception or overt reaction occurs the subject may be entirely unconscious of the steering effect of this preparatory attitude. Yet it was the attitude, or set, of the subject, not the stimuli nor the mechanical laws of association, that determined the reaction.

At the outset this phenomenon was observed primarily through introspective reports of cognitive processes. It was studied by Marbe, Ach, Watt, and others of the Würzburg school by a procedure involving the following experimental or theoretical concepts. There was first the task that was set and the instructions that were given by the experimenter (*Aufgabe*). Through the conscious acceptance of these there was developed in the subject a task-attitude (*Einstellung*). And secondly, there developed the operation of a selective mental

[5] Cantril revives Helmholtz' teachings and argues that purpose and the relation to ensuing action are factors that strongly influence what an individual perceives. He quotes from Ames the statement that "in a concrete situation, a perception is a potential prognostic directive for furthering of purpose by action." See references cited in the last two sections of Chapter 11.

trend or "determining tendency." This latter tendency governed the train of conscious content or response in a manner quite opposed to the routine laws of association. A "conscious attitude" was also found (or so it was thought). It represented an imageless experience, difficult to describe, which accompanied the mental trend.

The more direct bearing of set on perception is seen in a classic experiment performed by Külpe and Bryan and discussed by Külpe in 1904. The experiment was considered at the time to involve the process of "abstraction" and was related to the old question of defining the conscious elements. It was concluded from the investigation that *attributes* are all that occur in the mind at a given moment and that perceptions with different attributes could result from different instructions to the subject. Nonsense syllables of three letters, printed in different colors and given different spatial patternings, were shown tachistoscopically to the subjects.[6] On different occasions four different types of instructions were given, viz., to report on (*a*) the total number of letters, (*b*) the color of the syllables, (*c*) their patterning, and (*d*) the identity of the letters seen. The results were striking. The subjects reported, generally speaking, the aspects which they were set by the instructions to perceive. Their attempts, when asked, to report other features were far less successful, in fact, almost negligible. If a subject had been set to count the number of letters or to note their arrangement, he might not be able to report the colors at all and might believe that he had actually perceived no colors.[7]

Thus the stream of perceptual theory broadens. Instead of being limited to stable qualities and dimensions, to general laws of constancy, and to the association of elements, it now includes a predetermining, dynamic component, the attitude of the subject. This feature can vary with the situation, and even with the personality of the subject. The incorporation of this strand into perceptual thinking gave rise later to some important theory-construction. The terminology of the Würzburg school tended to drop away as modern findings gave more substance to *Einstellung* and the determining tendency. But as with the other strands of classical theory the full meaning of the phenomenon is still to be revealed.

[6] A tachistoscope is an instrument by which visual stimulus material can be presented to subjects at various controlled durations of exposure. For threshold work initial exposure durations as short as one one-hundredth of a second are sometimes used.

[7] The writer has been aided in conciseness of statement in this account by the able review of Gibson (1941).

NATIVISM VERSUS EMPIRICISM; LOCAL SIGNS

Do percepts and their physiological patterns occur immediately and in their full, veridical character the first time we experience a given stimulus object? That is, do they depend only on the native or congenital constitution of the organism? Or do they have to develop gradually, through a course of familiarization or training? These questions, which state the issue between *nativism* and *empiricism,* have been said to constitute one of psychology's dreary and futile topics. It is an old controversy, arousing much heat; and it is still far from settled. Perhaps it *is* a futile question; but it has certainly been a lively one. Evidently something important in the theories concerned was at stake depending upon the way it was answered. From the middle of the last century and down through the development of the gestalt and behavioristic psychologies the issue has been very meaningful.

It is not, however, an all-or-none issue, at least so far as nativism is concerned. Scarcely anyone, now or earlier, would be found on the nativist side with respect to all the phenomena of perception. The question acquires its significance chiefly in the areas of sensory qualities, dimensions, forms, and shapes. It arises also with respect to the constancies, which appear very early in life. Are all such perceptual achievements a part of the biological endowment or do they have to be learned? In these cases the inference of nativism seems somewhat plausible. Such aspects of perception, sometimes referred to as "autochthonous," are both universal and comparatively stable. They might be properties of the organism's native physiological constitution.

In order to bring the topic into historical perspective, let us narrow it still further. Many of the aspects of perception to which we have just referred involve the perception of *space.* Are spatial perceptions, then, nativistic or acquired? Stimulation from the world about us, acting upon our receptors, must be the immediate source of space perceptions. We must therefore think of the part played by these receptor processes. Though there are many other factors, in large part cortical, that enter into the perceiving of visual, auditory, and tactual-kinaesthetic space, there is a kind of common denominator in the stimulation of innumerable points on receptor surfaces—localized stimulations on the retina and on the cochlea of the ear, touch-spot distribution on the skin, end organs in the muscles and joints, and so on. It is from these innumerable points of excitation, leading to patterns of impulses in cortical networks, that our perceptions of space are built up, both in their immediate spatial localization on the body and, in a more complicated way, in the awareness of space around us in its three dimensions.

The question of whether spatial experiences are inborn or empirically acquired therefore becomes a question about the role played by these points of sensory stimulation and how that role originated. Are the "space-yielding" capacities of all these points of excitation based on their native endowment or character, or are they attained only through association and learning? In addition to their qualities (red, sweet, pressure, etc.) or their other attributes, it was supposed (for the matter could scarcely be explained any other way) that the sensations aroused at the various receptor-points also possessed some spatial indication or "sign" of their whereabouts. When an object touches the skin, for example, we not only have the phenomenological attributes of touch sensation; we know *where* we are touched. How is this *local* sign to be explained? Is it inherited or acquired? The answers given to this question constitute our *sixth* strand of classical theory. As we have seen, it is a divided strand.

Though the preceding statement presents the main issue, the case, as Boring points out, was not quite so simple. The earlier psychologists were both nativists and empiricists to some degree. Both sides agreed that the "mind" had innate capacities that transcended the senses. One of these *a priori* categories, as Kant had called them, was space. The mind apprehends all experiences through its categories of space and time. But though psychologists on both sides of the controversy agreed upon "spatiality" as a capacity of the mind and hence were all, to that extent, nativists, they disagreed as to how the spatial significances of particular receptor patterns came about.

The nativist doctrine was that the local signs were *intrinsically* spatial in character. The points of sensory stimulation were "directly labelled" in phenomenological experience as to their loci. Hering, for example, whose work appeared from 1861 to 1864, held that spatial signs were attached to the visual experiences arising from every retinal point. In fact there were three such signs for each point, one for each of the spatial dimensions. It was not necessary to bring in eye movements; the spatial aspect was immediately given. The nativists, however, had some difficulty in showing just how "given" visual space is organized.

Lotze, Helmholtz, and Wundt, all empiricists, held a different view. It was Lotze who, in 1852, originated the notion of local signs. He maintained that the signs that were connected with sensations, or were properties of them, were not originally endowed with a spatial character but had to acquire it. The process of acquisition involved muscular sensations and the associative combination or fusion of sensory components. Every tactual and retinal point had its local label. The experienced locus of the former depended upon its proximity to tendons, fatty tissue, or other conformation that affected the stimulation pattern of the spot touched. The aspect of sensory experience which carried the spatial quality was, for Lotze, the attribute of intensity; specifically it was the intensity of *muscular* sensation, an intensity pattern *specific for the spot touched*. For retinal points the local sign was given by the tendency of the muscles that rotate the eyeball to contract in such a way as to bring the image of an object falling on that point to bear upon the fovea. Every retinal point thus had associated with it an intensity of the muscular sensation involved in this specific eye-movement. With the continuous movement of a receptor in relation to a surface the successive local signs are experienced in proper sequence. Continuity and order in space, the basis of the perception of linear and surface dimensions, therefore resulted from this process. Here was a constructive theory concerning the manner in which the experience of space is built up. If not a complete motor theory of perception, it was at least a good beginning. Wundt elaborated further the role of kinaesthetic sensations from movements both of the eyes and the body, thus extending the explanation that the experience of spatial-continuity arises from the continuity of movement. He differed from Lotze in believing that the distinctive local characteristic of points was *qualitative.* Other investigators brought in associated ideas and visual imagery of the part stimulated.

Such was the issue before the beginning of the present era. In answering the question as to what has now become of nativism and empiricism Boring concludes that the gestaltists are the modern nativists and the operational positivistic behaviorists are the modern empiricists. The behaviorists assert that if the organism can respond to a stimulus pattern by correct orientations of its body, then it has correctly perceived the spatial relationships concerned. This procedure, of course, involves learning. Stratton's and Ewart's experiments (page 36) clearly demonstrated that retinal local signs could be acquired through practice. But in treating the matter wholly from the "outside," as modern behaviorists are wont to do, have we not lost all of Lotze's ingenious inferences about local signs? Even if we discount "sensations" as bases of signs, do not proprioceptive stimulations and returning afferent impulses have something to contribute, in quite objective physiological terms, to the understanding of spatial orientation? Cybernetists, in their feed-back mechanism, have certainly shown this to be the case. In what way are the gestaltists descendants of the nativists? Chiefly in starting their system from phenomenology, and in the belief that forms like "square" or movements like the phi-phenomenon are given immediately and as wholes in experience. The gestaltists' nativistic basis for space, however, was not distributed in the manner of local signs, but lay in the pattern of organization in the brain. But are not the gestaltists also losing something of the legacy of Lotze in not providing more of a place for the motor aspect and in not taking the whole round or pattern of behavior into account?

The nativism-empiricism controversy in the realm of spatial and other dimensions is far from dead. We shall consider it again in Chapters 12 and 13 where it will be seen to be revived by the opponents of a new movement in perceptual theory. Perhaps one of the main enigmas left by classical theory was the fact that these two antithetical viewpoints have continued so long side by side. We must either show the problem to be futile because it is meaningless or else try to solve it. If we do neither, it will probably continue to plague theoreticians as long as psychology lasts. Could it be, as has been suggested, that temperamental differences among scientists are reflected in this controversy? One hesitates to press such an *ad hominem* explanation very far. It may at least be noted that different backgrounds and different leanings in philosophy that might have reflected differences of personality could have existed among empiricists and nativists both in the earlier and the present time.

BACKGROUNDS OF CONFIGURATIONISM

The same possibility again presents itself in connection with our *seventh* and final classical strand which deals with the backgrounds of configurationism. There was something highly matter-of-fact, at times almost mechanistic, in the approach of the sensationalists and associationists. Though they dealt with awareness and ideas they tended to take them in "pieces" and to analyze or combine them in a rather mechanical fashion. This was true even when they considered that the synthesis added something to the parts combined. It is possible to view both psychology and nature as a whole quite differently. One could begin by seeing the aggregate from the start as a unified *whole*. One could place emphasis upon some unifying principle that appeared to operate among the parts from the beginning and served as a condition of the parts themselves. The aggregation could thus be brought about by a method less "bit by bit" and less mechanical than in the other view. One could proceed, as Wertheimer later said, by starting at the top and working from the top down. If one did this, one's attention would be drawn to the configurational aspects of the immediate experience and to principles of relationship latent in that experience. There would be a "givenness" in the total experience such as Hering attributed to his nativistic space perceptions. It is evident that such a view, though not necessarily a philosophy, was at least more hospitable to a certain kind of philosophical postulate than were the more piecemeal methods of the positivistic approaches.

Since we have started our discussion on the note of philosophy let us try to characterize the philosophic tradition within which the configurational movement arose. Generally speaking, this was the idealistic trend that appeared, largely in Germany, in the wake of the Kantian critique. That great work made men skeptical of the sources of knowledge because it showed that an important part was played by the experiencer in his perception of the world. This critical attitude did not, however, remain detached. It gave rise to divergent tendencies in philosophy and to the development of various systems which we cannot here trace in detail. Perhaps we can epitomize two broadly different approaches by referring back to some of the distinctions, made in Chapter 2, that were characteristic or at least involved. It was suggested in Chapter 2 that experience is roughly classifiable into two types. First, there is the class in which there is an element of encounter—the criterion of denotation or quasidenotation, as we have called it. Such experiences and their method of attainment were said in Chapter 2 to constitute "objective" physicalistic procedures because they gave the best assurance that the involvement of the observer and his method of reporting what was being described was reduced to the minimum possible amount. The second class of experiences comprises those which do *not* have a denotive aspect—nothing is here encountered. These experiences are not physicalistic; we have called them "phenomenological." In a broader treatment this class might be extended to include not only perceptual data but also "ideas" and mentalistic constructs of all kinds. The conceptualizations of rationalistic or metaphysical systems could thus be included.

Now regarding the distinctions made between these two forms of experience and their relative emphasis there have developed two general positions. *First*, one could say that the distinction is important and should be maintained, but that because the second class of experiences is lacking in objective status it should be disregarded in the work of science. All scientific inquiry should be denotive, physicalistic, and positivistic. One here maintains the distinction between the two types of experience merely in order to eliminate one of them. In the *second* view one would maintain that the distinction between the two types of experience is not fundamental. So-called objective, physicalistic observations, if direct, should, of course, be included— one would obviously not be on tenable ground in ruling them out. But having accepted them, no important distinction is to be made between them and any other form of experience. Perhaps they depend only upon certain special classes of sensations or upon a special way of interpreting certain phenomenological clues. All experience is the same—and all experience is really *phenomenological.* Thinkers of this class often substitute the word "phenomenal" for "phenomenological." All phenomena are phenomenological (i.e., mentalistic, or of-the-"mind," experience).[8]

It is this second general class of philosophical system, dating from after Kant, flourishing among idealistic thinkers in Germany and other countries, and culminating in phenomenological philosophies such as that of Husserl, that forms a part of the background of configurational experimentation and theory. Thinking of reality as essentially "mental" was compatible with the notion of a supersummative, holistic activity such as the perception of configurational wholes seemed to require.[9]

The history of the ideas leading up to gestalt psychology is usually said to begin with Brentano (1874). He held that mental processes are primarily *acts* or *intentions*, not passive contents such as sensations. Conscious data, or phenomenological "objects," are contents

---

[8] Thus Köhler (1938) uses the concepts of "phenomenal" and "transphenomenal" worlds, the latter comprising the physical order of nature but observable only by inference from phenomenal (phenomenological) experience and describable in terms that have been suggested by, and are consistent with, the latter. For example, the experience of "requiredness" typical of many phenomenal (phenomenological) states suggests the concept of "force" in the transphenomenal (physical) world. Köhler proposes a bridge between the two worlds in terms of a formal resemblance of certain physical concepts to phenomenological experiences. The present writer is proposing an approach to the physical world in terms of *denotational* experiences, and the building of physicalistic concepts upon that basis.

[9] There were other backgrounds also. In Wundt's idea of creative synthesis and in J. S. Mill's mental chemistry there was some recognition of wholeness, at least in terms of synthetic character. Wholes in perception are seen as providing something that is not found in the parts taken separately.

which "inexist" logically within the acts. Every act intends an "object" which in turn exists in the act, and such intention confers meaning upon the object. The true subject matter for psychology, for example, is not the passive sensory quality "red," but the *experiencing* or *sensing* of red. The contribution here made to the development of configurational psychology lies in the notion of an intending, creative mental process.

Another important thread was the doctrine of "form-qualities" (*Gestaltqualitäten*) with which the names of Mach (1886) and especially von Ehrenfels (1890) are associated. Von Ehrenfels developed the illustration of a melody. One can transpose a tune into a different key, so that all the tones are changed, and yet have the same melodic experience. And so also with geometric forms or patterns. In a square all the specific elements—lengths of lines, colors, size, and so on—that is to say, all the "fundamente"—can be changed while still leaving a form of combination (square) that is perceived as such. Von Ehrenfels regarded the "form" as a new element of higher order added to the sensory components. Meinong, developing a "theory of objects" (again mental or phenomenological objects), distinguished them as of a lower or a higher type ("Inferiora" and "Superiora"). The elements of a melody or a geometric form (lines, tones, extensions, and the like) are the "founding contents" that determine by their relationships the "founded content" or "superior object" of form-quality. The process can also go on to higher combinations. The bearing of the earlier form-quality discussion upon the theory of configurations is evident. By revealing that a form of combination is a set of relationships that is invariant among changes of the elements it conferred significance upon form in its own right.

There is a further way of looking at the matter that will show its relation to another phenomenon-class of perception. Instead of thinking of the invariant relationships as non-quantitative, that is, as geometric or temporal forms, let us conceive them for the moment as *quantities*, and as related to some changing scale. This is a possible way to regard them, for a transposed melody really represents the shifting of an entire group of pitches (quantitatively, frequencies) along the continuum of tones. The proportionality of these pitches to one another remains constant in spite of the shift of the set as a whole; and the result is that the same melody is perceived through all the transpositions. Or again, if we shrink or expand a square, or any figure, by contracting its total scale without altering the ratio of the sides or angles, we can then experience shape regardless of size.

It will be seen that form-quality, when treated quantitatively, belongs in the class of phenomena we have called *dimensional frame of reference* (Chapter 3). This phenomenon appears later as a basis of certain modern theories of perception.

Returning to philosophy, the man who contributed most directly to the configurational movement was Husserl. In his phenomenological system, published in 1913, he sought to "purify" all phenomenological "objects" by stripping from them everything that was not direct, immediate, experience. All questions of the origins or consequences of our impressions, all judgments as to realities, existences, or validities which they may or may not indicate, all systematic propositions or references to other objects in a scientific or natural context must be thrown out if we would reach the true nature of "being." By this method of "phenomenological reduction" we arrive at the true phenomenon. We could say many things, for example, about the color red: its name, the surface on which it appears, its associated wave length, its existence in the awareness of a perceiver, and so on. But only the direct experience can give us "red" itself and, as such, can serve as the point of reference, or fulfillment, of all those statements. Higher processes are not required in order to explain meanings, values, or conscious objects. Experience affords its own interpretation and validation. (Cf. Murphy, 1929, pp. 451–453.)

This philosophy supported configurationism in two ways: first, by providing a postulate, and second, by underwriting a method. To take the latter point first, it is evident that configurational experience is possible only when one sees the figure or pattern as a whole. Introspective analysis that breaks such experience into parts or attributes will destroy it. But analytical introspection brings in something that the introspector is doing to his experience; it is not the immediate experience itself. Hence it must, on the basis of Husserl's criterion, be ruled out. When dealing with figural phenomena only an experience of wholes will satisfy this criterion; experiences of wholes, then, must be what we observe and report. Herein lies the justification of the gestalt method of direct, unanalyzed introspection. Phenomenological philosophy also lent its authority to a helpful postulate. If one is to accept the evidence of direct experience as the most valid, one must believe that what direct experience gives represents the true nature of reality. That assumption was the main feature of Husserl's system. The assumption also included meanings. Meanings were directly present in the given objects as the "physiognomic characters" of gestalt, and they also appeared as the "demand characters" or valences of topological field-theory.

The scholars of the earlier period did more than supply the later configurationists with philosophical supports. They handed down some ingenious experiments and intriguing findings. One such source was the interest that developed, around 1890, in geometrical optical illusions. Schumann, early in the present century, anticipated Wertheimer by studying the combinings of patterns of dots and by formulating statements about the subjective and objective factors that gave rise to their groupings. He fixed upon the concept of "attention" as the combining principle. Benussi performed excellent experiments showing the great variety of ways in which such elements are subjectively combined. He believed that these configurations were accomplished by suprasensory, or "higher," acts and were therefore "mental" or "ideal objects," as contrasted with objects mediated by the senses ("real" objects). The term object is, of course, used here, as elsewhere throughout the configurational writings, in a phenomenological sense. Benussi investigated individual differences in the way in which objects were configurationally perceived, and hypothesized different types of perceivers. He thus anticipated the use of perceptual factors in the study of personality by almost half a century. There was also Katz who invented the "reduction screen," a device which cut out environing objects and gave rise to the perception of color as a film. This was an important phenomenological finding. Rubin (1915), whose work overlapped the beginning of gestalt psychology, made a number of significant observations on phenomenological figure and ground. The foundations were thus laid, both in philosophical ideas and experimental findings, for the systematic development of a concept of *dynamical gestalten.*

To be sure, the new theory of gestalt psychology changed the earlier interpretations. As for form-quality, an explanation in terms of an added higher element of sensory experience no longer sufficed. Elementarism had to be rejected and was replaced by the doctrine of the immediately experienced whole. The old laws of attention were found inadequate to account for the groupings of dots in Schumann's figures; and Koffka strongly denied Benussi's "higher processes" that were supposed to organize the objects mediated by the senses, asserting that configuration is *primary* in all experience, that experience is *self*-organizing. Basic changes were to occur through the idea of supersummation, through Wertheimer's bold statements about whole-properties as determiners of parts, through Koffka's forces of the field, through Köhler's demonstration of physical *gestalten* and concept of a steady state, and through speculation about a "brain-field" that is isomorphic to the percept. It came to be recognized that phenomenology alone was not enough. The long series of findings of perceived *gestalten* required the development of some physical or physiological theory as an underpinning. In this respect, also, the work of the classical theories was unfinished. There is no denying, however, that the beginnings we have inadequately sketched brought forth a new and broad theoretical system that was destined to influence psychology for a long time.

These seven strands of the historical development of perceptual theory thus found their subject matters in all the classes of perceptual phenomena. Sometimes there were several strands that dealt with a single aspect. Though most of the classical theories contributed something of value, they also bequeathed to later generations a legacy of problems and perplexities. We can recognize throughout them one recurrent theme. All were seeking a clearer understanding of the interdependence of the components, however we may conceive them, that make up the perceptual act. There were associationistic linkages of ideas or images, combinings of sensory elements or attributes, contexts of meaning with kinaesthetic content, determining tendencies acting upon set-selected content, and unconscious inferences from groups of sensory data. There were cyclical, movement-involving patterns of local signs, configurations, lower psychical objects founding higher ones, formal qualities arising from sensory combinations, creative syntheses, fusions, complications, mental chemistry. All these were attempts to explain the composition and dynamics of the perceptual aggregate, to understand, shall we say, the structure of perception. And we shall see that in the later approaches psychologists have continued to ask the same questions. What is the perceptual aggregate? How is it put together? How is it delimited? How does it operate? The diverse strands of the earlier approaches have extended down and ramified in many directions. Though in the next chapter we shall begin our account of present systems with gestalt, whose backgrounds were last discussed, it will be found that practically all the problems that were interwoven in the strands of classical thinking will reappear within the gamut of the modern theories.

ANALYSIS OF CORE-CONTEXT THEORY: THE TWO ORDERS OF
MEANING; "INSIDE-OUTSIDE" PROBLEM

On the whole the classical views of perception are now somewhat outmoded, and they were too specialized or undeveloped to warrant an attempt at their formal evaluation. Let us simply accept their contributions and their shortcomings on the basis of the brief impressions already gained. Titchener's core-context theory, however, came nearer to meeting our criteria than most of the others; and more than any, except perhaps the theories of the early configurationists, it attempted to deal systematically with the central problem of perception, the organization of the perceptual aggregate. Though the principle of linkage between perceptual elements, as well as the nature of the elements themselves, have changed since Titchener's time, context still seems a natural way of regarding perceptual integration and meaning for those who carry on the tradition of associationism. When critically viewed, moreover, the notion of an inside core and an outside context opens vistas not foreseen by its author; and quite apart from its relation to meaning it raises a crucial problem in theory-construction that is still unsolved. A more systematic appraisal of this theory and a following through of some of its implications will therefore be a fitting conclusion to this account of the classical legacy.

At first sight core-context theory seems parsimonious, logical, and in good agreement with the facts enlisted in its support. With respect to its completeness, it could perhaps be generalized to some phases of dimensionality, constancy, frame of reference, and set, though such extensions would need to be worked out and supported in detail. But even aside from its unsuitability to configuration, we could scarcely say it is a complete theory of perception. In the notion of context it tends toward logical or philosophical definitions, rather than toward denotive explanations. Let us now inquire how well, upon closer study, it meets the tests of consistency, experimental availability, and explanatory value.

The first difficulty arises from the questionable status of sensation as an element. If, as we have seen, sensations are nothing more than sensory attributes, then sensations as entities cannot be the core or context elements in the perceptions of objects. Percepts must be composed, rather, of integrations of attributes. Can this be so and still leave us with an equipment adequate for explaining object-character and meaning? Can one experience the perception of a tree, a man, a melody, or a play in a football game in terms of a core and context consisting entirely of sensory qualities, intensities, clearnesses, durations, and spatial extents? Would we not require some stipulations of design, boundaries, configurations, or arrangements of specific events as a kind of framework to which the qualities and dimensions could be attached? One could not proceed with the description of such percepts in terms of sensory attributes without *assuming* such characteristic patterns. For example, in order adequately to describe the awareness of a tree as spatial extendedness or the perception of a play in football or a melody as temporal duration we would need to have "end-markers" in space or time to give us the terminal points of these phenomena. Such "end-markers" are a part of the perceptual meaning; and since they are dichotomous rather than continuous features they could not be given to us adequately by mere degrees on an attribute dimension. Something would have to bring the temporal and spatial extensities to their ends in order to establish their amounts.

From another standpoint the core-context theory of meaning seems to suffer from certain logical defects that militate against its value as an explanatory system. To exhibit them is a rather subtle task. In order to make a logical analysis we shall need to use symbols for describing the core-context manifold. In core-context theory it will be remembered that the core was spoken of as a "focal cluster" or "group" of sensations. Let us call the physical stimulus-pattern giving rise to this focal group A. The physiological processes of the corresponding sensations together with their conscious or phenomenological aspect can be indicated by a. The psychological core, therefore, is a; it is the cluster whose meaning is to be given by contributions from the context. (For convenience we shall speak of the combined physiological and phenomenological aspects of the perception as "psychological.") Let us now turn to the context. It seems likely that the contextual items will also be clusters rather than single elements. Practically every stimulus source that affects us has more than one elementary component. We can, therefore, specify a series of groupings B, C, D, E, etc., as making up the context features from the stimulus standpoint, and a series of clusters b, c, d, e, etc., for the corresponding psychological aspects of context. The total manifold, therefore, is represented by A, B, C, D, E, etc., and a, b, c, d, e, etc.

One further matter of definition is needed. How far do the context clusters of this series extend? Do they go on indefinitely or are they limited? Experience tells us that the latter must be the case. Whenever we search for the meaning of something we find that we do not need to go on to contextual items indefinitely. There is usually a fairly limited group of clusters that are relevant to the thing and that give us its adequate meaning. Every phenomenon has its perceptual bounds. Let us, therefore, consider that our series is closed and ends with E and e. To repeat, then, in this manifold A and a represent, respectively, the outer physicalistic phenomenon and the psychological representations of that phenomenon (core) whose acquisition of meaning is to be explained; and the other letters represent context and contribute the meaning to the core, a; and in every case it will be assumed that the range of such context-clusters will be definite and limited. So much for the definition of the problem. Core-context theory requires two assumptions which we shall endeavor to test: (1) There is a definite core, cluster a, and there can be only one core; clusters b, c, d, and e are not cores. (2) The core by itself has no meaning. All of a's meaning must come from outside, that is, from context clusters b, c, d, and e.

Now in regard to the first point, it does not seem logical that in this closed manifold there can be only one core. It seems more likely that each of the clusters can serve, or has served at one time or another, as core, and that, as such, it has derived meaning from other clusters. It is true that there is a selectivity of attention that might determine which cluster would be core in any one act of perception. But in this case the meanings that lie in the contextual clusters and were acquired either in the past or the present must now be *present* and *active* to produce the perception required, even though they are not focal. An application of the "negative-causation" test (p. 76) would demonstrate this to be true. The size of the retinal image from a recognized object of constant physical size can give us, in part, an impression of the object's distance; but on the other hand, the impression of distance (from other clues) can also affect the perception of object-size that will accompany a given retinal-image size. In the first case the sensations from environmental clues to distance might be taken to represent the focal cluster, or core, a; while the retinal image-size could be a contextual cluster, b. In the second case the roles of these two clusters are reversed. This contextual interchange could hold even though we are interested at the moment in only one of these aspects. To take an example from language, we note that words in a sentence affect one another's meaning reciprocally. Take the sentence: "The man rendered thanks." Here some meaning is added to the core "rendered" by the contextual word thanks. If we had said "The man rendered a bill," the connotation of the term rendered would be somewhat changed. Similarly, if we take "thanks" as core and "rendered" as context, we see that some meaning has been given to the word thanks by the contextual word rendered. If we had simply said "The man expressed thanks," some of the connotation of the previous "thanks" would be lost.

Our first doubt with respect to core-context theory, therefore, is whether core and context can always be logically distinguished except through the selective process of attention, a process that merely points up a center of reference among meanings but does not contribute meaning itself. If we conclude that any cluster in the manifold can be a core in the sense that it has some presently employed meaning that is being derived from some other clusters, core-context theory is weakened because, with respect to any given context, there is nothing single and definite to be "contexted." That the clusters are all interrelated is clear. But would not some other way of expressing the matter be more satisfactory?

Now for the second point. Can a core-cluster by itself be devoid of meaning? Can all of its meaning be contributed by the context? Suppose that our manifold embraces only a and b; a is the core-cluster and b the contextual cluster. Remember, again, that the manifold is closed. Let us now say that a has no meaning by itself; all of a's meaning is contributed by b. We note then that b must have meaning or it could not give meaning to a. Where does b get its meaning? Here we would have to treat b as core and a as context and say that b derived its meaning from a. But this is an impossibility since a, in itself, has no meaning. If we had said that a derived some of its meaning from b, then we could turn about and say that b derived *some* of its meaning from a. This procedure would assume, of course, that each cluster has some meaning all by itself. Let us take a broader manifold, a, b, c, d, e, and again test the assumption that all the meaning of a cluster lies in some other cluster. We could then look for the meaning of a in b, of b in c, of c in d, of d in e; and then for the meaning of e we would have to come back (since the manifold is closed) to a or to one of the other clusters. Whatever course we might take, provided the manifold is closed, we would keep coming back circularly, looking for the meaning of some cluster in a cluster whose meaning we had set out originally to find. Meanings of clusters or elements in a closed manifold, therefore, cannot lie completely in some other cluster. The clusters must process *some* meaning entirely on their own. Since we have seen that core and context clusters are interchangeable, so that our demonstration does not apply to context items alone, it follows that some meaning must be present in a core-cluster all by itself. Again we have a contradiction of the theory.[10]

---

[10] Even if we regard the manifold as open with respect to a particular perceptual act, it cannot extend to an indefinite number of context-clusters since it will be limited by the range of observation and the past experience of the perceiver. The above argument against a core that is entirely meaningless by itself would therefore always apply.

Possibly one might seek a way out through a regressus-reduction. In order to find a core which does not possess meaning by itself one might think of taking a reduced manifold. The previous core, a, can itself be taken as such a manifold because, as we have seen, it is a *cluster* of elements. Suppose, then, that we take as a new core one of the *elements within* the old core and that we let the other elements of the old core make up the context. There is no real objection to this procedure on the grounds that it would lead to another such reductive step, and so on, continually; for we would always stop the regressus whenever we reached a grain of denotation below which perception does not take place. And, as a matter of fact, such limited reductions in our manifolds are continually being made and are an important part of our daily perceptual activity.[11] But the trouble is that *wherever* we stop we always find, by the preceding reasoning, that the core possesses some meaning in itself. The regressus-reduction procedure, however, teaches us something new and important. Suppose that in order to escape locating meaning in the core, which is against the rules, we have taken the core by itself and broken it up into a new context and a new and smaller core. We had at the start the core-context manifold a, b, c, d, e. *Now* we concentrate only on cluster a and dismember it into a new core and a new context. Let us symbolize this manifold as a', b_a, c_a, d_a, e_a. But it must be noted that we are doing this only logically. From the perceptual standpoint we probably have the old manifold, a, b, c, d, e, still on our hands (at least there is always the possibility of returning to it). The "negative-causation" test, also, would show it to be involved.

[11] For example, they occur when we look for and perceive the mechanism by which to wind the clock, or when we study the signature on a check or the detailed design of wallpaper. They also occur when we proceed toward the garden and look at a particular rose, or when in making our way through a crowd we recognize the face of a friend, or when in reading a paragraph we pause over the meaning of a particular sentence. In the last instance the same thing is true at a still less inclusive order when we fix upon the meaning of a particular word. An important case appears, at a more ideational level, when we contemplate the personality of an acquaintance. We can observe the individual in his social or occupational relations (collective or "outer behavior" contexts or aggregates); in this case we are aware of what is usually called his *traits*. Or, on the other hand, we can try to understand from clues from his outer behavior what sort of things he is *characteristically trying to do*, i.e., his "inside meanings" which we try to discern and which then become the inside meaning of our own percept or concept about him. These latter, inner, contexts or meanings the writer has elsewhere called *trends*. The trend-picture is nearly always different from the trait-picture, yet they are related (i.e., interstructured) in definite ways both in the acquaintance and in our (full) perception of him.

What is the result? We now have *two* perceptual manifolds, *one inside the other;* the new context for *a'* is set inside the earlier manifold *a, b, c, d, e.* We perceive, for example, the pattern (context) making up the rose, but we also perceive it within the context of the garden. How does core-context theory deal with such a complication as that?[12]

In view of the above analyses does it not seem again that the notion of context, which is really not very useful without a definite core, is here giving way to something else? While we recognize the important contribution of Titchener in showing that perceived meaning involves an interrelationship of items, the picture has now changed. The uniquely "contexted" core disappears, each cluster is both a core by itself and a context for every other, and the cores themselves break down, in closer perceptions, into included context-like manifolds. The view of clusters and their interrelationship to which our analysis has led, if translated into the language of the physicalistic or physiological world, would be a concept of *structure.* If a meaning within the organism were to be conceived as a dynamic patterning or structuring of the motions and events of actual physiological elements as they are brought by their mutual ongoings into some definite interrelationships with one another, we might then begin to understand it better. So-called contextual meaning would then cease to be a logical abstraction of core and context and would refer to something that is, at least in principle, denotable. We could understand, for instance, how there actually *could be* two manifolds or contexts (structures) and that one could be inside the other in the sense that smaller structures could be aggregated to form a single, more inclusive, structure. An entire manifold, such as the one we have symbolized as *a, b, c, d, e,* would then be conceived not as a core with a context, but as a larger structure composed, and composed entirely, of as many substructures as there were element-clusters within it; and each substructure, in turn, would be a structuring of its still more elementary clusters. The notion of core would now entirely disappear.

In the preceding critique we have tried to keep as close as possible to Titchener's conception of core and context. It might be objected, however, that the cluster-conceptions we used, and those we shall use

---

[12] Helson, also, has sensed a difficulty in the relationship of core to context. He has criticized the theory for not showing how core and context could be integrated in such a way as to transform core data in the many ways necessary to account for the facts of perception. For this and further criticisms see Helson, 1930 and 1951.

later, are more complex than those which Titchener intended as the basis of his theory. He regarded simple sensory elements or attributes, devoid of meaning, as the constituents of the focal group and of the contexting clusters. The clusters we used for illustrations already have some meaning. But so also must the contexting items of Titchener's theory if they are to contribute meaning to the core, unless meaning is assumed to be something that arises spontaneously out of the interrelationship as the gestaltists have maintained. This latter interpretation, to which we shall return in a moment, does not seem to have been Titchener's idea. As for using only the bare sensory attributes as the elements of clusters, we have seen that these are not enough to build the many complex meanings of the objects, events, and situations perceived in daily life. Titchener himself sometimes used words as examples of cores and contexts. And as for taking only elements that are wholly devoid of meaning, where shall we find such elements? Does not practically everything in experience, no matter how "elementary," have some meaning? Let us consider, however, the possibility that the meaning of core a is not *contributed* by context-item b, that is, that the meaning of a does not *lie in* b, but that it lies in the *relationship between* a and b. In this case we would be dealing with "pure" context, with a term that refers neither to phenomenological nor to physiological data, but only to a logical or perhaps merely verbal existence. We do not want to lose the whole empirical problem of meaning by forcing it into a philosophical mold. In fairness to Titchener it should be said that he did not claim for his context any existence or contribution *further than* such a "logical" meaning. He was counting, as we are, on the physiological processes to furnish the nexus between the element-clusters. But if our analysis has been sound, the hypothesis of a unique non-contextual "core" with "context" elements arrayed about it might have given the physiologists some trouble as a guide to neurological relationships within the organism.

The preceding analysis of context theory has been rather abstract. We shall now try to apply it, along with the structural reinterpretation, to a concrete case; and in so doing we shall come upon further difficulties with the notion of a non-meaningful core. Let us take as our object, A, whose perceived meaning is to be explained, a plant. The focal cluster of sensory elements, a, that constitute or underlie the experience of the plant itself is to be the *core*. We shall try to account for the perceived meaning of this core. Various other objects or events in the manifold are to serve as the contextual element-clusters, B, C, D, E, etc. For simplification we shall not carry a parallel

set of lower case letters, *b*, *c*, etc., but shall ask the reader to assume
that whenever we seem to be describing only the outer, or stimulus,
situation we are at all times signifying also the corresponding psychological processes involved in perceiving it. Let us now explore
the psychological context-manifold, that is, the manifold surrounding
the focal cluster, "plant." This manifold is, of course, aroused by the
stimulus-manifold that attends the physical object (plant), just as
Titchener's theory assumes. There is, first, the perceived fact that
the plant is set in the soil. The perceived element-cluster, soil, provides part of the context, and hence part of the meaning, of plant.
Further sensory context items are provided by the sunlight that falls
upon the plant and by the rain that sinks into the soil around it. The
plant also grows to a certain perceived height along the wall. Seeds
dropped from it or from other plants spring up nearby producing
perceived results. There is an ecology of plant life. Plants or plant-
products are widely used as food by animal organisms and are used
by human beings in many other ways. Plants also appeal to human
beings from the aesthetic standpoint. A woman might buy a plant
and take it to a sick friend in the hospital as an outward token of her
sympathy. With all such outwardly observable stimulus-properties
of objects related to the plant there are, of course, correlated the
contextual clusters *b*, *c*, *d*, etc., in the nervous system of the individual
who perceives them. These constitute a psychological (i.e., physiological and phenomenological) *context* which gives the core (plant)
a meaning, or, more exactly, a number of meanings. "Plant," then,
means something that increases in size, receives sunlight, gets
moisture from the soil, reproduces, furnishes useful products, gives
pleasure to human beings, and so on. All the physicalistic clusters
have their ready perceptual (hence physiological) counterpart in the
organism that perceives the "plant in context." Beyond these more
obvious contextual items a specialist might derive further meanings
by using quasidenotive methods to study the minutiae of the plant's
environment in its relation to the plant. His perceptions would here
have to be in terms of the reading of his instruments.

In all this manifold of plant-relationship-and-use one could sometimes shift one's ground and consider other element-clusters as the
core, of which the plant-cluster might become a partial context; as,
for example, in perceiving the meaning of market-stalls in which
plants are sold. Nevertheless, let us concede for the sake of argument that Titchener's scheme has thus far fitted fairly well. We have
a psychological core that is given meaning by a psychological context.
In passing let us note one important feature. The context as thus

far perceived is something *within which* the plant occurs. All the elements or clusters of the context are external to the plant itself and surround it. Such, of course, is the relationship that a context would *naturally* have to its core.

But it is now fair to ask the following question: Has the *full* meaning of the core (plant) been given by the context just described? The immediate answer, of course, is no. We have neglected to look for its meaning in a source that is very important—the plant itself. Here we are aware of a number of new and smaller element-clusters *within* the sensory pattern that made up the core-experience of plant. Among these are "leaves" and "stem." Perhaps some roots or blossoms are also visible. We might see still finer details such as veins in the leaves or stamens in the blossoms. All of these smaller clusters contribute, some of them in a very essential way, to the meaning, plant. If the perceptions of "leaves" and "stalk" are not psychological clusters that help to convey the perceptual meaning of a plant, then surely plant-meaning is nowhere to be found. It is obvious that the processes set up in the nervous system of the perceiver by these details or clusters of the stimulus manifold are a necessary physiological basis of "plant-meaning" to him, and that the "appearance" of such features is an inalienable part of the experienced percept. Again, finer explorations by suitable means would give further plant-meanings to the specialist in terms of "plant-metabolism" and the like. Such meanings, however, would be more ideational than perceptual.

What shall we call these new perceived element-clusters, such as those representing the leaves, the stem, and the roots, that form a part of the perceptual meaning of plant? To call them context would be confusing, for they are a part of the original *core;* they are sensory experiences that constitute the focal group that was to *receive meaning* from its context, not to be identified *with* context. On the other hand it must be admitted that this new group of element-clusters is certainly "context-*like.*" A meaning of the percept plant, and an essential meaning, is given by them; for if either the stem or the leaves were to be permanently or characteristically absent, plant-meaning with respect to the object before us would disappear. The florist could not have sold the woman a "plant" to take to her sick friend unless the woman's perception of the object in question included these features. But if we call these perceived clusters context, the problem arises that a core for this context is not in evidence. The plant as a perceived entity (our earlier core) disappears when we fix our attention on the separate clusters of this new context. It is broken up into its own element-clusters and becomes identical with this new contextual manifold. Have we then a *new* and *smaller* core, say the stem, that receives its meaning from the contextual items, leaves and roots? This solution is unsatisfactory for it will be seen that we could just as logically consider the leaves as the core and the stem or roots as contributing meaning to the leaves. What we really have is *a structure of interdependent parts,* both in the object and in our percept of it; we do not have a "core" and a "context." If we still use the term context (and let us continue to use it for the present), we are obliged to think of a context without a core. Yet this new (coreless) context is a *sine qua non* of plant-meaning.

Still keeping the Titchenerian terminology we now note a marked contrast between this new context and the one earlier described in terms of plant-relationship-and-use. The earlier described context was one that was, phenomenologically as well as objectively, *outside* the core or phenomenon whose meaning was to be accounted for. It was a context that the object (plant) was *in.* The new context is perceptually as well as objectively *inside* the phenomenon; it is a context that is *within the object.* In our abstract analysis we said that a one-step regressus or reduction might be made, dissolving the earlier core into a second new contextual manifold lying within the old. Here we see, in the concrete instance, that such a regressus-step has been taken. In order to achieve *full* plant-meaning we have had to do two things. First, we have had to take into consideration the *outer* context of the plant (soil, sunlight, its products, human uses, and the like); and second, we have had to descend into a restricted manifold, the plant itself, and view the context that is *inside the plant.* Here, then, we have a remarkable result, one that we never could have predicted from core-context theory alone. Since context gives meaning and since we have here two different contexts, the full meaning of our perceived object, plant, must have two meanings, one in each of these contexts. The plant has *two* separate meanings, or types of meaning, not *one.* It seems inescapable, then, that a full account of the perceptual meaning of the object must include (at least potentially) a consideration of both these contexts and their inherent meanings. One of them is an *outer,* or including, context, the other is an *inner,* or included, context; and the latter must be conceived as a context without a core. We thus have a context within a context, an inside contextual pattern set in the framework of an outside contextual pattern and constituting with the latter the total manifold.

And now let the reader ask himself whether this will not also be the case with respect to the full perceptual meaning of *any* object. Consider a book, a stone, a house, a mountain, a machine, a dog, or a man. Do we not always have to take into account the relation of the object to its surroundings, its outer results or use, if we would experience its *full* meaning? Do we not also have to consider the elements, properties, and relationships within the object itself in order to experience its full meaning? Do we not always have, at least to some extent or potentially, both an outer and an inner context? If the former is entirely omitted, the object appears "within a vacuum," a condition which is no more true of our perceptions than it is of physical objects in the world perceived. If the latter is entirely omitted we would have a contextual manifold with a hole in it; some meaning absolutely essential to the phenomenon would have evaporated. Recognition of objects would in this case be impossible. If we were to retain the context theory of meaning, it would thus have to be a "double-context" theory. All objects have inside and outside "contexts"; the perceptions of all objects have inside and outside meanings. This dual context-reference holds not only for the stimulus-situation and its manifold as physicalistically described, it holds also for that very reason, but within perceptually discriminable limits, for the physiological processes and the phenomenological percept involved in the perception of the object and its manifold. The general law of perceptual constancy with relation to the environment holds here just as in other aspects of perception.[13]

[13] So fixed are we on the notion of discrete perceptual objects to which, severally, we give our attention that there may be some reluctance to accept this point of view. The matter, therefore, should be more fully elucidated. Let us consider two instances: we can either watch the behavior of a football player in the outside context of the game, or we can minutely observe his members and their movements; or again, we can look at a pine tree as part of a pine grove or we can look at it as an individual tree with more attention to "inside" characteristics of the percept. Now what seems to have misled students of psychology is that there is a shift of the focus of "attention" or set as one passes from one of these contexts to the other; and so the two views are often regarded as quite separate percepts, each with a context and meaning that characteristically stands alone. This supposition, however, if we take the more "global" attitude that often occurs in daily life rather than this more reductive procedure, is frequently, perhaps usually, untrue. One can readily see that if it were not for the outside context of the game, the particular player's movements would lose much of their usual significance, even though the "game" is peripheral rather than focal in our attention. This is not true in the same degree in the observation of the pine tree. Still it is true to some extent. Inner and outer context both add *something* to each other's meaning. We must not limit our definition of the percept to the focal part of the field of attention or we shall truncate the awareness of meaning. We must have a "set" that is somehow sufficiently broad and integrated to prepare us to observe not only a certain object in its "inside" features, but also, **and at the same time,** its relation to various surrounding objects or conditions

But because of the serious confusion earlier demonstrated with regard to "core" and "context" the writer suggests that we now begin to lay aside the core-context terminology and think in terms of "aggregates," or, shall we say, of "structures." The notion of core is now unnecessary and misleading; and the notion of context is replaced by that of structure. The object and its manifold are, in this conception, resolvable without remainder into aggregates or structures. One structure is "inside" the other in the sense that it is *included within it*—it is really a part of the latter. The *including* structure can be thought of as made up entirely of such lesser aggregates serving as "substructures." For example, if the lady carries the "plant" to the hospital, the plant (i.e., the "inside context" or structure that constitutes the plant) is transported and remains fairly stable in the process. The plant, here, is a "substructure." It is structured into a larger pattern ("outside context" of plant) that comprises the purchase of the plant, the locomotion to the hospital, the handing of the plant to the friend, the friend's grateful expression and acceptance of the plant, and the lady's acceptance of the acknowledgment. The plant is thus a pattern of ongoings and events (really a self-closed pattern) interlaid within a more inclusive (self-closed) pattern of ongoings and events. It is an aggregate within an aggregate, a structure within, and constituting a part of, a larger structure. And correspondingly with the manifold of perception that would be involved in an onlooker who is watching the procedure. Both the inside and the outside structuring of the plant, as above described for the stimulus situation, would be represented in the organismic structure that constitutes the observer's perception. In this way both the inner and the outer meanings of plant are simultaneously fulfilled within the perceiver. Again the reader can generalize this illustration, if he wishes, to cover the perception of objects and surrounding manifolds of a wide range and variety.[14]

---

that give the object an outer-situational meaning. The reason for the difference between the two above cases is that in the football example "structure" is more apparent as constituting the relationship of the inner and outer contexts. In the pine-tree case the dynamic structure (i.e., interaction within the grove) is less perceivable. As for what goes on in the brain, structure (both "inside" structure and "outside" structure) is probably present in both cases.

[14] It could be applied, for example, to the apprehension of the personality of the woman who is bringing the plant to the hospital. We have the meaning that she is actually (outwardly) helpful or "giving" (trait description) with respect to others. We have also the (inner) meaning that she *characteristically tries* (if this is so) to give help or comfort to others (trend description). A *full* apprehension or meaning of the woman's personality would include both.

The preceding account of a possible approach to structure-theory in perception has been highly condensed and inadequate. But perhaps enough has been said to show that the idea that context can be translated into terms of dynamic structure is at least suggestive, and that it permits a statement both of stimulus-manifolds and of the process of meaning that is denotational in principle and consistent in logic. We hypothesize, first, that veridical perceptual meaning involves some physiological processes and phenomenological experiences of the organism that are representative of a corresponding order in the outer physicalistically experienced world; and second, that this order is to be found in the existence and operation of self-contained structures of events that are related to one another in various ways, one of the ways being the interstructuring of lesser, included, aggregates to make up greater, including, structures. We hypothesize, further, that this process repeats itself; more and more widely inclusive structures being assembled as we ascend into the so-called higher levels or orders of nature. This descriptive paradigm, which applies both to the physicalistic world and to the perception of that world, postulates (1) that every "object" is resolvable into a structure (inside-structuring of the "object") and (2) that the structure into which it is resolved is a part of a more inclusive structure (outside-structuring of the "object"). It also postulates that, corresponding to these two related orders of (perceptual) structuring, the perception of every object has both an "inside" and an "outside" *meaning*. We might even say (though a complete explanation would lead us too far afield) that the occurrence or operation, as within the organism, of these inner and outer structures *is* the meaning.[15]

Further reinterpretations of core-context theory can now be made, some of them parallel with details discussed by Titchener. The two perceptual structurings into which the object and its manifold are resolved can have different energy-levels in their operation, so that different persons, or the same person on different occasions, can be more aware of the inside than the outside meaning, or vice versa. The inner structure is usually the more stable and predictable, but the outer also may in certain cases have a high degree of predictability. All are self-contained and are composed of the dynamic ongoings of denotable elements and their interrelationships or events.' Outer

---

[15] A preliminary exposition of the writer's theory of event-structure will be given in the final chapter. The above portions of the theory are introduced here because of their bearing upon Titchener's context theory and also to give some background for various suggestions to be made later in connection with the review of the theories of perception.

structures ("outside contexts") in which the object may appear may sometimes be numerous; some may be relatively permanent, some shifting. The inner structure (the "object" itself) may remain practically the same through time. The two are not usually operative with an equal degree of energy ("conscious or attentive clearness"); one may be increased at the expense of the other according to circumstances. For example, if a professor of zoölogy were to say to his class "Today we shall study the physiology of the cockroach," ensuing perceptions would have a content consisting almost entirely of the inside meaning of that creature; while if one were to say to a housewife "There's a cockroach crawling in the kitchen sink," inside meaning would diminish and outside meaning would operate with considerable energy. It is important to note, however, that in both cases *some inside meaning* must be present. We would say, as Titchener said about his core and context, that the physiological bases of both areas of meaning are present and are potentially capable of being raised to the energic-threshold requirement.

Titchener's idea of the direct recognition of an object (core), in "old" perceptions, without the need of context, represents a case in which the inside structure is well above the threshold energy level, and this structure by itself is sufficient to give a meaningful recognition. The inner, or included, structure is practically always represented in some degree in its phenomenological counterpart which is fairly constant in form; and it is *necessary* as *physiological* structure if any meaning of the object is to occur. The outer, including, structure cannot do without the inner. The latter represents not a mere "embeddedness" within the larger structure, but an actual operant part; for structure is always dynamic throughout. The lady visiting her friend in the hospital could not take her a plant unless there were a plant to take; and the florist could not sell the lady an object that did not possess at least some of the recognizable features of a plant.

Finally, it should be noted that the structural analysis of objects and their perceptions will apply also to *situations*. Consider, for example, one's perception of the visible organization of operations in a large bank (the including structure), with the interaction of a particular teller and payee (included structure) set within it; or consider one's perception of a whispered inquiry of one worshipper to another as to the number of the hymn, a happening of a smaller structure that is interlaid within the more inclusive structure of a church service. Situations as well as objects thus have both an inside and an outside context or structuring and an inside as well as an outside meaning when they are fully perceived. (If, for example, we should apply this idea, at the conceptual level, to nations in the international scene, not making them "entities" but keeping them in terms of the dynamic interstructuring of structures of denotable elements, we would then have a better understanding of international relations.) This structural similarity of objects and situations is not surprising since an *object* observed at a scale of denotation fine enough to make its inner kinetics apparent would itself be a situation.[16]

Starting with Titchener's core-context theory we seem to have been striding with seven-league boots over unknown territory, far afield from Titchener's postulates and into realms that he would have said do not belong to psychology at all. These reflections of the present writer concerning the possibility of successive orders of perceptual structuring, though they seem to him plausible, can be offered at this point only as speculative. The reader can make of them whatever he will. The problem out of which they have arisen, however, is both clear and deeply significant. Whether one accepts the structural viewpoint or not, it has become evident, both from our analysis of the core-context theory and from the facts of everyday life, that behavioral aggregates, both perceptual and overt, have within their total manifold of patternings, contexts, or structures (call them what you will) this double inner and outer aspect.

This dual principal of aggregation, though a definite part of the perceptual meaning of objects, is by no means limited to perception. It extends to the entire behavior of organisms. Every act of behavior

[16] In order to make the preceding discussion of structure easier to follow the reader might be tempted to try to translate its concepts into the more familiar terms, "molar" and "molecular." The outer structuring of behavior seems like what one would observe from the *molar* standpoint as the "whole organism" interacts with its environment. The "inside structure" would be represented by the physiological details within the organism that "underlie" molar behavior, details to which the term *molecular* is usually applied. The reader is warned that if he takes this course he will be likely to miss the whole point of the discussion. In the first place, molar and molecular are terms that connote "linear" entities or agencies at their respective levels. They do not carry the clear idea of structure, much less the *dynamic* structure of ongoings and events into which the "mole" and the "molecule" are, in terms of the theory, actually resolved. Secondly, these terms cleave the total aggregate into "levels." They are "either-or" terms. One works *either* on the molar *or* on the molecular level, and no one has been able to put the two together. Event-structure theory, on the other hand, works in two or more orders *at the same time*. Its objective is to present not an inside *or* an outside view of the aggregate, but an inside *and* an outside view; and this under one unified set of principles—not under the rubrics of different fields of science. The terms molar and molecular are foreign to such a meaning as this. One would find neither mole nor molecule in a thoroughgoing structural interpretation.

has both its "inside" and its "outside" characteristics. The principle, in fact, probably applies in some way to every phenomenon studied by scientists. The very fact that phenomena are aggregates that are finite and self-delimited, though never totally isolated from other phenomena, renders their inside and outside relationships inevitable. Such relationships lie in the very nature of the physical world. Two points of view are thus always presented to the observer. He can take either the inside view of the aggregate (at any level concerned) or he can take the outside view. He can see either the "context" that composes it or the "context" that it helps to compose. How these two views can be reconciled, how the inner and outer aspects or relationships of the phenomenon can be simultaneously dealt with without dislocation or gap and explained in one consistent theory, is one of the most pervasive, difficult, and important problems of science. For later reference we shall call it the "*inside-outside*" problem. We have here the old question of the hierarchy of the sciences in a new guise. The atom, the molecule, the crystal, the cell, the organ, the organism, and society are all knit together in some mysterious way that can be understood only when the inside and the outside aspects or relationships of these several aggregates at their respective levels can be reconciled. Doctrines of emergence and terms like molar and molecular are only makeshift explanations that do not explain. The topic pertains to life, to behavior, to all forms of social organization, and to the universal and unending search for unity in nature. As such, it presents a problem of paramount importance in the construction of theories. We may be sure that it will cross our path again in our study of the theories of perception.

But we shall leave the problem, for the present, to return to the more familiar interests of the theorists whose perceptual systems we are now to examine. As for the further possibilities of the dynamic structural viewpoint, additional suggestions will be introduced by the writer from time to time, including many that will deal with simpler and more direct aspects of structural theory than the one we have been considering.

5

The Configurational Approach
Gestalt Theory of Perception

Any serious discussion of modern perceptual theories may well begin with gestalt psychology. This influential system had its rise from the study of perceptual phenomena and its greatest successes have remained in that area. Somewhat philosophical in its outlook, it is a theory of imposing intellectual stature and in some respects of elegance and beauty. It is most at home in the realm of configuration, and its adequacy as a general theory must rest on the extent to which configurational aspects are representative of the total phenomenon of behavior. The subject-matter and method of the theory have been, from the start, strongly phenomenological. The immediate experiences of the subject are the matter to be described and explained. For the purpose of explanation, however, facts and speculations about the brain and neural activities have been freely, even if not always successfully, employed. Although for many psychologists gestalt theory has "changed the face" of the whole science, and although it has brought to the attention of all a vast array of new facts and principles, one does not usually realize that it is not so much a finished theory as a broad way of looking at the facts of perception and behavior. It is a systematic orientation to psychology having a strong philosophical note and a set of apt and coherent formulations, rather than a basic explanation established by reference to a rigorously tested and proven model. Vigorous attempts at such explanation in terms of neurophysiology have been in the making, but their fulfillment lies in the future. The heuristic value of the gestalt doctrine as a way of looking at psychological phenomena, however, is so great that it has won a large number of adherents upon that basis alone. If one is willing to waive certain criteria, it is possible to conceive an astonishing number of psychological facts in terms of dynamical configurations, field forces, and wholes that seem more than the sums of

112

their parts.   One cannot do justice to gestalt theory in a single chapter.
We shall here merely try to bring out its main contributions for perception, returning to it again in Chapter 19 where further aspects
touching upon a special perceptual problem will be discussed.

BASIC CONCEPTS OF THE GESTALT SYSTEM

No less than one hundred and fourteen "laws of gestalten" have
been formulated by various writers.   These were brought together
by Helson in 1933.   Boring (1942) edited the list down to fourteen.
Although a reduction of a cool hundred is quite an achievement, let
us see whether, by making certain combinations, we can present the
fundamental ideas in a still smaller compass.   The following six
headings are more in the nature of basic concepts and principles than
of formally stated laws; they comprise in part postulates and in part
empirically established generalizations.

1. *The form-concept and isomorphism.*   The central idea of gestalt
theory is *form*, both in psychological phenomena and in nature
generally.   Form is a fundamental law; it is the way things appear to
the perceiver.   When one perceives an object that object tends, psychologically, to take on form; and forms establish themselves and
persist, independently of the stimulus, as a property of the perceiving
organism.   Phenomenological experience comes in *gestalten.*   Such
forms occur within the nervous system or brain as macroscopic states
or physiological configurations which are "isomorphic" (i.e., identical
in form) with the configuration of the percept to which they give rise.

2. *Wholeness-character and relationships.*   Though the form can
present itself as a pattern of parts its essential character is not a
linking together of such parts in piecemeal fashion, nor even their
assembly as interacting elements.   It possesses, rather, some pervasive
and unifying quality within the physiological state and the percept
as a whole.   The form always has a "whole-character" that transcends
the characteristics of the parts.   In this conception the view of the
perceptual aggregate was sharply changed from that of elementarism
and associative context.   The fact that it *is* an aggregate, that is, a
constellation of parts or elements, is minimized; and a microscopic
treatment of the aggregate is prohibited as destructive to the reality
of the total state.   The whole-character manifests itself in the relationships between parts as well as in changes produced in the parts
themselves.   The perceiving of relationships is an essential aspect of
wholeness in experience.

3. *Field and forces.*   The specific principle through which whole-

character operates in the perception of any object is that of a continuous set of influences throughout the macroscopic state or perceptual figure. These influences operate as combined forces with resultants and communicate changes from one part of the state or figure to another. The conception is essentially that of a field within a medium that comes to equilibrium, or sometimes of a system that reaches and tends to maintain a steady state; and the field interpretation is employed both at the physiological and the phenomenological levels.

4. *Flexibility, transformation, and transposition.* Such fields, wholenesses, or configurations are not bound in any one to one way to the proximal stimulus-pattern from the object. They follow laws that are intrinsic to the organism; and, being fields, they are capable of flexibility and transformation. The relationships which they preserve to the proximal stimulus-pattern may represent that pattern only topologically, that is, in the same way that a pattern drawn on a sheet of rubber that is later stretched out of shape is still preserved in its essential features, that is, in its "in-betweennesses" and "adjacences," even though all its metric properties have been changed. Certain invariants of perceptions are, however, preserved through changes of the stimulus-pattern. Among these are transpositions of the perceived object on the scales of various dimensionalities.

5. *Bounding features, symmetry, goodness of form.* The perceived configuration and its macroscopic physiological state usually have boundaries or "constraints" that delimit them and thus play a part in the work of the field-forces. A figure, as contrasted with ground, is self-bounded. The configuration and state tend to be self-closing and to be simple, balanced, and symmetrical. The tendency is toward "good" form.

6. *Organization.* There is organization within a configuration and with relation to its surroundings. The field is organized by its forces, giving rise to segregation, groupings, combinations into subsystems, and articulation. "Strong" *gestalten* may be produced by strong forces or firm articulation, and as such resist fusion or analysis and eliminate "weaker" or poorly articulated forms. Unbalanced or poorly articulated forms fuse more readily than well-articulated or "good" forms.

These six major themes, form, wholeness and relationships, field-forces, flexibility, bounding and symmetrically closing features, and organization cover most of the gestalt laws and experimental exhibits. They have thus far been demonstrated more unequivocally in the phenomenological than in the physiological realm. It is evident that they deal principally with one particular phenomenon-class in perception, namely, configuration. They are formal in character; but temporal as well as spatial configurations are included. Auditory rhythm, for example, is a configuration in time. We shall discuss the logic involved in the development of these formulations and their application to specific effects in perception.[1]

PHI-PHENOMENON; LAWS OF ORGANIZATION; EQUILIBRIUM OF FORCES

How gestalt theory was directed by the polemics of Köhler (1929) and Koffka (1935) against the analytical introspectionists, associationists, behaviorists, and "empirical" theorists generally, is too well known to require much comment. It was pointed out that the manner in which the integration of sensations, and of these with images, was achieved by the organism so as to produce a single unified perception was left by the elementarists as an insoluble mystery. As a matter of fact their analytical descriptions were in direct contradiction to the facts. For sensations or their attributes rarely come to us in an elementary state. If they do, they are probably artifacts of the method employed. It is only when we distort the direct experience by subjecting it to an unnatural introspective dissection that we can discover such a thing as a pure sensation or attribute. Instead of being a "bundle" of elements acquiring meaning through context or through some higher process of interpretation, the perception is an organized whole from the start. Particularly heavy was the assault upon the notion that properties of sensory experience follow in a one-to-one way the properties of the peripheral or proximal stimulus-pattern and that constancy in perception is gained by some added "interpretation" from past experience brought to bear upon these bits of sensory data. Perceptual constancies, the gestaltists claimed, are natively given, are experienced directly, and are a property of the organizing action of the nervous system. The mechanical-linkage laws of association were also shown to be inadequate to explain the selective process by which the organism learns. Behaviorism was criticized as committing the "stimulus error," that is, for reading into the stimulus all kinds of meanings that really derive from the configurational process within the organism.

[1] In almost any standard textbook of psychology there may be found, usually in the chapter on perception, drawings and other demonstrations that illustrate most of the above principles. Cf., for example, Dashiell, 1949, and Woodworth, 1938. For more complete accounts and examples of configuration see Hartmann, 1935, Ellis, 1938, and especially Koffka's scholarly treatise (1935).

Since the principles of gestalt psychology arose in the realm of phenomenology we can best begin with some crucial observations as to "how things appear" to the perceiver. The starting point, as most writers agree, seems to have been the studies of apparent movement reported by Wertheimer in 1912. If a fixed short line of light, a, is very briefly shown and then a similar fixed line, b, is briefly shown a short distance away or in a rotated position and following a very closely in time (say by $\frac{1}{30}$ second), the two stimuli will appear as two and as simultaneous. If the interval between the two exposures is relatively long ($\frac{1}{5}$ second), a and b are again seen as two, but as successive. At some interval whose duration is between these two intervals an appearance of *movement* is seen. The optimal interval for this effect is about $\frac{1}{16}$ second. One sees, in this case, a *single* line of light moving from the position of stimulus a to that of stimulus b. At a slightly longer interval, but still before successive appearance is reached, Wertheimer reported an experience of "pure movement" which takes the same course as the optical movement and connects the objects, but does not in itself seem to be a moving object. This experience he called "phi movement."

On the basis of these findings Wertheimer maintained that phenomenological movement is a primary sensory phenomenon, an experience that does not refer to any basic constituents. It does not consist of the displacement of a sensation as an object is moved in space through time. It is immediately "given" and is not reducible to terms of time or space. Phenomenological movement, under optimal conditions, may be indistinguishable from the perception of the movement of an object that is physicalistically moving. Hence all perceived movements can be interpreted as phi-phenomena. Movement is a veridical experience when there is actual physical movement and a non-veridical experience when there is not. Korte (1915) formulated the laws of optical perceived movement in terms of the distance between the stimuli, the time between them, and their intensity. Wertheimer went further, postulating a kind of "physiological short-circuit" in the brain that took place at a certain time and space relation of the stimuli and served as the substrate of the apparent movement. This parallelistic explanatory attempt was a forerunner of Köhler's isomorphic theory. Following the work of Wertheimer other investigators described other kinds of phenomenologically experienced movement, mainly of a non-veridical sort.

It can be readily seen how this famous experiment seemed to establish the validity of a phenomenological world of percepts that took place by laws intrinsic to the organism and did not bear a one-to-one relation with the stimulus-pattern on the receptors. The phi-phenomenon is a cortical, not a retinal, happening. The investigation also seemed to show that a perceptual experience has a whole-character that is not merely the addition of its parts (a and b), but is something entirely new (apparent movement). There was also a field-like effect in that an influence or excitation extended through the cortical medium from the locus of one stimulus-object's cortical projection to another. Finally this research was significant as com-bining the spatial and the temporal aspects of a configuration.

The gestalt psychologists set about trying to state the laws of "how things appear" in terms appropriate to such configurational interests. They affirmed that immediate experiences come organized in wholes; that certain items "belong" to one constellation rather than to another; and that experienced features are modified by being together. Wert-heimer stated the principles according to which parts combine into wholes—the laws of organization.[2] These include, among others, proximity, similarity, direction, good curve, uniform destiny or "com-mon fate," and closure. In viewing dots arranged on a page in clusters we see every cluster together, as a unit; one dot does not get drawn over into an alien cluster. If dots of various colors are scat-tered on a page, but there are a number of them of the same color, these *similar* elements tend to group themselves and may form a distinct pattern. The same is true of any identical items dispersed within a heterogeneous arrangement. In dot figures rows of dots proceeding in the same direction are grouped in perception. A line that forms a good curve within a figure will stand out as a unit. The principle of common fate may be shown by displacing upward or downward some of the dots in a row of dots. Those displaced will be perceptually grouped. A principle of "good continuation" can be illustrated by Köhler's demonstration of a sweeping scroll-like curve in which there is a slight hump or irregularity. There is an almost irrepressible tendency to push this irregular part in or out to make it follow the continuation of the curve, a phenomenon that Köhler called "requiredness" and generalized into a dynamic principle of phenome-nological *gestalten*. Closure can be exemplified by viewing a circle with a small gap in it. It tends to be seen as a true circle; and in a brief tachistoscopic exposure the gap may not even be seen.

In all these examples it will be observed that the whole has a character of its own which could never be realized by experiencing the parts separately. The nature of the configuration which the "wholeness" takes on, or to which the pattern tends, is said to be that

[2] See in Ellis, 1938, pp. 71–88.

of the greatest possible simplicity and clearness (either a simplicity of uniformity or a simplicity of articulation). It also represents, in figures, the maximum symmetry and regularity. The thought is expressed by saying that percepts always tend toward "as good a figure" as the circumstances, that is, the stimulus-pattern, will permit. This statement, one of the most important of the gestalt generalizations, is called the law of *prägnanz*. It has innumerable manifestations. To give merely one example, suppose one is looking at a circle composed of dots with one dot slightly out of line. The tendency is for the dot to appear pulled back into the circle making a regular figure. The example of the curve cited from Köhler could also be called a demonstration of *prägnanz*.

Though we have thus far been traveling only in the realm of phenomenology, all these phenomena forcibly suggested to gestalt psychologists a dynamic property of configurations. In figure perception, which has always been a basic experimental medium for gestalt, there is said to be manifested an interplay of "forces" of differing strengths internal to the figure, external to it, or along its boundary; and this interaction of forces is what produces shape. Where the external forces are weak and the internal forces strong, a simple, good figure is obtained by the internal cohesive forces coming to equilibrium. For example, in the region of the blind spot, or in after-images, regular contours are filled out and the corners of square projected images become rounded off. Where the external forces are stronger they will produce unities and good figure through segregating objects by pressing in along their boundaries until an equilibrium is again obtained. Equilibrium in all cases represents the balancing of the forces within and about the figure as well as the attainment of maximum continuity; and in this process regularity and symmetry are also attained. The fields of forces at work thus organize frameworks, contours, and boundaries. They set off figure from ground, give articulation to the figure, confer thing-character, and so on. Complex figures are either fused into wholes or segregated into "duo" or multiple patterns, according to the arrangement of the forces. Subsystems may be formed. Some figures may be "embedded" in larger ones so firmly that they are completely masked and it is impossible to observe them even though we know they are there. Phenomenological forces distort stimulus patterns, providing all kinds of illusions. Perceived meaning enters and is treated in two ways. First, it is assumed to be immediately given in the configurational experience, a view that is in direct line with phenomenological philosophy. This fact led Boring to say that the gestaltists do not have a theory of meaning. They take it "on faith"; that is, they make of it a postulate. But meaning is also treated, more specifically, in terms of configurational dynamics. It is defined, in part, as the coming of the percept-field to equilibrium; it is a property of the whole as it proceeds toward and attains organization, articulation, and goodness of figure. Though practically all the examples in the preceding paragraphs have been in the visual field it must be remembered that gestalt theory is a theory of *perception* and that its principles can also be exemplified in other sensory modalities.[3]

PERCEPTION OF THREE-DIMENSIONAL SPACE; RELATIONSHIPS AND GRADIENTS; CONSTANCY

Koffa's treatment of the perception of three-dimensional space may be cited as illustrating the dynamics of organization. The dimension of distance or depth, producing an appearance of solidity in an object, is obviously not given by the retinal pattern, for the latter is only bidimensional. It is a property of the field whose physiological existence must be inferred to be in the brain. And the field has not two dimensions, but three. A drawing of a hollow, or outline, cube is seen clearly and inescapably in three dimensions, not as twelve lines on a single plane. The third dimension is produced by the fact that "rotating" an angle in this dimension is the simplest method of perceiving it. "Flopping it over" in a third dimension of space requires less action than twisting the figure around and moving it up or down in a bidimensional plane. Field forces operate by the principle of least action and also in such a way as to produce symmetry. If one sets up a situation of apparent movement in the frontal plane (see earlier discussion) but interposes a line across the path of the movement, the movement will be seen to pass beneath rather than through the obstruction, thus producing an experience of the third dimension. This effect can again be interpreted as the simplest action, and it also preserves the "thing-like" identity of the interposed obstruction. The clue to stereoscopic vision lies in realizing that it is a process of forming objects, phenomenologically speaking. The organization by field forces produces an attraction and fusion of images falling on nearly identical points of the two retinas not because of their sensory similarity, but because such a fusion reconstitutes a simple organization in which one part of the figure is seen to be at a different distance from the observer than another, just as it would

[3] For a more complete account of organization and configurational dynamics see Koffka, 1935, Chapters IV–VII inclusive.

actually be in the physicalistic experience of a solid object. It thus seems that a process within the organism is organizing or "filling in" between stimulated points in such a way as to produce tridmensional space and with it a fairly faithful reconstruction of the physicalistic world (cf. Chapter 2). Such an interpretation, it must be remembered, is thus far only a program for a theory rather than a theory itself. Really to explain the matter some more definite conception of the organizing action of the brain must be offered.

It was said earlier that the perception of relationships was one of the problems with which gestalt theory is concerned. What *is* a relationship from the psychological standpoint? Köhler[4] answers this question by his and von Lauenstein's theory of "gradients." It is assumed that when two phenomenological objects differ in some respect their cortical correlates have a corresponding difference of physical state. In the medium of brain tissue lying between them a gradient may be set up according to the nature of the processes and their differences. Gradients are familiar in physics, as in the field gradient between different electrostatic potentials or as between objects of different temperatures. Under certain conditions currents of various sorts develop between the bodies or states concerned. Phenomenological relationships are explained by the existence of such gradients in the tissues of the brain. Stated abstractly, a "relationship" depends upon a situation involving two or more items, A and B, concerning which the following three statements are true: (1) A and B would both exist even if the relationship between them were not present; (2) the relationship could not exist without A and B; and (3) the relationship itself is of a different class of phenomena from A or B (for example, the temperature-difference of bodies is not the same thing as the bodies). It will be seen that gradients fulfill all three of these conditions or relationships.

To take a concrete example, imagine two vertical lines printed on a page, one slightly longer than the other, and about one-half inch apart. The longer one, on the right, projects slightly above and below the shorter one. Between the two lines we now have a "field" and a pair of "gradients." Suppose we connect the adjacent *ends* of the two lines at the top and also at the bottom by straight lines slanting from the longer line down, or up, to the shorter. There will then be a trapezoidal figure, and the connecting lines will describe gradients between the two verticals taken at their ends. These gradients, that is, the amounts of their slopes, will depend upon both the difference between the lengths of the vertical lines and their distance apart. If

[4] 1938, Chapter VI.

the vertical lines should be widely separated the gradient would be less steep. It would be reduced so that the figure would approach an oblong in shape. In order to maintain the same gradient at a greater distance than that with which we started the difference between the lengths of the vertical lines must be increased. The same phenomenon has been shown with respect to brightness gradients. Using the intensity-difference of visual stimuli at the just noticeable difference point (differential threshold) an experiment has been conducted to determine this threshold when the stimuli are presented at different distances apart in space. It was found that the greater the distance apart of the retinal points stimulated (hence the greater the cortical interval), the greater is the *difference* of the stimulus-intensities required to produce a just noticeable difference in the perceived brightnesses. A gradient for brightness, expressing a relationship between the two percepts, was thus demonstrated that conformed to the deductions from the earlier example of the lines.

Let us now return to the lines, and instead of moving them apart, let us merely increase their lengths—but let us increase them *proportionally*. We draw the connecting lines as before. We now find that though the size of the figure is increased, the gradients are the same. It is still a trapezoidal figure with respect to its "form." We now have a partial interpretation of the "form-qualities" of von Ehrenfels. A rectangle, for example, can remain a rectangle regardless of changes in size. Constant gradients have preserved at least a part of a constant formal relationship. A further development of the gradient principle might explain the stability of a melody or chord when it is transposed from one key to another. The theory also fits the phenomenon-class we have called dimensional frame of reference (Chapter 3). So much for the argument; but to make it finally effective the required gradients must, of course, be discovered in the brain.

Perceptual constancy provides a problem which any complete theory of perception must solve. Here we also have relationships, but in another sense. The constancy here is not one of a form that persists through changes of dimensions of a changing stimulus-object, but a tendency of the perceived configuration to agree in its dimensions with a constant distal stimulus-object, though the pattern of receptor stimulation is changing with changes in the conditions of observation. Koffka attempted to handle the problem of spatial constancies by such concepts as frameworks that tend to normalize, localization within a framework, invariants, and field-forces. The relation between retinal-image shape and the perceived orientation or slant of the object is the clue to shape-constancy. Shape as seen when the object is slanted is said to be the product of the forces of organization in a field of stress that result from the non-normal position of the object and the stimulus-pattern itself. The tendency to right the object that is perceived as tilted combines with the foreshortened stimulation pattern from the retina to produce the perceived shape that would be seen if the object were *not* tilted. Brightness constancy is explained by gradients, together with a principle called "appurtenance," or "belongingness." A black stimulus object given bright illumination in an otherwise dark room may be seen as white. When seen near a white paper, both being brightly illuminated, it appears black. In the latter case the black stimulus object is seen as at the bottom of a "white-black gradient." Its perceived brightness is determined by *this particular* gradient because it is *near* to the other object (white paper) that receives the same illumination. Objects that by proximity "belong" together appear as having a gradient between them. It will be noted that these explanations are again given in purely phenomenological and stimulus terms. To be complete they would have to tell us what is meant by frameworks, field-forces, gradients, and belongingness in terms of the nervous system.

MEMORY AND TRACE; RELATION TO LEARNING; WHOLENESS AND SUPERSUMMATION

The final theorem we shall discuss is one that links the perceptual activity with memory. In stating the first of the six major ideas of gestalt theory (p. 113) it was said that forms not only establish themselves but tend to persist through time. They are subject to memory-retention and recall. Here we must still more definitely leave phenomenology and postulate a basis in the process of the brain. For after the stimulus object disappears we are no longer conscious of the configuration; yet it may last "potentially" over considerable periods of time. Later, some stimulus-pattern may give rise to its recall. There must, therefore, have been a *trace* that was left by the original excitation in the brain. The stimulus-excitation is called the "process" in contradistinction from the "trace" that is left as a residue of this, or of earlier, stimulations. Because of the trace it is possible to recall names when we need them upon seeing faces, to experience temporal succession, to have experiences of temporal rhythm, to make comparisons between stimuli successively presented, or merely to "recognize" some stimulus-object we have seen before. In short, traces are necessary in order to deal with the whole topic of memory and the time dimension in behavior. Without this notion gestalt psychology could not aspire to be a general theory. Some physiological process in the brain through which the earlier perceived form is isomorphically retained as a residue is necessary as a basis of the trace-concept. In perception, insofar as it bears upon the recognition of meaningful situations, the matter is important. We must suppose that past experience with objects, or the physiological basis of that experience, has something to do with our present ability to recognize them and to make suitable behavorial adjustments.

What, then, is the precise nature of this physiological "trace" that remains in the nervous tissue? Nothing very definite is known. One might refer to analogies such as the "memory" of a wire that has been twisted so that it comes to a stable shape slightly different from the original. Here there are probably molecular displacements or deformations that persist through time. Koffka made two points about traces that are worth noting. First, the trace must exist in a different location in the brain from that of the stimulus-process. Otherwise when a succession of two similar stimuli is given there would be no way of recognizing the second as a member of a pair the first of which is recalled in imagination at the time the second is given. The experience that is recalled by imagery from the past must not seem as one with the present sensory experience. By introducing a *spatial* interval in the brain provision was thus made for an experience of *temporal* succession. Another way of saying this is that temporal differences in the environment are translated into spatial differences in the cortex. Second, without some kind of bridge from the trace-region to the location of the process, the past might be obliterated. We need stimuli to recall past experiences, and stimuli happen "in the present." Though a "memory" may seem to lie behind us in time, a neural process does not "exist only in the past"; a physicalistic experience is a "present" experience. There must, then, be some means of selective communication, through the intervening space-distance, between the stimulus-process and the trace. Presumably the forces of the field supply this connecting and reactivating influence. The field-excitation occurring in the space-interval between the stimulus-process and the trace-residue is also said to leave a trace. Traces themselves are not in consciousness; they are the physiological basis of conscious memories. The earlier experience is recalled by the field-excitation that is directed from the immediate stimulus-process toward the trace of an earlier process.

Another inference in gestalt theory is that traces must tend with the passage of time to become simpler, better organized, and of better, or more symmetrical, figure. Such terms as normalizing, sharpening, and levelling have also been used. In other words, traces follow the same dynamic laws as all configurations; organizing activity occurs within the trace. Experimental studies made to test this theorem have not been too convincing. Owing to the evaluative, non-objective character of such concepts as "simplicity" and "good figure" judges who have examined drawings made by subjects from memories of previously perceived objects have not agreed very well as to whether these configurational laws were being fulfilled in the successive reproductions.[5] It will be recalled that in Chapter 2 some reservations were made as to the dependability of purely phenomenological judgments.

The trace concept serves the purpose in gestalt psychology not only of recognition and memory, but also, to a limited extent, of the function served by association and habit in the more objective theories. In insightful learning traces are "transformed," acquiring meaning in relation to goal activity. Traces interact with their processes to create new results; and trace-systems become consolidated so that more influence may be exerted by them over processes than occurs in the reverse direction. Stereotyping of the perceptual activity may thus occur. Trace-systems may become available to processes in varying degrees, like habit-sytems ready to function. With the doctrine of traces we again have a concept that seems ideologically necessary, but one for which (at least thus far in our story) no firm or definite physiological theory has been advanced.

In their notion of traces gestalt theorists have thus provided a place for the retention of experiences. What traces can do, however, toward explaining learning in the ordinary sense is very limited. Though earlier configurations are given a present habitat in trace systems, and though traces can spontaneously change *themselves* according to the dynamic laws, the role of *accumulated past experience* as a factor in changing them is denied. Whether the configuration is one that occurs now for the first time or represents a trace from an occurrence that took place at an "earlier present," the continuity of past experience and environmental factors working through time have played no essential part in molding it. Since the percept has an indissoluble unity it could not have been acquired in the first instance by adding sensory units "piecemeal." It might take a little time before the *Gestalt* appears: but when it comes its advent is sudden. It is all or none. Learning would therefore have to be

---

[5] Recent experimental evidence, using a recognition method, seems to be negative. Cf. George, 1952.

a discontinuous, rather than a continuous, process. It is perhaps incorrect to say that the gestalt theorists, in minimizing the role of experience, have always opposed to it a doctrine of strict nativism. This doctrine was often implied, as in the citing of experiments to show that fully formed perceptions are present in young infants. What was insisted on, however, was that perception is organization from the start, or it is nothing. We do not get the pieces one by one, and then "learn" to put the whole together; the whole comes in experience in strict contemporaneity with the parts. (Some have even said that it comes earlier!) Insofar as past experience enters, it operates through the earlier providing of wholes that may later become organized into some larger configuration. This interpretation either reduces the significance of learning or else it makes of it something very different from the gradual acquisition of a habit envisaged by associationistic theories. It is a difference of view that underlies the wide cleavages characteristic of current psychological theory.

We have tried to show how the six major principles—form, wholeness and relationships, field-forces, transformation, good figure, and organization—all play a part in gestalt formulations of perception. To these were added perseveration through time, since this aspect is also essential to perceptual theory. Is there some one principle under which all the others can be subsumed? Possibly not; but if there is, at least, a *common bond*, it can be best stated as the idea of wholeness. Perhaps this theme has not been emphasized so much in later gestalt writings, having been superseded by the development of the idea of field. Still it has been of crucial importance in the past and is still assumed as a broad background generalization. It is maintained that wholes have unique properties. There comes into existence with the whole a kind of "supersummation" that is different from any mere addition, or "and-summation," of the parts. The whole is more than, or at least different from, the sum of its parts. It has laws of its own that do not belong to the parts either separately or in combination. The observations on which the formulations of gestalt are based show that in every case it is necessary to consider the whole, and that when the whole is taken into account some unique phenomenon—belongingness, figure and ground, articulation, apparent movement, prägnanz, three-dimensional space, transposed relationships, constancy, trace-recall, or the like—is sure to appear. If we dismembered the whole into parts, these phenomena would disappear.

Whole-character exhibits the principles of dynamic configurations, that is to say, it proceeds by the laws of organization which are assumed to be laws of the whole. From these conclusions it was but a step to giving to the whole, or at least to the laws intrinsic to it, a determinative role with respect to the parts, an ability to select and organize them and to impress upon them a character they would not have in isolation. For some gestaltists, though it seems a logical contradiction, the whole can exist independently of, or even before, its parts. It is in this assigning to the whole an independent existence and a role of determinative agency that gestalt psychology lies closest to philosophy.

THE SEARCH FOR PHYSIOLOGICAL BASES: ISOMORPHISM AND MACROSCOPIC BRAIN-FIELDS

The preceding account has taken its departure from phenomenological experiences. The phenomenology of configuration, and to some extent of frame of reference and constancy, have been kept in the foreground. Though we have frequently noted the assumption that there must be a physiological basis for configurational experiences the question of what that basis is has been passed over lightly. For purpose of exposition the account of the phenomenologically stated principles has been presented as though they comprised a separate, earlier chapter of the theory, and as though the physicalistic aspects form a later chapter. We must now correct this impression. Interest in physiological considerations started early among the gestaltists and has been developing steadily. Our separation of the two aspects, therefore, has been a logical rather than an historically accurate division. With the reader's indulgence, and in order to get the logic of the problem clearly stated, we shall continue for a moment to speak as though the phenomenological approach alone had held sway and as though no considered attempt at finding a physiological basis had been made.

Assuming, then, this frame of reference, which would really have applied only in the earliest stages of the theory, let us see what the logic of the situation would have been. We have seen that laws of organization had been stated. Forces were said to be in operation that established the contour and shape of a figure; and in coming to equilibrium these forces tended to mold the figure into the most simple and symmetrical form. Figure segregation, as against ground, was also established. Wholeness character, phenomenological fields, transposition, articulation, and the like had been demonstrated. But as thus far stated, the theory, though it had achieved some useful generalizations, was unsatisfactory. Though its introspective method had been improved by using direct experience, the theory still rested only upon introspection. Forces had been employed as explanatory concepts. But were these forces physicalistic or were they merely phenomenological? If the latter only, they could not be tested by objective methods. Many facts, such as the retention of skills, recognition, recall of earlier experiences, and the resumption of daily activities after sleep, pointed to the existence of organic factors that must be present and operative though they are not at the moment in consciousness. When we try to recall a forgotten name there is something that seems to beckon to us from the realm beyond our awareness. Though we have not yet recalled the name something tells us at once whether our attempts are right or wrong. This "something" must be a physiological process. Then too, without exploring this region it would be difficult to find a suitable anchorage for the laws of organization. They could not be laws of the "parts," for they could not then account for whole-character. They could not be entities that are *added to* the parts, for then they would be merely new *parts*. They must, therefore, be laws of the whole. But if one tries to locate this phenomenological whole, one meets methodological difficulties. It is not implied that the founders of gestalt theory recognized all of these inadequacies in just the way we have pointed them out. They were not slow, however, in deciding that something essential was missing from the theory; and Koffka relates how Wertheimer, in 1911, suggested a point of view that made it possible to develop the missing portion.[6]

To continue this analysis a little further we can recall briefly a part of the discussion in Chapter 2. Percepts of tables, trees, moving objects, conversations, and melodies, on the one hand, are direct experiences. They have a "phenomenological" reality. We know, however, that these "percepts" are not the same as the physicalistic experience of these objects or situations; they frequently exhibit discrepancies with respect to the latter type of experience. Moreover, acts of perceiving, themselves, in order to be objectively and fully described, must be stated in terms other than the experiences of the perceiver. Another person must observe the process physicalistically; he must note or try to investigate the stimulus-pattern on the receptors, processes in nerve fibers, connections made in cortical regions, and so on. These physiological items, since they are more denotable in principle and continuous, must not only be included, but must carry the main burden of explanation. The subject matter for the

[6] 1935, pp. 53, 56.

study and theory of perception must therefore include not one realm, but two, the phenomenological *and* the physiological.

Here we meet a dilemma. These two realms are descriptively distinct; formulations must stay in one of them or in the other. Yet if we are to give a full and connected explanation of perception, theory must somehow "straddle" and be applicable to both at the same time. A kind of "two-way" formulation must be invented.[7] The part played by physical (or physiological) data is what had to be added to gestalt theory; and the finding of a formula that would "straddle" and incorporate both realms in a single consistent system was the task that gestalt psychologists faced. It is clear, for reasons earlier stated, that one of the two worlds cannot be considered as acting directly upon the other. The two series must run along "in parallel" without interaction. If, in order to get on with the task, we can accept this dualism (which the gestaltists regarded as purely epistemological) we can then try to see how the straddling might be accomplished. Such an objective might be gained, at least in a certain rational sense, if we could show that the two orders of phenomena *obey the same set of "logical" laws* and that a single type of formal conceptualization might fit both. In this case the phenomenological and the physiological might both be regarded as the expression of some single deeper and more universal reality. (At this point, perhaps, a bit of metaphysics creeps into the picture; but it could scarcely be avoided if one is to attempt to get behind psychophysical parallelism.)

A thesis was therefore developed to the effect that whatever happens on the conscious, or phenomenological, side is mirrored by an exactly corresponding process, like it in all the gestalt properties of organization, in the brain. Presumably such a process would be found in the cerebral cortex. The gestalt theorists thus incorporated a postulate of *isomorphism*, as this view is called, as a basic part of their explanation of perception. Isomorphism means that all experienced order in both space and time "is a true representation of a corresponding order in the underlying dynamical context of physiological process." And organization, or the experience of a pattern as one thing, that is, as belonging together, always implies a corresponding dynamic unit (or whole) in the physiological processes. (Köhler, 1929.)

But in arriving at this postulate still another decision was, perhaps

[7] The old term "psychophysical" represents the traditional attempt to phrase both sides of the problem under a single concept. This term, however, has never conveyed much illumination and has been used merely as a matter of convenience.

unconsciously, involved. It was made so spontaneously that it hardly appeared to be a choice between alternatives, which it really was. We might arrive at an isomorphism of perceptual awareness and physiological process in either of two ways. We might take our clue either from the latter or from the former. That is, we could seek an isomorph in phenomenological experience corresponding to what we have discovered in brain action, or we could seek an isomorph for brain action from what we know about phenomenological experience. The gestaltists unhesitatingly chose the second method. Such a choice might perhaps be defended by the argument that we know more about phenomenology than we do about brain processes. However that may be, the decision to establish isomorphism in this way involved a certain burden of proof. Nature throughout the whole physicalistic order displays a considerable amount of continuity and regularity quite independently of the phenomenological experience of the organism. This regularity would, at least in part, unite both physiological and inanimate physical happenings under some common laws. And so if the gestalt principles of organization, good figure, and the like were to be manifested as laws of brain action, especially if they represent, as the gestaltists claimed, *universal* principles, they must also be expected to appear rather generally in the inorganic as well as the organic world. This was the burden of proof that Köhler assumed in his forthright, and to a considerable extent rewarding, search for "*physical gestalten.*" But there might also be a large amount of order in the physical world that cannot be adequately or fully described in such terms. Though Köhler · did succeed in pointing out many interesting "physical forms" that obey configurational laws, it would be going rather far to attempt to construe all physical principles, or even only the most pervasive, under this heading. Hence the decision to take the starting clue from phenomenology was, after all, a gamble. There would have been uncertainty, of course, in either way of proceeding. It is at such points as this that the philosophical preference or values of the theorist might enter (pp. 89–90).

Assuming, however, that we are going along with the decision of the gestalt school, the question that next arises is this: How can one use the known aspects of the brain processes that go with perception in such a way as to conceive an isomorphic relation between them and the configurational character of the percept? Let us first note that percepts are wholes, not parts in isolation. If we take the physiological processes as *microscopical* units, that is, as receptor cells with their specific correlations with neurons and as separate junctions of neurons at cortical synapses, we shall miss this point. The isomorphism of wholes will never be seen in such a one-to-one, piecemeal fashion. Experience is not something that is put together in a mosaic-like way; it does not appear as a bundle of molecular elements that are tied together. A percept is a *macroscopic* phenomenon. Therefore its physiological isomorph must also be macroscopic; it must involve an appreciable extent of cortical tissue. This idea was the contribution of Wertheimer to which Koffka had referred.

Considering the requirement in more detail it appears that what is further needed for the wholeness or macroscopic character of the percept is the provision that all the parts of the isomorph be bound together in such a way that a change in any one of them is accompanied by a change in the others. The physiological isomorph, like the percept to which it gives rise, must be a *configuration*. One part has to be "represented" in its influence at points where it does not actually exist. In order to avoid the old fallacy that things can act on one another through forces of attraction or repulsion "at a distance" there must be provided an actual medium in which a series of changes (or "representations" of the part concerned) can be propagated. For conceptualizing such a medium Köhler considered that the only possible model was that of the *field*, a concept well established in physics by the labors of Faraday, Oersted, and Maxwell. The notion is here provided of forces or "tensions" that are set up throughout the field when a disturbing influence (the stimulus) is brought to bear. These forces then come to equilibrium at a certain point or through a certain state of affairs; and in so doing they represent the propagation of changes through small steps in a medium. This model was considered as admirably suited for an isomorphic explanation of the configurational character of the percept. The effect of one part can be manifested at some distant place in the figure by the "field" of that part. Macroscopic electrical fields in the brain were thus hypothesized as explaining the facts of perception; and the hypothesis of cortical fields has come to constitute an integral part of the theory of gestalt.[8]

Certain issues were now cleared up in the relation between the percept, on the one hand, and the sensory stimulation received from objects on the other. The percept does not depend on the pattern

---

[8] Köhler in some of his writings has considered that the concept of a "steady state" such as characterizes open systems was a better formulation than the idea of a field coming to equilibrium. For a discussion giving the background for this concept see the first section of Chapter 18, and especially the footnote on the "candle-flame."

of points in the peripheral (i.e., retinal) stimulation; nor does it accompany some alleged one-to-one representation of such points in the cortex. It depends, rather, upon what happens in the macroscopic electric fields of the cortex after the afferent impulses are received at cortical projection areas. If there is a distortion in the percept in relation to the environmental object, that is, if the perception is non-veridical, then the cortical field is agreeing with the percept rather than with the object. In so far as the percept *is* veridical it is not adequately accounted for by the proximal stimulus pattern, for that pattern would change at different distances from the object and with different angles of regard. Thus the phenomenon of constancy, also, is to be explained, in some manner not yet fully revealed, by what happens in the cortical field. In the words of Koffka things appear as they do "because of the field organization to which the proximal stimulus distribution gives rise." (1935, p. 98.)

PHYSICAL *Gestalten;* KÖHLER'S THEORY OF STEADY ELECTRO-
CHEMICAL STATES IN THE CORTEX; FIGURAL AFTEREFFECTS
AND SATIATION

Seen from this standpoint the program of gestalt theory has consisted of three parts. First, it was desirable to show that the percept itself is really "field-like" in character. Second, there had to be elaborated some hypothetical model by which electric fields in the sensory or adjoining areas of the cortex could be conceived on the basis of the neurological and physiological facts already known, and to which the field-like aspects of the percept could be isomorphically referred. Third, and most important, it was necessary to show that gestalt-like physiological configurations based on field properties do exist in the cortex of the brain and that such brain-fields are associated in a necessary and intimate manner with percepts. The theory of dynamic *gestalten* had, of course, been already tested from a broader, more philosophical standpoint. At an early date Köhler was pointing out the presence of physical *gestalten* in nature, such, for example, as the tendency of electrostatic charges always to distribute or "shape" themselves in a way that would produce an equilibrium of forces over the surface or a conductor. One can change the *strength* of the charge in any way one wishes ("and-summation") without in any way altering this instantaneous tendency to assume the characteristic configuration. There was also cited the illustration of an oil drop surrounded by some liquid, and the play of forces external and internal to the drop whose balance gives it a symmetrical form. Many such examples of physical *gestalten* were available. In all of these the final distribution within the aggregate, the distribution that does not change further with time, is one whereby a form is reached in which forces act within or upon a smallest possible surface for a given volume (i.e., a sphere) and in which there is a minimum of energy capable of doing work. Such distributions represent both an equilibrium of forces and a simple and regular pattern.[9] Mach's dictum was cited to the effect that macroscopic physical states tend to develop in the direction of maximum regularity and simplicity and to become as stable as possible because in such distributions forces balance one another more exactly than in irregular patterns (Köhler, 1938, pp. 254–255).

The first and second portions of the program have been vigorously pressed, particularly in the direction of a hypothetical cortical model. It had been earlier proved by physiologists that as impulses reach autonomic nerve endings a chemical substance is secreted into the surrounding medium between the end of the nerve fibre and the muscle fibre which it activates. Assuming this same condition to hold within the ganglionic layers of the brain, Köhler (1938, 1940) envisaged in the cortex similar stationary chemical states maintained by the cumulative action of sensory nerve-impulses as these impulses come to the cortex in waves along the afferent neurons. These states will depend for their intensity upon the intensity of this chemical activity, which in turn depends upon the intensity of the stimulation. Thus, in the case of a white square seen on a gray background, the activity will be more intense in that cortical area represented by the square than in the part represented by the ground. Since ions are involved in chemical processes we may assume a concentration of ions inside the figure different from that in the ground outside as these parts are represented in the cortex. Since ions diffuse from regions of higher concentration into those of lower, one of these areas will become electropositive with respect to the other. Through this difference of electrostatic potential, which constitutes an electromotive force, a current is set up. The current passes circularly from the cortical region of the figure through that of the ground in the surrounding tissues, and back into the figure again. There is thus produced a "halo" of current around the boundary and all the way around the figure, and a field by which influences can be exerted from one part of the percept-area upon another. The self-distribution of electrostatic potential in the field, arising originally from optical sources and neural transmission to the brain, thus "segregates" the

---

[9] See, however, footnote, p. 138.

figure from its ground and gives it unity and homogeniety. The ground also is homogeneous but separated from the figure. Inside the figure, where the current is more restricted, it is more dense; while outside the figure it spreads more widely. Hence the ground, phenomenologically, is less vivid than the figure.

One of the deductions from the cortical field theory is based on the fact that when a current has been passing through a medium for some time its effects alter that medium. For example, chemical deposits may accumulate on the interfaces of cells; and polarization of membranes may occur that will alter or oppose the current's further passage in the same direction. To this obstructional effect, which has been called electrotonus, Köhler gives, for the purposes of his theory, the name "satiation." If the foregoing supposition is true, prolonged visual exposure to a figure should change its appearance (size, vividness, etc.), and the distance between two figures should be altered in consequence. An "old" percept should appear different from a "young" one though they may have exactly similar stimulus sources. Such effects have been demonstrated in experiments. This hypothesis permits a neat explanation, also, of the reversals of figure and ground that are seen when an ambiguous figure is steadily fixated for some time. Köhler and Wallach have published reports of experiments on figural aftereffects in which deductions from the theory seemed in general to have been verified.[10]

Demonstrations of such aftereffects are very interesting. The subject fixates his gaze on a point and an "inspection figure" is placed near the fixation-point. After prolonged looking this figure is removed and another stimulus, the "test-figure," is presented on or near the area that was occupied by the inspection figure. Since the subject's gaze remains fixated on the same point, the test figure can be used to explore the changes in the retino-cortical region that was previously stimulated. In this way satiation-effects and their distribution can be determined. Comparison of the perceived size of a test-figure placed on or near the region previously stimulated with that of an equal figure exposed upon an "unused" part of the retina will give evidence of the nature and degree of the satiation-effect. The test-figure is now seen as smaller in size. It is also found that the test-figure recedes in its perceived position away from the area previously occupied by the inspection figure (satiated area). If

[10] Köhler, 1940, Chapter II; Köhler and Wallach, 1944. Osgood and Heyer have worked out a different, statistical explanation of these phenomena based on more direct neurophysiological evidence provided by Talbot and Marshall. See Osgood and Heyer, 1952.

placed inside that area, it shrinks away from the boundary (satiation is greatest just inside or outside the boundary where the field of the encircling current is strongest). In similar ways "test-lines" can be made to assume non-veridical angles, and a straight test-line placed in a region formerly occupied by a curved line will appear as curved in the opposite direction. Corresponding aftereffects in the judgment of distances by *kinaesthesis* have been obtained.

All these phenomena Köhler considers as peculiar to object or pattern perception and as representing relationally determined processes in which satiation occurs. (Compare this statement with the definition of relationship that was given earlier.) That is to say, there is a difference of concentrations that determines a gradient and a current-flow in one direction or the other. There is, in figure or object perception, an electric current of diffusion whose distribution is governed by the shape of the boundaries at which parts of the system are in contact; and the pattern of current flow is thus actually determined by the geometrical properties of the object perceived. One important provision, however, is made by Köhler. We are not so naïve as to suppose that the distribution of the current or the shape of the field of the percept actually conforms in metrical fashion to the exact shape of the stimulus-object or to the proximal stimulation-pattern. The correspondence of the brain-pattern to the stimulus-pattern is only *topological*. That is, it has a "functional" geometry that preserves relationships of "betweennesses" and "adjacences" in the figure, rather than exact sizes, angles, or shapes. The tissue of the brain is also regarded as a volume conductor and the field established is in three dimensions: it applies to the perception of objects in depth as well as to figures lying in one plane. Temporal as well as spatial relationships can also be established in such a field. The degree to which various parts of the medium are affected by electrotonus (polarization effects) is directly related to the density of the current at those points, and this density diminishes as we go outward from the figure. The density of current-obstruction must occur in the same distribution, and it was shown to do so in the satiation experiments above described.[11]

APPLICATIONS OF KÖHLER'S THEORY; ITS EXPERIMENTAL AND PHYSIOLOGICAL TESTING

The cortical field-theory makes possible a meaningful interpretation of many of the phenomena of configuration. A field, of course, is

[11] Cf. Köhler, 1951.

continuous, and so is the percept of an object or figure; and by the fact that each part is able to exercise an influence through its field upon other parts the integrated wholeness-character of the percept is given an isomorphic physiological basis. A number of Wertheimer's laws of organization can be accounted for by the theory. Ground could appear to pass beneath the figure because of an overlying placement of the field of the figure. Strong gestalts, preventing the perceptual isolation of parts, can be ordered to intense field-currents. Vectors of actual, not merely psychic, forces inside and outside the cortical figure and along its contour can give it its shape. Equilibrium *via* Mach's principle will be attained as the opposing currents bring the system into the simplest and most regular configuration attainable under the constraints imposed by the stimulus pattern and the topographical neural framework. Transposition and form-quality can be accounted for by a gradient of electrical energy between the parts related plus the fact that the field process as a whole can be changed in intensity without altering the proportionality of the parts concerned. Trace systems can be explained as due to the persistence of the cortical field conditions after the stimulus object has been removed. An elegant theory, beautiful in its logical consistency, and explaining (if true) a large number of facts of perception. It is also parsimonious, not only in the general holistic concept of gestalt which unifies its postulates under a common head, but also because it introduces no new postulates except that of a general interneuronic chemical state at cortical synapses. In its accounting for the phenomenology of perception by an electrical field in a chemical medium it conforms to what such a field should be like and shows how its changes would proceed. The only question that remains is whether it conforms to known facts about the cortex of the brain.

Köhler and Held (1949) have made a beginning on the cortical problem by demonstrating experimentally that potential differences between the occipital visual cortex and the vertex of the brain do occur when a bright object is moved across the field of vision. The subject's gaze was fixated and the potential difference in the recorded curve was found to be greatest as the perceived object crossed the region of the fovea.[12] There is, therefore, at least the possibility that

[12] See also Köhler, 1951. Köhler discusses the possibility that these potential changes are due to the random or the synchronized distribution of nerve impulses. Such explanations are considered tenable only if it is implied that the impulses set up fields in which the external currents are no less important than those which run in the nerve fiber. A macroscopically steady field and potential are conceived in which a steady current develops and spreads through and around the active area.

electric brain currents do occur in the perception of objects. These findings, of course, do not establish the cortical field-theory since no attempt was made to correlate electrical field changes with the cortical boundaries or adjacences of the percept-figure.

In his conception of cortical electric fields Köhler has supplemented the otherwise one-sided system of gestalt by adding to it a property essential to all good theories, namely, the experimental availability of its concepts. Phenomenological wholes are vague in their reference; but the brain is something that can, within limits, be observed and even experimented upon. But in making its concepts available directly to experiment Köhler also made the theory vulnerable. Neurologists have pointed out that the cortical area upon which afferent fibers from the fovea are projected is magnified vastly out of proportion to the relation of the macular area to the rest of the retina. This condition would produce a corresponding distortion of the percept and loss of perceptual constancy. Complications would also arise from the fact that there are two hemispheres and from the fact that the infolding of the cortex, and probably transmission across sulci, would bring some functionally unrelated areas into closer contact than related areas. The fluid in the intercellular spaces, acting as a conductor, would disturb the field-currents of the region involved. Facts of brain pathology show that disturbances in perception which, according to the theory, should occur with tumors or in the destruction or removal of tissue do not occur.[13]

Still greater doubts arise from an experiment by Lashley, Chow, and Semmes (1951). The brain-field theory posits, on the one hand, a gestalt description of the percept, and on the other hand, the same sort of gestalt-like description of the cortical state. This cortical state, in order to explain overt reactions in perceptual discrimination, must be conceived as connected with efferent pathways and thus with the motor organs of the body. In problems of learning in which an organism has been trained to react *positively*, for example, to a figure shaped like a letter S and to *ignore* a figure in the shape of a cross, we must infer, first, that percept-fields set up by the stimulus-figures remain and operate as traces during intervals when these stimulating objects are not present, and, second, that these fields of the figures, as they persist as traces in the cortex, remain fairly constant over the interval. They must not suffer serious distortions; otherwise they will no longer tally with the incoming stimulus-process that is supposed to activate them nor make proper connection with the motor

[13] For a more detailed review of these criticisms see Lashley, Chow, and Semmes (1951).

pattern of the reaction. Hence if the fields (or their traces) were grossly disturbed in the interval between trials, the habit of reacting positively to one figure (S) and negatively to another (cross) would break down or would at least be impared. By producing a disturbance of the alleged fields in the visual area of the cortex and by noting the effects upon a previously established habit dependent upon visual figure-perception one could therefore get some evidence as to whether such fields exist. If the habit were impaired it would be an argument in support of the theory. If the habit were undisturbed, the theory could not be true. Since the hypothesized field is macroscopic and covers a considerable portion of the area where optic fibers are projected upon the cortex, it should be possible to introduce conductors which, by short-circuiting the field, would alter the flow of the current and thus disrupt the field-pattern of the figure.

Taking two chimpanzees, Lashley and his associates trained them to react in a simple discrimination problem to one or the other member of pairs of geometrical figures. After this learning had been accomplished they performed a delicate operation on the brains of these animals. In one of them they placed four gold foil "conductors" in the occipital lobe of each hemisphere. The strips were inserted along the surface of the cortex, outside the pial membrane, and running in different directions. In the other animal they pressed pins of the same metal vertically clear through the cortex (eleven in one lobe and twelve in the other). In both cases a considerable amount of the conductive material was in contact with the projection area of the macula. Within twenty-four hours after the operation the animals were retested on the visual discrimination problems. It was found that they had lost nothing in the retention of these habits, and their reactions to visually perceived objects about their cages were also practically the same as before the operation.

Though one might prefer to suspend judgment until other facts are obtained before joining Lashley and his associates in concluding that the *coup de grace* has been given to Köhler's ingenious theory, it is hard to see how electrical fields underlying figure-perception in the cortex could have been able to persist and to mediate a standard performance of a discriminatory habit under conditions such as these. On the whole such facts as we have at present concerning the actual functioning of the cortex not only offer no very extensive support for Köhler's theory, but raise some serious doubts as to its possibility. It seems, therefore, that the gestaltists' efforts to find a satisfactory physiological correlate for their highly developed phenomenological system, and more particularly their hope of sustaining an isomorphic postulate by means of a neurophysiological field-theory, have not yet been fulfilled.

OMISSIONS, DIFFICULTIES, AND SUCCESSES OF THE GESTALT THEORY OF PERCEPTION

Such then, is the present situation with respect to the gestalt theory of perception. In casting up the account we cannot, of course, undertake an appraisal of the gestalt system as a whole, but only of its contributions to perceptual theory. The coherence and unification of its concepts gives the theory a satisfactory parsimony and logic. Gestalt theorists have been on the whole rigorous and careful in their statements. The agreement of the theory with facts in the realm of its own phenomenological formulations is, of course, excellent; and the range of supporting facts which it has yielded through the stimulation of experiments is impressive.[14] On the physiological side the facts called upon to sustain it have been somewhat conjectural. The researches of Köhler and Held on brain potentials in object-vision are suggestive, but they do not carry us very far. In direct brain experiments or observations definitely adverse findings have appeared. It is fair to say that gestalt theory needs a support from physiological facts which the facts thus far have stubbornly refused to give. The virtuosity of cortical field-theory as an explanation of figural aftereffects and configurations can become convincing only when more direct indications support the supposition that such fields exist and are active in perception.

On the score of the completeness of coverage of perceptual phenomena there are some notable omissions. Configurational experiences are in general well handled, and the phenomena of frame of reference also receive attention. On both these topics some real illumination is provided. As for the constancies, though much is said about them in support of the general gestalt viewpoint, it must be conceded that Koffka's pioneering efforts were not too effective. Köhler, in permitting his brain-fields to be topological rather than tied to proximal stimulus-dimensions, has escaped the error of a literal brain topography. But the percept, in constancy phenomena, *is* fairly representative of the distal object. At the same time it is supposed to have an isomorph in the brain-field. If, therefore, the brain-field's topo-

---

[14] Some doubt, however, has arisen concerning the generality of the laws of organization and good figure (*prägnanz*). Exceptions to Wertheimer's principles occur in the phenomena of cortical satiation and visual aftereffects. Cf. Luchins and Luchins, 1953.

logical agreement with the stimulus-pattern cannot be guaranteed to give a *more than* topological (that is, a fairly accurate metrical) agreement with the distal object, how can the constancy of the percept with respect to the object be assured? How the brain-field does this is a mystery that has not been elucidated. It is only fair, however, to say that constancy remains a difficult problem, in the last analysis, for all the theories.

Sensory qualities and dimensions seem to have been slighted in the gestalt theory of perception. Much has been said about the fact that they are affected by field changes and are subservient to the laws of the whole; but these statements do not do them justice. How do we account for the *existence* of these phases of experience, and how can they be fairly recognized and given a part in the building of a configurational system? They are truly parts of direct experience whether we analyze them or not; they are not artifacts of analytical introspection. They cannot be explained by isomorphism since they are merely continuances or "spreads" of a homogeneous quality or dimension; and they are without form or articulation. Köhler has made an attempt to relate them to "specific energies" by way of chemical differences in the brain; but so far there is not much evidence for this view. In throwing out elementarism gestalt theory has not been successful in covering the phenomena of which the elementarists tried to give some account.

Perceptual set is recognized by gestaltists—it is even included among Wertheimer's principles of groupings. But it does not seem to have been well integrated into the theory. The prevailing state of the subject, and its atypical and individualized effect upon perception, have not seemed important in the framework of the universal, formal, and nativistically-oriented ideas of gestalt. As we shall see, the omission of motivational factors has been severely criticized by some of the other perceptual theorists. As for perceived object-character or meaning, we have a long story on our hands. The role of gestalt with reference to this topic will be considered in Chapter 19. We might note here that in the discovery of the distinction between film and surface color Katz was revealing something about the perception of *objects.*

As for the criterion of explanatory value, perhaps enough has already been said. The picture is not too satisfactory. Gestalt theorists themselves have acknowledged the necessity of finding a physiological underpinning for their dynamic concepts. Configurational field-theory and the "whole" are not very satisfactory as explanations so long as they cannot be located with respect to the organism. "Depicting" the object as fields in the brain has run into morphological and physiological difficulties. Can Köhler finally be vindicated? Are there cortical fields, but of some sort other than electrochemical? Or is field theory itself at fault as applied to perception? Will the whole concept of isomorphism prove in the end a tenable doctrine, or will it have to be given up? Can macroscopic brain states be found and correlated with perceptions, or must neurophysiologists continue to work at microscopic levels? Finally, is the mold of configuration itself large enough to fit all the facts that a complete theory of perception must explain? That it covers a broad and important area there is no denying; but is it broad enough? All these questions may receive an answer in the course of time. But until that time comes the explanatory potential of gestalt theory, so far as its physiological basis in the organism is concerned, must remain more of a hope than an accomplished fact. There are still further difficulties that bear upon explanatory significance. The neurological picture of the brain gives us everywhere a specificity of elements; we look in vain for something that would correspond to macroscopic fields or "wholes." This fact in no way detracts from the truth or importance of the gestaltists' demonstrations of a unique "whole-character" in perception. The failure of the physiological and anatomical facts to conform only makes us appreciate the difficulty of the problem. The same consideration applies to the specific character of efferent neurons and muscle fibers. How could *these* gear in with macroscopic wholes or fields even if the latter could be found in the nervous system?

Thus far our review seems to have given rise to an anomaly—almost a paradox. The influence of the gestalt theory of perception upon modern psychology has been great, and no doubt justly so. Facts concerning perception and behavior in general that were not previously dreamt of have been brought to light by its experiments and demonstrations. Principles have been stated that we have only to apply to everyday experiences in order to realize their appropriateness. New schools and procedures of psychology, both theoretical and applied, have emerged and flourished on the basis of gestalt teaching. And yet when the balance-sheet is drawn up we find empty spaces. Important phenomena within the field of perception itself are left out of account or inadequately treated. One wonders also how a theory can say so much that is true about phenomenology and yet give us so little in the way of fundamental explanations. Possibly we should ask again whether the configurational approach is broad enough, and whether phenomenology really *is* the key that will best unlock the doors. This much at least is true. When the doors are finally unlocked the view of perception and behavior generally that will be attained will be one in which the significant array of facts pointed out by the gestalt theory of perception must find their rightful place. The possession of these facts, made possible by the resourcefulness and courage of the founders of the theory, must help to shape the character of our ultimate understanding.

CRITIQUE OF THE DOCTRINE OF DETERMINATIVE WHOLES

The experimental availability of the basic gestalt concepts is a final criterion upon which some comment might be made. Here there are entries upon both the credit and the debit side. The way in which field concepts have been made denotive and available by referring them to the brain has already been mentioned. There is another fundamental idea, however, perhaps the most characteristic of the concepts of gestalt theory, that is not directly and unambiguously available and probably cannot be made so. This idea is the doctrine of the "determinative whole." It is true that much of the later course of the theory has not been so directly dependent upon this notion. Nevertheless the theory of a dynamic, supersummative "whole," operating by its own laws and affecting the parts, remains in the background. It was there before its isomorph was elaborated in the form of a configurational field in the brain; and perhaps it gave impetus to the entire theory of cortical fields. Since there is a chance that this might be true and that the wholeness doctrine might be responsible for some of the theoretical shortcomings we have noted, it might be well to examine it at closer range.

In every theory some starting point has to be taken; and in choosing such a starting point the investigator inevitably gives special weight to some particular class of data. And so it was with the founders of gestalt. We have seen that configurational phenomena impressed themselves strongly on that illustrious trio[15] as they worked in the Frankfurt laboratory, and that these investigators derived therefrom a system destined to have a wide impact. No doubt the influence of the gestalt theorists has arisen in part from the truth embodied in their descriptions of their phenomena. It is true that the parts of a percept are very seldom isolated in direct experience; they do occur together and are always interdependent in some way. Relatedness of the constituent parts or aspects is, in fact, a characteristic of every natural phenomenon; it is not peculiar to psychology.

[15] Wertheimer, Koffka, and Köhler.

But it is not so readily understood why gestalt theory took just the form it did with respect to the distinction between wholes and parts and the determining influence of the former over the latter. To the founders of the school this probably seemed a most natural distinction. Perhaps it did not seem an assumption at all, but something that was immediately revealed in the data. We should be cautious, however, about accepting any such conclusion. The whole certainly does appear differently from its parts taken separately. One can experience a *whole-character*. So far we have good phenomenology and the gestaltists were following the precepts of Husserl. But does phenomenology tell us that the whole is selecting, determining, or shaping its parts, or that it is operating by a set of laws peculiar to itself? Are we not here departing from the strict phenomenology of direct experience and entering the realm of inference *about* experience? Postulates are necessary in building theories; but they must always stand trial, later, in the court of facts. If the postulate happens to spring from a philosophical preference in which the postulater is involved, it might mislead him in deducing theorems from it to explain what he observes. Has this been the case with the doctrine of the determinative whole? Is it a postulate or a datum? If the former, has it led configurational theory astray; and what might have been the course of the theory had this postulate not been adopted?

In order to separate fact from possible inference we present below five propositions which, in our view, the facts did force upon the observers.

1. A percept is a phenomenological aggregate consisting of a number of items of direct experience.

2. This aggregate is self-contained and self-delimited from other aggregates: it its usually experienced as a more or less segregated whole.

3. The parts of the aggregate appear different when observed together than when observed separately, and the whole aggregate appears different from any one of its parts.

4. Elimination, addition, or change of parts is accompanied by a change in the appearance of the other parts and also by a change in the appearance of the whole.

5. When the aggregate is observed as a whole it appears to have certain whole-characteristics, such, for example, as unity, continuation, articulation, closure, tendency toward symmetry, and a "requiredness" among its relationships.

These five statements sum up the facts upon which a phenomeno-logical configurationism could legitimately rest. In gestalt theory, however, a further, or sixth, proposition was added. It was the doctrine that the "whole" referred to in the above statements is independent, dynamic, and causal. To it there was assigned an influence that was responsible for the changes empirically produced by changes of the parts and for the whole-character described in the last proposition above. There was assumed to be a whole which was something more than, or at least different from, the parts, even if the parts were taken as acting together, and which was to be distinguished theoretically from the parts. This whole was assumed to have laws of its own according to which it selects, acts upon, or organizes the parts.

The difficulty with this assumption, from the standpoint of direct experimental availability, is that we have no objective evidence that a whole is anything other than the parts, provided always that the parts are taken as they *exist and operate together*. A whole that is something more, or other than this, must remain an inference. It is perhaps an "impelling" inference, derived from striking differences in the phenomenology when the parts act together as compared with the phenomenology when they act alone. But it is still an inference. In questioning it, we are in no sense denying that there is a perceived unique "whole-character" that appears when the parts exist and operate together. We question only the assumption that this "whole-character" comes from something other than, or more than, this set of conditions, or that there is an "independent" whole, or that the whole acts to control the parts. If the reader is willing to play the role of an advocate of the latter doctrine, we can imagine the following conversation.

"It is going directly against the facts," the reader will say, "to claim that the whole is not something different from its parts or something that influences them. Take the figure on this card [any of the familiar illusion figures will do]. It gives me an optical illusion. When I look at the *whole* some of the parts appear slanted or changed from the positions that physical measurements would show. I can look at the *parts*, however; and, if I look carefully enough, the illusion is reduced, or it may even vanish: the parts now conform more nearly to the physical measurements. Surely the whole, *when I see the figure as whole,* affects the appearance of the parts."

"But take your pencil," we reply, "and point to the whole. Go further and actually touch it; that is, *denote* it, in our present sense of the term denote. Can you touch it without in that very act touching at least one of the parts? Can you denote or make any unique and unambiguous contact with this whole (as such) that you say is influencing the parts?"

"No, but that's not the question," the reader might quickly answer. "I'm not talking about the figure here on this card; I'm talking about what happens inside *me*—probably in the visual or adjoining areas of my cortex. The influence of wholes upon parts is something the brain must provide."

"Very well, but now suppose you could examine and deal closely with some such 'whole' process in the brain, a process involving neurons, parts of neurons, molecules, ions, or anything else you care to imagine that is making it possible for you to see the figure as a whole at one time and the separate parts at another. This process, shall we assume, has, like the illusion figure, a whole aspect or whole-character; and also, it has parts. Now if you could denote or make any kind of contact with this 'whole' process in the brain, do you think you would be denoting anything that could not, quite as legitimately, be called one or more of its parts?"[16]

Still continuing in his role the reader might respond: "Well, perhaps not. But all this is a mere quibble. Suppose I touch one or more of the *parts,* am I not then also denoting the whole? The denotation of the parts is also ambiguous. So what have you proved?"

"But there is a real difference here," we reply. "Let us examine the 'grain' of your denotation. If it is so coarse that you encounter, without realizing it, all of the parts at once, we would admit that you are denoting the whole; but it would be a whole that has, under the conditions stated, no recognizable parts. So here the question of wholes in relation to parts would not arise. But now suppose that your grain of denotation is so fine that you only encounter one of the parts, or perhaps several. Are you now denoting the whole? No, you are not, unless you change the meaning of the term denotation, or rather, *add to it an inference.* You might say that *'what'* you are denoting *'is'* the whole? In the words 'what' and 'is' you are departing from denotive procedures and bringing in a physicalistically unverifiable assumption *to supplement* your physicalistic [denotive] ex-

---

[16] Thus although Köhler might say that a macroscopic brain field, as a "whole," determines the physiological happenings that accompany the conscious percept, he is also careful to give explicit meaning, that would otherwise be lacking, to this whole by referring to molecules of chemical substances, ions, membranes, electric currents (*i.e.,* flow of electrons), or other elements that make it up. Motion and "shape of motion" are of course involved in the action of these elements. These parts and their motions must of course be taken *together.* In their concentrations and interworking as parts, they are absolutely necessary for understanding the field-concept of the "whole."

perience. You are getting your whole by definition, not by denotation. If you go further and say that the 'what' that you consider yourself to be denoting is a whole *that acts by its own laws upon the parts,* you are not even phenomenological, but have departed into metaphysics."

The reader might here contend that our argument is unfair; for when we say that we denote a "part," we also go beyond mere denotation in *calling it* a part. To this we would reply that we are quite willing to give up the term "part" and not prejudge the question of whether there is a whole of which it can be a part. But we maintain that with a fine enough grain of denotation one would always have a *plurality* of encounters within any manifold. We concede that we might not know that any one of these encounters represented the denotation of a "part" of some "whole." But what we *would* be able to say is that *if* this plurum of encounters we are making were to be *called* a whole, then in making any one of them we are denoting what would be called a *part*. Denotation is, in itself, always ad hoc and specific. At whatever level we take it, it conveys no direct evidence either of "holism" or of "partism." But if it is fine enough to reveal the fact that a *number* of different encounters are possible in the situation, so that someone can raise the question of what is whole and what is part, we always find in the resulting designation that it is the "part" rather than the "whole" which has been denoted.

As a final resort the reader might reply: "Well, maybe the whole is *not* something that is denotably different from the interacting parts, or in control of them, on the *card,* or even in my *brain;* but it is certainly so in my *mind."*

"Well and good. If you mean by mind merely that experience of yours [phenomenology] that you reported in connection with the card, we would agree that you experience a whole-character that is different from the part-characters. But if you imply that the 'mind' constitutes or *creates* a whole as a separate entity which acts upon the parts, are you not going beyond what either phenomenology or logic will give you? Even the gestaltists would not follow you down that road; for in talking about 'mind' they are seeking a definite physiological process that is isomorphic to an actual perceptual experience. Is it not clear by this time that the notion of deterministic wholes operating on their parts by 'laws of the whole' is a pure inference, a postulate rather than an observed datum?"

Is it a good postulate? All postulates are a gamble. But do we not usually try to choose them in such a fashion as to comport at least with such empirical indications as we do possess? The advocate of the assumption we are criticizing might not care for the tests to which we have subjected it. An idealistic philosopher would probably reject denotation and our criteria of objectivity as beside the point for arriving at dependable knowledge. Yet where would scientific inquiry be without them? It must be remembered that in order to be explanatory gestalt theory must not travel in the realm of phenomenology alone. Wholeness doctrine, if it is to relate to the full facts of perception, must somehow gear in with the physicalistically experienced world. The gestaltists themselves have striven to find principles that could operate isomorphically, that could apply to each of the two worlds. And to do this it is necessary to come to terms with the criteria of objectivity. Only by accepting as adequate the support of a philosophy that discounts these criteria, that employs mentalistic principles to cover everything, and that does not even use phenomenological description carefully, could we be made to feel that the postulate we are considering is a promising wager.

At this point we release the reader from further participation in this discouraging argument. And we shall not wait for some Aladdin to come along and rub his lamp to show us where "wholes" reside or how wholes operate by their own laws to organize their parts. We have pursued the question far enough to come to the following conclusion: If the inference is made that there exists such a thing as a whole which is distinct enough from the parts to have laws of its own and to be able to subject the parts to them, then this inference must rest upon a metaphysical assumption rather than upon observed facts. The concept of a supersummative agency or determinative whole is one whose referent is not available for empirical investigation. It is not consistent with the tests of objectivity, as we have defined them, nor is it required as a means of describing the phenomena of configuration.[17]

The other questions that were raised concerning wholeness-theory we leave for the reader to answer. Could the doctrine of determinative wholes be what has led gestalt theory, with its many admirable insights, astray? Could it be the reason for its inadequacies with respect to explanation? What kind of configurational theory might have developed if circumstances, or perhaps the philosophical mode

[17] The question might be raised as to whether we could not legitimately "postulate" the whole as an "intervening construct" that mediates between the parts of the sensory pattern in the cortex and organizes them. The gestalt theorists themselves have rejected this solution, and logically from their standpoint. To conceive the whole in such a manner would deprive it of its status as a whole; it would become merely another one of the parts in the aggregate. It would also be as impossible to denote as an "embracing" whole.

at the time and place of its founding, had not impressed the wholeness doctrine upon its founders as fundamental? What would have happened if, instead of the combining action of a transcendent whole, the tendency of *parts* or *elements*, when adjacent, to structure in relation to one another in characteristic ways had been taken as the postulate? Instead of conceiving structure as the result of the organizing activity of wholes one might have tried to think of wholes and whole-character as a by-product of structure. In that case one would have sought for laws of dynamic structuring in nature rather than for laws of dynamic wholes. Could patterns of denotable events, rather than laws of macroscopic forms, not serve as useful postulates in perception and in nature generally? Our purpose at this point is only to raise these questions, not to answer them. We turn presently to other theories of perception; but we can be sure that the story of the *gestalten* is not yet fully told. The achievements and perplexities of gestalt theory, its brilliant insights as well as its liabilities, will probably be with us for some time to come.[18]

[18] As an example of the striking contrasts that occur in perceptual theories the reader might be interested in comparing with this account of gestalt theory a treatment of visual perception by Gibson (1950). Whereas the gestaltists point out the necessary differences between the proximal stimulus-pattern and the percept, disclaiming a one-to-one correspondence, and attribute the "way things look" to the organizing forces of the brain-field, Gibson attempts to show that the differences between what the stimulation-pattern contains and what is perceived are not so great after all. It is suggested that an elaborate central organizing process may not be needed for the perception of three-dimensional space, the constancies, and the like; the total stimulation may contain all that is needed. Gibson's thesis is worked out in an exceedingly graphic and vivid survey of the patterns of stimulation that give rise to our visual world. For example, in spatial perceptions there are ordinal arrangements, gradients, density and textural changes, frontal and longitudinal surfaces, and invariants under transformations—all features of the stimulation-pattern itself and represented in the retinal image as higher-order variables of the stimulation. To account for all the phenomena of perception we can without going more deeply into the organism than the retina and its images would seem a desirable move in the direction of parsimony, and would tend to link up order in phenomenological experience more directly with the order of the physicalistic world. One must be on guard, however, against an oversimplification of the problem. The range of aspects of perception covered by Gibson's peripheral theory is too small to serve as a scheme for perception as a whole. The system is, in fact, intended by its author only as a theoretical treatment of perception in a limited area. The essential problems of configuration and other aspects still remain. See also Gibson's chapter in Dennis(ed.), 1951.

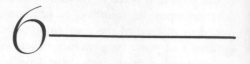

Topological Field Theory
and Its Relation to Perception

We must turn aside now to examine a school of thinking that is an
-offshoot of the gestalt movement. Though the adherents of this
school make use of fields and related gestalt principles they have no
direct concern about physiological bases or isomorphism. Perception
is a key word with them, and they regard fields as being perceptual
and cognitive, though they are not especially interested in perception
as an explicit organismic activity. *Field-theory*, as this system is
simply called, owes its origin and most of its development to the
genius of Kurt Lewin.[1] The name "field-theory," however, is not
properly definitive of the system, for the field implied is of a special
sort. It is phenomenological rather than physicalistic, though its
medium, as well as the actions going on within it, is again conceived
not as metrical but as topological in its spatial character. By Lewin
and his followers this theory has been expanded into an ambitious
program to cover not only perception but behavior in general, including, especially, motivation and goal-directed action. Though topological field-theory has made little contribution to the theory of perception in a specific sense, it is tangent to it in a number of ways.
Our treatment therefore will be in the nature of a digression that is
needed in order to trace the further implications of gestalt and to give
a background for some phases of perceptual theory later to be discussed.

THE FIELD AS A PHENOMENOLOGICAL CONSTRUCT: TOPOLOGICAL
AND HODOLOGICAL LIFE-SPACE

We have seen that the founders of gestalt theory, in order to increase the explanatory power of their system, sought to supplement

[1] 1935, 1936, 1938, 1946, 1951. See also Leeper, 1943, and Brown, 1936.

the materials of phenomenology with an isomorphic field-like counterpart in the central nervous system. The fact that phenomenological experience itself, without any consideration of its physiological accompaniment, has a certain field-like character had, however, been recognized from the beginning. This fact had led the gestaltists to seek its basis in a neurophysiological field. There was said to be, in other words, a "psychological," or more correctly, a "phenomenological," field. Though this concept is really only an analogy to the field-concept in physics, if one is content for the purpose of exploiting it to forego the support of physicalistic methods, one can develop it rather extensively in purely phenomenological terms. There is one point, however, that should be remembered. Phenomenological and physical concepts do not mix; there is only the possibility of associating them through the arduous conceptual procedure of isomorphism. If the theorist forgets that his field is purely phenomenological and introduces forces or bounding conditions of a physicalistic character, so that "psychic" and physical energies are made to interact, he will fall far short of the ideal of logical consistency, or else he will have to achieve a *tour de force* of explanation showing the operational equivalence of these two realms of experience in a manner that has never yet been accomplished.

It was the original intent of Lewin, or so it seems to the present writer, to develop a field-theory of a consistently phenomenological sort; and if we are sufficiently careful, his system can continue to be interpreted in this manner. The process, however, is not easy. It produces an unnatural strain upon our thinking, so that the tendency is to lapse into a mixed and uncritical terminology. Lewin himself seemed to be speaking often in terms of "psychical" forces and energies; and he evidently did not consider it necessary to distinguish these from the physicalistic uses and operational demonstration of these concepts that are necessary in the work of physicists and physiologists.[2] But we shall try, at least at the start, to present his system in terms of consistent phenomenological description.

The first point to note is that a phenomenological field is one that is experienced as extending *around about* the individual. It includes the phenomenological self, but it does not, in usual perceptual experience, lie within the self. We have an experience of the world about us and of ourselves acting outwardly toward it. We have practically no direct experience of what happens *inside* us, and certainly not of what happens in our brains. Ordinarily, no part of the phenomenological perceptual field lies within the individual. It must

[2] Cf. Ellis (ed.), 1938, p. 283 ff.

also be remembered that it is only the individual's *phenomenological experience* of objects and of himself among them that make up the content of the field. The objects as actually encountered or physicalistically experienced are not within its content. The field can be described only in subjective terms. For the purpose of such a field-theory the individual was regarded by Lewin as shrunken to a dimensionless "point-region" and was conceived as acted upon (phenomenologically, of course) by a set of psychical field-forces felt to be external to his own body. And he was conceived to be experiencing himself as moving ("locomoting") under the influence of these forces toward some "positive goal" or away from some "negative goal." The child sees himself as "going toward" a reward or "away from" punishment. The term locomotion was used, sometimes literally, but often figuratively, to describe the performance of the behavior act or act-sequence. Going through the steps of a problem in arithmetic is regarded as locomotion (or quasilocomotion) as well as going to the cupboard for a piece of pie. And again, to be entirely consistent, this description must be understood as the individual "experiencing himself" as moving, thinking, or acting, and not in terms of his actual movements or physiological processes, even though these are, of course, involved.

A concept of locomotion requires "space" through which locomotion can occur; and also, since a field means the influence of one thing upon another through a propagation of changes within a medium, there must be a medium that fills the space. The space in question was therefore phenomenologically construed as the "life space" of the individual, that is, the region in which he experiences himself at the moment as acting. The medium is whatever is perceived as lying within, or filling, that space. Since physicalistic dimensions are out of order, this life space was not regarded as having metric properties or determined directions for motions within it, but as *topological*. That is, it was regarded as capable of having at any moment any size or geometric shape whatsoever, so long as the principle of included-ness within boundaries was constantly recognized and there was afforded within it a continuous region, or connected regions, in which locomotion could occur. Thus the distance to be traversed in going to the pantry for food, the obstacles to be overcome, and the means of overcoming them (such, for example, as getting a chair to climb on, avoiding detection, opening the door, and so on) were not of any significance as to their physical dimensions, angular directions, metric properties, or similar aspects which might vary endlessly with the situation. The obstacles and the necessary manoeuvres were simply subregions of the total life space (the situation) that had to be gone through in reaching the goal (food). This ignoring of particular physical sizes, distances, and directions as not pertinent to the problem is possible since we are speaking entirely in a phenomenological frame of reference, that is, in terms of an adjustment which the individual experiences himself as making to whatever physical peculiarities the situation (phenomenologically) presents.

The life space was also *hodological;* that is, it was a space of pathways that had no fixed distances or directions, but only a kind of purposeful orientation affording a connection between the point representing the individual and some goal-region. The shortest possible hodological distance between these two points may not be that which is physicalistically the shortest, but may involve irregular "detours" around barriers; and the hodological direction toward the goal may lie in a pathway that leads for a time in a physical direction *away from* the goal.

PROPERTIES OF TOPOLOGICAL LIFE-SPACE: VECTORS, VALENCE, FIELD-TENSIONS, AND EQUILIBRIUM

For convenience we shall now drop our caution of stating the description in strict phenomenological terms and speak in the more familiar language used by Lewin, a usage in which this distinction was not carefully maintained. Logical consistency, however, requires that the purely phenomenological character of what we are talking about must always be assumed. The life-space is diagramatically symbolized as lying within a self-closing *boundary line,* the "Jordan curve." The life-space, thus graphically enclosed, might, of course, have any shape in the diagram; purely as a matter of convenience it is usually represented as oval. The boundary of this (oval) region on the one hand represents the surrounding constraints that are acting upon the individual and keeping him within the field, such, for example, as walls, or "psychological" boundaries such as rules, customs, prescriptions imposed by group membership, or any expectancies of others which define and give unity to the situation. On the other hand, the boundary also represents the outer limit of the objects or persons that the individual can use in trying to attain his particular goal. At some place (subregion) within this boundary the diagram shows the symbol of a *goal* ($+$ G or $-$ G) with respect to which the locomotion of the individual takes place. The individual himself is represented as a *dot,* or other small homogeneous symbol, somewhere within the life space. Behind this dot, or in front of it, is an arrow representing a *vector of force,* or a resultant of a number of forces, pushing the individual toward the goal if the goal is a "positive" one, or away from the goal if it is "negative." In the latter case the goal is considered as something to be avoided. The *strength* of the force toward or away from the goal is symbolized by the length of the arrow (vector strength), and the arrow's direction is to be regarded as hodological.

Within the life-space other details are depicted such as *barriers* to be surmounted or detoured around. These are usually pictured as heavy bars or other forms that lie between the individual and the goal. These barriers themselves exert a repelling force if "encountered," and the boundary also serves as a continual constraining influence. *Subregions* that must be passed through in order to reach or to evade the goal are marked off as cells within the life space. In general they represent different manoeuvres that must be made or successive topological positions that must be taken in order to reach or escape from the region of the goal.

As to the origin of the forces impelling the individual in the life-space field two sources seem to be required. First, a finding of gestalt psychology was employed to the effect that, phenomenologically, perceived goal objects have a "demand-character." Food is "inviting"; it seems to say "Come on." Punishment is "repellent," and things that lead to it seem to "force us away." Hence the goal objeots themselves exert field-forces and are said to have either a positive or a negative *valence*. But there are needs within the individual that must also be taken into account. We must be hungry in order that food shall seem attractive. These needs, however, cannot be shown diagramatically since the individual is represented as a mere point. "Tensions" are also referred to, sometimes as existing within the individual and sometimes as occurring in the field. The forces of the field, dependent upon the conditions just mentioned, are depicted as operating *externally* upon the individual and with respect to other conditions of the field.

Each part of the field is conceived, in accordance with general field-logic, as in communication with every other part; and any change in one of the forces will produce a change throughout the whole field. When any such change or upset of equilibrium occurs, as might be illustrated, for example, by the presence of a need (hunger) in a child and the sight of an apple high in a cupboard, the interplay of tensions (forces) of the field will yield a resultant force as a vector impelling the child to various movements and manipulations such as those involved in getting a chair, climbing upon it, seizing the apple and eating it—in short, to "locomotion toward the goal." When the goal is attained the field will then be again in equilibrium. An act of behavior may be defined as a locomotion in a field that has the result of so altering the field that all its forces are in equilibrium at a certain point (the point-region of the individual). And so we arrive at the principle of equilibrium, involving least action and a minimum of energy, which was the essential feature of the simplicity, symmetry, and good figure of gestalt theory.[3] When this condition of equilibrium is reached the paradigm is finished for the situation and action concerned. The organism is quiescent until a new situation with new field-tensions arises, that is, until the individual "comes into a new field."

It must always be remembered, however, that in order for the Lewinian theory to be consistent, field-forces must be regarded as mental or "psychic" rather than as physicalistic. They must represent the way in which the individual "perceives himself" as pushed or drawn with respect to valenced goal objects, or the way in which barriers or boundaries and their constraints are perceived or cognized by him. The field is phenomenological, not physical or physiological. On the basis of the postulates under which the field was established, comprising, as they do, "psychological locomotion," "demand-characters," "come on" aspects, and the like, no other interpretation of the field is permissible. This fact leaves completely open the problem of

---

[3] This conception of an externalized field did not appear in Lewin's earlier writings in so clear a form as is presented in the above outline. Needs and tensions within the individual were called into play without the external apparatus of a topological field. Frequently, also, it seems that the locus of the life-space field is left indeterminate. In Lewin's "plane of irreality" where the individual fancies himself in some imagined scene, or in the imagery by which the past or the future is projected into the present, it would be hard to say where these phenomenological fields exist. If they are within the individual's body (brain), they are not so localized by the individual. He imagines them as environments with himself phenomenologically situated within them. In other gestalt-like theories fields are employed that are represented as being within the individual rather than outside, that is, as fields having a physiological rather than a "pure experience" connotation, though sometimes these fields contain a liberal sprinkling of "inside" and "outside" physical objects mixed with phenomenological items of various sorts (cf. Tolman, 1949). When we ask *where* a given field is with respect to the individual we must always stipulate what we mean by "the individual" and by the term "where." Do we mean the individual as a phenomenological self which the subject perceives, or as a biological organism; and do we mean "where" in terms of phenomenological life-space or in the ordinary space of physical objects? These are some of the perplexities attendant upon the attempt to use a field-of-experience model for the depiction of behavior. For the most part current field-theory employs a life-space perceived by the individual out around himself as described in the above account.

the denotable events concerned and their structuring in the physicalistically experienced order. For the theory to attain full explanatory
significance there would therefore have to be added some kind of
isomorphism that would bring into play the operation of such physically experiencible elements as stimuli, receptor processes, afferent
nerve impulses, brain processes, efferent impulses, muscular contractions, and overt movements. This point, however, has been consistently overlooked in field-theory. The reason, no doubt, is that, when
we forget that the phenomenological-physicalistic distinction has to be
maintained, the Lewinian model appears superficially to be complete.
There is probably another reason, however, that will be mentioned
presently. The fact that the point *has been* overlooked renders the
explanatory value of the field model more apparent than real.

APPLICATIONS OF THE LEWINIAN MODEL

By the aid of this graphic and very ingenious device Lewin was
able, notwithstanding its theoretical limitations, to give a representation of psychological phenomena that has appealed to many as convincing and has been highly useful in the practical charting of behavioral situations. In portraying social episodes and relationships it
has been particularly fruitful.[4] Many such situations have been
lucidly diagrammed, showing the interplay of "forces," how the individual "detours," how forces issue from leaders in authority, how the
individual under a conflict of equal forces may "leave the field," how
he can be restrained by barriers from so doing, and so on. An attempt has been made to measure the "strengths" of the various forces
(if phenomenological forces can be conceived to have strength) and

---

[4] Cf. Gibson and Crooks, 1938, for an interesting application of field-theory to
the problems of automobile driving. In its description of the manner in which
the motorist experiences the boundaries of the field of free space (width of his
car *plus* an allowance) for passing, turning, and the like, this analysis is an
excellent example of a direct application of field-theory to the problems of
perception. The phenomenological field here loses its topological freedom, however, and becomes more veridical with respect to physicalistic checking. Social
situations have also been described, as, for example, when a man cognitively
expects his wife to enter a certain region of his own life-space field and she is
unexpectedly perceived as entering a different region. A cognitive reorganization
of the man's field is then required. At these points field-theory does approach
the status of a true theory of perception. Since, however, no attempt is made
to link the phenomenological field with happenings within the organism, we have
not regarded topological field-theory as sufficiently complete to merit a place
among the major theories that do attempt such explanations. It gives many apt
descriptions but they are in purely phenomenological terms.

to establish laws for making predictions about their interrelationships. Whether we consider these measurements to be indices of actual forces or not, the results of such investigations show the practical use that can be made of such data and the fruitfulness of the Lewinian model for suggesting hypotheses. The theory, it will be seen, provides a schema for a wide range of behavior. It therefore brings perception into its purview. Looking at behavior in this way, topics such as perception, cognition, thinking, and adjustment in general seem to coalesce into one process, namely, the manner in which the individual's field becomes organized. Behavior in general is interpreted as the reorganization of the individual's perceptual or cognitive field. According to the manner in which this field is organized the individual will *act*. Such a concept has been useful in the special and applied fields of psychology and is one of the most popular bases for current systems of social psychology.[5]

DEFECTS OF THE MODEL: CONFUSION OF PHENOMENOLOGICAL AND PHYSICALISTIC; EVERTING THE "INSIDE" CONTENTS

For meeting the requirement of a logically consistent, explanatory, and complete theory of perception, topological field-theory, for all its usefulness, leaves much to be desired. Because the physical and physiological bases of perception are ignored, or are concealed by shrinking the individual into a point-region, and because the perceptual phenomenon is placed in an "outside" field and each field is unique and occurs only "at the moment," it becomes impossible for the theory to explain how meaningful perceptions are built up or how the actual process of perception takes place. What is needed is an understanding of perception itself rather than merely a convenient formula for its role in human affairs. For a full understanding it does not help much to say that perception is "a sudden reorganization of the cognitive field." Or until the field concept can be put upon a basis broad enough to include physiological explanations it does not help to say that objects or events are perceived in a manner consistent with the existing "field." The general vagueness that results from phenomenological reference when taken without a physicalistic basis is a defect which the founders of gestalt theory tried sedulously to overcome.

This criticism brings us to a further explanation of why the need of

[5] Cf. Chapter 14. Phenomenology even without field-theoretical elaboration has been considered very useful in the study of human relations (MacLeod, 1947, 1951) and has been widely employed in counselling and clinical practice.

such a basis has not been adequately recognized. The reason, perhaps, is that physicalistic considerations have been brought into the theory surreptitiously and without raising the question of how they are to be articulated with the prevailing phenomenological scheme. It is unlikely that those who use the theory extensively think of locomotion merely as the phenomenological experience which the individual has of himself as moving or behaving. It is more probable that they regard it as his actual objectively described behavior. Lewin himself included bodily locomotion and figurative or "mental" locomotion in the same conceptual framework. Similarly, boundaries and inner field conditions are given in some instances a physicalistic and in other instances a phenomenological character. A "psychic" force is sometimes thought of as acting upon a physical object, and vice versa. Frequently one cannot tell whether the force is intended in a phenomenological or a physicalistic sense.[6]   And indeed, if one is not content to live in a world of pure phenomenology but wants to provide an objective account of behavior, it is hard to see how physicalistic considerations could be omitted. The attempt to put the two into *interaction* in a common field has, however, resulted in theoretical confusion. The fine consistency patiently wrought by Koffka and Köhler in their concept of isomorphism has vanished. Heuristic versatility has been gained at the expense of methodological care and exactness.

Associated with this confusion is another difficulty that is inherent in field-theory itself. In Chapter 4 an introduction was given, by way of Titchener's context theory, to the problem of the "inside" and "outside" views of a phenomenon. Lewin's system presents another example of this problem and the difficulty of its solution. To be consistent, topological field-theory, being limited logically to phenomenology, must, as we have seen, be rigorously phenomenological. Outer behavior as well as perception must be described only in those terms. Now when the behaving individual himself is brought into the picture as a part of his own field, that is, when we attempt to deal with overt behavior as Lewin did, phenomenologically, what is the result? We find that the individual's experience is always that of a field *around about* him. He perceives himself as acting within that field. But he does not experience anything that is going on *within* his own (phenomenologically experienced) body. His own internal operations are usually a complete blank. The phenomenological field is entirely an "outside" field so far as the experiencing organism is concerned. There is no "inner" field. Or, as *we* would say, the "inside" structure of the

[6] Cf. Lewin, 1951, pp. 72–74.

organism is not represented and hence cannot be considered in the development of the perceptual theory. This situation immediately creates a difficulty; for it it apparent to everyone, as it was to Lewin, that what goes on inside the individual physiologically must have a great deal to do with his perception and his outer behavior. One cannot afford to omit these inner aspects merely because they are not phenomenologically presented.

How was this problem solved in the Lewinian theory of the phenomenological field? It was done in a rather remarkable way; in effect, it was accomplished by everting the content of the inner physiological structure, giving it a *phenomenological* dynamism, and thus making it available as a part of the outside field. It is true that Lewin recognized that "valences of goals" and the like depend on conditions inside the organism. Food does not say "come on" unless we are hungry; "psychological" boundaries or barriers do not control or repel unless we inwardly react to them. But having made these admissions it was deemed permissible to neglect their implications and to organize the cartography of the field-model exclusively in outside-field terms. For example, though we know that demand-characters of objects spring from states internal to the organism, we can *depict* them as plus or minus "valences" possessed by goal-objects lying in certain *external* regions. Though group customs, regulations, and membership-character cannot exist without inner attitudes and meanings of the subject, we can conveniently project them as *outer* "*boundaries*" around the common life-space of the members. Though a detour solution of a problem may involve some kind of internal reaction, such as a change of tonus or an "anticipatory goal response," we can forget about this inside aspect and *represent* the detour solution as an *outer* "hodological pathway" which the organism as a whole, externally viewed, is to take. It will be seen that this procedure has the practical effect of turning the behavioral structure of the organism inside out, conceptually speaking. Dynamisms that are really internal are now depicted as *out around* the individual. Even though their inner source is still acknowledged, for purposes of the theoretical model (and that is what we rely upon for explanations) they are represented as in the outside field.

But there is a further result. We know that *some* parts or properties of the outer field actually *are* "out there" and have been there from the beginning. This is true both phenomenologically and physicalistically. The light-reflecting food objects, other individuals acting with respect to the subject, actual barriers placed in certain positions—all these are, and were, parts of the objectively described and denotable outer situation. What happens therefore is, first, that the inside physiological structure, which was phenomenologically a blank but was nevertheless present and active, becomes everted into the phenomenological environment and changed into "psychical" forces, forces which, though only phenomenological, are nevertheless conceived as pushing or pulling the organism; and second, that as the inside forces are thus everted and transmuted to phenomenology they become "mixed in" with the objects and forces that were already *physicalistically* present and active in the outer situation. This, at least, is the implication of the theory: it could not, of course, occur in fact. The final step can now be taken to unify the whole picture within the framework of an externalized field. The crucial elements in the inner structure of the organism having been shifted to the outside, the interior of the individual is no longer needed. Hence the individual can be "shrivelled up" to a "point-region" in the surrounding field and represented as entirely subject to the forces of that (outer) field. It is as though we were to take a stocking filled with some intricate mechanisms and turn it inside out, mixing those mechanisms with others that were outside, and should then shrink the stocking to negligible dimensions and reduce its role to that of being merely acted upon by the confused mass of outside influences. All semblance of the proper ordering of inside and outside structuring is now lost.

Far from being solved, the inside-outside problem now becomes a hopeless muddle. A consistent field-representation, with mixed life-space contents, has been gained, but at what a cost![7] If it should be objected that it is *we* who have caused the trouble by injecting

---

[7] A similar lack of logical realism is seen in a phrase that is used to describe what happens when an individual is caught between two equal and repelling forces (negative goals), such as a disagreeable task to be done and punishment if it is not done. (Lewin, 1951, p. 78.) Here, unless barriers are set up to restrain him, it is said that the individual will be likely to "leave the field." Let the individual be taken as a physical person, for only so will the theory have much applicability. Suppose also that the "field" he is leaving is an outer situation of a physicalistically describable sort. In this case we could say he is leaving the situation, but hardly that he is leaving a "field." Suppose, on the other hand, the field is regarded as purely phenomenological. *Now* the field, if it exists at all, must always accompany the individual wherever he goes. It is dependent upon him. In this case if it were said that the individual "leaves the field," what could be the possible meaning? What would there be for him to leave? We are implying by this phrase an "outside" situation with respect to the individual; he can leave a field because he is *in* one. When we try explicitly to define that field, however, we find that it is, at least in certain essential respects, *inside the individual.* If this is true, the individual *cannot* leave it.

physicalistic, "inside" elements into a picture that previously was phenomenologically homogeneous and "outer," we would reply that without bringing in these elements the scheme itself would be meaningless and quite inadequate for the explanation of behavior. The phenomenological field, as Lewin himself recognized, is *contingent upon* these inner physiological conditions. If one were searching for a theory of "structure" in perception or in behavior generally, this dire confusion of the inner and outer facts of the aggregate would take one as far away from such an objective as it would be possible to go.

DIFFICULTIES OF FIELD THEORY IN GENERAL:
THE INSIDE-OUTSIDE PROBLEM

The lesson here learned should be carried further. Topological field theory has been criticized on the ground that it is a poor analogy to the concept of physical fields from which it was borrowed. For example, in a true field the resultant of the forces operating can be determined at any space and time point, while in Lewinian field theory this is possible only at regions where behavioral contacts or events are taking place. No doubt such criticisms could be multiplied. But our present objection goes further than this. The trouble is not merely that Lewin did not set up the right kind of field, but that any field concept would have run into the very difficulty to which we have previously alluded. The inside-outside problem has been a stumbling block for physical field-theory as well as for psychological. Maxwell dealt with it, in the same way Lewin did, by taking a small, but still real, area within the field as a locus for determining the magnitude and direction of the field-vectors. But what about the region *within* that small portion that was taken? This region is not a part of the field itself; it represents only something that is acted upon by the surrounding field-forces. Does it have an "inside field" all its own? If it had, we should not know what to do with it or how to integrate it with the field outside. Hence its status is quite anomalous. For the development of the electromagnetic field theory and for its practical applications, the Maxwell expedient sufficed, because the point-region taken was so very small. It could consist of a theoretical minute "particle" that was given a vector magnitude by the forces of the field. The field or structure *inside* the particle was neglected by Maxwell just as it was by Lewin; but with vastly different consequences. The difference made by the use of an anomalous field particle in the manipulation of electromagnetic field constructs was negligible; but when, as in psychology, that "particle" is so large and important as to constitute the entire inside of the organism the difference may well become colossal. Within this particle lies something that psychological theory cannot do without.[8]

Even in Maxwell's case the solution of the inside-outside problem in physics was opportunistic and theoretically unsatisfactory. Einstein (1950) has recently proposed an answer in his new generalized theory of gravitation. The untoward result of this solution, however, is the obliteration of any sharp distinction between inside and outside. Since the field is now continuous, the concept of particle cannot play any fundamental part, nor can the concept of motion. The particle's inside and its outside are continuous in one unified field of space-time; and the particle itself represents only a limited region in space in which field-strength or energy is especially high. But if the "particle" or point-region that constitutes the *organism* were to be treated in this manner, psychology would disappear. When there is no line of demarcation between the inside and the outside of an organism the organism as an operational entity is gone and we have no psychological problem. Thus field theory by its very nature is lacking in the resources necessary to solve the inside-outside problem in psychology. It is a beautiful theory for formulating some of the facts of physics; but it does not fit the realm of organisms. So long as psychologists set themselves to deal with an organism perceiving or outwardly acting in a surrounding manifold the problem will remain and the need of its solution will be pressing. We should not censure the Lewinian school for ineptness in the handling of the field concept. Though we cannot regret and do not belittle their ingenious attempt, there was a disadvantage, at the very start, in having any traffic with field-theory at all. Whatever heuristic value field-theory may have for psychology will, in the writer's opinion, be found to be merely temporary as we face the problem of unifying the inside and the outside relationships of the aggregate into one conceptual scheme. Some other way to do this must be found.[9]

And so, in the last analysis, Lewin could probably not have done much better with the tools he was using. Field-theory, if it is applicable to the affairs of organisms at all, is either an inside or an outside view; it is not both. For Köhler it applied to regions in the cortex; it was an inside view of a part of the organismic aggregate. For Lewin it represented the organism in its phenomenological environment, and the organism was phenomenologically described as from

[8] For a statement of the physical problem see Einstein and Infeld, 1942, pp. 129–160; and especially 255–259.
[9] Another kind of solution will be proposed in Chapter 21.

the outside. In neither case did field-theory succeed in drawing together the two essential halves of the total picture. We hasten to add that Lewin himself was not content with this state of affairs. He was too good a psychologist not to recognize the need of giving an account of the "inside" of the individual in its own right. He therefore developed a set of formulations for the "topology of the person" (1936) and a description of "inner-personal regions." Such concepts included the dynamic dependency of inner regions, degrees of differentiation, central and peripheral strata, tension systems, and the like. But this topology of the "inner" person, though useful, was a different theoretical system from that of the outer topological field. Locomotion of the organism in such a manifold was operationally impossible on a reality plane, for the manifold itself was inside the organism. "Inside" and "outside" were both treated by Lewin, but in different theoretical frames of reference; and in neither case were constructs employed that dealt with physiological happenings in any direct way.

The point of this criticism stands out even more clearly when we consider fields of collective action. If we try to depict the field in terms of the motivational, perceptual, or cognitive processes of the individual, the social configuration is poorly represented. If, on the other hand, we consider the group as a medium in which "social" field-forces are playing upon the individual, we are at a loss to integrate with this field the energic resources that lie within individuals. *Inter*individual field-forces cannot retain their uniqueness as a collective field if they are identified with forces acting *within* individuals; and collective structure is therefore lost. Yet it is impossible to account for the energies of collective fields *unless* they are so identified. For where do social forces come from if not from the energies of individuals? What usually happens in practice, when such field-cartography is attempted, is a confusion of the two sources in which it is impossible to assign events unambiguously as belonging *either* to the inside *or* to the outside. The model then loses its realistic character and becomes a fictional enterprise. Topological field-theory does embody a profound truth, aside from the aspects we have been criticizing. It points out, as gestalt theory in general does, the interrelatedness and interdependence of all the elements and events in an instance of behavior or collective action. Whether our attention is centered only on phenomenological experience or on physicalistic observations as well, this interrelated character of the various parts of phenomena is one of their most significant features. Emphasis upon this fact has probably played no small part in the theory's usefulness. The field model gives a heuristic way of tying these elements together and a ready terminology for expressing relationships among them. But though it offers a convenient way of assembling these aspects through pseudoforces and other field constructs, the theory still fails to describe explicitly what takes place as individual behavior or collective interaction is going on. The model that is provided, because of its intermixture of phenomenological with physicalistic elements, and because of the confusion of inner and outer, cannot be directly checked against physicalistically observed facts.

POSITIVE CONTRIBUTIONS OF LEWIN'S SYSTEM

In fairness to Lewin it should be noted that his method of working was very supple and at times resembled the impressionistic approach of an artist. He took whatever lay at hand that would help him to construct a meaningful diagram of a behavioral situation; and it must be said that his constructions were often highly meaningful. Cartwright, in editing a posthumous collection of Lewin's papers (1951), regarded him as "one of those few men whose work changed fundamentally the course of social science in its most critical period of development." Though topological field-theory concepts are somewhat lacking in parsimony and logical consistency, and though we have seen reason to challenge them as to their direct experimental availability and explanatory value, Lewin's work nevertheless extended the generality of application of gestalt-like ideas and inspired a large amount of research. Such investigations yielded many facts that were capable of interpretation within his system. The current movement of group dynamics originated largely under his personal guidance. Topological field-theory itself added little to the fundamental theory of perception, its advocates being content merely to accept the work of other theorists, especially that of the gestalt school. But the gestalt notions of configuration and of fields coming to equilibrium that had had their rise mainly in the perceptual and cognitive area were extended by this movement to the phenomena of motivation, covering that subject in a more adequate way than it had been handled by gestalt. Lewin was also more liberal in his treatment of wholes, of subsystems, and of differentiation, making these ideas serve a broader range of behavioral facts. He did especial service by insisting upon the *self-delimited* character of aggregates.[10]

One of his greatest contributions, in the writer's opinion, lay in introducing, through topology and the Jordan curve, the notion of

[10] See in Ellis (ed.), 1938, pp. 283–299.

the behavioral aggregate as something that is highly flexible with respect to its spatial properties, as something that is unified and self-delimited and yet as possessing many possible degrees of freedom. Surely this is a conception that applies in some measure to the phenomena of perceptual activity as well as to behavior generally.

The concept of the field will appear again in our review of perceptual theories; and the topological system of Lewin was one of the factors that made field notions popular among many psychologists. Whether one agrees with the present writer or not with respect to the inadequacy of field-theory for psychology, its importance as a current movement cannot be denied. In particular, it must be remembered that Lewin was largely interested in the social scene; and the bearing of his work upon perceptual theory lay not in its substantive contribution to the understanding of perception, but in helping, through the dynamisms of field concepts, to make perception and cognition a basis for modern systems of social psychology. The "fields" within which individuals perceive one another and recognize the objectives and attitudes of their groups constitute an important theme in modern social science. From all this gestalt and field-theoretical background a new and somewhat divergent view of perception and its role has arisen. In a later chapter this development will be traced in some detail. Our excursion into the borderline area of field-theory is now completed and we return to the more representative theories of perception. We shall consider next a theory that stands in marked contrast to the whole tradition of gestalt.

7

The Association Approach
Cell Assembly and Phase Sequence

Having followed the development of configurations, macroscopic brain states, and fields, it is now time to return and pick up a thread of classical theory which the gestaltists had strongly opposed. The notion of a one-to-one linkage of specific elements to make up the aggregates of perception, memory, and habit was sharply challenged by the advocates of wholeness theory; but it by no means succumbed. The doctrine of the association of ideas, it is true, belongs mainly to history. We have almost ceased to talk about ideas at all. In the past, associative processes played a major role in psychological systems and entered into explanations of perception, as we have seen in the case of Titchener's context theory. Associationism is not dead, but its form has now been radically changed. The modern emphasis in learning is not upon the joining of ideas, but upon the linkage of stimulus and reaction; and many other variables and sophisticated laws have been brought in as a part of the process. In perception, modern associative theory again employs the principle of the linking of specific elements, but hypotheses must now work with something more explicit than "mental" elements or "ideas." An associative theory of perception today will either be an overt account of discrimination learning (Chapter 17), or it will deal with perception as the formation and perseveration of associative linkage-patterns among the elementary brain-processes involved in the perceptual act. And since linkage here means that specific items are joined in what the gestaltists would call "piecemeal" fashion, the contest of the two viewpoints still goes on. In this chapter we shall see what answer is given to the perceptual question, "Why do things appear as they do?" by a theory that follows the associative tradition and attempts, in defiance of configurationism, to explain the matter by the joining of specific elements, one-to-one, into neurophysiological combinations. Our

164

example will be Hebb's work on *The Organization of Behavior* (1949).

DIFFICULTIES OF EQUIPOTENTIALITY AND CONFIGURATION FOR ASSOCIATIVE THEORY; HEBB'S "FIGURAL IDENTITY"

Hebb has adduced evidence that the initial perceiving of figures is not so complete and organized a process as the gestaltists have claimed. Even in looking at simple outline figures there are aspects of perceiving that gestalt theory does not fit. Hebb maintains that perception in some of its most essential features is not an innate process; it has to be learned. A concept of natively endowed brain-fields activated by the stimulus-pattern and operating as immediately organized and integrated wholes does not conform to the facts. Instead of being a "spread-out," macroscopic sort of thing, with a field-like continuousness, the physiological ·basis of the percept should consist of finer units connected together in an "additive" way.

But in launching such a proposal one must contend not only with gestalt theory but with certain experimental findings which, though they do not comport particularly well with gestalt theory, are nevertheless antagonistic to the view just stated. If a particular perception is based upon the action of specific units, its function should be sharply localized. It should not be extended indifferently to large cortical regions or to the cortex as a whole. Lashley's epoch-making discoveries, however, (1929, 1942) have shown that the retention of a habit does not depend upon the particular sensory points in the cortex that were involved in the afferent excitations from the receptor pattern of that habit. It depends, within limits, only upon the amount of the cortex available for its performance. Any part of a given cortical area (such, for example, as the area of vision) might serve as effectively as any other part, or as the whole of that area, in the mediation of a given habit. This remarkable principle, which is known also to obtain between the two cerebral hemispheres, is called equipotentiality. It is but one of a number of functional equivalences found in the physiology of behavior. Though there are certain limits to equipotentiality, as well as variations in the size of "equipotential parts" in different areas and with respect to different learning problems, the principle is well enough established to pose a baffling question for perceptual theory. Since perceptions always involve sensory and discriminatory behavior, this principle means, in effect, that if a figure has come to be perceived through retinal stimulation and its projected pattern of events *somewhere* in the visual area of the cortex, this same appropriate physiological pattern must also be represented *everywhere* (that is, throughout an entire equipotential region) in the visual or other areas of the cortex. If the whole visual system is extirpated, visual habits will be lost; but it is impossible for a habit to be dependent upon *one part* of the system locally in contradistinction from another part.

A serious question is now posed for perceptual theories. How is it possible for processes that occur in this multiply represented or "everywhere-at-once" form to explain the perception of figures and objects, which, after all, are very specific, segregated things. Are there a *large number* of physiological bases for the perception of a figure scattered throughout a large cortical area, all *just alike?* If we employ a connectionistic model, is that model "multiplex" and duplicated in many regions at the same time? A similar problem arises for a field-theory of perception. How can the cortical fields be everywhere at once and yet sufficiently local to give segregation and definite boundaries to figures that are perceived? Such questions defy our attempts at logical understanding.

Both configurationism and equipotentiality are opposed to a theory espousing specific localization and intercommunication of the elements of a perceptual aggregate, an interpretation that Hebb proposed to defend. It should be clearly stated, however, that Hebb did not deny either of these opposing considerations; he only questioned their range of applicability. Phenomenological observations such as figure and ground and the equipotentiality findings of Lashley had to be accepted as facts. For Hebb the question was "whether gradients and fields are the only mechanism of selective neural action or whether they are combined with an equally important mechanism of connections and specialized conduction paths" (1949, p. 41). And he chose the latter alternative. His theory maintains that "a particular perception depends on the excitation of particular cells at *some* point in the central nervous system." On the other hand he not only acknowledged the great debt of modern psychology to gestalt theory, but accepted the presence of *some* innate organization in perception as the gestaltists had contended. There is therefore an element of eclecticism in his position.

Hebb shows fairly convincingly that the perception of simple outline figures means much more than the experiences of segregation, unity, good figure, and the like, upon which the gestaltists had based their theory. He recognized at the start the feature of "primitive unity," a purely sensorily determined wholeness of the figure and its segregation from the surroundings. Figure and ground belong to this class of properties of the percept; and this aspect of perceptual experience is native to the individual. So far there was complete agreement with gestalt theory. But in addition to primitive unity there is another, "non-sensory," aspect of figures in which prior experience plays an important role. This phase is seen, for example, in the fact that in concealed figures, though the organization of the whole conceals the part, we can perceive the part independently if past experience gives us a clue as to what to look for. Finally, there is in figure perception also the aspect of "identity." A figure seen can be later recognized and can be made the basis of an experience of selective similarity and generalization upon which a class-concept can be developed. Identity also means that the figure can be associated with other ideas or actions; it can also be named. It will be seen that in these distinctions Hebb is approaching what we have called the concrete-object character of the perception. The meaning that Hebb incorporates in the percept is thus more characterizing of the figure than was the gestalt-limited meaning or figure and ground, pragnänz, equilibrium, and the like. And with respect to this characterizing, identifying, aspect Hebb draws some conclusions as to the modus operandi of perception that are quite at odds with the views of gestalt.

GENETIC AND MOTOR EVIDENCE THAT PERCEPTION IS LEARNED; CONTRAST WITH GESTALT PROCEDURES

The argument is a genetic one. The primitive unity of a figure (i.e., seeing it as one segregated whole against a background) is readily attained not only by any normal person, but by those who, having been congenitally blind through cataract, see by means of an operation for the first time. It is also apparently attained by the normal rat and by a rat seeing for the first time after having been reared in darkness. It is presumably experienced also in earliest infancy. The case, however, is very different for the perception of identity. In this aspect the percept is by no means given at the start as an immediate, organized whole; it has to be gradually acquired. Citing the work of Senden and of Riesen, Hebb points out that newly seeing human beings (after congenital cataract removal) and chimpanzees reared in darkness, though they readily discriminate two figures when both are given together, and though they perceive unity in the primitive sense, are amazingly poor in the perception of figures or objects. They have great difficulty in recognizing figures and in having, with regard to them, an experience of identity. A course of patient learning is required to bring out the potentialities of the way things look. The human learner under these conditions goes through a process of separate attention to each part of the figure (certainly not a gestalt-like procedure) and only *gradually* arrives at an identification of the figure as a whole. Trained to discriminate a square from a triangle over a period of thirteen days, one patient still could not report their forms correctly without counting the corners. Without an extended learning period generalization of perception cannot be accomplished. Objects, also, whose names have been learned may fail to be recognized, i.e., named, when their previous surroundings have been changed.

It is possible, Hebb reasons, that a normal human infant goes through the same process. The immediate correctness and apparent utter simplicity of our adult perceptions of objects and forms may be entirely misleading as to the genesis and physiological basis of these perceptions. Very early in life, perhaps before the age at which the traditional gestalt experiments with infants were performed, there may have been this same piecemeal, repetitive, and summative process, demanding eye movements (anathema to gestalt theory) and many separate visual fixations; so that as adults we are able to perceive a square at a glance only by virtue of this earlier complex learning.

Motor aspects in the form of eye movements play an important role in Hebb's theory. Various lines of evidence support the view that perception involves a motor as well as a sensory activity. Though tachistoscopic speeds at which objects can be perceived seem to rule out eye movements as a means of the ordinary perceiving of objects, eye movements nevertheless facilitate definiteness and stability of perceptual experiences and imagery, as they clearly did in the case of the newly seeing patients to whom they were *necessary* for learning to perceive. Hebb argues that the capacity for recognizing patterns without eye movement is possible only as a result of prolonged visual training and improvement that goes on during every moment that the eyes are open from birth until adulthood is approached. Tachistoscopic studies of the process of reading show a piecing together, bit by bit, of elements already familiar, a filling in of the gaps by residues of earlier experiences, and an arriving at an end result consisting of a combination of familiar things, a reconstruction on the basis of experience. In the prolonged visual training of infancy and childhood "we learn to recognize the direction of line and the distance between points, separately for each grossly separate part of the visual field." In reading, the habit factor in perception with respect to definite parts of the retina is shown in experiments on the typographical line aspects of word recognition. From reports of the perceptions of newly seeing adults Hebb is inclined to explain both perceptual generalization and the apparent equipotentiality of a cortical region as the "sequel and product of learning." Pattern perception is specific and limited at first; it is generalized and made recognizable at varying directions of visual regard only with further practice. As for the gestalt theory of cortical perceptual fields Hebb argues that the necessity of accepting such a theory can be eliminated by the demonstration that perception is an additive, serial, reconstruction (rapid and unconscious for the normal adult) and that the perception of identity, that is, of distinctive wholes, depends upon a series of excitations from the parts of the stimulus figure.

The foregoing account, if read in conjunction with the rationale of gestalt-theory, shows clearly the influence of background postulates in the development of a theory and the consequent divergences of the product even when dealing largely with the same materials. We might say that for the gestalt theorists the isomorphic search started with two basis postulates: (1) the importance of using phenomenological description, provided by the introspective report of direct experience, as a basis for psychological theory, and (2) the dominant position of the whole as compared with its parts. Thinking of gestalt theory as a general psychological system rather than merely a theory of perception we can trace six steps of reasoning in its development, in each of which a position had to be taken. The decisions that were made were as follows: (1) to start with a set of specifications elaborated from phenomenological data, (2) to take the facts of *perception* as the basis for these specifications, (3) to use for this purpose the *configurational*, that is, the "whole-character," aspect of perception, (4) to devise a physiological model that would be isomorphic to the description of the configurational percept and would embody the idea of a dynamic whole, (5) to portray the model, in order to meet this demand, as macroscopic in size, and (6) to use as the specific design of the model the concept of an electrical field in the cortex, a choice best calculated to meet the requirements of the preceding steps. None of these decisions was *by itself* necessary. Each might have been different had the initial assumptions and the decisions preceding it been different.

In Hebb's approach we see that this is exactly what happened. He was more impressed by clinical, physiological, and behavioral data than by direct introspection. Discrete elements rather than gestalt-like wholeness were more to his liking as a postulate; and though he regarded wholes as significant, he insisted on seeing them as built up from the activities of parts. As a result we may note that his choices, corresponding to the six steps of the above reasoning, were all widely different from their gestalt counterparts. Unlike the gestaltists he decided at the start to do as little elaboration of the specifications of "direct experience" as possible and to go directly to the facts of cerebral anatomy and physiology. His starting points in phenomenology were so simple that they could almost be comprehended in the following statement: A triangle is perceived as having three angles and three sides and is recognized and identified for what it is. The next decision was that, in building the model, not only perception but other processes, especially learning, should be taken into account. As for the aspect of perception that *was* employed (stage three), this was not to be some abstract property, but the concrete identifying of the particular figure, which meant the utilization of its specific details rather than its primitive wholeness character. At the fourth step there was the decision that the model should represent, first, the development and joining of *parts*, and only after that the properties of the whole. This decision correlates with the next, namely, that we should look to microscopic neurological units, rather than to macroscopic regions of the cortex, for the stuff of which the model is to be composed. Finally, in keeping with all these requirements, there emerged (through working, however, with the same kind of experimental materials as the gestaltists—figure drawings) an associationistic model diametrically opposite to the field paradigm of gestalt.[1]

THE CELL ASSEMBLY AND PHASE SEQUENCE MODEL; "t"-ASSEMBLY; APPLICATIONS

The detailed character of Hebb's theory, a virtue from the standpoint of its explanatory value, makes it difficult to do it justice in a brief review. The working postulates are few and simple, but they were chosen after a careful consideration of the findings of neurophysiologists. Since learning (i.e., past experience) must be provided for in the perceptual process, a "dual trace mechanism" is postulated whereby the effects of short-lived reverberating circuits known to occur in the cortex can sustain a connection between neurons long enough to permit a lasting association to occur. This

[1] We are not, of course, implying that either Hebb or the gestalt psychologists actually went through six steps of a line of reasoning of just this sort or in the order here indicated.

more permanent connecting process is described as follows: "When an axone of cell A is near enough to excite a cell B and repeatedly or persistently takes part in firing it, some growth process or metabolic change takes place in one or both cells such that A's efficiency, as one of the cells firing B, is increased."[2] Probably this is brought about by the development of "synaptic knobs" on the terminal fibrils of the axone, increasing the area of contact and thus decreasing the resistance of the gap between the fibers. Metabolic changes and neurobiotaxis are also mentioned as possibilities. Typical transmission includes the convergence of two or more afferents upon the dendrites of an efferent, and extends from the sensory projection areas of the cortex into neighboring association areas. This last point is important. Since perception is considered to be an associative process involving learning we must think of its cortical organization or "assembly" as occurring not merely in the visual area (area 17) of the cortex, but also in the adjacent and more topographically random associative regions, such as areas 18, 19, and 20. Hebb is at some pains to show by neural diagrams how massive visual stimulation in area 17 combined with neural connections back and forth into an adjoining area, and involving convergence and summation, can provide the basis of the synaptic strengthening and facilitation of neural patterns in these outlying areas.

A group of cortical neurons functionally associated in this manner and involving sensory to sensory, as well as sensory to motor, connections is known as a *cell assembly*. The cells of such an assembly facilitate each other; and as the area of their contacts (through end-knobs) increases, the timing of their discharges becomes coördinated, the afferents gaining an increasing control through timing over the firing of the efferents. The cell assembly is conceived as a three-dimensional lattice-work, and in it there are frequently alternate pathways converging upon, or issuing from, a single synapse, thus giving a certain amount of equipotentiality in case some of the pathways are out of action. Because of the re-entrant character of the series a pathway can be used more than once in a given assembly action; hence if a neuron is in refractory phase and must be by-passed at the common synaptic juncture at one moment, it may be functional again at a later instant. A possibility is thus afforded for an almost indefinite reverberation of the structure that may serve as a basis of perceptual integration. Assemblies develop or change through "fractionation" or "recruitment" as some cells that lose their syn-

[2] See Hebb (1949), p. 62.

chronization drop out and others more compatible with the new timing of the assembly are brought in.

The cell assembly as thus defined is the unit of perception. It represents the physiological basis of the most simple percept. More complex perceptions are formed out of these assemblies by the same principles of mutual facilitation in conduction and consolidation in timing. There must, however, be a prolonged period of integration of the single simple assemblies before their association into larger perceptual complexes is possible; and there may be characteristic differences in perception according to the stage of organization which the units, or the larger complex, have reached. It is worthy of note that Hebb did not start with the naïve conception of a single neuron as the unit, or of a single synapse, but chose as the basis of the smallest perceptual activity a well-knit, self-contained, and continuously active *aggregate* of neurons, with synapses as the connecting points of the structure.

The next stage in the organization, then, is an assembly of these unitary assemblies. This process is the basis of the perception of a *complex*, and it involves what Hebb calls the *phase sequence*. At this point Hebb turns to figure perception as illustrative of his conception; and eye movements, or motor tendencies toward eye movements, come in as "vectors" along the lines or at the angles of the figure, thus producing facilitation between the component assemblies. Let us imagine a subject confronted by the outline drawing of a triangle.[3] As the subject looks at the triangle, he fixates a certain angle, A. This procedure gives rise to the beginning of an assembly, *a*, in the subject's cortex. There is now both a percept of A (foveal) and a motor tendency to look toward one of the other angles, B or C. A corresponding condition would be true if the subject should fixate the other corners and should thereby initiate assemblies *b* or *c*. Each of these three fixations, if repeated, builds up an irregular, diffuse neuronic assembly, embracing not only the proper corner of the figure but extending beyond it. The three assemblies *a*, *b*, and *c* (for the three corner-fixations of the triangle) are readily connected by motor activities (eye movements). In fact, there is a continual tendency to look from one corner of the triangle to another, a continual expectancy of what the new fixation will bring. Originally separately organized, the assemblies thus come, by occurring in close succession, to be interfacilitated. They can, however, also occur independently

---

[3] The reader will be aided throughout the following account by getting firmly in mind the image of an equilateral triangle with its lower left-hand point labelled A, its lower-right hand point labelled B, and its apex labelled C.

of one another. The lines of the triangle as well as the angles give rise to assemblies facilitating each other so that we really have *six* perceptual units in the complex.

As interfacilitation occurs (synaptic knob growth between the three assemblies), and as fractionation and recruitment (timing consolidation) proceed, there occurs, on the basis of these originally separate processes, the growth of a new *"superordinate"* system that Hebb calls *"t."* This *t* is "an assembly of cells whose activity is the perception of the triangle as a distinctive whole" (identity perception); and the whole in question is conceived as "other than the sum of its parts." It should be noted, however, that it derives its distinctiveness from the perception of the parts. On this latter point Hebb is clear and consistent in his opposition to gestalt doctrine. The whole (*t*) comes later than the parts (assemblies) and requires, as a precondition for its elaboration, the prior activity of those parts, just as the assemblies themselves require the repeated activity, in close conjunction, of the neurons of which they are composed.

One of the most interesting portions of the theory is that which describes the way in which the perception of a complex proceeds. In looking at a triangle, for example, we have seen that from the activating of assembly *a* (resulting from fixation on one angle, A) two incompatible eye movement tendencies are set up. One is toward angle B and one toward angle C. One of these two tendencies always stays below threshold, the other is supraliminal. The latter produces a change in fixation (a movement toward B or C, bringing into play assembly *b* or *c*); and from that latter fixation a similar fixation shift occurs either toward C or else back to A, and so on indefinitely. There need be no regularity in this process. We might, for example, have a fixation order of the series such as *a-b-c-b-a-c-a-b-a-*. When *t*, the assembly for the triangle as a whole, becomes organized, its activity does not replace that of the elements *a*, *b*, and *c*, but intervenes between them. Such a phase sequence, for example, might be: *a-b-t-a-c-t-c-t-b-*. Cancelling vectors of eye movement in such a series would hold the fixation constant. Thus *a*, *b*, and *c* facilitate each other, separately or in combinations, with intervening eye movements; and *a* may facilitate *t*, either through *b* or *c*. Or, in later stages, *a* might facilitate *t* when acting alone. Perception of the whole is thus momentary and alternates with the perception of the parts. Transiency is always a characteristic of the sequence: ". . . excitation in one of the assemblies *a*, *b*, *c*, and *t*, is an unstable equilibrium which moves readily into another phase. . . . The stability of a perception is not in a single persistent pattern of cerebral activity but in the tendency of the phases of an irregular cycle to recur at short intervals."[4] It is necessary only for reverberation in the assemblies to continue long enough to provide a temporal overlap between them.

The model of the assembly and perceptual complex, aided by this ingenious idea of an irregular shifting sequence, becomes the basis of Hebb's system of the organization of behavior. In the area of perception it aptly describes the gradual process (noted by Senden and Riesen) of the acquisition of figure perception by the newly seeing. The gestalt phenomenon of closure is interpreted as an activation of t, the superordinate assembly for the whole, which can occur even when the basic earlier assemblies are not all present. This would happen, for example, when a triangle is left open at the apex, assemblies a and b being given but c omitted. Abstraction and generalization in perception are illustrated by having two presentations of a triangle, one of them with the triangle alone and the other with the triangle inscribed in a circle. Though the neuronic convergences involved in the latter figure (where the circle touches an angle, for example, C, of the triangle) would tend in some cases, on a statistical basis, to disrupt the organized activity of assembly c, sometimes they would not do so; and the assemblies for the angle, that is, for all the angles, would persist and allow the figure to be recognized as a triangle in spite of its occurring in the setting of a different whole. In the latter case we could say that the organism has *abstracted* from a total complex; and by recognizing the similarity of the abstracted figure to the plain triangle it arrives at a *generalization* of the perception.

Beyond the field of perception Hebb regards his treatment of behavior as an attempt merely to generalize the ideas of this scheme, and to show how it fits other topics of psychology. He does not consider it a rigorous explanation of these other phenomena. One could hardly assign to his model, therefore, in its present stage, the status of full-fledged general theory of psychology. Many of his deductions from it however, and the supporting illustrations, are suggestive. Attention is the "central facilitation of a perceptual activity," as when assembly a facilitates (and also tends to select) b. When this occurs in advance of the corresponding sensory process for b, "expectancy" is said to occur. The facilitating process also serves as an explanation of association. Though more complex relationships can be learned by the higher than by the lower species at maturity, very simple relations are learned about as readily by the lower as by

⁴ *Ibid.*, p. 100.

the higher animals, and *first* learning (i.e., in infancy) is *slower* in the higher than in the lower forms. Learning consists of lasting changes of facilitation among the activities of specific neural elements. At maturity it concerns a complex of cell assemblies and elaborate phase cycles. It amounts here to a strengthening of facilitations rather than a setting up of new connections between unrelated activities. Prompt learning is based on the fact that the stimulus sets off well-organized phase sequences. To the extent that the environment controls the organized activity of the association areas and re-establishes the same pattern of cortical activities on successive trials, cumulative learning is possible. The same elements sometimes recur in different perceptions, so that two concepts having phases (that is, assembly-actions) in common can be associated. Ready-made links are thus provided needing only to be strengthened to establish association. Maze learning, presenting sequences of phases in which sensory and ideational elements (assemblies) are mixed, often shows irregularity and back-tracking. With each phase there is a selective influence on the motor system; and the phase sequence is dominated by the concept (or expectancy) of reaching a specific reward, as well as by the perception of the animal's present place in the apparatus. Conceptual complexes are always linked by activity of the cortical motor system.

The term motivation refers to the existence, direction or content, and persistence in direction, of an organized phase sequence. Pain may control learning by disrupting one phase sequence and leaving another undisturbed. "Pain stimuli" arouse pain experience only when their cerebral action is unorganized and interferes with other organized action. Metabolic changes, by altering the timing of the firing of neurons, tends to disorganize behavior. Lack of food is therefore a disruptive influence, producing restlessness. A learning process is required, originally, for transforming this disturbance into hunger as we know it in the adult. Hunger is not, therefore, a simple product of a need for food; it is to be defined as the excitation of a neural mechanism that controls eating. The mechanism that determines such behavior as eating or sex activity is phase sequence or "conceptual activity." As such it is subject to development through learning; and there are evidences that the regulation of food intake according to needs, as for example, in the rat, is not innate but learned.

Well-learned activities tend toward a "short-circuiting" in the phase sequence and readily "run themselves off." In order to maintain interest, therefore, a challenge in the nature of a conflict within the sequence is needed, and a domination by the thought process in rearranging the phase sequence. Novel sensory stimulation may offer such a check to phase sequence and demand a reorganization. Such a situation is important to the maintenance of a positive hedonic tone; and pleasure itself is defined as "a directed growth or development in cerebral organization."

Emotion is regarded as a disturbance in the timing of thalamocortical firing, a disruption, when the subject is awake, of established and operating phase sequences. This disruption may be produced by a conflict of phase sequences (having an ideational basis of the strange or unfamiliar), by a lack of sensory support for phase sequences (darkness, solitude, etc.), or by a metabolic change. Strong emotional disturbance of the unpleasant sort, however, has a coördinating aspect. It tends to put an end to the stimulation that aroused it and "to prevent the repetition of any line of thought that leads up to it." Mental illness is said to consist either of a long-standing disruption of time relations in the cerebrum or a lasting distortion of thought processes resulting from an earlier disturbance.

CRITIQUE AND EVALUATION OF HEBB'S SYSTEM

In evaluating Hebb's theory of perception two facts stand out as representing an advance over gestalt theory. First, more consideration is given to the question of *what* the subject is perceiving. Second, it is shown that the implications of gestalt theory as to the immediacy or innateness of all perceptual wholes are not supported by facts; and Hebb, in his own theory, has given to past experience and learning a needed place in perception. The working postulates of the theory are at least as parsimonious as those of gestalt, and its concepts are definite and experimentally available, at least in principle.

The most serious doubt regarding the agreement of the theory with facts comes from one of the sources with which Hebb himself was most concerned, namely, the facts of stimulus equivalence and equipotentiality of cortical action. The array of evidence on these points is so impressive that any perceptual or learning theory based on localized action and specific connections must face a considerable burden of proof. The hypothesis of "multiple representations" in the visual or other areas of the cortex seems strained; and the notion that equipotentiality in the brain is the result of learning on this basis seems a forced assumption. It is true that Hebb has allowed considerable leeway in the network of *alternate* pathways within a gross region of closely knit cortical tissue. In order to achieve the amount of equipotentiality that is present, however, and to provide the amount of overlapping of elements that must occur among different perceptions, these pathways would need to interlace in so thoroughgoing a manner that there would have to be some pathways representing every assembly or complex at all relatively small areas of cortical surface within fairly large regions. Interferences also would arise where the same assemblies are required in different phase sequences.

Associationistic or specific-connection models in general lack the flexibility necessary to account for equivalence, equipotentiality, and transfer of function. Gestalt theorists had called attention to similar difficulties as one of their reasons for abandoning attempts at explanation through one-to-one connections. For them, the neural architecture represented merely topographical frameworks and "constraints" within which the electrochemical field forces were obliged to act and which they probably could not alter except in a small degree. Hebb proposes a whole theory of perception in which a modification or relinking of these same frameworks is supposed to carry practically the whole burden of perceptual patterning. Either we must assume here the possibility of a disagreement of his model with facts or else we must acknowledge that it does not as yet possess the equipment necessary for showing how it works.

There are some further questions as to the explanatory power of the theory. One could wish that it had been worked out for a broader range of demonstration materials than merely an outline figure of a triangle. Gibson (1951) has criticized both Hebb and the gestaltists for assuming that an "outline figure" can be used as an experimental basis for drawing conclusions about visual perception in general. Solid-forms and surface forms, involving depth or slant, are realities; but outlines are only representations. How surface would be perceived in Hebb's theory is somewhat of a mystery. The perception of relative magnitude or other dimensional properties offer similar difficulties, though Hebb attempts to deal with the point (pp. 105–106). One wonders also how the perception of specific shape, as distinguished from the mere "threeness" of the sides of a triangle, can be represented by this linkage-model. The questions of the dimensionality and shape of a perception were answered in principle by Köhler with his macroscopic brain field isomorphic to the percept; but good evidence for the existence of such brain fields has not been forthcoming. Hebb is more realistic about the cortex, but his isomorphism is too abridged and sketchy in its relation to perceptual experience to be very explanatory.

The theory also is not free from the old, troublesome, whole-part confusion. Somehow many theorists seem to feel that they must provide some physiological basis for the existence of a whole that is more than, or other than, the sum of its parts. Yet, as brought out in our earlier discussion, no one has ever been able to state in terms that are both explicit and general what this supersummative whole *is*. In his derivation of the t-assembly Hebb maintains that it is a "superordinate" formation, that it is a *new* structure, not a sum or a hooking together of parts. Since it is conceived by him as a whole in its own right, Hebb prefers for it the notation t rather than the notation abc. The activity of this new formation is the perception of the triangle as a distinctive whole. The process suggested for t-elaboration seems to be as follows: "two determinate actions [as of assemblies] simultaneously would have a determinative effect, tending to excite specific transmission units, and . . . the action of these units would tend to organize in the same way that the earlier established systems were organized."[5]

If the writer has correctly understood this new organization to represent t, and to afford the basis of the distinctive wholeness of the figure, the following criticism could be offered. There is in the above theory more than one transmission unit excited by the component assembly activities, as, for example, by a and b; and these transmission units organize to give the physiological basis of the perception of a distinctive whole as contrasted with that of the perception of the parts. We thus have *a number* of units in the formation, mediating a perception of *one* unified, distinctive whole. By what token is this new formation, t, any better qualified to yield this unitary wholeness percept than the preceding assemblies would be if the latter were united directly into one complex, abc? In both cases we are making one thing out of several discrete and specific units joined together in their action. In order to have the experience of one unified whole that is something other than a number of parts joined together do we not need to have a cortical entity that is *one* unit and **not** an aggregation of several? Otherwise we must posit an intracortical "observer" standing back of the whole process to experience the *unum e pluribus*. To make an explicit and denotable whole that is more than the linking together of its operating parts would be just as difficult at one level as it is at another (cf. the discussion of wholes near the end of Chapter 5). Furthermore there is in Hebb's scheme no apparent reason why one should not have, phenomenologi-

---

[5] *Ibid.,* p. 98.

cally, a perception of the parts *a*, *b*, and *c*, and *alongside* these at the same time another equally vivid perception of the whole, that is, of *t*. This however does not occur: we perceive *either* the parts in their separateness *or* the parts as integrated into a whole, but not both at once.[6]

If the perception of a distinctive whole is made to depend upon this superordinate logic, the explanation of this aspect of perception would have to go a-begging. And this would be unfortunate since the important phenomenon of identity in perception was so ably stressed by Hebb both in his critique of gestalt and his own assembly theory. But perhaps this outcome is unnecessary. It may be that he was trying to explain something for which there is no need. It would seem that simply to affirm the integrated activities of *a*, *b*, and *c* (with the notation *abc*) as the basis of the perception of the whole would answer all rational demands. Differences of activation of the component elements, which would represent the situation when our attention is on the parts, might account for whatever *part* is more vividly perceived; while if the activation is fairly equal throughout, the figure as a distinctive *whole* would be perceived. This interpretation would also tally with the fact that we perceive the parts separately *or* the whole, but not both (separately) at the same time.

Turning from questions of agreement with fact, explanatory value, and logic, we may ask how wide a range of the phenomena of perception the theory covers. As we have seen, it gives some consideration to specific object-character, a phase that was lacking in gestalt theory. It presents, in part, some of the essentials of concrete meaning. It fails, however, to incorporate other aspects, notably some of the configurational features. Such experiences as boundary influences, good continuation, figural aftereffects, and the like are difficult to construe in terms of an assembly model. Hebb himself admits the truth of certain basic gestalt assumptions, as in the matter of primitive unity. This admission, though it reflects a tolerant and open-minded attitude, does not solve the theoretical problem. We are left with two ingenious, but totally different, schemes, both designed to give answers to the same general set of questions. Other phenomena of perception not adequately covered by the theory are sensory dimension, frame of reference, and constancy.

[6] As to the *activity* in this superordinate *t*-formation Hebb says that it "is best defined as being whatever determinate, organized activity results from repeated activity in the earlier-developed or subordinate structures giving rise to it. . . . " This is not too enlightening a statement of that "something more than its parts" which the whole is supposed to represent. (*Ibid.*, p. 98.)

We cannot leave the cell-assembly and phase-sequence theory without a more adequate appraisal of what its author has accomplished. The molar doctrine in psychology has served partly as a defense against the hazards of trying to explain behavior, in the present state of our knowledge, in terms of what goes on in the central nervous system. Yet Hebb, like Köhler, saw the necessity of such an attempt. The labor and discouragement involved in trying to link uncertain neurological details with the vast array of known psychological facts are great; but Hebb has faced them and has at least made a beginning. The theoretical difficulties to which we have referred have resulted largely from the forthright way in which he went to work. In attacking the problem by going directly to the cortical situation he found what every investigator finds, namely, that there are in the cortex no visible "fields," "total processes," or "supersummative wholes." The picture as it unfolds under the miscroscope is highly specific and vastly intricate. Neural arrangements seem to spell out specific connections on every hand. To bridge the gap between this microscopic, interconnected, aggregate and what is seen in the behavior of the whole organism with its perceived configurations, its unity, its generalizations, and its equipotentiality, is a problem that calls for almost superhuman ingenuity. And it is at this point that an associationistic model, to which we seem nevertheless directed by the facts of neural organization, appears too limited.

Yet there are some aspects in which such a theory has its advantages. Let us compare it for a moment with the gestalt position. In order to give their percept-bases a wholeness character, to let them be "suffused," as it were, with the nature of the whole, gestaltists have set up their concept of a cortical field. Though this notion seems to correspond with the phenomena of configuration it has not fared very well under experimental testing or general neurophysiological findings. Now the strong indications that motor elements enter into perceptions signify that we must take into account not only the sensory and association areas of the cortex but the motor centers as well, and beyond these, efferent impulses and muscular reactions with their returning proprioceptive impulses. Certainly we must do all this for the understanding of behavior in general. These motor elements must then be fitted into the configurational pattern of the gestalt theorists; hence presumably they too must constitute a field. And the field they constitute, moreover, must be in some way *continuous* with that set up in the cortex by the stimulations received from perceived objects. But the provision for such a continuity or communication of fields is lacking in brain-field theory. By enclosing the field in a chemical fluid in interneural spaces of the cortex, and by considering it all by itself, Köhler had been able to make some plausible comparisons between the phenomenological percept and authentic field-properties. But how we are going to extend this idea of a field in a continuous chemical medium in the brain so that it will cover outgoing impulses in efferent neurons and contractions of the muscles of the eyes, trunk, legs, arms, and hands? To say that the behavior of the *entire organism* constitutes a field is, in the absence of better field specifications than we have at present, to indulge in pure metaphor. Impulses to muscle elements, as well as the returning proprioceptive impulses, go on in particular fibers and issue from, or are projected to, specific locations in the brain. How can we tie up continuous, macroscopic fields in intracortical regions with such specific elements as these?

Here the Hebb model is on better ground. If we conceive the physiological basis of perception to be the organization of neural elements and their impulses, rather than fields, this problem offers no unsurmountable difficulties even though other difficulties, such as that of equipotentiality, remain. What Hebb has done is to reject the picture of behavior and of its cortical segment as a process having a "determinative" whole character. He has substituted for this the idea of an *aggregate of elements* joining together and operating together under definite physiological laws. Such a model has certain advantages in addition to the one mentioned above. The joining of the elements may *take time;* and repeated excitations of the elements may be needed throughout the early years or even later. If the aggregating occurs at a later period and takes an appreciable time and many trials, we recognize it as "learning." If it has occurred extremely early, or if it now occurs very quickly, that is, under conditions in which its repetitive or trial-and-error aspect cannot be observed, we call it perception. By this conception Hebb has not only been able to make a place for the learning process that is lacking in gestalt-theory and to incorporate perceptual data from clinical, physiological, comparative, and developmental psychology, but he has also provided a generalization that may increase the parsimony of psychological systems.

It is true that the model proposed is not sufficiently flexible; equipotentiality is not fully accommodated; some essentials of explanation are missing; and, as some critics have pointed out, it is too much controlled by cognitive aspects at the expense of motivation. Nevertheless the germ of a useful idea is there. The model comports well with trial and error manifestations in learning and thinking; and it provides for the energizing or disruptive effects upon the phase-sequences exerted by metabolic changes and processes involved in drives, pain, and emotional states. Though the model has many shortcomings in the field of perception and certainly cannot be called a satisfactory general theory, it probably goes further in suggesting the way *toward* such a theory than do other conceptions that lack its denotational clarity and boldness of design.[7]

[7] The foregoing critique has been concerned mainly with the perceptual aspects of Hebb's theory. For a critical review from a more general standpoint see Leeper, 1950.

For another theory of perception based on connectionistic principles see Householder, 1947. This author attempts to deal with discrimination, constancy, transposition, and other aspects on the basis of neural architecture and the principles of excitation and inhibition.

8

Motor Aspects
Sensory-Tonic Field Theory

Looking back over the aggregates of perception as thus far studied we recall that for *gestalt theory* there were (phenomenologically) contours, surfaces, segregated figures, figures differentiated from grounds, and the like. On the physiological side there was, for gestalt, the brain-field aggregate, comprising such items as neural topography, molecules in solution, ions, interfaces of cells, polarized regions, and electric currents. The aggregating of these seemed to involve whole-character, self-containedness, and unity. Specifically there were the laws of organization including closure and good figure. Physiologically the parts were held together as an electrochemical field in the cortex; and perceiving operated by the coming of the field to equilibrium or to a steady state. For Hebb the phenomenological aggregate consisted of perceived angles and lines that give a figure its distinctive character. From the physiological standpoint there were motor elements in the form of eye movements and, of course, nerve cells with their end-knobs at synaptic junctions. Aggregation and operation were accomplished by growth of the end-knob connections between neurons through use. Such interfacilitation, combined with timing of neural impulses, gave rise to the formation of neural assemblies and phase-sequences. Two sharply contrasting conceptions of the perceptual aggregate have thus resulted from these two systems.

Though we are accustomed to think of perception as the organization of sensory experience a little thought will show that the *muscular contractions* which play a part both in sensory accommodation and in general bodily adjustments to the object must also be important. Gestalt theory had minimized the role of the efferent side, and it seemed inevitable that motor aspects would eventually have to be added to the aggregate in order to supplement the purely sensory emphasis. At an earlier time Titchener had stressed the role of

183

kinaesthetic sensations and images as carriers of meaning. In Hebb's theory of figure-perception eye movements played an indispensable role. If we consider the matter more broadly we see that a large part of the way the world looks to us is determined by how we react or are set to react to it. One cannot eliminate the awareness of an apple as something to be eaten (or otherwise appropriately reacted to) from one's total percept of the object without losing a great deal that is significant. Such aspects as sensory qualities, dimensions, segregation, surface, contour, and figure when taken alone, do not supply the full perceptual meaning. As distinguished from such aspects, *motor* considerations also must claim our attention. They have even been so impressive that they have led to the development of purely motor theories of perception dedicated to the proposition that the perception of an object is merely "what you do with it." But there is a danger of narrowness also on this side. What we habitually do with an object will add important features to the way in which it appears to us; but such additions do not cover its full appearance any more than the dimensional or purely formal properties. The problem is how to include both aspects in some well integrated scheme.

LOGICAL STARTING POINTS OF THE WERNER-WAPNER THEORY: EQUIVALENCE AND INTERACTION

A serious attempt to unite the sensory aspect with the motor has been made by Werner and Wapner in their "sensory-tonic field theory of perception."[1] These authors were dissatisfied with the sensory approach of psychophysics because it ruled out the state of the organism, the role of objects in relation to the organism, and the part played by individual differences. To cover these omissions they developed their own theory. Concerning the terms "sensory" and "tonic" in the title of their theory some explanations must be given. The word tonic is used in a broad sense to include not only changes of muscular tension of a postural kind (tonicity), but also the larger, phasic contractions entering into actual movements. It applies to visceral as well as somatic muscular activity. The term sensory, particularly as used in contrast with tonic, harbors an ambiguity. On the one hand it can refer to a conscious experience, e.g., a sensory quality, a dimension, or

---

[1] This theory, originally appearing in the *Journal of Personality* (1949), has been republished in Bruner and Krech, eds., 1950, pp. 88–107. See also Werner, 1945; Wapner, Werner, and Chandler, 1951; Werner, Wapner, and Chandler, 1951; Wapner, Werner, and Morant, 1951; and Wapner and Werner, 1952. For a more recent and complete statement see Werner and Wapner, 1952.

sensory data "supersummed" into a gestalt. This is the meaning that is expressed by the term phenomenological. On the other hand sensory can mean the physiological system whose functioning accompanies the sensory experience, that is, the action of receptors, afferent neurons, and sensory cortical processes. Sometimes the word is used, though with danger of resulting confusion, to mean both. If we assign to sensory the strictly physiological meaning, the problem of integration with muscular contractions seems simpler.

The term motor, or tonic, as used in perceptual theory also has its ambiguity, though of a different sort. Either we must say that a sensory-motor interaction in perception occurs as the impulse begins to go out from the motor centers over the efferent neurons, or else we must say that the muscular reaction is made first and then proprioceptive (kinaesthetic) impulses, originating in receptors in muscles and joints as a result of the reaction, come back along afferent pathways to the sensory or association areas of the cortex and join there with the excitation received by way of the exteroceptors (eye, ear, etc.) from the perceived object, and that these two sensory processes acting together make up the physiological basis of the percept. This latter interpretation is the one that seems most probable. In this case tonic elements would not enter directly into the perception; they would be effective only as producers of kinaesthetic sensory components. All perception would thus really be sensory in its constitution, though because one class of the sensory elements has arisen from *motor* changes within the body we would need to consider motor or tonic factors as a part of the total perceptual process.

The problem Werner and Wapner faced was that of combining those two sets of factors (sensory and tonic) into one explanatory system. "How is it possible," they asked, "that intrinsically different elements, such as motor and sensory, can affect one another?" Or, as we might translate it for the sake of clarity: how can exteroceptive (e.g., visual) and proprioceptive (i.e., *non*-visual) elements interact? That they must do so is a necessary inference from facts presently to be cited; and the authors express the opinion that no organismic theory can be developed without such a concept of interaction.

Interaction between the tonic and the sensory would, they thought, be a permissible concept if both of the two following conditions were fulfilled. First, one would need a construct of a process that is "prior" to both the sensory and the motor aspects. What this requirement might mean is somewhat vague, but we are told that it implies the priority of some "total dynamic process" of which the sensory and the tonic are contributing factors or components. Though this total process can be analyzed into these two parts which, taken singly, have properties "alien" to each other, it must not be regarded as the mere "combination" or "summative result" of these two factors. The first requirement, then, was to set up a gestalt-like concept of sensory and tonic as a whole that is different from the sum of its parts and within which these (essentially alien) parts can interact as a unified system. The second condition was that sensory and tonic factors must have "common dynamic properties." Though different in their specific properties, they must nevertheless be equivalent *dynamically;* that is, they must possess some features in common that would enable them to contribute to the total dynamic process in an equivalent way.   It is implied that if such equivalence is provided, sensory and tonic factors *will* interact. The notion of equivalence here employed is similar to its usual meaning in psychology: things that are equivalent can be substituted for one another in a process without changing the end result.   For example, we speak of the equivalence of two stimulus patterns in evoking the same reaction.

It is difficult to see why equivalence in this sense was made a necessary and sufficient condition of interaction between the components of a perception.   In an interactive situation, at least of the type known as a mechanism, the parts that interact are usually *not* equivalent; one *cannot* be substituted for the other.   The reciprocal phases of contraction and extension of opposed muscles in motor coördinations are interactive, yet they are not equivalent in the sense defined above.   But in any event, the authors of the theory have rested their case for the possibility of interaction upon these two supports—the presupposition of a total dynamic process embracing both sensory and tonic, and the equivalence of these two aspects as parts of the total system.   The notion of a prior dynamic total process is of course a postulate; there is at present no direct empirical evidence by which it can be established.   Under this postulate the authors contend that the validity of their theory can be tested in terms of two requirements: (1) that it be shown that tonic factors interact with sensory factors in perception, and (2) that sensory and tonic factors are shown to be equivalent with respect to their contributions to the total dynamic outcome.[2]   We must add, finally, that perception is to be regarded not only in terms of the interaction of sensory and tonic factors, but as a *field* in which the body and the perceived object interact.   In this process the whole organic condition of the individual is important.   "The potency of tonic factors for perception would be obscure without appreciating that the state of the organism is part and parcel of perceptual events."

[2] See their article in Bruner and Krech, 1950, p. 91.

EVIDENCE OF THE INTERRELATIONSHIP OF SENSORY AND TONIC;
EXPERIMENTS IN "ROD-VERTICALITY"; "VICARIOUSNESS"

Werner and Wapner begin marshalling their evidence by showing
that the sensory and motor areas of the cortex are not so sharply
separated as was formerly thought.   Various cortical regions, e.g., the
visual, may be said to involve both a sensory and a motor function,
autonomic as well as somatic activities coming under the latter.
Sherrington and Lashley have concluded that a close relationship
exists between sensory and motor activities, mediated by tonus.
Unilateral light, tone, and tactile stimuli have been found under
certain conditions to produce increases of bodily tonus, as shown, for
example, in a tendency to fall toward the stimulated side or by a
"pointing past" the stimulus.   Mach had earlier concluded that localization in space depends on impulses aroused by eye movements.   To
take another example, when a subject in a darkened room is asked to
adjust an illuminated rectangle so that the left hand edge appears to
be in the median plane he displaces the edge to the right, an effect
which is due to the tonus loadings in the subject's musculature induced by light from the illuminated rectangle.

These facts, interesting in themselves, point to a probable interaction between sensory and tonic elements (that is, between visual and
non-visual, kinaesthetic, factors) in the formation of a perception.
They do not, however, give us any notion of how the interaction takes
place.   They show us nothing about the dynamic equivalence of the
sensory and tonic.   An experiment upon which the authors do rely
for this purpose may be described briefly as follows.[3]   The subject,
seated in a darkroom, is asked to give the experimenter directions for
moving a luminescent rod, pivoted at its center, into what appears to
the subject to be a vertical position.   In a preliminary series it was
observed that the rod, on the average, was given a tilt by the subject's
directives to the left.   This position, which represented the subject's
usual and non-veridical perception of verticality when no "extraneous"
stimulation (i.e., no stimulation other than that from the perceived
object) was given, was referred to as the control.   There were two
main parts in the remainder of the investigation in which two forms
of extraneous stimuli were unilaterally applied.   One of these was an
auditory stimulus (tone), the other was an electrical stimulation
applied to one side of the neck.   We shall discuss the results of the
latter procedure first.

[3] Wapner, Werner, and Chandler, 1951.

The subject made his attempt at vertical placement of the rod as before, but this time under the condition of the unilateral electrical stimulation of the neck musculature.   The result was that the rod was tilted in its placement to one side of the control position and in a direction with respect to the control that was opposite to the side of the neck receiving the excitation.   A corresponding effect was secured through stimulation of the muscle on the opposite side of the neck. These changes in the subject's perception were presumably attributable to the influence exerted upon the perception of verticality by proprioceptive impulses arising from an increase of muscle tonus, the increase being produced directly by the electrical stimulation.   The effect of unilaterally increased muscle tonus was therefore to superimpose upon the normal slightly non-veridical perception of the vertical another error, inclining the perceived vertical, with respect to the control position, toward the side opposite to that on which the tonus was increased.   In the other portion of the experiment the situation was as before, except that instead of employing an electrical muscle-stimulation the experimenters sounded a tone that was conveyed to one ear or the other by headphones.   Again the vertical was seen as tilted towards the side opposite to that of the stimulation.   It was also noted that the angle of tilt was the same as that which had occurred when the electrical stimulation was employed.   In the statement by Werner and Wapner of their theory it was implied that such a result is also attributable to a change of tonus distribution as between the two sides of the body, produced this time not by direct muscle stimulation but indirectly by way of an auditory stimulus. These experiments are cited by the authors as showing that "one cannot properly deal with perception without taking into consideration the concept of a field where interaction takes place between body and object." It was also said that the experiment "points to the equivalence of sensory (auditory) and tonic (direct muscular) stimulation; i.e., *both affect the organism in an identical way resulting in similar perceptual changes.*"

Effects strikingly similar to the above were found by Werner, Wapner, and Chandler (1951) for the influence of supported and unsupported bodily tilt upon the visual perception of verticality, and by Wapner, Werner, and Morant (1951) for the influence of acceleration and deceleration in bodily rotation.   In the first of these experiments it was found that the apparent vertical was tilted, in comparison with objective vertical, in the opposite direction from the body tilt of the subject, and that the degree of displacement increased with increase of tilt of the body. Unsupported body tilt, involving more extensive muscular reaction on the part of the subject, gave a greater effect on the perception of verticality than did supported body tilt. In the second experiment the apparent vertical was inclined in a direction opposite to that of the acceleration. The shift of the vertical under deceleration in one direction was like that of acceleration in the opposite direction. Wapner, Werner, and Morant conclude that various forms of stimulation, auditory, labyrinthine, and those from postural changes, affect and contribute to the "dynamic status of the organism." And this status of the organism comprises a continuous patterning of tonic processes that is a principal factor in the sensory-tonic field and "makes for perceptual shifts of an otherwise enduring stimulus object."

Another line of evidence in which the authors see a support for their equivalence theory is found in certain ambiguous experiences which they term vicarious. Vicariousness means that one thing serves functionally as a substitute for another with respect to an end product; and this, of course, also means equivalence. Let us take an experimental instance. The subject stands in the center of a striped cylindrical screen that rotates about him. In this situation two possibilities arise. In the first, the screen is seen as moving; and the subject turns his eyes, and sometimes his body, in the direction of the movement as he follows the screen by nystagmus movements of the eyes. In the second, the screen is seen at rest, motor activity of the subject's eyes and body stops, and he perceives an apparent motion of a fixation point in front of the screen together with an apparent motion of his own body in the opposite direction. With the perception of illusory (bodily) motion, physical movements in the opposite direction stop; with the emergence of actual bodily motion illusory motion ceases. In view of this evidence Werner and Wapner postulate that "the available 'sensory-tonic' energy may either be released through body movement or may express itself in perceptual displacement or apparent motion." It is to be noted that another postulate is implied in this statement, namely, the existence of something the authors call sensory-tonic energy. By referring to studies in psychopathology the authors further seek to generalize their theory. There is conceived to be a linkage between the symbolic and the primary levels of tonic activities in the organism. Attitudes and motives may be represented in the sensory-tonic state (particularly the viscerotonic) and through these mechanisms may be "projected" into the perceptions of objects.

WHAT INTERACTS WITH WHAT TO PRODUCE WHAT?
A CLARIFICATION OF THE EXPERIMENTAL SITUATION

In trying to assimilate the experimental findings to the theory as thus far presented a misunderstanding regarding the authors' intentions is likely to arise. From the theoretical introduction and experiments thus far reviewed the reader might have gained an impression something like the following: Werner and Wapner are proposing a theory which combines sensory and motor happenings in explaining the organism's perceptions. We all have experiences of objects through the exteroceptive senses. We also have, through the same sensory channels, some experience of the position of such objects. Here, for example, is the experience of the rod which the subject *sees* as an object extended in space before him. This is a direct visual and sensory experience: it must represent the "sensory" factor entering into the total percept that Werner and Wapner have hypothesized as being "sensory-tonic" in its origin. Now the experiments have shown that when extraneous stimulations or other conditions occur, of the sort which produce changes in tonus on one side of the body (for example, a unilateral shock or a sound delivered to one of the subject's ears), such changes in tonus *modify* the perception of the rod's position so that the position in which the rod now appears to be vertical is slanted away from its usual vertically perceived position. This influence, though evoked by some kind of sensory stimulation, is definitely muscular in its production and must therefore represent the "tonic" factor in the sensory-tonic couplet. Here then we have the two factors, the *visual* (sensory) experience of the rod as a qualitative and spatially extended object, on the one hand, and the *tonic* factor, introduced from extraneous stimulation, that modifies the rod's apparent spatial position on the other; and these two factors fuse or interact giving us the total percept of (i) a rod (ii) in an "apparently" vertical position.

As the authors of the theory have stated their case, the above interpretation would be quite incorrect. It does not accurately designate the sensory and tonic factors that are said by Werner and Wapner to be equivalent and interactive, or the end result toward which they interact. Though the above mentioned sensory and tonic factors do obviously interact, and it would seem highly desirable to build a theory that would deal with their interaction, they are not functionally equivalent; and it will be recalled that equivalence was for the authors the test upon which interaction was to be based and the principle by which it was to be explained. Functional equivalence means that both factors play the same role toward an end result so that one could be substituted for the other without changing that result. Clearly, as we have defined sensory and tonic above, this could not be the case; for if the extraneous *tonic* elements were omitted, i.e., substituted for by the sensory (visual) perception of the rod alone, this visual perception would not give, by itself, the experience of the rod as vertical when in the slanted position in which it was perceived as vertical under the extraneous stimulation; while if the *visual* elements (rod perceived as an object) were excluded there would be no rod-perception at all. Something is therefore wrong with our choice of the end result and its determining factors.

What then *is* the end result to which the authors are referring as a test of equivalence, and what are the tonic and sensory factors that are proved by their experiments to be equivalent in producing that result? The theory can be understood only if we take the end result not as having to do with the perception of the rod as an object, nor even with the rod as an object in a certain position, but only with the slant or position that the rod *is in*, that is, the angle of tilt that is necessary in order that it shall appear as vertical to the subject. And the test of equivalence we employ must be a test based upon contributions to this perceptual result of pure object-*position*.

All exteroceptive stimuli, as well as other environmental conditions, are regarded by the authors as productive not only of sensory but also of tonic effects. The rod itself, as a visual stimulus-object, produces both. This statement is proved by the fact that the apparent vertical will be characteristically misplaced by the subject, though in lesser degree, when there are no extraneous stimulations. Furthermore, the "starting position" (initial slant) of the rod has been found to have an influence upon the position at which he will finally experience it as vertical. And of course both the unilaterally sounded tone and the electric shock applied to the neck muscle on one side were seen to have tonic effects that influenced perceived verticality. So now the question of equivalence has shifted its locus of application. It is no longer the broader question of the equivalence or fusion of all the sensory and tonic elements, as such, in the perceptual act. It is the more specialized question of what stimuli or external conditions are equivalent in the sense that they produce *the same type of influence upon the tilting of the rod that is required to give the subject the experience of verticality*. The claim of Werner and Wapner is that in this special function sensory and tonic factors are equivalent.   They can be separately demonstrated to have the same effect upon perceived verticality.

But to what sensory and tonic factors are they referring?   They cannot mean the sensory visual experience or cortical process involved in the perception of the rod as an object, for that, as we have seen, does not afford equivalence.   The *sensory* factor to which they really refer may come, in fact, not from the object (i.e., the rod) at all, but from an extraneous stimulus.   In the experiment first cited above it was considered to be the auditory stimulation from the tone that was sounded into one of the subject's ears.   The *tonic* factor was taken to be the contraction resulting from the electric shock applied to the neck muscle.   This shock acted directly upon the muscle and presumably did not involve, or at least require, any sensory channel for its mediation.   Granting that the rod is perceived at all (a fact that seems to require some sensory factors other than that just mentioned), these two conditions, tone (sensory) and shock (tonic), were, as we have seen, functionally equivalent in producing perceptual displacement of the vertical.   They could therefore interact, at least in principle, combining their effects toward this common end.   It is upon this argument and this designation of sensory versus tonic that the authors seem to base their claim for the functional equivalence and interaction of sensory and tonic elements.   This kind of demonstration constitutes the main experimental basis for the hyphenated expression "sensory-tonic" that plays the title role in their theory.   If we define the sensory element as the tone (auditory experience) and the tonic element as the direct muscular effects from the shock, we can then assert that sensory and tonic factors are equivalent in their results (perception of the vertical); hence they can interact.   In so interacting, they can provide a common "dynamic status" of the organism that influences the manner in which objects are (spatially) perceived.   To be explicit, the theory is not a sensory-tonic theory of perception directly but a theory of the equivalence of certain factors in the formation of an underlying state (tonus distribution) which state in turn affects the total perception.   We thus have a sensory-tonic theory not of perception but of one of the conditions of perception.

Two questions arise, however, that suggest inadequacies in such a designation of sensory and tonic.   First, we note that although the auditory stimulus that produced a characteristic displacement in the perceived verticality of the rod was truly sensory, it probably accomplished this result through a series of neural events that culminated in a change in distribution of the bodily tonus-pattern. The sensory component is therefore effective *because it evokes tonus changes.*[4] But this is the very same reason why the direct electrical stimulation of the muscle was effective in producing an equivalent displacement of the rod. The only difference was that in the latter instance the effect was supposed to be directly upon the muscle rather than mediated through the usual afferent-efferent channels. Furthermore an electric shock, if applied to the skin of the neck, would undoubtedly produce sensory as well as tonic effects, just as the auditory stimulus did. Is it not somewhat gratuitous, then, to maintain that we have here *two kinds* of agencies working to produce effects upon perceptual displacement, and to classify these agencies in two separate categories, calling one sensory and the other tonic? By the time the effects of these two incitements are produced that feed back into the central nervous system in such a way as to affect perception they are *both* tonic. We do not therefore have an equivalence and potential interaction of sensory with tonic elements, except in an initial and superficial sense, but an equivalence of tonic with tonic. Such equivalence can hardly be used as a proof of the interaction of sensory elements, as such, with tonic elements or as the basic of a "sensory-tonic" theory postulating some prior dynamic state and "sensory-tonic" energy.

This consideration leads to our second question. The picture now before us of the equivalence and interaction of sensory with tonic incitements in the production of a tonic change affecting perception does not seem too clear-cut or meaningful. Ought not the emphasis to lie, rather, upon the equivalent effect of such tonic changes, however produced, upon the perception of verticality? Such changes affect the cortical areas involved in perception only as they are mediated by proprioceptive stimulations and their afferent impulses. We ought further to note that a rod's position can be perceived only if the rod itself is perceived. If the perception of position is not combined with the perception of the object that has the position, the percept in question cannot occur at all. What has become of the perception of the rod as an object (that is, the experience of its texture, brightness, color, meaning, etc.) in the Werner-Wapner theory? This problem, so far as we can determine, was largely ignored. It must now be raised again. We now have on our hands a different problem of interaction, namely, the question of how the proprioceptive (sensory) effects from the body-tonus changes interact in the

[4] An interpretation of this sort is suggested by the authors themselves (in Bruner and Krech, eds., 1950, pp. 96–97, 100).

central nervous-system with the direct visual (sensory) effects of the retinal pattern from the stimulus-object, and in so doing produce the total perception of (i) the rod (ii) in a vertical position. To be complete any sensory-motor theory of perception must provide some answer to this question. The focus of our attention must thus shift to the sensory or association areas of the cortex, and the interaction that seems to be demanded is not one of a sensory-tonic or even a tonic-tonic sort, but an interaction of sensory elements with sensory. Though the general equivalence of the tonic factors making up the dynamic state of the organism has been established and their effect upon perception proved (a valuable finding), we are still left with an overall problem: How do sensory factors in their unique and broader sense combine with tonic factors in the formation of the percept?

FURTHER FORMULATIONS: EQUILIBRIAL AXIS AND STATE; FIELD INTERPRETATIONS; BODY AND BODY-OBJECT BALANCE

By this time we have strayed far afield from the formulations of Werner and Wapner. Let us return to the theory as it has developed in their more recent work. In 1952 these authors published a more integrated and comprehensive statement in which certain matters were clarified, further evidence adduced, and some new constructs employed. In an effort to accommodate the recent findings of pro- jective personality research and of the effects of cognitive and moti- vational states upon perception the term tonic in the sensory-tonic couplet is now used more broadly. The problem which the authors have called the paradox of interaction now includes the question of how two essentially alien types of elements such as emotion, drive, motivation, and need, on the one hand, and exteroceptive sensory processes, such as visual and tactual, on the other, can influence each other or even fuse. In the main, however, the experimental demon- strations are still limited to the simpler motor activities such as the tonus-distribution involved in equilibration and the perception of the vertical; and the problem of resolving the dilemma of the interaction of sensory and (simple) tonic still dominates the theoretical outlook. We find the authors again asserting that the fundamental entity in perception is neither sensory nor motor, but some dynamic process prior to both, and that it may be brought to bear in a similar way by receptor-stimulation and direct tonic excitation ". . . with respect to the total perceptual process there is a functional equivalence between sensory and muscular factors." An attempt is made to weld the two elements still more closely together by the use of hyphenated terms. The authors cite evidence to the effect that "any stimulation, whether it comes through extero-, proprio-, or interoceptors, is sensory-tonic in nature." Instead of talking in traditional terms of an object stimulating merely receptors and sensory areas in the cortex, they speak of the stimulus arousing "*sensory-tonic*" *events*, events that involve the entire organism. It is asserted that "the perceptual properties of an object are a function of the way in which the stimuli coming from that object will affect the existing sensory-tonic state of the organism." The concepts of a sensory-tonic field, involving body and object, and of sensory-tonic energy are again employed.

It is clear, therefore, that the questions we have raised above are still to the point. Were the sensory and the tonic elements *really* differentiated in the experimental program so that their functional equivalence and essential unity *could* be demonstrated? Or do we have only the equivalence of the tonic elements that are evoked by varying stimulus patterns some of which are called sensory and some tonic? Have we explained perception as a total process or only the dynamic state of the organism that is one of the factors of the total process?

These issues are still unfaced in the article we are now reviewing; and attention is kept focused upon the organismic state produced by the extraneous stimulations and upon the way in which tonic effects received from the stimulus-object interact with the organismic state to influence the perception of spatial position. Concerning this latter problem, however, some new concepts are introduced which clarify the situation considerably and provide an important addition to the theory. The authors begin by stating that one cannot conceive of the verticality of a line in isolated space and independent of relationships to the body: verticality depends on the dynamic relation between the line's objective position and the current organismic state of the subject. We recall that all stimuli are considered as arousing impulses that have some effect upon tonus distribution in the body; and this holds for the stimulus-object to be perceived as well as for all the "extraneous" stimuli (sounds, body-tilt, rotation, electric shock, etc.) that are acting upon the subject at the moment and whose effects comprise the background organismic state. The stimulus-object (in this instance the rod) must itself be regarded as having not one, but two, effects: (i) the perception of the rod, with quality, brightness, meaning, and so on, as an object, and (ii) a change in tonicity of the bodily musculature. The latter, tonic, effect combines with the organismic state produced by whatever extraneous stimuli may be present in influencing the perceived spatial characteristics of the object.[5]

According to the authors, when the organism is subjected to stimulation from objects to be perceived one of two relationships to the organismic state will obtain. The stimuli may either interfere with the organismic state or they may not. Here the important concept of bodily equilibrium is introduced. Where the incoming stimuli do not interfere with or disturb the organismic state we can say that the object is "in balance with the existing body equilibrium." If they do interfere or are incommensurate with the organismic state, "there emerges a tendency in the organism to change its state in the direction toward establishment of equilibrium between body and object." One of the ways of re-establishing such a balance is to change the position of the object (as when the rod is shifted to an objectively slanted position in order to appear vertical). The change of state is thus reflected in the resulting perception of the object's position; ". . . the perceived spatial properties of the object are a mirror of these dynamic relations between the object stimuli and ensuing body activity." The perception, in its spatial aspects, is thus the result of an equilibrative tendency set up between the effects of stimulation from the object and the organismic state at the moment; and this tendency also represents an adjustment in the relationship between body and object—an attained equilibrium in the field that is composed of these two parts. When the body is erect a rod that is perpendicular will be seen as vertical because the stimuli from it do not interfere with the existing body equilibrium. If the body equilibrium should change, as for example through body tilt or through the sounding of a tone in one of the ears, the stimuli from the objectively perpendicular rod will be incommensurate with the new organismic equilibrial state and the rod will no longer appear vertical. It must now be shifted to an objectively slanted position in order to harmonize with the newly established bodily equilibrium and thus be perceived as vertical. Verticality of a line is therefore "that position of a line which is in tune with the existing body equilibrium."

The authors go still further in developing their concepts in the direction of field-theory. It must be remembered that the attainment of a state of equilibrium always involves a change of tonus distribu-

---

[5] Werner and Wapner might not distinguish these effects (i and ii) as sharply as this; and as we have seen they scarcely paid attention to the first at all. Such a distinction, however, is necessary in order to take account of all the phenomenological content of the perception.

tion in the body. When extraneous stimulations augment the neuro-muscular tonus on one side of the body, thus constituting a "primary" force, "counteractive" or "balancing" forces are brought into play upon the opposite side in order to restore the balance. These balancing forces consist of tonus increases on the side of the body opposite to that receiving the extraneous stimulation. From the balancing of these forces a new equilibrial state is set up, characterized by a new equilibrial "bodily axis." In the new state the equilibrial axis *becomes rotated toward the side of the balancing force.* This shift in the axis is what determines the apparent slant or verticality of the rod as perceived under the experimental conditions. The apparent vertical is tilted in the same direction as the bodily equilibrial axis is rotated. Opposed rotational vectors and axis-lines are used by the authors in diagramming these relationships.

It will be noted that the extraneous conditions employed in the experiments (electrical stimulation, tone, body-tilt, and rotation) were not objects to be perceived in the sense in which the rod was a stimulus-object. They played the role, rather, of stimulations that established the background, or organismic, state. The balancing vector and shift of the apparent vertical were a reaction to these separately initiated changes in the bodily equilibrative state: that is, they were a function of "body balance." Individual differences in the characteristic organismic state underlying body balance were found by the investigators, the displacement of the apparent vertical differing in degree and direction for different subjects. But if every stimulus has tonic effects as well as sensory, may we not expect that the perceived stimulus-object itself, entirely apart from the extraneous stimuli, will induce changes of equilibrial state and axis to compensate for any disturbing or unbalancing influences it may have produced? In other words, there may be a compensating vector and shift of the apparent vertical merely as a function of "body-*object* balance." In line with this expectation Werner and Wapner found that the position of the apparent vertical is influenced not only by extraneous stimulations, but by the starting position of the rod itself as the subject begins to make the adjustments for bringing it into a perceived vertical position. The apparent vertical, as a result, lies closer to the side to which the rod was originally tilted than to the opposite side. Thus there is a correspondence between the position of a line perceived as vertical and the equilibrial state of the subject, whether that state is induced by extraneous or by object stimuli. By this formulation the authors are able to explain figural adaptation, a phenomenon discovered by other investigators, in which a slightly

tilted line, as the subject continues to observe it, appears to be less
and less tilted until it finally appears vertical.

FURTHER EXPERIMENTATION: SUMMATIVE EQUIVALENCE OF
TONUS-INDUCING STIMULATIONS; SYMMETRIZATION AND
MINIMAL DISTURBANCE; GENERALIZING THE THEORY

With the conceptual equipment of balancing vectors and equilibrial
states and axes the authors attacked again the problem of functional
equivalence and interaction.   The task was to discover experimentally
the relation between the various stimulating conditions, both those
that were extraneous and those arising from the perceived object, as
their vectors contributed jointly to the equilibrial state and its effect
upon the perception of the vertical.   A general equivalence of these
factors in the production of such an effect had already been demonstrated in separate experiments.   If now they are combined in a
single experiment what will be the result?

It will be remembered that the direction of displacement of the
apparent vertical depended upon the side of the body that was stimulated by the extraneous stimuli or upon the starting position of the
rod.   If one changed these stimulations from one side to the other,
the direction of displacement also shifted.   It was thus possible to
use plus and minus signs to denote the direction of the vectors concerned.   If the hypothesis of functional equivalence is sound, it is
to be expected that, when the various stimulus conditions are brought
to bear upon the subject simultaneously, the perceptual result in the
displacement of the apparent vertical will be equal to the algebraic
summation of all the vectors involved.   This ingenious idea was put
to the test in an experiment that employed, in combination, the individual equilibrative state of the subject, the starting position, electrical stimulation, and body tilt.   Though it was impossible to quantify
the vectors for these conditions in an exact way, an indication could
be secured by noting the effects upon the mean adjustment of the rod
to the perceived vertical under experimental circumstances in which
all or most of the vectors had the same sign, as compared with a condition in which half of the signs were plus and the other half minus.
We should, of course, expect a maximum displacement of the apparent vertical in the former situation since the effects would be additive, and a minimum displacement in the latter where the effects
would cancel one another, with an intermediate displacement in
stimulus patterns between these extremes.   The results brilliantly
confirmed these expectations.   Thus it was demonstrated not only

that the vectors representing all these stimulating conditions (both for object and extraneous stimuli) were dynamically equivalent in the production of the equilibrial state that determined perceived spatial position, but that they "interacted" with one another according to their sign (and no doubt according to their magnitude) in attaining this result.

Two points, however, should be noted. The first concerns the meaning of the word interaction. This concept was construed by Werner and Wapner solely in terms of the potentiality of the various factors for producing a single summated effect: interaction means summation. The term, however, has another meaning which we must consider later. Secondly, the experiments did not clearly demonstrate a summation or interaction of *sensory* and *tonic* elements in the strict meaning of the term sensory as employed in our earlier discussion. In order to exert their influence upon the total equilibrial state *all* the conditions studied had to produce changes that were *tonic* in their nature. Equivalence, summation, and interaction refer really to tonic factors or their results, rather than to sensory factors as equivalent to, or summed with, tonic factors. These criticisms do not detract from the significance of the authors' discovery, but they are necessary in order to keep the problem in the proper perspective.

The perception of the median plane, that is, the direction "straight ahead," was found in the authors' experiments to follow principles similar to the perception of verticality. Brighter illumination introduced asymmetrically to one eye was found to shift the apparent median plane of the subject, as determined by pointing, to the side opposite that of the stimulation. In addition to this body-balance effect, a body-object balance can be demonstrated for median plane perceptions. The subject is asked to adjust a luminescent upright rectangle in a dark room in such a way that one edge (left or right) appears in the median plane, no extraneous stimulation being applied. When the subject in performing this task fixates the left-hand edge, so that the figure extends entirely to the right of the fixation line, his apparent median plane is shifted to the right, that is, toward the center of the rectangle; and the opposite tendency occurs when the right-hand edge is fixated. That is to say, the displacement occurs toward the side from which the stimulation from the whole outline or surface of the rectangle comes, an effect opposite to that observed in simple body balance resulting from extraneous stimulation. The shift of the apparent median plane toward the center of the figure is spoken of as a tendency toward "symmetrization" and reflects a trend to change the equilibrial state in such a manner that stimuli from the object will result in a minimal disturbance of the organism. (We recall that symmetry was one of the properties of "good figure" as enunciated by gestalt psychologists.) *Minimal disturbance* is now posited as a basic field-principle, of which verticalization and symmetrization are two manifestations.

From the foregoing constructs Werner and Wapner seek to generalize their theory to include configurational phenomena. They note that the organism employs its balancing vectors in opposite ways for extraneous stimuli (i.e., for stimuli that do not have object-characteristics such as spatial location and contour), on the one hand, and object-stimuli that do have these properties, on the other. We have seen in the former instance, for example, that perceptual displacement is toward the side opposite the stimulated side of the organism, while in the latter it is toward the same side. In the former instance (extraneous stimulation) *object*-body equilibration tendencies are absent; there is set up merely an organismic state of *body* balance irrespective of the presence or absence of perceived objects. In the latter instance, where an object to be perceived is present, *object*-body tendencies toward equilibration are established. In such interpretations the authors see a basis for an explanation of figure and ground, definite object-stimuli resulting in figure and the accompanying extraneous stimuli in ground-effects. The effects of ground stimuli, which do not have object properties, are also said to constitute a kind of "internal homeostasis," while those of figure, arising from object-stimuli, "refer to homeostasis of the field composed of object and body." An attempt is made, further, to explain the selection of figure versus ground by the principle of median plane displacement. When, in viewing a reversible figure-ground drawing, the subject concentrates upon one half of the picture he experiences a vectorial dynamic quality or force to one side commensurate with the shift of the median plane that occurs in the tendency toward symmetrization. For some types of figure this tendency is stronger (that is, median plane displacement is greater) than for others. Herein we might infer a tendency for the corresponding part of the drawing to be seen as figure (present writer's interpretation).

The authors believe that in these principles of "visual dynamics" we may eventually find the explanation of the phenomenological "demand qualities" or "physiognomic properties" exploited by the gestaltists.[6]

---

[6] At this point, and in their treatment of figure and ground, the authors seem to be trying to supply some of the sensory elements whose omission was noted earlier in the discussion, that is, the perceptual properties of the object itself as distinguished from its position. The problem, however, is still not adequately

They also conjecture that, by considering the tonic factors underlying perception as including viscerotonic as well as somatotonic effects, recent findings regarding motivational, directive, and projective influences upon perception can be incorporated into their theory. Some further evidence is also introduced in support of vicariousness and the postulate that the sensory-tonic energy can be released either through sensory or through motor activities. Experiments have indicated that the actual movement of the subject and his projected perceptual experience of a movement are inversely related. Subjects who are immobilized by being strapped in a chair while looking at a stationary point of light in a dark room have a greater tendency to see the light as moving (autokinetic phenomenon) than do subjects who are moving their arms continuously while making the observations. Following a situation in which motor activities are inhibited, observers tend to make more "movement" interpretations of a Rorschach card than when under uninhibited conditions. Pushing against a board before looking at drawings of mobile objects reduces the number of movements perceptually projected into the drawings.[7]

CRITIQUE AND QUESTIONS FOR FURTHER STUDY;
ACHIEVEMENTS OF SENSORY-TONIC FIELD THEORY

In reviewing the work of Werner and Wapner one has the feeling that we have here some novel and valuable experimental results and some ideas that should have a profound influence in shaping perceptual theory. In pressing their attack in various directions and in showing inescapably the role of motor factors in spatial perceptions, as well as in unifying their theory, the authors at times display great adeptness and masterful strategy. Yet as sensory-tonic field theory now stands there appears a discrepancy between its postulates and its line of experimental attack. There is also a certain lack of consistency, availability, and explanatory value in some of its concepts. The

recognized. For a recent extension of the theory to the influence of a figure's "directional dynamics" upon the apparent median plane, see Werner and Wapner, 1954.

[7] Most perceptual investigations and theories have specialized strongly in visual perception, the other senses being relatively neglected. It is gratifying to find that Wapner and Werner (1952) tested their general theory by experimenting upon the *kinaesthetic* experience of rod-verticality as affected by the extraneous factors of bodily tilt and rotation. The results conformed closely to the findings we have reviewed for visual perception. By this extension of their methods the authors have provided evidence that their theory deals with the perceptual process as such, and not with a single sensory modality.

experiments themselves have been imaginatively conceived, the experimental facts are convincing and in agreement with theoretical predictions, and the experimental program is unified; there is no ground for criticism in these respects. As to its generality, it has been shown to have some bearing upon sensory dimension, prevailing state of the subject, configuration, and perhaps frame of reference. The methods thus far employed, which involve mainly spatial placements and perceived motion, are too limited to allow the theory to be readily generalized to constancy, to object-character, or to an adequate range of the aspects of configuration and set.

The authors, moreover, have not formulated their position from the overall theoretical standpoint as clearly as they might. Though the results are clear-cut, we are not certain as to just what hypothesis they are supporting. A somewhat metaphysical urge (if we may call it that) to amalgamate sensory and tonic factors into some prior total process, or into some more elementary form of energy that expresses itself in alternative ways, seems to have complicated the straightforward meaning of the experiments; and the effort to fit the results into a rational design requiring equivalence of the sensory and tonic has imposed an unnecessary limitation. The background assumption of a single basic process underlying these two sets of elements does not seem necessary for understanding the authors' convincing demonstrations of equivalence and summation as giving rise to the equilibrial state and its effect upon perception; for it is not clear that the equivalence and summation are between uniquely sensory and tonic elements. And the introduction of such background postulates only leads to further complications. The same is true also of such hyphenated expressions as sensory-tonic events and sensory-tonic state. The meaning of sensory has not been adequately differentiated from that of tonic, the authors evidently preferring not to go into physiological details, especially those of a sensory or cortical nature, and remaining content with a mention of muscular contractions, tonus distribution, and a rather loose application of the field concept.

The treatment of vicariousness may be taken as another example of the handicap of a commitment to somewhat doubtful postulates. It will be remembered that the phenomena that were termed vicarious were characterized by a sharp contrast between actual motion or its perceptual content on the one hand, and an illusory experience of motion upon the other. These phenomena were cited by the authors as indicating a vicariousness, therefore an equivalence, of sensory and tonic factors. Equivalence, it will be recalled, means that one element can be substituted for another toward the attainment of a certain end result. But *can* we substitute one of these perceptual states for the other with respect to a perceptual outcome? One of them can *replace* the other to be sure. But it is difficult to see what could be meant by "substitution" in reference to a given result, since when one of these states is replaced by the other the result is completely changed. We have merely these two strikingly different sets of experiences, one excluding the other. The problem is similar to that of a sudden shift of contradictory meanings in an ambiguous situation. Werner and Wapner, as already mentioned, refer to a common "sensory-tonic energy" which takes now the one form and now the other. Such perceptual differences have also been conceived as related more permanently to extraversion and introversion and to other personality characteristics. The authors even mention the possibility that the energy-transformation concept of psychoanalysis may here emerge in such a fashion that it can be tested by experimental procedures. These speculations do not help much, since we still have the crucial question of what produces the alternation or dominance of an energy-form. We seem to be dealing not with energy alone but with the neurophysiological pattern in which energy is manifested, not so much with energy-transformation as with the constraints of the system in which energic events occur. Field-theory will not help us, for again we would have to explain the ascendancy of one type of field-organization over another.

A significant fact has been here overlooked. Although these so-called vicarious perceptual states seem to give evidence of interaction, the interaction is of an altogether different sort from that shown in the rod experiments. It is not an interaction of two components summed, by plus or minus effects, along a common continuum toward one particular sort of perceptual outcome. It is, rather, a mutually negating, all or none affair. The experience is always *either* that of true motion (veridical) *or* that of the illusion of motion (non-veridical). It is never, within a single percept, a matter of degree. What sort of a total dynamic process or field, in which energy distribution is by definition graded in minute steps, can encompass so disjunct and opposite a relationship as this? And how can two such mutually exclusive or antagonistic aggregates be regarded as equivalent and vicarious? Does it not seem, rather, that we have here two alternative and antagonistic "patterns of meaning," as we have when, in sitting in a slowly moving railway carriage, we misinterpret our own motion as the movement of a car on the adjoining track? The crucial question here is how we can describe these "meaning structures" in denotive terms and how we can explain their antagonistic interaction. Perhaps Werner and Wapner could supply an answer by pointing out that one of them contained more sensory elements and the other more tonic. This would indeed be an interesting hypothesis. But far from uniting these two "alien" factors, such an interpretation would seem to push them farther apart.

In considering the view of our authors on this question perhaps we can show what was meant by the earlier reference to a "metaphysical" tendency toward a monism of sensory and tonic.[8] The equivalence implied by the term vicarious was not demonstrated as the authors demonstrated it in the rod experiments. Obviously it could not be demonstrated since there was no single empirically observable end-result toward which the two states could be equivalent. There were two end results that were entirely different. The ability of the two states to summate algebraically could not be tested since they could not occur at the same time. The only way in which equivalence or vicariousness could be maintained was by *postulating* some prior total dynamic process or "sensory-tonic energy" of which the two perceptual states in question could be alternative expressions. If we assume that there *is* such a common substrate, then substitution or vicarious functioning, as between alternative sensory and tonic forms of this basic process, can be regarded as possible and used as a logical explanation of the phenomena in question. The postulate of total dynamic process or sensory-tonic energy having thus been set up, a theorem of equivalence can be deduced from it. Such a procedure is both usual and legitimate in theory construction *with one proviso*. The theorem in question must then be experimentally tested. That is to say, inductive procedure must follow and sustain deductive. The testing of *this* theroem, however, was, as we have just seen, operationally impossible.

The hypothesis of vicariousness, however, is somewhat tangent to the main current of the theory and hence not a fair gauge of its logic. Returning to the main line of investigation we can broaden our critique by asking the following questions:

1. What does one mean by elements or factors? What are the sensory elements with which the theory is concerned, and how do they relate to the tonic elements?

2. In speaking of an "event" in the above connection what do we imply?

---

[8] Perhaps this term is too strong. Certainly the clear-cut line of experimental attack by the authors upon their problem did not betray any tendency to stray from the path of empiricism.

3. What is a *sensory-tonic* event? We can understand how one event can be sensory (e.g., the stimulation of a receptor) and another can be tonic (the contraction of a muscle); but how can both these episodes be incorporated in the *same* event? If they are so incorporated, what would the "interaction" of sensory and tonic mean?

4. It is not difficult to accept the statement that functional equivalence makes interaction (of a certain kind) possible and that such interaction can be tested by the algebraic summation of the effects of whatever interacts. But what is it that is equivalent to, and interacts with, what? Does sensory interact with sensory, tonic with tonic, or sensory with tonic? Though the authors affirm that the last combination is the true one, the conditions of the experiments are somewhat equivocal. Is it the sensory factors that interact with the tonic, or is it the *tonic results* of sensory factors?

5. Does defining interaction in the quantitative sense of equivalence and summation cover the situation, or is some other form of interaction also needed to explain perceptual integration? For example, there is an interaction between afferent and central neural processes, between efferent nerve-impulses and muscle fiber contractions, and between the corticovisual processes of rod-perception as representing an "object" and those processes that underlie its "tilt." These interactions are all necessary in a motor theory of perception; yet it would be quite meaningless to *sum* the energies of the members of any of these interacting pairs. Nor are they in any sense equivalent. It is clear that we are dealing here with pattern-like relationships that cannot be adequately described in quantitative terms—a theme that has appeared before in our consideration of perceptual theories and will occur again.

6. What would the *total* percept be according to Werner and Wapner? It would seem that it must include the experience of the rod as an object and not merely the verticality of its position. Should it not also include the object that is adjusted to the median plane and not merely the median plane to which the object is adjusted? Can the perception of "objects" *in conjunction with* their "positions" be explained by organismic and equilibrial states?

7. What is sensory-tonic energy? What evidence have we of any energy directly operative in perception that is not the energy of receptors or effectors or of afferent, efferent, or cortical neural elements?

8. The vagueness that attends field concepts in psychology pursues us in the sensory-tonic field theory. The inside-outside problem again appears. Is the field in the cortex of the subject, in his entire organism, or between and including him and the world outside? Is

there both an internal and an external field as implied in the terms body-balance and body-object balance?   If so, how are they related? How does the field, if cortical, provide a means of combining the vectors of force involved in tonic equilibrative tendencies with sensory data from the object in such a way as to be isomorphic with the percept of a tilted *rod*?   We have seen the difficulties encountered by Köhler in attacking a much simpler problem.

Certainly it would not be fair to expect at this stage a satisfactory answer to all these questions.   It seems not unlikely, however, that by reshaping some of the basic logic of the theory, and, in particular, by giving up the idea that it is a theory which unites sensory and tonic elements as expressions of a superordinate entity, a more consistent and informative construction could be placed upon the experimental findings.   Sensory and motor tendencies in perceptions, or in individual personalities, may be united; or they may be contrasted or otherwise related in subtle ways; and Werner and Wapner may be here on the trail of something important.   But it may be doubted whether the explanation through a "total or prior dynamic state" will turn out to be the best interpretation.

In pursuance of our "perfectionist" policy in the examination of theories, the analytical portion of this review has been concerned mainly with certain logical difficulties of sensory-tonic field theory. Our criticisms of its consistency, availability of concepts, and explanatory value may have appeared rather exacting and unsympathetic. This, however, has been far from our intention.   It has seemed to the writer that the excellent work of Werner and Wapner and their associates deserves a better overall theoretical framework than has been provided.   It should be made to yield *more definitely* what it has to offer for the understanding of perception.   To point out such discrepancies where they seem to the writer to exist is one of the objectives of our present inquiry.

Too little has been said in this appraisal about the admirably conceived and ingeniously tested *experimental* hypotheses and the achievements in confirming them.   These will hold quite independently of the theory's more general postulates.   An important beginning has been made in the problem of bringing into the perceptual aggregate the much-needed component of motor elements. On the theoretical side itself, in spite of what has been said, certain generalizations stand out as novel, distinctive, and promising.   Not to appreciate the formulation and experimental demonstration of such concepts as organismic and equilibrial state and the discovery of a summative, lawful, and perhaps universal effect of motor tendencies upon the perception of objects would be both obtuse and ungrateful. These are, in the writer's judgment the *real* contributions of the theory; and they will probably stand, in the end, as more important than our strictures concerning the overall theoretical orientation.

The authors themselves have said that they regard the work of theory construction as a steady growth, a "dynamic interrelationship between scientific thought and empirical research." And their own accounts are modestly presented as a stage in a developmental process that will involve continual reformulation. In building or revising any theory of perception we must work, especially on the neurophysiological side, with many speculative unknowns in combination with other factors of which we have some knowledge. The foregoing criticism has been offered in the hope that it may help to focus the attack upon what we need to know and thus help, in the end, toward more clearly delineating the potentialities of this very significant contribution.

9

Motor Aspects (*Concluded*)
Set and Motor Adjustments
Their Relation to Perceptual Theory

The theory just considered has made a good beginning toward the incorporation of motor phenomena into the explanation of perception. But arising as it does from perceptions of verticality it deals mainly with a narrow range of tonic reactions and is limited to perceived spatial position and movement. Before a thoroughgoing theory of the motor phases of perception can be developed it will be necessary to take into account a larger range of motor facts and their relationship to a wider variety of phenomenological aspects. We shall now be concerned with the requirements of this broader task, with the materials with which it must deal, and with such beginnings as have already been made.

What *are* the motor activities that universally accompany perceiving? We are not referring here to the subsequent behavior, to what is ultimately done with respect to the object perceived, but to the motor aspects of the perceptual act itself. To one unacquainted with the subject it might seem that there are none: perception, in the popular view, is not really acting at all; it is just perceiving—pure sensory awareness of something. Could it not be described then, as the gestaltists imagined, wholly in terms of exteroceptive sensory organization? Werner and Wapner, with their demonstration of the effects of reactions to extraneous stimulations upon the percept, have already disabused us of that notion. In fact, all sorts of complex adjustments are going on in the perceptual act, adjustments both to the object focally perceived and to its surroundings. There are the muscular contractions involved in "giving attention," including the accommodation of sense organs and bodily position to the receipt of the stimulus energy, motor attitudes facilitating recognition or aiding

208

in the recall of previous sensory experience, "tensions" or "overflow" effects produced by the stimulus-field, occasional respiratory and perhaps circulatory changes, and tonic changes accompanying size-awareness, position, balance, and preparation for action. Some of these effects are subtle, requiring laboratory procedures for their detection and study. These and other motor accompaniments of the perceiving process, or shall we say motor parts of the perceptual aggregate, must be considered more closely in order to build a complete theory of perception or to make a start in canvassing the materials with which such a theory must deal. The manner in which all these elements of reaction enter into the perceptual process can perhaps be formulated under two concepts, namely, *set* and *motor adjustment*. These concepts are by no means distinct and will not be treated separately. Taken together they belong in the perceptual phenomenon-class that we have called the "prevailing state" of the organism. It is with this broadly motor aspect of perception, and particularly with its bearing upon perceptual theory, that the present chapter will deal.

The reader is cautioned, however, that the treatment will not be like that in the preceding chapters in which a major theory was carried through an extended analysis; for no comprehensive theory has yet appeared that synthesizes this array of facts. One must be content with presenting the pertinent findings and their diverse, and as yet unorganized, theoretical implications. The topic is included because some discussion of it is necessary in a book on perceptual theory. We need to appreciate not only finished theories but the task for theories of the future. A considerable portion of the chapter will therefore be devoted to the factual content of this neglected area; and we shall then discuss the work of one motor theorist who has made an attempt to relate the findings to perception. Another reason for this procedure is that we shall later consider an important system that presupposes the phenomenon of set. That theory does not adequately include the physiological bases of set; and the present account will therefore supply information by which it can be better understood. Because of the undeveloped theoretical state of the subject the writer will also take the liberty of introducing some interpretations or emphases of his own.

THE PHENOMENON OF SET

We do not usually perceive "out of the blue." Unless we are startled or confronted with an unexpected situation there is behind our perceptions, as we go about our daily affairs, a background state of the bodily musculature that is more or less relevant to the objects we are about to perceive. This condition renders the perception, or for that matter any organized activity toward the object, more rapid and effective. We should not limit this background state, in our thinking, to the motor organs; neural elements and other parts of the organism are also involved in the adjustment process. We must also remember that this phenomenon, which is called set, is not peculiar to perception. It enters into practically all types or phases of behavior. Let us review the situation, as a start, by recalling a few examples within a broader context.

Students in elementary psychology have long been familiar with the "rabbit-duck" figure, an ambiguous drawing which the perceiver can readily see either as one of these animals or the other according to the manner in which he "prepares himself." Perception of figure in reversible figure and ground designs is subject to a similar control. We can see an outline of a hollow cube with one side or its opposite nearest to us according as we set ourselves and facilitate our perception by shifts of fixation point. The following incident is taken from the recollections of a former college student who had been reared on a farm. Looking out of his dormitory window one day shortly after arriving at college, this young man was astonished to see a hen jumping up and down on the campus. A closer look showed that the object was a football. Here we have the "selection" of a percept apparently determined by a long-standing habit. All these cases illustrate set in the area of perception.

Let us consider examples from other categories. The runner in a race, in order to get a quicker start, crouches in a "prepared" position for the take-off. In waiting for a red traffic signal to turn, our usual impatience to get ahead quickly is expressed by a readying of the muscles of the foot for pressing the accelerator pedal. In approaching a green light that has stood for some time without change we have a similar preparedness for action upon the brake. Reactions in the laboratory can be made more quickly when a warning signal is given shortly before the stimulus is presented, a procedure that allows time for response-readiness to develop. In these cases we have sets for overt bodily action. We try to remember a name. In so doing we review the incidents in the past where we have been in association with the person concerned; we imagine scenes and try to reinstate the mood. Perhaps we are not successful at first. Later the name may "pop into consciousness" when we are not actively trying to recall it, probably because of the continuation of a state of readiness built up by the earlier activities mentioned. Set therefore operates in memory-recall. A similar phenomenon is seen in learning. A student sets himself to memorize a lesson in preparation for an impending examination. There is an initial period of warming up, of overcoming distractions, and of adjusting his body to the task, after which the work proceeds smoothly and quickly. The distracting influences now seem to be automatically shut out. Sets for mental work and problem solving are very familiar. In paying our bills, once we have gotten into the task we do not need to remind ourselves each time to *subtract*, rather than add, the checks drawn from the earlier balance; we do so automatically. Problems in multiplication and addition are more quickly done in an arrangement where one first multiplies for a whole series of problems and then adds for a whole series than when they are performed in a mixed arrangement. When an individual is given a number of reasoning problems of the same type and a model procedure for solution there is tendency, subject to individual differences, to follow the model consistently rather than to become aware of other possible methods that might be more effective.

The above examples tend to show that "being set" for a certain stimulus or for a reaction to it, and the effect which this setting has upon the ensuing or corresponding behavior, are phenomena that are practically as universal as behavior itself. The problem for perception is therefore bound up with the problem for other behavioral acts. Whenever we speak of an instance of behavior it is also possible to consider that there may have been a prior "set" for that behavior. May there not be some broad principles that explain the nature of set as a universal phenomenon? If so, then perhaps they could help us toward a more unified understanding of behavior in general. Attempts have been made to treat the topic in this synoptic fashion.[1] Success, however, has been limited by the ramification of the subject into many other topics that psychologists had regarded as already "salted down." Some, for example, would rather explain set as a part of the learning process than regard it as something that determines the course and efficiency of learning. Some desire to interpret the perseveration of reactions as due to learning rather than to the persistence of a set. Sets are regarded by some as habits endowed with a dynamic quality (mechanisms with "drives"). Intention may be something that is learned, so how can learning be due to intention? In many instances, also, set competes for recognition with theories of motivation. As usual, the already established compartments of psychology act as

---

[1] Cf. Dashiell, 1940. This writer refers to the problem of set as a "neglected fourth dimension" of psychological research.

barriers to a new and broader interpretation that would require a drastic shake-up of concepts. The obstacle to a satisfactory theory of set that presents itself at the start is thus one of definition—though inability clearly to define it may be, in turn, a symptom of the lack of an adequate theory.

Whatever set may be, it is largely covert in character. If one takes a molar viewpoint, refusing to look inside the organism at all, one is mystified. To say that the organism as a whole "sets itself" for a reaction and then carries it out, or to say that it "sustains its own behavior" while it is going on, is like saying almost nothing at all. Since the preparatory set is so much like the ensuing response it also seems strangely as though the organism reacts *before it reacts*. Or, in cases of the sustaining of a performance already started, it seems as though the organism paradoxically reacts *while it is reacting*. The experimental psychologist who is not quite so limited by the molar doctrine, but still not ready to involve himself in physiological details, might handle set by calling it an "intervening variable" or a "hypothetical construct." It is known only by its antecedents and its "fruits"; but these, at least, are observable and measurable. We know the task-instructions that may have included a suggestion toward adopting the "set"; and we know the stimulus and the past conditioning. We can then measure the ensuing response; and, through comparison with the results for a control group who were *not* set, we can determine the result of the organism's "being set" in terms of the speed or energy of the reaction. Set is thus known only by its effect upon the reaction which the organism is set for. This solution, however, is still unsatisfactory for an inquirer who is more interested in finding a theory that really explains than in formulations tailored to a somewhat opportunistic experimental design.

For the perceptionist the problem is crucial. Some degree of set is probably present in many, if not most, of the typical perceiving situations of daily life. We do not usually perceive "at random" but in accordance with some course of action that is being prepared or is under way. Though set is not regarded as a part of the percept itself, but rather as a condition of perception, the very fact of its ubiquity and its potentialities for facilitating or strengthening what is perceived would require that it be incorporated in any theory intended to have a fair degree of completeness. Taking set into consideration in its sensory as well as its motor implications (for it has both), and in conjunction with the actual behaviors for which it prepares and sustains the organism, we have an aggregate of adjustments affording an excellent basis for a theory of the motor aspects of perception. Nor is the concept devoid of clear and denotive empirical meaning. Though it has been confusing to the molarist, inadequately treated by the behavior-experimentalist, and somewhat slighted by the perceptionist, physiologists and physiological psychologists have provided a tentative account of it that makes much sense.

THE FACTS OF SET AS REVEALED IN
PSYCHOLOGICAL EXPERIMENTS

Before turning to that account it would be best to see what the experimental psychologists have discovered regarding set. To them, of course, belongs the credit for many significant discoveries of the outwardly observable facts with which physiological observations must be correlated. Some of the findings have already been touched upon in our earlier examples. They can be assembled more adequately in the following sixteen propositions, for most and perhaps all of which there is some support in the results of psychological experiments.[2]

1. The phenomenon of set involves, basically and characteristically, the following aspects: (*a*) There is *some preparatory or facilitating condition* of the organism that precedes, accompanies, or may even outlast the completely executed overt behavior or the act of perception. (*b*) Though the facilitating condition cannot usually be explicitly distinguished from the overt performance itself, or from the content of the percept, it has the effect, operationally, of making that process occur *with greater promptness, speed of execution, energy, or magnitude.*

2. In some instances the condition seems merely to *prepare* or *make ready* the full behavior process. In other cases it *sustains, prolongs, or enhances* it during its entire course. It may even last over after the full process is finished or between separate episodes in which the process recurs. In some cases all of these temporal relationships are evident. When the set is preparatory rather than sustaining (that is, when it is aroused before some necessary outer stimulus appears) an important difference naturally occurs between the circumstances of the set and those of the ensuing behavior. For example, one may be set to look for (perceive) a brooch, but the brooch is not yet present. Only when the eye falls upon the object does there occur a

---

[2] In preparing this and other accounts in this chapter the writer has found Gibson's critical review (1941) and Dashiell's textbook (1949) especially valuable. For the experimental literature on the propositions here listed see Gibson.

full performance of the perceptual act and the actual percept-content. Though the set was there beforehand and facilitated finding the brooch, it is necessary to introduce a certain external feature, the stimulus-object, in order to complete the perceptual aggregate. The runner is set on the mark, but the full behavior occurs only when the pistol (outer stimulus-source) is fired. In the case of a *sustaining* set the stimulus object has been present from the start, and the set facilitates the ongoing of the series of responses. This situation is illustrated by the perseveration of a set to multiply a series of figures rather than to add or divide. Because of the briefness of its time-span the perceptual act seems to belong to the class of activities for which sets are preparing rather than sustaining, though the possibility of a sustaining effect is by no means excluded, especially in tasks where a series of similar stimulus objects is being perceived.

3. The response always represents exactly the same behavior as that for which the organism is prepared by the set. When we are set we are set for a particular percept or overt act; and unless some unexpected circumstance intervenes, *that particular* behavioral aggregate takes place, or is sustained if it is already going on. One might even say that the "expansion" or "intensification" of the set *is* the act. (And therein, as we shall see later, may be the clue to its explanation.)

4. From this and the preceding propositions it follows that set will always appear as a *selective process*. The act implied in the set will be brought to complete performance; all other acts, barring intruding circumstances that might impel a change, will be excluded.

5. Sets thus stand in an *antagonistic* relation to one another and have a *negative* or *inhibitory* as well as a positive aspect. It is probably better not to regard sets as being inhibitory of their own related behavior, that is, as preparing the organism *not* to respond; for that would be like producing "nothing out of something." We are always prepared physiologically for *something*. To be prepared for nothing is to be not prepared. Sets are therefore to be regarded as inhibitory only with respect to *other* acts and their corresponding sets.[3] Sets in themselves are always "positive," never "negative." It might be inferred that the inhibiting set may sometimes be a set to avoid or

[3] For example, Freeman says that when a set is established by the instruction "*not* to lift the hand from the shocking plate when a shock occurs" what happens is a covert preparation to "press down" on the plate. Lifting is thus inhibited only by preparation for the contrary positive reaction (1948*b*, p. 216). A positive set to turn the head or eyes away from the place where an object will be presented might be what would be meant by a set "not to perceive" that object.

escape from something, and that this set has been conditioned to some cue from the object or situation to be avoided. Further commerce with that object, or sets for such commerce, would thus be inhibited by this avoidance set at the first appearance of the cue; but the avoiding set and reaction are *in themselves* positive, not negative. Sets to avoid something may turn out to be important in interpreting some of the experiments upon which perceptual theories, later to be examined, are based (cf. Chapter 13).

It is logical to suppose that one set will tend to inhibit another in proportion as the second involves a behavior coördination that could not be carried out by the effector system simultaneously with the first. In the traffic example the set to press on the accelerator pedal when waiting for the green light is directly opposed in a muscular sense to the set of lifting the foot from that pedal that occurs when a change from green to red is anticipated. The inhibiting of one of these sets by the other would therefore be a foregone conclusion. Since all sets for different behavior acts are, like the acts themselves, unique, they all probably tend to inhibit one another to some extent. An exception, of course, would occur for acts that are integrated into a single larger aggregate, as is true, for example, in acts of coördinated behavior. Insofar as motivation and learning enter, we would probably have to conclude that when two competing sets tend to be activated and to enhance their respective behaviors simultaneously the set which is "strongest" in respect to its motivational or learning background will prevail. The same would be true of the antagonism of sets in general, regardless of the sources of their intensities.

6. In preparatory and sustaining sets there is a *peripheral sensory* as well as a *peripheral motor* aspect. This aspect however is probably brought about, or at least accompanied, by the *motor elements involved in accommodating and in the holding of the accommodation of the receptor organ* (convergence and focusing of the eyes, turning of the head toward the source of sound, widening the nostrils, moving the tongue about, and the like). Such set activities are a part of the familiar process of "giving attention."

7. It follows from the preceding propositions that, other things being equal, when a certain preparatory set is in operation and the anticipated stimulus appears, the perceptual reaction corresponding to that set will occur more promptly than a reaction proper to some other stimulus which is presented simultaneously but for which the organism is not set. This phenomenon is known as *prior entry. When two stimuli occur simultaneously the one to which the subject is prepared to attend is experienced first.*

8. Since set is a property of the organism rather than of the stimulus it is possible to establish for the same series of stimuli *at different times* sets for quite different and mutually inhibiting types of behavior. *Two different sets built up at different times can facilitate two different percepts from the same stimulus pattern.*

9. Two general classes of preparatory set have been experimentally distinguished. These are sometimes known by the phenomenological terms *expectancy* and *intention*. In the first the set of the subject is mainly *sensory* in character. He "expects" a certain *stimulus* to appear and gets ready for it; his preparation for the response is not so strong or definite. Reaction times taken under this condition are spoken of as "sensory" reaction times. The second type or phase of set is one in which the subject is set strongly for the *response;* and the sensory aspect, that is, what the stimulus will look like or sound like, is neglected. The time required for reaction is here called the "motor" reaction time. Though both types of set tend to render the ensuing activity more prompt or vigorous, motor reaction time is usually shorter than sensory. In the "intentional" (or motor) situation we also are likely to have false starts ("jumping the gun," or players offside in football); or the overt activity may occur in response to a wrong stimulus. These two emphases on different parts of the set-aggregate expressed by the terms expectation and intention are of course matters of degree. Probably most set-situations comprise both, and they may be combined in different proportions.

In perception one would be likely to think of the prevailing preparation as being expectant and "sensory" rather than as intentional and "motor" in character. We are set for the "looks," "sound," "touch," or "smell" of things. It is probable, however, that there are in perception definite intentional elements as well, at least those of a generalized sort. Such sets are related to the nature of different classes of objects and to what one does with them or about them. Sensory-tonic field theory clearly demonstrated such elements in the perception of rod position. Examples cited in this chapter have also revealed that preparation for action is a significant feature of many perceptions. The inclusion of both expectancy and intentional aspects is not only demanded by the facts but is essential to the construction of a complete perceptual theory. Because perception-time is so short it may be that these two aspects fuse or are so close together in time that they are not capable of being separately recognized or experimentally analyzed. But in any case they are both phases of the same total process; they represent merely different emphases upon different parts of the perceptual aggregate.

10. *Preparatory sets may be long in preparing, or their building may occupy only a short interval.* In reaction-time experiments or other routine operations where there has been a general and rather lengthy background preparation for the activity it is sometimes necessary to establish a second, more immediate, set for the "release" of the action. For this purpose a *warning signal* is given at a short interval, usually from one to two seconds, before the stimulus is presented. The interval may be varied from time to time in order to prevent the development of a reaction to the interval itself. For any given reaction there is probably an optimal preparatory interval; and irregularity in the interval tends to lengthen the reaction time. Preparatory sets of a more complex or background type, however, may exist for a long time prior to the occasion for the behavior to be performed, and they may take a long while to develop. These may exist also as sustaining sets during and between the courses of prolonged or repeated activities. It would not seem unreasonable to consider personality characteristics that may endure through life as forms of behavior in which the individual is set for some individualized course of perceiving, thinking, or outwardly acting. As we consider all its temporal phases, it becomes ever clearer that set is not a separate process requiring some special psychological mechanism for its explanation, but a universal aspect of the behavior itself that shows itself within the time during which the behavioral aggregate is undergoing its structuring, whether that time be long or short. Both set and learning may turn out to be merely temporal dimensions of the probability of a behavioral aggregate's occurrence under varying conditions of outer situation and stimulus presentation. We shall see that the physiological facts lend support to such a view.

11. Getting set for an activity may be *either a voluntary or an involuntary matter,* depending on the circumstances.

12. *Sets can involve or be involved in learning,* both in the fact that they may control a course of learning either at the start or when appearing during its course, and in the fact that the subject may acquire a readiness to shift to alternative sets when conditions require. One can "learn" to adopt sets.

13. Though sets are specific as to their relation to the activities for which they prepare or sustain, and though they are unique, *they can also be generalized* if the activities concerned belong to a certain class. A set can be established to react to a list of words by giving free associations or by giving associations opposite in meaning to the stimulus-words. The first set is more generalized than the second, and the second is more general than would be the case if the subject

were instructed to respond with a *particular* word. Sounding the pitch by the leader of a chorus arouses a general set of tonality in the singers. Set is thus incorporated in the phenomenon of relationships, a fact which may also play a part in the transfer of training. A good example of generalized set in perception is found in James' illustration of the meaningless series of French words: "Pas de lieu Rhône que nous." If the general set for French is removed and replaced by telling the subject that the *sounds* represent *English* words, he may be able to perceive the meaning "Paddle your own canoe."

14. Though a set can be built up either consciously or unconsciously, and though one can introspect in regard to the bodily processes involved, *it is usually very meager in its phenomenological content*. We are not usually conscious of our sets. Sets of which one is not aware are frequently operative in one's thinking and acting. Rationalizing, or superficial reasoning by verbal analogies, can be set-prepared ("atmosphere effect"), and as such may not be conscious or insightful on the part of the subject. The pattern of motor adjustments present in normal perceptions is *physiological;* it is represented weakly if at all in phenomenological experience. Perhaps we could say that the motor phases are "projected" into the perceptual experience, though we would have to be content here with talking merely in terms of metaphors. It is perhaps more meaningful to say that the phase of the response that is called set, when considered apart from the direct effects of the stimulus object, is too weak, energically, to form the basis of a conscious pattern, though it still operates as a preparation for, or enhancement of, the ensuing activity. We could say that its energies, apart from the stimulus contributions, are "below the threshold" required for awareness.

15. *Sets can be built up and can become effective in a variety of ways.* For example, they can be established by the instructions for the task in hand. Immediate sets in reaction-time experiments follow upon the giving of a warning signal. On the other hand they may arise during the course of the task itself from regular and repeated conditions under which materials are presented (space and time order effects, "absolute impression," etc.), or by the general range of magnitude of the stimuli presented (see Helson's "adaptation-level" discussed in the next chapter). Sets can affect work curves. Being set for a long monotonous task seems to produce a decline in the curve after an initial high level. Shifts in the nature or conditions of a task may occasion marked differences in set, overcoming slumps in performance sometimes attributed to fatigue or satiation. Finally, sets

can be established or brought into play by bodily needs or emotions, or as long standing characteristics of personality.

16. Like the full reactions of which they are a preparatory or sustaining phase, sets that have been already established, but are at the moment "inactive" or unrelated to the existing trend of events, can be "evoked" or "aroused" by appropriate stimulus conditions. They will thus become "geared" to the existing situation and available for the enhancement of its perceptions or overt actions. A large range of circumstances, either "inner" or "outer," may serve as evoking conditions. As in other instances of "traces," "retentions," or "habit-acquisitions," sets can be "stored" for later use when not pertinent to the circumstances of the moment. This feature, as we shall see, becomes important in one of the recent theories of perception (Chapter 15).

Though sets do seem at times to exert a motivating influence, we should, in closing this account, insist upon a needed distinction. The concept of set does not adequately cover the topic of motivation. Frequently we have "reasons" for performing tasks that rest upon considerations other than those of how we are set. A coercive stimulus such as "hunger pangs," pressure inside the bladder, a threatened injury, a telegram, or a loud noise may provide energic upsets in the organism that must be brought to equilibrium. These energic increments can break through existing sets and bring about a condition in which the organism frequently acts with a minimum of preparation. They may also lead later to the establishment of sets of their own. Motivation, in other words, may be a factor that *lies behind* set. The complexity of behavior requires that we add these energic motivational elements to the operation of the aggregate of which set and set-formation are also a part and make suitable theoretical provision for them.

Though this situation holds also for ordinary perceptual activities the influence of direct motivation in percept-formation may be somewhat more limited. For some psychologists set *is* the motivating factor in perception in so far as perception is motivated. Other theorists, who believe in the direct effect of needs and motives upon perception (Chapter 13), would dissent from such a view. Probably the most tenable position is that *both* set and the stronger underlying motivation must be considered as parts of the total aggregate for any kind of behavior. In perception as distinguished from more overt behavior, however, there are strict limits to which a change produced by motivating factors can occur without making the percept so non-veridical as to reflect a condition of maladaptation to the environment. In overt action we can often *change, mold,* or *adapt* the environment to our needs; but in perceiving (perhaps in order to do this adapting successfully) there must be set up in the organism a fairly faithful facsimile of the environment as it is (Chapter 2). There are differences of opinion, however, as to the degree of "molding effect" that is normal or tolerable, and the whole problem must concern us in later chapters. One point which should not be overlooked is the suggestion that in the perceptual act itself there is a motive. It is the motive merely "to perceive," to get perceptual meaning with respect to the environment as it impinges on our receptors. Such motivation would, of course, be entirely consistent with veridical perception.

THE PHYSIOLOGY OF SET: FREEMAN'S EXPERIMENTS AND
ANALYSES; ENERGIC AND STRUCTURAL INTERPRETATIONS

Having considered the nature of set as seen by the experimental psychologist we now turn to the physiological aspects. At a comparatively early date Titchener gave an introspective analysis of a set-experience in which kinaesthetic elements loomed large, showing the importance of bodily attitudes, postures, and movements.[4] By the same token it was possible to introspect upon these muscular changes as "conscious" happenings only because of a return flow to cortical centers of afferent impulses from proprioceptors in the muscles, tendons, and joints, that is, from sense organs that were stimulated as the muscular reactions occurred. This feature, which is sometimes called proprioceptive "backlash," must be continually borne in mind as we study the phenomena of set, just as we found it to be necessary in sensory-tonic field theory. From the sixteen empirical facts of set previously reviewed we shall make up three questions upon which to concentrate for the physiological analysis. We shall consider (1) the patterning of muscular reactions involved in the set, bringing in as a corollary its selective aspect; (2) expectancy versus intention insofar as this question leads to the problem of whether the locus of a set is peripheral or central; and (3) the question of how muscular sets prolong or sustain the behavioral act. Freeman's useful experiments and assembling of the pertinent data will serve as a guide.[5]

[4] 1909, pp. 180–181.
[5] Freeman, 1939, 1948a, 1948b. See also Morgan and Stellar, 1950, Chapters XIII and XIV.

1. *The specificity and selectivity of set.* A set, according to Freeman, consists of (1) covert tensions in the skeletal muscles that precede (and also follow) overt reaction of those muscles and (2) the effects in the central nervous system of backlash from the proprioceptive stimulation attending these tensions. Such tensions exert a selective and determining influence upon subsequent overt responses. The tension-sets, as they are called, can be studied by small levers placed over the muscle, or better, by the recording of electric potentials set up in the muscle by its own activity. The arrangements of the organism are such as to produce a kind of narrowing down, or channelization, of these tensions in comparison with the external and internal stimulus-patterns by which they are aroused. There are many more afferent neural pathways from receptors than there are efferent neural outlets to effectors, so that were every afferent to require its own motor discharge pathway, ordered behavior would be impossible. The central nervous system provides, through "adjustor" mechanisms, for an orderly concentration of the neural flux into a smaller number of efferent channels. Diffuse postural tensions, representing general alertness, form a kind of background for this process, according to Freeman. Through learning, these become focused down into specific set "expectancies," the sets acting as selectors of efferent channels. The locus, intensity, and timing of such tension-states are factors upon which their control over the ensuing overt activity depends. The above account is, of course, largely hypothetical; but it will serve as one kind of physiological interpretation.

The entire tension-pattern at any given time consists of two parts. First, there is a *general*, or background, supporting function consisting of diffuse tensions in muscles other than those concerned with the particular activity. Second, there is the *specific* supporting function consisting of tensions in differentially localized muscle groups. This latter tension-region represents the immediate preparation and support for the ensuing or continuing activity for which the organism is set. It serves as the "focus" of the tension-pattern; and the focus of the preparatory tension-set tends, on experimental evidence, to be identical with the muscles whose tensions are involved in the full overt response. The general tensions in other muscles serve as background excitation in support, both peripherally and centrally, of the focal set. There is thus a gradient of activity from the focalized tension-region outward to the other bodily musculature. General tension-effects from the background excitation maintain the body in a state of tonicity during waking activity and provide a flow of returning proprioceptive stimulation constituting the "vigilance" of the central nervous system. Body-tonus is maintained in a self-completing, circular-reflex manner. Studies of the *general* tension accompaniments of specific tasks have shown that, within limits, they facilitate those activities, increasing the amount of work accomplished. There is, however, a range and an optimal point beyond which their increases lead to a *lowering* of the effectiveness of the performance. The more complicated and minutely organized the task (focal set and act) the less is the amount of general bodily tension that can be experimentally induced without impairment.[6] The pattern of covert muscular tensions aroused in a response to a warning signal is found to be more diffuse when the instructions call for a "sensory reaction" than when a "motor reaction" set is employed. Finger-movement reaction is most rapid when the tension is localized in the finger muscles and least rapid when it is localized in more remote muscles. When the instruction calls for a reaction by some part of the body not previously employed it is found that the focus of preparatory muscle tension shifts to that part. Reaction to a "startle" stimulus is focalized if there is preparation of some part of the body to "take it," but not otherwise. Considerations of timing, as well as the spatial location of focal tension-sets, enter into their formation and operation. The preparation of an aggregate of neural impulses and muscle-fiber contractions that leads to an overt response, being a dynamic occurrence, must be ongoing at a time when the outer stimulus is presented. We may conjecture that the activity is thus raised in energies to its full threshold level for performance. It is clear that these findings, together with reasonable inferences therefrom, support the generalization that sets, considered as the focal parts of tension-patterns, are specific to their overt responses, are selective, and constitute a preparation or a sustaining of the pattern of response.

2. *Is the locus of set peripheral or central?* We have seen that two different kinds of set are familiar in experimental work, namely, sets of expectancy and intention. Related to this difference is the following theoretical question: Is set mainly a peripheral and motor phenomenon, or does the phenomenon of expectancy argue for a central theory? According to the *peripheral* theory the set represents merely

---

[6] It is as though energies in other parts of the bodily muscular system could be recruited to enhance the operation of the focal aggregate; but when too much of this outlying energy is fed in, the capacity of the aggregate to use it is exceeded and a decline in the probability of the aggregate's operation, that is, a kind of entropy of the structure, results.

an implicit or anticipatory stage of the full response. The stimulus, when it comes, serves merely as a trigger to release the full strength of an activity already in progress. Freeman's criticism of this theory is that by being *too* specific it does not provide for the non-focal part of the muscular tension pattern. General postures may be facilitative in some degree of a whole class of responses. According to the *central* theory the preparation is entirely cerebral; motor effects are due simply to "overflow" from the central sources of neural action involved. Titchener, for example, spoke of a "cortical" set. Mowrer, Rayman, and Bliss (1940) reported an experiment in which the subject was set to react in an identical way (finger movement) to two stimuli of different types (light and tone). It was found that if a series was run for light followed by a series for tone, the reaction-time for a tone was longer than in series in which the responses had been only to tones. Since the same motor response (finger movement) was involved in both cases, it was inferred that the difference in reaction-time must be a function not of the preparation of the motor process, but of the "stimulus expectancy." Hence the set was central rather than peripheral or motor in its location. Freeman (1948*a* and *b*) criticized this interpretation, pointing out that the experimenters had not taken into account, or at least had not controlled, the motor preparation involved in tensions of the muscles of sensory accommodation, such, for example, as the tensor tympani of the ear. The shifts from one mode of stimulation to another did not permit time for an adequate preparation of this non-focal class of peripheral elements; hence the results for the two types of stimuli were not comparable.

Freeman has offered his own "dynamotor" theory involving both central and peripheral factors. Whenever a tension occurs in any muscle, sensory-accommodative or otherwise, there is a backlash from that muscle to the central nervous system creating a differential brain state that further lowers the threshold of the motor pathways through which the ensuing or ongoing response will occur. If the same overt reaction were to be elicited by several classes of stimuli, small changes in the tension pattern (such as are involved in sensory accommodation) would establish by backlash action "a central condition of lowered threshold for the stimulus about to be presented." The basis of central expectancy, says Freeman, "is backlash excitation from outlasting postural adjustments previously made to the stimulus anticipated." (1948*b*, pp. 226–227.) The process represents the motor set or adjustments involved in sensory accommodation, together with other postural changes induced by the stimulus object. We note also that it is circular in character, proceeding from muscular reaction through backlash to the central nervous system and out again as further facilitation of the response. On the way, in the brain centers, the so-called process of "expectation" may be said to occur. There is thus a cycle from exteroceptive stimulation, through central connections, to sensory accommodation or other movements of effectors, with returning effects of a circular-reflex character that bring the sense-organ into fuller contact with the stimulus. This accommodation persists as a postural adjustment holding the receptor in that position and thus prolonging the operation of the perceptual aggregate. Both peripheral and central regions are represented in this cyclical chain of events. Since this is so, the question of the role of central *versus* peripheral factors as the locus of set fades out, and another, more fundamental, fact appears. The percept or overt reaction and its set are seen as an aggregate of *interdependent parts;* and the set is a kind of *self-closing structure.* As the reader will recall, the same point could readily be made with respect to the pattern of happenings in sensory-tonic field theory. Returning proprioceptive excitation from unilateral stimulations closed the circle of the perception of an object's position in such a way as to make the angle perceived accord with the subject's equilibrial state.

3. *How do sets sustain or prolong the activities for which they are specific?* Behavior is not just movement. It is not merely a flitting of effectors from one point-contact with objects to another. If objects in the environment are to be related to the needs of the organism there are times when a steady unchanging relationship has to be maintained between the object and the organism long enough for certain adjustments to it to be made. In any system of motion among a number of bodies there may be occasions in which all of the bodies are moving relative to one another; and there may be other occasions in which some of them are "at rest" in respect to certain others, even though there may be *still* other members in relation to which they are moving. When one takes a drink of water from a glass there are relative-motion phases of the behavior as the hand reaches toward the glass, as the glass is raised to the lips and tipped, as the mouth opens, and as the water flows into the mouth and down the throat. There are also relative *non-motion* phases as the glass *remains* gripped by the fingers during the time in which it ascends and is tipped, and as the mouth *remains* open during the flow of the water. Both these apparent non-motion, or "rest," phases require muscular contractions *maintained through time,* even though no overt movement

is seen. (There is, of course, incessant motion at a microscopic or molecular level.) The maintenance of "rest" in relation to particular objects during a behavioral act presents as much of a problem for physiology as does relative motion. Both are really dynamically operating aspects of the behavioral aggregate.

When we speak of an activity being sustained or prolonged we can mean either or both of two things. (1) The activity may constitute a series of *repeated* acts, all similar. In this case there are repeated self-closing cycles of neural and effector action through time. Or (2) the activity may be extended through time in *one* cycle, either by the slowing of the movements or by the lengthening of the steady portions of the muscular contractions that do not involve overt change of position. For example, under 2, we could either make the movements of drinking slower, or we could hold the glass longer in any one position before proceeding to the next, thus relatively extending the "gripping" time. Whether the act is prolonged by repetition (more acts of the same kind) or by perseveration of one act, the important point is that circular patterns of neuromuscular events are always involved. The aggregate is a dynamic, self-closing structure.

This dual conception of behavior, one phase employing motion, the other the sustaining of position and contact, is pertinent to the problem of set. It leads us also to ask whether there is evidence for the two phases in corresponding arrangements within the body. And here the physiologists have given us at least a suggestive answer. There *are* two systems, or two portions, of the neuromotor mechanism, called respectively the phasic and the tonic, that are involved in just this way in behavioral activity. The *phasic* system is concerned with muscular contractions that are more intensive, extended, rapid, and short-lived. It affords a basis for the *motion* aspect of behavior. Its nerve fibers are assembled largely in the great pyramidal tracts descending from the cortex and crossing in their descent. This system is connected through cortical "adjustor" centers with the afferent fibers from the exteroceptors (eye, ear, and so on) which also cross on their way to the cortex; and it is concerned largely with "voluntary" actions in adjusting to the environment. The *tonic* system, on the other hand, is an arrangement in which a continuous flow of impulses is sent to the muscles, producing incipient tensions, or "tonic" contractions, rather than full contraction. Both systems, of course, have their impulses grouped in "volleys," but the motor activities of the tonic system are slower and more sustained than those of the phasic. They keep the muscle in a "state of readiness" for the latter.

The tonic system is thus obviously related to the steady maintenance of posture, position, and lasting contact. The efferent neural elements of the tonic system lie in the extrapyramidal tracts and connect with centers in the cerebellum. There are, of course, afferent fibers as well as efferent in the tonic system. These lead from the proprioceptors in the muscles to the cerebellum, and they are the pathways over which the backlash travels to the central nervous system. The fibers running from the proprioceptors to the cerebellum as well as those from the cerebellum back to the muscles are for the most part uncrossed, continuing on the same side of the body as that in which they originated. In the cerebellum there are also connections of the tonic system with fibers going to the cortex. According to some physiologists there are different types of muscle fibers that function in the two systems, the "red" fibers that have a large supply of sustaining energy and are involved in the postural (tonic) reactions, and the "white" fibers, less rich in metabolic resources, that are active in the phasic. It has been suggested, on the other hand, that there may be different kinds of constituents within the same muscle fiber for the two forms of contraction.

How tonic and phasic reactions are related is not known in detail. They may operate as a continuum without a sharp break, providing, in the various regions of the continuum, for differing proportions of the two contractile types. Or again, there may be some threshold arrangement between them. The writer would suggest the following interpretation of what happens. When an object remains in contact with the receptors (as in holding a glass while drinking) there would be a steady flow of afferent impulses, giving simply an extension of energy-increments through *time*. Then, when other sources of stimulus energy impinge momentarily or in larger units on the receptors, whether inside or on the surface of the body, there might occur additions to the energic fund in the form of briefer and more vigorous trains of impulses and contractions that represent *spatial* redistributions of energies through time, in other words, the phasic aspect of behavior as seen in the overt motion of an effector. Time distribution would thus give way to the spatial distribution of motion. In the nervous system generally we often see such an interchange between the temporal and the spatial aspects of activity. When this occurs the only way in which it would be possible for the *phasic* reaction to be sustained would be as a series of repetitions of the complete act. The self-closing aggregate would thus be structured upon a larger (macroscopic) scale. It would be natural to imagine that different neural pathways would be used in these altered space and time arrangements of the aggregate, perhaps with a threshold relationship between them.

In any case, the facts in hand concerning tonic and phasic enable us to obtain a much clearer notion of set. Through this picture of the tonic reaction-system we can now more readily conceive what may be involved when we say that a set prepares, prolongs, or sustains the full or overt reaction to the stimulus. And since the same muscle groups are involved in both tonic and phasic reaction-patterns we can also see clearly the reason for the specificity, or so called selective-action, of set. This point is important. Whether separate nerve-fibers are involved in tonic and phasic reactions or not, and whether there are distinct muscle-fibers or separate chemical constituents of fibers, the coördinated muscle groups that make up the patterns of reaction are the same for any given act of behavior in response to its appropriate stimulus. We are dealing essentially with the same arrangement of motor elements in both tonic and phasic systems. We can say, then, that tonic and phasic reactions are really not distinct entities, but are, for all intents and purposes, merely stages of the operation of the *same aggregate*. The "tonic" reaction represents only a less spatially extended and less intense form of the reaction overtly observed as "phasic."[7] A "set," as studied in the psychological laboratory or as seen in daily life, since it is considered to be based upon a tonic state, can thus be regarded merely as a partial aspect of the full reaction, whether that reaction be an act of perception or of overt adjustment. It can also outlast the overt movements or phasic stage, sustaining the steady contacts or positions which must be maintained between the various phasic portions of the behavior-act; or it can persist between successive full performances of the act. To say that a set is "selective" of its ensuing or facilitated behavior would, on this view, be gratuitous and misleading. The set is not a "selector" of the behavior; it is the behavior pattern itself as seen in an incipient or less energic state.

In order to complete the picture let us recall once more that sustaining means prolonging or repeating through time. At basic levels this must always mean a repetition of some self-closing process, a cyclical course of events. How else could an ongoing in the organism be temporally sustained? Whether the aggregate is in a stage of set or of full performance, we can regard this feature as constant. Some initial stimulus in the recent or more remote past has led *via* the central nervous connections to a motor response, as for example, in

---

[7] And both phases can be regarded, as suggested by earlier considerations, as self-delimited, *self-closing* structures.

limbs, hands, vocal organs, or the muscles of sensory accommodation. Proprioceptive stimulation in the muscles, tendons, or joints arising from that response starts impulses in afferent neurons leading back to the central nervous system. From there impulses produced or reinforced by this excitation flow out again into the musculature of the same effector organs. The contractions, so produced or reinforced, *again* set up proprioceptive backlash to the central nervous system— and so on. There is thus a circular process that can maintain itself for indefinite periods of time, that can, in a sense, become *independent* of time, until the internal condition of the organism or the environmental situation changes. The steady tonic contraction of particular muscle-groups as well as of the bodily musculature in general (Freeman's background excitation) is thus maintained, and in the particular instance the phasic reaction is prepared or sustained. It is even possible that there could be a reduction in the "circumference dimension" of the self-closing aggregate, of such a nature that the set-process could go on in the cortex alone (central theory of set).

Since tonic and phasic are the same in their cyclical "format" there is no reason why phasic contractions could not also set up their backlash stimulation, repeating the excitation of central neurons and thus tending to produce a repetition of the overt act. Without such cyclical arrangements of tonic and phasic systems the temporal continuities and coördinations of the behavioral aggregate would be difficult to explain. And if the process obtains for overt action it probably holds for perceptual reactions as well. This assumption, in fact, is necessary in order to account for the findings of Werner and Wapner. The reader is asked to bear this hypothesis of the self-closed aggregate in mind since we shall have repeated occasion to refer to it.[8]

The preceding account of the energic and dynamic-structural character of set has been shaped in part by the writer's own conception of behavior. Let us now add a few interpretations given by Freeman whose work has provided us with so helpful an orientation. Though the role of tonic reactions is here described a little

---

[8] Though we have not included vestibular receptors, glandular activities, volumic or humoral changes in the blood system, or other sources of inner stimulation in our hypothesizing of the set and behavior cycle there is no reason whatever for excluding them. The neurons also have their self-maintaining activities. In fact, the physiologists regard practically all kinds of tissues as having their "tone." The concept of the "dynamic structure" of energy in the organism thus takes on a pervasive aspect.

differently, the account will tally fairly well with what has been said. Freeman asserts that the tonic response represents a more enduring, diffuse type of adjustment, maintaining a continuity in the organism's behavior and serving as a basis for the quick, localized, phasic reactions. "From this standpoint *sets are to be regarded as specific patterns of the postural substrate in the process of becoming (or at least supporting) phasic reactions.*" Exteroceptive impulses produce their effects upon the background of such proprioceptive-tonic readiness. Being stronger, they may arouse the motor neurons and muscle fibers to a quick and full activity, but they do so *only with the aid of the tonic preparation.* If the afferents from the muscle are cut or rendered inactive by disease, and the tone of the muscle thereby lost, exteroceptive stimulation (as from the eye or ear) will produce little or none of its previous motor response. Postural adjustment thus antedates and sustains phasic adjustment. Exteroceptive impulses influence autonomous, tonically controlled processes, such as heartbeat and respiration, only within definite limits. Responses to pain stimuli mediated through the thalamus vary with the general neuromuscular state of the organism including the degree of set-expectancy for the pain. We may conceive of tonic sets as developing into phasic responses and phasic residuals as serving to form tonic sets.

Because of the excess and relatively diffuse spread of afferent impulses from exteroceptors, as compared with the smaller number and closer connection of proprioceptive impulses with the motor neurons to the muscles in which the proprioceptors lie, only those exteroceptive impulses that fit in with the timing, phase, and direction of the prevalent proprioceptive pattern and the tonic pattern from which it arises will be likely to be effective in producing a response. This condition is in accord with the "selective" action of sets and their ability to shift. Set phenomena are thus considered by Freeman to be "expressions of the limiting effects of proprioceptive-tonic aspects of response upon exteroceptive-phasic activity." Tonic patterns that arise from the general postural substrate make for economy of neuromuscular action. They prevent the organism from being always at the mercy of the most intense exteroceptive excitants and from making continual movements that are wasteful of energies. Tonic reaction-patterns are more economical in that they are slower in reaching their maximal strength and slower to subside. "Phasic-exteroceptive excitants come and go, but the stream of proprioceptive-tonic impulses is measured and continuous." The tonic pattern is thus well adapted to the task of preserving the organism's homeostatic balance and equilibrium.

CORRELATION OF SET WITH THE FACTS OF PERCEPTION

We now have at our command much information about set, both as seen in the experimental psychology laboratory and as explained from the physiological side. The task now is to formulate more definitely the contribution of this knowledge to the understanding of perception. Unfortunately we cannot review for this purpose any systematically developed theory, for none, to the writer's knowledge, has appeared. In spite of its universality in behavior, this aspect, generally speaking, has not been popular with perceptionists as an anchorage for their theories. Freeman has stated a motor point of view and a few perceptual principles that we shall presently discuss; but for the most part efforts toward a complete set-theory of perception have been merely programmatic. Since we do not have a well-rounded theory at hand let us try to see for ourselves how the facts of perception can be related to the findings of experimental psychology regarding set, on the one hand, and to physiological findings and interpretations on the other. A drawback to perceptual theories of a motor sort has been the fact that these aspects of the perceptual process are subtle and difficult to observe. Set manifests itself operationally in reaction-time or learning experiments by measurable differences in the observable outcome. In perception, however, except for special dimensional set-ups like those of Werner and Wapner, there is little we can outwardly note beyond changes of sensory accommodation and perhaps some slight effects upon respiration, general bodily position, and the like. The subject himself reports not his bodily changes or tonus levels, but what he sees or hears. In perceptual experiments, moreover, in which one would like to see what happens in a single act of perception rather than in a series, about the only type of motor phenomenon that can be dealt with is the *preparatory* set. Perceptual sets seem in daily life, also, to play more of a preparatory than a sustaining role.

But to proceed with the task. When we view the facts of perception in the light of set-phenomena and their physiological explanation the following suggestive relationships appear.

i. Perceptions, first of all, are always specific and definite, even when they are associated with generalized meanings. Unless there is a real basis of ambiguity in the stimulus pattern or a lack of learning background we do not vacillate between one interpretation of the perceived object and another. This fact is at least in conformity with the idea of a set as a particular pattern of motor adjustment prepared for dealing with an object or class of objects.

ii. Perceptions, like sets, are specifically related to their stimulus-objects. We perceive one thing at a time, or else, when a number of objects are seen, a clear perceptual act requires some grouping or organizing to produce a kind of unity. Parallel with this fact are experiments upon tension-patterns showing that there is, in relation to an act, a focal region of muscular tension and a gradient falling off to lesser tensions in remoter regions. The clearness-fields of attention and sharp vision possess a similar pattern.

iii. As for perceptual organization, we might note one of Freeman's principles to the effect that separate muscular activities in the same tension-pattern tend to vary concomitantly.

iv. The "prior entry" of percepts for stimuli to which the subject is prepared to attend has already been illustrated by sets for finding lost objects. This feature also can be ordered to a tonic state of readiness of the organism, specific in character, focalized, and precluding for the time the operation of other focal patterns.

v. Set antagonism or conflict might be seen in connection with the unifying forces within a figure that set it off against ground and in the many figures yielding reversible perspectives. There are also the striking cases cited by Werner and Wapner in which incompatible experiences of body-motion and motion of the surroundings alternately occurred. Though experiments have ruled out actual eye movements in viewing illusions and reversible figures, such exclusion may apply only to the phasic aspect of the response. It might be that the fundamental tonic pattern would be found to differ in the two ways in which the figure can be seen.

vi. Long-standing sets, peculiar to the individual, that seem to determine the characteristic content of his perceptions might be evidenced by the different ways in which a forest would usually be perceived by a hunter, a forester, a lumberman, and a paper manufacturer. These sets might be explained by a long-sustaining activity of tonic patterns maintained in the circular manner that has previously been described, and possibly reduced to a cortical locus of operation. The possibility of such explanations is at least not incompatible with known neural activities (reverberating circuits within the brain), interpreted according to our self-closing model of set-structure.

vii. Freeman calls attention to the possibility that the postural substrate may become abnormally "fixated," especially in cases of the persistent thwarting of motivations or needs. Backlash from postural tensions thus aroused might dominate the afferent inlets so that it would be difficult for exteroceptive stimulations to break through and produce shifts in behavior.   Such postural fixations might help to explain the loss of perceptual "contact with reality" as seen in some psychotic individuals.   Perhaps we could employ the same type of explanation to account for "autistic" perceptions and other types of non-veridical experience (see Chapter 13).

viii. The wholeness-character and unity of perceptual aggregates, as described by the configurationists, might be related to our principle of self-closing structurization of the set and the behavioral act.

ix. Expectancy-sets, which by the nature of the case must be prevalent in perceptual activity, find a place in Freeman's dynamotor theory of set.

x. Set is often involuntary; and so is perception in the sense that we do not usually "will" to perceive an object or to have it appear as it does.   We recall here that the tonic system is less involved in voluntary activities than the phasic system.

xi. The same may be said concerning the lack of the subject's awareness of the process that goes on in perception.

xii. We have seen, as in Hebb's theory, that learning may have something to do with perception.   Learning also enters experimentally into set formation and no doubt into the acquision of physiological tonic patterning.

xiii. Task instructions and warning signals are often used in perceptual experiments.   These facts are compatible with the building of sets and the time required for their establishment.   There is probably some correspondence here with the time required to build the appropriate tension-pattern in the muscles of sensory accommodation and perhaps in other musculature.

Our attempt to correlate the facts of perception with set as experimentally demonstrated and physiologically explained thus seems on the whole to have been rather fruitful.   It is surprising that perceptual theorists have not more fully exploited this rich source of information.

FREEMAN'S THEORIES OF MEANING AND MOTOR ADJUSTMENTS

In Chapter VII of his *Energetics of Human Behavior* (1948b) Freeman explains very briefly his ideas on the role of motor adjustments in perception.   These views appear under the heading, "The Response Basis of Meaningful Discrimination"; and the phrase "motor adjustments" seems to be used by him to cover all kinds of responses to stimuli and the tonic states and proprioceptive flux that are involved therewith. Since his interests lie in the sphere of "physiological determinism" he has no great concern with phenomenology. He criticizes both the gestalt approach and Lewinian field-theory. In an earlier publication (1940a), under the doubtful assumption that the latter was brain-field theory, he had maintained that certain of its defects and omissions could be remedied by introducing into the field the directive influence of proprioceptive backlash from motor adjustments.

The theorems of Freeman that we are to cite must be understood against a background of his general thesis of behavior as a part of the *homeostatic process* in organisms. This process represents the maintenance of a basic energy level by restoring physiological equilibrium after the latter has been disturbed. The basic energy level itself may vary with different conditions of the organism. From this energic level the subject in the Freeman experiments is "displaced" by external stimulations of a controlled sort. The resulting equilibrating sequence is defined by the *"homeostatic response curve."* It has three phases: (1) the internal arousal of bodily energies to meet the displacement (mobilization), (2) the external expression of the aroused energies by overt response (discharge), and (3) the return of the organism's energy system to its condition prior to the stimulation (recovery). Placing the concept of set in this context, and as a result of the analysis of muscle-tension experiments, Freeman says: "Set-expectancies are tentative and antecedent homeostatic adjustment acts, developed in response to minimally displacing stimulus cues and preparing the channelization of discharge through some particular response outlets which, if not so prepared, would function only through a greater displacement to general equilibrium." (1948b, p. 220.) The preparation of the channels of discharge prevents the excitation from the ensuing stimulus, for which the set has prepared the organism, from overflowing into "non-relevant discharge mechanisms." Hence it tends to conserve energy. Equilibrium would usually be gained in any case, even where, for example, the organism flees precipitously from a danger that might have been dealt with more effectively through acts involving smaller energy mobilizations and discharges. The *set* for such "more adaptive" behaviors, where it exists, helps to restore the equilibrium at lesser energic cost. We may assume that perceptual activities like other behaviors are to be regarded as conforming to the same homeostatic law.

Freeman's thesis is that motor adjustments (interpreted as above upon a homeostatic background) play a considerable part in perceptual activity; and he develops his point mainly with reference to perceptual meaning. Taking his illustrations from vision he begins by saying that the organizing of sensory excitation into meaningful patterns is largely due not to the objects themselves, but to reactions made to the objects. The residue of past reactions, such as ways of looking at, or moving with respect to, the stimulus-object, are essential parts of the excitation field. The point is illustrated by reference to earlier experiments (1929) with ink blots, in which different meanings were elicited under instructions to react to different side-details or by presenting the stimulus in a manner favoring different ways of looking. Such differences in angle of regard and response to detail are said to be the basis of the shift in meaning of reversible perspective figures. They are thus due to background motor adjustments and not to an interaction of the figure and ground portions within the field of visual excitation, as the gestaltists had claimed. Instead of seeing objects or figures as "unlearned wholes" or "global totals" because an analogous stimulus organization reflects itself through afferent channels directly in the brain, the child sees these wholes without learning because of backlash excitation from reflex motor adjustments which interacts in the brain with the exteroceptive stimulation from the object. Different types of global totals tend to condition different sorts of eye movements and angles of looking. Common objects have a characteristic spread and we react to them by looking in a particular way. The motor adjustments made in discriminating fine differences are, however, not the meaning per se; the meaning of the total excitation pattern refers, rather, to the source of the visual excitation.

Just where, or what, meaning is in Freeman's theory is a somewhat puzzling question. He does not want to refer it directly to the motor elements involved in looking, but says that the meaning of an object (such as a dog) is the "product of equivalent ways of looking at sets of equivalent visual objects." One wonders what he means by the word product. Such a statement also seems to place the existence of meaning in a purely logical category and to confine it to the sphere of abstract or "class" ideas, or perhaps to verbal symbols. Can there not be a meaning of a single concrete object? Would not the child who had never seen but *one* dog have a meaning with respect to that object whenever he saw it? If so, where would this meaning fit into the motor schema?

Perhaps Freeman resolves the situation by saying there is no (visual) perceptual meaning in the absence of these ways of looking or their surrogates, and that the more differentiated meaning-structures (concrete-object meaning) *are produced by a greater particularization of these reaction tendencies.* In other words the meaning of a single concrete object would result from a sufficiently fine pattern of ways of looking, the different ways no doubt being determined by the finer features of the object. Freeman's meaning theory, though suggestive, does not seem wholly satisfactory. Would there not be other types of response-adjustments that would be crucial for the meaning of an object beside ways of looking? It does not seem that our author is using the full resources of his own analysis of tension-patterns.

Looking at perception more broadly Freeman states five principles which are here presented in substance and with a change of order. Comments by the present writer are added parenthetically.

i. Perceptual integration always involves more than one mode of sensory excitation, though it is usually built around one particular mode. The one type of excitation, however, that is common to all perceptual integrations, and is universal, is proprioception resulting from muscular reactions that participate directly or are involved in the equilibratory (homeostatic) response. (Backlash from motor adjustments originally evoked by exteroceptive stimulation from the object thus enters into all perceptions. Here then is a principle upon which a motor theory of perception could be built.)

ii. Perceptual integration is always a selective response. Motor adjustments reinforce one group of sensory impulses to the neglect of others. (This principle clearly involves the concept of set.)

iii. The modal excitant, for example, vision, tends to become by conditioning a substitute for effects coming from other reactions that originally formed a part of the perceptual aggregate. Thus the "soft look" of velvet was originally contributed by motor and tactual experiences, but in time comes, by stimulus substitution, to be carried by the visual excitant. (The old metaphor "carried by" betrays how far we are from the goal of translating sensory qualities or meanings into physiological and motor terms.)

iv. The modal (motor) excitant in the perception provides other elements that contribute to the perceptual integration beside the basic adjustment-responses mentioned in i. For example, empathic motor reactions evoked by visual stimulations afford aesthetic meaning, as in the proper balance of the objects seen.[9]

---

[9] We may assume that *backlash* from the empathic responses is involved in the contribution of these responses. Freeman evidently implies that these elements *supplement* the motor adjustments that underlie the object's *meaning*. His theory attempts, as we have already seen, to deal with object-meaning, a problem which the Werner-Wapner theory ignored.

v. Perceptual integrations shift readily and displace one another. Different portions of the available afferent excitation are involved in these different selective groupings as the perception shifts. (Here we have the principle of antagonism and the inhibition of one set by another. Freeman, however, would include fatigue of the processes involved in the focal tension pattern as one of the important reasons for perceptual shift. Such a condition is said to underlie the phenomenon of reversible perspective.)

COMPARISON OF FREEMAN'S VIEWS WITH THE SENSORY-TONIC
SYSTEM; PROBLEMS STILL UNSOLVED

These five principles, which the author calls, respectively, modal focus, selection, surrogation, induction, and shift are significant for a motor theory of perception. Together with his preceding statements they deal with the selective, specific, holistic, and integrative aspects of perceptual phenomena, and with their shifting or mutually inhibitory action. There are many interesting parallels between Freeman's views and sensory-tonic field theory. Fully to utilize the physiological facts presented by Freeman we would need to break down the undifferentiated concept of tonic as used in the Werner-Wapner theory into "tonic" and "phasic," making clear what system the sensory-tonic theory was employing. The similarity, however, between the notions of organismic or equilibrial state, on the one hand, and Freeman's basic energy level, on the other, is apparent, except that the latter is broader. Just as Freeman "displaced" his subjects from their basic energy level, so Werner and Wapner displaced their subjects by presenting a rod out of alignment with their equilibrial axes. The subject's reactions in adjusting the rod to apparent verticality represented the "discharge" phase of Freeman's homeostatic curve. In reactions of this sort the subject exhibited such tendencies as body-object balance and symmetrization, which brought about a condition that corresponded to the "recovery" phase in Freeman's scheme. The whole procedure took place in sensory-tonic field theory according to the "law of minimal disturbance," which seems the exact analogue of Freeman's principle of energy conservation. The only difference is that the former idea was a field concept while the latter called upon physicochemical processes and metabolism. Perceptual shift, the last of the Freeman principles, though broader in coverage and non-dimensional, might include cases in which the equilibrial state of Werner and Wapner was changed by altering the extraneous stimuli that were influencing the perception. It may also be related to the "vicariousness" of the latter authors. Basic to both theories is the hypothesis that muscular contractions, tonic states, and proprioceptive backlash are universal factors in perception and play an important part in determining how the world appears to the perceiver. Such convergences of investigators, approaching perception from somewhat different viewpoints and with different methods, augurs well for the general soundness of the motor view.

It does not, however, prove the completeness of such a theory; for we must note that the two systems have not only common achievements but common shortcomings. Freeman's concepts point up a commendable effort to deal with object-character and meaning, aspects that were overlooked in sensory-tonic theory. But both theories have defects in this regard. Both theories, of course, assumed, or at least implied, that in the full perceptual experience, and therefore in the physiological processes, the sensory effects that are received from the object by the exteroceptors (eye or ear) must in some way be combined with the motor or tonic effects of the response into one unified whole. The explanation cannot be *entirely* motor; exteroceptive-sensory features must be included. The rod must not merely be seen as "vertical" (tonically induced aspect); it must be seen as a vertical *rod* (visually induced aspect). The velvet must not only have the softness previously experienced in pressing against it (kinaesthetic experience from motor reactions); it must also *look* soft (visual experience) and also look like velvet (color and other visual qualities). Werner and Wapner seem to have neglected the problem or to have side-stepped it by a logical slip in the construction they placed upon the terms "sensory" and "tonic" and their interaction. Freeman recognizes the problem and attempts to deal with it. But can we say that he has really brought about the wedding of these two "alien" factors? The principle of surrogation (iii) was an effort in that direction, but it left much to be explained.

The task of synthesizing these two portions of the perceptual aggregate, as the writer sees it, is the great problem that any motor theory of perception must face. No motor explanation of perceiving can rise to the stature of a complete theory until this problem is solved. Perhaps we have here a part of the reason why perceptual theorists have so largely shunned the motor elements. Gestalt-minded psychologists, who are phenomenological and therefore sensorily oriented, have found it hard to accommodate the motor components in their scheme. Now we find that psychologists who prefer a more objective or motor-oriented approach are having equal difficulty in incorporating the exteroceptive elements. Motor theorists might try to find an easier way out by not taking the sensory or phenomenological aspects too seriously. But if they do so their treatment will continue to be one-sided. A motor theorist of perception who omits the consideration of how things appear to the perceiver in the usual sensory meaning of that phrase would have little justification for introducing tonic or proprioceptive effects into the description of the percept. He might better give up phenomenological data entirely and join the behavior-ists in treating perception merely as a learned discriminatory response. And this, perhaps, could be stated as the objective of Freeman—up to the point where he speaks of the "soft look" of velvet and the aesthetic meaning afforded in the balance of the objects seen. It would scarcely be fair, however, to require completeness of Freeman's principles, since they were not put forward with any systematic intention but only as ideas bearing upon the "response basis of meaningful discrimination."

Turning for a moment to the problem of meaning, since that will concern us in later chapters, we may note that Freeman has taken more cognizance of this vital aspect than most other theorists. He de-serves much credit for the notion that the way in which the object is regarded or reacted to may play an essential role in its meaning to the perceiver. Some questions, however, are left unanswered. How an object is perceived "globally" is not explained by backlash from reflex adjustments to the object combined with the exteroceptive flux until some principle of integrated totality is demonstrated in these proprio-ceptive and exteroceptive sources. "Ways of looking at the object," which explain how *alternative* meanings are evoked, still leave us without a detailed statement of how any one particular meaning is brought about. How meaning, which is considered as motor in its source, can come to be "carried by" the exteroceptive senses is still a mystery. Finally we need some explanation of the transition between the original overt action or adjustment that affords the backlash and the subsequent and continuing *covert* meaning. How does the first lead to the second? How is the second intensified and externalized into the first? Are meanings the tonic residua of earlier phasic mus-cular patterns, capable of being raised again, when the stimulus is presented, to the phasic energy level? This would seem a logical and intriguing possibility; but it is not explicitly developed. One wonders why our author left out of his response theory of perception so much that he himself had clearly presented regarding the nature of sets, muscle-tension patterns, and tonic states. No doubt it is there, by implication, under "motor adjustments"; but further development would have been helpful. We have already seen how perception is linked to set and to the underlying tonic substrates of behavioral acts.

Would it not seem possible to go on from this point to the elaboration of a more complete motor theory of perception?[10]

THE UBIQUITY OF SET IN PERCEPTION

Whether this achievement will be possible or not, the fact remains that set is ubiquitous in nearly all forms of behavior; and the probability will remain that it plays a considerable part in the perceptual process. Its presence seems in some way implied in all the theories that have sprung from the investigation of the various aspects of perception. Set was employed by Külpe (Chapter 4) in his discovery of the conditions that led him to classify conscious elements as their dimensional attributes. It has appeared in psychophysical experiments as expectancy, absolute impression, and the like. Gestalt psychologists recognized set, though in general they played down the perceptual effects of motor adjustments. It would not be difficult to construe the configurational principles of closure, good-figure, and figure and ground as highly generalized sets of the perceiving organism. Set is shown in looking at illusion-figures, and strikingly in such phenomena as the size-weight illusion. Though such experiences are often construed, gestalt-wise, as due to influences of the total field, they also represent instances in which, through past experience of things in their usual relationships, we are set to perceive details in a certain way. In the theories we have still to examine we shall see the same general implication of set. When we become "adapted" to a certain level of intensities or other perceptual dimensions, so that a "frame of reference" is established, the process is one of being *prepared* to perceive or react in a certain way. Perceptual constancies, broadly construed, may be matters of set. They suggest the sustained

[10] One other presentation of the case for motor elements in perception may be mentioned. Sperry (1952) reviews the "mind-brain" problem and rejects both topographical isomorphism and "brain-coding." He reverses the gestalt view of the motoric as a system operating at the service of sensory (perceptual) equilibrium and maintains that sensory elements are subservient to motor adjustment or preparation for response, which is the brain's chief function. The anatomical difficulties that beset brain-field theory disappear, says Sperry, when we make the motor and premotor elements of brain-functioning the basis of conscious experiences. Unification of figure, the perceptual constancies, equipotentiality, sensory equivalence, and the perception of number and size, phenomena which offer difficulties for configurational and sensory theories, become more comprehensible when viewed as the functional adjustment of the cortex for motor activities adaptive to the situation. The author does not succeed, however, in explaining how sensory and motor elements are combined in the perceptual act.

preparation to perceive in certain ways when a certain class of cues appears to which we have become habituated. When we come to the motivational theory of perception, to the claim that much of perception is regulated by personal needs or values (a belief that has sharply divided perceptual theorists), we shall see that the concept of set, though discounted at first, may hold the key to the ultimate reconciliation of discordant claims.

The problem of set and motor adjustments thus ramifies into all phases of perceptual study. Though we have not yet fully understood it or discovered how to integrate it with the other aspects of perception, it is a topic that theorists cannot afford to overlook. Yet strangely enough, though everyone recognizes its ubiquity, it has played little systematic part in the development of the theories. In some cases it is even regarded as a disturbing factor to be eliminated by controls in order that the theory may have its say. A rich store of facts and principles, so far scarcely touched, is thus awaiting the use of theoreticians. There is one outstanding exception to the general neglect of set. In Chapter 15 we shall discuss a system that is founded directly upon this concept, though its full implications are not worked out. With what profit it has been employed by that theory we shall later see.

AN INTERPRETATIVE SUMMARY OF SET

In the absence of a formulated theory we must not allow these facts and ideas about set to slip from our grasp as we proceed with the theoretical problems of perception. Let us try to distill from them a few notions that will be useful. Since our task has been not merely to cite findings, but also to suggest their theoretical significance, the points that will now be listed by way of summary will include some of the writer's interpretations along with the facts. The reader can readily distinguish between the two and should do so in the interest of separating facts from theory.

1. Set is not distinct or separate from the perception or the overt act, but is, with some modifications, a lower, or *subthreshold*, energic level of the perception or act itself. If the set is preparatory rather than sustaining, its aggregate is less inclusive as well as less energetic than that of the full perception or overt act, in that it lacks the outer stimulus-element and the contacts of effectors with the environment. There is still, however, a state of readiness to react that has a physiological basis in the organism. This first feature of set implies an ag-

gregate of interconnected neural and muscular events having the character of a "format," or arrangement, that can operate at different energy levels. That is to say, the neuromuscular pattern of the act has a reality and existence of its own, even apart from, and to some degree independent of, its usual points of environmental contact.

2. The set, which is probably largely tonic, is, like the full or phasic stage of the aggregate, a *dynamic pattern*. The aggregate is also *self-closed* and *cyclical* in its operation. Backlash excitation and circularly reinforcing, repeating, or adjusting processes occur at both the tonic and the phasic level. This feature gives the set-aggregate a continuance through time.

3. The above two principles show that sets can act as preparations for the full perception or overt act, or as sustainers of those activities. This is true in the self-evident sense that a "subperformance" of an activity or aggregate that is already going on may be said to "prepare for" or "sustain" an ensuing or continuing operation of that same aggregate upon a more intensive scale.

4. Passage from the set stage of the aggregate to full performance means (i) the building up of the energies of the aggregate, (ii) the supplying of any missing stimulation or effector events that may be required, and (iii) the resulting attainment of a point in such energic increase and format-completeness at which the perception or overt act suddenly appears. This point is known as the threshold.

5. Sets, persisting through time, can be brought into immediate availability (i.e., "evoked") in various situations by stimuli or other conditions, external or internal, that have formed a part of their aggregates in the past or are otherwise related to them. They can occur as parts of larger or more inclusive aggregates; and they are related to learning and motivation in various ways.

6. Sets are particularistic and specific to their full perceptions or overt acts. Since they are merely a lower energic state of these same aggregates this could not be otherwise. Sets also inhibit the operation (i.e., reduce the energies or block the pattern) of other (antagonistic) sets.

7. Sets tend, other things being equal, to determine physiologically what objects are to be perceived, the speed or readiness of their perception, and, within limits, the content and vividness of the percept.

It will be seen that the above principles constitute in themselves a kind of set-theory of perception and behavior generally. We shall return to them for a further development of their implications in Chapter 16.

10

Adaptation-Level
Perceptual Norm
and Frame of Reference

The theories thus far discussed have not been directly concerned with perceived dimensionality. Spatial or other magnitudes were sometimes used, as in sensory-tonic field theory. They were not used, however, as ends in themselves, but to test the influence of other hypothesized factors upon the perceptual process. The work of dealing directly with sensory dimensionality was, of course, the primary interest of psychophysics. That movement, though important as a method, has not contributed much to the content of perceptual theory beyond the Weber and Fechner laws. Was there more in the matter of perceptual magnitudes or intensities that might have been brought to light?

The entire notion, in fact the very reality, of quantitative experiences implies comparisons. One experience must be compared with another in terms of "more than," "less than," or "equal." Scales have to be devised upon which the differently experienced magnitudes or intensities can be distributed. In Chapter 4 we saw that this task had been accomplished through the psychophysical procedures. The fact, however, that psychophysics gave only modest returns for perceptual theory suggests the following question: In psychophysical measurement has the full story of the dimensionalities been told? In confining attention to the mere correlation of the subject's report with the immediate stimulus was the study of the conditions of perceived dimensionality too greatly restricted? We have already seen some grounds for criticism of the psychophysical law. More particularly, we are now interested in *all* the conditions that might tend to affect or determine perceived dimensionality. We might well seek some formula more comprehensive than that of psychophysics to enable us to predict how large, heavy, firm, bright, high-pitched, or enduring the things or occurrences of our world will, under different circumstances, appear to be. Would not such an approach yield a more basic and precise understanding of perception? Under these more adequate conditions would not the dimensional aspect of sensory experience hold the possibility of a more interesting and rewarding approach to perceptual theory? The next theorist we shall consider believes that it would. But he sees this possibility in the light, also, of another aspect of perception that will presently be described.

The sensory experiences studied in psychophysics are stimulus-bound. They are based on discriminations of small intervals in a definite, controlled series of stimulus-presentations; and the capacities for the quantitative judgments required are considered as somewhat standard, that is, as pretty much the same for everybody, and as dependent upon fairly stable physiological conditions. From a phenomenological standpoint, however, dimensionalities in perception may occur that are not so closely bound to the immediate stimulus. For example, if one asks how low a tone has to be to be perceived by the subject as "low," the question has meaning even though it is wholly divorced from any objective tonal standard and though its answer may vary greatly from individual to individual or for the same individual on different occasions. No one can *directly* control or measure a percept. It has a right to be of any magnitude the individual experiences it to be; and the experience of its magnitude may at times vary considerably from what one might expect from measuring the magnitude of the stimulus. This does not mean that *no* measuring scale is being employed. It means only that the scale in use is, to a large extent, observer-involved. In such a situation perceived magnitude or intensity may depend to a large extent upon the subject's past, his immediate past chiefly, but also on his more remote past. It will depend also upon his range of experience with magnitudes or intensities in general. Under certain conditions individuals acquire a scale, or frame of reference, by which to judge; and this scale is subjective and personal to the subject. It is upon such considerations that Helson's concept of the "adaptation-level," the theory with which we shall be concerned in this chapter, is based.[1]

MEANING AND EXEMPLIFICATION OF ADAPTATION-LEVEL; THEORY OF POOLING AND WEIGHTING

Helson criticizes current perceptual theories for their lack of the quantitative formulations that are necessary for the mature develop-

[1] Helson, 1947, 1948, 1951.

ment of any science; and he suggests that his method and theory may help to supply this need. One of the salient characteristics of organisms, he maintains, is the tendency to categorize their experiences in terms of some kind of order. In both the simpler, automatic phases of activity and the realm of organized *gestalten* an order, established not by the environment alone but by the individual, is a rule of life and adjustment. The order that Helson is mainly interested in, however, is limited to a particular kind. It is a *dimensional* or *quantitative* order, such as that which comes into play when we judge distances, sizes, or other magnitudes, or employ a scale upon which we allocate the degree of beauty of objects or any of a hundred other attributes that are significant to us.

The way in which the organism achieves such an order is by establishing subjectively some neutral, indifferent, region in its quantitatively arrayed experiences. Using the whole gamut of stimulus-magnitudes to which he is accustomed as a "frame" for his judgments, the individual establishes an "average," really a small region of magnitude, as a kind of standard. Particular stimuli are then judged as large or small, heavy or light, and so on, according to their position with reference to this standard. Such a neutral region in the hefting of weights would be the small range of objective weight-values within which the subject reported that the weight seemed neither "heavy" nor "light," but "*medium*." It has been found, for example, that in a series ranging from 200 to 400 grams the neutral or "medium" stimulus is about 250 grams; while 475 grams is approximately the neutral position for a range of 400 to 600. Such "medium" judgments may have little relation to the arithmetical average of the stimulus series. This neutral or medium position is called the *adaptation-level* of the subject. Its significance lies in the fact that it is a kind of standard of reference above which (i.e., at a greater stimulus magnitude) a weight seems "heavy" and below which a weight seems "light." It represents the "centering" of the organism with respect to the stimuli confronting it, and is the "true zero of functioning." The position of this functional zero (adaptation-level) is said to determine the whole structure of the perceived field. (It is to be noted that Helson here attaches a meaning to the term structure quite different from that which we have previously used, in that he considers it not as an organization of the parts of the stimulus-object, but as an array of quantities of some variable attribute that is abstracted from the stimulus-object.) The adaptation-level idea, which is capable of being extended to perceived or judged variables of every sort, holds intriguing possibilities. When we think of the great number and variety of dimensionalities that can be experienced in the various sensory modalities, and the many possible "frames of reference," we see that such a concept may become important in helping to answer the question of "why things appear as they do."

The Helson adaptation-level must not be confused with the more familiar concept of adaption in which the effect is supposed to come only after a long period of adaptation to fairly constant stimulus conditions, with greatly reduced capacity for response at the end. For every moment of stimulation, in Helson's view, there is an adaptation-level; and this level changes in time and with the varying conditions of stimulation. "It is a function of all the stimuli acting upon the organism at any given moment as well as in the past." For every case of excitation and response it is as though a stimulus were acting which represents the combined effects of all the preceding stimuli and to which the organism may be said to be attuned or adapted. Stimuli that are near this value fail to evoke a response or else call forth neutral judgments, such as "indifferent," "doubtful," or "equal," depending on the context. "Positive or negative enhancement occurs as stimuli are above or below the adaptation-level." This level may itself be high, moderate, or low, depending on a number of factors in the stimulus-configuration. A stimulus far above the stimulus-range that is being employed in the series may raise adaptation-level so high that most of the judgments and stimuli will be below it and the majority of the judgments will thus be "negative." The opposite will be true with a stimulus far below the usual range. When the adaptation-level is near the middle of the series the positive and negative judgments will be about equal, except for the Weber-Fechner principle which tends to reduce the effects of the more intense stimulation thereby producing an asymmetry in the judgments.

How is this whole array of sensory experiences, past and present, brought to bear in establishing the adaptation-level? This is done, says Helson, by a process of *pooling* in which the organism arrives at some kind of average (though not an arithmetic average) of its magnitude-experiences in the dimension concerned. The process is not a conscious one, and series stimuli that are below the sensory threshold may be shown to have an effect. Pooling is therefore a physiological as well as a "psychological" phenomenon: it may occur even below the level where conscious judgments occur. Helson regards pooling as a basic characteristic of all organic functioning. Experiences received from three different classes of stimuli leave their effects in the pool, and each of them plays a part in the resulting adaptation-level. First, there are the stimuli of the regular series that is being presented. These may be either given as single presentations (absolute method) or paired with a "comparison stimulus" (comparative method). Second, there are out-of-series, or "background," stimuli, far above or below the range-limits of the regular series. These may be intercalated once, or on repeated occasions, and with effects as predicted by the theory. For example, the introduction of a weight of 900 grams raised the adaptation level of a series ranging from 400 to 600 grams from its former position of 475 grams to 550. Third, there are the residual effects from earlier stimuli or from conditions previously experienced outside the experimental setting. The effects of all these stimulations, pooled together, determine the adaptation-level. They may not, however, act equally, but according to their frequencies, proximity, affective value, or other characteristics. It is possible to devise formulas for assigning appropriate weights to such factors and thus to compute for the individual in a given experimental situation a suitably weighted average that will predict his adaptation-level in perceiving and judging stimulus-variables of a particular class.

The concepts of pooling, weighted average, and adaptation-level thus make possible a quantitative theory and a mathematical procedure. The adaptation-level, mathematically, represents a weighted geometric mean of all the stimuli judged. The curve formed by plotting dimensional judgments (ordinate) against stimulus values (abscissa) rises rapidly below adaptation-level and then more slowly above. Generally speaking, adaptation-level occurs in the lower portion of the series of stimulus magnitudes.

An interesting and significant fact revealed by the experiments is that the adaptation-level is altered through using a different constellation of series, standards, or background stimuli, so that the perceived magnitude of an identical stimulus may become different from its previous estimates; and this phenomenon is not merely a matter of intellectual judgment—the stimulus actually *seems* different. The strong effect of introducing a standard of contrasting magnitude into a series is shown by a remark made by one of Helson's subjects. He said that it was considerably less fatiguing to use the 900-gram standard than to judge the weights individually "because the weights are so much lighter now." Actually the total weight so lifted was 4500 grams greater per series than it was in the series used for the single method of judging. Such is the effect of the level, reached through pooling, of the individual's perceptual adaptation.

TESTING THE THEORY: METHODS; NEW FORMULATIONS OF
PSYCHOPHYSICAL LAWS; OTHER VERIFICATIONS

Here then is a theory of perceived sensory dimensionality that is broader than the older psychophysical formula which merely linked the subject's report of just noticeable differences to the constant-fraction increments of the physical stimulus. Can the new theory, in addition to its many other uses, succeed in incorporating the earlier psychophysical data? This would be a good test of its generality and versatility. To make such a test one would think in terms of adaptation-level rather than the psychophysical indifference point at the present stimulus level and would average in (though by a different weighting) the standard, or comparison, stimulus along with the series-stimuli. A brief consideration of this procedure as reported by Helson (1947) will show how this venture was undertaken and will also provide an introduction to the methods used in adaptation-level work.

The subject-observer was told that he would be presented with two weights in sucession. After lifting the *second* weight he was to give a judgment of it by stating to which of the following categories it belonged:

> very, very heavy
> very heavy
> heavy
> medium heavy
> medium
> medium light
> light
> very light
> very, very light
> (or other categories which the subject might add)

The subject was further told that after he had judged a number of weights he would be given another set which he would judge in like manner. After a number of observations had been made he was cautioned: "Be sure you judge each weight as it is and not as you think it should be." It will be seen that there was no absolute categorizing of the meanings of the end terms or the "medium" of the scale. The subject was left free to interpret them as he wished. For purposes of computation these verbal judgments were translated into a decreasing set of numbers, the very, very heavy category being 90, the very heavy category 80, and so on down to 10 for the very, very light category, with the medium category at 50. The results were presented as the average judgments of a group of subjects. It should be noted that, although in presenting each stimulus a "comparison" or "standard" stimulus was also given as in psychophysical experiments, the judgment made by the subject was not, as in psychophysical experiments, a comparison between the second and the first (or comparison) stimulus, but was in terms of an absolute scale for the second stimulus alone, as above shown. The role of the comparison stimulus was provided for in the predictive equation. It was treated as one of the items that make up the pool from which the adaptation-level is established. In some experiments, where a comparison stimulus was not used, the instructions were changed to suit the method of single stimuli. The stimulus-series were composed of five stimuli increasing by regular steps, but by different intervals in different series.

The mathematical procedure for handling the data of the experiment was developed from another work of the author in the field of brightness vision. That method, as applied to the brightness dimension, involved the taking of a weighted logarithmic mean of all stimuli and background in the field times a constant. The choice of a logarithmic function was in harmony with the Weber-Fechner law as well as with the well-known principle of diminishing returns in social and economic situations. For the visual problems the formula found to be adequate was as follows:

$$AL = K(A_0^3 \bar{A})^{\frac{1}{4}}$$

where AL is adaptation-level, K is a fractional constant, A_0 is the brightness of the background, and $\bar{A}$ is the logarithmic mean of the brightnesses of the samples on the background. Adaptation-level is thus a weighted geometric mean in which the background is loaded three times as heavily as the log mean of all samples in the field. This equation was rewritten in logarithmic form and the symbols changed so as to fit the psychophysical problem of lifted weights. The stimulus series *as a whole* was weighted more heavily (by a factor of 3) than the comparison stimulus. At the same time the comparison stimulus, or "anchor," was made to affect the adaptation-level in the equation to a greater extent than any one of the series stimuli. A change in respect to the constant, K, was also made. With the predictive formula thus adapted to the lifted-weights problem computations were made, from the experimental data, of theoretical adaptation-levels for different experiments. These predicted adaptation-levels showed on the whole, fairly close agreement both with the observed "medium" judgments and with the corresponding data on the "indifference point" of psychophysical judgments as taken from standard tables. It was thus possible to use the adaptation-level concept for predicting psychophysical data and hence for generalizing the psychophysical relationship.

Helson's experiments were also addressed to the testing of a number of additional theorems deduced from the general theory. These included the following deductions: (1) the predicted equivalence of absolute (single stimulus) and relative methods for determining the adaptation-level when the comparison stimulus is chosen at about the log mean of the series; (2) the minimum stimulus effective as a standard in shifting the adaptation-level; (3) the greater effect of a stimulus upon adaptation-level when it is used as a standard (or "anchor") than when it is used as a member of the series; (4) the predicted effect of various types of stimulus-distributions; and (5) the effect of practice and past experience. The findings from testing these deductions were in accord with the general theory.

In a later article (1948) Helson carried further the adaptation-level translation of psychophysics by deducing what the "just noticeable difference" from adaptation-level (ΔA) in the judgment of a particular stimulus would be. He derived the formula,

$$\Delta A = k(X_i + A)/2$$

where A is adaptation-level, k is the Weber constant (p. 70), and X_i is the particular stimulus that is being judged at any given time. The weighting, which is here equal for the immediate stimulus and the adaptation-level, was found adequate for a wide variety of data.[2]

GENERALIZING THE THEORY; A HYPOTHETICAL MECHANISM

Aside from the experimental and theoretical demonstrations just reviewed, a considerable body of evidence has accumulated in support of the theory of adaptation-level. In color vision Helson (1948) has shown that the neutral point, that is, the point at which the stimulus appears achromatic, depends on the pooling of the amount of reflectance of the colored illumination with the effect of degree of brightness of the background, and that below the neutral point the illuminated object may reverse its hue. Experiments with lifted weights have shown that adaptation-level depends upon series and background stimuli. Certain time-order errors of judgment are

[2] See Caldwell, 1953, for an attempt to combine Helson's theory, the formulas of Weber and Fechner, and certain other psychological laws into a "unified field theory."

explained by the adaptation-level, as well as some specialized effects exerted by background stimuli. Changes of "perceptual fields," with corresponding changes in judgments of stimuli, have resulted from changes in adaptation-level, a reorganization that made previously positive stimuli appear neutral or negative. Influences of social stimulation on individual perception and judgment, exerted in relation to the size of the group, show that social interactions, also, may pool. Individual differences in estimates can be readily explained by differences in residual of stimulus-experience, or by personal differences in the weighting of various parts of the stimulus manifold. It is possible, says Helson, to change an underestimator into an overestimator, or vice versa, by a suitable selection of series and background stimuli. The possibility arises that personality differences, sometimes thought to be due to genetic constitution, can be explained as due to exposure to stimulating conditions that build up differences of adaptation-level.

Adaptation-level theory, as thus far presented, is merely a statement of an interdependent relationship among certain variables. It could hardly be said to rise to its full stature as a theory of perception unless an attempt were made to make it more explanatory. Some explanation has to be offered as to why the effects of all the various stimuli "pool," and of how the phenomena of pooling and weighted averaging take place. We need an answer to our familiar question of how the various elements of the perceptual aggregate (in this case the physiological effects of the many stimuli, series, comparison, background, etc.) are assembled and made to operate together. First, we need to know how they can act together at all, that is, the structure of their operation; and second, we must explain why such interoperation produces the mathematical result of a weighted geometric mean. Helson suggests for this purpose the use of a theoretical model of negative-feedback type devised by Pitts and McCulloch (1947). The model in question has to do with the neurophysiology involved in the visual fixation or centering of geometric figures, and operates on the supposition that the superior colliculi of the brain "calculate" the retinal coördinates of the center of the figure and transmit this "information" to the oculomotor centers. Since this model and its relation to adaptation-level theory will be discussed in Chapter 18 we shall reserve further description and comment until that time. Helson concedes that further elaboration of the model would be necessary for specific problems in connection with the general framework of his theory.

APPRAISAL OF ADAPTATION-LEVEL THEORY

The theory of adaptation-level has decided merits, as the reader will probably agree. It greatly broadens our understanding of perceived dimensionality and introduces new life into the old problems of psychophysics. The pooling and averaging principle is somewhat suggestive of the statistical concept of laws that has been applied to good advantage in physics and biology. Helson's ideas not only contribute to our insight into certain classes of perceptual phenomena; they also imply the possibility of a new approach in broader fields of behavior wherever quantities or intensities may come into play. The theory seems logical, parsimonious, and in good accord, thus far, with experimental findings. We must suspend judgment, for the present, as to whether, by the aid of the cybernetic model, it can fully explain those aspects of perception with which it deals. That it is a complete theory of perception may be doubted; and its author makes no such claim for it. He intends it "not so much to displace other theories as to supplement and broaden them." And in this purpose he has surely succeeded. Adaptation-level theory applies to some extent to color constancy; and it is integrated with psychophysics, as we have shown, in various ways, as, for example, in the fact that Weber's law enters in the derivation of a formula for predicting the judgment of members of a stimulus-series. It applies directly, of course, to sensory dimensionality and frame of reference.[3] An application of the theory to choice response in the perception of relationships (gestalt transposition effect) has been deduced by James (1953).

There are, however, limits to the extent to which such a theory *can* be generalized to cover the diverse aspects of perception. The very advantage which its author claimed for it is also its limitation. Any method that is centered on the purely quantitative aspects of phenomena, no matter how important or how truly a part of the whole picture these may be, is bound to lose sight of much that is both general and significant. In finding something that can be measured and computed one may overlook realities that are both essential and definable, yet not expressible in quantitative terms. The figural properties of the gestalt psychologists, the distinctive character of figures stressed by Hebb, the concrete meaning of objects and situations, and the predisposing or inhibiting effects of bodily states or

---

[3] Some attempt has also been made to extend its coverage to perceptual problems involved in social judgments and social change (Helson, 1948).

sets upon the perception of objects as such—all these are phenomena that require some kind of explanation in terms other than, or in addition to, bare quantities and dimensions. And this is true notwithstanding the fact that the dimensional law of adaptation-level may also be holding good in all these cases. The perceived object or situation cannot be all dimensions; there must be some type of *aggregate*, or structure, in order to give significance to the dimension itself. It remains to be seen whether the Pitts and McCulloch model will supply such a design. Order in nature, if not something more than quantities along a scale, is not really order in a fully meaningful sense.

Another point that seems not to have been fully worked out is the question of the weighting that should be attached to stimulus values because of their recency or "salience" in the subject's experience. The strongly selective aspect of perception and perceptual set also introduces conditions that go behind adaptation-level, in that this aspect probably establishes the confines of the pool within which the sensory excitations summate or average. When the individual is "giving attention" to some stimulus manifold and we have a behavorial aggregate of "dimensionally judging," the relevant excitations may be expected to pool themselves according to Helson's law. But what happens with respect to energies impinging on the subject's receptors from *outside* the manifold involved in the judging problem? What becomes of the "irrelevant" stimulations? One suspects that these might *not* pool themselves with the others by this law nor affect adaptation-level in the same way. The attempt to make this question operational might lead to some interesting disclosures. The fact that the question is logically meaningful suggests that perception has an aggregative and structural aspect that is something other than dimension per se and that must be included in our theory in order to permit the adaptation-level concept to serve its purpose. In other words, adaptation-level, like all frame-of-reference manifestations, implies a judgmental structure; and to understand this structure may be one of the conditions of understanding adaptation-level itself.

PERCEPTUAL NORM AND FRAME OF REFERENCE; WORK OF SHERIF

Adaptation-level theory is one phase of a more widespread movement in psychology to which the term "frame of reference" has been applied. The demonstration of adaptation to cold or warm stimuli and the concept of "physiological zero" are an old and familiar illustration of the same phenomenon at an elementary sensory level.

Experiments on judgment have been conducted that show the effects of "anchors" in producing shifts of a subjective scale with resulting displacement of estimates.[4] Sherif and Cantril have extended the notion to the study of attitudes and personality, to behavior in groups, and to cultural and societal phenomena generally, thus making it a basis for a systematic viewpoint in social psychology.[5] Starting with a classic experiment in which the judgment of the extent of "movement" of a spot of light in a dark room was found to be influenced toward the average of the spoken judgments of a group[6] Sherif developed his theory of "social norms." Such norms were believed to function within the frame of reference of a group (or set of group judgments) and to determine the dimensional characteristics of the individual's percept.

Owing to the impossibility of checking phenomenological reports for their accuracy (cf. Chapter 2) it is uncertain whether this phenomenon of convergence toward the mean is strictly a matter of perception or a tendency, when in a judgmental situation occurring within a collective aggregate, to behave in a manner consistent with the behavior of others. The line between perception and judgment is admittedly hard to draw; but if Sherif's finding represented the latter, it might be considered as an evidence of a conforming tendency of individuals when in collective situations rather than as a phenomenon of perception in the strict sense of the term. The present writer earlier found this same convergence effect in the judging of pleasantness of odors and heaviness of weights in the collective, as compared with the solitary, situation (1924, Chapter XI). Here the subjects did not communicate, and so no "social norm" could have been established. They might have been in effect "conforming," however, in that they avoided extreme (i.e., socially improbable) judgments when working in the group.

But whatever we may call it, there is clearly established in collective situations (of a certain sort, at least) a tendency toward a uniform level of behavior for the group-members, or, as we might say, within the "framework of the groups' activities." And the phenomenon seems similar to Helson's adaptation-level in experiments on perceptual judgments. When communications occur among the group members

[4] For reference citations see Helson, 1948; also Postman and Miller, 1945.

[5] See Sherif, 1936, 1948; also Sherif and Cantril, 1945, 1947 (Chapter 3). For an excellent account of the phenomena of frame of reference see Asch, 1952, pp. 55–70. The relation of perceived position and motion to a framework is one of the many applications of the idea brought out in the reference last cited.

[6] The spot of light did not really move. The "perceptions" that were involved represented an illusory phenomenon known as the "autokinetic effect."

we might expect the convergence tendency to be increased. In such a situation, the series, background, and residual stimuli of Helson's experiments would be replaced by the individual's observations, past and present, of the behavior of others in the group. By a pooling and averaging of these evidences a "social norm" might be established in the individual that would affect not only his judgments, but his values, beliefs, and even his conduct, within the "frame of reference" of the group. Conduct and beliefs are judged as extreme (and therefore as unacceptable) in one direction or the other according to the degree in which they deviate from this collective norm. The parallel with adaptation-level in perception is therefore close. In the writer's opinion, however, the terms norm and frame of reference are in need of more explicit definition and denotation in order to qualify them for use in the construction of an explanatory theory.

The well-known phenomenon of "level of aspiration" is another example of a judgment made within a frame of reference in relation to some norm. It represents a prediction by an individual of his own achievement in some definite future task; and it employs as residuals a knowledge of his past performances, of his abilities, and perhaps of the performances of others. It also contains, under some conditions, a strong component of striving or some type of "ego-centered" reaction. This trend in social psychology could take us far afield from our present topic; but it also bears upon perception in the broader usage of the term in which distinctions between perceptual and cognitive processes are not made.

If we examine frame-of-reference theories closely we find in them a common weakness. So impressed were their authors by the relativity of behavioral quantities to the frame of reference, that they slighted the search for a theory of those *non*-quantitative aspects that are necessary to explain both the meaning of the frame and the potency of the central tendency that is called the norm. Those aspects were not altogether overlooked, but their treatment was inadequate. It was sometimes almost assumed that a "normative quantity," all by itself, can act to control perception. On the quantitative side in perception, Helson has gone far beyond other theorists in that he has analyzed the factors entering into subjective-scale judgments and has stated a mathematical formula by which to predict the dimensional judgments of an individual when we know the particular circumstances by which he is faced. In norm and frame-of-reference theories the operational meaning of the norm has always been much clearer than that of the frame. What Helson has shown, in clarifying this question, is that the dimensional frame does not constitute a pair of terminal magnitudes that establish between them a definite scale of reference. Such "frame" stimuli affect the judgment only through the part they play with *other* stimuli in determining the adaptation-level. The norm that lies within the frame thus becomes the focus of our interest, and the frame becomes merely the extreme cases in the statistical distribution. The problem of the frame, however, is far from solved and will probably take us eventually into regions hitherto unexplored. Perhaps it is not a frame of reference which we are seeking, but some general principle of structuring. Just as we observed that an understanding of the judgmental aggregate in behavior is necessary for a full comprehension of the perceptual adaptation-level, so we may also find that an understanding of collective structuring and its relation to individual behavioral aggregates is needed for an explanation of the dimensional "social norm." Whatever the answer may be, it is clear that the phenomena now called norm and frame of reference, as well as the more precise concept of adaptation-level, add another chapter to the fascinating, though bewildering, story of perception.

Functional and Molar Standpoints
Probabilistic and
Transactional Functionalism

What is it that gives order, in the quantitative sense, to our perceptions? How can we account for dimensional stability in the way things look? We have seen that Helson sought an explanation through combining dimensionality with the perceiver's level of adaptation. In this chapter we shall consider two other answers to this question, both of which seek to explain the stability of perception from the standpoint of its adaptive function for the organism. Egon Brunswik,[1] whose theory we shall first present, is, like Helson, interested in an order of a dimensional sort, but the stabilizing factor that most commends itself to him comes not from frames of reference, but from the constancies of perception. He seeks an anchorage in the environmental object which the individual is trying veridically to perceive. In both his system and Helson's there is a functionalistic note; for the attainment of some stability in the perceived world is one of the first requisites of a successful adjustment. Both theories envisage the formation of the percept as the combining of the elements of an aggregate. The nature of the aggregate, however, and the procedure by which this combining takes place follow different principles in the two theories. Adaptation-level implies a "molecular" basis of explanation; Brunswik eschews molecularism. In his work the "molar" viewpoint is employed as a basis for perceptual theory.

To introduce our account of Brunswik's theory let us first recall briefly the nature of constancy phenomena. A man seen across the street, half a block or so away, or at any intervening position appears to be about the same size as when he is seen a few feet away. Hence the effect of a constant size obtains within moderate distances regardless

[1] 1936, 1939a, 1939b, 1943, 1944, 1949, 1950. See also Bruner and Krech, eds., 1950, pp. 56–65; Ansbacher, 1937; and Tolman and Brunswik, 1935.

256

of the size of the retinal images in the perceiver's eyes, a pattern of
stimulation which of course varies greatly in size with the distance.
Similarly, objects hold approximately their true shapes in spite of
changes that differences in angle of regard and perspective-distortions
produce in the retinal image. Objects seen under illuminations of
varying wave length, if surrounding conditions are not cut off from
observation, retain for us to a considerable degree the hues they have
when seen under achromatic illumination. Here then, in what is
called "thing-constancy," is the manifestation of order that Brunswik
has used as the basis of his theory. How, in spite of an almost infinite
variety and shift of stimulus conditions, the individual perceptually
attains the objects of his environment in a stable manner, what kinds
of objects can be so attained and with what degree of accuracy—these
are the problems to which the theory is addressed.[2]

DISTAL RELATIONSHIPS; "INTERMEDIATE OBJECTS"; THE ROLE,
PROBABILISTIC WEIGHTING, AND COMBINING OF CUES

Constancy research, as Brunswik views it, concentrates upon
measured correlations between the environmental stimulus object and
the reactions of the organism, a correlation most important for life
adjustment. He criticizes gestalt and field theory on the grounds
of their incompleteness. They are interested only in that small space
in which some process occurs in the central nervous system, or in that
brief instant of time in which the cognitive topological field becomes
reorganized. Such a narrowing down of the perceptual aggregate
he stigmatizes as "a self-sufficient encapsulation of the perceptual
system." It will be recalled that Koffka had defined the process of
perception as the central organization to which the proximal stimulus
pattern gives rise, a statement that leaves out of account the more
distant object from which the stimulus energy originally comes.
Brunswik considers that constancy research is not really a part of
gestalt psychology and that such formalistic concepts as closure,
equilibrium, and prägnanz are not adequate to handle the distal
relationships involved in this phenomenon. For these latter we must
turn to the stimulus-object and its relation to the proximal pattern

[2] We should be on guard here against a possible misinterpretation. The word
"object" is used by Brunswik to mean some physical property such as shape or
size, rather than the complete object itself. In saying that an organism "attains"
an object he means that the organism perceives with approximate correctness
some property or dimensional magnitude of the object. For details of the history
of the constancy problem in size and shape see Boring, 1942, 255 ff., 290–299,
308–311.

of receptor stimulation. We must ask what the organism has to work with in perceiving size, for example, at varying distances, and how it uses such means as are afforded by the environment.

Perfect size-constancy, that is, exact correspondence between the phenomenologically perceived and physicalistically determined size of an object throughout varying distances, is not attained in perceptions. There is a sort of compromise between actual physical size, which is constant, and the size that would be inferred from the retinal image alone as that image decreases with increasing distance. The perceived size however agrees more closely with the physical than with the retinal-image size. Thouless (1931) spoke of a "regression to the real object," a statement that should be corrected to read "regression *toward* the real object." Brunswik (1933), however, preferred to regard the phenomenon as a transformation to an "intermediate object" (*Zwischengegenstand*). The fact that constancy is not completely attained is important in showing the nature of perceptual activity; and it is basic in Brunswik's system. Using all the data that are available, the organism, in conformity with the demands of biological adaptation, actively tries to "reconstitute" the object and comes somewhere near doing so. The process is not perfect or complete; but this does not matter, since the ordinary needs of the organism can be met if the object is only approximately attained. These considerations emphasize the fact that perception should be studied with a view to its adaptive function as a biological activity. Both Thouless and Brunswik developed formulas that dealt with the weight of each of the components in the regressive transformation and measured the tendency toward object-constancy that would result in a given case.

The problem, says Brunswik, can be handled only through a proper recognition of the role of "cues." In visual size-constancy, for example, these include the size of the retinal image plus various "distance cues," such as the muscular reactions of convergence and accommodation of the eyes, the disparity of the two retinal images, intervening or occluding objects, angular perspective, atmospheric effects, brightness, color, parallax of motion, and a number of others. These cues come from the distal object itself in combination with processes in the perceiving organism. The maintaining of veridical distal relationships with objects in the environment is dependent upon the trustworthiness, or statistical validity, of these cue-to-object relationships. This validity in turn is limited by the somewhat erratic nature of the environment, so that the attainment of distal objects is never better than an approximate or "probable" achievement. Brunswik therefore calls his type of theory, which deals with these environment-oriented relationships, a "probabilistic functionalism."

Such a probability of veridical perception is maintained by the following process. Where single cues lack trustworthiness, the organism effects a compromise between many of them on the basis of their respective probability weightings so as to assure as accurate an object-attainment as possible. Cues to distal stimulus-bodies can be arrayed in hierarchies and classified as good or misleading, etc., according to the degree of probability by which they are linked to the distal variables, that is, according to the likelihood that a given amount of the cue means a certain actual physical dimension of the body in question. In the face of the varying trustworthiness of cues the best the organism can do is to compromise between the cues afforded in the particular situation in such a way that its "posit" concerning the body approaches the best wager it can make on the basis of the combined probabilities, or past relative frequencies, of the relationships between these cues and the body. Cues of the lowest validity are given least weight in establishing the wager, and the greatest weight is given to cues of highest validity. The combined result of all these cues, each with its proper weighting, is the perception of the dimensional magnitude of the body in question. This perceived magnitude is the "object" as it is attained by the perceiver.

To indicate more definitely how this procedure takes place we may note that in the perception of the size of a body at a distance the "projective" size alone (area of the image on the retina) has relatively low probability value. Since the retina's image varies with the distance of the subject from the body in question, as well as with the size of the body, the distance must be known in order that a correct estimate of size can be given on the basis of the retinal image. The organism must therefore keep its reactions free from control by variations of projective size, a feat that can be accomplished by combining this property with *distance-cues* into a single unified whole or "gestalt." Thus the perceived size of a body may depend upon either a large retinal image combined with a cue for a short distance or upon a small retinal image combined with a cue for a long distance. In either case the *perceived* size will correspond fairly closely with the objectively measured size of the body.

The size of the retinal image itself is not really perceived or responded to as such; it is only the body-size which is attained as an object. That the organism centers itself, so to speak, by means of cue relationships, upon the distal object rather than the proximal (retinal image) is shown by the results of an experiment in which Brunswik correlated a series of estimates of the size of bodies (made with a naïve perceptual attitude) with the actual body sizes, and then correlated the computed size of the retinal images with the actual body sizes. The former type of correlation yielded coefficients approaching 1.0, while the coefficients of the latter type were between .2 and .7. That projective size, however, must enter as an element in the perceptual aggregate for size determination at a distance is, of course, obvious. Unless there were a retinal image of *some* size, there would be no occasion for a size judgment at all. Furthermore projective size exercises a persistent, though slight, influence all by itself. Size-constancy in perception is not perfect; bodies of a given size, instead of yielding a perfectly constant experience of size at varying distances, look just a *little* larger when seen near at hand than when seen farther off because of their larger projective sizes. Ratios can be developed to express the amount to which projective sizes interfere with the veridical perception of body size. Thus there might be a 95 per cent body-size constancy, and a 5 per cent influence of projective size by itself upon the perceived magnitude.

One factor entering into the probability appraisal may be a kind of wholesome distrust which the organism has acquired of *all kinds* of cues. For example, even the disparity of the two retinal images, a cue that usually gives us a reliable hint that we are looking into a dimension of depth, deceives us when it is produced by two flat pictures viewed in a stereoscope. Such facts may sway us toward allowing a slight influence to projective size per se in our perceptions of magnitude. This slight tendency to accept the retinal image at face value may "correspond to an actual slight objective probability that a large retinal image may be caused by a really large object [body] at various distances rather than by a really small object [body] at the same distances." A set of more or less generalized "implicit hypotheses" may thus be said to govern the perception. These have varying degrees of subjective certainty in accordance with which they will interact; and the perceptual result will be a kind of compromise among them.

Brunswik develops an interesting behavior-diagram representing the points of conceptual focus in differing psychological systems. We here attempt only an abridged verbal statement. On the left we can imagine the *distal object* (body); then, next toward the right, the *"proximal* object" (receptor stimulus pattern or projective size). Between the distal and proximal objects and centering about the latter are the various "cues" that receive weights as described. Next toward the right, after the proximal object, comes the central mechanism within the organism. Then, on the right hand side of that, follow the *proximal reactions* of perception or overt behavior. These are the "means" employed by the organism for securing the needed adjustment. The means, in turn, are followed by the *distal results* or "ends to be accomplished" by the organism in its adjustment to its surroundings, including changes which it makes with respect to the distal object.[3] The relation of means to ends in behavior follows the same principle of probabilistic selection and weighting with respect to the achievement of distal results that were employed in the cues-to-object relationship of the perceptual process. "Hypotheses" of probability that the end can be acheived by this means or that are employed. The scheme as a whole has, therefore, an interesting symmetry.

A PSYCHOLOGY IN TERMS OF OBJECTS

One of the tasks of an environmental psychology of this sort would be to discover the extent to which hierarchies of probabilities, both of object-cue and of means-end relationships, that exist in the environment are paralleled by similar hierarchies of probability-evaluation by the organism. In order to do this we would start by ascertaining the environmental probability-values for all the cues or means with reference to the usual life conditions of the organism as a universe to be studied. For example, we would want to find out what the correlation is, on the whole, between actual distance from observer to the object, on the one hand, and the number of intervening objects or the degree of atmospheric haziness, on the other. Brunswik reports certain exploratory results in the task of making such a purely environmental analysis. Features of the social environment are also included in these investigations, as in the judgment of characteristics of individuals' faces. For the purpose of such a canvass Brunswik points out that a revision of our practices of statistical sampling will be required. Instead of obtaining a carefully selected sample of the population of *subjects* we shall need to make samplings of populations of tests, environmental conditions, or typical life situations; and the usual requirements of statistical procedure, such as purposive selection or randomization, will need to be extended to the environmental domain. Another goal of probabilistic functionalism, or perhaps the same goal stated more broadly, would be to find out what

[3] From this point on we shall not try to distinguish between the usual meaning of "object" and the Brunswikian reduction of the term to a dimension or property. The reader can make the distinction wherever needed.

kinds of objects or distal end-results an organism is *able* to attain through perception or through action, and in all variations of circumstances, with a relatively high degree of accuracy. This work and the inventory resulting from it might be called a "psychology in terms of objects."[4]

THE MOLAR CONVENTION; STATISTICS AND CORRELATIONS VERSUS EXACT LAWS

There are certain methodological conventions employed in Brunswik's system that should be stressed. Is it important, one may ask, for us to study closely the details involved in all these cue-to-object or means-to-ends relationships? Do we need to know the physical or physiological trains of causes and effects in the sense-organs, and in the neurons and muscles, that mediate between the distal object and the end result or perceptual attainment of the object? Such "molecular" details, says Brunswik, are not properly a part of our study, at least not at this point. He would reserve them for the later investigations of psychologists. The proper way to start, he maintains, is to take the organism as a whole, in a "lump" fashion. We want to know *what* objects are attained; we do not care so much about *how* they are attained. In supporting this position our author makes use of the following argument. The cues that are employed in perception, as, for example, in size-perception, are not only numerous but highly varied. They even involve different senses (e.g., kinaesthetic and visual). Yet in spite of this difference, one type of cue may be readily substituted for another; and the object can be attained as well by using one combination of cues as by using another. The cues, in other words, are "equipotential"; and their particular characters or methods of operation are therefore not significant for the psychology of the organismic attainment of objects. Thing-constancy research is essentially molar and environmentalistic, not molecular, mediational, or physiological.

What the organism "as a whole" does in perception must, of course, remain a rather blurred concept. It lacks the precision of a more analytic molecular approach and is based, as we have seen, upon probabilities rather than certainties. Yet it represents the way in which the organism "focuses" upon the objects of its environment; and if we, too, take that same perspective in studying the organism, it

---

[4] The environment is even conceived as having among its events a "texture of causality" which the individual is able to perceive (Tolman and Brunswik, *op. cit.*).

will provide us, so Brunswik argues, with conditions that are truer to life than those in which the more exact or "nomothetic" laws of nature are sought. The case is similar to that of the study of the law of gravitation, in which there are so many disturbing variables that it is only under the most unusual and rigorously controlled situations that the nomothetic law can be demonstrated. As a second convention Brunswik therefore argues for the use of correlation series and statistics in psychological studies, as over against the search for exact laws. In their ultimate uses these two procedures may converge; but the former practice seems in better accord with the life situations of the organism. Probabilistic functionalism and the psychology of environmental objects thus constitute a unique approach to the problem of perception. They show us another way in which the problem can be viewed.

APPRAISAL OF BRUNSWIK'S CONTRIBUTION; AGREEMENT WITH FACTS

One feels in reading Brunswik the touch of an investigator who is trying to look at a complex psychological situation in the broadest manner possible, of one who has a high capacity for original thinking and is not afraid to throw off the limitations imposed by the tradition of exactness in laboratory procedure in order to take a new starting point from which facts essential for the understanding of life will not be missed. That the organism spontaneously and unconsciously combines many elements into a single unified impression, highly veridical when occasion demands, certainly seems to be a basic principle. We have seen how productive the notion of a spontaneous and unconscious pooling of the elements of the perceptual aggregate has been in the work of Helson. Something like it also occurred in the sensory-tonic field theory. The highly original and suggestive contribution of Brunswik is that such pooling can take the form not merely of a weighted mathematical average, but of a probability estimate. Physical studies dealing with the ultramicroscopic world show that a great number of our so-called laws of nature are really statistical resultants that emerge from a "swarm" of minute events which, taken one by one, are unpredictable—or perhaps we might say, to use Brunswik's term, untrustworthy. We may here be stretching the analogy too far; but, in any case, a law means prediction, and prediction is only a projection of the probabilities or frequencies of our past experience into the probabilites, not certainties, of the future. Though Brunswik's thinking is set in a functional and therefore somewhat purposive frame, it is interesting that the concept of probability, which is now looming so large in the physical and biological sciences, seems also to have a useful meaning in perception. Another strong point of Brunswik's theory is that it highlights an important but hitherto neglected aspect of the psychological aggregate, the objects and events in the organism's environment. The significance of these elements in relation to behavior should be better understood and incorporated more fully into our thinking.

The question of the theory's agreement with the facts need not detain us long. The theory itself is largely programmatic, with considerable stress upon methodology. It does not so much call for support from a body of knowledge already gained as it points the way to new methods of investigation. Its author, however, has conducted a number of experiments the results of which are in harmony with the demands of the theory. For example, a general agreement is found between the rating of distance cues in pictorial materials for environmental validity and the inferring of their corresponding subjective weighting by subjects in perceptual experiments in which the cues were brought into conflict. In another experiment in which rats were employed and in which Brunswik tested a variety of ambiguous means-end relationships, the rate of learning a means-end relation (which might be regarded as an indication of the weight the organism gives to the means in question) was found to vary with the combination of the relative frequencies (or probabilities) of the intra-environmental relationships tested. Though such demonstrations of the effect of probability of success upon the judgments or choices in perceptual behavior are necessary and need to be further developed, it is hard from an *a priori* standpoint to see how the facts *could* go against the theory. If most of our perceptions were not fairly veridical there might be more of a question. It is difficult to see how we could have veridical impressions unless our cues were weighted in some degree according to their trustworthiness. Holway and Boring (1941) found that, when all distance cues are eliminated except visual angle, apparent size varies with distance about as visual angle does: in other words, the size-constancy of the perceived object is lost. As the cues, differing in kind, are added, one at a time, the apparent size at different distances approximates more and more the normal constancy relationship. If these contributions toward constancy made by cues of different kinds did not increase as the probability that there is a reliable correlation between the cue and the distance to the object increases, constancy would be hard to explain.

CRITIQUE OF MOLAR AND FUNCTIONAL VIEWPOINTS IN PERCEP-
TION; INCONSISTENCIES OF MOLAR EXPLANATIONS

In applying the criterion of explanatory value to probabilistic functionalism some troublesome questions arise. Here the methodological convention of molarism and the functionalistic viewpoint present
awkward and perhaps unnecessary limitations. By removing from
the field of our interest those details which Brunswik calls molecular,
and particularly those that are located in the organism, we are reduced in our attempts at explanation to what happens at the boundary
of the organism and round about it. If gestalt theory is encapsulated
in the brain-fields of the organism, probabilistic functionalism is "ex-
capsulated"; and the perceptual aggregate available for experiment or
theorizing is certainly restricted as much in the latter case as in the
former. The whole picture, both inside and outside the capsule (our
old inside-outside problem), must be viewed in order to have a full
account. Brunswik states frankly that his theory is not concerned
with "explanation," but only with "description," and with that only in
a restricted or "lump-wise" sense. No criticism therefore can be
made of the theory insofar as it relates to what its author intended
it to do. It is certainly legitimate to limit one's self, if one wishes, to
external molaristic description such as that which is employed when
we say an organism attains an object or achieves an end-result. Our
objective, however, is not merely to criticize, but to take stock of the
present theoretical output by using standards that measure the extent
to which particular systems throw light on the whole problem of
perception. It is perhaps in place to point out that the terms explanation and description can be used in a sense different from that employed above. From our present viewpoint (Chapter 1), it should
be said that when we give what we call the "explanation" of a phenomenon we are not moving into a methodological area that is
different from description. We are only employing description in a
more highly generalized way and showing how the generalization ties
up with the particular phenomenon. From this standpoint the following question arises: Why, if we are interested in describing, should
we stop at the molar level of things; why should we not continue
with our description of the whole process until we really understand
how perception takes place?

The functionalistic orientation in psychology acts as a partner with
molarism in setting up a barrier to a full description of behavior. It
is likely to eclipse the detail of what is happening by putting it under

a blanket of "to what ends or purposes," or by being content with a statement of objects attained that are "significant for the organism's welfare." Brunswik says that questions of "what" are more important for psychology than questions of "how." A functionalist, however, is likely to construe both these terms in a manner different from that of an investigator whose main interest does not lie in function. "What," for the functionalist, in the connection we are referring to, means what end-products can be attained, what can be achieved by the organism. For one who describes in terms other than functional it means merely "what exists" or "what happens." The term "how" is likely to mean to the functionalist another function. It asks the question: How is something done by the organism or by some agency within the organism? It usually refers to some instrumentality, perhaps to some mechanism, by which the first, more broadly defined, objective of adjustment is carried out.[5] For the non-functionalist the meaning of "how," as illustrated in Chapter 1, is very different. It follows directly from his meaning of "what." It is only a matter of pressing further the question of what, of seeing *what happens* when the first what is stated in terms of more general principles of which the case before him provides an illustration.

In looking at the process of digestion one who takes a non-functional view does not consider it from the standpoint of its being a life-sustaining function of the organism; nor is he interested in it primarily as a means (or mechanism) by which the body carries on the necessary work of absorbing its food. Without denying the importance of such a viewpoint, he is merely interested in describing objectively, and in the most general terms, what happens when the aggregate of events that are referred to as digestion takes place. But he wants no barriers to his observation. He does not want to be stopped at the boundaries of the organism by the statement that digestion is a function of the molar organism. Nor does he want to be stopped at the surface of the stomach, or at any other point at which the functionalist might wish to stop and say, "There, that is the system or mechanism by which the function is carried out." He will always be ready to explore the inside as well as the outside structuring of any aggregate. If one takes the non-functional approach, the distinction between what and how is purely arbitrary. What happens in the macroscopic order leads us naturally and inevitably to what is happening in the microscopic.

Whether a functionalist is immediately concerned with the matter or not, there are many who would be eager to know what happens as

[5] Cf. Woodworth, 1948, Chapter 2.

this amazing process that we call the weighing of probabilities goes on—the process that is described functionally and macroscopically by saying merely that "the organism perceives its world with a constancy ratio of unity." This difference of viewpoint comes out sharply in the matter of cues. If one is a molar functionalist, his interest in the cues themselves and in the details of their interaction is likely to be short-lived. Of course, he would like eventually to see them reduced, perhaps by physiologists, to some sort of "intervening mechanism"— that unfortunate word again. But for the present, if the cues can be readily interchanged, with proper regard for the probable trustworthiness or utility of the ensemble, a functionalist's interest in them beyond that point is likely to wane. He is more engrossed in "end-results" than he is in "mediational processes." Certainly there are many psychologists who do not share this indifference regarding the operation of things that have equivalent functions. The discovery of the equipotentiality of cortical regions in habit-retention, for example, has not meant that we do not need to be any longer interested in the cortical mechanisms involved in learning.

It should be made clear that we are not here inveighing against a functionalistic approach. We are only making the point that there *are* these two ways of looking at the matter, each of which has its place. Functionalism, both in psychology and in the life sciences generally, is a viewpoint of the deepest human significance. The entire program of applied science is based upon this view. But more than that, with the skill of men like Brunswik functionalism is capable of being developed, as we have seen, in novel and fascinating directions and with due regard for both its scientific accuracy and its generalizing power. Functionalists, whose curiosity about nature is likely to be blended with an interest in the utility of what they learn, are perhaps not unlikely to assume that the non-functional point of view cannot, after all, be radically different from their own and that both will come out with complete agreement in the end. This might be true if what was regarded as the end was the same for both groups. If, however, as the writer suspects, the roads diverge, this happy ending may not be possible. The two groups may speak the same language, use the same terms, yet not fully understand each other. "Molecular," for the functionalist, will mean the minute details of a process that carries out some function toward an objective of organismic adjustment. For the non-functionalist the term will refer only to molecules—to an impersonal molecular process. To the functionalist "mediation" will mean a connecting link that is necessary for the transmission or carrying forward of a function. To the non-functionalist it will mean simply a link. A non-functionalist may suspect a functionalist of being "teleological" and of being unwilling to go to the bottom of things—perhaps not even decently curious; while in functionalistic quarters a man who is non-functional might be regarded as "cold" or, in any event, as a little "queer." The influence of the functional viewpoint in psychology has come to be so strong that some degree of lip-service to it has almost taken on the aspect of a respectable custom.

We have here a divergence which, in the interest of basic psychological theory, must be brought into the open and carefully examined. For the present the writer wishes merely to suggest that, in relegating to a subordinate position, even temporarily, the question of what goes on inside the organism, the theory of probabilistic functionalism has been needlessly deprived of an explanatory potentiality it might otherwise have possessed. We take note of the fact that Brunswik has acknowledged the desirability of extending our studies later in the molecular direction. We still believe, however, that there is here a deep cleavage, and that one should, in addition to expressing a functional interest, go back also to the beginning and work at the problems of perception from a standpoint in which considerations of function do not exercise a dominating influence or even materially enter. Otherwise, in trying to understand nature, we shall always be assuming that the most basic aspects of nature's plan are written in terms of the purposes that organisms, which are after all only a part of a broader natural process, experience. We shall therefore be always trying to pull ourselves up by our own human bootstraps. If taken by itself, functionalism has inherent limitations in the work of trying to formulate an adequate description or explanation of behavior. These limitations must, sooner or later, be faced.

When the *molar convention* is further imposed upon theory-building the difficulties increase, this time from a logical as well as an explanatory standpoint. We shall try to aim our discussion, however, not so much at Brunswik's theory as at the problem of perceptual theory in general. The molar viewpoint can be defined as the application to behavior of the gestalt dictum that the whole is more than, or at least different from, the sum of its parts, and that the parts if taken separately, even though all of them are taken, do not give us the reality of the whole. Let us consider, for example, the following simple description: the man runs. If we look at any part of the man separately, his shoulder, his trunk, or even a muscle of one of his legs, it cannot be said that that part "runs." A muscle does not run: it only contracts or extends. Running is a property or condition of the man as a whole. Here we have in a nutshell the essence of molar doctrine. Its application lies in observing and describing only what the man *as a whole* does; any finer observation, any formulation in terms of what the parts of the whole (muscle fibers, receptors, neurons, and so on) are doing is to be regarded as molecular and avoided.

We seem in our example to have come upon something pertaining to the whole, i.e., the descriptive term "running," that is pretty observable and definite. Does not this fact contradict our earlier statement in which we seemed to assert the indistinguishability of the whole and the parts? It will be remembered that our point was not that the whole does not exist, or that the aggregate cannot be experienced as a whole. We can look at a figure-drawing in such a way as to perceive it as a whole, or in such a way as to perceive its parts, just as we wish. And, similarly, in observing the behavior of an individual, we can at will observe either the man behaving as a whole or the action of the man's parts. We can see the man running or we can see his legs moving up and down. What we did say in an earlier connection (Chapter 5) was that it was impossible for us ever to make an actual, literal contact with any whole that was not at the same time a contact with one or more of its parts. That assertion still holds true for molar behavior, as one will discover merely by reaching out his hand and touching a person who is running. It holds also for visual as well as tactual observation at the relatively near distance at which organisms must be seen in order to describe their behavior.

But what does all this amount to, one may ask? Can we not observe the individual "*qua* whole"? Can we not attend to him as a complete behaving organism and proceed to make our studies and our records in strict molar fashion? It is obvious that we can. Such observation and record constitute a familiar, almost routine, performance in psychological laboratories. And can we not also state our *theories* in such terms? Yes, some influential theories of learning, as well as other theories, have been so stated. Though there are limits to the explanatory power of such theories, and though one has always to be on guard against the intrusion of "molecular" elements, it is clearly possible to pursue such a course. When we come to perception, however, the situation changes. For here the question of what goes on inside the organism obtrudes itself more insistently. Molecular details force themselves in and produce an inconsistency in our attempt to give a unified account, since they necessitate an operation on two levels at the same time. One might reply, however, that it is still not *necessary* to let them do so; if we are sufficiently on guard we can carry out a consistent molar description of perception. The functional approach will help us.

But let us look more closely. Out of the entire roster of perceptual cues that enter into the organism's attainment of visual size or distance at least five (convergence, accommodation, retinal-image size, disparity of the two retinal images, and the motion of near and far objects as projected on the retina) represent changes that *lie within the organism*. They *involve parts of the organism*, even though a distal stimulus situation is also involved in their production. In order, then, to be consistently molar, that is, to develop a theory that deals always and only with the reaction of the organism as a whole, we must leave this internal class of cues *entirely out of account*. Such an omission from the repertory, however, would seem to produce an unnatural division. It would also be an arbitrary limitation of the roster of items upon which the pooling or the probability of attainment of objects is based, and would therefore seriously hamper the theory. One might, of course, give up talking about cues altogether. But would this course not leave us in a barren state so far as the explanation of constancy is concerned?

But surely, one might protest, there ought to be some way in which we can talk about an organism reacting to its perceptual cues and still be molar. Is there no alternative? Yes, there is one, provided we can put up with an inconsistency. We can dodge the issue by *talking* as though these cues are not parts of the organism itself, but outside and therefore separable from it. One can then go on speaking about what *the organism* does in "weighing" or "combining" these cues with the feeling that one is not molecularizing the organism. In this case, however, we would be actually talking about a *part* of the organism (the larger part), though we assumed that we were talking about the whole. This assumed, but not actual, whole would be considered in perception as acting upon the parts (cues) which we had surreptitiously taken away from it. The organism would be attaining its objects by using parts of itself (its physiological cues) as tools. What, then, *is* the organism? It can hardly be said, moreover, that an organism that has been deprived of part of the normal physiological bases of visual perception affords a proper model for a perceptual theory. There appears, then, to be no way out of this dilemma except to give up the attempt to build a serious theory of perception upon a molar foundation.

It seems undesirable and unnecessary to encumber the probabilistic hypothesis with the molar restriction. Constancy in perception is so immediate and primitive a thing, and so far outside the subject's conscious or deliberate efforts, that references to *the organism's* "distrust" of its cues, or to their "evaluation" and "compromising" by an act of the organism as an agent, seem somewhat far-fetched. And perhaps our author intended such expressions as merely metaphorical or as a kind of intervening variable. We could try to think, in more denotational terms, of how the whole process of probability weighting goes on at the physiological level. Helson has endeavored to do this for the adaptation-level. The nature and operation of cues, instead of being relegated to the periphery of the inquiry, would then seriously challenge us; and to devise a theory that would explain the probability situation would enlist our greatest ingenuity. We might retain, if we wished, the molar statement of an organism reacting as a whole in such a way as to "attain its objects." We could thus have both a molar and a molecular view for different purposes. But we would have to be careful not to mix the two views, nor to bring them together, until we could properly do so by solving the inside-outside problem of the dynamic structure of the organisim's behavior. In the writer's opinion such a revision of statement and ultimate extension might remove the logical difficulties and place Brunswik's ingenious and valuable contribution upon a more consistent basis.

There are, of course, aspects of perception that probabilistic functionalism does not cover. While it has an answer for constancy and dimensionality, configurational features do not seem to be a part of its program, nor does the temporary state or set of the perceiver. Though it is said to be concerned with the attainment of objects, we have noted that it does not deal with objects in the full sense of the term, but only with dimensional or other abstracted properties. In particular, concrete object-character, or substantive meaning, has been left largely untouched. It is not clear how dimensional frame of reference would be explained. In the area of dimensionality itself we have seen that other theories, developed to meet other needs, have pointed to answers of a different sort. Quantitative order in perceptual experience has many varied aspects and has been approached from a number of standpoints. It will concern us again in the second functional theory to which the remainder of this chapter will be devoted.

TRANSACTIONAL FUNCTIONALISM OF THE AMES GROUP

Perceptional order and stability can be regarded not merely as a matter of the appraisal of cues, but also as a more dynamic relationship between the organism and the environment. When percepts are attained their attainment is likely to involve direct participation in some process of overt adjustment. Perception and action can be seen to have a close functional relationship. Such a trend in perceptual theory is represented by a group of psychologists who have worked with Ames at the Hanover Institute for Associated Research. The system which they have developed rests upon two pillars. The first of these is a series of very ingenious and striking experimental demonstrations developed by Ames.[6] The second pillar is a philosophical theory of *"transactions"* recently put forward by Dewey and Bentley. The former, empirical, support, in the writer's judgment, is the more important. The latter seems to be mainly a philosophic rationale for defining perception in a manner usefully related to the experiments. The pragmatic philosophy of Dewey and Bentley serves modern functionalism in much the same way that post-Kantian idealism provided a philosophical underpinning for gestalt.

The relationship between psychological transactionism and Brunswik's probabilistic theory is close. Both deal with the *dimensional,* or *positional,* aspect of perception; both are, in general, molar; both rely upon past experience; both give a strategic position to cues and their probabilistic weighting; both involve unconscious inferences or judgments of the perceiver; and both find for the percept a kind of intermediate ground, or existence, between the stimulus object and some activity of the organism. Although other perceptual theories have a functional note, sometimes a strong one, most of them are functional only by implication or as a kind of by-product. Both the Brunswikian and transaction systems, on the other hand, seek to use the functional aspects of perception as the central idea in its explanation. They can therefore be regarded as the functional theories of perception *par excellence.* The main difference between them is that, whereas probabilistic theory is concerned chiefly with the phenomenological "attainment" of perceptual "objects," transactional functionalism includes a more specific statement of the perceptual significance of action and purpose.

For the sake of concreteness we shall approach the main tenets of the transactionists, first, through a brief analysis of some of the experimental demonstrations.[7] Probabilistic and transactional func-

---

[6] A number of the more important, including apparatus-construction and method, have been admirably described by Ittelson, 1952.

[7] The sources here include Ittelson (*op. cit.*), Ittelson and Kilpatrick (1951), Kilpatrick (1954), and Ames (1951). Further accounts will be found in Kilpatrick (1952), Lawrence (1949a and b), and Ames (1953). The first of the latter group is a useful manual containing a compilation of demonstrations, researches, and papers on method and theory.

tionalism are both descendents of the Helmholtz theory of unconscious inference. In that doctrine it was said that the organism infers
the nature of the perceived object by judging (unconsciously) what
physical object, or set of object-dimensions or properties, would need
to be present in order to produce the present pattern of stimulation
upon the receptors. A possible implication of this statement might
be that there is a certain *unique* physical object or set of object-
properties that will produce such a stimulation-pattern, and that the
organism has therefore only one possibility of interpretation. If it
makes this inference, a veridical percept of the object will be attained.
What is perceived through unconscious inference would thus be determined by, or in accordance with, the physical character of the
object. The inferring organism exercises little or no initiative other
than inferring the "reality," unless he is tricked by conditions into
making a false inference. In the latter instance, the Helmholtzian
functionalist might disregard the percept as having little meaning
other than that of a "miscarriage" of unconscious inference.

As we saw, however, in Chapter 2 (pp. 42–43), stimulation-patterns are *not* always unique for the objects from which they come. It
is possible to arrange conditions in such a way that a number of physical configurations will produce an identical pattern of stimulation
upon the eye or ear. For example, one sound given in the median
plane may produce a stimulation-pattern equivalent to that afforded
by two equal sounds, one opposite each ear. Here the cues afforded
are ambiguous in their object-reference, and there is room for choice
by the organism as to what kind of external object or object-properties
will be inferred. Under such conditions the resulting percept may be
either veridical or non-veridical; and there is opportunity for the
operation of some process that is not so stimulus-bound, some activity
within the organism that may be more influential in determining the
nature of the experience.

That such a process is present and active, and that it can be demonstrated when the above conditions are fulfilled, are strikingly shown
by the Ames experiments. Ambiguous conditions of stimulation-ob-
ject reference are here freely exploited, and there results a rich yield
of phenomenological report from which theoretical constructs can be
elaborated. Unconscious inference, to which the transactionists now
give a different name, can thus become a more useful hypothesis. If
we are careful to make the stimulus conditions ambiguous and to provide the opportunity for a non-veridical report, it can reveal both the
presence and the nature of "assumptions" made by the subject regarding the "probable character" of the object. In this way we can

discover the part played by the subject's own past experience in developing and using such bases for his unconscious inference in a particular situation. The eliciting, by artificial or unusual conditions, of a non-veridical perceptual experience is thus used as a method for throwing light upon the more normal, or veridical, process.

How can a stimulation-pattern be set up on receptors that will be ambiguous, that is, that will be identical for different physical objects? This can be done in many ways. An identical stimulation-pattern can be produced by a short line at a short distance from the observer or a longer line at a longer distance. A certain increment or decrement of brightness (intensity) of the retinal image can be produced either by moving the object forward or backward under constant light or by varying its illumination at a constant distance. The *size* of the stimulation-pattern can be controlled either by distance or by actual change of the size of the object. By the use both of varied size and varied brightness an identical size *and* brightness pattern can be produced in different ways. Small balloons that can be inflated to different sizes and illuminated to different intensities are used to produce retinal patterns of these two variables and their combinations. A window frame that is trapezoidal[8] in shape and placed in the frontal plane of the subject can make the same pattern on the retina that is made through perspective by a rectangular window frame that has been rotated to a certain degree about its vertical axis.

Foreshortening provides an excellent method of producing ambiguous stimulation-patterns. When we remember that space around us is three-dimensional, while the retina is more like a two-dimensional surface, it will be seen that a long line that is slanted at an angle almost equal to that of the visual axis (that is, almost perpendicular to the frontal plane) will subtend the same angle on the surface of the retina as a much shorter line that is more nearly at right angles to the visual axis. Any number of object-configurations can be made by using this principle, all of which will produce the same pattern of stimulation upon the receptor surface. For example, in one of the Ames demonstrations the subject looks successively with one eye into three peep-holes in the compartment for each of which there is an arrangement of white strings. Each of the arrangements is different from the other, and one is quite helter-skelter. In each

---

[8] The "trapezoid" used in these experiments is a four-sided figure in which two sides are vertical and parallel, but of different lengths; and the top and bottom side, if the longer vertical side is at the left, slope downward and upward, respectively, from left to right.

case, however, the subject has exactly the same percept—he "sees" a *chair* of constant dimensions and appearance, and at a definite distance. Both retinal-pattern equivalence and phenomenological identity are here produced by extremely varied physicalistic arrangements.

Using the same principle, small distorted rooms have been designed for studying perceptual processes. In one of these the left wall is made larger than the right, the floor is sloping, and the rear wall is set obliquely with trapezoidal windows of different size. The interior of this room, however, when it is viewed monocularly by looking into it through a peep-hole at a certain place in one of its walls, produces upon the observer's retina the same spatial pattern as a normal rectangular room. Actually an infinite number of such rooms could be made, all identical in projected stimulation-pattern with a given "normal" room. There is, in these unusual situations, an almost unlimited opportunity for the assumptions concerning rooms which the subject carries about with him to play their role in his perceptions and to reveal their nature and origin through the errors of perceiving to which they give rise.

What is the perceptual experience of the observer who views these ambiguous stimulus arrangements, and how is it to be explained? Here are a few typical cases. (In general only one eye is used; though binocular additions and adaptations are provided in some instances.) The subject, seated in a dark room, is shown two points of light equally distant from him, one of them brighter than the other. (Actually the same retinal pattern could have been produced by points of equal brightness at different distances.) The subject here perceives the brighter point as being nearer than the other. What is the reason for this choice of unconscious inference as over against the alternative perception of unequal brightness at the same distance? We must here look to the subject's "assumptions." The explanation is given that the subject "assumes," on the basis of the "most probable" occurrences from past experience, that the two points of light are "similar," that is, of about equal brightness. He therefore perceives the one which is brighter as being nearer.

To take another case, the subject looks at two vertical lines that are of unequal length but at the same distance from him. The retinal pattern thus presented could have resulted either from two lines of the same length at different distances or from two lines of unequal length at the same distance. The former experience constitutes his perception because of his assumption that the lines are probably physically similar. If an object is placed so that, from where the observer sits, its edge is seen to butt against a board (though it does not actually do so), it will be perceived to be at the same distance as the board (assumption of "togetherness"), and this appearance will determine its apparent size according to the distance at which the board is perceived to be (which is, in turn, the result of an assumption regarding the meaning of certain distance cues). There are similar assumptions as to the distance of an object that result from its being known to be *what* it is, that is, as a familiar object of a known physical size. More weight is given by the observer to some cues than to others in judging distance. Size, for example, is more influential than brightness; and the overlapping of objects is one of the very strongest of cues. We see here an identity with Brunswik's principle of probability weighting.

All these indications or cues as to position, size, and distance, as well as the assumptions from past experience to which they are related, operate immediately and *unconsciously*. We are not aware of the assumptions which underlie our perceptions. But they are, notwithstanding, very tenacious and may sometimes persist even when we "know" the true state of affairs and realize that it does not justify the perception to which they lead. When the various cues of the stimulation-pattern are related to the same set of assumptions the result is a strong or "sure" perception; where they are related to contradictory assumptions the percept lacks surety, and action based upon it is more tentative.

The rotating trapezoidal window frame is a dramatic masterpiece of ambiguous stimulation, producing effects as uncanny as any to be found in the whole repertoire of perceptual illusions. Viewed monocularly at about ten feet away, the window, though actually rotating, is seen to *oscillate back and forth*. A small cube attached to one side, however, is seen to move in true circular fashion and, in part of its course, to leave the frame and float through the air, passing in front of the "oscillating" window and returning finally to the original point of its attachment. A straight tube of paper thrust through one of the apertures of the frame is seen in part of its course to rotate in a direction opposite to the movement of the window. When the two meet the tube is seen to bend about the window-frame and then, with further turning of the latter, to straighten itself out again.

In the first of these effects the assumption is operative that the window, like most windows in our experience, is *rectangular*. Since it is perceived as rectangular the physical difference in length of the two vertical sides is interpreted as due to perspective changes in the window when it is in a turned position. But the perspective indication will not "ring true" if the window turns completely around.

Reversal of direction at a certain point is phenomenologically required in order to make size and prespective changes "come out right" and thus tally with our assumption of the window's rectangularity. The rotating window is therefore seen not as rotating but as oscillating. The perceived circular travel of the cube, which is a veridical perception, is explained by perceiving the change in apparent size under the (correct) assumption of the movement of an object toward us and away from us. We see the tube "bend" because the cue of overlay is so strong. We must assume either that it does bend, or else disregard the fact that it overlaps the window frame and see it as passing through gaps in the mullions of the window (a less probable assumption). The tube, however, can be seen as "cutting through" the window frame if we are told that it is made of "rigid material." We thus hold on to certain presumptive aspects and relinquish others; and we perceive in accordance with these assumptive emphases. Those indications to which we cling are said to be the ones which, on the basis of experience, have the greatest "prognostic reliability" with respect to our own potential action in the situation.

The distorted-room effects are equally dramatic. The room itself looks perfectly normal (i.e., rectangular), since, as we have said, its pattern on the retina is identical with that of a normal room (and we assume normal rooms to be rectangular). Normal objects placed in the room, however, appear distorted or out of proportion. Under the assumption that the room at which we are looking is normal and rectangular we see a man looking at us from each of the two rear windows. Under these conditions the two faces ought to appear to be of approximately the same size. But one face is actually much nearer to us than the other and therefore subtends a larger angle on the retina. The assumption of equal distances to the plane of the rear wall of a rectangular room therefore makes this face, as compared with the other, appear enormous. Such an upset, if we wish to keep our poise and sense of order in a natural world, compels us to revise our previous assumptions. The process, however, is difficult because of the firmness and unconscious character of those assumptions. What is required in order that such a revision can take place? The solution of the problem brings into focus the important principle of *action*. Let us try to *act* with reference to the room by hitting a spot on the rear wall with a ball, or by tracing the border of that wall with a wand. At first we make many errors. But with practice we find that we can succeed and can gradually learn more about the true spatial properties of the room. We come now to a very important point. *As this overt exploration proceeds something very significant happens to our perception of the room.* Its appearance gradually changes, and we come to see it more nearly as it is—*that is, as a room that is distorted in certain ways.* Perceptual learning has thus taken place. The perception of the particular distortion in the room will even be transferred (presumably within time limits) to the appearance of a normal, or a (dissimilarly) distorted, room.

The transactionists point out that the alteration of the original percept cannot be due to the stimulus situation or to the retinal pattern from the object, for these do not change. Moreover, normal and distorted rooms alike present the same stimulation-pattern upon the retina. The alteration of the percept is due, rather, to the change in the perceiver's assumptions about his world, a change which comes about through the acquisition of new clues as a result of his own action. We now have new perceptions which can, in turn, be taken as the basis of further actions; and these actions will, in their turn, confirm or deny, in specific situations, the assumptions upon which they are based. The principle of the intimate relationship of perception and action, and of both of these to our changing assumptions, is generalized by the transactionists and is considered to typify the continuing process of life adjustment in a changing and somewhat unpredictable world.

Having traced the procedures by which the tenets of the theory were derived from the experiments, let us now try to state these principles in a more formal and connected fashion. The following list, arranged by the present writer, covers only the major propositions. It will be seen that in some respects they follow directly as interpretations of the demonstrations, while in others they are derived not from empirical data, but from philosophical postulates or normative considerations.

1. The true, or objectively described, nature of a stimulus-object or situation is not given to perception by the stimulus-object itself, nor by the proximal pattern of stimulation from the object as presented upon the receptors. The demonstrations with stimulation-patterns having cue-ambiguity show that the experience of the actual properties of the object must be provided, when it *is* provided, by the combined operation of the object and the *perceiver.* There is a "transaction" between the organism and the environment.

2. In this process of perceiving, the past experience of the organism plays an important part.

3. Basic to the process is the fact that the organism has built up certain *assumptions* about the world in which it lives. These assump-

tions, which are usually *unconscious,* are based upon the principle that that external object or situation which has in the past been associated most frequently with the particular stimulation-pattern (cues) now presented to the organism's receptors will be the most probable one on the present occasion. The process of making assumptions is thus one of attaching significances to indications, or cues, from the environment. Perception is the process of apprehending *probable* significances. Assumptions thus represent the "weighted average" of the individual's past experiences. They are, in general, valid; but as referring to particular occasions of perceiving they may sometimes be false.

4. These assumptions, whether true or false for the immediate circumstances, constitute the basis for the present percept. The percept will be in accordance with them. As the organism assumes, so it will also perceive.

5. The assumptions underlying perception are not only derived from actions of the past; they provide, through their resulting percepts, a basis for action in the present and future. Perceptions are "prognostic directives for action."

6. In those cases where the particular assumptions operating at the moment yield a perception that is false with respect to the environmental situation the disparity will be experienced as a "hitch" that occurs when one tries to *act* in the situation on the basis of that perception. The percept will be seen not to fit the case. Adjustive action, however, may be accomplished through training; and as this process takes place new assumptions are formed and a new and different percept is acquired. This process may go on indefinitely since environmental arrangements and their cue-patterns are always shifting. Perception may be regarded as "the product of the continual recording of the relatedness of things as defined by action."[9]

7. There are differences (as well as universal aspects) in the assumptions (and hence in the perceptions) of different persons, because of differences in past experiences.

8. All the presently existing assumptions of an individual, taken together, constitute what may be called his "assumptive world." It is the only world he knows, and it determines the way he perceives the (physicalistic) world at any particular time.

[9] In the statement of this and preceding propositions the writer has drawn upon an article by Ittelson (1951). The reference to action should not mislead the reader into thinking that we are here dealing with a *motor* theory of perception. "Action" is used in the overall *molar* sense, not as involving the modification of the perception by returning proprioceptive impulses.

9. Emphasis upon action in the foregoing propositions points to the further question of "action for what?" Behind all intentional or adjustive action lies *purpose*. Perception is the process by which an individual attributes to his immediate environment the significances which he has found from previous experience *to have furthered his purposes*. Though perception represents a mixture of uncertainty and of action on the basis of a faith that our assumptions are correct, and though we create out of "probabilities" a world of functional certainties or "absolutes," these absolutes are nevertheless subject to modification whenever actions based on them fail to fulfill our purposes. (Ittelson and Cantril, 1954.)

10. The reference to purpose in relation to action and perception leads to a further question: "What purposes are here involved?" The answer lies in the whole realm of the characteristic human values toward whose ultimate realization the immediate purposes of individuals are directed. Social relationships and allegiance to the values of reference groups are also to be included as determiners of purpose and attitude and, through these, of perceptions. The process of living can be construed as the achieving of the individual's values through the physical and social environment via action and the perceptual process.[10]

11. As for the specific nature of perception, it is to be regarded as a transaction involving both the organism and the environment. It is not the activity of the organism, independently considered as acting upon, or reacting to, the environment; nor is it the environment independently considered as stimulating or acting upon the organism. Neither the concept of "*self*-action" nor that of "*inter*action" successfully describes the phenomenon of perception. The proper term is "*trans*action." It is the "interoccurrence" or happening itself that takes place between organism and environment. Indeed, neither the organism nor the environment can be completely understood without taking into account this interrelationship. For any object, according to transaction theory, derives at least a part of its very nature and comprehensibility from its participation in a total situation.[11] Such a present participation, or transaction, which constitutes the essence of perception, has its roots in the past experience of the individual, and its implications extend into the future. The world of phenomenological experience is a world of significances provided by such trans-

---

[10] See Cantril (1947, 1948, 1950a and b), Cantril et al. (1949, Part III), and Hastorf and Knutson (1949).

[11] Cf. core-context theory and our reduction of it, in Chapter 4, to "inside" and "outside" meanings or structurings.

actions.   These significances, resulting from past transactions, the perceiver "externalizes" as the basis of his present and future action.[12]

Such, then, is the meaning of perception as seen from the viewpoint of the second of the two major functional theories.   We turn now to a brief appraisal.

CRITIQUE OF TRANSACTIONAL FUNCTIONALISM

The proponents of the theory just reviewed make no sweeping claims as to its validity or scope.   It is presented as having a certain manifest "reasonableness" and as offering a useful first approximation to the explanation of the phenomena.[13]   From a practical standpoint it seems very meaningful as an account of the function of perception in daily life; and it helps us to bring to bear, in thinking about perceptual adjustments, the ever-present pragmatic considerations of purpose and value.   From the standpoint of its adequacy as an explicit explanation of the perceptual process, however, it appears, upon closer examination, to be in somewhat the same position as Brunswik's probabilistic theory, and largely for the same reasons.   It is strong in the areas where that theory is strong, and insufficient in areas where the latter is found wanting.   There is, however, one exception to this statement.

As to the particular facts elicited in its support, the theory is on good ground.   The demonstration of the multiplicity of possible equivalent stimulus situations which necessitates the participation of the organism in perceiving, and the evidence that action plays an important role, are incontestable and striking.   As was the case with the probabilistic weighting of cues, it seems unlikely, also, that perceptual facts in general will compel us to reject, from a functional standpoint, the theoretical interpretations given.   We would not expect the perceptions of an individual to be either inverse or unrelated to his assumptions or his actions.   The conceptual scheme presented is also parsimonious and unified.   As to generality, it has answers, like Brunswik's theory, for both the dimensional and the constancy aspects of perception.   Ittelson, for example, (1951) handles constancy by

---

[12] The philosophical theory of transactions will be found in Dewey and Bentley, 1949.   A brief statement and a discussion of its application to perception are given in a series of articles by Cantril, Ames, Hastorf, and Ittelson (1949).   See also Ittelson and Cantril, 1954.   For a more direct application to the phenomena of the Ames demonstrations see Lawrence, 1949b.   A vivid case-study applying transactionism to perceptual attitudes is presented in Hastorf and Cantril, 1954.

[13] Cf. Ames, 1951.

treating it as the effort of the individual to establish and maintain a world "which deviates as little as possible from the world which he has experienced in the past." This is the world which has been built up through his assumptions on the basis of past experience; and it "offers him the best possible chance of acting effectively and continuing to experience the particular satisfactions which he seeks out of living." It is to be noted, however, that Ittelson embraces under the term constancy the many instances in which the percept is non-verdical, that is, in which it "deviates markedly from the objective world." By this extension, however, do we not lose a traditional and sharp significance for the term constancy that is important, even from a functionalistic standpoint? Perhaps at this point Brunswik is on surer ground.

In the field of configuration, another area in which we must test its completeness, the theory offers some suggestive interpretations through the "assumption of togetherness" and the close, interdependent, relationship of cues. A "frame of reference" is also provided. This occurs, for example, in the assumption of the rectangularity of the distorted room and the assumptions involved in viewing the trapezoidal window, assumptions that determine the way in which objects within, or associated with, the frame are seen. The perception of objects also shifts when these "framing" assumptions change. This frame, however, is of a different type from those considered in Chapter 10; and it is not clear how it would explain gradual and average adaptations at the more sensory level, such as those described by Helson. Set and prevailing state of the perceiver are covered to the extent that one can consider assumptions to be sets, or that individual differences of assumptions reflect characteristics of personality. It would be difficult, of course, to deduce some of the phenomena of set and its relation to action and motivation from the purely spatial demonstrations employed in transactional functionalism. Set, rather than assumption, seems to be the more generic concept. It is true that both set and assumption are unconscious, both include facilitative and antagonistic relationships, and there are many other points of similarity. In regard to object character or substantive meaning, the theory, in its present spatially oriented form, has little to offer. It *employs* object character in its demonstrations of the fact that "what an object is" is related to its apparent location and size (dimensional properties); but it does not *explain* object character. On the whole, however, it must be conceded that transactional functionalism has some capability for generalization and is broader than the functional system of Brunswik.

The test of direct experimental availability of concepts finds the two theories in about the same status.   As long as one sticks to the molar point of view, the organism as a whole affords denotation at a gross level of contact.   In the transactional theory it is possible to give to assumptions and significances the status of an "intervening construct." A "hitch" can also be operationally defined in terms of observable elements.   When it comes to a finer grain of denotation, however, these concepts, like the probabilistic weighting of cues, are elusive. So also are "participation" and the exact character of the transaction-matrix that is said to involve the organism and environment.   Where denotation is lacking, the explanatory usefulness of a theory suffers. How does the percept, which is a phenomenologically experienced item, or an assumption, which is both unconscious and non-denotable, *steer* action, a molar observable having clear physicalistic properties?   Or, stating the matter in reverse, how can action act upon and alter assumption and perception?   How do assumptions "ascribe signifi-cances" to cue-patterns?   Or again, what references exist for such terms as "purpose" and "value" that will enable us clearly to describe their operation in the perceptual process?   It will be noted that we have placed these concepts near the very end in our earlier listing of the theory's propositions.   The transactionists also seem to have developed them in the same sequence (references cited)—perhaps because of their lack of denotational reference.   Purpose and value seem to be "afterthoughts" rather than considerations that are basic to the theory's systematic explanatory development.

It has been said that the concepts of "assumption" and "hitch" are capable of operational definition.   A difficulty arises, however, from the standpoint of operational logic that is worth noting.   Though the theory is intended to apply to perception generally, its experimental case is founded only upon non-verdical instances.   "Hitches" are in-volved as verbal or manual discrepancies of action are experienced. It is these hitches that constitute the observable operations through which the (non-veridical) assumption is inferred and in terms of which it is defined.   But this very operation by which both *veridical* and *non-veridical* assumptions are presumed to be established cannot, by the very nature of things, occur in the veridical case.   We are thus left with the necessity of defining the latter by the *negation* of an operation (i.e., "no hitch").   This is operationism, as it were, in reverse.   It might be argued that in *veridical* instances the *smooth performance of the act* which is based on the perception, and which is certainly a positive and not a negative thing, is the operation by which the concept of assumption is defined.   If we take this view, we have the concept of assumption defined by two different operations.

Although this procedure is legitimate and is often used in science, in order to prove that the separate operations *are defining the same concept* we need to combine them in an overall investigation and test the consistency of the results. Such a procedure is here clearly impossible since the two operations are *antithetical*.

It is not implied that assumptions are not active in veridical perceptions, that is, in cases in which there is no hitch, but only that some more positive way of demonstrating them is needed. And for this purpose some more explicit referent for the term will be required. If, as the writer suspects, the phenomena referred to by the term assumption turn out to be identical with the phenomena referred to by the term set, a physiological referent would then be available (cf. Chapter 9); and, as will be seen in later chapters (15 and 16), a movement which joins forces with the later concept might go far. It might be very profitable to construe the findings of transactional functionalism as a special case of the manifestation of the (physiologically based) set of the organism. The ambiguous stimulation-pattern renders the percept ("expanded set" of Chapter 9) less bound to a specific stimulus-object and therefore gives the (non-veridical) set of the perceiver a greater opportunity to come into play and to reveal itself through verbalization or manipulative action. This treatment of the Ames demonstrations would be less apt to invite anthropomorphic connotations than would the use of the term assumption.

The theory's present lack of denotability at finer levels is somewhat of a handicap in its explanatory work. By substituting function for denotation as a methodological criterion it leads to the same dilemma or inconsistency that was observed in the original Helmholtzian doctrine (Chapter 4). If we stay at the molar level, neither the probabilistic nor the transactional theory gives us much of a conception of what actually occurs when perception takes place. We must rest content with the explanation that a perception occurs through the functioning of an assumptive process of, or within, the organism, that the organism unconsciously appraises the probability of (its own) cues, that it weighs and averages its past experience, and that it develops new assumptions from the results of its own action. The notion of assumption implies the functioning of some agency; and the agent, in the activity of perception, must act, in part, upon or through himself. Though this conception is not entirely satisfactory, *still it makes some sense from a practical standpoint.* The assuming agent with his attained perceptions is at least before us, even if we cannot fully understand how he operates. When we descend to the "molecular" level, however, our troubles begin to increase. Here there is no referent for an assumptive process at all. We look in vain for a "probability weigher," an "inferrer" or an "assumer" among the neurophysiological elements or processes of the organism. Some concept of a quite different sort is needed if we would understand perception in intraorganismic terms.

Such is the dead end to which we come in all doctrines through which a process is wrapped up in a package of "function" and offered for sale at the counter of theoretical explanation. As long as we think functionally and use our purchase instrumentally and in a practical manner as we use our watch for telling time, without being too "nosey" about its contents, the doctrine has a meaning. But as soon as we become curious and open the package, or begin to pry into it, we find that there is nothing there at all. The doctrine refers to "outside" or molar utility and to nothing more. We need to be provided, as in the case of the watch, with some sort of dynamic pattern or structure of physicalistically describable occurrences that will give us an understanding of what happens in perceptual activity. To such a structure the notion of function could then be attached. But when we are able to do *this*, the "functioning" of the perceiving organism will be seen as identical with the operation of that structure. There will be no need for both concepts. Whether we describe perceiving in terms of functioning or as a dynamic pattern of events will then depend upon whether we have some ulterior pragmatic interest (some "broader" function that perception is considered as serving), or take the immediate, disinterested, and explicit attitude of descriptive science. If we take the latter view the "broader function" of functionalism becomes merely a more inclusive structure in which the dynamic structure of perceiving operates as a part. (Cf. the last section of Chapter 4.) Another way of stating the matter is that, from the standpoint of a denotationally oriented science, the functional explanation is only a temporary expedient to be used until we can discover some more explicit and objectively describable way of treating the phenomenon.

But here the supporters of transactional theory might object, contending that the type of functionalism which they propose leads into no such blind alley as that described above. The argument might run as follows. On the one hand, the writer has been speaking of the assumptions and perceptions of an isolated organism (agent) with relation to an environment that is distinct from itself, or of the result for the organism of the action of an external stimulus-object upon its receptors. This formulation represents interaction. On the other hand, the writer has been speaking of activity *within* the organism and has shown concern that no assumptive process or "assumer" was to be discovered in that quarter. Such a search for the bases of perception in the organism betrays a belief in *self*-action. Dewey and Bentley, however, have shown that there is a better way of looking at natural phenomena. It it more enlightening to regard them not as self-actions or as interactions, but as *trans*actions. As Ittelson and Cantril (1954) point out, both the "perception" and the "object-as-perceived" are parts of a total life situation. Neither exists independently of that situation. The parts of such a situation "owe their very existence as encountered in the situation to this fact of active participation." They do not appear as already existing entities that merely interact.[14] These authors quote Bentley to the effect that "We do not . . . take the organism and environment as if we could know about them separately in advance in our special inquiry, but we take their inter-action [i.e., *transaction*] itself as subject-matter of study." One might carry forward the argument, therefore, and maintain that it is foolish to look for the basis of perceptual activity merely "inside" the organism; and it is equally useless to look for the nature of the (perceived) reality either in the stimulus object or in the stimulation-pattern. Both sides of the relationship must participate to give us an apprehension of our world if we are to have an instance of perception at all.

The language of this formulation gives one the impression that it does escape the Helmholtzian dilemma. Our only problem lies in understanding the language. For one thing, we are not clear as to the two elements or phases that are said to be participating in the total situation or set of transactions. Ittelson and Cantril call these, respectively, the "perception" and the "object-as-perceived." But the object-as-preceived is not the physical object; it is really the same thing as the percept. If this is so, placing the "perception" and the "percept" (phenomenological aspect) in contradistinction and repre-senting each as participating in a total life situation with the other seems obscure to say the least. Bentley brings in the organism and environment as parties to the transaction. Presumably these are physicalistically conceived entities. Here the object is provided for (in environmental terms); but it is the physical object, not the "object as perceived." The organism here referred to is also taken in a molar sense. Where, then, would the stimulation pattern on the organism's receptors and the phenomenological percept, both of which should be considered in studying perception, fit into Bentley's scheme? What part does the stimulation-pattern play in the set of

[14] *Op. cit.*, p. 3.

transactions as seen by Ittelson and Cantril? Does the transaction occur as light rays from the object impinge on the retina of the eye, or as the *acting* organism makes contacts of some sort with the environment as in the distorted room experiments? Or does it occur in both these places? Is transaction, then, simply encounter—i.e., interaction? If not, what is it? Such questions must be answered before the philosophical theory of transactions can be made sufficiently definite to serve as an adequate explanation of perceptual phenomena.

Let us press the matter a little further. Even if the parts of the total situation do derive their "very existence" (as encountered in the situation!) from their participation, there must be some *other* aspects of their existence that are *not* so derived. That is to say, they must also exist independently. Otherwise everything would be participation with no one to participate. We must have some more enlightening way of identifying the elements of the perceptual aggregate than to say merely that they exist as participating parts of a total set of transactions. A "total situation," or "total set of transactions," is something with which we can scarcely operate in an investigation that requires experimental controls. No doubt Bentley would admit, in defining the transactional point of view, that there are *some* things about both organism and environment that can be studied and known about in advance of our inquiry into the nature of their interrelationship, even though the fact that in their relationship they contribute something *to each other* is undeniable. What, then, *is* this residual nature or property of the parties to a transaction? How can we describe that "self-level" of existence and show how it is integrated or, shall we say, "structured," into the more inclusive, overall, and containing situation?[15] Here again we come face to face with that old enigma—the "inside-outside" problem. The reader might wish to recall our attempt to resolve it in the structural interpretation of core-context and meaning as given in the last section of Chapter 4.

It is by no means implied that the theory of transactions is untenable or that it is without value for the explanation of perception. But it has not yet been rendered sufficiently explicit to meet the denotational needs of the problem. At least this is true of the manner in which it is employed by the transactional functionalists. If transactions can be kept upon the plane of physical events, such, for example, as contacts or encounters between minute particles, and if we can thus get rid of that non-denotable or ambiguously denotable

---

[15] Cantril and his associates themselves are not ready to reject self-action and interaction. They cite instances of the former and close the first installment of their article by leaving the matter open (Cantril et al., 1949).

nemesis of functionalistic theory, the agent, a way might be found to reinterpret perception as a dynamic structure of ongoings and their interconnecting events. In that case we would not need to speak either of self-action, of interactions, or of transactions; for we would not speak of "actions." Some of the details of such a view and its implications for perception will be presented in Chapter 21. Perhaps, in the discussions of set and meaning that are to come in that and other chapters, we shall learn more about that mysterious but strategic entity, the perceiver's assumptions.

The theory of transactional functionalism, in spite of its logical difficulties and its present shortcomings with respect to experimental availability and explanatory thoroughness, stands as the most able and comprehensive statement of the functional viewpoint that has yet appeared. Regardless of what one may think of the ultimate value of functionalistic explanations, the new and arresting insights into perceptual phenomena which its proponents have given, the careful systematizing of these insights, and the devising of ingenious experiments for their further development are contributions that greatly enrich the content of the field and enhance the scope and interest of perceptual investigation. Students of perception will long be grateful for contributions such as these.

12

Transition to Motivational Dynamics
Critique of Dimensionalism
Nativism versus Empiricism

We come now to an interlude in our account of the theories of perception. In the next chapter we shall find that a new and different accent is added. In briefest terms this new movement is based upon the hypothesis that dynamic factors such as the needs, values, and personality characteristics of the individual have much to do with the way the world appears to him. The somewhat revolutionary idea is introduced that motivational elements affect not only the way a person thinks and acts, but also the way in which he actually perceives the objects in his environment. To understand the situation confronting this movement we must try to unravel certain tangles that have by this time appeared in the methodological strands of our subject. In establishing their claim, the motivational theorists have had to combat the assumption that the more traditionally established theories were adequate to account for all the facts of perception. In the first place, we have seen the stress that had been placed upon figural properties and the concept of field. Gestalt theorists had asserted that the central problem for perception lay in such phenomena as wholeness-character, organization, and good-figure. Field theory, both cortical and phenomenological, was an extension of this general idea. The Hebbian theory, though it departed from field notions and treated figural problems in a more localized way, was still centered about the perception of a figure. Although, as we have seen, there are significant features of perception that are not accounted for by gestalt principles or the study of figural experience, these traditions have been so strong in certain quarters that their claim to completeness had to be dealt with by the proponents of the new theory.[1]

[1] No attempt has been made to follow a strict historical sequence in the discussion of the perceptual theories. Though some had their rise earlier than others practically all the major theories we are presenting are contemporary.

A more subtle problem, however, arises in connection with another strand of methodological background, the problem, namely, of dimensional attributes and their role. Dimensionalism, as embodied, for example, in psychophysics and as later carried on in sensory-tonic field-conceptions, adaptation-level, and probabilistic theory, has a tradition older even than that of gestalt; and the clash between it and the motivational theory reveals issues that are fundamental to the whole theoretical outlook.

In approaching this question it will be helpful to distinguish between two theoretical uses that have been made of dimensional experiences reported by subjects. The first is what we might call a "means-use." In this procedure estimates given by the subject of such attributive properties as size, direction, brightness, and so on were used to test some hypothesis that was not itself quantitative, either in its import or its formulation. Gestalt theory, where the emphasis was figural rather than quantitative, and sensory-tonic field theory are examples of this class. In the former, the perceived length of a line contrasted under two conditions of observing could have been used to prove the influence of a total configuration upon its parts. In the latter, an alteration in the angular dimension of perceived verticality was employed to test the hypothesis that motor factors exert an influence on perception.

The other usage of dimensionality is that in which the quantitative experiences and the estimates given by the subject constitute both the starting point and the central problem of the theory. The explanation of perception is here primarily a matter of finding a stabilizing law of sensory magnitudes; and the theory is essentially a dimensional one. Its aim is not to use quantities or perceptual magnitude-estimates to test some hypothetical model, but to formulate lawfully the obtained series of perceived quantities. We may call this viewpoint the "end-use" of dimensionality. Psychophysics and adaptation-level fit into this classification. The explanation of perception is here considered to be achieved primarily by the formal statement of quantitative covariation-laws. Thus in psychophysics the independent variable is the stimulus series, used discretely; in adaptation-level it is a weighted average of series, background, and residual stimuli. Both these systems are concerned mainly with the quantitative relationship of these variables to the dependent variable of perceived dimensionality. The question of whether nature has such a character that a basic theory can be most adequately expressed in quantitative form, or whether something that is *non*-quantitative is also essential and must be stated in order to give the quantitative laws their full meaning, raises a deep-lying issue that has not been adequately recognized. There are difficulties peculiar to either emphasis; and the ultimate solution must be some theory that provides an adequate place for both.

The attitude of the theorist toward problems that arise in the use of dimensional quantities (and it goes without saying that quantification cannot be dispensed with in any field of science) will be different according to whether he belongs to the "end-use" or the "means-use" school of thought.[2] For the former, since perceived magnitude or quantity of some sort is of the essence, there will naturally be an effort to state its conditions and its laws in terms of some strict and univocal system. It must be objectively "bound" in some way so that it can be predicted by equations. This type of theorist will also be sensitive to, and perhaps resist, attempts to tamper with dimensionality by those who are using it only as a means of testing their particular hypotheses and are not paying due attention to the specifications under which, according to the end-users, it should be employed. The end-users of quantitative reports in perception will also be likely to be more "sensorily minded" and to be on guard against the intrusion of "higher processes," such as inference or judgment, into the estimate of magnitude. But for the same reason it is more essential for their theory than for that of the instrumentalists that the definition of dimensionality be firmly anchored in unequivocal operational procedures. We shall presently see the difficulties that have arisen from this requirement.

For the instrumental, or means, users of quantity, on the other hand, the rules give somewhat more latitude—merely because of what they are trying to do. Since they are not hypothesizing some principle that is tied in a one-to-one way to dimensional considerations, they are more at liberty to employ quantitative procedures without implying a necessary univocality, in different experiments, of the perceptual dimension they happen to be using. So long as the results show that the factors they *are* hypothesizing are making a difference of some sort in the quantitative aspects of the perception there will be some evidence in support of their hypothesis. This liberty, of course, is only a temporary one. Ultimately they can give their theory full explanatory value only by showing how the factor they are hypothesizing produces these quantitative differentials; and that, of course,

[2] For example, learning theorists of the Tolman school use quantities in an instrumental way: they are "means-users." For the Hullian theorists, who are "end-users," quantities and their combination in equations become the heart of the theory itself.

will involve knowing what perceived dimensionality *is*. A similar statement, of course, should be made for the end-users of quantities. Perceptual theorists who belong to the motivational school are to be classified among the means-users of dimensionality. Their hypothesis is that motives, needs, and values affect perception, and they turn to the quantitative aspects of the percept merely in order to establish their point. The operational requirements that follow from our distinction of the two uses of dimensionality must be taken into account in order to understand and evaluate the disagreement that has arisen between the motivationists and the older dimensionalistic group.

AMBIGUITY OF THE DIMENSIONAL CONCEPT: A PROBLEM IN OPERATIONAL DEFINITION

As an illustration of some of the difficulties of dimensionalism, apart from the distinction just made, let us examine more closely two perceptual theories, those, namely, of Helson and Brunswik. Both are based on the effort to describe and account for certain quantitative aspects of perception; but the differences in the operations by which they define the dimensional concept produce, to use Bridgman's term, a "penumbra of uncertainty" regarding the concept itself. The subject, in the procedure of Brunswik's thing-constancy, is set to attain as objectively accurate a perception as he can of the dimensional variable given him by the object. Though he is told merely to say (or otherwise demonstrate) how large the object looks to him, his attitude is veridically oriented; the experience is to a large degree "object-bound" (though not proximal-stimulus-bound). In adaptation-level procedure, on the other hand, there is no effort on the part of the subject to see how closely he can make the magnitudes as judged by him tally with the corresponding physical magnitudes of the stimuli. Then, too, in Helson's type of experiment the subject attends more abstractly to some "pure" dimension—highness or lowness of a tone, heaviness of a weight, and so on. In the Brunswik setting, on the other hand, though the reactions are given in quantitative terms, the procedure is not so purely dimensional; the object itself looms more largely in the subject's experience. The judgment relates to a dimension of this thing or that. In the thing-constancy form of procedure the question is, in effect: How many inches in height or how many grams in weight does the subject estimate the object to be? Does he, for example, experience it as three inches in height, or as weighing 100 grams? In determining adaptation-level, on the other hand, the upshot of the question is: How large, under the present and past circumstances, does the subject consider three inches *to be*, or how heavy, in terms of his experience in the experimental sessions, *is* 100 grams? Finally, in Helson's setting the elements of the perceptual aggregate are all of the same kind, e.g., the effects on the organism of a single variable like weight; whereas in the Brunswik problem the cues are of many different sorts—they may even belong to different sensory modalities. In both theories the dimensional estimate must rest on some kind of combination of all the elements. But we have seen that the combining in the two cases was based upon different principles. The experiences received from the stimulus pattern were all of the same direct nature with respect to the dimension in Helson's experiment; hence they could be dealt with by direct computation. In Brunswik's problem the "cues" were heterogeneous; the magnitude experience was not directly the same as any of them. It had to be given, theoretically, by an unconscious weighting and combination of probabilities.

All these differences are here nicely ordered, and the two types of experiment are well differentiated. But nature seldom if ever follows such a procedure of laboratory segregation. It is quite possible that the subject may be in a magnitude-perceiving situation where *both* the adaptation-level and the principle of thing-constancy are (theoretically) operating. Will one theory then override the other, showing itself to be the more general? Will both principles be able to operate together? If so, how? Are their effects algebraically additive? If not, how are they to be combined? Are adaptation-level effects demonstrable only when all the cues for the thing-constancy are held constant; or will thing-constancy fall into the framework of adaptation-level?

Suppose the subject is judging the brightness of a patch of black paper seen under varying intensities of reflected white light. Let us assume, however, that he is viewing the patch through a hole in a screen that shuts out all details of background, illumination, and other environmental features. At a certain range of illumination-intensity the patch will appear as gray, not black. Since we have eliminated all the accompanying clues by the use of the screen, thing-constancy cannot operate; probabilistic functionalism has nothing to go on except the intensity of light reflected to the retina by the patch of black paper. Presumably, with a distributed series of illumination-intensities, an adaptation-level of brightness of a corresponding series of judged "grays" can be established. At least this will be true if the adaptation-level principle is general. This level will then determine whether, with a given illumination, the "gray" patch will be judged as "light," "medium," or "dark," or as of some other brightness on a scale containing these categories.

Suppose now that in the midst of this adaptation-level experiment the reduction-screen is suddenly removed. To add a touch of the dramatic let us say that a gust of wind blows it over. All the details of source of illumination, background of the patch, and so on are now visible. At one stroke the cues are thus restored and the conditions required to give perceptual constancy *via* probabilistic functionalism are presented. Brunswik's theory now comes into play. What then will happen to Helson's adaptation level? Will brightness constancy (Brunswik's theory) now immediately assert itself through probabilistic functionalism, so that the patch will always be seen as black (maximum darkness value) regardless of the reflected illumination and regardless also of whatever degree of illumination had been previously established as the adaptation level? If so, then the same stimulus that might have been judged as a "light" or a "medium" gray a moment before will now be judged as "very dark" (i.e., black), in apparent violation of the adaptation-level principle. Or, on the other hand, will adaptation-level prove stronger than constancy and the probabilistic weighting of cues? Or again, will some kind of compromise in judged brightness occur? If so, how is it brought about?

The outcome, of course, is properly a question for experiment to decide. If constancy were not achieved, then we would conclude that its law had failed, even though the proper conditions were provided, owing to the prior operation of another law. But is a law that succeeds in one compartment of experience and fails in another really a law? Can two quantitative laws, which, after all, are merely statements of the covariation of variables, block each other in this fashion? Let us suppose that it is the other way: adaptation-level holds sway in the first part of the experiment, but brightness-constancy supersedes it the instant the screen falls over. The same dilemma again confronts us. There is a logical possibility, of course, that the perceived brightness might be a compromise between that required by constancy and that required by adaptation-level. But such a result would pose a still deeper question: How is this compromise effected in the organism? How, indeed, can we devise a single theory that will predict any one of these three possible results? How can we achieve a generality of statement that covers both adaptation-level and brightness constancy in the same total situation?

We might try, from the results of the two component experiments, to work out a completely general equation, or at least a set of curves, from which we would be able to predict the degree of perceived brightness under various conditions. (In order to do so we might have to include results taken from many other types of perceptual experiments.) But there is another method that suggests itself. We might try to construct some kind of theoretical model, requiring of course a considerable knowledge of the physiology of perception, the object of which would be to explain what is happening in the optic tract and the whole sensory-motor system when brightness is perceived and judged. Having this model-construct in hand we would then try to deduce quantitative theorems that might be tested, provided we had sufficient ingenuity and equipment. It is important to note that the second proposal contemplates at the outset *some* considerations that are *not* quantitative in character. Quantities, of course, may definitely enter later; but if we do not think at the start in some terms besides quantities (as for example, in terms of concepts of how certain parts are integrated and work together) we can never construct such a model.

If we take this second course, the establishment of one univocal quantitative law of *dimensionality* (though we might hope that one could eventually be established) would not be our primary or immediate objective. In fact, the direct search for such a law might, at the outset, be a hindrance. Our essential business would now be the hypothesizing of what is aggregated with what as perception takes place, and by what kind of interactive, dynamic process. Only when such questions were answered would questions about the covariation of the quantitative aspects of the process be useful. When such questions *were* answered the whole matter of dimensionalities and correlations of quantities, and the hope of establishing a general quantitative law, might take on a new meaning and possibility. In pursuit of such an inquiry the use of dimensional data becomes instrumental for later model-checking rather than an end in itself. We become means-users rather than end-users of dimensionality.[3]

Our critique of dimensionalism, however, does not end here. For the sake of simplicity we did not raise, in the preceding discussion, the question of whether the actual experience of dimensionality in the Helson experiment was really the same as the experience in the Brunswik setting. That is to say, in reporting the apparent size of a

---

[3] It might be objected that our hypothetical example is unfair, in that the subject, in Helson's part of the experiment, would be judging film color, whereas in Brunswik's part he would be judging surface color. Helson, also, has already demonstrated that his theory can deal, at least in part, with color-constancy. But even so, the illustration will at least serve to indicate that sensory dimension can fluctuate in such a manner as to suggest that it may be dependent upon circumstances that are *non*-quantitative in character.

house, would the "largeness" of the object, if judged as "large" in an adaptation-level experiment, be the same kind of experience as the "largeness" of which the same subject would be aware in observing in a constancy experiment? Does size mean the same thing to the individual under these two sets of circumstances? We assumed earlier that size (i.e., largeness) was always the same experience, and that it was only the report of "*how* large" that might differ in the two cases. But how do we know this is true? All we can do is to accept the introspective report of the subject after he has observed in the two situations. Such a report, being based upon purely "private" operations, would represent a procedure that has been much in dispute. And besides, the subject might feel his own judgment to be very uncertain upon such subtle matters. If we were to follow the rule of those operationists who require "publicly" observable operations for defining concepts, we would have to eliminate all reference to *consciously perceived* magnitude. We would have to conclude that these two magnitude-concepts (that of adaptation-level theory and that of thing-constancy) were *different*, because it was necessary to use quite different kinds of operations in evoking and reporting the experiences concerned. In seeking to set up a theory in which quantities are the starting point and dimensional formulation the primary objective we are thus embarrassed at the outset by the fact that a perceived dimensional magnitude is not one thing, but two. The only alternative would be to sacrifice the operational standard or to weaken it to the point where it would be ineffective.

But why stop with these two types of experiment? Looking back over the theories of perception we see that dimensionality has appeared in other guises. In psychophysics, where it was put to an end-use, the perceived magnitude was considered theoretically to be bound closely to the proximal stimulus; and the operations included paired comparison in series and a verbal report of the subject. In gestalt psychology where a means-use was stressed, series were not usually regarded as important, and binding to simple stimulus-elements was avoided. Verbal or other reports of perceived dimensional quantity under specified configurational conditions were typical. In the sensory-tonic field theory such operations as placing a rod in a position that expressed the subject's subjective impression of the vertical were employed; and the dimension involved was the angular deviation from a standard position. In constancy experiments a flexible operation in which the subject made his own size-matching or equating of a comparison object to the thing as perceived was often practiced; and we shall see that this procedure is favored also in the motivational experiments. The operations in most of these experiments differed in one way or another from the operations employed in others. Some encouraged veridical report, others did not. In some the response was verbal, in others it was given by overt manipulative or discriminatory reactions. Can we say, then, that the experience of a given dimension, to which for want of better knowledge we assign a certain verbal label, is the same in all these types of experiments? Have we one dimensional magnitude or *five?* The elusive character of phenomenological data and its complete lack of direct experimental availability make it difficult, if not impossible, to answer this question.[4]

Even if we had the answer, the way to an adequate dimensional theory would not be easy. If there is only one type of experience for a given dimension, we would need to discover some one formula that would predict all these unique and often conflicting results in different experimental situations. If dimensionality is something that differs with the setting, it must be brought to some common denominator, or else the values in a set of related equations will be equivocal. We see again the difficulty in attempting to devise a complete theory of perception in which the postulating and testing of some law (or group of laws) regarding perceived dimensionality is taken as the primary objective. Our intention here is not to discourage the pursuit of such an objective, but only to indicate the need of tempering present claims regarding the inviolability of dimensional laws as previously formulated, on the one hand, and of weighing the assertion, on the other, that special conditions have been discovered requiring the addition of new laws of dimensionality. If we do not actually know what a perceived magnitude is, such questions, at this stage, seem to lose much of their significance. The reason for discussing the matter here is that in the motivational theory, which we shall presently examine, dimensionality is one of the issues upon which the theory turns, as well as one of the chief points around which controversy has centered.

GENERAL ASPECTS OF THE MOTIVATIONAL THEORY

In preparing for our account of this theory let us consider some of its further implications. Its starting point might be said to be in

---

[4] A parallel instance, the blame for which, however, cannot be ascribed to phenomenology, is to be found in Hull's behavior theory of learning (1943b). Four different ways of measuring the manifestation of "reaction-potential" are employed in that system.

our sixth category of perceptual phenomena, in the fact, namely, that the prevailing state of the individual helps to determine the way the world appears to him. Quantitative findings and dimensional differences are then used as a means of testing the theory that has been elaborated upon this basis. In its elaboration, however, the theory goes considerably beyond the influence of prevailing set or state as it was described in our initial list of aspects (Chapter 3). By endeavoring to show that motivation and past experience, under certain conditions, not only determine selectively what is perceived, but also can modify the speed, accuracy, or vividness of the perceptual act and even the perceived dimensions of the object, its authors have invaded the domain of those to whom dimensionalism represents a law too strict and sacred to be exposed to the winds of such transient circumstances. Whether humorously or with a touch of something else, the movement has come to be called, in certain quarters, "The New Look."

The theory itself is a functional one, though its functionalism is not that of the broader, biological sort embodied in Brunswik's probability theory. In the latter conception the emphasis was placed upon a process by which adaptation of organisms to their environment was universally assured, and this by means that were typical and common to the species. The theory now under discussion considers, instead, the individual organism in its uniqueness. There are the temperament and personality characteristics of the individual, the emotion prevailing at the moment, his changing need within the shifting situation; and always there is some aspect of the way the world looks that is likely to be determined by the value to the individual of perceiving it at the moment in this way rather than that. Need and value are not defined as necessarily instrumental to the soundest health and survival. The functionalism here contemplated is at times more like that in psychoanalysis, where a belief or an attitude may serve a purpose in the individual's life-pattern even though that pattern involves repressions and a failure to face realities. A way of perceiving, in other words, may be either veridical or non-veridically slanted according to the personality interests or the momentary needs of the individual.

Clearly such a theory of perception must be closely related to objects and occurrences that have a content beyond that of mere figure and dimensionality. In order that the percept may be dynamically connected with the interests of the organism the concrete character of the object or situation perceived, that is, its full meaning, must always be implicit in the experimental setting; and it is so included in all the investigations on which the theory is based. Though reports of how bright or large an object appears, or a determination of how quickly it will be perceived, are used in testing the hypothesis, dimensionality itself is important only as it is related to the fact that the object so perceived has a certain meaningful urgency or value for the individual. All this of course implies a further hypothesis: past experience with the objects perceived must be assumed to play an indispensable role. This condition of a dynamic value-relationship to the individual limits the experimental program to those instances of perception in which it exists or can be set up. The program, however, does not thereby diminish in importance. Its field of application, its exponents contend, is still very broad because of the large number of times such a situation occurs in daily life. From a theoretical standpoint, even if it rarely occurred, the question would still be important; for in order to be general a theory of perception must account for the atypical as well as the typical occurrence.

ISSUE OF EMPIRICISM VERSUS NATIVISM REVIVED; PRATT'S ADMONITION

Anyone who stresses, as determining influences in perception, the earlier life-experiences of the individual must expect sooner or later to run afoul of the doctrine of nativism (Chapter 4). And the motivational emphasis in perceptual theory is no exception. It has been vigorously opposed by those psychologists who consider perception to be an immediate, uncontaminated process grounded in physiological laws and present in the individual from birth. Nativism versus empiricism is one of the most venerable of psychological controversies. How one resolves it depends partly upon whether one takes a broad view and considers all the phenomenal categories listed in Chapter 3 to be truly "perceptual" or whether one wishes to restrict the phenomenon-class to such aspects as sensory quality, dimensionality, constancy, and configuration. If we admit frames of reference, prevailing states, and meanings as a part of the process, there is no denying the large part played in perception by past experience. In such a view no sharp line is envisaged between the cortical excitation set up by the receptors and afferent neurons, on the one hand, and the physiological elements representing traces, meanings, and even interpretations and judgments, on the other. In support of this view we have the fact that, except under unusual conditions, the latter are not introspectively separated from the former in the total perceptual experience.

The case for past experience, familiarity, and learning in perception has been made by appeal both to common observation and to experiment. Duncker (1939) found that the remembered *usual* color of familiar objects tends to enter the percept when such color is not given by the particular stimulus object itself; and Henle (1942) found lower thresholds in perceiving regular letters than in perceiving their reversed mirror images. Hilgard has presented an able review of phenomena indicative of the role of experience and learning in spatial perception as seen from a functional standpoint.[5]   Even when a new percept is suddenly gained, the process may be fundamentally the same as that of learning. Woodworth (1947) has contended that a perception is a response that has been learned like any other habit. The "will to perceive" is the drive or need, and this becomes satisfied (reduced) the instant the percept is gained, or, in gestalt terms, the instant the field is brought to equilibrium. This drive-reduction (or equilibrium-attainment) provides the necessary reinforcement, and the situation represents a true case of single-trial learning. Wertheimer himself included past experience or habit as one of the (minor) factors that influence organization. We have noted the importance of earlier experiences, and the necessity of learning, in the cases of delayed perceptual acquisition reviewed by Hebb, as well as the fact that adaptation-level is based upon experiences of the immediate and recent past.

Nativists tend to discount such evidence or to explain it away as the result of some process other than perception. One of the reasons for their tenacity is the fact that perception is such a swift, and for the most part unerring, activity. It has little surface resemblance to conscious trial and error or to the cumulative process of learning. Even in cases where some meanings from earlier experience must be present, the perception itself is so devoid of the usual earmarks of learning that it seems natural to classify it as part of the organism's native endowment. The opponents of empiricism are especially emphatic when it comes to configuration, constancy, and sensory dimensions. In both gestalt theory and psychophysics the effect of familiarity with the object has been discounted, and constitutional or "autochthonous" factors have been given precedence. When we consider the bare question of the size, weight, or intensity of objects as directly experienced, it does put us under some strain to believe that such attributes are altered by a particular stock of past experiences, or especially by the needs or moods of the moment. Since the great bulk of our perceptions are both prompt and fairly veridical from the

[5] See Blake and Ramsey (eds.), 1951, Chapter 4.

start the only appreciable effect that differences of experience or motivation could have upon them would be in the direction of falsifying the report of the perceived world or in producing a delay in perceiving it. Such eventualities would seem highly maladaptive. We can well believe that dimensional distortions of objects would occur *in retrospect* or upon the witness stand; we can see how an interpretation that is at odds with the facts can be arrived at through *reflection* upon what the senses give us. But can the pattern of central sensory excitation itself be so distorted by earlier experiences that there is a change in the size, weight, distance, color, or shape in which objects are actually experienced?

We can readily understand how, when two men go into a restaurant and one of them is interested mainly in wines while the other is interested in food, the attention of the former might be drawn to the wine-list first, while the latter might perceive first the list of entrees. We have here merely the principle of selectivity under the influence of a dominating set or interest—a phenomenon that has long been recognized. But will the wine-list as experienced by the thirsty wine-lover appear *larger* or *brighter* to him than his experience when he chances to look at the rest of the menu—and the reverse for the man who is hungry? If both men look through a thin curtain into the kitchen and see there some blurred object, will one of them be more likely to perceive it as a bottle of wine and the other as ham-joint? Or from still another standpoint, have we some inner mechanism, developed from past experience, that enables the percepts of things we value to come more quickly and veridically into our awareness than percepts of neutral or distasteful objects? If we were to entertain such questions too seriously, we might seem to be challenging our confidence in our own mental stability.

Pratt (1950) has argued forcefully against the influence of past experience in visual perception, particularly in the realm of sensory dimensionality, and has defined perception in such a manner as to exclude the effects of meaning in the sense that is important to motivational theory. He lists three criteria for nativism, viz., universality of the percept, its occurrence among the very young of different species, and evidence that the percept is "stimulus-bound" (as, for example, in the discriminations involved in establishing Weber's law). Upon the last-named criterion he lays greatest stress. Pratt asserts that the well-known effects of experience, as seen for example in the learning process, are concentrated toward the motor, not the sensory, portion of the stimulus-response arc. Knowledge and past experience are said to play relatively unimportant parts in size-perception, a phenomenon that depends primarily upon visual cues, visual angle, and related processes in the optic system. He is pointed in his attack upon the theory, current in certain quarters, that size-constancy depends upon our knowledge of what the object is, as, for example, when a man seen across the street is said to be *recognized as a man* and therefore judged to be "man-sized." The results of Holway and Boring (1941) are cited to show that in size-constancy no appeal to past experience or object-meaning is needed, since the degree of perceptual constancy here attained is a function merely of the number of visual cues that can be called into play. And the experimental observations involved can, according to Pratt, be interpreted merely as an instance of Weber's law in respect to apparent size. The findings of Hastorf (1950), purporting to show that the perceived distance of an object may depend upon what the observer conceives the object to be, Pratt reinterprets as probably due to a shift in the judgmental frame of reference. He reduces the experience theory of size-constancy to an absurdity by pointing out that this phenomenon is limited to relatively near objects. A man 500 yards away is seen not in the stature of a man, but considerably smaller. Why would our knowledge that he *is* a man not operate here as well as at shorter distances? This trenchant critic concludes by maintaining that most sensory and perceptual dimensions fall in the category of results that can be adequately accounted for in terms of stimulus-correlations rather than in the category which require non-stimulus hypotheses. "That is to say, sensory and perceptual dimensions are stimulus-bound. The exceptions are so uncommon that when they seem to appear they should be scrutinized very critically, if not incredulously."

One might agree that Pratt is probably right in rejecting the easy explanation of size-constancy as due to object-meaning. The conclusion that no appeal to past experience is needed, an inference drawn from the results of Holway and Boring, does not seem quite so obvious. Though size-constancy is found to increase with the number of available cues, may not past experience have played a part in assigning to each of those cues some meaning? We do not refer here to the gross and more obvious meanings involved in a knowledge of what the object is, but to the possibility of some subtler, but acquired, meaning-process that might have to do with the distance one would have to traverse to reach objects associated with such and such distance-cues, when taken in relation to other possible motor experiences such as manipulating or spatially circumscribing such objects. Then too, if our critic of empiricism is to be taken at his word, he will have to look at the results of Helson and of Werner and

Wapner "very critically" and perhaps "incredulously"; for those dimensional results were certainly not stimulus-bound in any one-to-one sense.

To be sure, Pratt says that his categories of perception must be taken only as operationally defined. But would it not be fair to ask this critic, who is himself one of the founders of operationism, why, if we are interested in a complete study of perceptual dimensionality, the operations of Helson and of Werner and Wapner are not as acceptable as those of psychophysics? And finally, should not the "penumbra of uncertainty" that we have shown to surround the concept of dimension itself impose some restraint upon those who, like our critic, regard psychophysical dimensionality as a property so definite and inclusive that other theories must be tailored to its design? According to Pratt "many if not most objects of perception are . . . stimulus bound"; and "phenomenal characteristics which are held in place by external stimuli do not as a rule yield to palpable change or distortion as the result of past experience." Taking a rather narrow view, in which one attempts to separate sensory factors in perception from cognitive elements and ignores the fact that early experiences might have contributed to the binding effect now ascribed to the stimulus alone, one can perhaps agree with these statements. It will be noted, however, that there is still a loophole. Though stimulus-binding is said to be "the rule," it is conceded by implication that there might be some occasions in which it would be absent.

This discussion, of course, resolves no issues. Our purpose has been merely to present the origins and assumptions of the motivational theory and to show the theoretical situation into which it has been launched. Nativism has many arguments and much apparent common sense upon its side. The way for the motivational theory, or, as we shall now call it, in the phraseology of one of its exponents, the "directive-state" theory, will not be easy. To make their point its advocates must reconcile empiricism with nativism, grapple with the slippery problem of dimensions, and carry perceptual theory forward into the unexplored domain of object-character and meaning. They also must go beyond the commonly accepted position that familiarity, set, and previously learned habits operate selectively in perception, and show that the needs, emotions, and values of the individual can enter directly into the perceptual act in such a way as to modify the character of the percept itself.

13————

The Directive-State Theory
of Perception

Turning to the theory more directly we shall for the present concern ourselves only with its general position. After that we shall review its supporting experiments and the investigators' interpretation of the findings, coming finally to a more complete grasp of its scope and explanatory principles. The directive-state concepts are still in an uncrystallized state. They represent not so much a definite or complete system as a viewpoint stated in a number of ways by its adherents and relating itself not only to motivation and personality, but to cognition, learning-theory, and clinical diagnosis, as well as to various other fields.[1] Obviously a program based largely upon the non-veridical aspects of perception cannot be complete in itself. The attitude of its proponents is that the ultimate theory is in the making, but that when it is finally stated it must be broad enough to embrace

[1] Bruner and Postman have outlined the general approach (see Dennis, ed., 1948; and Bruner and Krech, eds., 1950). The volume edited by Bruner and Krech, a symposium on perception and personality, gives a picture of the theory from a number of standpoints and contains a good deal of experimental material. In a chapter entitled "Perception, Cognition, and Behavior" Bruner and Postman present a program, discuss the systematic and methodological problems involved, and summarize the more pertinent investigations. In Blake and Ramsey (eds.), 1951, will be found a discussion of the non-veridical aspects of perception (Chapter I). In the same work (by Blake and Ramsey) Bruner gives a later statement of his (and Postman's) position, Miller reviews theories and experiments dealing with unconscious perceptual processes, and Rogers discusses the changes produced in percepts through client-centered psychotherapy. The relation of personality to perceptual theory and experiment is treated in the same volume by Frenkel-Brunswik and Klein (see also Klein and Schlesinger in the Bruner and Krech symposium). A somewhat different statement of the motivational perceptual theory, in terms of "autism," can be found in Murphy, 1947, Chapter 15. For a valuable outline of hypotheses that should enter into a complete theory of perception (including the directive approach) see Murphy and Hochberg (1951).

not only the older views on perception but the newer findings on the influence of the motivational state of the perceiver. In accepting their share of the responsibility for an ultimate, unified system the directive-state theorists are also outspoken in their criticism of the earlier approaches.

PRELIMINARY STATEMENT OF THE THEORY: AUTOCHTHONOUS VERSUS BEHAVIORAL DETERMINANTS; "FORMAL" VERSUS "FUNCTIONAL"; CRITICISM OF GESTALT

Bruner and Postman divide the determinants of perception into two sharply contrasted categories, the "autochthonous" or "structural" on the one hand, and the "behavioral" or motivational on the other. Corresponding to these, they outline two contrasting programs of experiment and theory, the *formal* and the *functional*. Autochthonous determinants include the stimulus, the effects of stimulation upon the receptors, the afferent neurons, and the sensory cortical areas. They represent the innate and relatively unchangeable endowment of the individual for the activity of perceiving. The so-called stimulus-binding of sensory dimensions (Pratt) and the facts of psychophysics are based upon autochthonous factors, as are also the laws of perceptual organization of the gestaltists. Theories based upon such conditions are said to be "formal." The behavioral determinants, on the other hand, are related to the control of the "higher-level" processes. They have to do with the way "in which perceptual functioning is imbedded in and interacts with other forms of psychological functioning." Included in this category are the needs, tensions, values, defenses, and emotions of the individual, and of course his past experience generally. Such factors are involved whether they are elicited by the momentary stimulus and context or represent a stable part of the individual's personality. Taken together they form a *central directive state;* and a theory that takes them into account is said to be a "functional" theory. The older, formal theories are alleged to have neglected these behavioral determinants. The experimenter tried his best to control them, that is, to hold them constant so that they would not enter into the experiment and distort the effect of the purely autochthonous determinants. Experimentalists of the directive-state approach view the matter differently. They maintain that their task is to vary also the behavioral determinants, treating them not merely as something to be controlled but as independant variables. In this way it will be possible to gain information regarding their effect upon the organization of perception.

The polemical aspect of directive-state theory has developed largely in opposition to the gestalt school. Its advocates, like those of some other theories, have found gestalt principles inadequate for explaining perception. They charge that gestalt psychology "snubs the perceiver" who is himself a part of the total field. It is also charged that gestalt theory side-steps or underemphasizes the organism's creativity, and that it neglects the role of defense and motivation in general. Minimizing the part played in perception by past experiences and expectancies of the future, gestalt theorists, in their concentration on field organization, are prone to overemphasize the immediate present. Luchins (1951) has published an able reply to these criticisms, questioning the worth of the distinction between "formal" and "functional" and pointing out that the latter term has many meanings and needs clarification. The sharp separation of the categories of autochthonous and motivational was likewise challenged. Bruner (1951) has in turn replied to Luchins. His answer brings out some attempts of the directive-state theorists to show the place within a single system of both the behavioral and the autochthonous factors as well as the familiar effects of set and past experience. Of special interest is his statement that the autochthonous factors operate as "limits" that are built into the nervous system. They are bounding features which determine that a set can go so far, but no further, in influencing an act of perception.

THE PHYSIOLOGICAL AND EXPERIMENTAL PROBLEM; "MARGINAL" PERCEIVING

From the physiological standpoint the process of perception, broadly defined, extends itself along a continuum of increasing complexity. It ranges from simple receptor excitation and afferent impulses at the one extreme, though cortical processes having to do with figural properties, constancies, and adaptation levels, and through the physiological accompaniments of object-recognitions and meanings that involve "traces" and associations, to those cortical integrations that are connected with judgments and with the grasp of entire situations in their significance to the individual. All these activities may, moreover, involve returning proprioceptive impulses from motor reactions or changes of tonicity. In the view of directive-state theory, the above account of the physical bases of perception is not yet complete. We must add the physiological correlates of drives, emotions, needs, and values, and the enduring conditions of temperament and personality. This entire outline, of course, is mainly a logical device.

Somewhere in this whole aggregate of events the quantitative aspects of perception, time thresholds and perceived dimensions, are determined; though where or how we do not know. Nor do we know through what possible stages or mechanisms the motivational or "behavioral" factors might enter to produce their effects upon these properties of the percept. It is at this point that theory-construction becomes a significant undertaking. The theoretical objective just implied is an ultimate goal of directive-state theory. But before we can come to it we must know for certain that motivational or behavioral determinants do influence perception. We must discover effects which are clearly attributable to them. The task of experimentation thus defines itself as the immediate problem, and we shall turn to some of the conditions that such experiments involve.

First, a word is needed concerning the subject's report and the setting in which it is obtained. If the hypothesis dealt merely with the influence of familiarity or present set in ordinary perceptual experiences, there would be little that would require investigating. Such influences upon perception are already well known. Or if we were interested in learning problems in which set, in the form of perceptual selectivity, plays a facilitating role, we would again be travelling over familiar ground. All such determinants merely "prepare the way" for the perception of a certain kind of item; they are not thought directly to influence the character of the percept. The demands upon the directive-state hypothesis are, however, more exacting. In order to test this hypothesis we must discover the direct influence of some specific need, value, or interest upon the content of the subject's perception; and we must segregate this influence from the effects of mere familiarity or the set of the task. The experimental controls therefore must be more extensive and rigorous. Though we cannot, and should not, eliminate the factor of object-meaning, we must also remember that we are trying to study *perception* rather than complex and purely cognitive activities. These latter processes, though they are often hard to separate from "pure" perception and indeed form a part of the whole perceptual activity, should be reduced to a necessary minimum; otherwise they may mislead us in drawing conclusions as to what is actually perceived. It will be seen that much of the issue may later turn upon how broadly we wish to define perception. But in any case, the task imposed by the hypothesis requires that we get as close to true perceptual process as we can, that we try, as it were, to "catch it in the very act." Tachistoscopic techniques and fine controls of stimulus, reactions, and timing are necessitated by this direct attack.

One more experimental condition remains to be discussed. Since we are getting down to the very fundamentals of perception and since that process, under the control of the autochthonous determinants, is in general highly veridical, any changes in the percept tending to prove the existence of a distinct motivational effect would, in the normal course of events, have to be distorting, and hence probably rather slight. For that reason, such evidence might be difficult, if not impossible, to obtain. The directive-state investigators have solved this problem by placing the perceptual activity under some disadvantage, that is, by making it occur under "marginal" conditions. If, as Pratt says, phenomenological characteristics that are held in place by external stimuli do not readily yield to change or distortion, we might provide an opportunity for motivational determinants to change or distort them by artificially reducing the definiteness of the external stimulus pattern and thus weakening the control exerted by it. Is such a procedure legitimate? If the results were to be taken as indicative of the role of behavioral versus autochthonous factors in the normal perceptions of daily life, of course it would not be. There are, however, some occasions in ordinary life where stimulus conditions are weakened and rendered less binding upon the percept and a complete theory of perception will have to cover these exceptions as well as the more typical experiences.

The weakening of stimulus-binding in perceptual experiments has been accomplished in a number of ingenious ways. There is, for example, the technique of the so-called unstructured stimulus situation, a procedure exemplified by the showing of pictures or objects through a ground-glass screen or with dim illumination. Ambiguous drawings and reversible figure-ground patterns have also been used. Or again, one might present so many objects in the field of vision that accuracy of report as to their character or number would be hampered. Temporal as well as spatial limitations can be imposed. Perception, though it is a very quick process, requires *some* time to develop. By presenting materials tachistoscopically with such brief exposures (a few hundredths of a second) that uncertainty results, motivational influences can be given a chance to facilitate, inhibit, or modify the percept in the process of its formation. In the matter of dimensionality, also, stimulus-binding can be weakened. In some of the more traditional psychophysical experiments, employing the method of just noticeable differences, the percept is continually "bound" by the procedure of comparing the magnitude of a test-stimulus with that of some objective standard. But if instead of estimating the object in terms of some fixed, externalized scale, the subject is free to "adjust" his estimate of magnitude more directly to his experience (so called "production" method), as, for example, in regulating the aperture of a diaphragm-opening, a motivational state may have a better chance to operate and will be more likely to show itself in the results. Using devices of this sort it has been possible to test the theory that directive states influence perception. One can determine their effect upon what is perceived, upon the speed or accuracy with which it is perceived, and upon the dimensions in which it is perceived.

EXPERIMENTAL EVIDENCE FOR THE THEORY OF A DIRECTIVE-
STATE: FINDINGS ON SIX HYPOTHESES

The studies we shall now examine are merely a selection from the literature; numerous others could have been cited. Those selected, however, form a representative group that give the hypothesis its most definite support. Though some of the experiments were performed by psychologists who might not classify themselves as advocates of the theory, such experiments should, however, be here included, since they form an important part of the theory's empirical basis. In order to bring out the salient points for our later and more detailed presentation of the theory the results of all these experiments and their alleged bearing upon the question at issue will be here taken at face value. It should be borne in mind, however, that many criticisms of them have been advanced, a point to which we shall later return. The material can best be presented under the six following propositions or special hypotheses. They will deal, respectively, with (1) the effect of bodily needs on what is perceived, (2) the effect of reward and punishment on perceptual content, magnitude, and speed, (3) the influence of values on speed of object-recognition, (4) needs and values as affecting the dimensionality of the percept, (5) personality as a perceptual determinant, and (6) the effect on perception of the emotionally disturbing nature of the stimulus-object.

1. *Bodily needs tend to determine what is perceived.* Levine, Chein, and Murphy (1942) presented to subjects who had been deprived of food for varying lengths of time a number of ambiguous drawings of objects, including pictures of food. The drawings, some of which were colored and some in black and white, were exhibited behind a ground-glass screen. The subjects were asked to try to verbalize an association for every picture. The results showed that for achromatic drawings the number of times some article of food

was mentioned in connection with a picture increased after three hours of food-deprivation and increased still further after six hours. There was, however, a *decrease* at nine hours of deprivation. For chromatic pictures the number of "food" responses increased at three hours, but a decline set in at six hours. A control group who were shown the pictures on a series of occasions shortly after eating exhibited no such trend toward increase of food responses. It seems therefore that this special hypothesis was given some support. At least for the shorter periods during which a bodily need was felt, that need did seem to determine what was perceived under marginal conditions of perceiving.

2. *Reward and punishment associated with the perceiving of objects tend to determine what is perceived. They also tend to determine its apparent magnitude and its speed of recognition.* The effect of punishments and rewards upon what is perceived was demonstrated by Schafer and Murphy (1943). These investigators used, as stimuli, ambiguous or alternative figure-ground relationships. Drawings were prepared consisting of an irregular line drawn vertically through a circle in such a manner that either half of the circle could be seen as the profile of a face. The two faces were then cut out so that they could be separately presented. First, a training series was run in which the two pictures were presented to the subject separately. Each time a certain one of the faces was shown, the subjects were rewarded; and with each presentation of the other face they were punished (reward and punishment consisting of giving or taking away small sums of money). Proper controls were established by using two such stimulus-pairs and by varying the punished and rewarded members for two groups of subjects. After the training period the pictures were reassembled, and the two parts, joined into the complete circle, were shown to the subjects tachistoscopically with an exposure too brief to permit a perceptual alternation of figure and ground. A marked tendency was found for subjects to perceive the face for which they had received a reward during the training series, that is, to perceive this face as "figure"; while the other portion of the circle was not experienced as a face but only as "ground." This effect persisted up to the sixteenth trial when a different set intervened. Reward, as contrasted with punishment, therefore seemed to determine which of two alternative percepts would be attained. The subjects apparently had "learned" what to perceive.

The dimensional part of the proposition was tested by Proshansky and Murphy (1942). Subjects were asked to judge the length of sets of lines in a semidark room. A "long" set and a "short" set were used, together with an "intermediate" set. Every time one of the long lines was presented, the subject was rewarded, and every time a short line was presented he was punished (rewards and punishments as before). After a training period of this sort had been completed, a test series was run in which the subjects estimated the length of the lines again, but this time without reward or punishment. Again the effect of reward and punishment is seen. The average length-estimates of all the lines was greater in the test period than it had been in the training period; while a control group, who had received no reward or punishment in the training period, showed no such tendency. Thus the magnitude that was perceived did not obey Pratt's dictum of stimulus-binding, but was apparently determined by the satisfaction that had previously accompanied the perception of lines of greater length. A similar result was obtained in the estimation of weights, reward and punishment accompanying light and heavy weights respectively. The behavior of the subjects, according to the investigators, revealed that they were not merely "learning what to say" as a line was presented, but were actually trying to perceive the objects each time in a veridical manner. Smith, Parker, and Robinson (1950) have reported a similar investigation in which subjects were asked to estimate the number of dots in a cluster. The experiment was conducted as a contest in which prizes of ten and five dollars were awarded, the subject receiving one "scoring point" for each dot on a card when that card was correctly judged as to the number of dots it contained. Motivation toward realistic perception was thus employed; but against it there was pitted the desire for a higher score in order to win the prize. There was found to be an initial tendency toward overestimation by the experimental group as compared with the control.

Turning to the question of the effect of a reward associated with a perceived object upon speed of recognition of that object, we find that Rigby and Rigby (1952) confirmed this hypothesis. Their method was to "reinforce" certain capital letters by giving the subjects (children) candy when these letters turned up in a block-tossing game. Other letters were not reinforced; and for some letters candy was taken away (negative reinforcement). It was found that the more a positive reinforcement for a letter occurred the shorter was the tachistoscopic exposure time required for its perception. Negative reinforcement effects, however, did not differ from the effect of mere frequency of occurrence of the letter.

3. *The values characteristic of the individual tend to determine the speed with which words related to those values are recognized.* Postman, Bruner, and McGinnies (1948) administered the Allport-

Vernon Study of Values to twenty-five college students and secured their scores on the six value-categories—theoretical, economic, aesthetic, social, political, and religious. The subjects were also shown thirty-six words tachistoscopically, six words being meaningfully related to each of the value categories. These stimuli were presented with an increasing duration of exposure, beginning with .01 second and increasing until the word was correctly perceived. Five trials were given at each tachistoscopic speed. It was found that the higher the value to the individual of the value-category to which the word was related the shorter was the exposure period at which the word could be recognized. This special hypothesis therefore seemed confirmed by the shorter duration thresholds of the "valued" words. The incorrect responses given by the subjects before recognition of the words was achieved were grouped for analysis into several classes as follows: those which represented the same value-area as the stimulus word ("covaluant responses"), those which represented an area opposite in meaning ("contravaluant responses"), and "nonsense" responses. Stimulus words related to high-value categories for the subject brought out more covaluant reactions than words related to categories of low value, while stimulus words related to low-value categories yielded more contravaluant and nonsense reactions. Hence even the subject's "hypotheses" concerning words exposed more briefly than threshold duration showed a tendency to be consistent with the area of his higher values and inconsistent with his lower values. Using the same stimulus material a similar result with respect to recognition threshold was obtained by Vanderplas and Blake.[2] These investigators, however, employed as a measure of threshold the intensity of sound at which a *spoken* stimulus-word could be recognized (auditory perceptual threshold). They thus demonstrated the effect of the individual's values upon the acuteness of perceptions in an additional sensory modality.

4. *The value of objects to the individual tends to determine their perceived magnitudes.* In a somewhat more complete form this hypothesis may be stated as follows: The perceived dimensional properties of an object are altered (accentuated) by the relevance of that object to some need of the individual. This dimensional proposition was tested by Bruner and Goodman (1947). Ten-year-old children estimated the size of coins by altering a circular spot of light so that its area seemed to them to be equal to the size of the coin. In order to do this the subject turned a knob on a box which controlled, by

[2] See Bruner and Krech, eds., 1950, pp. 252–266.

means of an iris diaphragm, the size of a spot of light thrown from behind upon a ground glass screen. Coins in the denominations of one, five, ten, twenty-five, and fifty cents were used, also gray cardboard discs of the same sizes. It was found that the estimated size of every coin was larger than its true size and that the overestimation increased with the value of the coin from one to twenty-five cents, but dropped with the half-dollar. These effects were not found with a control group who estimated the size of the cardboard discs. In order to test the hypothesis with respect to individual differences in the value placed upon coins (behavioral factor of "need") an experiment was conducted in which the size-estimates made by ten children from well-to-do homes were compared with those of ten children from poor homes. In the case of every coin the "poor" children overestimated its size on the average more than the "rich" children. In an experiment where the subject was not given a coin to match but was asked to *imagine* one and to match its size from memory, overestimations similar to those for the condition of "coin-present" were given by the poor children, but to a lesser degree. Such overestimations were given by the rich children only for the half-dollar.

This experiment has been criticized on the ground that where the groups used are so small they should be more nearly matched with respect to all variables other than the one to be tested, which was in this case the psychological organization that carries the meaning of being well-to-do or poor. Ashley, Harper, and Runyon (1951) repeated the experiment. They solved this problem by using for both rich and poor groups the *same* subjects! To accomplish this remarkable feat they changed the "psychological organization" of the subjects from "rich" to "poor," or vice versa, by suggestions given to them in an hypnotic state. Adult subjects were used. They were hypnotized to a given criterion and were then told in some detail that they were affluent or that they were hard-pressed economically, as the case might be. Still under hypnosis, they were put through the Bruner-Goodman experiment using coins up to the twenty-five cent denomination. The results on the rich-poor hypothesis were in full agreement with the findings of Bruner and Goodman. Size-estimates made by these same subjects *before* they were hypnotized had been found to be approximately equal to the physical size of the coins. Under hypnosis the subjects when in the "poor" state (so-called state of "need") made their estimates consistently larger than their normal estimates, while in the "rich" state they made them consistently smaller. When metal slugs were estimated instead of coins and the subjects were told (at different times) that the slug was composed of "lead," "silver," "white gold," or "platinum," the size-estimate of the slug increased for both "rich" and "poor" with the value of the metal of which it was alleged to be made, the judgments of the poor again exceeding those of the rich for all metal-types. Estimates of *remembered* sizes of coins were similar to those in the Bruner-Goodman experiment but more consistent. Both "rich" and "poor" regularly overestimated, the latter more than the former; and for the poor the overestimation, more consistently with expectation, was greater when the coin was absent than when it was present. If the value and need can be regarded as capable of being instituted by a frame of reference hypnotically induced, the relation of these factors to perceived dimensionality seems clearly established by this experiment.

Lambert, Solomon, and Watson (1949) also thought that differences in the life-histories of subjects that might have a bearing upon the valuation of objects should be better known and controlled. The mere fact that a child comes from a poor or a well-to-do home does not tell us definitely what his attitudes or felt needs regarding coins will be. These experimenters reasoned that if they could take an object that originally was neither familiar to, nor valued by, the subjects and could give it a value by experimental procedures, they could be sure of the life-histories of their subjects with respect to that object and could know that the experiences of all the individuals regarding it had been uniform. Their subjects were nursery-school children. The object used was a poker chip. It was given a value by the fact that the chips, having been "earned" by the children as payment for cooperating in some simple task, could later be exchanged in a slot-machine for candy. Using the Bruner-Goodman type of equipment, size-estimates of the chip were made by the children in a pretest, that is, before it was used as a token that could be exchanged for the reward. Size-estimates of the chip were made again after ten days of rewarded use as tokens, again after extinction of the work activity by stopping the reward, and finally after reinstating the reward. Estimates were also made by a control group who were rewarded by candy directly after the work sessions without the mediation of the poker chip. Overestimation of size of the chip was general; but after ten days of reinforcement of the chip by the reward there was a significant rise in the overestimation as compared with estimates made in the pretest. Then there was a significant drop in the overestimation after extinction, and again a significant rise after reinstatement of the reward. No significant differences for these estimates occurred in the control group. An induced meaning of value thus seems to have increased the perceived size of the valued object.

Extending the logic of this sort of experiment to the field of symbolism, Bruner and Postman (1948) had subjects estimate, by the diaphragm technique, the size of discs bearing a dollar sign (as a positive value-symbol) and of discs bearing the Nazi emblem, the swastika, as a negative value-symbol. They found that a disc containing the former was judged larger than a disc containing the latter, though both were judged larger than one containing a neutral design. From these results it was tentatively inferred that whatever is *important* to the subject, whether positively or negatively, is likely to "loom larger" in his perception.

The studies so far described were concerned with monetary tokens or with symbols representing objects that might be acquired through their use, rather than with the valued objects directly. Will the same results appear when the latter condition is employed? Beams and Thompson (1952), using seventy children from ten to twelve years of age, showed to each of them an object of food for which the child had previously expressed strong liking or disliking, and asked him to estimate its size by adjusting a kodochrome image of the object by moving a sliding screen. The distance to which the screen was moved by the subjects was measured and a comparable set of measurements were secured for a "life-size" (i.e., veridical) adjustment. The difference between perceptually estimated and life-size adjustments was then computed for both the liked and the disliked articles of food. Finally, the difference between these two difference scores was obtained and was found to be significant. Overestimation of size occurred with the liked but not with the disliked food objects. Affectivity, as a special variety of value, seems to play a part in the determination of perceived magnitude. There is, however, one difficulty with this experiment as a study of perception. The food-object was not in view at the time when the subject made his size estimates. He moved over to another position in the room for manipulating the screen adjustment. The accentuation-effect may therefore have occurred with respect to the *memory* of the object rather than in its actual perception. Had there been an actual matching of screen-image to food-object with both in the field of vision, the effect might not have occurred. Such, indeed, is the position taken by the authors. It will be seen later that another pair of investigators (Carter and Schooler), using careful controls, were able to confirm the Bruner-Goodman findings only with respect to the *memory* of coin-size.

5. *The personality characteristics of the individual predispose him to perceive things in a manner consistent with those characteristics.*

This hypothesis is not as crucial as some of the others for the theory of directive state. Though it is clearly in line with that theory, it represents a combining of directive-state procedures with independently established methods of clinical experimentation. Since it is impossible to review here the extensive literature in this field we shall give only a few of the more pertinent observations. Taking a broad view of perception, the wide and successful use of projective techniques may be regarded as a confirmation of the proposition as stated, though, as we shall later observe, its precision in hypothesis-testing is limited. Traits of extraversive or introversive activity are considered to be associated with the amount of "empathic movement" seen in ink-blot tests. There is some evidence that a tendency toward illusory visual experience of motion, as contrasted with perceived bodily motion, is related to differences in personality. Witkin found that people who had difficulty in visually extracting an imbedded figure from its context also found it hard to separate their own bodies perceptually from a tilted environment so as to determine their position with respect to the vertical by gravitational cues alone. Such a finding suggests a general personality factor underlying spatial perception.[3] Frenkel-Brunswik[4] found evidence that ethnically prejudiced individuals, who may also have a general "intolerance for ambiguities," display a lack of flexibility in classifying the members of a transitional series of pictures. Similar differences of rigidity or flexibility have been manifested in estimating sizes or weights when the series to which the individual was becoming adapted was changed without warning.[5] Such individual differences can be taken as evidence that the personality of the individual may determine, within limits, the way he perceives, or at least judges, his world.

A more systematic way of approaching the question is to take measurable variables that reveal individual differences in perceiving and correlate them with certain aspects of personality that might play a role in their determination. Thurstone (1944) employed factor analysis to identify basic variables underlying perceptual differences. Cattell and Wenig (1952), using normal subjects, investigated a special class of perceptual variables familiar to clinical psychologists, namely, the "projections" of the individual's characteristics that reveal themselves in what he says in interpreting or telling a story about a picture. These authors prefer to call such projections "misperceptions." Employing thematic-apperception pictures that might yield

---

[3] Studies reported in Bruner and Krech, eds., 1950, pp. 145–170.
[4] Bruner and Krech, eds., 1950, pp. 108–143.
[5] Klein and Schlesinger in Bruner and Krech, eds., 1950, pp. 32–47.

various types of projection, measurements of the variable of misperception were obtained for a number of hypothesized "misperception processes" evoked by pictures expressive of the drives of dominance and sex. The subjects were asked to give an interpretative response, but selectivity was invited with respect to a number of alternatives. There were also obtained measurements of the strength of the subjects' sex and dominance drives, a set of non-misperceptive measures of processes believed to *underlie* misperception, and measures of six characteristics from a personality test. Forty-eight variables of this sort were submitted to factor analysis.

As a result there were isolated the following eight factors upon which misperception, as defined by the authors, was found to depend: self-assertive "erg" or drive (dominance), mating drive (sex), cognitive disability (from deficient intelligence or lack of information), autism, rationalization, phantasy, "true" projection, and general neuroticism. Cattell and Wenig do not speak of these items, for the most part, as personality characteristics, but simply as factors in the misperception-process. The last named, general neuroticism, was a second-order personality factor. There are, however, unitary tendencies found in what is broadly called projection; and it seems not improbable that they bear some relation to the consistent personality pattern of the individual. The two drives, sex and dominance, named above as factors underlying misperception, are clearly personality variables. Certain characteristics of personality appear to be associated with particular misperception *processes:* sex drive, anxiety, and perhaps dominance seem to go with fantasy. Rationalization tends to go with "superego strength," and true projection with paranoia. High "libido-strength" is associated with phantasy, rationalization, and projection. There is evidence that the amount of misperception is proportional to the amount of drive as manifested in the tests. This last finding runs counter to the claim of some clinicians (experiments to be later mentioned) that misperception is proportional to the strength of *unconscious* motivation but not to the intensity of drives that are overtly expressed. Studies of this sort illustrate a systematic method of exploring the influence of the individual's characteristics upon the way he perceives his world. That there is some relationship between the two is evident.

6. *Verbal stimuli that are emotionally disturbing or threatening to the individual tend to require a longer recognition-time than neutral words, to be so misperceived as radically to alter their form or meaning, and to arouse their characteristic emotional reactions even before*

they are recognized. This proposition, the most challenging of all the directive-state hypotheses, was tested in its various parts by McGinnies (1949) and by McCleary and Lazarus (see Bruner and Krech, eds., 1950, pp. 171–179). McGinnies presented a series of eighteen words tachistoscopically to his subjects (eight male and eight female college students) beginning with an exposure of .01 second and increasing by steps of one one-hundredth of a second until correct recognition was achieved. After each exposure the subject stated what he thought the word was. Eleven of the words were of a "neutral" character; seven were "critical." The latter were words of an unpleasant or socially tabooed character, such as "bitch," "whore," and "raped." The galvanic skin response (indicating autonomic reactions) was taken, with electrodes placed on the palms, after each presentation of each word. The results were striking. Duration thresholds for the recognition of the critical words were longer than those for neutral words, and the galvanic skin responses were greater for the prerecognition presentations of the critical words than for the prerecognition presentations of the neutral words. An analysis of the misperceptions or "guesses" showed that for neutral words there were more cases in which the word as perceived was structurally similar to the stimulus word than was the case for critical words, and that for critical words there were more instances where the word as perceived was structurally dissimilar or of a nonsense character. All the predictions of this special hypothesis therefore seemed to be confirmed.

McCleary and Lazarus, in order to eliminate the effect of certain uncontrolled variables in this type of experiment, employed ten five-letter nonsense syllables in place of meaningful words. For five of these an unpleasant or disturbing effect was established by accompanying a one-second exposure of the syllable with an electric shock. Through a series of this sort a galvanic skin response, showing autonomic or emotional disturbance, was conditioned to each of the five crucial syllables. After conditioning had been established all the syllables were presented at tachistoscopic speeds that ranged from extremely brief up to approximately threshold. The galvanic skin response was measured, each time, between the instant of exposure of the word and the subject's report of what he saw (the report being delayed sufficiently to permit the recording of the GSR). No shock was used here; but because of the prior experience of the subject the conditioned autonomic responses persisted throughout the test-period. Considering only syllables that were wrongly perceived, i.e., that were reported at *subthreshold* exposures, it was found that the galvanic skin response was greater for the previously "shocked" syllables than it was for those that had not been accompanied earlier by shock. Even though the exposure was too brief to permit a correct perception, the word elicited the autonomic (or emotional) response that had been conditioned to it. The authors conclude that "at tachistoscopic exposure speeds too rapid for conscious discrimination . . . the subject is still capable of responding in a discriminatory way."

The results of this remarkable study seem to show that there is a very rapid and unconscious, but nevertheless "veridical," level of perception that goes on at the same time as the slower and less accurate process of consciously perceiving, and that with exposures below the ordinary threshold of visual perception this rapid unconscious activity gives us, in quite appropriate emotional terms, the significance of an object which, though it stimulates us through our eyes, we do not visually perceive. Such a possibility does violence to our settled habit of conceiving the organism as a being that is stimulated, then perceives or recognizes, and then reacts. Could it be that meaning from past experience is a deep-lying physiological process or ensemble of events geared in with bodily activities, and that *conscious* perception is only a superficial part or manifestation of this meaning-ensemble? This interpretation, in any case, would enable us to get away from the anthropomorphic notion of some inner perceiving agent that first "cognizes" and then sends out the appropriate signals for response.

DIRECTIVE-STATEISTS' INTERPRETATION OF THEIR FINDINGS; "PERCEPTUAL DEFENSE"

Though, as we shall see, interpretations of the experiments differ, findings of the sort we have reviewed in these six special hypotheses are the groundwork upon which directive-state theory is based. Let us see what the investigators themselves have said about them and how the results were spelled out into a set of concepts and a rationale for the theory. In some instances, as new findings came to light, generalizing constructs were hypothesized on the spot. In other cases older concepts were furbished up and put to work. It was assumed that a "mechanism" of some sort mediated between the motivating conditions and perceptual reaction, producing the observed effects upon the latter; though the nature of this mechanism could be only a matter of conjecture. By Murphy and his collaborators the process was spoken of as "autism." It was a kind of wishful perceiving, or cognizing, in the direction of need-satisfaction.

Bruner and Goodman inferred from their results a process which they called "perceptual hypothesis." It might be set up by any need or demand internally or externally imposed upon the organism. If the hypothesis is "rewarded" by the attainment of a corresponding percept, it may become "fixated." At the same time it becomes stronger, with the result that perceptual objects habitually selected become more vivid or greater in apparent size—in other words, they become "accentuated."

From their experiment upon word-recognition thresholds Postman, Bruner, and McGinnies formulated three mechanisms through which values come to determine perceptual selection. First, value-orientation lowers the threshold for acceptable stimulus objects (*selective sensitization*); second, it raises the threshold for unacceptable objects (*perceptual defense*); and third, it induces the observer, even at speeds so great as to lead to misperceiving, to perceive the object as something that lies at least within the same value-area as his preferred hypothesis (*value resonance*). Perceptual defense was illustrated by the fact that stimulus words related to categories whose value for the subject was *low* not only had higher duration thresholds, but evoked more prerecognition responses of a "contravaluant" type. Words relating to high-value categories were more quickly perceived; and they produced at subthreshold speeds more "covaluant" prerecognition responses. For example, the word reverence presented to a religious subject called forth, at a one-hundredth of a second exposure, the covaluant response "divinity." The total vocabulary of the theory does not end with the three mechanisms above listed. It has grown into an impressive array of intervening constructs including such terms as "availability," "normalization," "dominance," "assimilation," "compromise-formation," "vigilance," "primitivation," "hierarchy of thresholds," "schematization," and "degree of personal relevance."

A deviant branch of the theory is represented by Klein, Schlesinger, and Meister (1951) who question whether a broadside concept of accentuation through need or value is appropriate or adequate, and maintain that the non-veridical in perception is a function of the personality of the individual. Their own repetition of the Bruner-Postman experiment on the size of symbols yielded not a clear-cut general tendency, but consistent individual differences. Hence we must take into account not merely value, but the valuer. The determining influence may not be blanket categories of needs, but the manner in which the individual is organized to cope with his needs. To the list of constructs given above these authors add such phrases as ego-structure, limits of tolerance of error, differences of ability of perceivers to minimize "irrelevant" factors like need or motive, and preferred perceptual attitude.

The most daring exhibit of the theory and the winner of all honors for revolutionary outlook is the concept of *perceptual defense*. It is also the one that offers the greatest theoretical difficulties. We have for some time been accustomed to psychoanalytic mechanisms of repression, wish-fulfillment, and rationalization as influences that distort the way we *believe, feel,* or *think*. When however this "functionalistic" idea is extended to the *perceptions* of normal college students in looking at words in a tachistoscope, we have something new. The inference here is that the subject represses, delays, or distorts his percept of something that he has not yet seen so that he will not see it. We have already mentioned the hypothesis of Postman, Bruner, and McGinnies concerning the raising of the duration-threshold for non-valued words and the injection of contravaluant and non-relevant responses in the misperception of these intruders. In the experiment of McGinnies, the subjects, faced with unpleasant tabooed words, not only were slowed in their recognition-time and led to give structurally dissimilar (defensive) reactions, but they also exhibited a telltale emotional reaction. It was as though they had recognized the words in exposure-times too short for them to be recognized!

We have seen that evidence of autonomic discrimination without awareness was found by McCleary and Lazarus for shock-paired nonsense syllables. These authors maintain that they have demonstrated a level of perceptual activity different from that of perception in the ordinary sense, and they suggest that we call this process "*subception*." McGinnies interprets his results as "representing conditioned avoidance of verbal symbols having unpleasant meanings to the observer." Certain cues from the inimical stimuli are "appropriately evaluated by the central nervous system" even though the afferent impulses from them do not become fully integrated to the point of recognition of the word. Perhaps cortical integration is delayed by some thalamic process that mediates a concurrent autonomic reaction. Avoidance of "further anxiety" is provided through the incompleteness of the cortical integration and the raising of the perceptual threshold. Perceptual defense thus manifests itself in the resulting failure to recognize the word.

The difficulty with any theory of "perceptual defense" is that if we do not understand it in a functionalistic manner, under the teleological concept of agency, we are unable to see how the word "defense" is appropriate; yet if we do think of it in this way the weirdest kind of nonsense results. If the defending agent is something inside the individual that controls perceptual activity, we have a manikin-theory. If the defense is carried out by the perceptual process itself, we would have to believe that a physiological process operates in such a way as to prevent itself from operating. Critics have not been slow to point out the inconsistency involved in perceiving something before one perceives it. Behind the perceiver we must postulate a "pre-perceiver." ⌊Referring to the experiment on word values, Hochberg and Gleitman charge that this kind of interpretation implies a "Pure Ego," one who "initially cognized the percept, then rejected it," and that "the need theorist can unify his battalion of needs only by placing them at the disposal of a small simulacrum of the organism, almost an organism in miniature, placed somewhere within the 'personality.' "[6] Such an approach seems to reduce psychology to an "homunculus situation," with a tendency to relegate problems to a "never-ending, concentric series of homunculi." Bruner and Postman are themselves aware of the difficulty. The experiments, they say, "suggest to the guileless investigator the image of the superego peering through a Judas eye, scanning incoming percepts in order to decide which shall be permitted into consciousness."[7] Before we conclude that psychological theory has fallen upon such an evil day as this we must scrutinize more carefully the methods of these experiments. If something then remains to be explained, it will be the office *par excellence* of some good theory to take us out of the morass of anthropomorphic functionalism and give us some hint of what is happening in the organism. As was remarked in the first chapter, important theories grow out of intellectual crises.

One requirement for an overall theory (assuming that the directive-state interpretation of the experimental work is sound) is that we find some way of clarifying the relation between autochthonous and behavioral factors in perception, or as Murphy might put it, between realism and autism. In Bruner's reply to Luchins it was stated that the autochthonous elements set limits within which the behavioral elements are constrained to act. But on the other hand, it had been found that behavioral determinants influence properties of the percept that had been regarded as autochthonous. Schafer and Murphy found that the aspect of the total percept that has been accompanied by rewards is seen as figure. It is also the contention of the directive-state theorists that dimensional properties of percepts, previously considered the sole domain of the formalists, have been altered in a

---

[6] Bruner and Krech, eds., 1950, p. 184.
[7] Bruner and Krech, eds., 1950, p. 25.

number of experiments by the factor of need or value. How this two-way action occurs and what sets the limit as to how far behavioral determinants can go are matters that are shrouded in mystery. The possibility that "suppressor areas" in the cortex, under the activation of autonomic impulses, might function in the control of sensory phenomena has been mentioned by Klein and Schlesinger.[8] Murphy and Hochberg (1951) suggest that the veridical phase of the percept is the work of the exteroceptive stimulus pattern, while the autistic or non-veridical aspects are due to afferent impulses from proprioceptors or interoceptors. Increasing the latter, therefore, while weakening the organization of the former, will enhance autistic or need-motivated perception. This interpretation seems plausible, but it does not go very far.

In seeking to explain accentuation, Bruner and Postman have invoked Helson's adaptation-level. In the matter of size, for example, it may be assumed that this level for valuable or needed objects is, under certain conditions, higher than for indifferent or neutral objects. The "trace system," in the gestalt concept of memory, is similarly affected. Valued objects therefore have a higher adaptation-level in memory. In judging the dimensions of a valued object the stimulus is assimilated to this high level and in consequence appears large. It would also seem in point to invoke the sensory-tonic field theory; for Werner and Wapner hypothesized that the need-state of the organism, represented in viscerotonic changes, may, by projection, affect the properties of the perceived object.

All these ideas clearly imply the role of past experience in perception. In terms of gestalt theory, recognition, a process involved in the perception of objects, must always bring into activation through the stimulus a "trace" of a similar experience in the past. Such traces (or memories) are organized systems which, for Koffka, had a localization in the brain that was distinct from the locus of the stimulus-process. In Köhler's theory traces are simply cortical fields whose activity continues after the stimulus has ceased to act. Recognition requires some kind of communication between the incoming stimulus and a trace; and this process assumes importance in trying to explain the results of experiments upon word-recognition, such, for example, as altered threshold and the misperceptions associated with the value or the disturbing character of the stimulus. In attempting such a theory one can assume, first, that a given stimulus-process can communicate with, or "mobilize," many traces; but that the "availability" of the various traces for mobilization may be

[8] Bruner and Krech, eds., 1950, p. 38.

different. Some communications may have lapsed through disuse, or some traces may have become unavailable because of the punishment or deprivation to which their activation had previously led. Other traces, however, may be highly available. Moreover they may be "indiscriminately" available, as classes, to a broad range of stimuli. Shifting over to a behavioral, stimulus-response terminology (for Bruner and Postman believe the explanation holds as well in the parlance of behavior-theory as it does in gestalt), we can say that there is a broad gradient of stimulus generalization for the stimuli with which we are concerned.

We now make the final assumption that motives, need-states, and expectancies of the organism produce characteristic changes in availability of different traces or response systems. It is this differential availability of classes of traces or responses that accounts for the phenomena observed in the tachistoscopic perception of words of differing values or of emotionally disturbing character. Thus Bruner and Postman sought to rid themselves of the demonology that had crept into the concept of perceptual defense. It is not necessary, they said, to assume that veridical report is the only kind of response the subject is capable of making to a stimulus word. There may be many possible response tendencies that can be "tripped off" by a presentation of the verbal stimulus; veridical report is only one of these. Other reactions, affective in nature and leading to avoidance responses, may also be tripped off. All these responses moreover may have *different thresholds*. A *generic* affective or emotional reaction aroused by the tabooed word might forestall perceptual closure (recognition) for the stimulus word and lead to disorganized or contravaluant responses. From this general line of reasoning the perceiving superego and the Judas eye seemed no longer necessary. In their "Theory of Cognition," a later development of the notion of hypotheses, Bruner and Postman have made a significant advance over these earlier attempts at explanation. This part of the story, however, will be reserved for a later chapter.

EXPERIMENTAL EVIDENCE AND LOGICAL CONSIDERATIONS AGAINST THE THEORY

In beginning our appraisal of the directive-state program we would do well to recall its principal conditions and objectives. The material we have just covered has been concerned with attempts to formulate a theoretical system for explaining the results of the numerous motivationally oriented experiments earlier described. It was assumed in these attempts that the experiments themselves were valid, that the findings were reliable, and that their interpretations were both logical and inevitable. We cannot begin at this point with our critique of the theory, for these assumptions raise some questions. Though the results as we have reviewed them appeared convincing, careful study of the matter by other experimenters and critics have produced some doubts. The actual findings can probably be accepted as statistically sound—only reliable experimental differences were represented in the summaries given. But were the experiments valid as tests of the special hypotheses to which they were directed? Were they adequately controlled so that the hypotheses they were confirming were always the same as those the investigators intended? Could the results be as logically explained by some other theory without the use of the directive-state formula? Have other investigators obtained the same results? Since the field of investigation is new and experimenters have not yet reached stable agreement, these questions, relevant to the testing of all theories, must here be given special attention.[9]

The first of the experiments, that of the Levine, Chein, and Murphy on food-perceptions produced by hunger, has been criticized on two grounds. First, the subjects were asked not to report what they "saw," but to "verbalize associations" with the blurred pictorial stimuli, a process similar to that of finding a meaning in ink-blots. Though we cannot draw a sharp line between perception and associated imagery and interpretation, it would have seemed more convincing, for an hypothesis making specific claims about perception, if the report had been restricted more definitely to what the subjects *saw*. Second, the effect of hunger on perception markedly *decreased* in passing to the long (nine-hour) period of deprivation. The results in toto, therefore, did not support the hypothesis; and additional, somewhat opportunistic, hypotheses had to be developed to explain the discrepancies. Still, the findings for the three- and six-hour hunger periods remain as something to be accounted for. There is some evidence that hunger affects the character of "perceptual associations," though we are handicapped in stating a law that accurately and meaningfully describes their relationship. In contrast with the "autistic" finding of these investigators it should be noted that Brozek, Guetzkow, and Baldwin (1950–1951) found no reliable effect of

[9] For additional criticism of some of the directive-state experiments and of the theory itself see Pastore (1949), also a reply by Chein et. al. (1951). See also Luchins, 1950–1951.

semistarvation on the number of perceptual food-responses to Rorschach stimulus cards.[10]

In relation to the second experimental proposition, the study of Schafer and Murphy dealing with the effect of reward and punishment on the perception of figure and ground has been repeated by Rock and Fleck (1950) with negative results. These investigators also discovered a disturbing effect (novel appearance of the two faces when placed together) that constituted a criticism of this general procedure. Smith and Hochberg (1954), however, found that administering a shock with the presentation of one of the two profile faces decreased its tendency to be later perceived. This result supports the conclusion of Schafer and Murphy with respect to the effect of *punishment* on figure-ground perception. The work of the Rigbys on perceptual thresholds under reinforcement has not so far been challenged.

We turn now to the third hypothesis, that of Postman, Bruner, and McGinnies on the speed of perception of value-related words. As is often true in pioneer work, an important disturbing variable was here left uncontrolled. Howes and Solomon (1951) demonstrated that the briefness of duration of visual perceptual thresholds for words is positively related to the frequency of occurrence of the words in ordinary language usage. It is thus a function of word-familiarity. Noting the stable relationship between word frequency and visual duration threshold, Solomon and Howes (1951) predicted that "differences between the duration thresholds of words representing extreme differences in *value-rank* will be small compared with differences between the thresholds of words representing extreme differences in *word frequency* according to the Thorndike-Lorge word counts." Using a procedure essentially the same as that of Postman, Bruner, and McGinnies, they tested this prediction and found it to be fully confirmed. Though there was a slight tendency for words of

[10] It might be objected that our presentation of the case for the autistic perception of objects related to bodily needs was incomplete. A number of experiments and many observations have been reported that show the preoccupation of people suffering hunger-states with ideas of eating and food. These investigations, however, have not for the most part been studies of perception, but were at the level of associated ideas, picture or word completions, or, in one case, of imagery aroused in looking at a blank screen. Attempts to verify, in controlled experiments, the actual perception of stimulus-objects as having a form and character dictated by a bodily need that has undergone deprivation are rare.

higher value-ranks to have lower thresholds than words of low value-ranks, the tendency was not as systematic as it had been in the results of Postman, Bruner, and McGinnies. These investigators also found that when stimulus words were divided into frequently and infrequently used classes by the Thorndike-Lorge word count the *frequent* words showed little relationship between value-rank and duration threshold, while for *infrequent* words this relationship was much greater and was significant at the extremes of value-rank. Postman and Schneider (1951) repeated their original experiment using the frequency controls of Solomon and Howes and obtained substantially the same results as the latter.

These facts show that, for words commonly used, the subject's value-areas and involvements have practically nothing to do with his speed of recognition of words relating to those areas. His threshold is merely a reflection of the probability of word responses in the general population. But how about the words that are infrequently used? Here opinions differ. Postman and Schneider maintain that the correlation between value-rank and shortness of duration threshold that was found here is a real support for the directive-state hypothesis. Their claim is that with a longer period required for recognition of infrequent words selective sensitivity to different value areas has a chance to become effective and therefore operates to reduce the threshold for high-value words of the infrequent category. Solomon and Howes contend that with infrequent as well as with frequent words recognition threshold is still merely a matter of familiarity. This factor operates with infrequent words in a more personal or idiosyncratic manner. Subjects who are high in a certain value-area have probably used words relating to that area more often than subjects whose interests lie in other directions; hence they will recognize them at shorter duration thresholds than will other subjects to whom they are not so familiar. This interpretation, in the light of our present knowledge, seems better than that of Postman and Schneider in that it is more parsimonious. It makes use of a principle already established and does not require the invoking of mechanisms of whose nature we are entirely ignorant. Postman and Schneider, however, cling to the importance of personal values, maintaining that even if the frequency of usage of words does account for their low recognition thresholds, the values of the subject will have underlain the frequency of his past usage of these words. Such a view, though reasonable and convincing in itself, really undermines the directive-state position; for that hypothesis was oriented toward the effect of values operating immediately upon the act of perception and not merely in past experience or upon the frequency of past activities or habit formation.

If the case for the hypothesis that word-value influences perception should be lost (and it is hard to see how it can be clearly sustained without new evidence), there would then be no occasion for a theory to explain *how* word-value affects perception. This denouement would mean that the concepts of perceptual sensitization, perceptual defense (as based upon these experiments), and value resonance would, for the present at least, have to be abandoned. Doubts would also be raised concerning other earlier experiments based upon the word-threshold method.[11]

The fourth experimental proposition, which concerns the effect of needs or values upon perceived dimensions, would appear at first sight to be well fortified through the four supporting investigations previously reviewed. There is, however, some conflict between these results and those of other investigators. Carter and Schooler (1949) repeated the Bruner-Goodman experiment on coin-size estimation with certain changes prompted by the need of more rigorous methods. They failed to confirm the findings of Bruner and Goodman except in the non-perceptual area of memory for coin-size. Inconsistent results for different age groups is seen in a preliminary report on the coin-size problem by Rosenthal (1951). Klein, Schlesinger, and Meister (1951) repeated, with extensions, the Bruner-Postman experiment of judging the size of discs bearing symbols. Notwithstanding the fact that the symbols had strong positive or negative value for the subjects, neither intensity of valuing nor degree of value attached to particular symbols had any consistent influence upon error of size-estimation. Individual tendencies either to overestimate or to underestimate in general were found to occur independently of the value of the stimulus figure.

Since our preceding review of the size-accentuation experiments was written, Gilchrist and Nesberg (1952) have published a beautifully controlled study which would seem at first sight to clinch the argument for perceptual accentuation. They chose for their accentuated dimension not size but "illuminance," that is, the amount of light which the object seemed to reflect, or, in more ordinary terms, the brightness of the object. The subjects, who had gone without

---

[11] In the more recent word-recognition experiments investigators have usually been careful to control word-familiarity by the Thorndike-Lorge frequency counts.

food (or water) for a varying number of hours, were shown projector-images of food (or liquid) objects at standard voltage illuminances. After the picture had been exposed for 15 seconds the light was turned off for 10 seconds and the picture was then shown again but at an illuminance different from the standard. The subject's task was to adjust, by turning a knob in front of him, the illumination of the image so that it would appear to him exactly equal to the standard illuminance previously used. It was found that as the need for food (or water) increased, through an increasing time of deprivation, the subject's adjustment of the illumination of the need-related picture steadily increased. A control group who had taken their meals and had drunk water at the usual periods showed no such tendency. Slides presenting homogeneous stimulation-patterns, or articulated figures not related to the needs in question, produced no such over-estimation. It was thus found that the apparent brightness of the object is increased if the object is related to the satisfaction of need; and its brightness accentuation is directly proportional to the need.

There is one difficulty with this experiment which, unfortunately, is crucial for perceptual theory. As in the Beams and Thompson experiment the subjects were not looking at the standard object when they made their matches. The light had been turned off, and the same picture was then used for the illuminance adjustment. No stimulus to be matched was present. The matches were therefore based on "remembered" rather than on perceived brightness. It was a case of immediate memory, of course, but still memory. The question therefore arises whether the subjects were retaining and duplicating through the adjustment an actual accentuated percept which they had experienced ten seconds earlier, or whether their prevailing need-state led them to distort the memory image or at least to produce an illuminance that would be in some way consistent with their energic state, even though in so doing they would be exaggerating what they had previously actually perceived. A perception of standard and reproduction in the same field of vision at the same time, if the method had permitted such a procedure, might have yielded more veridical estimates. That need states and emotions may affect memory-processes dimensionally has long been suspected, but it is another matter to prove that they affect the dimensions of percepts. Perhaps they do, but a method of showing it is extremely difficult to achieve. As for experiments of the type performed by Gilchrist and Nesberg we should remember that while directive-stateists are allowed the privilege of making their stimulus-objects indistinct and marginal they are not permitted to abolish them from the perceptual situation altogether when estimates of their dimensions are to be made. An experience without a stimulus-object is not a perception.

Questions now begin to arise about the other experiments, those, namely, of Bruner and Goodman, of Lambert, Solomon, and Watson, and of Ashley and his associates. Did the subjects make actual perceptual matchings in which both standard and variable stimulus patterns were equally attended to at the same instant, or did they pass from an inspection of the former to an adjustment of the latter in such a way that the standard impression was maintained only in terms of a memory image or of some bodily set that was subject to modification in the interim? Of course, if memorial accentuation through the energizing effects of a need state occurs, it is in itself a highly interesting phenomenon and must find a place in psychological theory. But the question concerning the magnitude of the *percept* does not yet seem to be fully answered. *Are* perceptual dimensions, as Pratt says, really stimulus-bound? Are there exceptions? If so, how far from the stimulus dimensions can they deviate? The situation is not yet clear. Although some striking experimental results have appeared there are probably many who feel that the burden of proof still lies with those who reject stimulus-binding as the rule and attempt to supplement it with motivational determination.[12]

The findings for the fifth experimental hypothesis, the influence of personality characteristics upon perception, are difficult to evaluate with respect to directive-state theory. There is no denying the progress that has been made in individual study and clinical diagnosis through tests that measure or classify various aspects of perception. Work with projective tests has had a long and fruitful history independently of the current of perceptual theory to which it is, in one manner or another, related. As a general proposition it seems likely that insofar as the stimulus situation permits, and within the range of the non-veridical that does not seriously disturb the adaptation of the organism to its surroundings, normal individuals do tend to perceive in a manner consistent with their personal characteristics and their

---

[12] For a further critique of the size-accentuation hypothesis see Bruner in Blake and Ramsey (eds.), 1951, page 139. Bruner and Rodrigues (1953) have sought to resolve the differences between the Bruner-Goodman and Carter-Schooler experiments by a new investigation. They conclude that the causation of size-accentuation is complex and that the resolution of the experimental discrepancies is still far from complete. Their main finding demonstrated a "relative," as opposed to an "absolute," overestimation for coins. That is, as the value (and size) of the coins increased, their overestimation increased more markedly than was the case for the discs.

differences of temperament and constitution. This point has been stressed by Werner and Wapner, by Klein and Schlesinger, by Witkin, and by many others. Psychopathic individuals in whom thematic apperception tests or other methods indicate the presence of repressions show tendencies for increased perceptual thresholds for pictures or auditory stimuli related to the areas of these conflict disturbances; while others who do not repress seem to be more, rather than less, sensitized to areas in which their stronger impulses lie.[13]   But as we shall see later, the inference of perceptual defense which seems here supported is subject to some variations of interpretation.   Concerning the question of whether personality elements affect perceived dimensionality, there is some positive evidence from the studies of Klein and his associates and also from findings on the perceptions of the verticality of objects or of the body.   Some of these results, however, are subject to the type of criticism of dimensional experiments that has already been presented.

As a test of the essential directive-state position, research in the field of personality is on the whole less satisfactory than that in other areas we are discussing.   In the first place, the directive-state program, at least as originally conceived, postulated broad nomothetic laws concerning the effects of motivation upon measurable aspects of the percept.   In clinical work and personality studies that use directive-state procedures the emphasis is upon individual differences. Direct and unequivocal evidence for a *general* theory of perception can scarcely be expected from such a quarter.   Second, few of the methods of classifying or measuring perceptual variables in clinical and personality diagnosis are sufficiently precise or well defined for a quantitative testing of the motivational theory of perception.   Do the answers in a Rorschach test, for example, reveal actual object-perception in the narrower sense of the term perception; or do they reveal associations, imagery, or interpretation—or do they perhaps reveal a composite of all these processes and others besides?   Is not the emphasis here upon meaning-classifications and qualitative considerations rather than upon magnitudes and thresholds?   And similarly for tests of thematic apperception: Is the individual who acts as subject merely perceiving, or is he also interpreting?   If he is doing both, or if perception *is* interpretation (which we must be prepared to admit), how can we relate this complex situation to the exacting demands of the directive-state propositions?   How non-veridical is a subject's report in his interpretative story of a picture?   Whose interpretation could be taken as a veridical standard?   What kind of a

---

[13] Cf. Eriksen, 1950, 1950–1951, and Lazarus, Eriksen, and Fonda, 1950–1951.

continuum could be set up among such qualitative materials as pictorial "thema" that would provide the quantitative testing which the hypotheses require?

Finally, it should be noted that the directive-state hypothesis, in order to be true to the claim of motivational versus autochthonous determinants, must envisage a demonstrable effect of need states or motives set up *in the immediate situation* and their direct influence upon the perceptual act.   If the hypothesis is true, such immediately controllable effects should be found.   Personality studies of perception, on the other hand, deal with background conditions, long-standing sets or characteristics of the individual that can scarcely be modified or controlled in the experimental situation.   In view of all these considerations it would seem that evidence from the field of personality, though it has been included within the directive-state program because of its obvious affiliation, is not really a critical test of the theory.   It seems justified therefore to give it less weight in our appraisal than we give to the other hypotheses.

We now come to the sixth and final proposition, which has to do with subception and perceptual defense.   We recall that McGinnies found a rise of recognition threshold for emotionally toned as compared with neutral words.   Concerning this investigation Howes and Solomon (1950) have advanced two trenchant criticisms.   The first deals with the lack of control of the frequency or familiarity variable with respect to the words used.   The second alleges, that, under the conditions of the experiment, the subjects may have been retarded not in perceiving the tabooed words, but only in reporting them.   The so-called defensive delay in word recognition might have been due to the withholding of the report because of embarrassment in the experimental situation, a setting that included not only the "dignified professor" but a young lady assistant.   From the standpoint of social psychology the failure to control this feature seems an obvious error. The heightened galvanic skin response to tabooed words could be interpreted in a similar manner (embarrassment in the social situation), as could also the dissimilarity of the critical "prerecognition" responses from the stimulus word that evoked them.   McGinnies (1950) has replied to Howes and Solomon, but not too convincingly on the matter of withholding.   For details of this spirited and somewhat ribald discussion the reader can consult the references cited. It is of course possible that the interpretation of this experiment as revealing defensive perceptual tendencies was correct.   Further experimentation, *provided it can be conducted with adequate controls*, is the only way in which the question can be answered.   The investigation of McCleary and Lazarus might be cited as a study in which the use of nonsense material forestalled these two criticisms of Howes and Solomon. It does indeed escape both. But in the report of this study, as earlier cited, there was no evidence to show that the conditioned response to the shock that had been given with critical syllables operated as a *defense against their recognition*. In fact, the "shocked" syllables were correctly recognized more frequently than the non-shocked. The experiment definitively tested only the hypothesis of autonomic discrimination without awareness. The findings, therefore, do not establish the case for perceptual defense.

It should be acknowledged that in work with mental patients there have been found differences in perceptual indices accompanying, and diagnostic of, different types of needs and apparently related to repressions; and that in some cases differentials on thresholds for words or pictures related to such disturbances have shown a defensive character.[14] The question arises, however, whether such findings reflect something that happens in the perceptual act itself or a different sort of reaction. The term perceptual defense is misleading in that it suggests that defense is accomplished *through* perception (i.e., through the abortive character or self-retardation of the perceptual process), an interpretation that raises the dilemma of a subconscious, preperceiving perceiver. If we could consider that some fractional stimulus-element in the situation, rather than the complete and meaningful stimulus pattern, can, in short exposures, lead the subject *to avoid perceiving anything further with respect to that stimulus pattern* until long exposures give him no escape from perceiving it, the matter could be more simply explained. It would not be a case of "perceptual defense," in the sense of raising the threshold, but simply of an inhibition of perceiving that has been conditioned to certain (actually perceived) cues. We shall return to a fuller consideration of this problem in another connection.

Returning to the experiment of McGinnies, which we said should be repeated with better controls, it should be noted that such an attempt has already been made in a study by Cowen and Beier (1952, 1954). These investigators used, instead of a tachistoscope, blurred typewritten copies of the critical and non-critical words. They were arranged in booklets for each word, in which the typing became clearer as successive pages were turned. The experimenters recorded the number of trials (pages turned) and the time required for the word to be correctly reported. As a check upon word familiarity they correlated threshold magnitudes for correct recognition with the

---

[14] Cf. the experiments of Eriksen and of Lazarus et. al., *op. cit.*

Lorge word-frequency count. The resulting correlation coefficient was found to be zero. A second problem was to control the social setting. This factor they apparently identified with the conventions surrounding polite communication with a member of the opposite sex. They sought, therefore, to determine whether any raising of the threshold that might occur for the critical words represented merely a delay in the reporting, in the presence of a member of the opposite sex, of words that had already been perceived. For this control both male and female experimenters were employed equally for both male and female subjects, and a comparison of results was made between like-sexed and opposite-sexed experimental situations. It was again found that the crucial or "threat" words required more trials to decipher correctly than did the neutral words; and this was true whether the subject and experimenter were of the same sex or of opposite sex. No significant differences were found as between like-sexed and opposite-sexed situations. The authors thus concluded that their results were not due to the social factor, but showed the operation of a process of perceptual defense.

But does this experiment really settle the issue? It is true that the delay of reporting the correct word could not have been due to a difference of the sex of the subject from that of the experimenter to whom he reported. Inhibition of report was also probably lessened by the fact that the experimenter read to the subject, before the experiment, a list of words containing those that would later be used as stimuli. Nevertheless some inhibition against reporting the tabooed words might still have occurred. In the "polite" society of *either* sex one may not wish to reveal that he has been consciously entertaining a word of such an unconventional character until he is pretty sure that he has seen it and the experimental conditions permit no escape. Nor does the fact that post-test inquiries showed very few cases of (conscious) inhibition, or that the subjects were said to be "sophisticated," guarantee that inhibition of report had not taken place.[15] We cannot suppose that the subject upon entering the laboratory becomes an "experimental robot," laying aside segments of his behavior that have become habitual in the presence of those who form a part of his daily environment. The writer has elsewhere called attention to the possibility of broad social attitudes, or sets, that may be active in the presence of human beings generally (1924, pp. 320–321). The experimenters in the present study have probably

[15] In connection with an earlier study (1950–1951) the authors themselves suggested the possibility of delay in giving the report and noted that some evidence in this direction had been found in the introspections.

oversimplified the problem of controlling the social factor. It is indeed possible that it cannot be controlled by any method short of turning the whole experiment over to the subjects and trusting each subject not only to do the perceiving, but to report to *himself* and to pool his results anonymously with those of other subjects. Perhaps it could not be controlled even then. Words like "penis" and "whore" might not "threaten" the subject so much when he sees them all by himself as when he is in the presence of, and in communication with, another person; and this might be true not as a perceptual matter, but because of the danger of a breach of the amenities that might arise in an act of communication to which the presence of another person is a standing invitation.

At the risk of betraying certain tendencies in himself, and recognizing that there might be individual differences in such matters, the writer would say that he is not at all sure that if one were to come upon such words written on a piece of paper lying in a field in which one was taking a solitary walk, one would not ordinarily be intrigued rather than "threatened." Perhaps the defense that has appeared in all these experiments is a matter of behavioral interaction in a social situation, rather than of perception. Or, if it *is* a matter of perception, it might be perception only in a social situation, where the thing that menaces us is not the stimulus-object but our own cognizance of that object while in the presence of others. This, of course, might still be called a case of perceptual defense if it involved the blocking of the actual percept as well as the communication; but it would place the problem in a new framework. The same analysis might hold for the clinical case where strong repressions, such as those holding in check an aggressive tendency, seem to be raising the perceptual threshold for related stimuli. For after all, the reason for such repressive restraints upon ourselves is usually, in part at least, a social one; and we would naturally be on guard against revealing to others, that is, to "society," any percepts that might betray such tendencies. If one wishes, one can say that the experimenter represents to the repressed subject a projection of his own "superego" or his "social self." We would then have a case in which "part" of the subject refused to admit to the other part (and to the experimenter) that it had perceived the word. But all such speculation seems idle in view of our lack of experimentally available referents for these concepts.

Let us turn for a moment from these unprofitable "agency" concepts to another kind of interpretation. From the preceding analysis the reader will recognize in another form our old problem of the "inside" versus the "outside" (Chapter 4). The psychology of an individual has two aspects; it "fronts," as it were, two ways. There is the internal viewpoint, the operations of "dynamic structurings" that go on inside him, and there is the outward-facing aspect, the individual conceived as structured into a social group or society. The situation is not unlike that of ballistics in the physical world. A ball that is thrown has a characteristic trajectory as a whole (gravitational structure of space-time); but there is going on within it at the same time a complicated dynamic process involving molecular and atomic cohesive action and vibrations. That is, there is also an "inside" structure. We feel that these two structures must be related, but the ordinary principles of mechanics do not show us how. In the behavior of an individual (organismic structure) who is operating within, and as a part of, a larger, collective, structure the same kind of problem arises. How are the inside and the outside structures of the individual related?

We encountered the problem in Lewin's system where he tried to solve it through a denial of the inside structure by everting it, making the individual a point, and by mixing the inside features with the outside components of the topological field. This problem, which Lewin failed to solve, is basic to any theoretical program of social psychology. To apply it to our present discussion of perception we would ask whether the delay of the report for tabooed words is something that occurs because a structure that is *in the individual,* that is, the perceptual structure, yields a percept-meaning so adverse or negatively relevant to the collective structure which the individual is *in* that the outer enunciation of that meaning is inhibited as long as possible; or, on the other hand, is the individual's involvement in the "outside" or collective structure so strong that not only does he hesitate to speak the negatively related word but his "inside," perceptual, structure fails even to "perceive" it?[16] The collective or outer structure of the individual and its control are often very strong. But so is the inner, perceptual structure. Without an acute and fairly accurate capacity to perceive our world we could not survive. Are we so constructed that we jeopardize or reduce this capacity in order to satisfy the conventional expectations of those with whom we associate?

---

[16] The latter interpretation, however, would not be equivalent to admitting either a preperceiver or an act of perceptual defense. It might mean only that the individual has habitual generalized *sets* for perceiving that which is socially approved, and that these sets are antagonistic (Chapter 9) to sets for non-approved perceptions and tend to inhibit them. The whole matter will be further clarified in Chapters 15 and 16.

Here we have a nice question, one that carries us into realms beyond the present experiments and calls for a deeper analysis of the whole problem. We cannot settle such issues at the present stage of our knowledge; we can only hope to lay the groundwork for later inquiry. Returning, then, to the appraisal of the directive-state experiments, we can conclude our discussion by wishing the proponents of perceptual defense good speed and hoping that they will be able to find more rigorous methods and better controls than they have in the past. Again we concede the possibility that the "defense" findings may represent some true perceptual phenomenon. What the advocates of this view must do, however, is to devise techniques that will really prove the point and lead on from there toward a discovery of how the process works.[17]

WEIGHING THE EVIDENCE: EVALUATION OF THE DIRECTIVE-STATE MOVEMENT

This re-examination of the experiments supporting the directive-state hypotheses leaves us in considerable doubt. Many of them, if viewed by themselves, seem to point in the direction of the general thesis, and often in a striking manner. But when problems of control, of interpretation, and of variations in other findings are considered, the matter becomes less certain. Let us leave to one side the hypothesis dealing with the effect of personality, since, as earlier noted, it is not a crucial test. Of the five remaining experimental propositions none has succeeded in attaining both universal agreement on the findings and a method that forestalls ambiguities of interpretation. Let us examine them in order.

[17] Howie (1952) contends that the results of perceptual defense experiments can be explained more simply as due to the dominance of some perceptual set, a possibility to which we shall later return. He criticizes the defense theory on the ground that it is biologically non-adaptive. By defending itself against stimulation the organism closes the door to the perception of realities and thus tends, through the Freudian pleasure principle, not toward adjustment but toward the "goal of death." See also Luchins, 1950–1951. Both Howie and Luchins call attention to the inconsistency of directive-stateists in employing the two concepts, "perceptual vigilance" and "perceptual defense." In some experiments an increase rather than a decrease in sensitization or accentuation has been found for threatening stimulus objects; and the two terms just mentioned have been applied, respectively, to these two opposed effects. There is here no ground for the building of a consistent theory. If perception defends us against perceiving, it cannot render us more alert and effective in the perceptual act. The practice has apparently been to choose between these two principles according to the way the results turned out. But see also Postman's reply (1953) to Howie's objections.

In the *first,* though Murphy and his associates found effects of hunger on the number of food-responses reported, the results were not supported through the use of another method. They were also inconsistent for different periods of deprivation and had to be harmonized through ad hoc hypotheses not subjected to testing in independent experiments. In the *second* proposition (on the effects of reward and punishment on figure and ground, magnitude of lines and weights, and perceptual speed for rewarded stimuli), though quite a number of experiments gave positive results, one investigation was negative. On the whole this hypothesis seems better supported than most of the others. In the *third* proposition, word-value in relation to threshold and other recognition features, Postman, Bruner, and McGinnies found significant differences between valued and nonvalued areas of word-reference. Other investigators, too, have discovered such differences. It is doubtful, however, that the influence of value and affect, if present, can be separated in these experiments from the effects of word-frequency or familiarity. Owing to individual differences in familiarization, this criticism may hold even for words that are infrequently used, and in cases where the lists have been equated by standard word-frequency tables. The *fourth* hypothesis, dimensional accentuation of need-related objects, has four experiments in its favor; but there are three in whole or in part against it. Bruner and Postman, moreover, discovered size-accentuation for both valued and disvalued objects, a finding that complicates matters. It is also difficult to prove in these experiments that the dimensional change results from a need or motivational state rather than from some meaning-factor (to be discussed later); and there is the further point that two of the positive studies, and perhaps others, involved immediate memory rather than perception alone. In the *sixth* and final proposition, on the hypothesis of perceptual defense, though consistent results have appeared, it has not yet been possible to control completely the disturbing effects of the social environment. Prerecognition reactions of an emotional character to syllables previously accompanied by shock have been demonstrated; but this fact alone does not confirm the defense hypothesis. Time differences in reporting crucial and non-crucial words at brief exposures have been found among patients having repressed areas of conflict. These delays of recognition, however, might have been due to avoidance factors operating in some manner other than by a slowing of the perceptual activity per se, and the problem of controlling the experimental-social factor again arises. Though the concept of perceptual defense is coming into common use, experiments are not yet sufficiently controlled to show clearly the meaning of the results obtained. That the subject's behavior in the perceiving situation is affected is clear, but it is difficult to be sure that the effect is truly perceptual.

From the standpoint of special types of investigation rather than experimental propositions, there are three procedures whose results or methods have not, to the writer's knowledge, been contested. The first two pertain to the effects of reward and punishment. They are the procedure used in the study of the Rigbys on duration-threshold for letters whose perceptions have been positively or negatively reinforced, and that of Proshansky and Murphy on the estimation of lines and weights following punishment and reward in training series. The first of these seems capable of interpretation as the establishing, by prior reinforcement, of a set, thus making the positively reinforced objects seem to "stand out" and reducing their recognition time. Here set, rather than value or motive, might be the strategic factor. This interpretation, of course, does not preclude the possibility that motivation was *indirectly* active in establishing the set. The second of the experiments might be related to a similar attention-set, or to an adaptation-level toward greater length of lines or greater lightness of weights. The level of a whole class of stimuli might thus have been raised. Again, there is the *possibility* that motivation to secure the reward may have entered; but it does not seem *necessary* to assume this in order to explain the results.

The question, of course, will arise as to why punishment did not produce a similar attention-set in these experiments. The withdrawing of candy or pennies might very well have served, like the bestowing of these as rewards, to establish an attention-set. This time, however, the attitude created, if any, may have been one of indifference toward neutral objects or toward objects that did not fulfill a certain (reward) type of set-expectancy. It seems better, however, to think of such objects simply as devoid of a (positive) set for recognition and report. In tachistoscopic experiments the troublesome question of a preperceiver does not arise when the reaction is one of positive or facilitated perceptual recognition. The set, as shown in Chapter 9, is selective and automatically reinforces the perceptual process for the stimulus-object for which it prepares. Metaphorically speaking, the ground is prepared for the reception of a certain stimulus-pattern or pattern-type. If the ground is not so prepared the stimulus-pattern acts more slowly upon the nervous system and recognition takes longer to accomplish. In cases of actual avoidance of the percept (defense), if such occurs, the concept of set (a contrary set) also covers the matter if we are willing to accept the hypothesis of cues. But perhaps it is not necessary to raise the question of the "punished" stimuli at all. It will be remembered that in the Rigby study definitive results for the negatively reinforced letters were not obtained; while in the Proshansky-Murphy investigation a set to see the lines as long would automatically have prevented their estimation as short.

Social psychologists will be quick to point out another possibility in the interpretation of these experiments. The relationship between experimenter and subject could have determined the emphasis which the subject placed, in his sets, upon different stimulus objects, according as they seemed to be implicitly characterized as important or unimportant by the experimenter. This unintended suggestion of experimenter-appraisal could have been communicated to the subject *via* the "rewardings" and the "takings away" in the earlier training period. It is as though, in giving a reward, the experimenter were to say "*these* are the stimuli to which you should pay special attention." It would not be necessary for the subject to believe that the experimenter "valued" the rewarded objects, but only that he apparently wanted them to be emphasized in the subject's set. In the line and weight experiments such an inference of the attitude of the experimenter might have helped to induce longer or lighter estimations. Here again, we would have to consider the subtle, but no doubt appreciable, influence of the "outside," or collective, structure in which the individual is at the moment involved. It would seem that this consideration might outweigh the reward value of the small amount of money associated with the longer lines. The situation could still be regarded as a learning process, reinforcement coming from the realization by the subject that he had satisfied the experimenter's expectation in the social structure. But once this disturbing collective structuring of the individual is introduced, would we be sure that he had learned how to *perceive*, or only how to communicate? Proshansky and Murphy have rejected the latter interpretation on the ground that later reports from the subjects gave no evidence for it; but in view of the fact that the formation of sets in collective as well as solitary situations is usually unconscious, the rejection is not altogether convincing.

The third of the experimental procedures which thus far have yielded uncontested findings is that of McCleary and Lazarus, the results of which led those investigators to postulate a subthreshold process of "subception." Autonomic discrimination of the stimulus object at exposure-speeds too great to permit its recognition, if further confirmed, might take its place as an important and theoretically challenging phenomenon. But as we have shown, it is related to the concept of perceptual defense only in a tangential manner. The fact that the "shocked" syllables were more readily recognized than the "unshocked" would argue for an energizing effect of emotion within the perceptual aggregate quite contrary to that implied by perceptual defense.

In the preceding analyses we have been employing earlier established concepts such as attention, set, and adaptation-level, as well as other considerations only indirectly related to the postulate of motivational perceiving as announced by the advocates of directive-state theory. Since these explanations have seemed adequate to account for the phenomena, the bringing-in of the directive-state postulate would seem unnecessary. It will thus be seen that unambiguous support for the hypothesis that needs, values, and motives directly affect perception has not been forthcoming from the group of experimental procedures whose results and methods have thus far been least subject to question.

What, then, should be our final appraisal of the directive-state thesis upon our first criterion of theory-evaluation? Is it broadly supported by the facts? Are the facts presented in its support deducible from it in a clear and univocal way? There have been later confirmations as well as contradictions of the directive-state findings on various hypotheses, and this consideration should be given due weight. In some cases of mainly negative experiments a *portion* of the findings were in the direction of the hypothesis. There is much in the experiments that is suggestive and in line with the directive-state contentions; and there is every indication that the investigations should be pressed further. Fair appraisal is at present rendered difficult in a number of ways. Different methods of attacking the problem often give different results. Changes of procedure, though indicated for the purpose of better control, still leave us in some doubt as to the processes that are active when conflicting results are obtained. For this reason, and because different experimental conditions may have subtle and uncontrolled effects upon the subjects' attitudes, the situation is not clear. We do not always know what hypothesis we are testing. Investigations or experimental propositions other than those reviewed might have supported the thesis better. The writer concedes that a possible subjective bias may have entered into his selection of the cases we have studied.

All things considered, however, it seems fair, in the writer's opinion, to say that the hypothesis that needs, values, and other motivational factors operate directly as determinants of perception, affecting the quantitative aspects and character of the percept in the manner predicted by the experimental propositions, has not yet been definitely confirmed by the experiments. There are indications that this *may* be true; but although some marked and characteristic changes have accompanied the introduction into perceptual experiments of conditions productive of motivation, we are not certain that these changes are always perceptual or that they are typically the result of the motivational aspect of the interpolated conditions. Nor have they yet been shown to be sufficiently uniform, stable, and predictable through repeated investigations to permit a lawful statement of their relationship to the variable of motivation. If the hypothesis were to be stated in some other fashion perhaps the imposing output of the experiments might tend unequivocally to support it. But it is also highly probable that further experiments will be necessary if any single hypothesis is ultimately to be sustained. Investigations will be needed that are focused upon essentials already brought to light under experimental and logical criticism and implemented by newly devised and more adequate controls.

Since the hypothesis that motivational state influences perception, or at least the question of what effect it produces, is still in an unsettled condition, attempts to formulate a theory explaining *how* this effect is produced must be uncertain in that they are elaborated only upon the insecure and sometimes conflicting evidence the experiments have thus far yielded. For this reason it would not seem profitable to enter upon a systematic stock-taking of the particular theories already advanced. These have been presented at length in earlier pages and we shall leave them without further comment.[18]

There is nothing inherently illogical or improbable in the directive-state proposals. On the contrary, we might well expect that large increases of energy (motivational or otherwise) in any of the aggregates of behavior might alter the timing and dimensions of the latter in some lawful way. Provided one recognizes that most perceptions are in the main fairly veridical, it would seem logical to suppose that *some* effects of motivating conditions, which are so critical in the learning

---

[18] Some attempt, however, will be made to evaluate them in the general summary in Chapter 20.

A movement is already under way toward a broad reformulation and reorientation of the central hypothesis. It will soon be our task to follow this development and to suggest further related hypotheses which might fit more adequately with the present experimental situation.

process, would show themselves also in the act of perception. Psychological theory is tending toward an increasing awareness of integration among all aspects of the organism's behavior. The ultimate question might not be whether motivational states enter or are related to the perceptual act, but in what way they are related to it—how we can find a place for them along with autochthonous principles, and the extent and manner in which they enter into or modify the laws upon which the veridical perception of objects depends. With better controls and sharper definitions the experimental movement of directive-state may ultimately succeed, and a systematization may then be in order. Such an eventuality, however, would be not unlikely to involve a reformulation of both the theory and its experimental hypotheses as perception becomes better understood. The experimental program in this field is developing and changing rapidly, and some basic modification of its position may soon be forthcoming. An important step, already taken in that direction, will concern us in a later chapter.

Before a final restatement is achieved, however, we may see further diversification, uncertainties, and schisms among the theories of perception. Though they have pressed their attack vigorously, the directive-state theorists have been on the whole neither dogmatic nor oversanguine in their expectations. They have opened a new and fascinating field of study, but they do not maintain that it will provide in itself the key to a unified and general theory. Though not all who have applied the directive-state rationale to their special fields have shown such caution, most of the investigators whose work we have been reviewing have recognized the great complexity and diversity of theory in all domains of psychology, a diversity which directive-state theory, because it deals only with a limited class of perceptual phenomena, is the more obliged to take into account. Bruner and Postman in concluding their earlier methodological article have said that in the study of directive factors in perception increasing linkages must be made with other areas of behavior theories. Since the latter are discordant one may expect that perceptual theory will become correspondingly riven. According to these authors we may see ten years hence an article in some prominent psychological journal entitled, "There Are Six Kinds of Perception."[19]

The failure of directive-state experiments to provide clear-cut confirmation of the hypotheses as originally stated does not diminish their theoretical importance. Indeed, as we come to realize that the hypothesis requires revision and that we must grope our way further

[19] Bruner and Krech, eds., 1950, p. 30.

among the data for new ideas, the significance of the experimental contributions becomes increasingly clear. Though the results have been sometimes divergent and their import uncertain, reliable findings in particular experiments have revealed unexpected phenomena that show both the need and the possibility of exploration in an area about which all too little is known. Whether interpreted as due to set, to adaptation level, or to motivation, the reinforcement effects upon dimensional estimates, thresholds, and figure-ground selection discovered in such experiments as those of Proshansky and Murphy, Smith and Hochberg, and the Rigbys are challenging. Even though it may not be "defensive" in its significance the "subception" phenomenon reported by McCleary and Lazarus is something to be reckoned with, something that might help to shape the course of future ideas concerning behavior. Accentuation estimates for size or brightness of valued objects, first noted by Bruner and Goodman but found also by others, are striking discoveries even though we are still uncertain as to what they mean. Whether perceptual testing in clinical psychology can be used to test a theory of the specific effect of motivation or can serve only as a diagnostic procedure, it has extended our horizon concerning the total integrated behavior of the individual—and in this behavior perception plays an important role.

Through all these experimental efforts there runs the consistent thread of motivational influence, emotional stresses, drives, valuational emphases, and conflict states—in short the significant theme of the energies of human behavior. Though the experimenters have not always been able adequately to isolate them, to identify their sources, or to spell out their specific consequences for perception, striking evidence of the presence of these energic changes in connection with perceptual situations has in one way or another made its appearance. Whether such changes reveal the operation of perceptual laws or not, their incorporation into systematic conceptions will lead in the end to a more unified and adequate basis for psychological theory. In bringing such phenomena to light the contributions made by directive-state theorists have been outstanding.[20]

[20] Since the preceding account was written, several investigations have been reported throwing further light upon the directive-state hypothesis. Wispé and Drambarean (1953) have studied thresholds of word-perception for words related not to values, but to biological needs (hunger and thirst). They found that words related to these needs were recognized more rapidly after a period of food and water deprivation than immediately after eating and drinking. The relation however was not linear, since the recognition threshold for these words did not decrease after a 24-hour, as compared with a 10-hour, deprivation. The authors interpret their results in terms of stimulus-response learning theory and

METHODOLOGICAL CRITIQUE OF ACCENTUATION EXPERIMENTS:
PHENOMENOLOGICAL AND OPERATIONAL DIFFICULTIES;
AMBIGUITY IN THE CONCEPT OF VALUE; MOTIVATION
VERSUS COGNITION

Though no useful purpose would be served by attempting a detailed criticism of the original directive-state theorems it will be worth while to examine two characteristic and troublesome problems encountered in their method. These difficulties, which have contributed to the uncertainty regarding the conclusions, bear upon the availability and explanatory value of the concepts employed; and both can be illustrated from size-accentuation experiments. The first deals with the dependent variable of perceived magnitude, the second with the independent variable of value and the related concepts of motivation and meaning.

What is the methodological status of perceived accentuation? The problem is a knotty one. Neither the percept nor perceived magnitude

---

the "hypothesis" theory of Bruner and Postman (see Chapters 15 and 17), rather than in the more subjective framework of the effect of "needs" on the perceptual threshold. Among the prerecognition responses, reaction-words signifying acts *instrumental* to need-satisfaction, as distinguished from needed objects or "eating" and "drinking" words, decreased at the 10-hour and increased at the 24-hour deprivation. This result is related to an earlier finding of McClelland and Atkinson (1948) to the effect that responses pertaining to acts instrumental to obtaining need-satisfiers increase as the need increases.

Bricker and Chapanis (1953) attacked the problem of McCleary and Lazarus using "guessed" responses to tachistoscopically presented nonsense words, but without shock-reinforcement. They found that after the first wrong guess fewer trials were needed to perceive the stimulus correctly than would be expected by chance. They interpreted their results as signifying simply that "incorrectly perceived tachistoscopic stimuli convey some information." Applying their findings to an interpretation of the McCleary and Lazarus experiment they maintain that the information conveyed prior to recognition comes from partial aspects or cues within the word. They thus reject the notion of "subception" and the implication that an unconscious determination of behavior can be operating under conditions where recognition is impossible.

Howes (1954a) argues that, by making certain reasonable assumptions, the McCleary-Lazarus data can be shown to be predictable from the experimental condition on the basis of *probability-theory* much more adequately than by the "subception" hypothesis. Lysak (1954) reports a "punishment" experiment analogous to the setting for perceptual defense, the results of which are said to support an interpretation of response-withholding rather than of defense against perceiving. Eriksen (1954), however, presents arguments in favor of the defense concept, especially with respect to individual differences in defensive reactions.

are in themselves directly available for experimentation. One can define them operationally only in terms of the stimulus conditions and the verbal report, or by manipulations of some apparatus by the subject. Since a percept, being purely phenomenological, has no physical size, measurements can be applied only to the matching device which the subject tries to equate to his perception of the object. We could, if we choose, apply strict operationism and say that the perception or the percept *is nothing but* the verbal report or manipulative response as it follows the presentation of the stimulus-object. Thus we would define perception entirely in terms of externally observable and measurable factors (cf. pp. 52–54). But to do this would be to answer the question originally posed by our definition of perception by eliminating it. We would not be interested in explaining why things appear to the subject as they do, because we would not be concerned with their appearance at all. We would be interested only in measurements of an object and a diaphragm, and in the stimuli and movements by which the subject adjusted the latter to the former. We could add to these observables, if we chose, the statement that perception is an unobservable "intervening variable" lying between the stimulation and the matching response. But we could say nothing further. If, on the other hand, we want to treat the *experience* of perceived magnitude lawfully, if we want to keep the percept, we are then confronted by some troublesome questions.

When, for instance, a subject adjusts a diaphragm to the perceived size of an object, or a projector-image to the size or illuminance of an object previously viewed, how do we know that he is reacting merely to size or brightness? How do we know that his "size"-*perception*, as distinguished from his overt adjustment, is an experience only of size? In psychophysical experiments the monotonous and meaningfully meager character of the stimuli control this feature; but in directive-state experiments the very *lack* of its control becomes an inseparable feature of the method. The object must not be neutral, but must have some challenging meaning to the subject.

We must, therefore, ask such questions as the following: In making his adjustment, is the subject making a "whole-souled" effort to match the stimulus exactly as he has *perceived* it; or does there creep into his reaction an unconscious tendency to make it conform to some attitude, idea, or feeling that he has *about* the object, such as its monetary value, its emotional significance, or his need of an object of that kind? Is the matching operation geared in a one-to-one way with the percept, or do other considerations enter? Does he, at the instant of matching, *perceive* the object's dimension that he leaves upon the instrument, or does his adjustment express in part his idea of how large or bright the object, being what it is, *ought* to look? Since the percept is phenomenological and private no one can tell, possibly not even the subject himself. These facts cannot be revealed by the observable operation and quantitative results, no matter how ingenious and careful the procedure employed.

Should such an extraneous set as we have just indicated be present, would it fuse with the visual experience (cf. the motor theory of perception) in such a way as to make an exaggerated adjustment *visually appear* as equal to the object—would the dimensions of object and diaphragm be *perceptually* the same? Or would the adjusting operation, under the influence of a set toward the object's character or meaning, prevent the subject, in spite of good intentions, from carrying out the instructions of reacting only on the basis of perceived size? Such an inquiry becomes especially pertinent when the experiments rest, as at least some of them do, upon memorial rather than direct perceptual matching. For even an instant of immediate memory could permit such a factor to enter the adjustment of the apparatus and give a spurious result. Unless we knew that the subject then looked back at both the standard and comparison object, *perceived both* at exactly the *same* instant, and then made a readjustment, we would have no way of being sure the error had been eliminated. Such time factors in comparisons are, however, difficult to control; and so intrusive is the aspect of meaning that neither the experimenter nor the subject might be able to say that a purely perceptual experience of equality had been attained.

These questions are fundamental to any decision as to the claims of directive-state theorists regarding the relation between value or need and perceived dimensionality. Yet who is in a position to answer them? All we know is that the subject, when asked to match the aperture of a movable diaphragm to objects, makes openings for supposedly valued or needed objects that are larger than the physical size of these objects. And so we are *forced* back to the standard of outwardly observable operations even though these operations leave us in the dark about important matters.

This discussion illustrates the limitations pointed out in Chapter 2 with respect to phenomenological data. In spite of the gestaltists' endorsement of introspection as the reporting of immediate experience, the method falls short of the physicalistic standard of accuracy; for we cannot always be sure as to what the immediate experience is. Though the adjusting act *seems* to be an objective matter, the processes on which it is based and therefore the resulting measurements are observer-involved. There is no encounter of the subject with a testing instrument which *in turn* encounters the object to be described. Overt operations, though acclaimed as the basic criterion of scientific objectivity, do not, in the perceptual experiment, denote, identify, or even guarantee the existence of the referents of the concepts they are called upon to define. It might seem better here simply to admit the unavoidable limitations of perceptual experimentation insofar as it involves phenomenological data, no matter how the percepts are reported. This discussion at the same time points out the limitations of the molar approach and the impression that we can solve our problems by intervening variables tied down at both ends to the observables of stimulus and response. The fact that the subject as a "whole organism" observably manipulates a diaphragm or screen-image in a certain way cannot tell us the story of his perceptual, ideational, or memorial processes. The overtly observable response is likely to involve merely the outer elements of some aggregate-phenomenon that cannot be analyzed until we find a method of exploring the remainder of the aggregate that lies inside the organism. Until we recognize these limitations and develop finer methods of study, even in the face of great difficulties, our chances of acquiring the knowledge necessary for basic theories seems rather slight.

Even if true perceptual accentuation could be established, our present lack of a denotable basis for dimensionality would restrict the explanatory significance of any theory that might be proposed. Perceived size, brightness, and the like are to the subject just what they are—simple, indivisible experiences. They bear no earmarks showing what increments might be contributed to them by one set of elements or another. There is no way of determining what would be provided by the sensory stimulus pattern, and what would be added by cortical integration, motor activities, emotional processes, drives, or the physiological bases of cognition and meaning. Nor do we know when or how dimensional contributions from such sources might enter the percept. If we assert that the so-called dimensional effects of motives may be due merely to the physiological accompaniments of "interpretation" that are *added to* the physiological basis of the percept, how can we draw the line, with our present externally limited operations, between the "judgmental" and the strictly "perceptual" part of the total aggregate? How, also, can we explain or envisage the "additive" process? Or if, with the directive-state theorists, we say that no such line should be drawn, that it is all "one perceptual process" within which dimensionality is being controlled by motives along with other determinants, how can we prove this assertion or give a rational account of the matter unless we can explain in physiological terms what perceived dimensionality is and how it *could be* so affected?

Notwithstanding all these difficulties, it must be conceded that the results of some of the experiments are challenging. Though accentuation effects were not found in some of them, and though in some they seemed to apply more to memory than to perception, the overestimations when present were often pronounced and statistically reliable. Distortions of the actually perceived size or illuminance of valued objects might really be occurring. If it occurs in the "memory-trace," as seems highly probable, it might also appear in the original perception. It would not seem strange that the large increases of energy induced in the perceptual aggregate by the presence in that aggregate of disturbances from need states might affect the cortical physiological pattern of the percept in such a way as to accentuate its physical dimensions, thus giving rise to changes of perceived brightness or size. Our problem, however, is to devise some method by which we can *know* that this is occurring and some testable theory as to how it might occur.

Turning now to our second problem, that of value and motivation, we note that an aura of the spectacular has surrounded at least a part of the directive-state program. The motivating circumstances have sometimes been exaggerated out of their proper proportions. Although the hunger states and the electric shock were real enough, the few pennies that were given or taken away from college students in the figure-ground and line-estimation experiments could hardly be called effective rewards or punishments. The tabooed words of McGinnies and the swastika on the Bruner-Postman discs, however inhibiting the former might have been to communication, were probably not actual personal threats against which the subject needed to defend himself to the point of stultifying his perceptual capacities. If the immediate value-connotations of words can so act upon the perceptual process as to raise or lower thresholds of ability to perceive when we are trying our hardest, would not the organism be paying too high a price for the indulgence of its affect? It may be stretching the point to say that college students hypnotized into a "poor state" had their reactions to coins of small value determined by actual, or even by psychological, "needs," or that children from poor homes would necessarily react to coins with a sense of need, while rich children would react without such a sense, and that this difference would be what determined the magnification of perceived size. To inject the *social* character of values into the picture, as is sometimes done, with the implication that there are specifically and purely social determinants of perception, that because perception is often the awareness of socially valued or confirmed objects it is "social" in its nature, seems to the present writer both untenable and confusing.

Instead of tying the phenomena to such long-range inferences would it not have been better to have interpreted them more simply in terms of the differentiated meanings involved? Let us take again the case of accentuation. In the discussion that follows we shall waive the question of whether this is a perceptual or a memorial phenomenon. What we shall say concerning the effect of value on dimensional estimates would be equally true whether we regard such effect as a spurious intrusion of an attitude or as a true perceptual alteration. To explain this effect we could assume that a particular background, giving a certain basis of familiarity, or a special setting might introduce a particular frame of reference that would otherwise be lacking. The stressing of some accompanying feature (pennies or candy) might raise a whole series of estimates to a new level. Or again, value as employed in these experiments may have operated, where it did operate, not because it represented the needs or interests of the individual, nor for "social" reasons, nor because of some doubtful "cultural" association of value with size, but because it served as a kind of meaning-indicator.

To show the implications of the last statement let us examine and try to clarify the psychological concept of value. What has not been clearly recognized in the directive-state experiments is that this concept has not one, but two, distinct meanings. Though an attempt to distinguish them may seem somewhat involved, it will be worth while to try since it will lead to new insights into the whole problem. The *first* meaning of value as applied to an object (and it may apply to some objects or classes of objects more typically that to others) refers to the fact that the object, as given, completely satisfies a characteristic need. The need may be one of many different classes. It may be either a need of a consummatory type, such as that for food or water, or of an avoiding type, such as a need for escape. But in any case, the object has "value" because it fully satisfies that need. Under this value-concept what does the *measure* of value of an object refer to? It does not refer, as might be thought offhand, to the "degree" to which the object will satisfy the need. It depends, rather, upon the strength or intensity of the particular need that is (fully) satisfied. The longer we have been deprived of food, the greater the value to us of a "standard and complete meal." We mean by this a meal such as would bring any state of hunger to satiation. Immediately after we have been fed, the value of that meal, under the meaning of value here employed, falls to zero. Or, if different needs can be compared as to intensities (or energies), the object that will fully satisfy the most intense of the needs will be the object of greatest value. It will be seen that the nature of the valued object is here kept constant—its properties, amount, or dimensions are not changed; and furthermore, it is assumed that the need will be fully satisfied each time this object is employed and no matter how strong the need.

In comparing the values of different, but constant, objects, we here vary the needs, either qualitatively of quantitatively, and see which need each object will fully satisfy. The value of a (constant) object or class of constant objects is thus defined as the characteristic or average strength of a type of need, or total mean strengths of different types of needs, that the object will satisfy fully. For example, A has a characteristic or average state of unsatisfied hunger between periods of eating. He also has a characteristic state of wanting to manipulate tools and build things, a want that is unsatisfied between periods of work in his handicraft shop. Are the energies (energic imbalance) characteristic of his hunger state on the average greater in amount than the average energies of his wanting-to-manipulate state? If so, then a full meal (to satiation at the time) will have more value for him than a period of handicraft work of such length as to bring the manipulative want, for the time, to satiety. To take another instance: Because of time difference between meals, or because of motivational differences, A has a characteristic or average state of unsatisfied hunger between eating-periods which is much greater than the unsatisfied hunger of B between eating-periods. If the same "standard full meal" is set before each of the individuals at the customary time of eating for each, it will evoke a greater value-experience in A than in B. In ordinary terms, we say that A appreciates his food more than B because he is hungrier when he gets it. If both A and B were reduced to the point of starvation, the value-experience of the full meal would probably be the same for both and probably higher than the corresponding maximal value of most other objects. In practice, difficulty might arise in attempting to measure this kind of value of food (or of any object) for different individuals upon the same scale. We must also be careful not to confuse value-experience with biological requirement, for the two may at times be different. The example will, however, suffice to show the meaning of the term value we are here illustrating.

We may call this meaning of value the *end*-value of the object, since it is measured in terms of the consummated end or ends which it (as a standard object) makes possible. Obviously the concept of motivation is closely linked with this meaning of value. Motive could be defined, at least in part, as the tendency of an organism to acquire and use objects of a class that have end-value; and again, the *strength* of the motive to get the class of objects will depend upon the intensity of the need that will be fully satisfied by them. It is true that the word motive is often used more broadly; but the above definition is at least clear and possible. The term end-value and the related, or perhaps identical, concept of motivation may be said to represent the strength or potency of the *"involvement"* of the individual in a need-fulfilling situation, that is, in a situation in which objects are to be used for the bringing to equilibrium of the disturbances set up by the energies of a need-state. Value as thus defined seems to have been the independent variable of the "rich" versus "poor" accentuation experiments. Upon it the degree of magnification of perceived size was believed to depend. At least this was so in such comparisons as those which Bruner and Goodman made between the estimates of the rich and the poor boys. The value of a certain coin to the poor boys was assumed to be greater because their need for what it would buy was assumed to be greater. For the same reason the motivation of poor boys toward securing such a coin was deemed to be stronger than that of rich boys. The poor boys were, in the terms just used, more "potently involved" in the type of situations in which money in general served as a medium for need-fulfillment, because the energics of the (unfulfilled) needs in those situations were greater for them than for the rich boys. At least that was the assumption.

We turn now to the second meaning of the term value. Here the reference is not to the strength of a need to be fully satisfied, nor to motivation as we have defined it, but to *the degree in which the object will satisfy a standard, or constant, need.* In measuring *this* value we do not take a standard object to be appraised in terms of the strength characteristic of a need it will fully satisfy; we take instead, a *variable* object having a particular allocation upon a scale of degrees of "need-fulfilling potentiality" upon which a *series* of variable objects of the same or comparable class could also be arrayed. The need that these objects are to satisfy in different degrees is not considered, as in the previous case, to be variable, but is regarded as constant; while the degree, or better, the *proportion,* in which the different objects will *reduce* this original need-strength to a lesser amount is variable. It is this proportional variable which represents the value of the object in the sense of our second definition. Another way of stating it is that the object whose value is to be rated is judged in terms of the proportion of the maximal energic disturbance produced by the need-state that its use will bring to equilibrium. The more fully the object will satisfy the need, that is, the greater the fraction of the energic upset it will "equilibrize," the greater will be its value. We can refer to this concept as the *means*-value of the object; or, if we are careful not to become confused, we can call it the "value-meaning" of the object. If one prefers more subjective terms than those of energies, one can say that the means-value, or value-meaning, of an object represents the *"degree of positive relevance"* which that object has to a particular need-fulfillment situation in which the individual in involved. Means-value, as thus defined, is specific to the situation in which a need is to be satisfied; through its treatment as a proportionate index in need reduction it enables us to compare means-values, or relevances, of the same objects for different maximal involvement situations.

Applying our second definition more concretely, we would note that "value" might in some cases be merely or mainly a matter of the relationship of the object to some standard end-seeking situation. Thus, if a person did not value money at all (end-value of money or of the things money will buy), he might still be able to value it in the other sense (means-value). That is, he could, if the occasion required, evaluate its buying power upon a scale of reference. Value, as the term is loosely used, may at times be more determined by the perceived relevance of the object to an ulterior goal or need-fulfillment situation than by our own involvement in that situation or our striving toward that goal. It all depends on the meaning of the term value that is operating on a given occasion, or upon how much that meaning is operating as compared with the other meaning. Insofar as this is true, instead of saying that the "motivation" is determining perceived size, it might sometimes be more accurate to say that size-accentuation occurs merely as an expression of a situational relevance which the object is perceived to have, that is, as an expression, perhaps an *experience*, of its means-value. We say this because means-value seems to reflect some sort of cognitive set rather than the influence of a "motive" or "need." The situation might also involve motor tendencies; it might carry within it an indication of how much one can do with a given object, relative to an habitual frame of reference, in securing a generalized class of results; it might determine "how far a certain piece of money will go," and the like. A given coin would probably "go further" in buying the type or quality of commodities required by a poor boy's standard of living than in buying those consistent with the standard of living of a rich boy. Such "meaning-sets," representing means-values, might affect (though we do not yet know how) the memory-image of the coin and perhaps even its perceived dimension. It would seem more fruitful in such cases to speak not of need or motivation, but of the "value-meaning" of the stimulus object. Considerations of this sort might have suggested different, or at least supplementary, postulates, less heavily charged with motivation, urgency, or need than those employed by the directive-state theorists—hypotheses that were less dramatic and more appreciative of perception as simple cognitive meaning against a frame of reference operating as an habitual set.

We are by no means implying that the influence of motivation as we have defined it should be excluded in the interpretation of experiments or the setting up of hypotheses. The "end-value" of the frame of reference as a whole, representing the subject's involvement in the situation, might also have an effect upon the percept. Indeed such a possibility must be made the subject of experimental inquiry. A miser who valued money just for itself, or a person who strongly valued the things money will buy, might give a higher size-accentuation of coins in general than an individual (say an ascetic) to whom neither money nor what it would buy had any appreciable importance. It can be seen, however, that the problem would here be different. For the purpose of determining the influence of such end-values on perception, controls would have to be employed of a character different from those used in determining the effect of means-value. And again, it is possible, indeed likely, that in experimental as well as practical-life situations *both* experiences of value may be entering. They might then produce a combined effect upon the estimate of size or other dimensions.

As suggested above it does not seem appropriate to link the concept of motivation with value as presented in our second definition. Though the term motive has been used in many senses, its relationship to what we have been here describing seems indirect. The process involved in experiencing means-value is more intellectual or cognitive than motivational. Means-value enters into perception as an awareness of a relationship or relevance which could perhaps be more clearly experienced with a certain *detachment* from the press of the involvement in the situation to which the object to be judged is relevant. Such detachment may have existed in varying degrees in the subjects of the directive-state experiments. There is no way of being certain of the extent to which it entered.[21] Of course, the complete psychological situation undoubtedly comprises both these meanings of value, and in all probability they operate together in connection with perception. But the analysis we have presented also suggests that they may have a certain amount of independence. In any case, it seems clear that in order to arrive at a *full* understanding of the effects of need-related situations upon perception, "end-value," or motivation as we have defined it, and "means-value," a more cognitive process, must be differentiated in the experimental conditions. We must distinguish the way in which the basic involvement in a need-fulfilling situation affects the percept from the manner in which the percept is affected by the relevance of the object to that situation. The first of these influences is strongly saturated with need and motive. The second is of a different character; it does not stem directly from the strength of an existing need and may vary independently. The directive-state theorists apparently did not recognize this distinction, or else they did not consider it practicable to follow it up experimentally.

Unless these two value experiences are controlled, or their joint effects successfully predicted in the perceptual outcome, we cannot say definitely whether accentuation phenomena are the result of strictly motivational, as opposed to cognitive, factors, or whether they are in part the result of one set of factors and in part the result of the other. At least one could not call the influence purely motivational unless one subsumed cognition under the process of motivation, a confusing procedure at best. Perhaps one might hold that the experiments have already provided such a control in the size-perceptions of coins of *different denominations* by subjects having the *same* end-values for money in general, as in the case of the rich boys alone or of the poor boys alone. Here end-value, or motive arising from strength of need, is assumed to be constant for the group taken, and means-value alone is varied. Such a group of subjects would then differentiate the effects of value-meaning for different coins on a common frame of reference rather than the absolute value of that frame as a whole. This claim can be accepted as showing clearly that means-value is playing a part, just as we anticipated it would; for the size overesti-

---

[21] It might be argued that the need-strength, or end-value, *determines* the means-value experienced. When we are very hungry we might misjudge a less than standard meal or a coin of relatively small denomination as possessing more means-value than it has. Common experience, however, is against this view. Experiments with the lower animals show that they can react on the basis of degrees of mean-value independently of end-value.

mation increases (though not always consistently) with denominational value for rich and poor groups alike.

But so far we have no way of knowing whether this is the *only* effect operating and whether the influence of end-value, or of motivation in our strict sense, has been ruled out. It might be replied that further aspects of the results show this not to be the case. For the experiments that gave positive results, and they were in the majority, demonstrated that the overestimations made by the poor boys on single coins were consistently higher than those made by rich boys on the same coin. Do we not see here that the influence of end-value, of motivational involvement in the situation of need-fulfillment through money, is clearly at work? This seems likely, but we still cannot say *how much* it is at work; and we cannot even be *certain* that it is at work at all. As earlier observed, it is not improbable that the *means-value* of each of the coins is greater for poor boys than for rich (a given piece of money has to go further for them). This factor (means-value), rather than the difference in end-value, might have produced the consistently higher overestimation by the poor boys on single coins *as well as* the increase of overestimation with denominational coin-value for both groups. Thus means-value might have been the only influence at work.

Before reaching such a conclusion, however, let us look back at the experiments of Beams and Thompson and of Gilchrist and Nesberg (pp. 315, 328f.). The former, we recall, employed size estimations of projector images of desired and undesired food objects, while the latter used illuminance judgments of need-related objects under different conditions of need strength. Though we have earlier said that these experiments may have depended on memorial rather than perceptual matching, they may still have significance for the present discussion. In both these studies the means-value of the object to be estimated was fairly standard. The stimulus object was a replica of a need-related (or desired or undesired) object. The relevance of the object to the need-fulfillment situation, at least at a symbolic meaning level, was high. It was also constant and it did not depend upon a characteristic state of deprivation or standard of living as might have been the case with the coins. Yet under these conditions differences in size or illuminance overestimation varied markedly with the need-state, that is, with degree of involvement in the (potential) need-fulfilling situation. (We are here interpreting the food preferences of Beams and Thompson as an indication of need or involvement.) In the Gilchrist-Nesberg study, moreover, the overestimation increased consistently with the strength of the need-state.

It seems then that in these experiments end-values did produce an effect on the size-estimation of the object, at least with respect to its memory-image. This conclusion does not imply that means-value (relevance) was not also entering into the estimate. It probably was; but it was controlled by being equalized for the need and non-need cases, so that the effect of *end*-value could be demonstrated even though its influence as a single factor could not be separately measured. Because it could not be separately measured we see again the limitation of the method for testing the hypothesis, or at least for giving us a full understanding of what was happening.

At this point the reader might be tempted to say that we are making too much of the distinction between the two types of value. We have seen some evidence that both can influence the dimensionality of percepts. Why not adopt a functional viewpoint and say that the experience of value, no matter how it is gained or what it represents, is a factor that can affect perceptual activities? But surely we sense an important difference between a situation in which persons of widely differing degrees of hunger view and estimate the dimensions of satisfying food objects and one in which individuals having a similar need-state, or perhaps very little need-state, estimate the size of coins of different denominations. One of these situations brings out clearly a motivational factor; the other is more nearly judgmental or cognitive. Directive-stateists were banking mainly on the former type of situation as a pillar in their theory. Are we going to let them down by watering down their independent variable into a means-value experience that may have any degree of need behind it, a value-meaning that might be exerting its effect independently of the degree of need? Good theory demands such distinctions as we have been making.

Then too, if we take the position merely that value (as a kind of philosophic term without a referent in the organism) determines perception, important questions are left unanswered. Shall we assume that there is in the organism some entity (or "function") that receives value-information from either a motivational or a cognitive source and translates it into a common effect upon the percept? Do we not want to know what is happening as these sources of information or their "translator" are said to function? What *is* value in the organism? Perhaps we should call value a meaning rather than a conscious experience. If so, what is meaning? We must answer that question before we can talk about "information." How is the meaning we call value related to set? What types or conditions of perceptual aggregate, conceived in physiological terms, can give meaning? What types can represent end-value as distinguished from means-value? And what happens in the many cases in which the operations of these two are joined as components in a combined result? Can motivation and cognition be fitted into a single common pattern of events? The fact that the two kinds of process give a similar result (equivalence) does not indicate that we do not need to study their differences. This sort of functional view would seriously limit our search for knowledge about the organism and its behavior (cf. pp. 266–267).

Or again, it should not be thought (because the distinction we are making is subtle and requires the use of careful logic or because means-value and end-value usually operate together) that the distinction is unlikely to be represented in the psychology of the subject as he estimates the valued objects. To say that he is not conscious of any such distinctions within himself as means-value and end-value and that therefore he, as a molar being, will not govern his perceptions by any such considerations is to invite an anthropomorphic confusion of the whole organism with its parts. It is also to assume wrongly that the operation of meanings and judgments must be a conscious and deliberate process. "Physiological" calculations more subtle than these are made unconsciously by organisms, and often very rapidly. This we have seen to be true from the work of dimensionalists such as Werner, Wapner, Brunswik, and Helson. Sets for reaction, as noted in Chapter 9, are unconsciously selective and they can shift about. They can also act together, when not incompatible from a motor standpoint, to facilitate a composite response in a certain direction (cf. the summation of effects of "extraneous stimuli" in sensory-tonic field theory). There is ample ground to infer that means-value and end-value may represent separate processes, distinct but related in their operation, whose effects can enter into the memory estimates of the size or brightness of objects. Perhaps they enter also into percept-formation. If such an inference should be sound, then in experimental settings that involve means-value and end-value in combination, unless better methods of control than those now used are invented, we cannot decide whether the results are dependent upon one of these variables or upon the other; or if they depend upon both, we cannot tell the degree to which each is involved. To say the least, the strictly motivational hypothesis of directive-state theory will be left cloudy until this issue is cleared up.

Much of the failure to distinguish the two value-variables has no doubt arisen from the term motivation as used as the independent variable of directive-state hypotheses. Does "motive" represent only end-value, as we have said; or should it be extended to cover means-value as well? Since directive-stateists are functionalists (of a sort) they would probably object to our attempt to confine the concept to a mere energizing activity, that is, to make it the dynamic of the need and involvement situation and nothing more. There has been a tendency to regard motive as a process that not only drives the organism, but also *steers* it in a given path toward the solution of its problem. Popular parlance brings out this thought. We speak of the motive behind a man's act not merely as his spur, but as something that can be read from the course which the act takes (why it is this act and not another). Motive has an intentional quality. Like the overt act, the percept is "steered" by the energies of needs or motives. Motivation represents a directive-state.

But in extending the concept in this way perhaps we fail to preserve distinctions that ought to be recognized. We may be missing the very essentials of the structure of behavior. To be sure, by treating motive in an unanalyzed, all-inclusive way we can make it *appear* to be an independent variable adequate for all the tasks envisaged in the preceding discussion. But in stretching the term to cover both the basal behavior-energies and the cognitive activity of means-evaluation are we not in danger of setting up an anthropomorphic agent? We know that *an organism* is both stimulated (receives energies from external and internal changes) and also that *an organism* chooses its line of conduct. It accepts or rejects; it evaluates. If we say merely that there is a "motive" that is responsible for these two lines of activity, we are either identifying the motive with the organism, in which case we are stating a tautology, or else we are reading into the organism a small copy of the organism itself. Such manikin methods, substituted for explicit explanation, only serve to conceal whatever is going on.

To relate the issue to our present problem, when we assume a motive to be something that not only energizes but directs behavior we are giving to it not only the energies that arise from involvement in the need-state, but also the capacity to judge means-value, to assess the relevance of a stimulus object to that state. We have no evidence that there is any such dually endowed process within the organism. Energizing and means-appraising or supplying seem different in their manifestations, just as the electric motor and the machine it runs are distinct, though related, aggregates. One does not say here that the motor steers the machine or determines the *way* it operates, though obviously it may determine, along with other factors such as the machine's own inertia, the *speed* at which it runs. Likewise, the degree of basic need-state in the organism may help to determine the dimensional aspects of an object that is judged through a different, though connected, process to be relevant to that need state. So, too, a means-value structure might help to determine the dimensional aspect. There is no necessity either to attribute the relevance-judging power itself to the need-condition or to establish a higher entity (directive motive) that straddles or encompasses both. We may have here two structures or substructures of the perceptual aggregate that are tangent or connected in some lawful energic interrelationship. If we choose to cover both of these by the word motive, we may be able to sustain our hypothesis; but in this case the hypothesis itself might be largely verbal. We see again that the logic of an unanalyzed "intervening variable" tied at the ends to something that is outwardly observable, though it may enable us to conduct experiments, does not really show us what the experiments signify. Finer differentiation is required, and here an intelligent theory might serve as a guide.

The whole problem calls for new methods of study. Since an object that satisfies a need usually has both an end-value and a means-value, and since these processes are hard to get at with our present techniques, it may be difficult to isolate their effects experimentally or to observe directly how they interact. If that is true, the directive-state hypothesis would still need to be revised in the interest of providing a more inclusive formulation as to alternatives and sharper definitions of motivation and value. To do nothing more than this, however, would be little more than a respectable way of giving up the problem. Even though the effects of the two variables cannot be isolated in the result, it might still be possible, through knowing how much of each was *entering* the situation, and by having some good theory about their interaction, to predict their combined quantitative effect in the perceptual outcome. In other words, we might come to know more about the effects of end- and means-value processes on perception if we could set up conditions in which these two values could be under quantitative appraisal, and if in setting up our *theory* of their relationship we had a "hunch" that came somewhere near the truth. Confirmation of a prediction made upon the basis of such an hypothesis would then support our explanation and appraisal of the parts played by the two factors. This is the hypothetico-deductive method of modern science. Again we note that such a theory and its accompanying experiments could clear the ground regardless of whether we consider accentuation to be a truly perceptual phenomenon or only a memorial or attitudinal effect. The psychological bases of means and end values could be operative with respect to judgment and attitude as well as with respect to perception in the narrower sense. It goes without saying that in order to develop such a theory we would have to give up the "molar commitment" and employ concepts involving as fine a grain of denotation as might be needed (cf. pp. 27–28).[22]

We leave the problem now to return to it in the final chapter where such a theoretical construction will be tentatively suggested. These two problems, the true character of accentuation estimates and the experimental meaning of value and motivation, have for the present helped to show us what a complex and subtle task the directive-state hypothesis has had to face and some of the difficulties of interpretation by which the program is beset. Though the issue is still open and the experiments have provided many new and challenging possibilities, much remains to be done before the hypothesis itself can be sufficiently clarified and methods developed for a final unambiguous solution.

[22] For another model in which cognitive or means values and motivational or end values are distinguished, though under different terms, and are related to behavior in the Bruner-Goodman coin-matching experiment, see Tolman, 1952.

14

Directive-State (*Concluded*)
Perceptual Theory in Social Psychology
Roads That Diverge

Though our analysis of the directive-state hypotheses is now completed there remain to be considered certain aspects of the movement
as a whole and its place in psychological theory. We have noted
earlier a tendency within the movement toward its reformulation and
certain directions in which future experimentation might be expected
to develop. In the next two chapters we shall discuss some of the
lines of revision now under way, and shall suggest, in harmony with
these efforts, the outline of a possible restatement. Before passing on
to that task it would be well to consider the theoretical position of the
directive-stateists in a somewhat wider setting. For insofar as their
contentions might turn out to be true (and we have seen that the case
for them is by no means closed) there arises an *impasse* in the search
for a unified theory of perception. We seem to have come to a fork
in the road. Let us try to mark out the directions in which the older,
more established views and the newer motivational dynamics seem to
be heading. But in so doing we shall see that there are other divisive
tendencies that may well be studied and that must be followed in
order to see the problem in its broadest scope. In our inquiry we
shall therefore discuss some other current views of perception not too
closely related to directive-state, but still possessing something in
common with it.

THE CLEAVAGE IN PERCEPTUAL THEORY

It must not be thought that the conclusions to which our detailed
criticism of directive-state theory has led would be accepted by most
of those engaged in the movement. Need and motivation are still

regarded in their own right as directing influences upon perception. As we have seen from the beginning, directive-state theory was iconoclastic. It broke sharply with the tradition of psychophysics and also with that of gestalt. Its emphasis has lain not upon perception as a universal process, as a means of biological adaptation to a common environment, but upon the way the *individual* perceives his world. This way represents the manner in which he is sensitized to perceive for reasons of his own. Without rejecting autochthonous perception the advocates of the theory insist that its laws be modified. Veridical perception is to a certain extent assumed, but what they are interested in are the cases in which the percept appears to be distorted or changed by the present motivational state or personality of the subject. Their functionalism is different from that of other theories. It is charged with motivation, emotionally centered, and defensive of the interests of the individual. For life adjustments in the more general sense it is probably as likely to be maladaptive as adaptive. Perception is valued not as a process of accurately structuring a representation of the physical world, but as a means of diagnosing and understanding the perceiver. The other schools had struck pretty close to "pure" perception and to its determination either by the laws of the stimulus relation as expressed in psychophysics, adaptation-level, or constancy, or by processes of organization that dealt with simple configurational aspects. Directive-state theorists have thrown off the restraints of stimulus-binding and formal organizing principles, have placed the subject under marginal conditions of perceiving, and have permitted all the "higher" process—association, judgment, interpretation, cognition—to be brought freely into play. On the basis of what they found in these marginal and non-veridical areas they have proceeded to challenge the earlier formulated principles and to demonstrate their inadequacy. Perceptual dimensions and thresholds, the home areas of psychophysics, are the battleground on which the issue has been fought.

As a correction of the established principles, or in competition with them, directive-state theorists have introduced various "perceptual mechanisms." Such mechanisms have featured perceptual selectivity, a process which had already been recognized; but they have also gone much further. They have implemented special effects which, because they were different among individuals and on different occasions, were by that very fact deviations from the laws of veridical perceiving. Under the influence of the prevailing need or motive the perceptual act could accentuate, retard, accelerate, resonate with values, or compromise, as the case might require. It could even defend the individual against itself. These views have not always been stated in this loose, metaphorical fashion. Attempts have been made to exclude anthropomorphic interpretations and to find a basis in accepted behavioral theory. But however stated or explained, these newly imputed, specialized mechanisms of perception present a sharp contrast with the earlier and more uniform autochthonous laws. There is a wide divergence in interests and emphases.

FURTHER DIVERGENCES: PERCEPTION AS A DYNAMIC PRINCIPLE
IN CLINICAL AND SOCIAL PSYCHOLOGY; OBJECT
PERCEPTION VERSUS SOCIAL COGNITION

This cleavage has had consequences outside the field of perceptual investigation and has influenced the course of perceptual theory as employed in special fields of psychology. A number of clinical and social psychologists have espoused the directive-state view, pretty much in its original form, and have given it a place in their systems.[1] Clinicians, already familiar with projective techniques and their perceptual implications, are beginning to find the directive-state armament of demonstrations and concepts an open sesame to diagnosis and a rich field for clinical experimentation. Misperceiving and its mechanisms seem to afford an avenue to the central regions of the personality. Some social psychologists have found the new perceptual psychology useful as a paradigm for explaining social adjustments, stereotypes, loyalties, and conflicts. Ethnic prejudices have been interpreted as stereotyped attitudes, some might call them perceptions, based upon personality deviations of the prejudiced individual. Directive concepts have sometimes taken on the guise of field-theory or frame of reference; and the social field, or the collectivity as a "reference group," has provided the motivational forces or the norms by which the perceptions of individuals are thought to be controlled (cf. Chapter 10).

Modern social psychology, though it is maturing, is still a young science. It has many approaches: some are behavioristic, some phenomenological. Field theory plays an important part in some instances. Motivation, learning, perception, cognition, and personality are all variously stressed as bases in general psychology for the explanation of group behavior. In at least one subschool of the science, however, the theoretical groundwork for social relationships and action is

[1] Cf. Krech, in Helson (ed.), 1951; Sherif, 1948, Chapter 4; and Haire and Grunes, 1950.

coming to lie primarily in the field of perception; and this movement brings the work of those concerned into the scope of our present interest. In the tendency of social psychology toward perceptual explanations the findings of the directive-stateists, as suggested above, have had some influence. They should not however be regarded as the only, or even the primary, factor. By defining perception in a very broad manner social psychologists have been able to tie it up heuristically with a wide range of collective phenomena. But in so doing they have moved, in the same general direction as the directive-stateists, away from the traditional current of experimentation in the perceptual field. They have therefore contributed to the divisive tendency of which we have been speaking. If one is to base one's discipline in a special field upon a particular psychological process, one will be likely to form some concept of that process most serviceable to that subject and will invent or accept some special theory about it even though such theory may not be sharply delineated. Because of this fact it becomes necessary to consider the way in which those who have built systems of social psychology upon such concepts have come to think about and employ the term perception. We shall here undertake no extended review, but merely try to sketch the outlines of a position frequently held and proceed from there to a consideration of the problem created for perceptual theory as a whole.

In general it may be said that such systems of social psychology, like directive-state theory, regard perception as a process that is regulated by some conditions other than the stimulus-pattern. But in this case the ultimate dynamic of control resides not so much in inner motivation as in the outer or collective order. The latter operates *through* motivational channels, to be sure; but social forces are an outer controlling agency. Sometimes the whole process is regarded as cognitive in a phenomenological sense; sometimes the determinants are said to be in an "objective" cultural pattern, in "norms" of the group, or in other sociological constructs. In the more detailed systems, the collective order as perceived by the individual becomes a field; and his own motivations are translated into, or at least linked up with, the forces of that field (cf. Chapter 6). The action of these forces therefore constrains the individual to perceive or to "cognize" the situation or the object in a manner consistent with the field, that is, in a way that will bring the field to equilibrium. The equilibrium of the field is, however, "dynamic"; it is subject to changes that take it to higher or lower levels. The phenomenological field of social field-theory is therefore the specific medium for the operation of the perceptual process. Finally, it is believed that perception, which has thus been redefined as social perception, in turn directs the individual's action and thereby reacts back upon and changes the social scene. As a man perceives his (social) world so will he act toward it. This result is sometimes said to come about as a "reorganization" of the perceptual or cognitive field. For some the study of human relations thus begins (and perhaps ends) with perception. Social psychology becomes "encapsulated" to use Brunswik's term, in a field of societal factors acting upon, and in turn influenced by, perception. As in gestalt and field-theory generally, the motor aspects and their necessary connection with the perceptual process are neglected. We do not know how the motor system (that is, social behavior in the overt sense) comes to play upon the percept-field or how perception operates through motor channels to direct social action. Such systems of social psychology are therefore inclined to be one-sided. Half the picture is omitted.[2]

In all such theories it should be remembered that perception is not sharply distinguished from cognition. And we have earlier seen that there is no convincing reason why it *should* be so distinguished. The treatment here, however, is exceptionally broad. Perception may be used in such a societal or social-field context to cover almost everything that enters into the individual's apprehension of the complex situations that comprise his social living. It may include not only his seeing or hearing of the other members of the group, but his awareness of their relationships, their values, and their attitudes toward him. Perception is nothing less than the individual's understanding of the social situation in which he is placed. Here we are a long way from simple figure-patterns and configuration, from psychophysical stimulus-dimensions, and from the constancies of shape, size, and color. We are far removed from the simple organismic effects on perception contemplated by sensory-tonic field theory and adaptation level, even though it might be possible to demonstrate some of these effects in the sphere of social perceptions. Stimulus-binding is now reduced

---

[2] For a development of this general viewpoint see Chapter XIV, by Krech, in Helson (ed.), 1951; also Krech and Crutchfield, 1948. Attitudes, which are closely allied with perceptions, also play a prominent role in such systems. See also Rohrer and Sherif, 1951, Chapters 1, 2, and 7.

Krech (1949, 1950a, 1950b) has recently formulated a unified theory which attempts to break down the distinctions between perception, learning, and motivation, combining them all as part-aspects or parameters of organized "dynamic systems." The theory is given a physicalistic basis in the nervous system. Though it is not directly concerned with social psychology and is too detailed to go into here, readers with an interest in the possibility of conceiving behavior as a structural phenomenon will find these articles stimulating.

to the lowest possible point. The problem of how the percept relates itself to the stimulus pattern becomes lost in a sea of cognitive meanings and social evaluations with which the stricter laboratory theories of perception are powerless to cope.

This extreme perceptual-cognitive view of the social order could scarcely have arisen had there been an equal recognition of collective action as an *overt behavorial* phenomenon and of perception as a universal process of biological adjustment to a world of common natural objects of a non-social as well as a social sort. It is as though a perceiving process were thought to be at work in society quite different from that found in psychophysics, space-perception, and the study of constancies. For perception is now made equivalent not merely to the way specific objects or happenings appear to the individual, but to the way in which he intellectually grasps or conceives highly complex situations, many of whose elements, as stimulus-objects, are not present at all. Where the perception is bound so little by the stimulus and is thought to be so pervasively controlled by socially oriented motives, roles, and social norms, the latitude given for individual and group differences, for deviating and hence non-veridical awareness, is very great. Sherif's classical demonstration of the collective influence upon judgments of motion, for example, was made by using a stimulus situation that was of necessity non-veridically reported by the observers. Where social norms, pursuant to this paradigm, are made a basis of the social order, since the members of each group or society will perceive under their proper norms quite differently from other groups, the perception of some *must* be non-veridical; or else we are so entrammeling the object-percept and submerging it under ideas for which there is no denotable referent that the terms veridical and non-veridical, important in perceptual theories of the past, have scarcely any meaning. The same is true of approaches like that of Asch (1952) that are so thoroughly phenomenological that physicalistic checks, though not discounted, appear to play little part in the description of the social order. Hence even where, as with Asch, such systems are not founded on misperception or directive-state theory, they subtly change the meaning of the term, perception by slighting the veridical–non-veridical distinction, so that a denotational study of the social process is not encouraged, while the term perception itself is given a quasiphilosophical and subjectively oriented meaning.

We are not saying that the weighting of perception upon the cognitive or interpretative side is illogical or improper, but only that it creates a sharp rift in perceptual theory. The practice represents a moving away from perception as the way things appear to the individual under stimulus-controlled conditions; yet in such moving away no responsibility is assumed for establishing a bridge back to the realm of the veridical testing of experience.   All this means that the great store of knowledge which earlier laboratory studies have yielded, tracing carefully the relationships between the percept and the stimulus situation, has little or no place in the newer view.   The perceptual movement in social psychology is scarcely true even to its gestalt origins; for the founders of gestalt, though they gave up stimulus-binding, carefully predicated an isomorphic basis in the cortex that was related not only to the percept but to the stimulus pattern of the object that acted as its outer source.   The application of the term perception in social disciplines has thus shifted from mere object-awareness, physical-world relations, and biological adaptation to a cognitive and perhaps even phenomenological *modus operandi* for collective activities and role playing, and for concepts of self and society, cultural significances, and the alignments and conflicts of human associations.   Perhaps one might protest that social psychologists' use of the term is only a legitimate extension of its more restricted laboratory use.   But though this may be true, a great deal of confusion has arisen from the extension, and, as we shall presently show, much explaining has to be done in order to show that the two uses actually belong upon the same continuum.   Perception is really in danger of becoming a word with two meanings.   The laboratory perceptionists and the social psychologists are scarcely speaking the same language.   The gap between the two views that began with the experiments of the directive-stateists, or even earlier with phenomenological centering, has thus been widened in the special psychological fields.

It would, of course, be arbitrary to say that only the stimulus-bound features can be regarded as the content of the percept, that meanings, associations, and cognitive interpretations must be excluded.   We cannot bound the percept in so tight a fashion.   But if we are going to put together the actual object-experience with this complex mass of associated ideas and cognitions so that the two form one total act of integrated perceptual behavior, does not *someone* have to take the responsibility for a clear and reasonable statement of what the essential principles of perception *are* and for a theory of how all these elements can be interrelated in one total, unified aggregate?   Do we not have to develop some objective, physiological explanation of cognition and motivation and also of the learning of processes involved, an explanation that might then be integrated with a physiologcal account of the sensory aspects of perception? At this point both the perceptual and the cognitive theories of general and social psychology are lacking. No one has discharged this duty or even seriously assumed it. Both the social appliers of perceptual theory and the autochthonists are content with their own definitions of perception however inadequate they may be. Sensory perceptionists and cognitive perceptionists have merely gone their separate ways. The problem of unifying perception and cognition into a more general interpretation has been neglected.[3]

Such a condition cannot be wholesome either for perceptual theory or for the fields to which it is applied. All psychologists need basic definitions that are broad enough to cover all the phenomena with which they are dealing or could reasonably be expected to deal. They all need such glimpses of the truth as a broad and unified theory, supported by experiment, alone can reveal, glimpses which, because they *are* true will be equally true and important for all. There should not be one theory of perception for the traditional laboratory perceptionists and another theory for directive-stateists or social psychologists. The solution, as the writer sees it, does not lie in polemic, nor in experiments which, though carefully conducted, are addressed only to the testing of the one or the other of the present views. A point seems to have been reached at which the only answer lies in the constructing and testing of new and more general hypotheses, employing all the elements that are necessary for a complete coverage and shaping toward some general theory that will incorporate the truth that lies upon both sides, but that will show it as a unified and lawful whole. There seems little doubt that such a theory will have to be broader than perception, or than any one area of psychology.

DIRECTIVE-STATE VERSUS AUTOCHTHONIST CLAIMS

Our digression into social psychology and the diverging currents of thinking has led us away from the issue in the more limited province of directive-state theory and its contentions against the formalists. Shall we return for a final appraisal of that argument and of what must be conceded on both sides? Let us begin with the directive-

---

[3] Two recent exceptions, however, have appeared. Krech and Calvin (1953) have produced some experimental evidence that so-called perception and so-called cognition are phases of the same continuous process. Ability of individuals to achieve organization shows itself as perceptual ability or as intelligence according to the type of test procedure employed. The "Cognition Theory" of Bruner and Postman (Chapter 15) is another exception.

state position. First, in view of the many suggestive findings of the experiments, even though they do not all meet the test of agreement with other findings or methodological requirements, can we now say that percepts are as closely stimulus-bound as they were formerly believed to be? We should, of course, scrutinize the experiments carefully, as Pratt advises, just as we scrutinize all scientific experiments. But can we any longer view them "incredulously"? Even though the findings are not yet clear and reformulation may be needed, the theory seems to be on the track of something important. We have also seen that the attempt to divide psychology into isolated compartments, to say that certain processes, being stimulus-bound, belong to perception and others do not, and that therefore certain kinds of laws are *a priori* admissible for one group of processes but not for another, is not a fruitful procedure. Should we not concede that the directive-state experiments have at least opened possibilities not before entertained? The individual perceiver adds something to the process that should no longer be neglected. Motivation as a part of that contribution may turn out to be important, even though we cannot yet appreciate its relation to value, formulate its laws, or determine how far it can go in steering perception away from its usual veridical course. It may be true that the older quantitative laws are inadequate and will need to be restated.

But having taken this position should we not be equally tenacious of the truth upon the other side? For after all, perception is, we may be pretty sure, a biologically adaptive process. Though organismic functionalism cannot go as far as we would like it to go in explaining *how* phenomena occur, it is a pretty good guide as to the sort of outcome to be expected in the lives of organisms. If the physiological aggregate involved in perception did not yield in most cases a fairly faithful restructuring of our world, we could not long survive. No one questions the importance of the fact that we usually perceive our environment very much as it is when physicalistically encountered. On the side of interpretation and cognition, which we concede cannot be sharply separated from the more sensory aspects, the case may be different; for since we lack a denotive, physicalistic approach to these features we cannot treat them objectively, and there is as yet no standard for determining what the veridical would here be. Nevertheless, an adequate theory of perception would always give due recognition to the fact that the perception of physical objects and happenings, including the outward phases of the actions of others, is usually fairly, even highly, veridical. Directive-state experimenters may be able ultimately to show that there are significant exceptions and that these arise from the influence of motivation. But a good theory of perception would then not only have to account for these cases, but would also have to show why they are, and must be, *exceptions*. And there would still be the vast number of instances where motivation was not significantly present, or, in any case, was not appreciably influencing the percept. Psychophysical relationships, configurational aspects common to all, space-perceptions, the constancies and many other facts that demonstrate an ability to deal effectively with our physical world would still comprise the major content of our subject. Even illusions that are common to all would tell against the universality of the motivational theory. Coming back to the theme of the veridical, it is to be concluded that a successful theory of perception would have to place stress on the way we usually perceive objects essentially as they *are*, as much as, if not more than, why we sometimes perceive them as they are *not*. Though special contingencies must be provided for, the foremost requirement, obviously, would be the formulation of laws that cover not merely the classes of exceptions but also the general rule. All this should be conceded by those whose interests lie in the directive-state position and should be a caution to those who might have hopes of making that position a basic one in perceptual theory.

RESPONSIBILITY OF SOCIAL PSYCHOLOGISTS IN THE FIELD OF PERCEPTUAL THEORY

On this score perceptual social psychologists also could be reminded that, in spite of their inference that social field-forces, cultural standards, and collective norms determine perceptions in particular ways, if it were not for the innumerable cases in which they do *not* do so but in which the percept has the same stable, uniform, and veridical character for all human organisms, intelligible communication, enduring groups and institutions, in short, any semblance of ordered social living, would be impossible. Furthermore, it must not be thought that this rule applies only to the perception of physical objects and technological equipment. Consider the perceptions involved in the interactions within a bank, an office, an army, a government—or even in a family. If the physiological basis of these did not yield a fairly accurate percept of what one's fellow beings do and say, these groupings or institutions could not exist. Veridical perception of a *social* sort is the *sine qua non* of all enduring collective structures. There are, it is true, cultural significances that are also required for the full understanding of these behaviors. But if the fundamental aspect of the percept that comes to us through sensory channels were not fairly veridical with respect to physicalistic experience, the cultural meanings themselves would fail. Insofar as culture has any demonstrable existence apart from the individual it can be acquired by him only through adequate perceptions of the behavior of others or their material products. Veridical perception, free from influence or alteration by cultural norms or social fields (even though supplemented by them), and the physiological structures by which such perceptions are accomplished are therefore just as much the business of the social psychologists as of the autochthonous laboratory worker. He cannot neglect his responsibility for sharing in theory-development along this line without leaving his own science upon a weak and unrealistic foundation.

Many social psychologists no doubt recognize this principle, and probably few would explicitly deny it. It has been pointed out that the awareness of individuals that they have a common, realistically experienced, physical world is one of the factors that make for a sense of social kinship and solidarity. But should we not go further? What we are here urging is that social psychologists, in building their theories of perception, assume their share of the responsibility for reconciling and integrating their "social-perceptual" concepts, fraught with all their deviations and special cognitive loadings, with the common and mainly veridical character of the basic human perceptions. They should see both aspects and learn how to fit them together into a single unambiguous account of perceiving. Though we may wish to keep our definition of the percept broad, covering the many processes that have to do with the way the world in the fullest sense appears to individuals, the price of such desirable generality is high. It requires us to come to terms with the problem of theory-construction, to develop not merely a definition, but an *explanation* that is broad enough to encompass these diverse and often contradictory phases. It will not do to assume that the task has already been done, that since everybody knows what perception is the social psychologist can just go ahead and use it. There is, as the writer sees it, no escape from this theoretical obligation. When social psychologists prepare to meet it they will be on their way toward a theory of perception adequate for their own perceptual tasks. If the problem is to be solved, the phenomenology now characteristic of much of the gestalt- and field-oriented social psychology will probably have to give some ground to a more physicalistic approach in which definitions and procedures can be better controlled; and the prevailing concept of social perception must undergo a considerable supplementation upon the side of overt action and the objective denotational description of individual interactions and collective aggregates. Social psychology cannot be entirely a matter of perception, cognition, and phenomenological fields.

THE OLD VERSUS THE NEW; VERIDICAL AND NON-VERIDICAL; NEED FOR A UNITY OF OBJECTIVES

But let us leave social psychology and return for a final look at directive-state theory. Do the findings for this theory help to resolve the issue we have been examining? Does the evidence, such as it is, that percepts are controlled by factors other than the stimulus and autochthonous processes give adequate support to the perceptual social psychologist's position? We cannot accept this view, in the first place, because directive-state theory as it stands has not yet been firmly established. Second, it encounters the same difficulty as the blanket perceptual process of the social psychologist: it fails to show how the various parts of the aggregate can operate together. And finally, since the directive-state hypothesis is based on non-veridical perception its contribution would be too one-sided to lay the basis of a general theory. The directive-stateists themselves made no claim to providing the key to a full understanding.

But there is some danger that the schism between motivational and autochthonous investigators and the enthusiasm of the former over new perceptual discoveries may lead to the neglect of some fundamental problems, particularly the problem of unifying the knowledge that is being gained. It must be remembered that we have before us also a great array of facts of another character, facts won by long and arduous efforts. Admittedly the older knowledge must be integrated with the new as soon as the new knowledge has taken on a dependable form. But does this mean that the implications of the earlier question that was asked of nature should be forgotten? When we asked "Why do things appear to us as they do?" that question, though requiring extensive search into the processes of the organism, implied the problem of why phenomenological experience was on the whole so adequate a representation of the physical world. If we take a generic-functional view, we have here a function that can be second to none in the life of the organism. One has only to read the account of the theories reviewed in this book to realize that we are far from the solution of the problem of perception as a universal and essentially faithful restructuring in the organism of the world by which it is surrounded. Should not this fundamental process still engage us and remain central among our curiosities? Though the lure of the individual anomaly and its diagnostic meaning be great, it would seem unwise to sidetrack this basic problem through peroccupation with a more limited issue or imagine that we can solve it through a study only of its deviant forms. If we try to explain the veridical by the non-veridical, the typical by the atypical, we shall not only probably fail, but shall also be relinquishing in large measure the quest of science, the effort, namely, to describe in terms that are always as general as possible. This caution is necessary even though it is conceded that the occurrence of *individual* patterns of meaning, unique personalities, and characteristic differences in the perceiving process are also wide-spread and important facts—facts whose full significance we also hope eventually to understand.

In all this admonition there is no thought of criticism of the lines of experimentation now being followed. Each investigator must proceed in his own way. We are making a plea only for a broadening or reorientation of theory that will prevent a rigid academic view-point, on the one hand, or a devotion to a special or practical interest, on the other, from crystallizing prematurely into theories that will have to be made all over again. Psychologists of all persuasions might work better together toward some common viewpoint, a view that will ultimately explain both the veridical and the non-veridical, the broadly adaptive along with the deviant and wishful, the generic along with the individual, the physicalistic norm along with the social —a view that will combine perception, cognition, motivation, personality, and learning into one coherent system. But whether we are directive-stateists or autochthonists, clinical functionalists or formalists, social psychologists or laboratory perceptionists, this objective counsels us, in our coöperation, to keep all roads open. Though the roads now seem to separate we may hope that with a concerted facing of the problem they may eventually converge upon the goal. There are signs, moreover, that this converging might not be too long delayed. Perhaps we shall see some of its possibilities in the next chapter.

15—————

Directive-State Reformulated:
Hypothesis-Theory
and the Revival of Set

The saying that criticism is the life of science is nowhere more clearly illustrated that in the reaction of psychologists to the theory of directive-state. The "New Look" has been attacked, as we have seen, from many quarters; and as a result its claims are being pruned to bring it nearer to the facts as they now appear. It is now beginning to take on, in consequence, a new vitality. Scientific theory, under criticism, may lose some of its spectacular quality; but the new life given it is one in which the theorist, though chastened after his period of unbridled revelry, is left on surer ground.

> A sadder and a wiser man,
> He rose the morrow morn.

That there was "pay dirt" somewhere in directive-state theory seemed clear, but it needed sifting. The principle leaders in the endeavor to sift out the dross were Bruner and Postman. Their reformulation, as stated in their "cognition" or "hypothesis" theory, accommodates itself to the valid earlier criticisms, broadens the outlook, and gives the whole movement a more promising experimental direction. The present chapter will be devoted to a review of this important contribution.[1]

Let us first ask what was wrong, specifically, with the directive-state program. What has come out of the experiments or the discussion that, in a fairly general consensus, would call for a restatement? First, there was some ambiguity and contradiction in the results.

[1] For details of the theory see Postman in Rohrer and Sherif, eds., 1951, Chapter 10; also Bruner in Blake and Ramsey, eds., 1951, Chapter 5. The account that follows has been drawn largely from Postman. The authors acknowledge their indebtedness to Tolman and Brunswik (1935) with respect to the development of their concept of "hypothesis."

Investigators sometimes differed as to findings. It was shown also that there were many deviations in "directive" perceptual phenomena that were due to individual differences and that seemed to imply a dependence upon the personality of the subject rather than upon a uniform law. Instead of the clear-cut propositions canvassed in Chapter 13 what seemed to be tested was often the motivational pattern of the individual. There were experiments, of course, in which this was not true; but even here the data may have obscured this important aspect since they were usually presented in pooled form. A third point was the lack of a good operational criterion for perceptual defense. Can perception really be a defensive process; or is there merely an alternation or choice among different possible percepts? If there *is* defense, what is being defended against, and how? These and other questions arose from the lack of adequate controls or the failure of methodological analyses. Fourth, in order to keep to the spirit of directive-state theory an opportunity had to be provided for the operation of needs, motives, and values; but it was also necessary, and at times very difficult, to determine *how* these factors operated in the perceptual process. Especially important, as a fifth point, was the lack of proper recognition of the *cognitive* phase of percept-formation. *Relevance* to need, or instrumental significance, as well as need or motive itself, might be highly significant. Sixth, all these considerations highlight the past experience of the individual. What has he perceived in the past and how do these experiences provide a readiness to perceive a certain object in a given way? Though the theory had recognized this aspect little provision was made for it in the conduct of the experiment itself, and this failure of provision confused the interpretation of the results. And finally, something needed to be done about the ad hoc multiplying of novel "mechanisms" by which directive-stateists had tried to explain their findings. A more parsimonious set of concepts was to be desired, having closer affiliation with already established principles.

ORIENTATION TO HYPOTHESIS-THEORY: EXAMPLE FROM
THE SOLUTION OF AN OVERT PROBLEM

The basic idea underlying the reformulation by Bruner and Postman was that all cognitive processes, whether they take the form of perceiving, thinking, or recalling, represent "hypotheses" which the organism sets up, or that are evoked by the particular situation. These hypotheses, in perception at least, are largely in the background and are usually unconscious. They require "answers" in the form of some *further* experience, answers that will either confirm or disprove them. Adjustment of the organism to the environment proceeds by this process of hypothesis-confirmation or rejection. The answer, if the hypothesis is confirmed, comes into consciousness as some kind of percept, image, idea, or memory that is suddenly attained and that fits into the expectancy-pattern, or supposition, of which the hypothesis is composed. If the added items, whose source is provided either by the environment or by "memory-traces," do not fit this pattern of the hypothesis, the percept is not clearly formed, the idea for solution of the problem is not yet gained, or the memory-item is not yet recalled. The process then continues. One tries again with a new hypothesis and with its testing by sensory or memory material that is being provided.

The forming or arousing of hypotheses in the situation concerned, together with the receiving of information related to them, their testing, and their ultimate confirmation or rejection through this information, constitute the processes of thinking, perceiving, and remembering. When we perceive, think, or remember we are evoking and testing organismic hypotheses. We have long been familiar with the term hypothesis and with its testing as employed in a purely logical sense in scientific or philosophical inquiry. Bruner and Postman propose that we use the same term as the name of a postulate to be used in describing the *actual psychological process* involved in all cognition. Hypothesis-confirmation is the process that invariably takes place, no matter whether the hypothesis to be confirmed is as complex as a principle of physics or as simple as the assumption or expectancy that the object one is looking at is an "apple." We have always the background or prior *hypothesis*, and we have some added *information;* and the cognitive process is an interrelating or matching of the two.

As a starting point let us describe this procedure not in perception as such, but in an imagined case of a thought-problem involving overt action. We are seated at a table. On the opposite side sits a man engaged in putting together a jigsaw puzzle. The puzzle is nearly completed; a half-dozen pieces still lie on the table before him. ·He picks up a piece and looks at it and at the unfinished pattern. We might say that he seems to be "summoning some kind of hypothesis." Finally, with an air of decision, he moves the piece toward a certain gap in the unfinished puzzle. We could now say, from a similar experience and behavior of our own, that he has definitely formed an hypothesis, namely, that the small irregular fragment in his hand will fit into a certain opening of the pattern. This conjecture was perhaps gained through two factors; the appearance of the gap, which constitutes the basis of his hypothesis, and the information apppropriate to that hypothesis which he received from the piece.   Let us suppose that his assumption is correct; the piece when tried is seen to fit exactly.   We could now say that the hypothesis has been "confirmed." The act has now become "stabilized" and completed, and the man can turn to another part of the task.   Borrowing from the terminology of perception, we would say that the hypothesis the man had held was "veridical."

But suppose the piece does not fit; that is, the hypothesis is "non-veridical."   In that case the hypothesis, to use Bruner's and Postman's convenient term, is "infirmed" by the non-fitting of the piece and hence is rejected.   The man may then look elsewhere in the un-finished pattern to find the right sort of opening for the piece he is holding.   That is, he may develop a *new* hypothesis.[2]   If that, too, fails, still another hypothesis will be summoned; and so on until the piece is placed and the act stabilized.   The whole procedure could be described as one of successive "trial and check."   In each case of a further trial the man might, though not of necessity, be guided in his choice of hypothesis, that is, in what hypothesis is "evoked," by an apparent likelihood that the information given by the piece will be positively relevant, or supporting, to the particular hypothesis chosen. If it is *negatively* related, that is, contradictory to the hypothesis, we can say, to put things in backward fashion, that the hypothesis would not have been so likely to have arisen.   If it has arisen, it will be infirmed.

But besides this relation between the hypothesis and the information from the puzzle-fragment, is there anything else that might enter to influence the choice of the hypothesis or to increase the strength or certainty with which the man holds it?   Yes, there is, for one thing, "past experience."   In other situations with another puzzle the man may have been dealing with a gap that looked something like the present one and with a piece that resembled the one in his hand. Though the present hypothesis might be non-veridical in this instance, still the number of times it had been confirmed in the past might now serve to strengthen it and make the man tend to cling to it.   Another influence might have been the fact that the pieces below the gap suggested that the horizon in the picture should come at that place. Hence a blue sky would be hypothesized and a piece that is colored

[2] It is, of course, also possible that he will keep his attention upon the same opening and look about for another piece that might fit it.   In that case we could speak of the awareness of each new piece that is tried as an hypothesis.

blue would be called for to give confirmation. We would then have another hypothesis in addition to that determined by perceived shape. We might say that this latter hypothesis gave "cognitive" support to the former. Or again, a group of bystanders might all agree that a certain gap in the puzzle was the place for the piece or called for a certain piece; and this consensus might add weight to the man's belief in the correctness of his own supposition. Here we have a "motivational" strengthening of the hypothesis through "social consensus." Finally, let us suppose that the solving of the puzzle has proceeded until only two pieces remain to be placed. The task will now be easier. We note that the man will probably feel greater certainty in the hypothesis which he holds for the penultimate fragment or gap than he did for those preceding. Reduction of the "number of hypotheses" that can arise will tend to fortify a given hypothesis.

Now it might be that the hypothesis first formulated or evoked was the correct one. The apparent relation between the pattern of spatial information given by the piece and the gap might have been sufficient in itself to have evoked it. If this had been the case, confirmation would have come with the first move and all the other influences toward further strengthening the hypothesis would have been "beside the point." It would be as though they were not present. But if we suppose that the first hypothesis was *not* veridical and that a series of further hypotheses might also be untrue to the physical facts, then it is conceivable that the other influences could be operating to keep a wrong hypothesis "alive," or to strengthen each of a series of non-veridical hypotheses in turn. Such an effect would show itself through more erroneous trials. A wrong hypothesis, if strong and persistent, might lead to more than one futile effort to place the piece in a certain location. The greater the strengthening which (wrong) hypotheses have received by cognitive, motivational, or other factors, the greater the number of trials and errors that will be necessary to induce the man to give them up. Each trial, however, means that some *information* about the piece in relation to the puzzle has been gained. Hence we can say that the greater the number or strength of non-veridical hypotheses that are active the greater will be the amount of contradictory information necessary to "infirm" them.

The psychological situation involved in almost any complex problem is likely to be of this sort. Hypotheses are formed. They are then confirmed, or else they are infirmed and change rapidly. Information relevant to the hypothesis is continually being utilized to confirm or infirm it. Such information helps both to evoke an hypothesis and to test it. Other factors, however, can enter. Motivation, the way the individual rightly or wrongly "cognizes" the situation, the accumulated effects of past trials, the number of choices apprehended —all these can serve as enhancing and supporting factors for certain hypotheses, making them more easily confirmed or necessitating a greater acquisition of contradictory information in order to disqualify them.

This account of problem-solving in attacking an overt manipulative problem is closely analogous to the paradigm by which Bruner and Postman describe the process for perception. There are differences, to be sure. The puzzle solver operates by perceptions of many kinds *in the course* of his manual solution. He also moves the pieces about, and the gaps to be filled and pieces to fill them lie out there on the table as well as (by some sort of representation) in his brain. For the "mere perceiver" of an object this is not true. The gaps that enter into his hypothesis-pattern lie only in himself; nature does not permit gaps in the object. Moreover the mere perceiver, in checking his hypothesis, does not move any external object about; all the "moving," all the use of information in hypothesis evocation and checking, goes on in his own organism. The hypothesis and the information to be related to it are not like the physical margin of the gap in the jigsaw puzzle; they are *not* denotable by the perceiver. Phenomenology alone makes up his experience of the situation. From this there follows the important consequence that a non-veridical hypothesis as well as a veridical hypothesis is capable of being confirmed. We can have an hypothesis that requires an *illusory* perception of an object for its confirmation; and when that illusion occurs hypothesis confirmation occurs. Such a state of affairs is manifestly impossible in the validation of hypotheses involved in the overt puzzle-solution. Another difference between the two situations lies in the extraordinary rapidity of the perceptual process as compared with the manipulation of the jigsaw puzzle. We shall see, therefore, that in spite of categorical similarities in the two processes, the perceptual model has to be elaborated in certain directions that would not be appropriate for the model of overt problem-solving. Still, the analogy will be helpful in many respects, as would indeed be required if the hypothesis-model is to be regarded as general for cognition.

FORMAL STATEMENT OF HYPOTHESIS-THEORY: THE COVARIATION THEOREMS

Our greatest help in understanding the Bruner-Postman theory will lie in the clue the authors themselves have given us, that is, in the concept of set. The psychological and physiological content of this notion has been developed in detail in Chapter 9. The first point to note is that we seldom perceive anything "out of the blue." We are usually *eingestellt,* or set, in some particular way. *And this set is the hypothesis of which we have been speaking.* We have "perceptual expectancy" hypotheses from past experience that tell us what objects to look for and, to some extent, how these objects will be likely to appear. The situation itself is "earmarked" in some manner that brings these sets very rapidly into play. That which was happening to the man in his systematic hypothesizing as he surveyed the gap in the puzzle is like what is happening in each of us in the simpler process of perception whenever an object and its surroundings present a stimulus pattern upon our receptors, except that in the latter case the process of "set-arousal," or "hypothesizing," is less conscious and may extend over an amazingly small period of time. As a rule in perception we have sets that are long established through previous perceiving activity and may be already almost at the point of full operation when we enter a situation. In this case only a little further "arousing" or "evoking" of them is required. Organisms, according to Bruner and Postman, carry about with them such predispositions, expectancies, or sets that serve to select, organize, and transform "information" that comes to them *via* the sensory input from the environment. Such "stimulus-information" takes the form of "cues" or "clues" that serve both to broaden the range of hypotheses and to confirm or deny a specific hypothesis. The hypotheses are said to be "evoked" by the arousal of central cognitive or motivational processes depending upon environmental conditions.

If the information from the clues confirms the hypothesis, there results a stable perceptual organization. If it does not, there is a change in the hypothesis until one is set up that *is* confirmed by the information, so that a stable percept is again attained. There is thus a cycle of "trial and check," "trial and check." The strength of any given hypothesis depends upon the frequency of its past confirmation, the number of alternative hypotheses, and the motivational or cognitive support it has acquired from attendant circumstances. All these points will be seen to present a close similarity to the process as depicted in our illustration of the man solving the puzzle. To pursue the theory further, there are some laws of covariation between certain variables that will take us to the heart of the matter. The first of these is as follows: *The stronger the hypothesis, the greater is the likelihood of its arousal, and the less the amount of appropriate and supporting stimulus-information that will be required to confirm it.* A very strong hypothesis might be confirmed with scarcely any supporting information at all. When appropriate information is lacking the perceptual organization tends to be determined directly by the dominant hypothesis. *Where the hypothesis is weak a large amount of appropriate and supporting information is necessary for its confirmation.*[3] Though Postman in his statement of the theory (*op. cit.*) does not employ the inverse of this theorem for "contradictory" information, use is made of it by Bruner (*op. cit.*) and it is developed elsewhere in the literature.[4] This addition must be considered a part of the theory and is required to make the point of some of Postman's illustrations. It can be stated as follows: *The stronger an hypothesis, the greater is the amount of contradictory stimulus-information necessary to infirm it; and the weaker it is, the less contradictory stimulus-information is needed to infirm it.* Contradictory stimulus information is thus related to tendency toward hypothesis *infirmation*, and in direct covariation with hypothesis strength, while supporting information is related to hypothesis *confirmation*, and in inverse covariation with hypothesis strength. The hypothesis-theory has been extended to remembering; and in this case, as distinguished from perceiving,

---

[3] It will be found that some of these last statements are limited with respect to their application to overt problem-solving as in the puzzle situation. The statements about confirmation, for example, could apply only to a certain class of overt-manipulation hypotheses, namely, veridical ones; for only these could be confirmed in problems of objective encounter such as the puzzle situation. This is not true of perception. Misperceiving, for example, a phenomenon that is central in the directive-state program, is a case of confirming a non-veridical hypothesis.

[4] Blake and Vanderplas (1950–1951). There is some confusion of terms here. Postman (*op. cit.*, p. 251) uses the term "appropriate" to cover information that will either confirm or infirm an hypothesis, but does not develop the implications of the "infirming" type, and a logical confusion is implied in regard to the way it operates (*op. cit.*, top of p. 252). Blake and Vanderplas use the term "inappropriate information" for this class and clearly state the inverse theorem that will presently be cited. Bruner uses the term "relevant" for information that will either confirm or infirm the hypothesis and characterizes postively relevant (confirming) information as having various possible degrees of "reliability." This latter usage is confusing in that we do not always know whether reliability is attributed to the confirming of a veridical or a non-veridical hypothesis. Furthermore, information may have different degrees of reliability for *infirming* an hypothesis. "Degree of relevance" would seem to be the best translation of "reliability." We could then distinguish two types of relevance: positive, or supporting the hypothesis, and negative, or tending to infirm it; and both positive and negative relevance would be matters of degree. We shall here keep the term "appropriate" to cover information that is either positively or negatively relevant to the hypothesis, and shall distinguish the two types of relevant information as "supporting" (positive) and "contradictory" (negative) to the hypothesis, respectively.

the trial and check is against "trace-information" rather than against stimulus-information.

HYPOTHESIS-STRENGTH; AMOUNT OF STIMULUS-INFORMATION; "DETERMINERS" OF HYPOTHESIS-STRENGTH; CONSENSUAL VALIDATION

The above account states the hypothesis-theory in its main outlines. Let us follow a few of the details of Postman's presentation together with some of the related investigations. One limitation of the theory is that, beyond saying that an hypothesis is a set, its authors do not give us much information about it from the physiological standpoint. Methodologically, however, they do succeed in giving it a status that meets a requirement of current experimental procedure, namely, the ever-popular intervening or hypothetical construct. Hypothesis is operationally defined, on the one hand, by the entire pattern of stimulus-information the subject receives and its attendant conditions, and, on the other hand, by the subject's responses concerning what he experiences. If certain lawful relations are found to exist between these two, or more particularly between the perceptual report and various stabable antecedent conditions (motivation, past experiences, etc.), we say that this result is explained by the operation of an intervening "hypothesis."

Closely associated with the notion of hypothesis and providing one of the main factors in such lawful relationships is the important variable of "hypothesis-strength." It is related, on the one hand, to objectively determinable conditions such as a setting that provides motivational or cognitive elements, repetitions of the perceiving act, or alternative choices. These conditions are postulated as *determiners* of hypothesis-strength. Hypothesis-strength is *defined*, on the other hand, by the amount of appropriate stimulus-information needed to confirm or infirm the hypothesis according to the principles earlier stated. This measurement gives an "operational anchor" for hypothesis-strength at the response end of the activity. The strength-determining conditions can usually be controlled; the measurement of the stimulus-information needed to raise a percept "above threshold" and to make it inhibit and replace another is already a familiar part of laboratory procedure; and the covariation formulas, stating how amount of hypothesis-strength, as measured by the amount of stimulus-information needed for confirmation or information, is related to the determining conditions, provide theorems for experimental testing. The new formulation thus affords a strategic reorientation and blueprint for further research. A number of experiments have already employed the above design and more will doubtless follow.

The *amount* of stimulus-information required for confirmation or infirmation is given directly by the number or length of exposures of the object that are required, by increases in illumination, or by similar methods. The meaning of stimulus-information itself, that is, of information appropriate to a given hypothesis, is stated by Postman in these terms: Suppose that an organism has an hypothesis that a certain type of object will appear or that a certain event will occur. We now try to show in "independent defining experiments" what stimulus variations or organizations are related to the discrimination of the object or event hypothesized. For example, in an hypothesis concerning the size of an object, the secondary cues to distance, which can be demonstrated in independent experiments, can be called appropriate stimulus-information.

But what about the cases in which all the necessary cues or elements are given at once in full strength and the percept is instantly attained, as indeed occurs in normal veridical perception and in the example of size-perception just mentioned? The fact that percepts are usually attained immediately and completely troubled Postman a little and seemed to throw him back upon the concession that the theory is little more than a restatement of the older unconscious-inference doctrine. In the present writer's opinion it is not necessary to go back to manikin interpretations. Why not regard all the sensory elements entering into the perceptual process as providers of stimulus-information (that is, as structured energies) no matter whether they are all made effective for perception at once or are parcelled out as in a series of brief tachistoscopic exposures? Hypotheses, as well as their confirming additions of stimulation from the object, may be regarded as accumulations of information (i.e., energies). We could thus, in our usual veridical perceptions, have hypothesis-establishment and confirmation coming immediately at "one trial." But it might also be true that the individual carries about with him long-standing hypotheses (at low energy level or incomplete) as to how the sizes of objects ought to look, hypotheses that are based upon earlier stimulus-information and are not "confirmed" until stimulus-input from an immediate, present object is provided. When such input is provided and in the amount usually present in our daily adequate perceiving conditions, the threshold for the full performance of the aggregate could be suddenly reached and crossed. The perception would thus seem to come "at one trial." On either of these interpretations the usual perceptual process would thus be merely a limiting case of the Bruner-Postman covariation theorem, in which only one installment of stimulus-information is necessary for confirmation. Laboratory experiments, in which stimulus-input is given not in large installments, but in "bits" by repeated or lengthening tachistoscopic exposures, enable us experimentally to separate the stage of hypothesis-confirmation from the subthreshold state of an existing hypothesis that had been previously built up and is now "evoked" by the present setting. In ordinary life, perceptions are accomplished so quickly that the fact of the earlier establishment of the hypothesis (or set), its evocation by the present circumstances, and its confirmation all seem to run together.

Hypothesis-theory, according to Postman, is concerned with the specification of hypotheses, the description of conditions that govern their formation, the analysis of information related to them, and the elaboration of a suitable model for describing their operation. The theory is developed by a further treatment of the conditions upon which the strength of an hypothesis is said to depend. The first of these is *frequency of past confirmation.* Since such frequency is assumed to make for greater hypothesis-strength and strength is measured by the inverse of the amount of appropriate stimulus information needed for confirming, we would predict that the greater the frequency of confirmation of the hypothesis in the past, the less of appropriate information is needed to confirm it on later occasions. Through feeding stimulus-information into the organism, bit by bit, in a series of rapid tachistoscopic exposures, it should be demonstrated that the specific hypothesis which is "aroused" among a number of possible ones, that is, aroused with a smaller amount of information than is required by the others, will also be the one that has been most frequently confirmed in the past. This expectation would follow from the assumption that the stronger an hypothesis is, the more readily it can be evoked. Once aroused, further input of stimulus-information will then *confirm* it. Blake and Vanderplas have performed an experiment, to be discussed later, which used hypothesis-strength depending on frequency to test the role of strength in relation to hypothesis *infirmation.*

The second of the "strength" conditions is the *number of alternative hypotheses available.* This aspect is *inverse* to hypothesis-strength. A lone hypothesis is stronger than one that occurs in the same perceiving situation with a number of others. The larger the number of hypotheses operating in a given perceiving situation the more of appropriate stimulation is required for confirmation of any one. "Monopoly" by a single expectation and extreme multiplicity are the limits of the range. The larger the number of alternative hypotheses, the less probable it is that a given unit of stimulus-information will confirm any one of them. The hypotheses "compete against" one another, and the strongest one that fits the information is the one that is confirmed. The operation of this principle is shown in experiments where the subject is not told beforehand which of a number of possible attributes of the stimulus he will be asked to report upon. Here the range of alternative hypotheses is wide and his perceptual discrimination of any given attribute is relatively low.[5] The same is true when words belonging to a number of different classes are presented. When the number of alternative hypotheses is reduced by the setting or the instructions, veridical-hypothesis confirmation, as shown by the number of correct reports, comes more frequently or with shorter exposure of the stimulus.

The third condition of hypothesis-strength is *motivational support*. The stronger the motivational backing of an hypothesis, the less the amount of positively related stimulus information necessary to confirm it, and the greater will be the amount of contradictory information necessary to *in*firm it. Under motivation we think of the consequences that confirmation or infirmation of the hypothesis may have for the individual. Either punishment or reward may be expected to operate to strengthen hypotheses and thus reduce the amount of positively related information required. The theory is thus no longer one of wish-fulfillment, need, or positive value; we must be careful to note that *any* motivational or emotional disturbance, whether its hedonic tone is pleasant or unpleasant, may serve to strengthen an hypothesis and to lead to its readier confirmation. Postman inclines also toward an "instrumental" view of motivation. Instrumental hypotheses are stronger than non-instrumental hypotheses. In the field of emotions, personal values, and personality characteristics, experiments of the type we have reviewed in Chapter 13 are cited as evidence of the smaller amount of stimulus information necessary to confirm motivationally supported hypotheses and thus to attain percepts related to value or need-states. But there is also a tendency for objects accompanied by negative reinforcement, or punishment, to strengthen and sensitize hypotheses.

The fourth and last condition of hypothesis-strengthening is *cognitive support*. The more firmly an hypothesis is embedded in a larger organization of a cognitive sort, the less will be the amount of appropriate information necessary to confirm it, and the less subject will it

---

[5] Cf. the account given of Külpe's experiment in Chapter 4.

be to change in later experiences. By a "larger cognitive organization" the author means a system of related hypotheses which are governed by a common set of rules or principles. The topical reference of a paragraph that one is reading might, for example, be a support for a number of specific hypotheses in a common cognitive context. Another example is the finding that it takes relatively more time to perceive a reversed letter as reversed when it occurs in a meaningful printed word than when it occurs in a series of unrelated printed consonants.[6] The hypothesis in this case is that all letters shown in (real) words are presented printwise, and the context supported the hypothesis more strongly in the case of the meaningful word than in the meaningless series of letters. The stronger the cognitive support for the hypothesis the greater the amount of contradictory information necessary to infirm it. Incongruous playing cards, for example, hearts printed in black, are recognized for what they are much more slowly than normally printed cards. The hypothesis that hearts will appear as red is supported so strongly by the more general context of playing cards appearing always in their proper colors that much contradictory information is necessary in order to induce the subject to see these hearts as "black."[7]

A related principle stated by Postman brings out in another way the fact that hypothesis-strength is an important factor in confirmation. The less the amount of supporting stimulus-information available, the greater is the tendency for the perceptual organization to be determined by the dominant hypothesis. An experiment is cited in which pictures of objects normally varying in hue *from red to yellow* were cut out of the same gray paper and presented on a blue background under a sheet of glass, so that they all appeared (to the experimenters), by simultaneous contrast, to be of the same unstable orange color. The subjects were asked to adjust a variable color mixer to the hue they perceived each of the pictured objects to have. Under these conditions of poor stimulus-information the subjects showed the marked influence of their strong habitual hypotheses about the colors of these objects, adjusting the color differently but incorrectly toward the red or the yellow according to the hue with

[6] Postman, Bruner, and Walk, 1951.

[7] The author comments that the distinction between motivational and cognitive support may be only a temporary one. He cites with approval the view stated by Krech to the effect that a dynamic system related to our experience in looking at a lopsided figure is under the very same kind of tension as a system related to looking at a steak after several hours of food deprivation. This effort to unify psychological theory recalls Köhler's principle of "requiredness" and reflects the influence of configurational theory.

which the object is usually seen in nature. When more definite stimulus-information was given about the cut-out pictures by using an *orange paper* for all, instead of the unstable induction color, and by permitting simultaneous comparison of the objects, this effect of the dominant hypothesis was reduced. The color matches now tended toward the veridical, involving the same (orange) hue as a match for all the objects.

As a final principle, Postman states that hypotheses are sometimes confirmed by a method which he calls "consensual validation." Here he seems to leave the perceptual aggregate as dependent solely on the organism and invokes a more inclusive order of phenomena, the social group. In the absence of appropriate stimulus-information, says Postman, the consensus of members of a group may serve to validate an hypothesis. Sherif's work on the establishment of "social norms" in the autokinetic phenomenon (pp. 253–254), in which the subjects judged the illusory movement of a point of light in a dark room, is cited as an illustration. The judgments of the amount of movement, which were spoken aloud, tended to converge and stabilize near a mean or norm, a fact which is taken by Postman to indicate the confirmation of an hypothesis by consensus.

Though this interpretation sounds plausible one would be inclined to say that the group here affords the basis of something much broader and less well understood than the above formulation implies. On the one hand, as the author himself elsewhere notes, the process of socialization consists of building into the individual a set of hypotheses for perceiving in culturally approved ways. In other words, social consensus is a *source* of, as well as a means of validating, hypotheses. Yet on the other hand, the specific way, or *modus operandi*, by which such "outside" hypothesis-providing and checking act upon or through the perceptual process is left quite vague. We note that the social consensus theorem appears strangely out of line with the other theorems of the author. Frequency of past confirmation, motivational and cognitive support, and number of alternatives available are all matters that seem to reside in the single organism rather directly, or in its operations with reference to its immediate surroundings. With consensual validation, however, we suddenly transcend this organism-bounded, psychological sphere and enter the field of interstructurings among individuals, the sphere of the "group." Another order in the hierarchy of phenomenal aggregates is thus reached. If, throughout the rest of the theory, hypothesis-confirmation is achieved by sensory-input built into meanings inside the individual's brain, we are now at somewhat of a loss to understand confirmation as taking place by meanings already established in other persons and conveyed to the subject by the cultural symbols of language. A corner seems to have been turned without our seeing how we turned it. Problems arise that call for further understandings if we would carry hypothesis-confirmation with profit into the "consensual" realm.

Once before, in the discussion of perceptual defense, we have noted that marked but elusive theoretical complications arise when the collective aggregate enters the environment of an individual's perceptions of group-related objects. There seems to be some connection between his "inside" operations and his "outside" structuring as a member of a group, a connection that exerts a definite effect upon his outer behavior and might conceivably, within limits, affect his perceptions also. This would be most likely to be true, so Sherif thought, when the stimulus field has no definite anchorage-points, as in the case of a spot of light in an otherwise completely dark room. Without attempting to say whether there is an effect exerted by operating in a collective aggregate directly upon perception, we still recall that the question of its *possibility* arose in connection with the hypothesis of perceptual defense. Though we have criticized social psychologists for "overdoing" social relationships in the field of perception and for the highly perceptual trend in social psychology generally, we must concede that the relationship of the collective pattern of action to what is happening inside the individual, and vice versa, though not well understood, is probably very close. It goes, at this level of phenomena, to the very heart of the more universal "inside-outside" problem that came to light in dealing with core-context theory in Chapter 4. But we are very far from understanding it.

Returning to hypothesis-theory, we now have the following equipment for dealing with the problem of perception: (1) the notion of hypotheses (perceptual sets) and their checking; (2) the definition of hypothesis-strength as the amount of information required for confirmation or infirmation; (3) the four determiners of hypothesis-strength; (4) the four covariation theorems by which hypothesis-strength may be predicted for experimental purposes in terms of the determiners; (5) the principle of competition of alternative hypotheses (the strongest that fits the information will prevail); and (6) the principle that in the absence of appropriate or decisive stimulus-information a dominant hypothesis may determine what is perceived. How well do these definitions, theorems, and principles serve as a reformulation of directive-state theory? Do they give greater facility and sureness in interpreting the earlier findings? Do they resolve contradictions and clear away ambiguities? In answering these questions we shall also refer to other experiments that have been conducted as more immediate tests of hypothesis-theory.

CLARIFICATION OF THE TRANSFORMATION CONCEPT

We observe, first, that the entire problem has shifted in meaning. The *hypothesis*, now, is always the determining factor; needs, values, and motivational states that were central in the earlier theory become merely one dimension of the strength of an hypothesis or set. It is only as these motivational factors influence some hypothesis concerning how things may be expected to appear that they can affect perception. In hypotheses there can be expected also to be a considerable amount of *cognitive* organization, as is, in fact, implied by the term hypothesis itself. The hypotheses, then, not the needs or motives directly, are the factors whose influence we must consider as the first task in the revision of directive-state theory. Since they are, for confirmation, inverse to the amount of stimulus-information, they will show themselves most clearly in the perceptual outcome when the latter is reduced; and the same will be true of the effects of the determiners of their strengths, i.e., repetition, motivational and cognitive support, and the like. Hence the marginal perceiving conditions described in Chapter 13 are again pertinent. These conditions are construed under the new theory as providing "substandard" stimulus-information which may permit hypotheses, if they are strong enough, to achieve confirmation in their own right; and strong, motivationally aroused, hypotheses such as those involved in directive-state experiments presumably can utilize information that is of a "lower grade" than that required for the confirmation of less potent hypotheses. But in utilizing it, since it is vague or ambiguous, transformations may sometimes be made in it that make it *appear more consistent* with the hypothesis. Hence in directive-state and hypothesis-theory experiments slanted misperceptions or prerecognition responses may sometimes occur as confirmations, in marginal conditions of perceiving, of non-veridical hypotheses that have been strengthened by needs or motives. Poorly defined stimulus content also gives an opportunity for various alternative hypotheses to arise and for the dominant hypothesis to be singled out.

In order better to apply hypothesis-theory to the experimental situations we need to make some distinctions in the use of its terms beyond those that are made in the theory itself. In speaking of the "transforming" or "organizing" effect of hypotheses upon marginal information, as Postman does, something new seems to have been introduced. This formulation does not sound like the principle of "trial and check" that was earlier enunciated; for the hypothesis in these cases is made ascendent over the information rather than the reverse. The situation is more like stimulus-*de*formation (by the hypothesis) than like checking and shifting of the hypothesis to accord with stimulus-*in*formation. It more nearly resembles the gestalt concepts of "organizing forces of the field," "closure" and the like, than it does trial-and-error testing. This change of meaning in the relation of hypothesis and stimulus-input is to be found in Postman's own statement of the theory as well as in its application to experimental work.[8]

We need to clarify this question before proceeding with the review. It is seen from the experiments that *either* a veridical *or* a non-veridical hypothesis may achieve confirmation, according to the circumstances. In the former case we would note that the stimulus input is either a faithful one-to-one copy of the stimulus pattern and is not much altered in the cortex, or else that, if it *is* altered or transformed, then it is transformed in such a way as to preserve a fidelity to the distal object. A notable example of this last type occurs in perceptual constancy, a process that actually tends to correct the deviations of the proximal stimulus pattern in such a way that a more veridical percept of the object is attained. Transformation may thus work *toward* the veridical in perception as well as *away* from it. The *latter* effect of transformation applies to the autisms, distortions, or

---

[8] Compare Postman, *op. cit.*, p. 250 (lower half) with pp. 251 and 260 (middle of page). The author speaks, on the one hand, of hypotheses as something that the organism "checks," for purposes of acceptance or rejection, against stimulus-information, and on the other hand, as themselves "transforming" stimulus-information. These two statements are contradictory. Perhaps the relation is at one time that of "checking" and on another occasion that of "transforming." Indications, in that case, ought to be given as to different types of percepts or perceptual activities in which the two uses, respectively, function. A way of combining the two ideas might be to say that in some cases the hypothesis is checked directly against stimulus-information whose transformation in the cortex has not led to a "deformation" of the percept; while in other cases the stimulus-information is transformed by the hypothesis into what amounts to a deformation, and is then used in that state to check the hypothesis. This process seems redundant in that the transforming of the information into some experience that "fits" the hypothesis would render further checking unnecessary. But we can tentatively accept this proposal in order to try to generalize the mechanisms employed by Postman. Bruner uses a still different term to indicate the work done upon the stimulus-input by the hypothesis. He speaks of this as the "maximization" of certain informational cues. This, however, would seem to be a process more of selection than of transformation.

accentuations found, or alleged, in directive-state experiments. In all those cases where the transmission or transformation of information is in the direction of a *veridical* hypothesis-object relationship we shall speak of such input as representing stimulus-*information*. In those cases where the hypothesis is *non*-veridical with respect to the object and changes, i.e., distorts, the stimulus-input to accord with itself, we shall use the term stimulus-*deformation*. These terms are used for convenience rather than with any sense of physiological exactness; the actual processes, of course, are very obscure.

We can say now that checking by stimulus-*information* will confirm *only veridical hypotheses;* for stimulus-information as we have defined it is positively relevant only to veridical hypotheses. Checking by stimulus-information is, moreover, the *only* way in which veridical hypotheses can be confirmed. Stimulus-*deformation*, on the other hand, may confirm (i.e., be positively relevant to) *non*-veridical hypotheses, and checking to such stimulus-deformation (if we can still use the term checking) is the only way in which non-veridical hypotheses can be confirmed. Stimulus-information is negatively relevant to non-veridical hypotheses and tends, if it is obtruded through insistent presentations of the stimulus-object, to *infirm* them. Stimulus-deformation, also, may also infirm a non-veridical hypothesis, as when, for example, we cease to see a white sheet as a "ghost" and see it as a "white horse" instead. Here the stimulus-deformation required for validating the hypothesis of white horse is negatively relevant to the hypothesis of ghost. Stimulus-deformation *would be* infirming with respect to veridical hypotheses if it occurred in that connection; but since the hypothesis is veridical it would not, by definition, act to deform the stimulus-input. Confirming or infirming an hypothesis by the stimulus-input is now seen as a somewhat more varied and complex phenomenon than in the authors' account of their theory; but these concepts as we have refined them become more meaningful for a theory of perceptual dynamics, especially with reference to the distinction between veridical and non-veridical hypotheses.

RECONSTRUCTION OF DIRECTIVE-STATE LOGIC AND THE EXPERIMENTAL CASE FOR HYPOTHESIS-THEORY

Among the directive-state experiments to be recast in terms of hypothesis-theory let us consider, first, the type in which the question of *what* is perceived is asked. In the autistic-perception experiment of Levine, Chein, and Murphy, the food-deprived subject might be said to have a motivationally supported hypothesis to the effect that what is to be shown under the ground glass will be an article of food. Here, pursuant to directive-state theory, we rely on the meagerness of definite stimulus information and the corresponding freedom of a dominant, motivationally supported hypothesis to determine the perceptual organization; and the process in this case would be a deformation of what little stimulus-input *is* received so that it will be positively relevant to, and therefore help to confirm, the non-veridical hypothesis of "food-object." Blurred details of the picture might thus be seen as "filled-in" portions compatible with a "food" hypothesis. Another investigation, conducted by Minturn and Bruner (1951), tests the effect of a *cognitively* supported hypothesis in bringing about perceptual closure and determining what is perceived. Subjects were trained in viewing a series of two-place numbers, a series of capital letters, and a "mixed" series. Three sets, each composed of a different type of cognitive organization, were thus established in the subject. After each training series a capital letter B was presented with the curved part slightly separated from the vertical so it could be seen either as a B or as the figure 13. At such subthreshold testing exposures the earlier training on the *letter* series led to more perceptions of the stimulus-object as a B, while pretraining on the *number* series led to more perceptions as a 13. Training on the mixed series gave an intermediate result. If this was a true perceptual phenomenon rather than an accommodation of the subject's report to the apparent expectancy of the experimenter (effect of the collective order of the individual's structuring), it would show the influence of a cognitively based hypothesis in transforming, or in some cases deforming, ambiguous stimulus-input in such a way that it confirmed the hypothesis.

Another type of question asked in directive-state experiments was "*How quickly* is an object perceived?" Here we have the experiments on duration-threshold for words related to personal values and the experiments on perceptual defense. Tachistoscopically speaking, the question "how quickly" is translated into "With how little stimulus-exposure or sensory-input to the organism?" A very brief exposure means that few elements of the stimulus have time to be active and that little effect is produced on the receptor. With longer exposures more of the stimulus material becomes effective. In the original directive-state hypothesis it was assumed that the positive value to the subject of the area of meaning to which the word belonged would increase the speed of perceiving it, that is, only a small amount of stimulus-information would be needed. *Negative* value or dislike of such meanings, or emotionally toned words of an unpleasant or tabooed character, would be predicted to decrease the speed of recognition. Under the hypothesis-theory this assumption is altered, the prediction being liberalized. In a study by Postman and Leytham (1950–1951) it was pointed out that the threshold may be lowered (as well as raised) in the presence of inimical stimuli. It has also been found that accentuation phenomena have occurred for both positively and negatively valued objects. Discarding the older concepts, such as wish fulfillment, vigilance, and defense, Postman and Leytham now suggest that *any* motivational support (either positive or negative, either of reward or of punishment) will strengthen an hypothesis so that it will be confirmed with a smaller amount of positively relevant stimulus-information. (We here use the meaning attached to "stimulus-information" by the experimenters.)

This view is a great improvement; it brings together previously inconsistent findings under a single formula. It is also less teleological, since motivational upset may be regarded simply as an energic change regardless of its hedonic tone.[9] Furthermore, Postman and Leytham stressed, in word-value experiments, the predictive importance of the frequency of past confirmation of the hypothesis. If motivational support has been constant, the ease of its arousal and confirmation will depend upon the *frequency* with which it has been aroused and confirmed in the past, and this regardless of whether such motivational strengthening as it *has* received has been of a positively or negatively valued character.

So much for the *a priori* aspect of the Postman-Leytham study. These investigators employed brightness threshold for the perception of words in order to measure the amount of stimulus-information required for confirmation in veridical perception. The stimulus words were the names of personality-traits that had been rated as "desirable" or "undesirable" by the subject. It was assumed that both these types of terms had about the same motivational significance to the subject, though with opposite feeling-tone. Since the hedonic direction of the motivation was expected to make no difference it was anticipated that the recognition thresholds for these two classes of trait-terms would be about equal. The motivational part of the theorem was not quite proved since the disvalued class (undesirable traits) was recognized more quickly than the positively valued. But this fact at least disproved the assumption that perception was a wish-fulfillment process.

----

[9] This view is also consistent with findings in other fields. Studies on remembering have revealed that *both* pleasant and unpleasant episodes are recalled more frequently than those of a neutral character.

The theorem of the strengthening effect of frequency of past confirmation was tested in a roundabout way. Self-ratings and ratings of the subjects by acquaintances on the traits were obtained. It was assumed that in cases where a discrepancy between these ratings existed the subject had heard the trait applied to him less frequently in the past than in cases where the ratings by self and others were close together. Difference of rating was therefore taken as a sign of relative lack of past confirmation of an hypothesis of the subject respecting his possession of the trait. It was found, in agreement with the prediction, that a higher recognition threshold tended to hold for the trait-terms that showed discrepancy of rating. It was found, moreover, that this result was not due to any weighting from the tendency of having rated one's self as lower or higher than the estimates of one's acquaintances on undesirable or desirable traits.

Though we might wish that the experiment had involved fewer assumptions the results were fairly well in accord with the investigators' predictions. The effect of the motivational variable in strengthening a perceptual hypothesis cannot be identified with wish-fulfillment and defense, nor with a selective sensitizing for stimuli of positive value and an excluding of stimuli having negative value; for both positive and negative consequences serve to strengthen the perceiver's hypothesis. Whether the percept will appear to be wish-fulfilling or defensive, on the one hand, or veridical, on the other, that is, whether it is to be confirmed by relevant stimulus-deformation or by relevant stimulus-information, will (other things being equal) depend on the comparative frequencies with which confirmations of these respective types of hypotheses have occurred in the past. Motivation (of any sort) and frequency of past confirmation may both affect the strength of hypotheses.

It will now be seen that while an opening is left for motivation to operate the authors have fully adjusted to the criticism of Solomon and Howes (1951) concerning the uncontrolled variable of word familiarity. They have done so by incorporating the frequency or familiarity factor in their own system and basing their predictions in part upon it. The interpretation given by Postman and Leytham of their results is also noteworthy as one of the clearest expositions of the role of set that has appeared in the whole sequence of directive-state studies. As such it helps to give hypothesis-theory the definite stamp of a "set-theory."

Blake and Vanderplas (1950–1951) have tested one of the covariation theorems of frequency by using auditory intensity-threshold for word recognition (another sensory modality). Their method, however, dealt not, as in the preceding experiment, with the confirmation of veridical hypotheses by increased stimulus-information, but with the infirming of non-veridical hypotheses, based on previous stimulus-deformation, by increasing the negatively relevant stimulus-information. They sought to test the "inverse" theorem that the stronger an invalid hypothesis is the more "inappropriate" information will be necessary to infirm it.

Specifically, their problem lay in determining whether a word that had been earlier misperceived in a series, that is, a word that had given one or a number of confirmations of a (non-veridical) hypothesis would require a greater intensity of stimulus (more stimulus-information) to cause it to become *correctly* perceived than would be required for the veridical perception of a word that had been correctly perceived on the first trial. If it *would* require a greater intensity, then the inverse theorem supporting the hypothesis-theory would be upheld; for it was assumed that the fact that the non-veridical hypothesis had received a number of past confirmations would mean that it was a stronger hypothesis. In this case the "invalid" hypothesis was that which underlay a word-misperception that had previously occurred. It had been confirmed in the past by one or more cases of actually misperceiving the word that way and should therefore be on the average stronger than the hypotheses underlying the initially correct perception of other words which were presented only once and therefore had not had the benefit of a previous confirmation in the series. The "inappropriate information" that was to be used to infirm the non-veridical hypothesis for the misperceived word was, of course, merely more intense presentations of the stimulus word. To clarify the above statements by an example: If at low auditory stimulus-intensity the stimulus-word "feeble" was heard and responded to as "steamboat," then, according to the theory, it would require, at a later presentation, a greater stimulus-intensity to be correctly perceived as "feeble" than it would have required had it been perceived as "feeble" upon the first presentation.

The results of the experiment bore out this expectation. Hence, if the amount of negatively relevant stimulus-information required to "infirm" is taken as a measure of hypothesis-strength, we can now say that the more frequently an hypothesis has been confirmed in the past the stronger it will be. The Bruner-Postman covariation theorem of frequency was thus supported.[10] From this experiment it appears

[10] Advocates of Guthrie's contiguity theory of learning might say that the experiment merely demonstrated the principle that an association "last formed" gains strength by virtue of its *being* the last formed. Hypothesis-theory and associative learning theory here seem to converge as they do at a number of points.

that prior non-veridical perception significantly raises the threshold of stimulus-information necessary to produce a veridical percept of the object. Having once perceived erroneously we tend to stick to the false impression. Misperceptions thus become stereotyped.

Some further observations of these authors show the need of adding to the Bruner-Postman statement the distinctions we have previously made with regard to "stimulus-information." In the illustration cited above they say, for example, that, since the hypothesis for "steamboat" is strengthened, other hypotheses are relatively weakened. The veridical information from the exposed word feeble that *might* have led to its correct perception as "feeble" does not have a chance to "get through"; and so "steamboat" continues to be confirmed by the meager information that *is* received. Furthermore, such evidence as exists in the printed word feeble is *made to appear* appropriate (i.e., positively relevant) to "steamboat" and hence continues to confirm that hypothesis. The non-veridical hypothesis, steamboat, is of course responsible for this effect. We might say that it distorts the sensory input and then "checks itself," as it were, against the distorted rather than the veridical criterion. It tends to "monopolize" whatever in the stimulus is positively relevant to it and to minimize whatever is negatively relevant. This interpretation, which seems plausible in a general way, is clearly in agreement with the distinction earlier made between stimulus-information and stimulus-deformation. The transformation of the stimulation-input that goes on in the cortex in this case represents a *de*formation of the stimulus-input rather than actual *in*formation about it or about the object. To go on calling all the cortical transformations of stimulus-patterns by which hypotheses are confirmed stimulus-"information" would therefore be misleading. In order to justify the "inverse" or "infirming" theorem of hypothesis-strength and frequency under the Postman-Bruner theory we need to break down the term stimulus-information into the two terms stimulus-information and stimulus-deformation, as previously suggested. This distinction is necessary in order fully to account for what happens in the experimental situation.

Turning back to the covariation of hypothesis-strength with frequency of past confirmation one wonders whether a significant factor has not been overlooked in this experiment and in a preceding one. The testing of the covariation principle seems, in these experiments, too much limited to the experimental situation. Capital letters like "B," figures like "13," and the misperceptions of words in the Blake-Vanderplas experiment had probably been hypothesized and confirmed or rejected many times in the subject's perceptions of the past.

No doubt after each series of occasions when these items had occurred there were left sets to perceive them in certain ways varying with the conditions. Would this fact not require a more extended canvas of past confirmation and infirmation in order to determine the frequency with which a given hypothesis had been confirmed in the (entire) past of the organism? The effect of frequency *within the experimental series* has been demonstrated; but such frequency, in the perspective of the longer life experience, might perhaps be more logically interpreted as *recency*.[11]

Continuing with the reformulation of the directive-state propositions concerning threshold we come to the mooted question of perceptual defense. Here hypothesis-theory again liberalizes the situation. The delay in correctly recognizing the crucial or tabooed words that is present, or alleged, in these experiments is said by the hypothesis-theorists to result not from the repression of what is unpleasant or inimical, but from the dominance of "alternative" hypotheses that are strong and persistent. These dominating alternative hypotheses, that are "socially approved" but in this instance non-veridical, could have acquired their strength through any one of the four strengthening conditions previously discussed. One might, for example, take a leaf from the book of Solomon and Howes and say that the misperceptions of crucial words given at rapid exposure speeds were confirmations, through stimulus-deformation, of non-veridical hypotheses that had been strengthened by frequent confirmations in the past in situations in which they were veridical. Tabooed words, in contrast with these conventionally approved words, are usually played down both in conversation and in print and are therefore less frequently seen or heard. Since these non-veridical word-hypotheses are therefore stronger than the unsavory veridical hypotheses, they would be confirmed by less of relevant stimulus-transformation (deformation); and longer exposures of the stimulus-word (increasing stimulus-*information*) would be necessary in order to infirm them. Hence the higher threshold for veridical responses to the crucial words.

Thus the disturbing muddle over perceptual defense seems to have been cleared up and we do not need a preperceiver or a "Judas eye." Hypothesis-theory has again shown its usefulness. One cannot help feeling, however, that certain questions are left unanswered. In the first place, since the authors did not properly exploit their own conceptual basis for their theory in the phenomenon of set, they failed to recognize that different sets (i.e., hypotheses) are, in the same situa-

[11] Recency of stimulus-word exposure has been found to be correlated with a lowering of recognition thresholds. Postman and Solomon, 1950.

tion, not only "alternative" but *antagonistic*. One *precludes* the other. Though conflict is an unsatisfactory term, it is one that refers to a state of affairs important both in perception and in behavior generally. If two percepts or their corresponding sets are in conflict (or antagonistic) with each other, it is reasonable to suppose that the stronger will prevail, that is, that it will establish a "monopoly." So far, the Bruner-Postman theorem of alternative hypotheses covers the ground. But does this fully describe what is happening? Should we not also inquire *why* the two perceptual acts *are* antagonistic? Is it merely because one has greater motivational, cognitive, or past-frequency support than the other? Suppose they were equally strong as a result of these strengthening influences; it might still be that in a certain experimental setting one would be carried out and the other inhibited; and it might be that the one carried out would be the one that is considered to be socially approved in that particular setting. For example, to say that non-critical words are less "played down" socially than tabooed words and therefore are more frequently confirmed as hypotheses at once raises the question of why this is so.

To explain this circumstance we need some better answer than custom or cultural determinism, explanations that merely beg the question. The writer has earlier suggested that the speaking of tabooed words represents episodes of behavior that are negatively relevant to the ongoing collective structurings that comprise the social relationships of the individual. The reasons why this is so would take us a long time to trace and would lie far ahead of our present story. Nevertheless such an idea at least gives us a possibility of understanding the inhibition of verbal behavior patterns, and perhaps of their corresponding perceptual sets, without invoking superorganic assumptions, group norms, customs, or other entities whose referents are non-denotable. Attention is again called to the "inside" and "outside" aspects of human behavior structure and to the general similarity and connectedness of structural relationships in the organismic and collective orders, with consequent possibility of effect upon the social behavior of the individual and perhaps upon his perceptual processes as well (pp. 335–337, 340, 389). Any such interpretation requires that we see competing sets, or hypotheses, not merely as "alternatives," but in some manner that involves the dynamics of their interaction. But apart from these as yet unexplored questions Bruner's and Postman's reformulation of perceptual defense is undoubtedly a decided improvement over the earlier formulations.

We come now to the directive-state proposition that has to do with the *dimensions* in which objects are perceived, that is, with the problem of accentuation. It has already been shown that exaggeration of magnitude, though related to value and motivation, is not dependent upon a positive value or liking of the object in question. Negatively valued objects are sometimes accentuated. What is needed is to put the matter again in terms of hypothesis-strength, as dependent on some combination of the strength-producing factors and on the stimulus-input received. Bruner theorizes that accentuation depends upon hypothesis-strength; but he recruits that strength in a new way, namely, by *combining* two or more hypotheses with respect to the perceived object. In the overestimation of the size of coins he assumes that one hypothesis deals with actual expected coin-size. It is, we may infer, a veridical hypothesis and has received its strength throughout many past confirmations. The other hypothesis predicts or expects a "linkage between size and value" which Bruner claims is widespread in our culture. That which has value is expected to look large; and the greater its value the larger it should look. Is this hypothesis veridical or not? Possibly it is for our culture-objects in general, though there would be a great many exceptions. But the coin accentuation phenomenon *itself* is surely non-veridical: any hypothesis that is confirmed by seeing the coin larger than it is must be a non-veridical hypothesis. Hence we must say that this second hypothesis, being non-veridical in respect to the coin, requires stimulus-*de*formation to confirm it. According to Bruner, since size-"information" tends to confirm both these hypotheses there is a "joint maximization" by the subject of size cues with a resulting accentuation of perceived size.

Though it seems reasonable that hypothesis-theory, as here exemplified by some kind of expectancy-set regarding the coin, may help us toward the explanation of accentuation, this *particular* explanation seems dubious. First, we must assume that stimulus-information and stimulus-deformation can work in the same direction. Second, we have no evidence to prove that in other cultures in which there might *not* be a linkage of size with value an analogue of the coin-accentuation phenomenon would not occur. If the phenomenon should be related to what we called in Chapter 13 the "means-value" of the object, and indirectly also to "end-value," and if accentuation is produced by an energic increase in either of these parts of the perceptual aggregate or in their sum, we would then expect accentuation of valued objects to be a phenomenon universal in all cultures; for means-value and end-value apply to human behavior everywhere. Third, Bruner's dual-hypothesis theory, employing culture, would not generalize to the accentuation of the brightness of food objects that was found (at least memorially) by Gilchrist and Nesberg—that is, unless we made a case that what is "valuable" in our culture is also physically *brighter*. One would probably not wish to carry on such ad hoc assumptions indefinitely.

Finally, we might ask whether references to cultural peculiarities are really useful, in an ultimate sense, in explaining behavior? The only denotable evidence we have of culture, aside from cultural objects, is the way in which individuals in a given region act, speak, think, judge, feel, and so on. To use cultural homogeneity to explain behavior is thus to explain behavior by itself. If there is a linkage of size with value in the individual's behavioral pattern and also in the "culture," we need to find the reason why they are so linked. Otherwise we merely turn over a problem that is essentially psychological to the sociologist. But let us note that although Bruner's particular explanation of accentuation seems doubtful, or perhaps incomplete, a better explanation along other lines might not be at all inconsistent with the hypothesis-theory. The theory, broadly interpreted, might in this field also be found adaptable to helpful solutions.

As a final problem in directive-state theory we recall the proposition that an individual's personality influences what is perceived or the mode of its perception. Bruner (*op. cit.*) insists that a personality-oriented theory must have means whereby it can account for individual differences of perceiving. Hypothesis-theory provides such means in the possibility of exploring the differences in hypotheses, as to both kind and strength, that different individuals habitually employ. And the task for the investigator involves a concentration upon those environmental cues or stimulus-inputs which are relevant to such hypotheses. When we find out what hypotheses are being consistently confirmed in the subject's perceptual experience we shall know a good deal about him as an individual. Bruner outlines some of these possibilities in an intriguing manner, carrying the search for personality-relevant cues far beyond those of size or brightness into the field of personal and social adjustments. Thus the perception of the "warmth" or "coldness" of people, their intelligence, or their sincerity, as well as cues of racial stereotyping, might all be related to the confirming of hypotheses peculiar to the personality of the individual perceiver. Or again, the anal-sadistic, the compulsive, or the narcistic individual might, by virtue of his strong prevailing hypotheses, be sensitized for their confirmation by small stimulus items that the average person would overlook and might be incapacitated for the normal stimulus transformations of a more veridical type of perceiving. The self-concept (self-salience, self-potency, etc.) is particularly important as a set to which various ways of perceiving the objects and persons of one's environment might be related. Hypothesis theory again provides a useful framework. It affords a means for identifying and studying the basic trends of personality; and it suggests that the phenomena of perception and personality may be closely connected.

GENERAL APPRAISAL OF HYPOTHESIS-THEORY

This review of the Bruner and Postman revision of directive-state theory leaves one with a sense of progress. The main defects of the earlier assumptions have been rectified. Inconsistencies that appeared in the experiments under the previous formulation have been resolved. Criticisms have been faced and, where valid, have been met by basic changes in the system. By including motivation among the hypothesis-strengtheners the theory retains something of its original directive-state orientation. It is thus accommodated to such directive-state findings as may finally be established, without however being committed to unwarranted or unsound assumptions. By incorporating the frequency of confirmations as a condition of hypothesis-strength the authors provide a needed place in perceptual theory for past experience and learning. By including cognition in a similar role they make a place for the perception of relationships that are so important in value theory and for the interests of the gestalt theorists and social psychologists. In stressing the importance of alternative hypotheses they pave the way for a more basic treatment of perceptual blocking and conflict, and for a more intelligible interpretation of the alleged phenomenon of perceptual defense. Perceiving, thinking, and remembering are brought together in a single framework. And finally, the authors have brought principles of measurement and co-variation laws into the picture. Instead of using quantities to bolster alluring but vague functionalistic conjectures such as "perceptual defense" and "vigilance," that may shift in an opportunistic manner, they have established a dimension along which the amount of stimulus-information needed varies, and have used this dimension as a measure of another, the strength of the hypothesis. Hypothesis-strength is further related to significant background conditions of perceiving, under testable covariation-theorems that are consistent with known psychological principles. Upon the side of pattern or rationale, the theory replaces the earlier ad hoc explanations with the broad concept of set. In short, the system is now consistent and workman-like. It has a conceptual equipment that organizes and invites research and puts the older methods into a more useful frame of reference.

We have still the task of evaluating hypothesis-theory as a general theory of perception. From this standpoint there are some weaknesses as well as some strengths. It seems well supported by existing experimental findings, though some areas are yet to be explored by investigations designed directly to test it. Aside from clarifications needed concerning stimulus-transformation and the inverse theorem, the theory is now logically consistent. Its parsimony has been improved through the reduction in the number of mechanisms and their replacement by set.

Something is missing, on the side of experimental availability, in the process called "hypothesis-checking" and in the explanatory equipment of the theory as a whole. Hypothesis-information and testing is a molar conception. It made sense to us in our opening illustration of the man whom we watched as he was assembling the jigsaw puzzle. It was the man as a whole who hypothesized and then checked his hypothesis; his neurons or muscle fibers did not form or confirm hypotheses. How can we pass from this molar level to an explanation of what must be going on *inside* the organism during the perceptual act? This we must do if we would come upon anything that is explicit or denotable in the perceptual process. The explanatory deficiency of the hypothesis-concept if taken at the molar level lies in the fact that it tells us very little we did not know before. It has, in some ways, even less meaning; for unlike the molar aspect of the problem of overtly manipulating a puzzle, perceptual hypothesis-checking is largely confined to what goes on inside; and the term hypothesis is not a good guide when we enter the network of neurons, the realm of receptors and muscle fibers, and their intricate pattern of interconnections. How, then, can we find a better statement?

Bruner and Postman themselves have at least suggested an answer. Their answer lies in the concept of set. Through this concept they have opened the way to finding more experimentally available definitions and explanatory theorems that may eventually show how the process roughly called "hypothesis-testing" takes place. Functional statements may then give way to a clear account of what is happening. But these investigators have only opened the way; they have not followed it. Our criticism is that they did not avail themselves of the resources which their own theory, with its fertile suggestion of set as the basic principle, had made accessible. A theorist should at least be as explicit as he can about his intervening construct; he should not leave it to conjecture, hanging end-bound between two observable outer anchors, if he has the knowledge and opportunity to do otherwise. Intervening-variable logic was invented only as an apparently necessary substitute for knowledge and a "passing-device" for our ignorance. We do know a great deal more about set than Bruner and Postman have brought into working relationship with their theory (cf. Chapter 9). Perhaps one reason for this oversight is the stated intention of the authors not to concern themselves with the energic aspects of their problem, but to talk instead about "information." Nevertheless, although they did not give themselves to a search for the needed organismic details, in sensing that a perception is like the confirmation of an hypothesis and that the confirmation of an hypothesis, in turn, is like the fulfillment of a physiological set, they have perhaps contributed to the theory of perception even more richly than they knew. But though hypothesis-theory has latent within it a great deal of explanatory potential, the system as left by its authors is at present unexplicit and somewhat anthropomorphic rather than truly explanatory. The *set*-theory of perception that underlies the formation and checking of hypotheses has still to be worked out.

As for its completeness in covering the various aspects of perception, hypothesis-theory, though not without merit, has still some distance to go. It does deal with dimensionality in perception, though, like directive-state, from a limited standpoint. Postman points out that some of its problems are essentially the same as those of configuration and constancy. There is a gestalt emphasis upon the cognitive side, and, somewhat confusingly, a continuity learning-theory implication upon the side of motivational strengthening and confirmation through past trials. The authors themselves have predicted that perceptual theory might be internally divided just as psychological theories in general are riven (p. 343). Hypothesis-theory, to become general, must apparently be made to bring strange theoretical bedfellows into harmonious relationships. It is possible to view frame-of-reference phenomena as general dimensional hypotheses pertaining to a whole group of related experiences. The question of whether the theory can be generalized to explain meaning in perception will be considered in a later chapter. On the whole, though there are some possibilities of extension of the system, the above approaches to generalization are as yet only schematic.

There is one conspicuous limitation that seems to be placed upon the theory with respect to completeness, a limitation which was found to be inherent in the original directive-state position and concerned us also when we were discussing the divergent tendencies of perceptual theory. Like directive-state theory, hypothesis-theory is occupied more with non-veridical or the "special-case" perception than with veridical or typical. Its rationale and experiments are still largely concerned with the conditions under which a non-veridical hypothesis is confirmed or infirmed or a percept is speeded or delayed through individualized or marginal circumstances.   In its present state there is still no considered and effective attempt to accommodate it to the "antochthonous" laws of veridical perceiving as a form of biological adaptation.   Though set and hypothesis are affirmed as basic principles of perception, the hypotheses are still selected and experimentally treated as dependent upon the history or immediate circumstances of the particular subject.   Stimulus *de*formation still plays a considerable part.   Though the theory may unify these "special-case" perceptions and interpret them admirably, it is as yet undeveloped with respect to the broader, more generic, task.

But here again, we are by no means saying that it cannot be so developed.   Perhaps one could say that the necessary implications are already present in the theory.   There are veridical sets as well as non-veridical, sets characteristic of the species as well as those peculiar to individuals.   And probably the authors intended no restrictions of their concepts to individualized or special cases.   We do not need to confine experiments or theorizing to situations in which a non-veridical hypothesis is confirmed, or is infirmed by being made to give way to a veridical one.   We can study veridical hypotheses and their confirmation in their own right.   We do not need to limit our attention to the individualized type of set, or to a set recently established by a particular training series; we can go on to the more permanent and general.   By the aid of such a broader development of the concept we may hope eventually to bring these different types of perceptual activity under one coherent explanation, to arrive at a point where the roads begin to converge.   The opportunity to extend their theory further in this direction than they did was probably overlooked by the authors only because they were still concerned with their responsibility for the special problems of directive-state.   And so they have brought us, like Moses, to the edge of the promised land, but they have not yet taken us across the border.

Regardless of how we rate the completeness or generality of hypothesis-theory it has achieved one objective in which other theories have largely failed.   It has brought the aspect of the prevailing state or set of the organism into a basic role in perceptual theory.   The rich yield of information on set and its relation to perception had hitherto been left to wither on the vine.   Though many perceptual theorists had implied set in their formulations, or had dealt with it in some of its specific manifestations, none had been adept in bringing it into a fundamental theoretical position.   With Bruner's and Postman's formulation this phenomenon now has a chance to come into its own. Though these authors have said relatively little that was explicit about set, what they *have* said, and especially the fact that they have developed a system of concepts that tallies in a general way with its characteristics, has been sufficient to fix the idea and to start a very promising trend of thinking.

16

Beyond Hypothesis-Theory
Toward a Structural Theory
of Set Dynamics and Interaction

In the preceding chapter it was noted that although hypothesis-theory gave a perceptual model based upon set, it did not show *specifically* how the model or the experimental findings exemplify the characteristics of sets. The present chapter will attempt to supply some of these details. Entering, temporarily, the scene of theory-building ourselves, we shall try to translate the language of "hypotheses" into some of the more explicit concepts which the facts of set are capable of providing.

Let us begin by reconsidering some of these aspects, from Chapter 9, in connection with the general logic of hypothesis-theory. The "hypothesis," as we have seen, is a set; and a set is a state that is preparatory for, or facilitative of, some definite act of behavior—in this case, a perception. In fact, it is an incipient stage of the act itself. The set may have varying degrees of strength; and it facilitates the activity in corresponding degrees of strength, speed, or intensity, all of which are manifestations of energy. The energy of the set, then, is the strength of the "hypothesis." As we saw in the earlier chapter the sequence of preparatory and completed action has two parts. *First,* there is the set itself, which is internal to the organism. It is a condition that frequently occurs prior to the complete act and may continue between separate episodes or repetitions of the act, thus facilitating and sustaining a whole series. Its counterpart in hypothesis-theory is the notion that hypotheses are carried about in the organism ready for immediate or sustained use. *Second,* there is the stimulus from outer objects or events whose energies are added to the set, thus increasing the energy of the total aggregate until it rises above threshold and perception or overt action occurs. In a preparatory set these added stimulus-energies are a *necessary condition* for the full performance of the activity for which the organism is set.

THE DUAL ROLE OF STIMULUS-INPUT IN SET

We should regard such exteroceptive stimulations, however, as having *two* effects, both necessary for threshold attainment. First, they afford elements or events that are needed, in a non-quantitative sense, to complete the "format" or structure of the aggregate; second, they increase the total *quantity of energies* in the aggregate. To take a crude analogy, when a carpenter, following a blueprint, sets a beam, say the last beam, at a certain place in a house which he is building, he is doing two things: (1) He is completing the *structure* of the house—and this fact can never be adequately expressed by using only quantitative terms that represent *amounts* of energy or any other kind of variable; structure always involves a *non*-quantitative concept. And (2) he is increasing the *supporting-strength* of that structure. Here quantities and variables are essential. It will be seen at once that building a house requires *both* these facts; neither one, alone, is sufficient. This analogy, however, is imperfect owing to the (apparent) static character of the house. We must imagine the set-perceptual aggregate to involve continual, but self-closed, ongoings among all its elements and continual events occurring at a microscopic level among those elements. Viewed in this way every act of behavior, as well as every set-stage of an act, requires two features in its descriptive model: (1) a "format" or "kinematic" aspect (geometry) of motion, connectedness, and events and (2) a "dynamic," or energic, aspect. The energy concerned, in other words, never occurs merely as a quantity or a purely scalar entity; it is always *structured*. It is the fact that the dynamic structure of behavior has been overlooked that has made set a phenomenon so difficult for psychologists to explain.

In hypothesis-theory the added items of stimulus-input, analogous to the beam the carpenter is placing, are called "stimulus-information"; and their description is couched in cognitive, molar, and somewhat telic terminology as "informing" to the individual concerning the validity of his hypothesis. This functional aspect is not considered in the more rigorous set-theory interpretation we are here giving; elements of structure and increments of energy are used instead. As we have previously represented them, the exteroceptive stimuli from the object give rise to one or the other of two classes of effects through their afferent impulses and transformations in the central nervous system; they provide either stimulus-information or stimulus-deformation. Each of these contributes to the energies and pattern of its proper set in the manner described above, according as the set provides a place into which one or the other of the two types of effects will fit.   When this happens, and the energies of the aggregate are thereby raised above threshold, the "hypothesis" represented by the set, whether it be veridical or non-veridical, is said to be "confirmed."   On the other hand, if the exteroceptive contribution does not fit the structure of the set, that is, if it is of the "wrong" pattern like the non-fitting piece in the jigsaw puzzle, it will detract from the operational energy of the set and, if its own energies are great enough, will reduce the set-energic level below threshold.   When this happens the "hypothesis" is said to be "infirmed."

The threshold therefore represents the point at (or just above) which, with increasing set-energy and format completion, the percept suddenly appears, and just below which, with decreasing set-energy and incompatibility of the input with the set-structure, the percept suddenly disappears.   To say that the percept disappears, however, does not mean that the object vanishes; it is merely perceived differently. The earlier percept gives place to a later one whose set-energies and structure, under continued or increased contributions from the stimulus-object, are now being raised to threshold requirement.   In hypothesis-theory positively related stimulus-input tends to "confirm the hypothesis"; in the more basic set theory it merely adds its energies and pattern-element to the ongoing aggregate that is already operating at a lower energic, and less complete, level.

TRANSLATION OF HYPOTHESIS-THEORY INTO SET CONCEPTS; ILLUSTRATIVE CASES

So much for the general statement.   Before proceeding with its application to directive-state experiments let us look at a few examples from familiar situations.   Just as the runner is set on the mark, anticipating the pistol-shot that will raise the energies enough for the set to pass over into full overt action, so the perceiver in the perceptual experiment sits with his eyes fixated on the tachistoscope awaiting a stimulus, or perhaps one of a class of stimuli, that will raise the energies of the perceptual set above the threshold where a full and conscious percept will be attained.   And just as the leaping forward at the firing of the pistol is exactly the act that the structural patterning of the nerves and muscles of the runner was prepared to accomplish (were incipiently accomplishing), and just as the pistol-shot was "congruous," i.e., capable of being intercalated into this setting, so the type of stimulus-object exposed in the tachistoscope is congruous with the perpetual set-structure of the subject.   In hypothesis-theory we say that the stimulus-information in these cases is "appropriate or supporting to the hypothesis." "Hypothesis-supporting" really means that the stimulation-input "fits" the set-structure, and the energies of the whole aggregate are thereby raised.

Let us consider another example to illustrate further this feature of so-called "selectivity." We are set, let us say, to find a brooch we have lost. Suddenly our eyes fall upon it and we perceive it almost instantly. The "brooch hypothesis" (an expectancy of an object that has a certain glittering appearance) is "confirmed." In a parallel sense, as soon as the pistol is fired and the runner leaps forward we might say that his "hypothesis" ("I must spring forward at the pistol-shot") is confirmed. Hence, just as the set-structure of the runner is selective for the sound for which it is prepared and leads only to a certain kind of response when that stimulus occurs, so perceptual sets are selective of certain stimulus-inputs and prepare only a certain kind of response (i.e., a perceptual response).

But the runner sometimes leaps forward before the pistol is fired. "False starts" are sometimes made. Similarly, if we are very intent, we might "perceive" the brooch before there is any brooch to perceive. The set in this case, having high energies, is near the threshold point and the aggregate is somewhat unstable. Expressed in terms of hypothesis-theory this case would be an instance in which, in the absence of stimulus-information, a dominant hypothesis alone can sometimes "organize the perceptual situation." A related case would be one in which our gaze falls upon a shiny bit of broken glass and we "clearly perceive" it to be the brooch, only to be disappointed upon a longer or more careful examination. The hypothesis in this case was that an object which is about to appear will be the brooch, and it was non-veridical. The illusion of perceiving the brooch might be spoken of in hypothesis-theory as the work of the hypothesis in "transforming" the stimulus-input into "information consistent with the hypothesis." In the preceding chapter, we have called this an instance of hypothesis-confirmation by stimulus-*de*formation. What this process of deformation may be in terms of the physiological facts of the set and set-operation no one is as yet prepared to say. The runner might make a false start upon hearing a train whistle, though it is doubtful whether he would actually perceive the whistle's sound as the pistol-shot. The difference seems to lie in the fact that his set is more predominantly one of a "motor" rather than a "sensory" kind (p. 216), and the motor events of the aggregate are not so susceptible to deformation as the sensory.

With regard to the illusion that a bit of broken glass is the brooch, it has been said above that a non-veridical hypothesis is momentarily confirmed. But as more stimulus-information is received this hypothesis is infirmed.[1] What is meant by this expression in terms of motor-adjustment theory? It means that the physiological pattern of the set will not "accommodate" the further details of the stimulus-input that are being received. The set to perceive the "brooch," with its motor component, might, for example, be a tendency to pick the object up, pin it on one's clothing, admire it, and so on. In structural theory we would say that the details of stimulus-input from the bit of glass would obviously be "antistructurant" to any such set-structure as this. A different format of neuromuscular events is involved in what is done with a "rejected" fragment; and, in the face of increasing stimulus-input that "gears in" with a "rejection-set," no "transformation" of that input could make it retain its fitness for the "brooch" set.[2] The physiological aggregate of the brooch-set, having thus lost the support of stimulus-energies because the (increased) input is now negatively relevant to it, sinks below the energic threshold. This means also that a phenomenological percept that was experienced an instant previously now vanishes. One sees not the brooch but a bit of glass. And so it was with the many experiments in which, through stimulus deformation, non-veridical hypotheses, as for example in tachistoscopic word-perception, were temporarily confirmed, and then later rejected as more of the stimulus-input became active through the lengthening of the exposures. The account given in this paragraph will serve as a restatement in set-terminology of Bruner's and Postman's monopoly and hypothesis-shift.

Let us take another example. We sometimes "perceive" an acquaintance a little distance away though our hypothesis so to perceive may be non-veridical. Still the hypothesis (set) may be very strong, and as we advance and get ready to speak to our acquaintance, this hypothesis may be said, temporarily at least, to have a "monopoly." Further stimulus-input is received, and the hypothesis that "the person is so and so" becomes infirmed. We may be called upon, however, in order to prevent our embarrassment, to attain a new percept, a more veridical one. So a new hypothesis (set) is quickly activated or aroused. Perhaps the individual before us, though someone other

---

[1] We note, incidentally, that infirmation in perception is something that happens only to non-veridical hypotheses. The bare stimulus-input, itself, coming as it does from the actual object, must always have a "veridical" character. If the hypothesis is veridical, it will not deform this information away from physicalistic fact. The information will therefore only tend to *confirm* the hypothesis.

[2] The physiological basis of antagonistic sets was discussed on pp. 214–215.

than we thought, is still someone we know; or at the very least would have the set-meaning "a human being" or "person," with reference to whom, as to all human beings, a certain consideration and a certain dignity of bearing are expected. In any case the added stimulus-input that proved negatively related to our first set leads to the arousal of some other set. It leads, in other words, to an "hypothesis-shift." Should it *continue* to do so, as when we struggle to recall the identity of a person we have not seen for some time, the process becomes one of repeated "trial and check" until a set happens to become available with which the details of the stimulus-input are fully compatible and the set- aggregate is thereby raised in energies to full perceptual recognition. In terms of structural theory we could say that the new set represents a broader structuring that brings into the total aggregate of the present situation, as a part or substructure, a structurization earlier set up with respect to the individual in question.

It would be well to note in all these instances how clearly motor elements enter as essential parts of the aggregate. We are set not merely to perceive but to react in appropriate ways to the expected object. The discrimination of the brooch is scarcely separable from what one is set to do with it. The person we mistakenly accost must, after all, be *dealt with* in some way. These considerations remind us that set was earlier discussed as involving patterns of muscle-tensions and proprioceptive backlash from those patterns (Freeman). They also support our earlier attempt to carry over the hypothesis-concept to sets within a *social* situation where overt behavior comes into play, and to the preparedness for what others expect us to do under our "hypothesis" of so acting as to appear worthy and acceptable within a collective aggregate. As soon as we begin to translate hypothesis-theory into the language of sets and motor adjustments we see that it must be broadened. Perception cannot be sharply limited to the use of stimulus-input merely as "information" by which to confirm or deny a purely "cognitive" proposition. Perhaps this is only saying that perception cannot be isolated from the total structural matrix of the individual's behavior. From this standpoint "hypotheses" must be regarded as parts of a broader design that sometimes renders the term itself inappropriate. We have "hypotheses" not merely to see or hear, but to do; sets for some kind of *action*, not merely sets for drawing conclusions. And all these processes are a part of the total aggregate and probably form an essential part of the perceiving activity through exactly the same logic of set-structure and its energic enhancement that has been used for perception in the narrower sense. The recognition of this fact makes the term hypothesis, as used in the experimental program, seem too narrow. Perhaps Bruner and Postman would agree to this further liberalization of their term. It would have the advantage of helping us to understand why most perceptions are, by the nature of the case, fairly veridical, and would permit the facts of set to be enlisted more extensively in the formulating of a truly general theory of perception.

In the shifting of alternative hypotheses the strongest hypothesis that fits the stimulus-"information" at the moment will be the one to prevail. Since stimulus-input can be construed as energies, is this not about the same as saying that the dominating aggregate will be that in which the summation of the set and the congruent input energies is greatest? And this thought brings us, finally, to a set-consideration of the conditions that underlie the strength of hypotheses. The strengthening effect of frequency of past confirmation we can translate into the fact that sets, both for perceiving and overtly acting, can be built up through training. As to the effect of the number of alternative hypotheses, it is reasonable to suppose that when a number of set-aggregates have, at a given moment, equal potential congruence with the stimulus-input the energies of any one are relatively low with respect to the total and therefore relatively ineffective. As for motivational strengthening, we have two alternatives. Either we can consider that energies from need-states, emotional reactions, and the like are an aspect of the physiological aggregate of the set itself, or we can consider them to be the energies of "tangent" aggregates, structures that are connected with and help to energize the structure of the set. *Cognitive* support probably represents the tangency of other set-structures that are in a relationship of "means-use" to the original set within a larger, more inclusive aggregate (cf. the closing section of Chapter 13).

The task of showing that the operation of hypotheses is basically the operation of sets has thus been simple and straightforward. Seldom do we find a heuristic model that fits the theoretical situation so well as the rationale of hypothesis-theory fits the fact of set. But let us test the agreement further by examining some of the implications of set-theory for the sequence of experiments that led from directive-state to hypothesis-theory.

TRANSLATION OF DIRECTIVE-STATE AND HYPOTHESIS EXPERIMENTS INTO SET CONCEPTS; VERIDICAL SETS

To be sure, we have seen reason to question the validity of some of these investigations as proofs of the theorems they were intended to test. In this analysis, however, it will perhaps be justifiable to see how far set-theory can go in interpreting such findings as are at present considered valid as well as those that might be found in the future to take the same direction. It is also reasonable to ask how set-theory can be related to the actual data of the experiments regardless of whether it be construed as involving attitudes, memory-recall, or effects in social communication, on the one hand, or as evidences of actual perceptual phenomena, on the other.

The most obvious characteristic, that of facilitating, speeding, or strengthening the perceptual behavior for which the set prepares, can be found both in experiments showing the ability to perceive at shorter tachistoscopic exposures where a set has been established, and in the determination of what is seen at very brief exposures. It is illustrated by the experiment in which the threshold was lowered for letters that had been "rewarded" on previous exposures; and it appears again in the tendency to see a particular part of a drawing as figure and the other part as ground after corresponding reward or punishment. We see it once more in the failure to recognize reversed letters in meaningful letter combinations. It would seem logical also to call the accentuation of perceived dimensions (size, brightness, etc.) a facilitating effect. In numerous experiments certain motivational or cognitive conditions (tangent set-structures) may have helped to strengthen a judgmental set-structure, as a result of which a set-relevant object was reported as being seen as of larger size or greater brightness. If sets are structures that have energies, it would seem not unreasonable to think of enlarged or intensified perceived dimensions as the direct increase of energies of the set-aggregate's operation. The "hypotheses" in all these experiments also operated like sets in their general preparatory, sustaining, or enhancing action; and the states concerned could have been either a long or short time in building. A readiness to perceive numbers, induced by a short period of practice, prepared the subject to see a broken B as a 13. The sets that were expanded into perceiving gray cut-out pictures of objects in the natural hue of those objects, or the personality patterns that underlay Cattell's characteristic forms of misperceiving, could have been a lifetime in the process of building. The "storage" aspect of sets is illustrated in all these cases. Sets established in the laboratory for more temporary use are usually sustained throughout the tachistoscopic series.

Many of the directive-state or hypothesis experiments have tended to reveal a selectivity for certain kinds of stimulus-input, or a specificity of the result, in accordance with the hypothesis. Such features are characteristic of sets by their very nature. The number- or letter-perceiving sets built up in the Minturn and Bruner experiment predisposed the subject to see the stimulus as a number in one case and a letter in the other. In the perceived, or perhaps remembered, brightness accentuation of food-objects, experimenters found this effect for food-deprived subjects, who were probably more set to be aware of food items, but not for the recently fed subjects; and they found that pictures of objects other than those of which the individual had been deprived were not accentuated. In another experiment size-accentuation (perceptual or memorial) was selective for the kind of food preferred. In these latter cases the original directive-state assumption of a direct effect of need or value upon the percept can now be replaced by the "hypothesis" interpretation, which, in turn, can be explained by a theory of the high energies of certain set-aggregates that have been further increased by the energies of their congruent stimulus-objects. The lowering of the perceptual threshold for need-related objects also follows naturally from the fact that the energies of the set to perceive them have already been increased through structural elements or tangent set-structures of "motivation."

Diverse sets are frequently antagonistic to one another. The energic increase of one precludes the enhancement of the other. This feature was regularly shown in the many directive-state experiments in which non-veridical percepts of an object were replaced, with the lengthening of exposure time, by veridical percepts. Among these are the dramatic, but contested, experiments on perceptual defense. Probably we are not dealing here with sets *not* to perceive something, but with sets to perceive "something else." This, as we have seen, was Freeman's opinion, and the same thought is reflected in Bruner's and Postman's "alternative-hypothesis" explanation. It still leaves unexplained, as we have earlier noted, the *reason* for the antagonism among the particular alternatives; and it fails to do justice to the possibility that antistructurant sets may actually affect one another's energies inversely. Learning is known to be a factor in the building of sets and is so recognized in the "past confirmations" of hypothesis-theory; and learning entered into some of the directive-state and hypothesis experiments with marked effect upon the results. The "format" of the set may be thought to "accumulate" energies through time and past trials. This feature would make the hypothesis that was most frequently confirmed the strongest in its residue of energy in the set-structure as that structure persists between its enhancements, through stimulus-input, in time. Sets in general can be established or made available in a number of ways, and this was also true of the conditions that underlay the directive-state effects. The various ways in which states were induced that seemed to lead to accentuated size-judgments (values, rewards, hypnosis, and the past history of the individual) are examples. So also are cases of cognitive involvement and of conflicts or repressions. All these considerations accord with the view of sets as structured aggregates operating in relation to other structured aggregates. Set energies, being subthreshold with respect to the full performance, are relatively "involuntary" and unaccompanied by consciousness. And we note that introspective reports from the subjects seldom revealed the awareness of any predispositions to perceive, a fact which probably delayed the theoretical recognition of the importance of set and was sometimes used by investigators to discount the possibility that certain sets had been operating in their experimental results.

Our reanalysis of the investigations has thus proved instructive. Indications of set-aggregates and their dynamics occur throughout their entire range. It seems that Bruner and Postman, in pointing out that set lies at the basis of their reformulation, have aptly summarized the meaning of the whole directive-state movement. It is now no longer necessary to invoke the direct action of needs, motives, or values upon perceptual organization, nor to invent mediating motivational "mechanisms" that "communicate between percepts and traces" or that select, organize, and mobilize the traces for specific recognitions or misperceivings. The set-structure, as built up by past perceiving episodes, is the trace; and into it may enter the energies of motivational states, but only as one set of factors among numerous others. We are no longer led to assume a valuative or protective process of "threshold-raising" or "lowering" through the unconscious impact of "threatening" stimuli. The energies and interaction of sets, together with the stimulus-input by which they are further activated or degraded and the covariation laws relating these factors, will account for the facts observed. Directive-state phenomena are really the phenomena of perceptual set. They express the conditions of set-formation and operation; and any theory intended to explain them must ultimately be a theory of perception as the activation or expansion of perceptual sets.

Set itself is a covert and subtle process. In ordinary perceptions, where abundant stimulus-information is given at the very start, the perceptual activity is so quick and reliable that the presence of deviant or individualized sets to perceive, which are after all largely unconscious, are likely to escape notice. Set-evocation, enhancement, and the crossing of the threshold to full perception occur as one continuous and extremely rapid process.   What has happened in directive-state experiments is that, through the shortening of the exposure-time or other marginal conditions that reduce the input, these special, non-veridical sets have had a chance to reveal their presence.   This they have done in a differential manner, each set producing its own fleeting, but highly characteristic, influence upon the tentative or abortive performance and leaving its subtle impress upon the phenomenological report.   The set-gamut or "set-spectrum" of the individual is thus spread out to the experimenter's view.   In most daily perceptual activities, however, essentially veridical sets and percepts are the typical condition.   Another difference is that veridical perceptions are not merely stimulus-bound, they are "response-bound" as well.   The perceptual adjustments of daily life are associated with more complete motor activities than are required in the laboratory reports of perceiving subjects; and these activities have to come to terms with the environment in a realistic way.   Probably no one, rich or poor, has been hampered by Bruner's and Goodman's coin-size illusion in picking out a coin to put into a slot-machine.   In directive-state experiments, however, where physicalistic checks are taken away and the subject, for example, merely adjusts a diaphragm to the "phenomenological" size of the object, there may be an opportunity for the play of special, non-veridical, sets that might have been strengthened by the energies of tangent motivational or cognitive aggregrates.   The exploration of this little-known realm is the unique contribution which the directive-state theorists have (perhaps unwittingly) made; and it probably accounts for the novel and surprising character of their findings.

Given typical conditions of perceiving and of reacting in his environment, the individual's perception, barring certain standard illusions, is ordinarily very close to the veridical.   This is partly because a generalized set of overwhelming strength, the set to perceive accurately and to respond effectively, overtops all other general sets for perception or action.   It is also because *veridical* hypotheses (sets) are by far the most often confirmed in daily life and are the *only* hypotheses that can be *consistently* confirmed.   Where such a set is not raised to threshold level by adequate stimulus-input, opportunities for the enlisting and enhancement of *other* sets, as determined by the conditions of "hypothesis-strength" and "stimulus-transformation," may come into existence.   Alternative sets evoked by, and tallying with, various atypical features of the stimulus-pattern may come into play within this twilight zone of substandard perceiving.   Some unity is now beginning to appear in perceptual theory.   For we see that there is one identical principle that enters into both veridical and non-veridical perceptions. Set operates in perception *generally*, notwithstanding the fact that its results will differ according to different organismic and environmental conditions. Herein lies the possibility of a general law for perception. Perhaps we can now begin to see a convergence of the roads, a closing of the rift between the older and newer theories of perception.

A SET-DYNAMIC THEORY OF HYPOTHESIS CONFIRMATION AND INFIRMATION; TRANSLATION OF THE COVARIATION THEOREMS AND EXPERIMENTS

In carrying hypothesis-theory over into the more definite conceptualization of set what has become of the useful quantitative formulations of its authors? Do the theorems by which one can predict the amount of stimulus-information needed to confirm or infirm an hypotheses still hold? Can these also be translated into set-language? This objective, in the writer's opinion, can be accomplished without difficulty; and its achievement will add explicitness and clarity to the Bruner and Postman statements. To bring this about, however, we shall need to lean heavily upon the structural interpretation which the present writer has introduced.

Let us, as a start, restate the paradigm at which we arrived in the points listed at the close of Chapter 9 and have developed further in the first section of the present chapter. We shall also introduce some symbols for the various aspects that will later be used for the development of formulas. In all that follows it should be borne in mind that this effort is wholly tentative. We are merely trying to help along a theoretical situation that is still obscure and has many unknowns. We have hypothesized that a perception and its corresponding set are operations of essentially one and the same structured aggregate of physiological elements and events. With certain exceptions, the "format," or structure, of the perception and that of the set are the same thing. The passage of the set into full perception involves (1) the addition of certain items from the stimulus-object or from effector contacts with the environment, items that complete the *structure*, and (2) such increase of *energies* in the aggregate, or structure, as may be afforded by the items just mentioned. The full perception (or the behavior act) is thus merely the completion and energic expansion of the aggregate as seen in its set-stage. This process, however, means that an energic threshold is crossed so that the perception-stage (or the overt act) occurs suddenly and in its full character. But the aggregate can also "shrink" or be rendered incomplete by the withdrawing of the environmental events and energy-input, or by the impact of incongruous features of the stimulus-manifold. That is to say, the threshold may be crossed in a *descending* as well as an ascending direction, and a (non-veridical) percept may disappear.

Since one basic aggregate is present throughout the whole process let us call it the "set-perception aggregate" and symbolize it by the letter a. This one identical set-perception aggregate has, then, two energic (or completion) *stages*, that of the set (or "set-aggregate"), which we shall call s, and that of the full perception ("perception-aggregate"), which we can symbolize as p. If we are using the symbol "a" without further stipulation, we note that there are two successive conditions of the aggregate in time, which we can call a_1 and a_2, respectively. In cases where the relevant stimulus-input is *increasing* until total energy level crosses the threshold and leads to the attainment of a percept, a_1 represents the set-stage of the aggregate and a_2 its perception-stage. Where the relevant stimulus-input is *decreasing* or is made *negatively* relevant, so that a percept previously experienced is lost and another takes its place, a_1 represents the perception-stage of the aggregate and a_2 the set-stage. Implied in this formulation is the principle that both the perception-aggregate and the set-aggregate can persist through time. The former lasts only as long as the stimulus-object and its positively relevant input is present. The set-aggregate, or better, the set-*stage* of the aggregate, even though deprived of actual stimulus energies and environmental contacts, persists and operates indefinitely according to circumstances. Its operation, of course, is at subthreshold level. That is to say, it has a more restricted, but still essentially the same, dynamic structure, or "format," that keeps it integrated and active, though it lacks the energic density and completeness to attain the threshold level at which the percept appears. This subthreshold operation is made possible, theoretically, by the fact that the set-perception aggregate is always regarded as *a self-closed structure of ongoings and events. Continual circularity (or repetition) via proprioceptive or other circuits in the nervous or neuromuscular system gives it a certain independence of time (pp. 227–228).* The set-stage of the aggregate therefore represents a kind of "storage" state of the perception or act which can later be expanded to its full energic and completeness dimensions (pp. 241, 414).

Turning to the stimulus-input (which we shall call i), we find this to be of two kinds: first there is the input which, through its transmission and through whatever central transformation occurs, still "yields correct information" regarding the object. We shall call such input "denota," symbolized as d. This term, of course, does not mean that the cortical energies implied are denotable by the subject, but only that the features of the object from which they come are veridically perceived—that is, their phenomenological description agrees with the physicalistic and denotive description of the object (Chapter 2). Second, we have the stimulus-input whose central transformation under the influence of the set *distorts* the perception of the object, making the phenomenology non-veridical with respect to the physicalistic facts. This type of input we shall call "deforma," indicating it by the symbol df. There arises also the question of the type of relevance ($+$ or $-$) of the denota or the deforma to the set-perception aggregate. Notations for these will be provided later.

Thus far, all our concepts and symbols *could* be taken as referring only to the structural format of the aggregate and its input rather than to their quantitative aspects. We can introduce the latter by using E as a symbol for "amount of energy" and subscribing to E the various stages or parts of the manifold as above described. In this connection the strategy of considering the aggregate as a self-contained, self-closed, structure will be apparent. If any manifold of types or classes of events, such as A, B, C, D, E $\cdot$ $\cdot$ $\cdot$, etc., goes on indefinitely in a "linear" way, practically nothing can be said about its total energies or the contributions of its various parts. If, however, the event-format is *cyclical*, as in the afferent-efferent-proprioceptive-backlash circuit or in the internal "reverberating" sequences of the brain, the energies form a system and can then be handled. If A and B make up the relatively self-contained energies of a system, C, then as soon as we know the amounts of C and A, we at once know the amount of B. This fact will be of immediate assistance in the translation of the Bruner-Postman theorems, for the energies of the set-aggregate and the stimulus-input are the parts that make up the total energy of the system. Noting, therefore, that the energies of a set-perception aggregate just after stimulus-input has been received are always equal to the energies of the aggregate just before the input was received plus the energies of the input, let us start with an aggregate (set) of very low energy and keep adding to it (as by lengthening tachistoscopic exposures) more and more of the stimulus-input. Such additions will both increase the energies of the aggregate and expand its structural format by the inclusion of more details of the total structure as contributed by the stimulus-object. Letting E represent energy, a_1 the set-aggregate at a point just before the introduction of the next installment of stimulus-input, a_2 the same aggregate just after the installment is received, and i the stimulus-input, we have

(i) $$E_{a_2} = E_{a_1} + E_i.\uparrow$$

This equation will hold good, theoretically, at any value of E_{a_2} and regardless of whether a_2 is at the percept, or still only the set, level of energy. E_{a_2}, in the condition we are employing, is of course to be considered as increasing (indicated by arrow at the right). Of all the values E_{a_2} may have there is only one that is of interest to us at this point. This is its value when just barely above the threshold level, a quantity which can be indicated as $E_{a_{T_+}}$. Since operationally the theorems of hypothesis-theory must always rest upon the fact of bare threshold attainment or loss, this point is all we need. We can therefore state that

(ii) $$E_{a_{T_+}} = E_{a_1} + E_i.\uparrow$$

By this step, then, we indicate that a_{T_+} must be an aggregate sufficiently high in energies to yield a phenomenological percept; while a_1, the same aggregate just before the receipt of the stimulus-input, must have been at the set stage. Substituting, then, the subscripts p ($=$ perception) and s ($=$ set) for a_{T_+} and a_1, respectively, we write

(iii) $$E_p = E_s + E_i.\uparrow$$

It is now time to make a decision. Shall we regard the set-perception aggregate, that is, the perception and its set-stage, as veridical or non-veridical? In the empirical instance this is of course readily determinable by noting the subject's report of the stimulus-object. Suppose we consider the case to be one of veridical perceiving, and indicate that fact by italicizing the subscripts, making them p and s. This done, we now can make a discrimination as to the kind of transformation of the stimulus-input. Owing to the decision just made, i.e., that a percept is going to be attained that tallies closely with the (physicalistic) object, it is evident that i must be represented as "denota" (see earlier definitions). Since the input, i, is transformed into denota we symbolize it as d, which is also italicized since it represents stimulus-elements in their service to *veridical* perceiving. And so the final form of the equation is

(1) $$E_p = E_s + E_d.\uparrow$$

To make the formula logically complete we could change the last term on the right to $E_{d.\overset{+}{R}\to s}$. Such symbolization would show that the stimulus-denota, d, are "positively relevant" to the set aggregate or structure, s, and that their energies are therefore to be *added* to those of the set. But since stimulus-denota are *always* positively relevant to a veridical set-perception aggregate the symbolization is here unnecessary.

Equation 1 expresses the principle of set-dynamics for the threshold attainment of a veridical set by the addition to it of the energies of stimulus-denota. It states the energies of the perceptual act when a Bruner-Postman hypothesis is said to be "confirmed" by checking against stimulus-information in the special case where the set-perception aggregate is veridical: s, or set, representing the hypothesis and d, or stimulus-denota, the stimulus-information. The symbol p represents the perception, whose attainment is the confirmation of the hypothesis. The values of the various subscripted E's spell out the dynamic or quantitative aspect. Confirmation of the hypothesis is represented by the fact that, through the incorporation of the energies of d into the energies of the set-structure, s, the structure as a whole is raised to an energic level, E_p, just above the threshold, and a perception, p, occurs. The attainment of the phenomenological percept (as reported by the organism) is the "confirmation of the hypothesis."

We can always take the left side of equation 1 as a constant, since in hypothesis-theory and its experiments we are dealing with a constant point that is just barely above threshold (minimal input needed for confirmation). That the right side of the equation exactly corresponds to the Bruner-Postman covariation model will at once be seen. The greater value of E_s (strength of the hypothesis or energies of the set), the less will be the value of E_d (stimulus-information, energies of stimulus-denota) that is needed to make the right hand side equal the constant superthreshold value E_p. The lower the value of E_s, the greater is the amount of E_d that will be needed. In other words the stronger the hypothesis, the less of stimulus-information will be needed to confirm it; and the weaker the hypothesis, the more of stimulus-information will be needed. Suppose that $E_s = E_p$, making the value of E_d equal to zero. This condition corresponds to the Bruner-Postman theorem that if a dominant hypothesis is sufficiently strong it may determine the perceptual organization (produce threshold attainment) in the absence (or extreme weakness) of stimulus-information. Such a situation would, however, represent only a limiting case. It is not ordinarily realized in the confirmation of a veridical hypothesis, since some input from the stimulus has to occur in order to assure us that the perception will be veridical, or in fact that there will be a perception at all.

In hypothesis-theory, E_p being always a constant established by the experimental conditions, the experiments themselves are directed toward testing the theorem of the inverse or reciprocal relationship of E_s and E_d, where E_s is rendered measurable in terms of the various ways of assessing hypothesis-strength. E_s, the energy of the set (hypothesis), is made operational by using some one of the four factors upon which hypothesis strength is postulated as depending, namely, frequency of past confirmation, fewness of alternative hypotheses, and motivational or cognitive support. The equation, moreover, is construed not in terms of the simple logic of energy-summation we have employed, but as a means of proving the theorem that hypothesis (or set) strength *does* depend, severally, upon these four factors. Thus the quantity E_d, representing the amount of input required for confirmation, is *defined* as the measurement of the strength of the hypothesis; or rather, in this case, the *reciprocal* of E_d is regarded as the direct measure of hypothesis-strength. By taking comparison groups of subjects and results produced under different amounts of past training, motivational stresses, cognitive embeddedness, or the like, the experimenters measure in this way the strength to which the hypothesis is enhanced by these several conditions. If an inverse relationship is found between the amount of the strengthening factor that "produced" the set (E_s) and the length of tachistoscopic exposure (E_d) necessary for correct percept-attainment (p), as predicted in our equation 1, the theorem that the factor in question strengthens the hypothesis is regarded as supported. For example, the greater the number of times the hypothesis has been confirmed (perceptual threshold attained) in the past the stronger the hypothesis (E_s) is believed to be; and this belief will be proved correct by finding that a lesser amount of stimulus-information (E_d) is needed to confirm it by bringing about the perception, p. This theorem was supported in the experiment of Postman and Leytham (*op. cit.*). A more convincing proof will be found in the next chapter in the neat demonstration of Solomon and Postman that length of stimulus-exposure required for the veridical perception of words varies inversely with the past training of the subject in perceiving the words. Equation 1 should be tested, if possible, by using all four of the strengthening conditions as correlates of E_s. The writer doubts, however, that it can be unambiguously demonstrated for any factor other than frequency of past confirmations. This position is taken because we are here dealing with a *veridical* hypothesis, and the evidence from past confirmations of such hypotheses is so frequent and overpowering that motivational, cognitive, or other supports would be subordinated to it in their effects.

Let us now consider the set-dynamical statement of the case for the confirmation of a *non*-veridical hypothesis. We here remove from p and s the italics that represented veridicality. We also note that E_i (equation iii) must become E_{df}, the stimulus-input being "deformed" in the direction of the set. This change is expressed in Postman's statement that hypotheses can "transform" stimulus-information. The deforma, therefore, must be indicated as positively relevant to the set ($\overset{+}{R} \to s$) in order to build up the energies of the latter, additively, to threshold level. So now, instead of equation 1, we write

$$(2) \qquad E_p = E_s + E_{df, \overset{+}{R} \to s}. \uparrow$$

What we have said with respect to equation 1 applies also for equation 2. Regardless of whether the set-perception aggregate is veridical or non-veridical, or whether the stimulus-input is transformed into faithful denota of the stimulus-object or into deformation patterns, the covariation theorem should still logically apply. The only difference is that this time the subject comes out with a percept that is untrue to the physical object. This equation, too, can probably be tested by using as surrogates of E_s each of the four conditions postulated as strengtheners of hypotheses. If the stimulus-input energy is zero and the set-energy, E_s, is large enough to equal the perceptual threshold, E_p, the set (hypothesis) could lead directly to the attainment of the perception. In these limiting cases, which are really hallucinations, the situation is unstable and the distinction between set and perception breaks down. Where $E_{df} > 0$ the percept will involve an "illusion."

The testing of the covariation theorem as expressed by equation 2 must take a roundabout form. It is difficult to guarantee that any past training or any motivational or cognitive supports that can be devised by the experimenter will continually strengthen the tendency to hypothesize a situation in a particular *non-veridical* way. It is, in other words, hard to build up definite and *determinable* non-veridical sets under laboratory control. The device is therefore used of taking a set that has been veridical in the usual past experience of the subject and arranging an experimental situation in which it becomes non-veridical. In the preceding chapter we described an experiment in which subjects tried to match the (vague) color of cut-out pictures of objects that varied in hue, naturally, from yellow to red. The hue as physically given in the cut-outs was the same for all pictures; but owing to the long-established set to see the objects in their natural colors differentials in the estimated hues appeared in the matchings. Here we can say that a set, s, which was non-veridical *in this situation,* had high energies owing to the great frequency of its past confirmations. Since, *therefore,* E_s in equation 2 was large, not much energy of stimulus-deforma positively related to the set was required in order to raise it to the threshold-level for the (non-veridical) perception. An unstable orange-like "color" had been produced over the gray cut-outs by simultaneous contrast with a blue ground; and this meager but "appropriate" stimulus-input yielded the central deformations necessary to raise the non-veridical set-level above threshold for the various objects. $E_{df, \overset{+}{R} \rightarrow s}$, though small, was still adequate. Under better stimulus conditions in which *denota* more characteristic of the actual situation (orange paper used in the cut-outs) were afforded, this non-veridical hypothesis was infirmed by stimulus-input that was now "inappropriate" to it; and a different hypothesis to which the stimulus-denota were positively relevant ("the objects are all of the same color") was confirmed. Though the testing of equation 2 has not been thorough or well controlled, it would seem reasonable that the greater the energy of the non-veridical set (E_s), the less would be the energy of the relevant and deformed stimulus-input ($E_{df, \overset{+}{R} \rightarrow s}$) that would be required to bring the aggregate above threshold.

So much for the confirmation of hypotheses; now let us turn to their infirmation. We are now to start with a set-perception aggregate already above threshold level. The subject is already perceiving the object, for better or for worse. We must now introduce into the manifold some stimulus-input whose central transformation is *negatively* relevant to the perception that is holding sway. Such negatively relevant input is, of course, to come from further exposure to stimulation from the same object. (We cannot change the object without producing a situation that would be meaningless for our problem.) Such input, however, will probably be *positively* relevant to some *other* (antagonistic) hypothesis about the object. How can stimulus-input be negatively related to a given set-perception aggregate? The only clear meaning this statement can have is that it tends to disrupt the "format" or structure of the set or perception into which it is intruded. Dynamically it has energies, just as the aggregate has; but these energies must work in structural directions or connections that are opposed to those of the aggregate. This consideration would mean that its energies will cancel and *diminish* those of the aggregate, and will do so in direct proportion to their own amount. Hence they must be subtracted from the aggregate's energies. Going back to symbols of the type used in equation i, we note that in the present case (hypothesis infirmation) the energy of the aggregate just after the stimulus-input is presented (a_2) is now *less* than its energy just before, that is, less than the energy-level at a_1. Subtracting the energy of the stimulus-input from the energy of the aggregate at stage a_1 we therefore obtain the energy now remaining in aggregate at stage a_2. Thus

(iv) $$E_{a_2} = E_{a_1} - E_i.\downarrow$$

Again, we are interested in the value of the resulting aggregate, a_2, only when it falls *just below* the threshold level, since that is here the strategic point for the testing of hypothesis-theory. We therefore construe the formula as follows:

(v) $$E_{a_{T_-}} = E_{a_1} - E_i.\downarrow$$

The aggregate in stage a_1, that is, before its energy was reduced by negatively relevant stimulus-input, was the perception. *After* its energy is reduced and it becomes a_2 it is merely a set, for it is now below threshold. The energy of this set is indicated as $E_{a_{T_-}}$ in equation v. Substituting the proper symbols, we have

(vi) $$E_s = E_p - E_i.\downarrow$$

We now take note of the fact that the stimulus-input, in the case we are considering, is always negatively relevant to the set-perception aggregate from whose energies it detracts. Whence

(vii) $$E_s = E_p - E_{i, \bar{R} \rightarrow p}.\downarrow$$

And we must also ask whether the set-perception (s, p) is to be regarded as veridical or non-veridical. Let us first *suppose* that s and p are *veridical*. The perceptual stage of the aggregate will then have to be reduced to the level of s by a stimulus-input, i, that is negatively relevant to it; and i must take the form either of denota or deforma. If i represents *denota*, the presence or increase of E_i could not reduce E_p below threshold, for s and p are (temporarily) assumed to be veridical, and denota are always positively relevant to such a set-perception aggregate. E_i, however, cannot be assumed to represent the energies of stimulus-*deforma*, since deformations could have been produced only under the influence of a non-veridical hypothesis, and the aggregate (s, p) was assumed to have been veridical. By this reasoning it will be seen that our question is answered; s and p in equation vii must represent a *non*-veridical aggregate. Veridical perceptions cannot be infirmed by adding further stimulus-input from the object, because such stimulus-input, to be negatively relevant to the aggregate, must be deformed by some influence which the aggregate, being veridical, does not possess. *Non*-veridical perceptions, however, *can* be infirmed by further stimulus-input, because that input, if it is in the form of denota, will be *ipso facto* negatively relevant to the aggregate. We therefore also infer that the stimulus-input (E_i) consists in this case of stimulus-denota. These considerations bring us to the third of our main equations:

$$(3) \qquad\qquad E_s = E_p - E_d.\downarrow$$

It will be observed that s and p are not italicized because they are non-veridical. The relevance subscript ($\bar{R} \to p$) for d is not needed since stimulus-denota are always negatively relevant to a non-veridical aggregate.

In following the logic of this equation it is necessary to realize a shift in terms in our translation of hypothesis-theory. *The hypothesis is now represented not by s but by p.* The change is fully justified by the fact that a set-perception (or a perception-set in the case of infirmation) is always basically the same aggregate. Moreover it is only by considering the hypothesis as representing the attained percept that a test of its infirmation is possible; one cannot obtain observable evidence of the infirming of a set. E_s being now a constant, just below threshold, we can find on the right side of the equation the Bruner-Postman theorem for the infirming of an hypothesis. It is seen that E_p and E_d are here not inversely, but directly, related. That is, the stronger the non-veridical hypothesis, E_p, the *greater* is the amount of stimulus-information, E_d, that must be supplied in order to reduce the aggregate to the subthreshold level, E_s, that is, to infirm the hypothesis. If $E_d = 0$ and $E_p = E_s$, we again have instability, the percept being on the verge of being lost, and the aggregate fluctuating between the set and the percept stage.

The general situation expressed in equation 3 is illustrated by the host of familiar tachistoscopic experiments in which a misperception (pre-recognition response) gives way, as exposures are lengthened, to a veridical reaction. To establish a non-veridical perception under control for purposes of experimentation is difficult; but the ingenious experiment of Blake and Vanderplas (*op. cit.*) was intended to accomplish the feat. The hypothesis-strengthening factor chosen to represent E_p was frequency of past confirmation. Non-veridical word-hypotheses, having occurred and been confirmed as (mis)perceptions (p), were assumed to have acquired more strength for their *next* confirmation than that originally possessed by "first-time" veridical word-perceptions of the experiment, for which only one exposure was given. According to the theorem, therefore, E_d, which was a measurement of the stimulus-input required for *infirming* these non-veridical hypotheses or misperceptions, should be greater than the input required for bringing about the originally veridical perceptions. The facts bore out this expectation.

But there is another way in which a non-veridical hypothesis (perception) can be infirmed. Suppose that after having perceived the object non-veridically the subject should shift his set to a new, non-veridical set-hypothesis after the manner of equation 2, so that new stimulus-deforma would be developed that would be positively relevant to this new set but negatively relevant to the old. One non-veridical aggregate would then be reduced below threshold by a negatively relevant stimulus-input that was positively relevant to another non-veridical aggregate. The equation for the first of these aggregates would then be

$$(4) \qquad\qquad E_s = E_p - E_{df,\ \bar{R}\to p}.\downarrow$$

This effect would have occurred in an experiment in which the subject gave up one misperception only to follow it by another on the next trial. We can state this equation only as a logical possibility since it would no doubt be too subtle to be subjected to the experimental control necessary for its testing by the covariation theorems.

Through these analyses we have found that the logic of hypothesis-theory can be meaningfully translated into our physiologically based concepts of set-perception aggregates, stimulus-inputs, and threshold, all conceived in a self-closed *structural* and *energic* design, and that when quantitative theorems are deduced from this model they correspond closely with those derived from hypothesis-theory and the findings by which the latter is supported. The four structural-dynamic equations, with their hypothesis-theory equivalents, are presented in a convenient form in Table I.

All these equations are variants of the basic forms

$$(5) \qquad\qquad E_P = E_S + E_i \qquad \text{and} \qquad E_S = E_P - E_i \qquad (6)$$

where E represents energy; P any perception, veridical or non-veridical; S its corresponding set; and i whatever transformation the stimulus-input takes on in the central nervous system. The *total* of energies of the aggregate after the $\overset{+}{R}$ energies of the stimulus-contribution are taken into the structure is, if above threshold level, represented by E_p in equation 5; P being the perceptual stage of the aggregate. The *net* or *remaining* energies of the aggregate after the R energies of the stimulus-input are subtracted from the structure is, if below threshold, represented by E_S in equation 6; S being the set stage of the aggregate. Equations 5 and 6 are, of course, identical. By reverting to equations i and iv the same ideas can be seen expressed still more generally, that is, for all energic values of the aggregate regardless of threshold.

Table I. Formulas Translating Bruner's and Postman's Basic Covariation Theorems into the Energies (E) of Sets (s,s), of Perceptions (p,p), and of Stimulus-Inputs (d,df)

I. FOR VERIDICAL HYPOTHESES   BRUNER-POSTMAN FORMULATIONS

   Confirmation

   (1) $E_p = E_s + E_d$

   The greater the strength of an hypothesis (s,s), the less of appropriate stimulus-information (d,df) is needed to confirm it.

II. FOR NON-VERIDICAL HYPOTHESES

   Confirmation

   (2) $E_p = E_s + E_{df,\ \overset{+}{R} \to s}$

   Infirmation

   (3) $E_s = E_p - E_d$

   (4) $E_s = E_p - E_{df,\ \bar{R} \to p}$

   The greater the strength of an hypothesis (p), the more of inappropriate stimulus-information (d,df) is needed to infirm it. (This theorem applies only to non-veridical hypotheses.)

THEORY OF ANTAGONISTIC INTERACTION OF SETS;
APPLICATION TO "PERCEPTUAL DEFENSE"

It might be profitable to carry these speculations a bit further. One important aspect of the directive-state problem, as we have seen, centers in the perceptual (or perhaps social) situations that have given rise to the issue over perceptual defense. Bruner and Postman have handled this matter by their principle of alternative hypotheses, with certain socially acceptable hypotheses that are stronger, through more frequent use, than those corresponding to the "threatening" or tabooed stimulus-words. Under conditions of the limited stimulus-information afforded by a short exposure, these are aroused and confirmed by stimulus-deforma first, and must be infirmed before the weaker but veridical hypothesis (for the tabooed word) can come into play. In terms of set theory we have argued that this explanation is incomplete and that the situation is probably more dynamic. On the principle that set-aggregates are structures that are selective, and that like all structures they cannot operate to advantage when negatively relevant stimulus-input is coming in, it would seem likely that antagonistic sets, such as those that are surely present in the perceptual-defense experiment, do not merely await their turn to be activated and brought to threshold in the order of their respective strengths, but detract from one another's energies and thereby lessen one another's probability of being raised by their proper stimulus-inputs to threshold level.   Such a decrease in probability of threshold attainment for a given set-perception aggregate would be manifested through a longer stimulus-exposure required for recognition of the related stimulus-word, and might be mistakenly regarded as a case of the individual defending himself against perceiving the word whose aggregate energy was temporarily at a lower level.

Let us then imagine that the stimulus-word is "raped," and that the subject has two antagonistic sets (hypotheses) with regard to the perception of this stimulus, or at least with regard to socially communicating it.   Both of these sets, which we shall now describe, are highly generalized and contain a preparation to "do" as well as to "perceive" (pp. 217f., 412).   The first set or hypothesis represents the tendency to perceive and react in a manner fitting to the "polite society" of the subject's usual or present environment.   There would here be a general set to make out of the stimulus-input (stimulus word) something that is socially approved.   With this set-aggregate prevailing, i.e., stronger at the moment, the word "raped" is flashed at very brief exposure.   There is, let us say, a deformation of part of this very meager input under the influence of the set, so that the word as seen (or at least is reported) is "rapid."   Let us refer to this set to perceive in accordance with the *amenities*, and to its corresponding stimulus-deforma and non-veridical perception, by the use of a superscript, A, placed above the symbols for these items.   It will be helpful here to return to equation i and express this situation in rather general terms.   In the equation $E_{a_2} = E_{a_1} + E_i$, E_a will represent the energies of the amenities-set or hypothesis, E_i the energies of the stimulus-input (deforma) positively relevant to a_1, and E_{a_2} the energies of the aggregate in its later energic stage when E_{a_1} has been increased by the addition of E_i. E_{a_2} will then represent the accumulated tendency toward perceiving the word non-veridically, in keeping with the amenities situation, as "rapid."   Since there may be a conflict, however, we must note that whether a_2 represents an attained perception or not will vary with conditions presently to be discussed. With these definitions in mind we can state the equation as

$$(\text{viii}) \qquad \overset{A}{E_{a_2}} = \overset{A}{E_{a_1}} + \overset{A}{E_i}.$$

We must now observe that another set or hypothesis is probably present. Let us refer to it as an "experimental" type of set. The subject under this condition "sets himself" to react at once by trying to perceive the word as nearly as possible *as it is*. Perhaps the experimenter does not *stress* the desirability of a veridical report, but only asks the subject to report what he sees. This, at least, he is expected to do and not to *withhold* or *conceal* the fact that he has perceived the word in a certain way. We may suppose that the subject is an honest, coöperative, and perhaps scientifically minded individual, and perhaps also one who is eager to give a good account of his perceptual ability. Even if the experimenter does not stress accuracy of report, the very conditions of the laboratory experiment (apart from the amenities aspect to which we have referred) seem to imply it. Open-minded objectivity and alertness seem to be required. The subject's attitude may even be that this is a kind of perceptual test, and that he is not to expect any particular class of words. Since accuracy at short exposures is a requirement (even if self-imposed) he must take in every detail of the stimulus, giving himself over to the exact pattern of stimulus-elements that is flashed before him. (Our descriptions of the two sets have been given in somewhat anthropomorphic terms, but perhaps the reader can make allowances.) The subject in this second case is set, as it were, to employ only stimulus-denota, and to check any *specific* hypothesis regarding the word that might arise under this general set strictly in terms of its conformity with the denota received from the stimulus-object. Let us call this general "experimental" set, or hypothesis, "X" and use this symbol as a superscript.

We shall now trace the consequences of this general experimental set in connection with the general amenities set. The word "raped" is flashed, beginning with very brief exposures. At the faster tachistoscopic speeds not enough denota are received to represent the stimulus-pattern correctly. Positive relevance of whatever denota there are to any specific set or hypothesis in view is not yet adequately established because of the fact that the general experimental set (X) requires not that *some* word be reported, but the *correct* word. What happens, therefore, is that in the earlier and shorter exposures a specific set-aggregate under the general *amenities* set (A)—for the subject has both sets A and X—has a chance to be activated and perhaps even brought to threshold level by stimulus-deforma that are relevant and induced by it. But as the durations of the exposures lengthen in the succeeding trials more stimulus-denota come into play to permit the evoking and checking of an "experimental" hypothesis; that is, they add their energies to a specific set-aggregate for the veridical word under the general experimental set. This set-aggregate then becomes more and more energized and completed until it finally crosses the energic threshold and the word is veridically perceived and reported. This situation is represented by again writing equation i, but this time for the set-perception aggregate X, as follows:

$$\text{(ix)} \qquad\qquad \overset{X}{E}_{a_2} = \overset{X}{E}_{a_1} + \overset{X}{E}_i.$$

In this equation $\overset{X}{E}_{a_1}$ is the set, $\overset{X}{E}_i$ the stimulus-denota. Whether the resulting energy of the aggregate E_{a_2} will be high enough for a perception to occur again depends on conditions, specifically, upon the antagonism between the general set-perception aggregates A and X. In the A and X equations as stated we have not taken the trouble to use symbols differentiating veridical and non-veridical, nor have we divided E_i into denota and deforma. The reader can easily remember that the superscript A means a non-veridical set-perception, while superscript X indicates veridicality.

We are now in a position to use our formulas, speculatively, to predict the outcome of the antagonistic operation of the two general sets; for we assume that they are in some degree operative in the subject concurrently. The equations presented above are predicated on the basis of the single, uncontested operation of each set with its proper stimulus-input, apart from any interference by the action of the other. Assuming that in reality such interference occurs, we need a symbol to indicate the expected energic outcome of each aggregate (a_2 stage) *under this antagonistic or conflict condition.* Let us acquire such a symbol by writing the term for the outcome-energies of the aggregate as a small letter e instead of the capital E used for non-conflict conditions. Thus $\overset{A}{e}_{a_2}$ and $\overset{X}{e}_{a_2}$ become the terms we wish to quantify under the condition of set-antagonism. What then are the equations for these terms? Since we postulate that as one of the aggregates becomes increased in energies it withdraws energies in the same proportion from the other, we would say that

(7)
$$\overset{A}{c_{a_2}} = \overset{A}{E_{a_2}} - \overset{X}{E_{a_2}}$$

and

(8)
$$\overset{X}{e_{a_2}} = \overset{X}{E_{a_2}} - \overset{A}{E_{a_2}}.$$

Substituting from viii and ix for $\overset{A}{E_{a_2}}$ and $\overset{X}{E_{a_2}}$, we have

(9)
$$\overset{A}{e_{a_2}} = \overset{A}{E_{a_1}} + \overset{A}{E_i} - \overset{X}{E_{a_1}} - \overset{X}{E_i}$$

and

(10)
$$\overset{X}{e_{a_2}} = \overset{X}{E_{a_1}} + \overset{X}{E_i} - \overset{A}{E_{a_1}} - \overset{A}{E_i}.$$

In equation 9 the net strength of the set-perception aggregate for the "amenities" set, $\overset{A}{e_{a_2}}$, that is, of the aggregate which, if it increases sufficiently in energy, will lead to the perception (or at least reporting) of the word "rapid" instead of "raped," is thus predicted by subtracting from the total energies of this aggregate when not under conflict (sum of the two terms on the right side with superscript A) the total energies of the aggregate (when not under conflict) for perceiving the word veridically as "raped" (sum of two terms superscripted X) as these quantities stand at the particular tachistoscopic exposure-period for which the prediction is made. The net strength of the set-perception aggregate for the "experimental" set, $\overset{X}{e_{a_2}}$ (equation 10), that is, of the aggregate which would lead, if sufficiently increased, to the verdical perception of the word as "raped," is given in a corresponding manner, and again as for the status of all the E quantities during the trial for which the prediction is made.[3]

[3] It should be noted that stimulus-denota and deforma from E_i may not have the same input-rate and that they may not be equal or linear functions of the exposure time. Furthermore the strength of the sets $\overset{X}{E_{a_1}}$ and $\overset{A}{E_{a_1}}$ might change and change differentially from trial to trial owing to activating stimulus-input incidental to the progress of the experiment or changes in the situation. The "expectancy" of tabooed words may also represent an increase of the X-set strength.

It will be noted also that if equations 9 and 10 are added, $\overset{A}{e_{a_2}} + \overset{X}{e_{a_2}} = 0$. This fact does not imply any violation of the law of conservation of energy. The addition is only a mathematical exercise and does not represent anything that can happen in the perceiving organism. Energies of the operation of antagonistic sets *cannot be added* since their neuromuscular arrangements are such that they always detract from each other.

If known experimental values could be substituted on the right side of equations 9 and 10, we could then predict the strength of the tendencies for the subject to perceive or report "rapid" or to report "raped" at a given moment during the experimental series. Inspection of these equations shows that upon their solution with actual values some one of the three following conditions will always be true. Either $\overset{A}{e_{a_2}}$ (aggregate for "rapid") will be found to be a positive quantity and $\overset{X}{e_{a_2}}$ (aggregate for "raped") an equal but negative quantity, or $\overset{X}{e_{a_2}}$ will be a positive and $\overset{A}{e_{a_2}}$ an equal negative quantity, or the value of both equations will be zero. We can disregard the equation which is negative, merely considering, since energy cannot be negative, that all its energy has been given over to the other (antagonistic) aggregate. The value, then, of whichever of the dependent variables, $\overset{A}{e_{a_1}}$ ("rapid") or $\overset{X}{e_{a}}$ ("raped"), is positive will be taken as the strength of the tendency, at the given time, for that perception to be attained to the exclusion of the other. (We must remember again that these values may shift as exposure times, that give the value of E_i, are lengthened.)

But will the perception for the equation that has the positive value actually be attained? We now have to postulate a *threshold-energy* value. If the energy of the positively valued set-perception aggregate (e_{a_2}) is above this threshold, the corresponding percept (or report) will occur. If it is below, the corresponding percept (or report) will not occur though there may still be a set for that perception. If the value of the equations is zero, there will not be a set of any strength for either word. Immediately the question arises as to what becomes of the energy in this latter case. The writer would propose as the answer that this energy remains "unstructured" or "unclosed." Neither the set-aggregate nor the perceptual aggregate will avail themselves of it. It remains as a number of random or "ungeared" events in the organism and may perhaps underlie the experience of complete inhibition or frustration. Another possibility might be that it is displaced through a cycle of emotion.

To all the above analysis, however, *we must now add a note of caution.* In view of the failure to control the social factor in these directive-state experiments (Chapters 13) we still do not know whether what the experiments yield, in the case of a crucial word, represents a report, at the given input-level, of what the subject perceived, or only what he *chose to report.* It would be safest, for the present, to regard $\overset{A}{E_{a_2}}$, in equation 7, as representing the energies of an aggregate which is *still undetermined* as to whether it indicates a perception or only a (social) verbal reaction, and to follow through with the same thought in construing the meaning of $e_{a_2}^A$ and $e_{a_2}^X$. Of course, the set which results in the report corresponding to E_{a_2} also contains a component of "set to report" as well as "set to perceive." We would not expect in this case, however, that either of these two parts of the set-pattern would be fulfilled by anything but veridically oriented details of the verbal material; hence there would here be no discrepancy or ambiguity as between perceiving and reporting.

This interpretation of set and of set-interaction in perception is, of course, highly speculative and schematic. But it does at least have the value of showing that it is possible to theorize about obscure problems in terms of the energies of sets, stimulus-inputs, and their interrelationships, and to conceive of interactions and inhibitions among perceptions, without calling upon questionable anthropomorphic or manikin assumptions. Such theorizing might help to build a bridge from the known to the unknown and to guide exploration along new empirical lines. It has also been an attempt, in terms of the writer's structure theory, to take up the problem where Bruner and Postman left it and to render their fruitful concept of hypotheses more explicit in terms of the organism.

Let us hope that the remarkable ingenuity shown by laboratory perceptionists may some day lead to ways of testing equations like those we have just suggested. Psychologists have tried repeatedly to get rid of the preperceiver connotations in the earlier directive-state terminology. If the "defense" experiments could be adequately controlled and if, then, the equations we have developed were to be experimentally proved, or indeed if any other good empirical demonstration could be given in energic terms that would handle their obtained data in a rational manner, we could then feel that the last rites of perceptual defense would finally be said and the ghost of the preperceiver would be *permanently* laid. It is not that we are superstitious, of course, as one often hears said when a person hesitates to light up "three on a match," but only that we would "feel a little better" than if we tried to exorcise the demon by theoretical incantations alone.

With these poignant reflections we shall close our long discussion of directive-state, hypothesis-theory, and set. The pursuit of the elusive perceptual process into the interior of the organism has been like a long and perplexing dream. Some may feel a little disappointed on waking to find that those remarkable mechanisms that were thought to direct our perceptions and to limit our phenomenological horizons according to our personal needs and values seem no longer necessary. It may be disillusioning to find that the heralded revolution in perceptual theory and the new "laws" that were to maximize the individual perceiver are already being modified in accordance with a unifying principle that is more universal and more revealing. But perhaps the reader will agree that while some might be a little sadder, we are all nevertheless a little wiser.[4]

[4] Some experimental support for the postulates employed in this chapter is seen in a study by Wherry and Rethlingshafer (1954). Having first established in their subjects, by instructions, a set for a given reaction to a given stimulus, they gave further instructions introducing, in the same experimental series in which the first set was still active, a second set for a *different* stimulus-reaction combination. The result was an increase in the reaction-time required for the release of the original set. The second set was said to have had a tendency to "disrupt" the first. Stating the matter in terms of energies in the structural theory, we might say that where the format of set-structure A is antagonistic to that of a simultaneous set-structure B, an *increase* of the energies of operation of either A or B tends to *reduce* (proportionally) the energies of the other (as indicated in equations 7 to 10). These investigators regard their experiment as a demonstration of the "structural nature" of set.

17

Perception and Theories of Learning
The Behavior-Theory Approach
Embarrassment of Rival Formulations

The history of human thought, set in a continual flux of discoveries, presents an exciting drama. Progress comes in waves. A way of thinking about certain phenomena is gradually developed which, though it has inaccuracies and limitations, is fairly workable for a time. Then come new discoveries and the shortcomings of the earlier view become more apparent. A better conception must be found. Sometimes there is a lag in the development of the new theory, leaving men in a state of tension and suspense. Or sometimes the newer view does not dawn all at once and there is a clash between its emerging statement and earlier cherished conceptions. At times, under the influences of rival hypotheses, or in the discrepancy between the knowledge of nature that men have relied upon and the facts revealed by new discoveries, it seems that nature is not only enigmatic but inconsistent. An intellectual crisis then arises. One recalls the situation at the time of the famous experiment of Michelson and Morley on "ether drift." Not only was common thinking molded by the ether concept up to that time, but the equations of the physicists seemed to demand it. Upon it rested men's understanding of such fundamental matters as wave-motion in space, electromagnetism, and the nature of light. Doubts had arisen, however, because of the relative nature of all motion and because the question of the presence of a "fixed" ether through which the earth moves had never been experimentally tested. Then came the experiment which showed that the ether-conception was unsound and had to be given up. Mathematical theorists tried to save it, but in vain. The very ground beneath a large part of the understanding of physical nature was shaken. Physics demanded an ether theory; yet it could not have it. Finally Einstein resolved the crisis, but only by a theory that radically changed all our notions of space, time, motion, and matter.

437

Seldom does intellectual crisis in science attain such cosmic proportions. Nevertheless in every field, and in every topic within a field, this well-known drama seems to repeat itself. In the theories of perception we observed how an early system of introspective analysis of mental phenomena was developed; and for a while it seemed that the notion of "conscious elements" as the units of which the "mind" is composed was the only answer to the question of why things appear as they do. Later, logical considerations began to show this view to be unsound. The newly discovered configurational aspects entered the scene and "elements" had to be given up. There arose a conception of wholes, relationships, and supersummation. Patterning, rather than what is patterned, seemed to be the essence of mind. Field conceptions began to appear. Yet this solution, in turn, gave rise to an issue. To many, analytical and synthetic methods, as adopted in the procedures of other sciences, still seemed good. We still must sum up intensities, energies, and strengths of association; we cannot "supersum" items without violating physical laws and making measurement seem meaningless. Yet the evidence of configuration, of wholeness and organization in nature, was too strong to be rejected. Two necessary but apparently incompatible ways of looking at the facts thus had to exist side by side. Was nature, then, inconsistent in the field of perceptual phenomena? It was also seen that configurationism had achieved its successes at the cost of practically ignoring the motor side of the organism. The failure properly to accommodate motor elements and learning was embarrassing for gestalt and field theory. The discoveries of men like Werner, Wapner, and Freeman have shown that the motor aspect is present in perceptual happenings; yet how can we combine such "alien" factors as sensory and motor phenomena? Again a gap was produced by experiments that theory failed to bridge. Out of this crisis arose sensory-tonic field theory, an ingenious but not wholly satisfactory solution.

Of late we have witnessed one of the most dramatic episodes in the history of perceptual theory. Perceived dimensions were traditionally supposed to be firmly rooted in psychophysical theory and autochthonous principles. But recently this idea has been assailed. As we have seen, it has been claimed on the basis of experimental evidence that conditions internal to the organisms, such as drive, value, or need, can affect the way in which the physical world appears, even in its supposedly stable quantitative properties. Phenomena appeared that seemed to suggest, at least to many, the presence of a functionalistic preperceiver who selected the sensory data that were to be permitted the right to organize as perceptions. Here was a crisis indeed. If this sort of thing was perception, then most of the knowledge gained from the earlier study of stimulus-percept relations must be an illusion, or at best insecure. But the situation was even worse than that. Nature itself looked, for the moment, quite illogical; perceptual defense was a contradiction in terms. We have seen how, by the aid of hypothesis-theory and the physiology of set, we have been able to make some progress through that impasse.

But now another issue is arising. Perhaps it could not yet be called a crisis; but it has a foreboding character. If present trends continue, we shall find that the rift that has occurred in another great area of psychological study will show itself also in the field of perception and that perceptual theory will be split into two rival camps. This impending crisis arises from the fact that the phenomena of perception are beginning to be claimed, and rather successfully, as a legitimate field by workers in a wholly different branch of psychological inquiry. We may soon have on our hands two entirely different theoretical systems for explaining the phenomena of perception—and the irony seems to be that each may achieve a fair measure of success. The road of science is hard. First we have no explanation for a phenomenon; then we have two! A pattern of happenings might conceivably be produced in different ways at different times; but how could it be produced in different ways at the *same* time? It seems as though nature plays a game of inventing devices to confuse the investigator. The present chapter will be devoted to this latest of our theoretical troubles and to an analysis of the rival theory that is now making its appearance.

The interloper, as the reader has probably surmised, is the theory of learning. It is not the whole of learning theory, however, but only one of the two great schools that are at present rivals in the field. The impending crisis over the rival claims of perception and learning has been long a-brewing. It has been foreshadowed by the fact that no one except nativists, gestaltists, and field-theorists has been able to talk about perception without bringing in, directly or by implication, the part that learning and past experience play in its genetic aspect. There is no need to go back over this ground which is already familiar. Suffice it to say that some acceptance of learning has been inevitably involved in the study of many of the aspects of perception.

REVIEW OF BEHAVIOR AND SIGN-GESTALT THEORIES OF LEARNING

As is well known to students of psychology there are at present two main varieties of learning theory. In order to show their bearing on our problem let us review their characteristics briefly. They are distinguished by Hilgard (1948) as the "association" theories and the "field" theories, and by Spence (1951) as the S-R theories and the S-S theories.[1] The first type, the associationistic, or S-R, theories are best represented by Hull's objective theory of behavior (1943b, 1951, 1952). Behavior-theory, as Hull's system is called, is based upon the notion of the linkage of a stimulus or stimulus-pattern to a reaction and the gradual strengthening of such a connection. Learning, then, involves the increasing of "habit-strength," a concept symbolized, to show its linkage nature, by $_sH_R$. This strengthening takes place through repetitions (trials), *provided* that such repetitions *are accompanied by "reinforcement,"* that is, by instances of the reduction of a need-state or drive. Such a reduction represents a state of affairs (reward) that accompanies or is produced by the (correct) response. These increments of "reinforcements" of the linkage between stimulus and response are an essential condition of all learning.

Reinforcement of habit-linkages may be secondary as well as primary; that is, it may be provided by conditions *associated with* the original reducing of a drive or need-state as well as by the reduction of the need-state itself. The conception is mechanistic; it excludes such notions as cognition in the usual sense, as well as all considerations of phenomenology. It deals with "stimulus-traces" that become associated through conditioning with motor reactions, with additive composition of part elements, with algebraic summation of habit tendencies or "excitatory potentials," and with the transfer of common elements from one situation to another. It has no use for wholes, *Gestalten*, or supersummation. Stimulations are not merely focal but are generalized in their effects for response.

In addition to habit-strength there are a number of other factors that influence the potential for reaction, that is, for the actual performance of the act that is being learned. Habit-strength, in making its contribution to reaction-potentials, becomes multiplied by the amount of drive (D) that is active at the moment. The degree of intensity of the stimulus also has an effect. Incentives or rewards have their weight. "Inhibitory potential" and "behavioral oscillation" *detract* from reaction-potential, and in predicting performance their effects must be subtracted. The "momentary effective reaction-potential" $(_s\dot{\bar{E}}_R)$, as finally constituted, must exceed a hypothetical threshold level in order to become effective. Reaction-threshold is thus recognized in learning theory as well as in perception. The

---

[1] Useful condensed versions will be found in the references cited.

resulting response, which includes, among other things, the effect of the amount of learning that has taken place up to that moment and provides the test of the theory, is measured on a dimension of one or more of its four attributes. These are its amplitude, its latency, its resistance to extinction, and its probability of evocation in the situation concerned.

A good many hypothetical "intervening variables," such as habit-strength, drive, reaction-potential, and reactive inhibition, lie between the ends of the chain, S and R. They are justified by being tied at their antecedent and consequent ends to outwardly observable and measurable conditions. By means of all the measurable factors and by using assumptions and experimental results relating habit-strength or reaction-potential to such factors as the number of reinforced trials, timing of the stimuli, stimulus generalization, amount of drive, and so on Hull describes, with the further aid of constants, the curves that the response-measures reveal when plotted against the continuum of trials in different circumstances and under the influence of the several experimental variables. The theory thus deals with functions, equations, and curves showing covariation of different factors in habit-acquisition and performance. It is quantitative by its very nature, dealing always with amounts in which certain outcomes can be expected. Habit-strength and the ultimate reaction-potential vary with a number of factors, such, for example, as number of reinforced trials, stimulus generalization or compounding, time-interval occurring between the unconditioned stimulus and the reaction, and delay in reinforcement. The theory interprets learning as a bit-by-bit, gradual, and continuous acquisition, through reinforced repetitions, of the strength of a linkage between a stimulus and a reaction.

The second type of learning theory, which has been loosely described as the S-S or field type, is illustrated by Tolman's "sign-gestalt expectancy" theory.[2] Whereas Hull's S-R behavior theory employs conditioned-response logic and is a development of the pioneering work of Pavlov, Thorndike, and Watson, field-theory systems stem mainly from the ideas of gestalt psychology and are affiliated with Lewin's topological field conceptions. In these systems notions of a goal achieved or a field coming, through the behavior act, to equilibrium are the dynamic principles. These are in marked contrast to gradually acquired connections between a stimulus and a reaction.

[2] See Tolman, 1932. The references to Spence and Hilgard cited above contain useful brief accounts. For some of Tolman's later views see references to his writings for 1948, 1949, and 1952.

In fact relatively little is said about the stimulus and response as such. As Spence puts it, this type of theory employs an S-S rather than an S-R linkage; that is, sensory components are not thought of as linked with responses but as integrated with other sensory components in a kind of pattern or field relationship.

One of the earmarks of such systems, including that of Tolman, is to be found in the term *cognition*. The organism acquires the "knowledge" of how to use pathways or other tools to reach certain goals, such knowledge being in the form of means-end relations that are "perceived," "cognized," and "remembered." The organism learns meanings and relationships rather than the specific movements to be made in the situation. (The theory, however, tells us little about the exact nature of the relating processes involved.) In Tolman's terms the animal comes to recognize certain objects in its environment as "signs" that suggest expected relationships to goal objects ("significates"): hence the phrase "sign-gestalt expectancy." He distinguishes three classes of such cognitions: (1) those connecting primary goal objects to drive satisfactions (cathexes); (2) those relating some environmental object to the primary goal object, thus establishing "subgoals" (equivalence beliefs-); and (3) those that deal with sequences among events in the environment that set up expectancies of objects to come and relations between such future objects (field expectancies). In connection with field expectancies one might refer to experiments on place learning, which are believed to have demonstrated the setting up of "cognitive maps," as it were, in the animal's brain. Expectancies can also be regarded as "hypotheses" which are confirmed (learned) through the success in goal-achievement to which they lead.

A corollary of sign-gestalt theory is that the transfer of what is learned (cognitive expectancies) from one situation to another is not limited to identical elements and is readily and widely accomplished. It makes possible, for example, the correct solution of a problem when a frequently used pathway is blocked but other pathways are available. Another corollary is that the sign-gestalt expectancy is relatively independent of the drive or motive under which is was acquired. Thus learning, as experimentally shown, can be accomplished, though it is not outwardly evident, under one set of drive conditions where motivation is either practically absent or is provided by an "irrelevant" drive, and can later show its effect in marked manner when the drive to be reduced is made relevant to the cognitive pattern or sign-gestalt that has been learned. Such an effect is said to demonstrate "latent" learning.

Though in his later writing Tolman concedes that certain types of cognitions are reinforced by need-reduction his position in general rejects reinforcement and the law of effect as laws of learning. He has regarded motivation, rather, as a condition of performance of that which is independently learned. It does, however, enter into the general learning situation in certain ways. Drive-states produce tensions and lead to "demands." Such demands can be operationally treated—for example, in terms of the length of time of food deprivation. Demands incite or activate the animal in the learning situation; and they may be primary, as in the case of demand for drive reduction, or secondary, as in the case of objects that are instrumental to drive reduction (food, pathways leading to food, etc.). Such secondary demands are a function of the cognition (cathexis) that the object will lead toward the reduction of the primary need; and the cognition depends, in turn, on previous training or experience in the situation. Motivation enters the learning process in still other ways: (1) by leading to an emphasis on certain features of the situation or response that are important in the cognitive pattern, (2) by laying the basis for the confirmation of hypotheses through goal-attainment, and (3) by preparing the organism to *perceive* relevant aspects of the stimulus situation.

Such concepts as demands, cognitions or cathexes, equivalence beliefs, field expectancies, behavior readiness, and the like constitute the intervening variables of Tolman's system. Their anchorage to outwardly observable variables on the stimulus and response sides is, in some cases, not very close; and Tolman has not developed and tested definite equations for predicting relationships in learning. Though he posits certain laws such as "belongingness" in relation to a sensory organization and association by contiguity (involving frequency and recency) as a basis for acquiring cognitive beliefs or expectancies, his system is not yet stated in terms of quantitatively expressed laws. For one thing the nature of the theory itself discourages their use. Equations deal with quantities that covary over a range or continuum, and Tolman's system does not view learning in this way. The learning or performance which it anticipates would need to have its amount indicated by discrete quantities that go with the particular configuration of the problem. Though Tolman did announce an earlier program for studying the covariation of various aspects of the learning situation, the trend of the experiments of his school has been of a somewhat different character. One point should be especially noted. Sign-gestalt theory predicts that the acquisition of whatever is learned will be a fairly sudden, discontinuous process. In field-theory terms it represents a definite all-or-none organization, a coming of the field to equilibrium. The cognition of a situation means, by its very nature, a momentary, complete grasp of the relationship or relationships involved. One does not learn one element now and another element (or "increment") on the next occasion. If cognitive patterns were to be regarded as acquired "bit-by-bit," as in behavior-theory, one of the most significant distinctions between the two systems would be lost.

Both systems are supported by a large amount of quantitative experimental work. Tolman's theory, in the absence of specific functions of covariation, uses quantitative results merely to demonstrate the soundness of the sign-gestalt conception ("means-use" of quantification, cf. Chapter 12). Hull, on the other hand, built his theory upon the demonstration of functions and curves of quantitative relationships. Aside from these his theory would have little meaning. We have called this the "end-use" of quantification in theory-building.[3] Both theories are behavioristic; they eschew phenomenology and introspection. Both are molar to the extent that it is possible for any theory to be molar and really tell us anything about what is happening in the learning process. Tolman first tried to adjust to the molar restriction, which he himself inaugurated, by a set of constructs of a non-denotative and somewhat teleological sort that could not be referred to any locus in the organism without implying manikin assumptions. Later, he sought to escape molarism by a variety of items such as maps, compartments, channels, images, + and − charges, needs, perceptual readinesses, and belief-value matrices, constructs which are somewhat obscure as to localization but are sometimes placed within the nervous system of the organism. Hull escaped by formulating, at points where non-quantitative, explanatory concepts were needed, such mechanisms as "afferent neural interaction" and "drive stimuli." Such concepts clearly imply happenings of some sort within the organism. In those cases where Hull did not escape in this manner his intervening constructs became convenient verbal labels for mathematical formulations useful in expressing lawful relationships between outer observable conditions.

[3] This characterization does not mean that Hull regarded quantities as ends in themselves, but only that the relationship of the measurable variables entering into a learning situation was the heart of the theory. The theory ignored relationships that were by their nature incapable of statement in quantitative terms, though, as we have seen many times, such relationships exist and are highly important for theory-construction.

RELATION OF THE TWO TYPES OF LEARNING THEORY
TO PERCEPTION

Brief and inadequate as these accounts of the two major learning theories may be, they make clear two points. First, they are incompatible. They give two contrasting pictures of learning, each covering the phenomena with a greater or less degree of success in a different way. For some phenomena behavior-theory seems to give the best rationale; for others field or cognitive theory seems better. Presumably, since they are both addressed to learning there must be some way ultimately of bringing them together; but so far no adequate formula for this purpose has been found. The second point is that the two types of theories represented by our examples from Tolman and Hull are different as to their relationship to the theory of perception. Taking the cognitive, expectancy, or field type first, we are struck by its similarities to a number of perceptual theories. Its line of descent goes back largely to gestalt psychology which was primarily a theory of perception. Just as the sudden acquisition of a cognition is expected in field-theories of learning, so the process of attaining a percept is a very brief and all-or-none affair. Though Tolman's rats could not introspect and he claimed to have removed all traces of phenomenology from his system, the cognitive constructs which he employed often seemed to fit a phenomenological frame of reference better than a physicalistic framework.

The associating of afferent or sensory components into meaningful aggregates has been a way of looking at perceptions that goes back to the earlier days (cf. Titchener's context theory). The notion of the field also has characterized a number of perceptual systems. The behavioral and perceptual readinesses of Tolman are suggestive of perceptual set. We have repeatedly noted also the impossibility of clearly separating perceptual from cognitive processes. These two merge in the Bruner-Postman hypothesis-theory, in modern social psychology, in directive-state assumptions, and in the perceptual judgments required by some of the dimensionalists. So far, therefore, as learning theories of the Tolman type are concerned, perceptual theorists need have no fear that they will "usurp" the field of perception or give it a different orientation. They are already in it. From the standpoint of field or cognitive learning-theories it may be said that perception is a necessary aspect of learning itself. Indeed it might almost be said that learning *is* perception.

The theme of S-S linkage, or sensory organization, that makes learning theory at least in part a theory of perception has been developed by a number of writers. Lashley (1942*b*) holds that "when any complex of stimuli arouses nervous activity, that activity is immediately organized and certain elements or components become dominant for reaction while others become ineffective." The former, only, those for which the organism is set, are associated in any trial of a learning series. Gestalt principles in part describe this type of neural organization. Lashley contends, on the basis of investigations, that in discrimination experiments it is the *relation* between the two stimuli that determines the reaction rather than the greater reinforcement of one of the stimuli, as Hull and Spence would have it.[4] The interpretation of the process of generalization is another point of controversy. This process is sometimes described as the tendency for a given response to be associated as a gradient of habit-strength with stimuli that lie, on a dimensional continuum, *near* the original training stimulus, as well as to be associated with the latter specifically. Behavior-theorists Hull and Spence have attributed this effect to the spread of associative connections. Lashley and Wade maintain that it is due to a variable stimulus threshold and is a function of differential training with two or more stimuli lying along the continuum. Instead of finding that generalization values form a smooth curve upon the continuum of their evoking stimuli with its mode centering at the original stimulus, Razran (1949) discovered that the subjects (animal or human) employ in conditioned response experiments a kind of categorizing or stepwise "rating scale." There are, in other words, "degrees of *similarity*" by which generalization effects are controlled; and this categorizing depends more upon the state of the organism than upon the physical stimulus dimension. Thus the fact that a given conditioned response may occur to neighboring tones on a continuum of pitch as well as (though to a lesser degree than) to the exact tone to which it was originally conditioned would be interpreted to mean that the subject was reacting on the basis of recognized steps of similarity of the neighboring tones to the original tone. Such a procedure clearly resembles an act of perceptual judgment rather than a gradual or continuity principle of behavioral learning.

The relating of sensory processes has been shown in still other ways. Leuba (1940) spoke of "conditioned sensations" that were manifested in his work on posthypnotic hallucinations. Brogden (1939) discovered the phenomenon of preconditioning, in which, when a stimulus, A, was presented with another and different type of stimulus, B, and B alone was *later* conditioned to a response, the presentation

[4] Cf. Lashley and Wade, 1946.

of A alone, still later, would evoke that response. This phenomenon, according to Hilgard, suggests the presence of an intermediating "perceptual response." Birch and Bitterman (1949, 1951) have drawn together many lines of evidence showing that there are numerous instances of learning for which Hullian behavior-theory does not account, since stimulus equivalence in eliciting a response may occur under circumstances where the usual conditioning and reinforcement requirements are not met. They postulate as the basis of a theory of learning a *sensory-integration* process, supplemented by an additional selective modification of the *response*. Spence, on the other hand, has challenged some of these lines of "evidence" and has presented analyses construing them under the S-R continuity theory. Woodworth (1947), a defender of the perceptual view, has argued that it is the *perception* that must first be reinforced in a conditioned-response experiment before conditioned-response learning can take place. In discrimination experiments the distinction is to be made between stimulus-objects, not between motor responses. The conditioning experiment really represents the establishment of a new perception. The case for perceptual and cognitive learning has also been well stated by Hilgard (1948, Chapter 12).

Turning from this scene to the relation of behavior-theory to perception a very different picture is presented. The most cursory inspection of this theory shows that it is at odds with the work of perceptual and S-S learning theorists and with their traditional method of attack. Meanings, perceived relationships, and cognitions, as such, are eliminated. Phenomenology and field concepts are ruled out. The perceptual patterning, if treated in this system at all, must be reduced to the habit strengths and reaction potentials of discriminatory responses. What the subject is "aware of" and how the world is perceived or cognized are of no concern. The subject's report is treated only as a reaction that makes some kind of adjustment to a situation requiring the behavioral differentiating of objects. What the S-R learning theorist would be interested in in the usual perceptual experiment would not be the strengthening of "perceptions," the integration of sensory processes, or learning to perceive relationships, but the acquiring of a consistent tendency to speak, or otherwise react, to a certain stimulus object in a certain manner. Though "incorrect" ways of reaction would at first occur, like the "errors" in learning experiments, and might persist for a time, the behavior theorist would predict that with a sufficient number of trials the "correct" response would come almost invariably be made. The correct response would also, by the same token, come to be the response that was most quickly given. This "perceptual" habit-connection would be expected to conform to the usual laws of continuity learning and reinforcement.

We are not concerned in this view, with any central neural process underlying a sign-gestalt or percept, but only with such synaptic connections as are necessary to afford the right pathway between the stimulus and the reaction. Instead of saying that learning involves perception, or is perception, it would thus be said that perception is (or is based upon) learning—and upon learning as interpreted by the associationistic theory. The learning theorists of this school would not help to develop "perceptual" theories; they would *take over* the phenomena of perception and treat them from a different standpoint. To make its potentialities still more apparent we should remember that Hull's behavior theory is broader than the area of learning; it comprises potentially an entire system of behavior. This fact portends that its concepts may become widely available in the attempt to interpret the phenomena of perception. Though the movement may still be in its early stages it has already made some headway. Let us trace some of these developments and their consequences.

TRANSLATING PERCEPTION AND HYPOTHESIS-THEORY INTO BEHAVIOR-THEORY

First, we may note that the simpler perceptual concepts such as those of psychophysics can be translated into the language of overt behavior (Graham, 1950). A psychophysical experiment means an "instruction stimulus" followed by a "discriminatory response" of the subject. The instruction accompanying the presented stimulus restricts the reaction to some specified attribute-continuum such, for example, as brightness or heaviness. It is a selection of a given class of discriminations. The psychophysical curve then represents a function describing how this restricted set of responses correlates with the operations involved in the systematic varying of the stimulus-object along the attribute-continuum chosen. A hypothetical equation is given by Graham relating the response to factors of stimulation, conditions of the organism, number of presentations or trials, and time. By holding some of these factors constant we can investigate the effect of others in the making of the response. By holding the response (dependent variable) constant we can study the interrelation between the other (independent) variables, as, for example, between the increment of stimulation necessary for the constant response of "lighter" or "heavier" to be made and the amount of stimulation already present.

Turning to more complex levels, we note that Berlyne (1951) points out a relationship between gestalt wholes and Hull's principle of "afferent neural interaction." In the latter concept neural traces resulting from stimuli that occur together modify each other, producing an effect like a shift along continuum of generalization. Mental or perceptual "satiation" in a task (as found by Karsten) is to be related, says Berlyne, to Hull's reactive-inhibition principle according to which any reaction carries with it, through an internal state it produces, a potentiality for its own termination. We may regard perception as a response to a stimulus, though it may be *either* a muscular *or* a purely neural (i.e., central) response. Imagery, a component of symbolic processes (and of perception), is to be ordered to Hull's "fractional anticipatory goal response." According to this latter principle a fractional part of the response characteristically made to a stimulus, for example, to a goal-object, can come to be performed separately from the total reaction and in the absence of the original stimulus-object. For example, chewing or swallowing movements in the rat might occur at points of the maze *preceding* the arrival at the goal-box and the food. This particular "anticipatory" reaction moves forward in time in the series of acts to be learned. It can act as a *stimulus*-producing response, that is, it helps to stimulate further reactions through its proprioceptive backlash. It thus can "represent" the object (goal) when that object is not present and can serve as an anticipatory "symbol" of it. This idea of a stimulus-producing response enables us to see the interpretation Berlyne places upon perception. A perception, he says, is a response to an outside stimulus-object that produces further stimulation of (i.e., stimulation within) the organism. This stimulation then leads to the appropriate overt response to the object. The perceptual response is thus another intercalated intervening variable that lengthens Hull's chain of constructs. It takes place in the middle of the series intermediating between object and final outer reaction and has a momentary effective reaction-potential of its own.

The effective reaction potential of this (inner) perceptual response gives an exact definition, according to Berlyne, of the phenomenon of *attention*, which, of course, is a constant feature of perceptual activity. His argument here is as follows. Just as Hull's concept of momentary effective reaction-potential includes the effects of habit-strength, drive, stimulus intensity, inhibitory potential, and oscillation, so attention is known to depend upon these same five characteristics. Moreover, a response to a stimulus receiving a high degree of attention will, by virtue of its high reaction-potential, show high probability, amplitude, and resistance to extinction; and it will show a low latency and a selectivity. These same features are among the behavior correlates of a high intensity of attention. And for our present purpose we may add that they are features also characteristic of a perceptual set (Chapters 9 and 16), though Hull's equations themselves do not specifically distinguish set from overt response.

A definition of the process of perception, therefore, *can* be rendered in the logical form of behavior-theory. The question now arises as to whether one can take a "perceptual" theory of perception that has been already formulated and translate it into behavior-theory terms. We shall find that this, too, can be done—at least in some instances. Hull himself made some reinterpretations of field concepts. Let us take hypothesis-theory as an example, though it is admittedly an especially favorable case. In making the translation we are not, of course, assuming that the specific comparisons will always represent an exact equivalence, or that they will cover the whole ground or be entirely free from logical difficulties.

Starting, then, with the hypothesis itself, this concept becomes in behavior-theory an S-R connection, or habit. Stimulus-information becomes both the condition of response-evocation in past trials in which learning to perceive the object was taking place and the present evoking stimulus in a test series. Hypothesis-strength can be translated either into habit-strength or into the broader concept of momentary effective reaction-potential. The four independent variables on which hypothesis-strength depends are, as we recall, frequency of past confirmation, motivational support, cognitive support, and the number of alternative hypotheses available. We shall take frequency of past confirmation first. Confirmation of an hypothesis, which for hypothesis-theory means the attainment of the percept, becomes, in behavior-theory terms, the evocation and performance of the reaction. In a perceptual experiment this evocation and performance would mean that the subject speaks a word or makes some other reaction as a differential response to the stimulus-object presented. Hypothesis-confirmation would also have a touch of reinforcement if we were to regard the "need to perceive the object" as a drive to be reduced by the perceptual response. Frequently of past confirmation as a source of hypothesis-strength thus becomes equivalent to the number of past reinforced trials or evocations of the act, a primary function on which behavioral learning-theory depends. Hence there is a good parallel with respect to this factor in hypothesis-strengthening. Motivational support, or consequences for need-satisfactions, another factor contributing to hypothesis-strength, could be interpreted in S-R theory both as the background condition of reinforcement and as the amount of drive; and through the latter, or through both, it contributes to reaction potential.   Motivation thus strengthens an hypothesis in the same way that drive supplements or "uses" habit-strength in the performance of the act.   Cognitive support of hypotheses may correspond to a number of things in behavior-theory.   It seems related to afferent neural interaction, to fractional anticipatory goal-response, and to secondary reinforcement, all of which have their effects in building up habit-strength or reaction-potential.

The number of alternative hypotheses available would be interpreted in behavior-theory as the number of S-R connections to the stimulus which have an approximately equal reaction-potential.   The determination of the response, among a group of competing responses, occurs according to the relative amount of reaction-potential possessed by the competing members.   This statement corresponds to the Bruner-Postman principle of "monopoly" in which the confirmation of a stronger hypothesis precludes the confirmation of weaker one.   Thus all the conditions that strengthen "hypotheses" and enable us to predict from them the exposure-durations necessary for their confirmation find their correlates among the factors by which Hull would have predicted effective reaction potential and the degree of evocation of the (learned) response.   In perceptual experiments the report of the subject *is* the response.

Where the response (report) is non-veridical to the stimulus-object this occurrence might be explained by behavior-theory as due to stimulus generalization.   Under conditions of brief stimulus exposure, a situation in which we may suppose that the generalization gradients have not had a chance to become stabilized, the response "surprise," normally elicited by the stimulus word surprise, might be called out by a stimulus-word near to, or "resembling," that word on a continuum of variations in sound.   Thus it might be called out, for example, by the stimulus-word "surmise."   Misperceptions (at least in certain cases) might in this way be accounted for by behavior theory to the complete ignoring of both phenomenology and meaning.[5] We note, further, that both hypothesis-theory and behavior-theory require a concept of a threshold.   As for the measurement of the strength of the tendency for the response to occur (hypothesis to be confirmed), hypothesis-theory employs one of the very measures used by behavior-theory for determining the tendency to response-evoca-

---

[5] See Solomon and Postman, 1952.

tion. This measure, which is called latency, is a measurement of the time elapsing between the presentation of the stimulus and the occurrence of the response; and it is represented in perceptual experiments by the length of the period of exposure of the stimulus that is required for its perception. Latency can thus be regarded either as the duration-threshold of a perception or the reaction time of an overt response. Finally, just as hypothesis-theory has convariation laws expressing the relation between hypothesis-strengtheners and amount of stimulus-information required for confirmation, so behavior-theory has curves and equations stating the relationships between the variables of learning conditions and the measures of reaction-evocation.[6]

[6] Because of such parallels as these, adherents of the S-R behavior-system might claim that hypothesis-theory had been assimilated into learning theory, and that since the latter is more objective the formulations given by hypothesis-theory are relatively unimportant. This attitude would be both unsound and unfair. Even if behavior theory does afford a more objective and mathematical statement, we shall see that it has definite limitations at points where perceptual theories, including hypothesis-theory, afford more stimulating and far-reaching suggestions. This is notably true with respect to the role of hypothesis-theory as an entree to the concept of set, an important aspect of behavior that is largely ignored by behavior-theorists. It might be said by the latter that set is merely a case where the reaction-potential is below threshold. This statement would be quite logical and would give set a recognition in behavior theory. But that it would not do full justice to the matter is readily seen by recalling the treatment of set given in Chapters 9 and 16, a treatment which fits the pattern of hypothesis-theory very well but not at all the pattern of behavior-theory. Though our set-theory comports with hypothesis-theory it cannot, like the latter, be translated into Hullian terms. If the reader doubts this statement, let him go back to Chapter 16 and make the attempt. The reason why this is true is that the structural-dynamic theory of set, though it, too, has its quantitative statement, is a deliberate attempt to conceive in denotive terms what happens inside the organism when perception takes place, an undertaking which behavior-theory as sedulously avoids. A *perceptual* approach to the problem, such, for example, as that of hypothesis-theory, because it relates itself directly to internal, central considerations of the *pattern* of the perception, may give us some inklings of *what to look for within the organism* that are more revealing than those which the equations of objective behavior-theory, with its molar commitment, can provide. Such inklings may suggest theories like the structural theory adumbrated in Chapter 16 which, though admittedly difficult to test by the denotational techniques at present available, is fully as objective in principle as behavior-theory. We note also that learning theory did not lead to the discovery of the facts on which hypothesis-theory and other perceptual theories were based. These phenomena were not available and could not be gathered into the fold of learning until the perceptionists had pointed them out. It is true, as this chapter will show, that the ingenious logic of behavior-theory can extend itself to incorporate many of the aspects of perception. Nevertheless, the points brought out in this footnote should be borne in mind in order to keep a proper balance.

EXPERIMENTAL AND LOGICAL ATTACK OF SOLOMON AND HOWES UPON THE WORD-VALUE-THRESHOLD HYPOTHESIS

To translate the concepts of one theory into those of another is one thing, but to test the second theory by applying it to obtained experimental results is something a little different. Does behavior-theory succeed in predicting the results observed in an hypothesis-theory experiment? What we are asking, more broadly, is whether a phenomenon that has always been regarded as *perceptual*, for example, the duration-threshold of word recognition, can be formulated experimentally as well as theoretically under a system that is built not upon perceptual concepts, but upon the concepts of learning. There is at least one important line of investigation in which this has been attempted and with some success. The field concerned is that of linguistic behavior. The perceptual word-recognition experiment was here reconstrued as a situation of responses to verbal stimuli, and the prediction was made that the lowness of the word-recognition threshold (latency) would be found to be primarily, if not wholly, a function of the frequency with which the individual had used or reacted to the word concerned. That is to say, this perceptual phenomenon (word-threshold) was alleged to depend upon the number of past (reinforced) performances and therefore to represent merely a case of habit-formation, the strengthening of an S-R bond. A review of the experiments through which this assumption was supported will take us into another exciting episode in the development of perceptual theories and will illustrate the struggle of competing systems.

It will be recalled from an earlier chapter that Solomon and Howes produced an effective criticism of the work of Postman, Bruner, and McGinnies on personal values as selective factors in word-perception. Their method lay in showing that these results might have been predicted by the frequency of usage of the stimulus words employed. We now return to this theoretical issue and its related experiments. In 1951 Howes and Solomon had performed an experiment published under the title "Visual Duration Threshold as a Function of Word-Probability." In their introduction they pointed out that perceptual studies involving the measurement of the optical conditions under which linguistic responses occur (e.g., visual duration or recognition thresholds) are evidently based upon *linguistic* as well as optical operations. Their work, they said, showed that one aspect of linguistic responses, namely, the probability of usage of the word, has a marked effect upon its visual duration threshold; yet, as they indicate, the conventional concepts of perceptual theory give no interpretation of this variable. The problem of this investigation of Howes and Solomon was to discover what relationship exists "between the relative frequency of occurrence of specific words in the English language and the visual duration threshold necessary for correct report of those words when they are tachistoscopically exposed."

The measures of frequency of occurrence of the words used were taken from the "Lorge Magazine Count" and the "Lorge-Thorndike Semantic Count." These frequencies, converted into logarithms, were used separately in computing the results, and their geometric mean was also employed. Sixty words were presented, with the usual method of successively increasing durations of exposures, to twenty subjects. Practice effects were controlled by presenting the words in different orders to different subjects; and recognition thresholds were computed from the data in three different ways. The nine correlations between word-frequency and duration threshold for recognition that resulted from this experiment ranged from − .68 to − .75, covariance of frequency with duration threshold accounting for an average of 50.9 per cent of the total variance. Certain empirical corrections for physical characteristics of words and letters raised the correlation range, making it − .76 to − .83. It was clear from this study that the exposure time required for the correct recognition of a word is an approximately linear decreasing function of the relative frequency with which the word, according to standard word-count tables, occurs in the (printed) language. If frequency with which a word appears in ordinary print is a sign of its familiarity to the subjects, we can say definitely that the more familiar the word the more quickly it is perceived.

In the same year Solomon and Howes brought out their critique of Postman, Bruner, and McGinnies. This study, whose results have already been outlined in Chapter 13, again argued for the dominance of word-frequency as a factor in lowering the visual duration threshold for words, and the discussion was supported by data from a repetition of the Postman-Bruner-McGinnies investigation. What is of interest to us here is the way in which the authors discussed the nature of word-perception and an experimental program for its study. They begin by deploring the loose use of terms to which perceptual theorists are prone. Concepts like "seeing," "distorting," and "selecting" are employed in ways that are often "private" and "imprecise" and that give rise to vague ad hoc explanations. From an operational standpoint it is clear that perception should be defined in terms of specifiable stimulus and specifiable response properties, for example, by reference to what the subjects *say* or *do* in a situation established partly by optical operations and partly by verbal-instructional operations. It is unfortunate, the authors comment, that the present tendency is to interpret perceptual behavior only from the standpoint of a situation which is defined only in terms of "private phenomenology." The authors propose to take the overt responses of the subjects into account; and they are interested in a class of responses that are called *linguistic* and that possess an operationally definable variable of frequency of occurrence. The perceptual concept that is to be considered and that is based on such linguistic operations is called the *visual duration threshold.* It is defined as "the duration for which the printed form of a word must be exposed in a tachistoscope, under a given set of instructions, before a subject will emit that word." We note that nothing is said here about "seeing."

Since the experimental results of the Solomon-Howes critique were earlier reviewed, we here note merely that they confirmed their previous investigation concerning the relation between the frequency of a printed word and the speed of its recognition. In order to make this relationship meaningful from the standpoint of an associative theory of learning, since the association must be made between a stimulus and response, it is necessary to assume that the words which appear often in magazines and the like will be words which are often used (i.e., spoken) by individuals who read these materials. We would have to assume that the subjects had, on numerous occasions, articulated these words, audibly or subvocally, in response to their presentations as printed stimuli. With this assumption (and it seems not unreasonable) we can draw the conclusion that the lowered threshold for words that are more frequently used in the language is a direct indication that word perceptions may be treated as learned language responses to linguistic stimuli. Solomon and Howes avoid making the above assumption, but their treatment of their experiment is along that general line. For some *indirect* experimental evidence supporting this inference, see Howes, 1954*b*. That the words which are *known* to have been used most frequently by the subjects themselves *are* the ones for which the perceptual threshold is lowered was proved in another experiment to which we shall refer.

Recognizing that the Thorndike-Lorge word-counts do not constitute a satisfactory independent variable since we cannot be sure that frequency of a word in these counts means frequency of the subject's use and since we cannot vary frequency of usage with respect to a given subject, Solomon and Howes discuss methods of manipulating frequency experimentally. One of these is to establish artificially differential frequencies in a laboratory situation and then observe their effects upon perceptual thresholds for those words. In this connection the authors refer to an experiment in which the subjects were first required to pronounce Turkish words, completely unfamiliar to them, a different number of times. The same words were later presented tachistoscopically; and the results conformed to those of the experiments in which the Thorndike-Lorge frequencies were used. This control seemed to clinch the argument that duration thresholds are an indicator of the degree of strength of the S-R connections for the words concerned. From another methodological viewpoint the authors infer that the relation between word frequency and duration threshold of perception may be a case of the general relationship between the "probability of evocation" of a response and the "latency" of its occurrence. In behavior-theory the probability of the response and its latency are assumed to be two manifestations of the same thing, viz., habit-strength (or reaction potential). Hence in this interpretation, also, the basic inference is that a stimulus-response connection (habit) involving linguistic behavior has been learned. In concluding, the authors say they are aware that frequency of use is not the only property of a word that is related to its duration threshold and that they do not wish to overemphasize the response-aspects of perceptual data. Nevertheless, the die seems to be cast for the treatment of word-perception as a frequency-based response to visually presented stimuli. Though the authors admit emotional factors as possible determinants of the reaction, such factors, they say, could operate through the building of frequencies of particular words in the life history of the individual. In this way they would affect frequency and duration threshold just as do other antecedent conditions of learning. There is as yet no evidence that they influence the tachistoscopic situation directly or apart from their earlier effect on frequency.

The experimental case of Solomon and Howes is carefully drawn and their argument sounds convincing. If perception is strengthened in the same manner as any habit, perhaps it is, after all, only a habit. By implication, at least, the whole position of those who desire to study perception in its own right and after the traditional manner of "how the world appears to the individual" seems to be threatened. As a result of the findings of Solomon and Howes one begins to wonder whether the objective-behavior logic and the S-R theory of learning might not eventually account for all the phenomena of perception for whose description a satisfactory operational criterion can be devised.   To be sure, it is only in linguistic behavior that this experimental entree of behavior theorists into perceptual phenomena has as yet been gained.   But in view of the fact that language responses are so widely used in perceptual experiments as a means of conveying the "report" of the subject, their behavioristic treatment might lead to an increasing invasion of the time-honored precincts of perception.

We can draw a fanciful analogy by imagining the following scene. A fair is being held in a certain town and the inhabitants are planning a race of toy balloons.   They prepare the field by sending up, attached to strings, a large number of red balloons and an equal number of blue balloons.   The blue balloons are theories of perception, or perception-like theories.   The red are the balloons of objective learning-theory.   The plan for the morrow is to release all of them together and see which will "go the furthest."   Everything being in readiness the workers retire for the night.   At daybreak two small boys sally forth undetected.   Equipped with blow-guns, darts, and a stock of red balloons to be inflated, they make their way to the field. . . .   Several hours later the populace, having breakfasted, come forth to witness the event.   They rub their eyes with astonishment.   Gone are all the blue balloons, the balloons of perception.   In their places, bobbing and waving, is a sea of one uniform color—red.

We do not think that Messrs. Howes and Solomon are really such bad boys; but they are extremely mischievous.   Their pranks are capable of causing perceptionists some tense moments as they see their cherished phenomenology and perceptual mechanisms being reduced to fodder for the Hullian grist-mill.   Not content with exploding the beautiful theory of perceptual value-areas, the miscreants began aiming their darts in other directions.   They would have shot down some important personality concepts and a highly respected and useful scale of personal characteristics if Adams and Brown had not come to the rescue.[7]

[7] Solomon and Howes attempted to apply their associationistic reasoning to the Allport-Vernon Scale of Values whose scores had constituted the independent variable of the Postman-Bruner-McGinnies experiment.   They argued that a more frequent usage of, or familiarity with, the words in a given value-area on the part of individuals whose main interest lies in that area will predispose them more readily to respond to and check the scale-words related to that area in taking the values test.   Such an interpretation would permit *both* the value-rank of the word, as established by the test-area of the subject's interest, and the duration threshold necessary for its perception to be derived from the same source, namely, the strength of the association between linguistic stimuli and (covert) linguistic responses.   This statement of the case, if true, would be ex-

Speaking seriously, it is fair to say that the assault of Solomon and Howes aroused some feeling in the ranks of the perceptionists. Postman and Schneider (1951) argued eloquently. It may still be valuable, they said, to search for laws that apply not to stimulus and response in general but only to a limited class of events. A reasonable distinction can be made between perceptual and other types of responses. "The history of perception is long and rich, and most of the time investigators have seemed to be in substantial agreement as to what constituted their field of study." In order to mark out the area peculiar to perception Postman and Schneider fell back upon the concept of set. It is the differential setting of the subject to respond to objects and events, together with specific dimensions of discrimination, that provide the hallmark of perceptual responses. Variations in response produced by variations in these factors are regarded as perceptual responses, and their laws are the laws of perception. The writers declare their unwillingness "to solve the theoretical problem by absorbing the study of perception into a general scheme of stimulus-response analysis in which the concepts of perception and perceptual organization disappear, with directive factors and stimulus factors treated as conditions of *response* probability." It is admitted that a portion of the variance in perceptual responses can be accounted for by laws of response not peculiar to perception; but this statement still leaves room for effects that are truly perceptual. What the subject does in a perceptual experiment is a resultant *both* of his perceptual predispositions and his repertory of verbal responses. Adams and Brown (1953) were more vehement. They resisted the attempt of Solomon and Howes to define "mentalistic terms like perception" by careful specification of stimulus and response properties and public operations. They asserted their belief that it sometimes pays psychologists to use phenomenological observations and to think in terms of so-called vague, mentalistic events like afterimages when talking

---

tremely disillusioning. Not only would the dependent and independent variables of Postman and his associates collapse into one variable, rendering their experiment meaningless, but the awful thought arises that personality characteristics as well as the concepts of perceptual theories might eventually be reduced entirely to associative habit-strengths based upon frequency of the past occurrence of an S-R connection. If such a trend should continue, all differentials of "meaning" in psychological processes might be lost, and everything in psychology might telescope finally into the S-R theory of learning—which, of course, is precisely the outcome which advocates of that theory contemplate. Cogent objections to this interpretation of responses to the Scale of Values have, however, been raised (Adams and Brown, 1953); and it is doubtful that Solomon's and Howes' inference can be sustained on this point.

about afterimages. They challenged their opponents to show the peculiar merits of operationism as spelled with a capital "O."

THE EXPERIMENT OF SOLOMON AND POSTMAN: THE CASE FOR WORD-FREQUENCY ESTABLISHED

In spite of these defenses the strength of the behavioral position on the particular subject of frequency of past usage as a determiner of perceptual response seems secure. It is attested also by the fact that Postman himself teamed up with Solomon in an experiment on the frequency principle. In their joint report of two carefully controlled experiments (1952) these investigators put the finishing touches on the proof that frequency of word usage in the subject's own history, not merely in population indices such as the Thorndike-Lorge counts, leads to a lowering of recognition threshold. Relative frequency of word usage was "built in" experimentally and its perceptual effects were then tested by tachistoscopic presentations of the words. The subjects were directed to go through a pack of 100 cards each containing a pronounceable "nonsense" word and read and pronounce each word carefully.[8] There were only 24 *different* nonsense words in the pack; but they were repeated in differing numbers of times ranging, at intervals, from 25 down to 1. Ten "core" words were then taken from the twenty-four, and mixed with twenty other words, half English and half (actually) nonsense. Tachistoscopic presentation of this list was then made. By differentially exercising the "nonsense" words by having a subject read them different numbers of times the experimenters had, as we have seen, "established associations of differential strength between the visually presented verbal stimulus and the response of reading or saying the word." The results fully sustained the earlier studies. *Recognition thresholds were again found to vary inversely with frequency of prior usage.* The indubitable effect of practice in perceiving a word, as shown by changes in the recognition threshold, definitely puts the problem in the general area of learning. Speed of recognition shows how well the perception has been learned. Is it necessary to assume that it shows any thing else, or that it obeys special "perceptual" laws that are of a *sui generis* character?[9]

[8] The "nonsense" words were really words selected from a Turkish-English dictionary.

[9] In one respect the work thus far reported does not fully test the behavioral learning theory of recognition threshold. No systematic use of the *principle of reinforcement* (drive reduction) was made. Reece (1954) supplies this missing

ARE PERCEPTUAL PHENOMENA EXPLAINED BY THEORIES OF
PERCEPTION OR BY ASSOCIATIVE LEARNING THEORY?

Such, then, is the evidence that visual word-perception, contrary
to tradition, can be studied and systematized in a predominantly objective fashion, ruling out phenomenology and treating the whole
phenomenon as the connection of a verbal response to a visual verbal
stimulus. The experiments show that perception can be treated like
any other act that is learned or is in the process of being learned.
From this the conclusion might conceivably be drawn that the laws
of perception are likely to coincide with the laws of learning, and
that where we have, as in Hull's system, a learning theory that extends
itself to a general accounting of behavior, perceptual theory will ultimately be remodelled to fit that system. Whether we agree with such
a conclusion or not, we must admit that the learning theory approach
to perception is beginning to make case for itself. One might as well
concede that it has probably entered the field to stay and will doubtless attain further successes.

Solomon and Postman say that for the analysis they have undertaken it makes little difference whether we conceive this learning
process in terms of S-R connections or S-S patterns; and a hint is included as to further methods for deciding between the two. The
way is also held open for using the measured effect of frequency as a
"base-line" from which to measure the possible further influence of
emotional, valuative, or need-related variables—the old direction-
state hypotheses! In spite of the liberty allowed for interpretation
in terms of contending systems it is to be noted that such theoretical
analysis as is presented leans toward the side of behavior-theory. An
explanation of competing responses at short exposures is given in
terms of stimulus generalization acting in combination with strengths
of associations established through frequency of repetition. There
will be an interference with low exercise-frequency words by words of
higher frequency, and it will be manifested in tendencies for the
guesses to be high frequency words. "If the actual stimulus word is
a low frequency word, effective stimulus fragments will elicit
erroneous 'guesses' until the amount of effective stimulation becomes
great enough upon successive exposures to reduce the numbers of

---

feature in reporting an experiment in which it was found that nonsense syllables
previously associated with an electric shock will be more readily recognized if their
recognition permits an escape from the shock.

competing word responses." Hypothesis concepts seem here to be held in abeyance, weak and strong hypotheses being replaced by habit-connections of low and high associative strengths, respectively. But this restraint on "perceptual" concepts is only temporary. The authors give the reader a choice, in this same case, either of considering the increase in effective stimulation as "limiting the range of competing hypotheses" or of interpreting the effect as a "restriction of stimulus generalization."

Here then we have the strange spectacle of S-R learning theory coming into play, but alongside it, and from quite another lineage, hypothesis-theory still carrying on. This housing of the two theories in the same phenomenon is the more arresting since it contrasts the viewpoints of the two authors within the same article. At the very moment that the balloons of learning seem supreme we are reminded that hypothesis-theory and set also gave us a very intelligent way of looking at perception. The balloons of perception now reappear. It would seem that each of the authors wishes to be tolerant of the natural proclivities of the other for the sake of their common interest in the frequency theorem. There is a congenial spirit of "live and let live." But a plurality of peacefully coexisting theoretical systems for explaining the same phenomenon, though it may suggest a virtue of brotherhood important for daily living, is scarcely the way to achieve the goal of parsimony in science.

We need to take careful stock of this situation. The writer does not believe that Solomon and Howes have shot down the perceptual theories, nor is there any immediate danger of the behavior-theorists doing so. And no doubt the reader will share this opinion. Our allegory was overdrawn in order to sharpen the issue. The balloons of perception are still afloat, though some of them may rise to greater heights than others. Before behavior-theory can take over the phenomena of perception some new insights into theory-construction will have to be attained, and by that time behavior-theory itself may have changed. As it stands the theory is resourceful enough to have given the perceptual theorists some pause. But as soon as we grant that the S-R theorists have done fairly well, but at the same time maintain that "perceptual" theories have not been replaced, a problem confronts us that may assume critical proportions. For we now have two broad and highly elaborated types of theoretical system standing side by side and explaining, or claiming to explain, the same phenomena.

Solomon and Postman (*op. cit.*) do not seem troubled by this fact; they seem, if anything, to regard it as a good omen. They point out that by using operations typical of perception experiments (threshold determination) they have attacked their problem in terms of concepts derived from verbal learning. So far so good. But they go on to say that "the phenomena of word recognition can play a strategic role in the rapprochement of theories of perception and verbal learning." And again, that their results, "provide a theoretical bridge between learning theory and perception theory." Can we share their feeling of optimism over this prospect? How much of a rapprochement is taking place between two theoretical systems when the steps in each system are shown to be parallel at almost every point with those in the other (as we have seen was the case with hypothesis-theory and behavior-theory) and when both give a fairly good accounting of the same phenomenon, but when, at the same time, the concepts, mechanisms, and dynamic principles by which they operate are so foreign to each other as to be in a separate universe of discourse?

Neither the concept of hypotheses and their confirmation nor their physiological equivalents of set-aggregates, stimulus-inputs, and energic threshold attainment are in any recognizeable way like stimulus-response linkages. Motivational support of hypothesis patterns only superficially resembles drive and the reinforcement of connections; and stimulus-information and its confirming action is far afield, as a conception, from behavior-theory's stimulus and reaction-evocation. Even though the appearance of the percept at threshold exposure is, like the evocation of a response, an all or none affair, and though the hypothesis, like the habit-linkage, might get strengthened gradually up to that point, we can scarcely picture it doing so as a stimulus-response connection. The pattern-like, or "structural," format fits the case of hypotheses better than does a synaptic juncture in a linear, open-ended chain. We might sum the matter up by saying, in the older terminology, that cognition is still cognition and S-R linkage is still S-R linkage; and for all we can now see they are destined to go their separate ways for some time to come. We should also remember that hypothesis-theory is based upon the concept of set; and set is a process that is not identical with learning in that it can both establish the conditions of learning and, on other occasions, determine which of a number of learned reactions will take place.

As we look back over the theories of perception reviewed in this book how different their concepts appear from those of molar associative learning theory. Phenomenology, isomorphism of phenomenological and physical, relationship of the stimulus complex or proximal stimulation to the brain-pattern, contexts, configurations, brain mechanisms, cortical and topological fields, organismic states, tension-patterns, phase-sequences, inner directive tendencies, hypotheses—what have all these to do with the molar orientation, measured stimulus and response variables, and chains of quantitative constructs of the Hullian school? Some day we shall know perhaps, but not now. The *seeming* parallelism of the perceptionist's and behavior-theorist's approach and their convergence upon a common field of inquiry may prove to be a good thing *eventually*, but *now* it confronts us sharply with a problem that must be solved if psychological theory is to advance. This problem is how to find an answer that will be *univocal*, a statement that is not merely as satisfactory as competing formulations, but so much better than competitors will, of their own accord, disappear. This result cannot be reached by "bridges" between conceptually incompatible alternative systems. If each of two theories has the *right* answer, and that answer is explicit, no bridges between them will be needed, for they will be identical. The fact is that we are now about to have on our hands, in perception as in learning, two elaborate but widely different types of theoretical system, each addressed to the same set of facts. We can think not merely of the Bruner-Postman theory (as over against S-R learning theory) but of "perceptual" theories of perception in general. We have in this broader sense the embarrassment of two rival types of formulation, one of which might prove in the end to be about as good as the other. And the irony is that the more highly perfected each becomes the more we shall feel that two are one too many.

What does all this mean for the future of perceptual theories that have been fashioned along the more traditional lines? We shall not attempt to answer this question or to make a prediction. It is clear, however, that the problem of perceptual theory has now been broadened. We can no longer view it as separate from that of learning. The aggregate that we have been calling perception is now becoming an aggregate of *behavior*. It must be considered as a physiological process or pattern developing and strengthening through time and performances, as well as one that underlies immediate experience. Instead of saying either that perceptual phenomena are strictly "perceptual" or that they are fundamentally the operations of "learning" we could say that perceptual theory and learning theory are two different ways of looking at the same facts. We might hypothesize that *all* psychological theories concern, in the end, one unified aggregate, the behavior of the organism. Or we might take a slightly different approach and say that, although there is only one fundamental aggregate to be studied, different theories may have dealt not with the whole aggregate but with its different parts or aspects. The time periods or phases in which they have viewed its operation may have been different; or one may have stressed its spatial aspects and another its temporal. One may have used quantities to demonstrate something about it that was basically pattern-like or *non-quantitative*, while another may have emphasized the quantitative, covarying relationships which it also reveals. If this were true, the question might arise as to why, since nature is presumably consistent, these partial theoretical systems could not be articulated into one harmonious view. The answer is immediately forthcoming from the difference of the starting assumptions, concepts, procedures, and methodological rules under which different groups of theorists have worked. Those who would combine their labors into one complete system must learn to speak the same language. Perhaps, then, the solution lies not in trying to translate these two great competing systems of present-day psychology into each other's concepts nor even in trying to synthesize them, but in developing a fresh set of *common* concepts and starting anew. This solution seems to the writer, at least, to be the most promising.

EVALUATION OF S-R LEARNING THEORY
AS APPLIED TO PERCEPTION

That the various S-S, field, or cognition-like theories have not succeeded in becoming general for all the phenomena of perception has been shown by implication throughout the preceding chapters. Furthermore such *perceptual* theories have not included a sufficiently detailed account of the role of learning. Some have almost completely discounted the evidence that past experience is an important and gradually accumulating determinant of perceptual behavior. Both perceptual theories and the cognitive theory of learning have been criticized for their lack of precise quantitative formulations. Though such theories have gone further than behavior-theory in trying to provide some kind of graphic or structural model of the learning or perceptual processes, the models they have produced have been lacking in explicit reference, explanatory value, and generality, and perhaps in some cases in agreement with the facts.

On the other hand, in spite of the perceptionists' trepidations over the work of Solomon and his associates, one could scarcely say that the S-R learning-theory approach is as yet a truly general one, or feel certain that it will go the whole way in taking over the problems of perception. Though its advent in the field does bring a desired knowledge of certain relationships and their equations, and though it draws the past history of the organism into the picture, there is still a serious question as to its completeness or coverage. Furthermore, in Chapter 2 it was pointed out that although phenomenological experience is less satisfactory for scientific description than "publicly observable" data it is still a legitimate part of that total field of experience which it is the business of scientists to describe. What, for example, shall we do with experienced qualities? Or again, can S-R principles handle such matters as perceptual constancy, perceptual set, and a shifting dimensional frame of reference? Though we do not say it is impossible for them to do so we are moved to ask whether behavior-theory possesses a stock of descriptive concepts that are sufficiently flexible to deal with such subtle matters? It has seemed possible to tuck away under the Hullian principles a surprising number of psychological facts. But when we try to fit cognition, sensory organization, motor influences in perceptual selectivity, meaning, and the configurations of the gestaltists into afferent neural interaction, stimulus compounds, and fractional anticipatory goal-responses are we sure that we can cover these facts in all their nuances, or that concepts having so little connotation other than numerical quantity and covariation will explain the many obvious and general *non*-quantitative features of these integrative relationships? Certainly the array of perceptual theories embraces many phenomena that would seem to be lost if we were to approach them only from the standpoint of stimulus and response (even if the response be covert) or as the frequencies, reinforcements, or reaction-potentials of stimulus-response connections.

A further limitation of S-R learning theory with reference to perception lies in the nature of its postulates and methods. As we have repeatedly seen, a good explanatory theory of *perceiving* requires that we consider what lies within the organism as well as what can be seen from the outside, and that we try to assemble all the elements of the aggregate into some kind of coherent and dynamic scheme. By their essentially molar approach, theories of the S-R type are excluded from this sort of inquiry. Their intervening variables are usually only "logical" constructs; they do not attempt to describe or to state explicitly the kind of happenings within the organism to whose measures or quantities they refer. The "operation" of the variables, for the most part, is described in purely quantitative terms. In spite of laudable standards of caution in speculation, there is something fictitious in using the adjective "intervening variable" (for it *is* an adjective), or even the term "variable," as a noun. There is, strictly speaking, no such thing as a variable in this hypostatized sense. To say that there is an intervening variable at work is like saying there is an intervening "tall," when we mean a tall man. It is obviously necessary to know what the term tall refers to. We have to be able to *denote a man* and to know what a man *is* in order fully to understand the reference of the statement. Unless something denotable is encountered or is included by quasidenotation and explicit reference in the theory, the intervening "variable," which is only a dimension or attribute of that something, will have little or no explanatory meaning in the sense in which we have used the term explanation in this book. It will serve merely as an abstract set of numbers, derived from calculations made from other data that are more concrete.

This methodological criticism is made notwithstanding the writer's admiration for Hull's system, for its rigor of statement, its quantitatively predictive accomplishments, and its remarkable adaptability to many psychological situations. It should also be said, in fairness, that Hull did provide some concepts in his system that were of a physiological rather than a purely quantitative sort and that he himself believed that we should try to find the denotable correlates of his intervening variables. We are here criticizing only the tendency to use non-denotational concepts extensively in building an elaborate system without giving an equal consideration to the denotational and, at the same time, essentially non-quantitative aspects that are present in behavioral phenomena and are necessary for their explanation. At this point, however, we are touching in a brief, inadequate, fashion, and perhaps somewhat dogmatically, upon a question whose full and fair discussion would require a much more extended treatment. The reader, of course, will follow his own judgment as to whether he considers this criticism to be valid. It will serve, in any case, as a closing caveat for the present chapter, an admonition that the threatened embarrassment over rival types of formulation in the field of perception may be arising from the fact that there is as yet no one type of formulation that is all-sufficient.

18

The System Viewpoint — Cybernetics
Its Psychological Implications
and Contribution to Perceptual Theory

But if the drama of scientific thinking has brought intellectual crises, it has also brought the insights that produced them as well as those by which they were sometimes removed. The gestalt discovery of the significance of configurations came when traditional introspectionism was approaching sterility. The crisis over dimensionalism and motivational dynamics led to a new realization of the significance of set. The behavior-theory approach, in tending to devaluate phenomenology, gave still another way of looking at the aggregate and contributed to it a dimension of growth through time and trials. But the last two decades of molar tradition, in which the covariation laws of behavior have been developed to a high degree, are beginning to bring forth a new crisis. It comes from the growing realization, in certain quarters at least, that not much further progress can be expected in psychology until we know more about what is going on in the organism when psychological processes occur. Molarism was a good doctrine for the purpose of establishing a much-needed standard of objectivity; but both phenomenological report and the measurement of overt responses to stimuli come to the end of their tether. We must now have better theories of what is going on "inside." As if to meet this approaching crisis a further sign has appeared upon the horizon and in an unexpected quarter. It is too early yet to say what insight it will give. But the movement is making progress; and with this, the last of the major theories we shall discuss, the current of thinking will again be seen to take a new direction.

Though the theory has backgrounds in common with the main course of psychological thought it leaves the familiar pathways of perceptionists and learning-theorists and to some extent the tradition of psychology as a whole. Its inventors, in the first place, were not psychologists; they were mathematicians, physiologists, and engineers. And the initial impetus of the movement did not come from organisms at all, but from *machines*. The new discipline is called cybernetics, a term that derives from the Greek word for helmsman—that is, one who "steers." Its rise is a part of the amazing modern development of technological communication and control. The success achieved in building automata that are able, at least in principle, to perform almost any kind of intellectual task, no matter how involved, have turned men's thoughts toward applying the principles built by human beings into their machines to the more thrilling adventure of explaining human beings themselves. A curious reversal this. First the product is created by its designer; then the designer is explained in terms of his product.

Though in some quarters this hypothesis may seem strange, indeed a little repugnant, it is rendered less unacceptable when we reflect that at the very least it compels our attention to an important, but difficult, aspect of psychological theory that has never been adequately stated. Psychologists, as a rule, have hesitated to enter the mysterious realm of the nervous system. They have waited for neurophysiologists to solve their problems, and have, for that reason, been forced to be content with theories that stopped far short of a full understanding. Now the mathematicians have taken the engineers by the hand, and joined by a group of adventurous physiologists, have proceeded boldly into the regions where psychologists have feared to tread. Their common aim has been the understanding of human physiology, neural and cortical organization, and behavior through the "communications" that take place within the organismic system and the mechanisms of "regulation" and "control" that such a system reveals. There is little doubt that these efforts have contributed to the development of an understanding of the nervous system and have given neurophysiology a new impetus. How far they can go in helping psychology remains to be seen.

One of the most propitious phases of the movement is the fact that it integrates many fields of endeavor, breaking down earlier departmental barriers. Its participants have included not only the original nucleus of physicists, engineers, mathematicians, and biologists, but also statisticians, psychologists, psychopathologists, students of linguistics, and social scientists. Pioneers and leaders in the enterprise are Wiener[1] and Von Neumann, mathematicians, and Rosenblueth, a

[1] Wiener's *Cybernetics* (1948) presents the logical and mathematical bases of the theory, together with applications in neurology, psychology, psychopathology and social science. Later references will cover extensions of the principles.

physiologist. McCulloch and Pitts, on the side of neurophysiology and mathematical logic, were also associated with it almost from the beginning. Other outstanding scientists have participated in the experimental program and the series of conferences extending as far back as 1942.

The specific contributions of cybernetics to the study of perception are as yet relatively few, but they are important. In order to acquire the background needed to understand them and also to appreciate the framework within which further perceptual contributions might be expected, it is essential to review the movement as a whole. This task will take us for a time away from our immediate topic of perception; and the reader should be prepared for this necessary broadening of our range of interest both in the review of cybernetics and its psychological implications and in the critique at the end of the chapter. The specific perceptual theories will be presented in due course and can then be understood and evaluated as a part of the total picture. We must first, however, give attention to a certain general background conception, viz., the concept of a *physical system*.

CHARACTERISTICS OF OPEN SYSTEMS: IRREVERSIBILITY; STEADY STATE; NEGATIVE ENTROPY

The complex of elements and events making up an act of behavior, to which we have given the general name "aggregate," has been referred to by theorists under a number of names. It has been spoken of, for example as a configuration, a pattern, an organized whole, a field, an assembly, or a mechanism. Still another term, one which we also have used on occasion, is "system." The system-concept, like the notion of field, has received special development in various areas of science, and both these ideas have attained considerable generality as explanations of natural phenomena. There are various ways of defining the concept of a system. It is sufficient for our purposes to associate the term with any recognizably delimited aggregate of dynamic elements that are in some way interconnected and interdependent and that continue to operate together according to certain laws and in such a way as to produce some characteristic total effect. A system, in other words, is something that is concerned with some kind of activity and preserves a kind of integration and unity; and a particular system can be recognized as distinct from other systems to which, however, it may be dynamically related. Systems may be complex; they may be made up of interdependent subsystems, each of which, though less autonomous than the entire aggregate, is nevertheless fairly distinguishable in its operation. The above definition is perhaps only a restatement of the picture of the aggregate that we have carried along through all our discussions. It will help us, however, to focus upon some details of system-models that have been forthcoming from the physical and biological sciences. The system view is different from the gestalt conception of the whole in that neither supersummation nor the effect of the whole upon the parts is implied. It is different also from the concept of field in that no continuous medium is implied, and we do not find that every spatial point is characterized by a strength and direction of forces. We think, rather, of a self-contained set of discrete motions or events, as in the case of integrated mechanical actions, moving or colliding particles, energy-states, or chemical interactions.

Two types of system have been distinguished, the closed and the open. An ideal closed system would be one into which no energy is received from any outside source and from which no energy is expended to its surroundings. Such an aggregate as this probably does not exist in nature. In chemistry, systems have been studied that are sometimes said to be closed in that the reactions taking place in them form a self-contained manifold leading to chemical equilibrium. A certain compound, for example, in a container may, at a certain temperature, split up into its constituent atomic parts; but there may be also a tendency at the same temperature for these atoms to recombine into the molecule. Such a chemical process is said to be *reversible*. These reactions involve a vast number of molecules and there is no way of predicting what particular molecule will split up, what molecule will remain intact, or what dissociated atoms will recombine. All that we have are averages in the proportions in these different phases. But at a given temperature a point will be reached in which a balance in the directions of the reactions occurs; that is, the number of dissociated atoms and of whole molecules of the substance remains constant. The system is then said to be in equilibrium. The going toward equilibrium has taken place through time; but when equilibrium is reached and there is a minimum of free energy the condition of the system as a whole is relatively static and "independent of time." Should the temperature be changed, the proportions will shift and a new equilibrium will be established. Heat, according to the theory, is given off or absorbed, as the case may be, in these changes, an effect that "compensates" for the shift of the point of equilibrium. The system may thus be said to preserve itself through a range of disturbing temperatures. (Cf. Humphrey, 1933.)

In contrast with such relatively closed systems are the "open" systems that characterize living cells and organisms (though organisms too may have some equilibrial systems of the closed sort). Open systems are those through which there is a continuous flow of component materials. There is a continuous input from the environment and a continuous output of products of the system's action. The system is of such a nature that after any disturbance of the input, or step by step in association with it, its constant and time-independent character may be restored and maintained, and a restabilization of its output may occur. But it is never in true equilibrium; it maintains what is called a *steady state*. The state is "steady" as to component-types and proportionate quantities; but it is far from static or motionless. It is in a condition of ceaseless activity and change of the specific materials involved. A simple example of an open system with a steady state is afforded by a container holding a quantity of water into which water is being pumped, but which also has an outlet from which the water flows at the same rate. The walls of the container and the molecules of water are the system's elements, and by their interaction a steady state of water level is maintained although the particular molecules of water are continually changing.

In organismic systems the constancy is maintained by complicated chemical reactions and by certain physicochemical principles. The homeostatic processes of the body, maintaining, in the face of environmental changes, a constancy of hydrogen-ion concentrations, blood volume, sugar content, temperature, and so on, are examples of steady states in an open system. The system, as it were, "defends its own existence," so that whenever any disturbance occurs something happens in it to make the new state differ as little as possible from the previous standard (principle of Le Chatelier). Chemical equilibria in closed systems, as we have seen, are based on reversible reactions; but the steady states of open systems are, in many of the component reactions entering into them, *irreversible*. The reactions go in one direction only.

A steady state is maintained in the organism by the fact that degradative processes in the cells are being continually compensated for by synthetic or anabolic processes. This work, of course, requires energy; and so we find that an organism requires nourishment merely to exist, that is, to maintain itself in a steady state, quite apart from the energy that goes into effective work upon the environment. As von Bertalanffy[2] puts it, energy is not needed for the preservation of a closed system, nor can energy be obtained from it. It merely remains in equilibrium until disturbed. A system, to perform work, how-

[2] For this account of systems the writer is much indebted to Bertalanffy's illuminating summary of the theory of open systems in physics and biology (1950).

ever, must not *be* in equilibrium but continually on the way toward attaining it. That is to say, it must maintain a steady state. Hence an *open*-system arrangement, with potential energy that can be made "free," is a condition necessary for the continuous working capacity of the organism. In addition to the self-maintaining properties mentioned, open systems have the characteristic of "equifinality." This expression means the ability to attain steady states that are independent of the initial conditions, as, for example, in the growth and maturing of plant or animal organisms.[3]

[3] The open systems of organismic and behavorial activity are sometimes called "quasiclosed" systems. The terminology is largely a matter of the emphasis desired. An interesting discussion of the "living" system of the organism and its behavior (especially in the field of learning) can be found in Humphrey (1933). This account needs, however, to be supplemented by more recent work. See also Köhler, 1938. Readers interested in the study of open systems should not fail to consult a stimulating article by Brillouin, 1949. Ashby, 1952, has developed a system-model of the brain on somewhat different lines from the cybernetic theory with which we are concerned in this chapter.

In order to contrast the principle of equilibrium with that of a steady state Köhler uses the candle flame as an example of the latter. Though the flame, upon lighting the candle, comes to, and maintains, a fairly constant size and shape (equifinality?) its status is by no means one of equilibrium; for such a condition would mean, according to the laws of thermodynamics, that the free energy of the system had been reduced to the lowest possible point. If we light the candle, the flame at first is small, but it grows quickly to its normal size. Holding our hand near it we find that during this initial (growing) phase the heat and light emitted are quickly increasing. This energy of course comes from the flame, but before that it is represented as potential energy in the candle, that is, as "food" for the flame, that passes up the wick. During its "youth" the flame attains higher and higher amounts of energy, so that in its final steady state it contains and emits a maximum of such energy, thereby departing from a condition of equilibrium as far as it possibly can. If we consider the burning candle and the surrounding atmosphere as a larger unlimited (but therefore "closed") system we see that the potential energy of the whole system (as stored in the candle subsystem) is continually being reduced. An equilibrium with the surroundings would therefore be ultimately attained (second law of thermodynamics) unless the store of food in the candle could be continually replaced. However, since the flame of the candle is the only way in which this potential energy reduction can take place, the system will lose its potential energy the more quickly the more of it passes into the flame. For this reason the flame contains continually a maximum of potential energy. To put it somewhat teleologically we could say that in order to achieve the energy dissipation required by thermodynamical principles the working part of the entire system that is provided by the open system of the candle maintains a steady condition that seems opposed to the law. It seems opposed, however, only while we are considering it within its own confines or region. This situation is also typical of living organisms. They remain in steady states, but only so long as a food supply is available.

We have seen that some systemic processes reverse their course. By a procedure of splitting up, parts of a molecule act independently as atoms; by chemical combination they come together again and form molecules. This reversal of process, however, is characteristic only for closed systems. In mechanical systems such as the automobile we can also reverse the spatial direction by shifting gears; that is, by altering the arrangements of the system. Both these cases, however, consist of the reversal of direction in a continuous, ongoing time. A system can never be so reversed that its events and the motions connecting them are reversed in *time order*, in other words, so that things run backward. We can put our shoe on or we can take it off. But we cannot "un-put" our shoe on. If the time sequence of the events and the motions connecting them were reversed, the shoe which we previously dropped to the floor would leap up to our hand, and the effects of forces in producing movements would precede the accelerations that define the forces. Since time is really defined through changes which involve motion, any such reversal of a system's operation would be equivalent to a reversal not in direction *through* time, but of time itself. All this is merely another way of saying that nature works according to certain invariable laws, and time itself may be regarded as a directionality from past to future which is essential in order to give these laws an intelligible statement. Time is a part of the law itself. In this sense then *all* systems are *irreversible*.[4]

This fact can be expressed in still another way. The laws of classical mechanics were applied to single bodies. If the body was large and complex, the location and speed of its center of gravity could give the quantities necessary in the equations. In dealing with macroscopic phenomena it is now recognized that laws like those of the earlier mechanical system apply not to single particles, but to the average of a whole swarm of particles which constitute the aggregate. The combined position and velocity of none of these particles, taken individually, could be observed with certainty, nor could the course of any one of them be predicted. The laws of modern quantum physics are, in other words, *statistical* laws. Considerations of prob-

[4] We must qualify the above statement with respect to such relationships as the motion of planets in a solar system. As Wiener (*op. cit.*, page 42) points out, if a motion-picture film of the motions of the planets were run backward, it would still be a possible picture of planets obeying the laws of Newtonian mechanics. Wiener contrasts this situation with a film of an atmospheric turbulence run backward. Time reversal of events in the latter phenomenon would look altogether wrong from a physical standpoint. Whatever may be said of reversibility in such instances as the planets, it is clear that in a vast array of natural phenomena, including those of organismic activity, the time order or continuity is not reversible.

ability and averages must therefore come in, and we enter the realm of thermodynamics whose laws express the most probable distribution of minute particles.   There is here a certain relationship of the attainment of this distribution to time that is inexorable; and time, which in such a system is now bound to natural laws of a statistical character rather than to astronomical observations, is again seen to be irreversible.   The following illustration will elucidate this principle.

A teakettle of boiling water set in a pan of cooler water, or merely taken off the fire, cools, i.e., loses heat, while the water or air around absorbs heat from the kettle, growing warmer.   That the water in the teakettle should grow still hotter would be an outcome which, though its possibility could not be logically disproved, would be so highly improbable that it can be discounted.   The second law of thermodynamics states that there is no continuous self-sustaining process by which heat can be transferred from a cooler to a hotter body.   In terms of probability this is the same as saying that a system always tends toward its most probable state.   In the case just mentioned, barring the presence of separate contacts with other bodies of differing temperatures, the two bodies will come eventually to the same temperature so that no heat will be transferred from one to the other. The system will then be in equilibrium.   To consider what equilibrium means in this case let us note that when it is attained the random or "heat" motion of the molecules in the two bodies will have the same average velocity.   There will not be a greater concentration of high or low velocities in one body than in the other.   If there originally *were* such a concentration, as was the case when the kettle was first removed from the fire, we could speak of it as "organization" or "order" in the system that comprised the kettle and its surrounding bodies.   Heat, in this case, would be definitely ordered, "classified," or "graded" within the different parts of the system.   When the system reaches equilibrium (most probable ultimate state) this organization or order is lost.   It is replaced by a random distribution of molecular velocities.   Randomness, the most probable outcome, is equivalent to "disorganization" or "disorder."   If a system has many internal regions of contacts, i.e., many places where events happen, instead of one general region of contact as in our example, the randomness in the system's coming to equilibrium will be spread throughout all these regions of the system.   There will then be no concentrations of potential energy ready to be released and making the system capable of doing work.   When complete equilibrium (disorganization) has been reached it is said that the maximum *entropy* for the system has been attained.

This tending toward entropy (maximum disorganization or disorder) is, so far as we know, a universal law of nature. But in order for it to be demonstrated one of the conditions is that the system must be *closed*, that is to say, it must be isolated from the possibility of receiving energy from other sources or of giving it out to other bodies or systems. If the kettle of boiling water and the basin of cooler water surrounding it were to be exposed to other contacts from which energy was continually being received and to which energy was being expended, the system would be *open*. Though practically all systems that one could study would be open in this sense, the universe as a whole may be conceived as a closed system; and within it, therefore, there must be supposed to be a continual entropic process in which the organization of systems in which energic exchanges occur is being continually degraded, complex organizations broken down into simpler ones, until the whole universe approaches an "entropy death," all energy being irreversibly converted into heat (random motion) at a low temperature. So invariable is this trend in all systems toward the most probable, random, state that it may be regarded as an infallible way of identifying the direction of time from past to future. The entropic process is "time's arrow." Such a thermodynamic conception of time is arithmetical, statistical, and local for the process concerned, rather than astronomical or metrical.

But if this were all there were to the matter of entropy, living creatures would soon disappear from the earth. Although the entropic process never becomes reversed but keeps going on, at least to some extent, in all systems, there occurs in *open* systems a remarkable state of affairs that affords for the time being, and in certain parts or aspects of the system, an arrest of entropy. The degree of advancement toward entropy in a system can be measured. If we measure a system proceeding toward entropy, the quantity so obtained (let us call it S) will be regarded as having a positive sign. But suppose there is an arrest of the entropic process in some part of the system. S then becomes a measure of the degree to which the system or that part of it can be regarded as "staying away" from entropy. It can thus be called "negative" entropy and written with a minus sign. Entropy taken with a minus sign is a measure not of disorder but of order.[5]

[5] The equations are as follows:

$$\text{entropy} = k \ \log \ D$$

where k is the Boltzmann constant and D is a term that gives a quantitative statement of the disorder of the body in question. The statement for negative entropy is

$$-(\text{entropy}) = k \ \log \ (1/D)$$

Where does such an arrest of the disorganizing or structure-disintegrating process come from? What is the source of this negative entropy? According to Schroedinger (1946) it comes from the food that organisms take in. They "feed on" negative entropy by importing organic molecules, using their (organized) energies, and giving back the simpler products to the environment. Thus open living systems can avoid coming to equilibrium and can maintain instead a steady state by taking in materials rich in free energy. The most probable state is kept for the time being from being actualized; they can avert the increase in entropy that is the fate of all closed systems. The total change of entropy can be written (Prigogine's formula) as

$$dS = d_eS + d_iS$$

where d_eS denotes change of entropy by (food) import and d_iS the production of entropy due to irreversible processes in the system. The term d_iS, in accordance with the second law of thermodynamics, is always positive. The term d_eS, however, may be either positive or negative. Hence the total change of entropy in an open system *can* be negative. The second law of thermodynamics is not really violated if we look at the open system *plus* its environment; but it does not hold when we look more narrowly at the system itself (cf. footnote on p. 472 discussing Köhler's illustration of the candle flame). Steady states in open systems are therefore not characterized by maximum entropy, but by the approach to minimum entropy production. Entropy may actually decrease in open systems; and they can thus maintain steady states of activity.

MACHINES AS OPEN SYSTEMS; MACHINE AND ORGANISM

We seem to be here a long way from the subject of machines and electronic computing devices and from their relationship to the organism. But the connection is at once seen when we realize that many of these man-made systems have certain remarkable similarities to open, organismic systems. To be sure they do not take in their negative entropy and maintain steady states *in the same manner* that organisms do. Their energies all come from an outside source rather than, in part, from within the system. They do not regenerate damaged parts nor show a resistance to disruption such as organismic systems possess. Nor are they capable of reproducing their own kind. Nevertheless the following points of similarity between these machine-systems and the open system of the organism can be noted. (1) Like organisms they have a continual input and output, and something that happens in between.   (2) They operate in an irreversible flow of time of a thermodynamic and statistical sort.   (3) As we shall see, they contain mechanisms whereby patterns of ongoings comprising order or organization (negative entropy) can be stored for future use.   (4) They are capable, through certain subsystems, of maintaining something that strongly resembles a steady state, as, for example, in their pursuit of an object that continually changes its position, in a regulation of their dynamics somewhat comparable to the homeostatic processes of the body, and in the maintenance of the form of a pattern while its specific contents change.   (5) The cybernetists deal with "information," a quantitative concept into which energic units are translated.   Information put into the calculating machine always tends to narrow the range of probability, that is, the number of alternatives to choose from in arriving at a solution.   In holding in a direction opposite to that of randomness, information thus resembles negative entropy.   To follow out the analogy with organisms, information is the order that the computing machine "feeds on."

In view of all these similarities to the organism, and in spite of obvious contrasts, is there not some plausibility in the cybernetists' claim that the principles upon which complex machines operate are also the principles that are at work in organisms?   In any case we are dealing in both instances with what may be called open systems; and the system-approach to aggregates will therefore be found useful in considering what the cybernetists have to say, first, about their machines and the principles of their construction, and second, about the explanations of organismic processes, including perception, which they believe these mechanisms provide.

Let us first consider some general comparisons between organisms and machines.   One common feature of organismic and machine systems is the fact that each has an "input" and an "output."   The input of organisms consists of stimulus-energy, food, water, air, etc.   Their output is seen in the product of, or work done by, the effector mechanisms.   The system's internal operation, connecting input and output, consists in the most generalized sense of metabolism.   In psychology the input we are most interested in is energy from the stimulation of receptors; the output here concerned is the coördination of the action of effectors that is known as behavior.   The detailed internal arrangements and operations of this system constitute the main problem of non-molar psychological theories.   Machines are parallel with organisms in a number of these respects.   Working energy or power and raw materials are inputs; and converted power, mechanical or other services, or finished products are their outputs. But there are also special additional inputs in the form of events that serve to *regulate* or *control* the main production-output, its rhythm, its rate, and so on. These inputs usually operate through some subsystem of the machine or through an attached computing device. These special energic units thus supplied to the machine are called "information"; and they are analogous to the stimulations received by the organism through its receptors. Through them, as they affect the working of the machine, the machine's output is controlled in a manner analogous to the action of the neural mechanisms that control behavior. Just as the organism is bombarded by many random stimuli that do not become effective toward the output, so the input of every machine includes some random energic events, called "noise." Information, whose input stream is called the "signal," represents negative entropy (or organization); the random disturbances of noise are entropy. A part of the task of the machine-designer is to make the ratio of noise to signal in the machine's output as small as possible. And similarly, the adjustment of the organism through perception, reasoning, or learning has the result of reducing the proportion of random, uncoordinated, or disorganized behavior.

Cybernetics, as we have said, was an inevitable outcome of the modern age of great power utilization, technology, and mass production. In an earlier generation, as Wiener points out, the emphasis was upon discovering how to acquire and use the large sources of power needed for rapidly developing industry. That having been accomplished, the task is now becoming one of the automatic regulation and control of the machines that use the power. Just as greater than human energy was needed for production, so now greater than human speed, constancy, and precision are needed in the specialized control mechanisms that keep the machines steady or that work out intricate problems pertinent to their enormous task. Thus, for example, the loom as a power machine performs the physical work of weaving a fabric; an "information" machine controls the pattern that is being woven. Terms like communication and information are here used in a very broad sense. Not only do human beings communicate with and control one another, within the societal organization, by word of mouth, telephone, telegraph, and the like; but by treating energic quantities or physically controllable unit-events as "information" we can be said to "communicate information" to a machine; and within the machine one part or subsystem can "communicate" in a similar manner with another. Through all this communication of information the parts of the machine are synchronized to the demands of the task, its motions are steadied, its rate of output is controlled, and the work of "society," insofar as it is dependent on these technological devices, is coördinated toward useful ends. Finally, the cybernetists believe that the same process of information, communication, and control occurs in the organism itself and that the internal controlling arrangements of human systems, as represented in the brain and nervous system, are similar in principle to the organization of the modern computing machine.

ANALOGUE AND DIGITAL COMPUTERS; CODING; "MEMORY"; INFORMATION

Communication is a temporally extended affair. The message, as Wiener says, is a discrete or continuous sequence of measurable events distributed in time. It is therefore treated by the statistical procedures dealing with time series. How is information, as a series of events in time, provided, transmitted, and brought to bear upon machine-processes and in the work of solving problems of regulation and control? This question is answered by considering the two main types of automatic computing devices now in use.[6] The first type is called the analogue machine. The data fed to the system are here analogous in form to the control problem which the machine is to solve. They consist of some direct physical quantity such as an electric voltage, the degree of rotation of a shaft, or the amount of compression of a spring. A simple example of this principle, though it is scarcely a computing machine in the full sense, is the flyball governor that holds an engine to a constant speed. "Information" regarding the engine's speed reaches the governor from the speed of rotation of the shaft on which it is placed (input of the governor subsystem). The output of the governor subsystem, as the whirling balls fall or rise by changes of centrifugal force, is the motion of a rod that connects with the throttle of the engine. The relation of input and output is determined by the physical construction of the governor. Since it is a direct relationship of speed of rotation, the action of the governor in controlling the speed of the engine can be said to be "analogous" to the problem of the engine. Computers based upon a similar plan of operation are employed in connection with control devices attached to many machines.

The other type of computer is the digital or numerical machine. For this machine the data or information must be expressed not as

[6] For a non-technical account from which the following statements are largely drawn see an article by Ridenour, 1952. See also Wiener, *op. cit.*

physical quantities, but in symbolic form as numbers.   Some operator has to render the data into numerical form before it is fed in.   The machine then processes this information according to the rules of arithmetic or by some logical scheme and delivers its output in numerical form.   From the standpoint of automatic control the digital computing machine suffers some handicaps.   The physical problem must be formulated for it, and the results of the computer's computation must be rendered back into a form that enters into physical relations within the machine to be controlled.   The machine's problem is not directly inherent in the nature of the computer.   Even though the time required for these operations may be reduced to a few seconds it may still be too long for very rapid tasks, as, for example, that of guiding directed missiles.   The analogue computer, on the other hand, works along hand in hand with the physical processes of the machine and can give its answer continuously.   Nevertheless there are strong advantages also on the side of the digital computer.   "Play" and "noise" are practically eliminated, and there is no specific limit to the complexity of the problem it can handle.   The digital machine also can be far more accurate than the analogue.

It is upon the digital computer that the primary strategy of cybernetics rests.   Let us consider the main parts of such a system and their operation.   We shall here follow a model whose principles were worked out mathematically by Wiener.   There is, first, the part where the "information" is fed into the machine (comparable to receptors in the organism).   Instead, however, of feeding numbers in the usual decimal system of ten digits a code is used that is based on a scale of two, the digits being 0 and 1.   A mathematical set of rules called Boolean algebra makes it possible to perform arithmetical operations with these digits and to use them in place of the more extended number series.   In the arithmetical subsystem of the machine the digits in this binary code are combined to give the usual results of arithmetical processes, addition, multiplication, and so on.   Electronic relays are the switching devices that give the operations for the two symbols. By being on or off they give, respectively, a "yes" or "no" answer. Thus every contingency that arises in the machine's operation demands merely a new set of choices of contingencies, 1 or 0; and these choices depend on two things, first, a fixed set of logical rules, and second, the decisions that have already been made.   At each stage each of the relays assumes a position (on or off) dictated by the positions of the relays of the bank at a previous stage of operation.   The operations are ordered in time by a central clocking device, or else they are controlled by not permitting one process to take place until its antecedents have been run off. The sequence-control procedure can be regarded as "instructions" that must be fed into the machine along with the information. Thus without any human interference the machine performs many thousands of ordered logical operations, condensing into minutes solutions of problems that would require human being days to solve, and delivering the processed information back to the operator through its "effector" mechanism.

In any extended calculation there is need in the machine, just as with the human calculator, for retaining certain portions of the information, or steps in the process, for later use. In other words, there must be in the computing machine a mechanism for "storage." A subsystem of the machine provides this function; and it is called, just as in the organism, the "memory." Memory subsystems are further divided into two classes (a distinction without analogy in the organism). There is first the short-term memory that is needed to hold only during a particular operation, as, for example, in the steps in a multiplication problem, after which it is erased to clear the machine. Then there is the long-term memory which serves as a file to retain information that may be needed later or throughout the entire run of the problem. The first type of memory can be provided by closed circuits in which the impulses keep travelling around in a sequence until the circuit is cleared by events from outside. The long-term memory of the machine can be provided, as one method, by condensers in conjunction with scanning devices. Still more permanent records can be obtained by the use of punched cards or by magnetic tape and the forming of magnetization patterns of molecules in iron wire after the manner of the wire recorder. The memory subsystem is connected with the arithmetical unit so that the information thus stored can be released for use as appropriately timed impulses arrive from other circuits of the machine.

A key word that has recurred throughout the preceding account is "information." It may strike the reader that this term has been used in a peculiar way. Can we say that an array of numbers that is fed to a machine, stripped as it is of all meaning except the digits themselves, is really very "informing"? Furthermore, if we could look through the machine as it operates, we would nowhere see information, in the usual sense, being passed along and worked upon to give a result. We would witness only the flopping on and off of the switches or states of vacuum tubes that serve as relays in an intricate network, or the circuital arrangements for currents in storage devices. We see plenty of manifestations of energy (in small amounts), but nothing that we could call information. Yet the pattern of activation of the relays, we know, is directly related to what we would call decisions or choices. And, since decisions must be based on information, these events therefore *function* as the handling of information. Logical rules apply to them, and the whole process will result in a calculation that has important bearing upon a practical human problem. Thus, in effect, the machines are continually concerned with the recording, storing, processing, transmission, and use of information. Though energies are involved, they are extremely slight for any one relay operation. It is the *patterning* of the operations, rather than their energies, that counts. As Wiener says, it is not useful to think of information as energy; information is just information.

One thing is clear, however. No matter how we define it, information, to be of any use in cybernetics, has to be capable of being associated in a one to one way with physical devices where events go on. This fact requires that it be as sharp and definite as these events. In other words it must be expressed in amounts, as numbers of units. The units must all be equal so that they can be added to give the total amount of information in a given situation. In short, we must make information measurable. How can this be accomplished? In the first place we must define it by giving it a very restricted connotation. If we were to listen to a lecture on a scientific subject telling us something we did not know, it would not be possible to say *how much* information we had received, since we would have no scale of units that could be applied to such kind of content, or in fact to any content where the boundaries of fact are unknown. We must therefore abstract from the unique content of what is said. What then is left? There is a further possibility if we are willing to limit ourselves to a particular class of situations in which the term information applies only to some message that will enable us to make a choice between clear-cut, known, alternatives. If all the alternatives and their probability as based on past experience are *known*, we can then have a basis for calculating how much information is conveyed to us by a particular statement or a segment of a message. The amount of information conveyed would be measured by how much it reduces (proportionally) the number of alternatives from which one must choose. In order to have a constant fraction or ratio of reduction it has been decided that every time the existing number of alternatives is reduced to *half*, one unit of information will have been gained. This unit is called a "bit" of information.

Suppose we are seeking a reward that is hidden under some one of sixteen boxes. We receive a message-segment telling us what box it is under. The possibilities are now reduced from sixteen to one, and the problem is solved. How much information did that message-segment convey? Let us suppose that we receive a series of message-segments reducing the numbers of alternatives in each instance to halves by delimiting successively smaller groups of boxes, any *one* box of which may conceal the reward. The first segment reduces the number of possible boxes (originally sixteen) by half, to eight. This segment therefore gives one bit of information. The second segment reduces the eight, by half, to four, giving a second bit. The third segment reduces the number from four to two, providing a third bit. And the fourth segment reduces the two to one, yielding a fourth, and final, bit. Four bits of information are therefore contained in the original message which told us the exact box to look under. If we had started with eight boxes and received a message-segment correctly identifying the box, that message-segment would contain three bits of information, and so on. The numbers of alternatives existing at the time of receiving each of the message-segments were, respectively, the fourth, third, second, and first powers of 2. But we have seen that 4, 3, 2, and 1 also state the amounts of information contained in message-segments that identify the correct box at their respective levels of number of alternatives. Hence we can express the meaning of our unit by saying that the amount of information contained in any given message-segment that reduces the number of choices to one is equal to the logarithm to the base 2 of the number of alternatives which can occur in the given context. More generally, the amount of information in a message that reduces k alternatives to k/x is $\log_2 x$ bits.

Recall now that in the binary system used in the computing machine above described there is always a choice between only two alternatives. The message dictates that the relay will be "on" or else that it will be "off." The reduction of the two choices (by half) to one thus requires one unit of information. In the binary system of the machine, therefore, the amount of information operative in any one decision is always just one bit. The term bit has been invented as a condensation of the two words "binary digit." Communication is a process of the continuous elimination and narrowing down of the totality of all possible messages until we arrive at the one message we wish to convey. Each succeeding symbol reduces the number of possible messages by a quantity proportional to the number of different symbols that *might* be sent. We now begin to see how the quantification of information can be made to apply to the demands and capabilities of machines in which simple choices between two alternatives are continuously made. The alternatives "off" or "on" can be made to apply either to a single pair or to states in which a group of pairs may be disposed with respect to the possible permutations of off and on within the group. Since information always makes possible a choice based upon a lesser degree of chance, that is, of randomness, than would occur without it, it can be regarded as *negative entropy*. It tells us something that is improbable or unlikely to occur in nature on the basis of pure chance. Specifically, it is the logarithm to the base 2 of the reciprocal of the probability of the state.[7]

NEGATIVE FEED-BACK, OSCILLATION, TRANSFORMATION AND INVARIANT, SCANNING: THEIR RELATION TO PERCEPTION

Returning to the machines for communication and control let us consider certain principles of their operation, beyond those already discussed, which may have a bearing upon organisms and their perceptual activities. These topics can be subsumed under the concepts of feed-back, transformation and invariant, and scanning. Let us begin with feed-back.[8] This principle, most simply stated, is a special case of one of the fundamental properties of all systems, namely, the interdependence of the parts. As one part of the system increases or decreases its speed or its amount of action in a certain direction, another part with which it is dynamically connected correspondingly changes its operation. The latter part, in turn, is connected back with the first part so that its own changes of speed, direction, or energy will have the effect either of further increasing the changes of the first part in their original direction or of reversing their direction, according to the manner in which the connection is made. The first of these effects is called the positive feed-back and the second the negative feed-back. The latter is a device *par excellence* for keeping the machine in a steady state of running as the flow from input to output goes through it. In terms of mechanical design a part of the energy of the output is "fed

---

[7] Information-theory is a rapidly growing branch of cybernetics. For a good non-technical discussion the reader can consult an article by Miller (1953) from which some of the details of the present account have been drawn. Some applications for psychologists are there developed with reference to psychophysics, mental testing, and and the natural redundancy of information in the idiom of a language. A bibliography of interest to students of psychology is given in this article. Aborn and Rubenstein (1952) have investigated the relation of the amount of information conveyed to immediate recall. See also King, 1952. MacKay tries to broaden information theory by the inclusion of scientific information content and adds a somewhat technical glossary (see Von Foerster, ed., 1952, pp. 181–234).

[8] For further details of various items in the following account see the clearly written article by Tustin (1952). More technical discussions well be found in Wiener, 1948, Chapter IV, and Trimmer, 1950, Chapter 8.

back" to the machine in such a way that it re-enters as input, but as input having the special function of regulating and controlling the operation of the whole system. In communication parlance it is said that the feed-back mechanism receives information from the working parts of the machine, either by the analogical or the digital principle, and transmits this information back to the working parts in the form of "orders." The amount of information that is "fed back" to the main part of the system is always the *amount of departure from the desired condition*. The feed-back mechanism is thus a buffer-system (really a subsystem) having its own input and output, but operating purely as a control device in tangency with the main line of the machine's productive activity. Its function is to correct the many fluctuations that are bound to occur in the running of any complicated mechanism and to keep the machine smoothly operating with a minimum loss of efficiency or damage.

If we were to attempt to write down all the uses to which the negative feed-back principle had been put, we should find the list very long. One of the earliest and simplest examples is that of the governor of the steam engine. The opening or closing of the throttle of the engine is brought about by the collapsing or rising of balls whirling on a shaft, which shaft in turn has been accelerated or decelerated by changes in the output of the engine. Other examples, mostly modern, include the regulation of the flow of liquid in a pipe, the household thermostat, the volume control on a radio, the regulation of temperature and flow in chemical factories, the steering mechanism of a ship, the control of guided missiles, gun pointing, and the guiding of fire at moving targets as in antiaircraft defense. Barrett and Post (1950) have used the terms teleostatic and teleodynamic to designate two types of feed-back mechanisms that are represented in the above examples.

From all this it will be seen that one significant feature of feed-backs is the relation of their use to the purpose of the designer or operator of the machine. First, the human agent, in designing the mechanism, singles out some variable aspect that needs, for practical or economic purposes, to be controlled (speed, volume, direction, etc.). Then, as an operator, he sets the adjustment so that a certain desired amount of this dimension will be maintained by the feed-back mechanism. For these reasons feed-back subsystems have been called *servomechanisms*, a term that has become widely used in control engineering. The feed-back principle, however, is now recognized as prevalent throughout many natural and socially evolved, as well as deliberately constructed, systems. The organism, as we shall see, exhibits many feed-back arrangements, and so do social systems, as manifested, for example, in the interdependences of the various elements that fluctuate in business cycles.   Moreover, if it occurs in the "outside" region *between* autonomous systems, rather than "inside" between subsystems *within* a system, negative feed-back (so-called) may operate for the destruction as well as the maintenance of organisms.   Animal populations such as those in which one species preys upon the other, as in the case of the lynx and the rabbit, show cycles of relationship of increase and decrease in their populations that are based upon this principle.   If we are aiming to give the principle of feed-back the importance it deserves as a universal arrangement in nature, the use of the teleological term "servomechanism," and perhaps of "feed-back" itself, is therefore quite misleading.

Of great moment in feed-backs is a characteristic called oscillation. As a relatively self-closed subsystem, interlaid within the total system of the machine, the negative feed-back mechanism is subject to self-excitation.   For example, in an artillery feed-back, if the gun's inertia while its alignment is being corrected carries it beyond the position of correct alignment, the new deviation will cause the controller to swing it back, and with an error in the opposite direction due to inertia. Unless some corrective is used the gun will thus continue to swing back and forth without settling into position.   Or suppose that an input fluctuates in value, as it is likely to do.   Then the output will also fluctuate, but there will be a discrepancy.   The fluctuation of the output will usually lag behind the input if only because of the delay involved in transmission.   The greater the frequency of variation in the input the farther behind the output is likely to fall.   Oscillations that occur in any part of the feed-back mechanism will be likely to be propagated around the feed-back loop until they affect the original quantity.   Thus, under certain conditions, the oscillations may become self-maintaining in negative feed-back systems.   In order to reduce the oscillation, designers sometimes introduce a device that will change the phase of the output, giving it a time-lead over the input in the cycle of feed-back recurrences.   Oscillations in some degree are a regular accompaniment of feed-back arrangements and are demonstrated, along with some of their correctives, in organisms as well. Too great an oscillation represents a "pathological condition," a defect in the feed-back mechanism.

Like the reverberating self-closed circuits in the "memory" of the computer, feed-back is a *circular* process.   It is a cycle of events which runs partly through the regular power sequence in the machine of input to output and partly in the reverse direction from output, through a "feed-back loop" or other connection, back to input. We might say that it is a cyclical structure "tangent to" the structure of the main operation. It is important to note that circularity is one of the cardinal principles of cybernetics. We might control the temperature of a house in a certain manner by merely using the outside temperature. Suppose that the outer temperature is registered upon a thermometer in the living room, and that this thermometer, in falling, activates a draft mechanism that increases combustion in the furnace and raises the temperature of the room. Here we have control, but not a true automatic control for maintaining a *steady* temperature; there is no feed-back. The furnace would have to go on heating the room and perhaps the whole outdoors once the drafts had been opened. The "structure of happenings" is here wrong. By introducing a thermostat that provides a closing of a cycle we change matters. When this is done not only does the reading of the thermometer depend on the warmth of the room, but also the warmth of the room depends upon the reading of the thermometer. This illustration points up our earlier statement that cybernetic strategy, despite the fact that it speaks continually of "*amounts*" of information, rests also upon *structural* principles. A crucial fact in the design is the way in which the successive events are so disposed in space and time that they return circularly to the event-region from which they started.

Let us turn now to the principle of *transformation* and *invariant*. It should be noted that computing machines afford, in a sense, an internal replication of a state of affairs in their environment. Information is given concerning the various quantities characteristic of a phenomenon at a particular time and place; and the machine computes an outcome that represents some summation, average, or prediction that may be expected to hold good with respect to the external phenomenon. The similarity of this situation with the operation of the organism in perceiving is clear (cf. Chapters 8, 10, and 11). In perceiving, the organism also has to reconstruct a representation that will be fairly veridical with respect to the outer facts (Chapter 2). These considerations mean that in both organisms and machines some kind of substitution or transformation is required. The relays of the machine are not the actual environmental events; they operate instead with a numerical code or symbolization that gives "information" about those events. The occurrence or non-occurrence of the event is *represented* by an "on" or "off" signal of the relay. And similarly the action of neurons (being either fired by impulses across synapses or not fired) is a kind of code that is substituted for environmental objects and happenings. As an "object," say a figure or a dynamic situation, is represented in the machine or in the cortex something must therefore happen that preserves the essential characteristics of the relationships presented in the stimulus-situation.

The problem can be approached by applying to the processes in the machine or organism the logic of transformations and invariants. A given patterned representation of an object may be said to pass through a set of transformations in which each element of the pattern will "go into" another. The situation is analogous to the case in which, when we move a block of wood in a straight line in a set of three coördinate axes, each point in the block acquires from instant to instant new coördinate values previously occupied by another point. Another instance is seen when the planets of the solar system change their coördinates in our space frame during the day, or when the zero point of our own coördinate system is moved, or again, when in inflating a balloon or magnifying a square we see that the points or elements change their location and distance apart. There may even be distortion, as in the case where we draw a circle or a square on a sheet of rubber and then stretch that sheet so that it fits over some irregular wavy surface. In the last example we see that not only position, but metrical constancy of proportions, is lost. Let us consider a still different case. The image of a table top on the retina, or as projected on the brain, when the table is seen from different angles must partake of some distortion with respect to the object owing to differences of angular perspective. Perceptual constancy overcomes a part of this distortion for phenomenology but not quite all. Such distortions are also familiar in optical illusions. The gestalt theorists have tried to explain these effects by the action of brain-fields, and we met them again in the stimulus deformations of hypothesis-theory.

But in spite of these changes as the pattern goes through a series of translations, rotations, or other types of transformation, there may remain certain relationships that do *not* change. If a block is moved in space or is rotated about one of its edges, it still retains for us a constant set of dimensions. If we look at an object through the microscope, though it is "blown-up" in scale, the *proportions* represented by distances between its elements remain the same. Even in a circle inscribed on a sheet of rubber that is then distorted so that the circle is pulled out of shape there remains something that is constant. For if we draw another circle inside the first before stretching the rubber, that second circle stays entirely inside the first no matter what distortion is imposed. There thus remains an equality of a "topological" sort. Now where we have a set of transformations such that every transformation has an "inverse" also belonging to the set, and where the resultant of any two transformations belonging to the set also belongs to the set, that set is known as a "transformation-group." If a certain quantity attached to all the elements transformed by the transformation group remains unchanged when each element is altered by the same transformation, whatever that transformation may be, that quantity is called an "invariant of the group" (cf. Wiener, *op. cit.*).

We have here, then, for perception, an approach to the problem of detecting an equivalence in percepts under different sensory conditions. It is illustrated by the case of a physical object seen from various positions, by the identity of the percept when the eyes become fixated from any starting position upon a given object, by the equality of an interval in a melody or chord when it is transposed to a new key, by the sameness of shape when size is changed, and by many other constant relationships of this sort. There is in all these cases some characteristic quantity or "figure" that remains invariant. In terms of the operations of the systems there is a certain sameness of output that continues for every particular input from the object perceived, regardless of whatever variations the object and its input may present. These invariants were recognized by Pitts and McCulloch (1947) as the basis of "ideas" or "universals" that remain constant in perception or imagination amid the flux of particulars of the stimulation. This hypothesis will be presented later in greater detail. A parallel is also drawn for the operation of the machines. To quote from McCulloch:[9] "For any figure in the input of a computing machine it is always possible to calculate an output invariant under a group of transformations. We calculate a set of averages, for all members of the group, of numerical values assigned by an arbitrary functional to each transform of the information conceived as the distribution of excitation at all points and times in an appropriate manifold."[10]

Turning to our third special topic, we shall try to describe an interesting device, related to transformation-groups, that works by a principle called *scanning*. Generally stated its operation is as follows: A beam of minute particles, say electrons, is made to pass very rapidly over a region containing a manifold of events representing the trans-

[9] See Jeffress (ed.), 1951, p. 53.

[10] It should be stated that the writer's equipment for handling the more technical formulations of cybernetics, including some that are to follow, is limited. He is endeavoring merely to present a general account for those not yet familiar with the theory. Readers desiring to employ cybernetic concepts in any systematic manner should consult the writings of Wiener, McCulloch, and others cited.

formations of a group. Not merely a plane surface but every region of a group space can be represented by a "group-scanning" process. Though not every point of the region is covered, the scanning beam can come sufficiently near to every point to yield a good sampling of the manifold. If the scanning is fine enough and sufficiently representative of the dimensions of the region, the information collected and sent back by the beam may even constitute a close likeness or image of the original transformations; and, since it can represent *any* transform of that group, we have here the basis for identifying the "universals," or invariants, of the group. A scanning process of this sort that passes through the cortex is hypothesized by Pitts and McCulloch as providing the basis for form perceptions. The mechanism of their scheme will be considered later.

We have an example of scanning that can be understood in less formal terms in television. The sending device, or "image-orthicon," focuses the incoming light from the scene as an image on a mosaic-plate of photoelectric elements. The light image there sets free a large number of electrons to form an electron-image in the space behind the plate, the number of electrons at any point being proportional to the intensity of the impinging light. In a target plate in this space positive charges are produced by the arriving electrons. Behind the target plate a sharply focused travelling beam of electrons controlled by an electromagnetic coil sweeps rapidly across the back surface of the target. Near the target some of the electrons unite with the positive charges, but the "unused" electrons are turned back through the tube to a collector. Where the beam strikes a highly charged part of the plate (representing bright illumination in the image) more electrons are absorbed and fewer are turned back. Hence the flow of electrons back into the collector varies in time as the brightness of the point over which the beam is sweeping. It is so arranged that the travel of the beam of electrons over the target plate is orderly and in the form of lines from left to right and top to bottom of the plate. A total of 525 lines are traversed in each full trip and within a time interval of $\frac{1}{30}$ of a second. Hence a complete picture is formed thirty times per second. If we assume that movement is occurring in the scene televised there will be a slightly different picture for each full journey of the beam. The flow of electrons into the collector is the same as an electric current and when amplified becomes the video output signal (changes of current strength) of the image-orthicon tube. By means of the modulation of radio "carrier" waves the signal is transmitted to the antennae of the receiving set.

The television *receiver*, or kinescope, is an electron tube with a broadened end serving as the viewing plate. In the kinescope the radio signal becomes again the video signal and is discharged as an electron beam from a travelling electron gun that moves synchronously with the scanning beam of the sending station. The beam in the kinescope traces 525 lines on the rear of the viewing plate in exact synchrony with the sending apparatus. A fluorescent screen on which it strikes gives out light when struck by the electrons in an amount proportional to the strength of the beam as regulated by the video signal. These light spots glow for a few thousandths of a second and combine to produce the effect of the picture. Constant scanning of the light pattern from the scene in the image-orthicon allows motion to be shown in the image; and the inertia of the human optical apparatus "fills in the gaps" between picture elements in successive pictures so that there is continuous perception of the changing scene.[11]

As so frequently happens in physical phenomena, this remarkable invention shows the equivalence of distribution of events in space with their distribution in time. A static or moving scene spread out through *space* is collected as "information" which, because it is gathered point by point by a moving electron beam, takes on a temporal pattern of current-pulsations and is carried along the lead-wire and in the radio waves as a signal stream in *time*. Then, at the receiving end, the pattern of information is spread out again in space; and in the changes that occur within the time through which the successive frames appear, *motion* within that space is also transmitted. Patterns of events ordinarily involving both space and time because of the motion involved can thus be "kept alive" in either their spatial or their temporal "habitat." To put the matter in terms of transformation groups we can say that the whole "sampling" set of transformations in the televised scene is here unfolded before the viewer, and for all practical purposes exactly as it is occurring at the sending end.

Let us now turn to perception and imagine that a process similar to that at the receiving end is happening in the organism. Perhaps we can see an analogy. Transformations are occurring in the brain that are parallel, even though not perfectly parallel, with those in the world outside. Outer perceived objects and motions are reconstructed within ourselves. Let us imagine that instead of the usual television drama we have a figure of a constant shape expanding and contracting through all possible sizes, or a given chord being played in different keys up and down the musical scale. We now have a basis for

[11] The preceding account has been adapted from an article on television in *The World Book Encyclopedia*, Field Enterprises, Inc., Chicago, 1953.

understanding the forms of gestalt and the universals of Pitts and McCulloch. Because the whole continuous set of transformations is run off in the cerebral mechanism, such a mechanism could now have the data for computing, as the scansion process goes on, a common or constant figure as an invariant of the group. This invariant quantity would then solve the riddle of our being able to hear the chord as the same interval through variations of its pitch or to see the square always as a "square" no matter how large or small it is. Group scanning might be a part of the mechanism that could bring all this about. *We have only to find such a mechanism in the brain!*

Returning to the machines we can also add a note concerning the *memory* for universals. An electronic storage tube is similar in principle to the television viewing tube. Its frontal surface is subdivided into a great many small points in which electric charges appear. Such charges are the results of earlier computations by the machine. (Let us think also of self-closed repeating circuits in which storage takes place.) By scanning systematically over the points where these charges occur, information constituting a message can be re-collected and used in the solution of problems. "Ideas," as universals in the *organism*, are also not bound to the time at which their originals occurred; they can be stored for use in memory recollection, imagination, and thinking. These comparisons, though they by no means establish a proof, show us the intriguing possibilities for perceptual theory that are afforded by the cybernetic approach.[12]

So much for our rather sketchy review of the principles operative in mechanisms of communication and control. It is not our present aim to extol the well-known prowess of modern electronic computers, or to dwell on the well-considered claim that they can surpass human abilities in any task, no matter how complicated, that is governed by logical rules. It is more to our purpose to note that the simple view of a physical system as a "black box," to which we would be limited if we could do no more than measure the input and output, has been greatly extended. We have new insights in the form of such inner devices as relays, information units, physical "decisions," networks, reverberating circuits, storage devices, feed-backs, oscillations, transformation groups, and scanning circuits. The theory of systems,

---

[12] Lashley, in a provocative article, has suggested another use of the scanning principle (see Jeffress, editor, 1951). He has assembled considerable evidence to show that in a complex act, such as typewriting a word, the elements (letters) may at first be cortically prepared for action in no regular order. Some cortical scanning device that releases these reactions in their proper sequence seems to be indicated.

at least those of an electronic or mechanical character, has grown to an imposing stature.   But it is high time that we turn to the organism to see whether it, too, has such equipment and whether these principles of cybernetics can be used to explain behavior and to illuminate, in particular, the problem of perception.   We shall consider in this connection both the known facts and the theoretical interpretations.

PARALLELS BETWEEN COMPUTERS AND ORGANISMIC PROCESSES; "TELEOLOGICAL MECHANISMS"; REPEATING CIRCUITS; MEMORY

Certainly in their general features the organism and the computing machine have much in common.   Like the machine, the organism has an input and an output, and its central nervous system, with some ten billion neurons acting as a "switching apparatus," corresponds to the interior mechanism of the machine.   Both have "receptors" into which "information" is fed: sense organs in the organism and photoelectric cells, radar systems, microphones, and the like in the machine. In both cases there are "effectors": motors, solenoids, and the like in the machine, and muscles and glands in the organism.   Both possess arrangements for integrating, storing, and transferring "information" along the way between input and output.   The storage feature and re-collecting devices of the machine have their counterparts in the organism in the physiological mechanisms through which memorial retention, recognition, and recall occur.   In both instances there are "messages" not only from outside but from effector operations of the system itself *via* returning pathways.   These are delivered by negative feed-backs in the machines and by the kinaesthetic receptors and the proprioceptive afferents in the organism.   The nervous system and the computer both operate on a relatively small amount of energy; they are not power mechanisms but "systems of communication" concerned with "messages" and the use of "information."   Both have a markedly structural character in which circular arrangements rather than straight-line operations play a predominant part.

It has been pointed out that the nervous system is admirably equipped to act as a digital mechanism since its neurons, like the vacuum-tube and electromagnetic relay, operate in an all-or-none manner.   The neuron does not transmit its effective impulse in degrees.   Either it fires or it does not fire.   Its firing is determined by its state immediately preceding the receipt of excitation (whether it is in refractory phase from a previous excitation or not) and by the number of branched axone terminations of preceding neurons that feed into it, a condition that is related to the total strength of the impulse received. Neuron relays therefore resemble those of the machine in that there is either an "on-phase" or an "off-phase"; and there are only these two phases. The situation seems well adapted to the transmission of information by the two digit categories, 0 and 1, of the binary number code. Just as grid biases modify the tube's timing, so the after-potentials of neurons are important in regulating the passing on of impulses through modification of synaptic excitability. According to Hoagland (1949) there is in the organism, as well as in the machine, a master internal timing device. Summation of impulses at the synapse in the organism has been compared with the use of amplifiers in the machine, and inhibitory impulses, in part, with mechanisms for damping oscillations. So far, therefore, there is pretty good agreement. The processes of the organism, which include metabolism, are of course far more numerous and varied than in the machine; and though the neuron system itself might act as a digital transmitter and organizer there are many circuits controlled by nervous activity that involve, at certain places, the analogy principle. For example, part of the reflex-circuit involved in regulating blood-pressure is digital (neuronal, and, by involvement of specific muscle fibers, muscular) while part is analogue (humoral). The latter part consists of a continuous hydrodynamic change in the pressure in the blood vessels. Information given by this analogue source to the nerve-elements is transmitted by afferent impulses that are again (digitally) directed back from the central nervous system to modify the tensions of the vascular muscles. In such an arrangement of digital and analogy operations combined in the same circuit there is a marked difference between the organism and the computing machine; and this difference may be important.

With regard to negative feed-backs we find a strong resemblance between the modern control devices and the organism. Organisms seem to be replete with them. In perceptual studies we saw that there were closed cycles involving returning proprioceptive impulses in set and motor adjustment. The cybernetists have developed the principle still more broadly. All the basic homeostatic processes controlling the physical and chemical properties of the blood-stream have been regarded as negative feed-backs. The moment that some change occurs in which blood quantities or constituents are altered or the temperature of the body raised or lowered some "information" regarding these changes is sent back to the central nervous system whence outgoing impulses are directed, in proportion to the amount of deviation, to bring the body back to the homeostatic level. Heart rate, vasomotor reactions, breathing rhythms, reciprocal inhibition of antagonistic limb-muscles in locomotion, and the maintaining of posture by returning conduction through the cerebellum are examples of a similar circular control.

If reflex mechanisms include negative feed-backs, what about voluntary action? Here the cybernetists have a field day. It would be hard to find striped muscular reactions in which there are not involved returning proprioceptive impulses, resulting from bodily movement, that "feed back" through the central nervous system to regulate the coördination as it is going on. When the pathways from the proprioceptors in muscle and joint are out of action, as in locomotor ataxia, well-coördinated behavior becomes difficult or impossible. These controls work negatively as they do in the machine. We do not have a discharge of efferent impulses that takes us directly to the goal. The process, instead, is one of rapid trial and error in which deviations from the objective are fed back by proprioceptive afferents, and motor impulses proportionate to the error are sent out, redirecting the movement back toward the goal. This process continues, and the effector thus comes ever nearer the goal-object until the goal is attained. As Wiener puts it, once we have "willed" to pick up a pencil we may say roughly that we do so by corrections of our *deviations* from picking it up; and the amount by which the pencil is *not* picked up is decreased at each successive stage. Visual afferents enter the feed-back process, but sometimes kineasthetic end-organs alone may be involved.

We now have something that bears upon the age-old question of agency and purpose. Much has been said by cybernetists about this matter under such captions as "teleological mechanisms."[13] The carrying out of our "purpose" to pick up the pencil is here given empirical meaning, for the negative feed-back mechanism seems to be its very physical embodiment, spelling out the operation of "goal-directed purpose" as the effectors, under feed-back regulation, come ever nearer to the goal (negative feed-back over the target). Mechanism is not *opposed* to teleology but is really the *same thing*—provided the mechanism is equipped with negative feed-backs. The philosopher Northrop (1948) has acclaimed this formulation as a means of bringing the purposive idealists and the hard-headed, positivistic behaviorists into one camp. If the problem of teleology could be solved in this simple manner, and if all the anthropomorphic explanations of behavior from Helmholtz down to directive-state theory could thereby be purged, there would indeed be cause for rejoicing.

A profitable source for knowledge of feed-backs in behavior lies in the study of oscillations. Rosenblueth and Wiener studied the

[13] Cf. Rosenblueth, Wiener, and Bigelow, 1943.

frequency of clonus contractions under stretch stimulation in the leg muscle of the cat and attained results in harmony with their prediction based upon this principle.[14] Oscillations support the inference that feed-back is occurring, since, as accompaniments of the behavioral mechanism, they become marked in its degenerative changes. Some evidence of this sort has been accumulated, as, for example, in a pathological condition called "purpose tremor." Neuroses, with their reiterative character of obsessions and compulsions, have been attributed to defective feed-backs or to feed-backs that have become positive, producing oscillations or self-perpetuating excesses that may sweep other brain cells into their orbit and dominate the behavior of the patient in an inescapable vicious circle. Barrett (1950) has considered three of the major psychoses from the standpoint of defective feed-back mechanisms. It was stated earlier that one way in which engineers control oscillation is by advancing the output ahead of the input so that time lag that might lead to oscillation is eliminated. Quite remarkably, there appears to be just such an arrangement in neuronal conduction, where excitation is, of course, rapidly rhythmic or pulsating.

Further extensions of cybernetics to the psychopathologies have taken the form of explanations in terms of a clogging of the system by circulating memories so that what remains of the system for the active routing of messages becomes overloaded and, like an overloaded telephone system, may break down in times of stress. A computing machine does not carry its reverberating memories along in this troublesome fashion. It is cleared at the end of every problem; or if it goes into a circular spin, it can be cleared immediately in as clean a fashion as Locke's *tabula rasa*. Not so the poor human being whose physiological memory system can be completely cleared only by death. The fit of the cybernetic model in the fields of motivation and emotion is not so well established as it is in some of the above applications. Wiener has regarded emotions as communications that are not directed to any particular place in the mechanism. They are messages labelled "to whom it may concern"; and it is hypothesized that hormones circulating in the blood-stream are their carriers. The enhancing or inhibition of behavioral processes is provided by an "affective tone totalizer," operating with feed-backs, in connection with local processes and their affective tone mechanisms. The organismic bases of such mechanisms is, however, a matter of conjecture.

When it comes to retention and memory, there are some definite neurological facts to which the cybernetic principles can be better

[14] Wiener, *op. cit.*, Introduction.

linked. The circular mechanisms employed in computing machines for storage of information have an analogy in the central nervous system of the organism. Lorente de Nó (1938) provided this knowledge by his famous discovery in the cortex of circular arrangements of neurons so connected that the excitation of one (A) will lead, through others (B, C, D, etc.), back to the re-excitation of the original neuron (A). The circuit can thus repeat itself indefinitely (but subject to certain conditions) as long as the cortex is active. Outlying neurons, connecting as afferents, can bring impulses into the circuit; and other neurons, efferent from it, can carry impulses away. There are thus in the brain re-entrant, reverberatory circuits, or, as they are sometimes called, "regenerative loops," that correspond in function to the memory-storage unit of the machines. In order to adapt the model to the equipotentiality of many different parts of the cortex for retaining the same memory Lashley has suggested that signals reaching the brain may reverberate extensively in a great number of rhythmic local circuits. These patterns might be reduplicated all over the cortex, ready to respond to their appropriate stimulus signals. The concept of memory-trace as stated by Koffka and used by many other students of perception has thus received a new and striking development.

There is an important logical consequence associated with the reverberatory principle that should not be overlooked. In the repeating circuit we have something that is definitely self-closed: *it comes back upon itself.* (Perhaps it would be better to say that it is *quasi-self-closed* since it retains some connections with elements outside the circle.) As a system that comes back upon itself, it is not merely something that has an input and an output; it becomes a *unit of structure.* It is an example of the general type of dynamic structure to which we have referred many times in the course of our discussions. There are strong theoretical advantages of such an arrangement over the open-ended stimulus-response model that has frequently appeared in psychological theory.[15] In the latter conception a "habit" can be only a linkage in an open-ended chain. It is dependent to a greater extent than the circular pattern upon a particular outer stimulus that leads over into a particular response. In the *circuital* model the so-called habit can attain, as a dynamic structure that is repeating itself, a certain autonomy apart from its receptor and effector connections. It operates in an independent manner *through time;* and it is not so closely bound to space-points as is the linear conception.

[15] For example in the diagrams employed by Hull, Spence, and other behavior theorists; see the works cited.

Moreover it can operate readily in structural integrations with other such circuits, thus forming more inclusive aggregates. A simple, linear, connection is merely a link. We cannot "handle it." It is used and then the linkage has nothing further to support its existence.[16] In its transient and unsubstantial character it is something like the hole in the doughnut. The circuital model, however, is like the doughnut itself. Being composed of a *closed chain of elements*, not just a connection or link *between* two elements, it becomes something more definite for experimenters and theorists to work with.

The cybernetists have construed the advantages of the model in still another way. By giving it autonomy through time and freeing it from its moorings to particular stimulus and response events it can be made to serve as the physiological basis for abstractions or "universals"; for these also must be free from time and space particularity. As McCulloch puts it, a train of circularly repeating impulses can preserve the form of the fact without having reference to the particular moment when it was sensorily experienced.[17] Form-qualities are one type of such universals, for, as we know, they transcend the particular receptor pattern made by the stimulus-object of the moment. Thus we come back through a new door to an aspect that was considered earlier under the head of transformations. The reverberating circuit can also underwrite "ideas," that is, abstract concepts that are attained and stored for use in processes of thinking.[18] Incompatibility or conflict in perceptual and ideational processes, which we found to be important in the motor and set theories, is provided for in cybernetics by the mutual antagonism of circuits. Swallowing and drawing a breath are mutually inhibiting neural arrangements that share common

---

[16] This would not be true, of course, if the link were thought of as some physical material or condition that exists at particular synapses and that could mediate the habit connection or inhibition by alterations of its resistance. It is difficult, however, to reconcile such a view with well-known facts, such, for example, as the temporal and spatial variability in the behavior pattern for a given act, the use of the same neural pathways for different learned acts, and the phenomenon of cortical equipotentiality. These facts, of course, would also produce difficulty for the circuital model if specificity of neural elements in behavior were a required condition. This difficulty, the writer believes, can be overcome by a theory of "probabilities" in connection with the neuronal structuring of behavior acts (see Chapter 21).

[17] See discussion in Northrop, 1948.

[18] Again there has been some rejoicing in the philosophical camp (Northrop, *op. cit.*). It has been inferred from these formulations that universals or ideas have an immediate physiological reality. They can be checked against experience from particulars and revised if need be, or they can emerge into particular actions on the efferent side and play a real part in the affairs of men and society.

elements in a part of their courses.   Thus the nerve net also embodies the possibility of selection, choice, and decision.[19]

But a troublesome question about memory-retention now arises. The machine differs from the brain in that it can be cleared of all memories at the end of the run of a given problem. Its long-term memories can be retained, if desired, on punch cards; but it is capable of being reduced very simply to the state of having no immediate memory. The brain cannot be cleared in this fashion; the entire course of life is like a single run of the machine. Some provision for long-standing memories must be made, analogous to the long-time recorders of the machine; another memory-mechanism has to be found in addition to the reverberating circuits. These latter continue to operate only so long as the cortex is active. What, then, happens during sleep, or in cases of excessive fatigue or inhibition? We do not lose our universal ideas or forget our invariants of perception over night. These must not only reverberate in the waking cortex ready for immediate use but must also be filed in "deeper memory" storage. Here, say some of the cyberneticists, we must look to more permanent modifications in the plastic material of the nerve cells themselves. How many such bits of information, either particular or universal, do we store in a lifetime; and what is the mechanism employed? For this purpose our 10^{10} central neurons are not enough. We need a number of elements of the order of 10^{13} to 10^{15}; for, according to calculations, there are about this number of bits to be preserved in the lifetime of a human organism. Such considerations impel us to descend into the realm of the protein molecules within neural elements. If these can be the vehicles for remembered bits we shall have so many that nothing needs ever to be forgotten. Much that is still unknown is involved in such an explanation. It must be admitted that we do not yet have a secure basis for explaining long-term memory.

CYBERNETIC THEORIES OF PERCEPTION: THE PITTS-MCCULLOCH MODELS

Let us now turn to perception. In earlier pages there were discussed at some length the logic of cybernetics as related to perception and some of the theoretical formulations suggested (transformation groups, invariants, and scanning principles). We come now to a more direct attack upon the problem. How can such mechanisms as are known to exist in the brain be enlisted through cybernetic

[19] McCulloch, 1946.

methods to help explain how things appear to the perceiver? For such insights as have been gained we are indebted mainly to McCulloch and Pitts;[20] and the topics investigated relate to the phenomena of frame of reference, form-quality, and perhaps constancy in a very broad sense of the term. Three general models have been proposed by these authors for attacking three different problems, dealing in each case with some invariant of perception. The first of the problems is concerned with the question of how the perception of forms is preserved through differences in the locality of their initial stimulation-patterns on the retina and through eye-movements of fixation. The second problem deals with the recognition of a constant chord-interval played at different pitches. The third attacks the question: how is constancy of shape in a figure perceived regardless of variations in its size? Really, only two models are involved, since the third problem is solved by topographical variations of the second. We shall here stay as close as possible to the phraseology of the authors while at the same time trying to give an account that will be meaningful in fairly simple terms.

The first problem, as we have indicated, lies in the field of visual reflexes. Of these there are a number, as, for example, the focusing of the lens, the convergence of the eyes, and the volume control of light entering the eye. The last named has the effect of freeing the retinal-excitation image of the irrelevant particularity of amount of illumination. All these reflexes are said to operate by the negative feed-back principle. In general, the visual reflexes tend to bring any object that attracts attention into a standard condition or orientation, so that the image formed varies within as small a range as possible. When an object enters the field of vision at the periphery, the eyes turn so that it becomes centered at their foveas. The mechanism by which this is accomplished is formulated in the model of Pitts and McCulloch with which we are now concerned.

First, let us state the known physiological facts. There is afferent neural transmission from the retina to the superior colliculi on the back of the midbrain. From that region there is a relay to the oculomotor centers; and from there impulses are sent out to the muscles that turn the eyeball. The surface of the colliculus has been mapped for the projection upon it of retinal points; and these projection-points have been found to be well coördinated with the eye movements that fix the gaze in certain directions. It seems then that there is a

[20] See Pitts and McCulloch, 1947; McCulloch, 1951; and Wiener, *op. cit.*, Chapter VI. Also McCulloch and Pitts, 1948; and McCulloch and Pfeiffer, 1949.

definite routing of the "information" which is received by the colliculi. Considering for the present only one eye, let us now imagine that upon the retina we have laid two coördinate axes, a vertical and a horizontal. The fovea, that is, the retinal point of fixation or direct gaze, is at the origin of this coördinate system. Now when the object, say a figure drawn as a square, enters the field of vision on one side and the information is transmitted to the superior colliculus, the colliculus, according to the theory, computes by double integration the lateral and vertical coördinates of the "center of gravity of the distribution of brightness" of the object's retinal image with respect to the coördinate system just described. (We remember that in cybernetic theory the brain acts in the capacity of a computing mechanism). This information is then transmitted from the colliculus to the oculomotor nuclei whence impulses are sent to the appropriate eye-muscles, serving as "orders" to contract and move the eyeball in such a way as to reduce these coördinate distances (i.e., to decrease the vector concerned). The colliculi supply this information *at a rate proportional* to the coördinate values as they change from instant to instant; for we remember that in a negative feed-back the corrective information sent varies as the deviation of the effector from the goal. Hence, as the eyes turn and the center of brightness of the image with its diminishing coördinates approaches the origin of the coördinate system (fovea), the eyes slow down. They finally stop when the visual axes point at the center of brightness of the object, that is, when the object is centered at the foveas. In this process invariants of translation are maintained. If our object, the square, appears anywhere in the visual field, the eyes turn until it is centered, and the form of the square remains always the same. Here then we have a universal of a sort; for the image is now rid of the particularity of the place on the retina at which it first appeared. Thus we could say concerning the region of initial stimulation: "There was some place such that it was this or that percept."

This principle is extended to reflexes in general. Every reflex brings some input or "apparition" through a series of values representing positions, intensities, or other variables to some final position or value of the variable, a position that is seemingly established by the constitution of the organism. By this process there is removed from the image some fortuitious specificity. There is selected from many possible positions or states some final one. This process is referred to by McCulloch as the "reduction to the canonical position." In general, the process is one of computing invariants for all members of some group of transformations. But here, in the case of reflexes, a question arises. As the eyes move, translating the figure from the periphery onto the fovea, we do not really perceive it in intermediate positions. The eyes move rapidly without perceptions of the object occurring in transit; and blurring of the image is thus avoided. It is, therefore, only the final, or canonical, position that should count in the averaging process by which the invariant is computed. This matter is handled by assuming that for reflexes the cerebral circuits (that is, the functional) actually assign the value of zero to all transformations except the last. Pitts and McCulloch support their model by a mathematical analysis, by histological drawings (in general agreement with the theory) of the layers of cell-networks in the part of the brain involved, and by a diagram of the retinal, collicular, and muscular connections.

The mechanism just described is the one which was employed by Helson as a neurological basis of his theory of adaptation-level (Chapter 10). Some points of appropriateness for adaptation-level can readily be recognized, though they may be clearer when we discuss another transformation-model which stresses the values of the whole series rather than just the end, or canonical, position. Just as the cybernetic model involves an integrating over a range of values and the computing of invariants as sums or averages for all members of a group of transformations, so adaptation-level is also computed as a (weighted) mean of stimulus-inputs varying through a given range. We might say that judgments of light, heavy, medium, and so on are stripped of isolated particularity and are referred to a "canonical" value or standard for the *group* experienced, a value given by this averaging process. Directly in line is the statement of our present authors that the nervous system averages over time whenever a series of sensory impulses arrives whose frequency measures the intensity of the continuous variable stimulating the receptor from instant to instant, and that it also averages in space when there is a continuum of more and more sensory elements that are being added (McCulloch and Pitts, 1948). As a standard built up by experience over a range of values and independently retained through time, the adaptation-level could be said to act as a sort of universal. Though the reflex considered by this Pitts-McCulloch model may seem a bit afield from usual perceptual problems, theoretical convergences such as that between its authors and Helson illustrate what was earlier referred to as the potential value of cybernetics for perceptual theory.

We now turn to the second model. This will be treated as the case of recognizing a given chord when it is played in different pitches. It deals with the perceived relationships of gestalt and the transposition effects or form-qualities of von Ehrenfels. When we hear a chord played we perceive not only the specific tones but the interval (or intervals) between them; and this interval, if kept objectively constant, becomes recognized as such even though all the specific tones are changed. In order to visualize the geometry of this model let us imagine that we have, in a vertical plane before us, a sheet of coördinate paper ruled by horizontal and vertical lines into small squares. Suppose also that a heavy line is ruled across the bottom of the sheet. Now imagine a number of parallel slanting lines, in a sheaf an inch or more wide, running upward diagonally across the sheet from the lower left-hand corner to the upper right-hand corner. Let the diagonals intersect the lines forming the squares at approximately the corners of the squares. What we are now looking at represents very crudely a cross-section of the general directions or "lay" of neurons in the primary auditory area of the cortex in the general region of its fourth, or receptive, layer. The lines, of course, are only a starting scheme to help us imagine how the neurons lie and the general courses of their axone fibers: let us not hold to this "graph-paper" analogy too closely.

Since we are looking at a cross-section of the cortex let us think of the horizontal lines as the *edges* of "sheets" or *"mosaic-layers"* of the cell bodies of neurons. The axones from the cells making up these layers extend downward and are represented (in direction only) by the vertical lines of the coördinate paper. Think of the whole model as in three dimensions with some vertical lines (axones) coming down from each horizontal mosaic-layer separately, like strings of moss hanging from boughs that interlace in horizontal planes, one plane above another. The cells of these horizontal layers are the receptive cells to which auditory impulses are brought by the ascending afferents (the diagonal lines). But we shall also consider that the horizontal or mosaic layers contain many associative fibers that run transversely in the plane of the layer, connecting all the cell bodies in the layer. This feature should be kept in mind. The heavy line at the *bottom* of our imaginary figure represents a sort of basal mosaic onto which the descending axones of the receptive cell-bodies in the mosaic-layers project. Let us return now to the *diagonal* lines. These represent the course of axones of afferent neurons relaying impulses upward from the auditory mechanism of the inner ear. Suppose that we consider several of these diagonal neurons as conveying impulses from the several tones of a particular chord. Each of the diagonal neurons may be considered as excited by a different pitch, so that a constant distance between any two of them means a constant pitch-difference, or interval, regardless of what specific pitches the fibers may represent. It will be seen that as these sensory impulses ascend they intersect the successive mosaic-layers of receptive cells upward and from left to right. Since the diagonal afferents run parallel to each other, keeping the same distance apart, they arouse the same spatial pattern of excitation in each of those layers successively upward and from left to right; and, as the cell bodies of those layers are excited, this pattern of impulses is projected through their axones vertically downward upon the basal mosaic. What is believed to happen in this basal region will be later discussed in more detail.

Owing to the way the figure is drawn the *pattern* of excitation will thus move from left to right in the successive mosaic layers along a continuum of pitch as the afferent auditory impulses ascend along the diagonal tracts. This very crude visualization will help us to grasp the principle of how a constant pattern of relationships, that is, an auditory "form," can be translated intact along a basal continuum by a succession of neuron-impulses set going by a specific patterned stimulus-input. Let us now turn to the diagram of Pitts and McCulloch shown in Figure 3.

The main features of our imaginary model will be recognized immediately in the upper part of the figure. Six mosaic-layers of receptive cell-bodies are shown, the cell-bodies connected within each layer by the horizontal, associative fibers. The small circles represent cell-bodies with their axones extending from them. The further courses of the axones where they are broken off to simplify the diagram are shown by arrows with a barb on one side. The small cup-shaped endings at the cell-bodies are axone terminations of the preceding neurons where they are in synaptic relation with the cell-bodies (or dendrites of cells) indicated by the small circles. Non-specific and associative afferents from other parts of the cortex or lower brain ascend at the extreme left side of the diagram and make synaptic connections with the horizontal associative neurons which, in turn, interconnect the cells within each mosaic-layer. From the cell-bodies of the horizontal layers axones extend downward. There are here columns consisting of many vertically placed cells carrying the impulses downward toward the base of the region and connecting with pyramidal-cells (cell-bodies shown as small black triangles) whose axones (broken off in the diagram) leave the region as associative efferents to go to the "secondary" auditory region of the cortex or to other parts. This completes the model except for the essential feature of the incoming specific afferents that bring the auditory impulses from the ear. This information is relayed to the cortex from the medial geniculate body, and the specific afferents carrying it (marked $+$) slant upward, as shown, through the cortex, making connections with the cells in the receptive layers. Three such fibers are shown in detail and others are indicated by the shorter arrows. It will be seen that the cells of the receptive layers (mosaics) receive

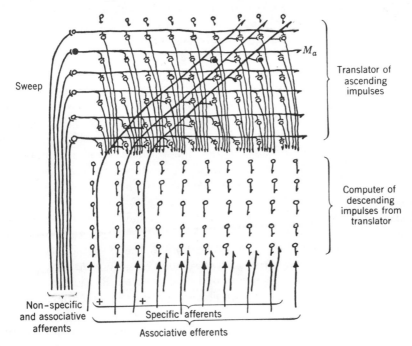

FIGURE 3. Hypothetical diagram of cortical neural network involved in hearing a chord independently of pitch. Impulses of some chord enter slantwise along the specific afferents, marked by plusses, and ascend until they reach the level M_a in the columns of the receptive layer activated at the moment by the non-specific afferents. These provide summation adequate to permit the impulses to enter that level but no other. From there the impulses descend along columns to the depth. The level in the column, facilitated by the non-specific afferents, moves repetitively up and down, so that the excitement delivered to the depths moves uniformly back and forth as if the sounds moved up and down together in pitch, preserving intervals. In the deep columns various combinations are made of the excitation and are averaged during a cycle of scansion to produce results depending only on the chord. (From W. Pitts and W. S. McCulloch, "How We Know Universals: The Perception of Auditory and Visual Forms," *Bulletin of Mathematical Biophysics*, 1947, 9, 132. University of Chicago Press. By permission of the authors, editor, and publishers. Legend is by the authors; title of figure added by the present writer.)

both the afferent auditory impulses and impulses from the transverse network of associative fibers. By the aid of the latter, impulses in the receptive layers can be summated and neural discharges synchronized. The secondary auditory cortex to which the pyramidal fibers lead is similar in arrangement to the primary except for having some larger pyramidals that connect with more distant motor areas.

Two important features in the operation of the model remain to be stated. Pitch is mapped upon the cortex in such a way that as we go from one end of the auditory region to the other the cells in the receptive layers represent continually higher pitches. In the diagram it can be assumed that the pitch of the receptive cells in the mosaic-layers is becoming higher from left to right. The same, of course, would apply to the function of the vertical columns descending from the receptive layers. There is evidence, moreover, that octaves are laid out over (approximately) equal cortical distances, as they are on the keyboard of a piano. Thus far the authors have been able to establish a very good fidelity of their theory to the known anatomical and physiological facts of the cortical auditory mechanism. They present additional drawings of the neural architecture of the cortex that show a similarity with the model. A fellow-neurologist, in fact, mistook their model-diagram for a picture of the cortex in the region concerned. The remaining feature, however, is more conjectural, at least as to its physiological identification in the brain. The theory requires that there be some sort of scanning mechanism that passes rhythmically up and down through the network described by the model. A fairly rapid wave of change in electric potential providing pulsations of impulses through successive neural elements or layers would answer the purpose. The word "sweep" on the left of the diagram might refer to the presence of such a scanning operation, which is thought to take place through the non-specific and associative afferents of the cortex. So much for the general anatomy and physiology of the model. Now let us see how it is believed to work in the perception of auditory form.

Figure 3 shows that for each receiving cell in each mosaic-layer there are two connecting afferents: (1) the specific auditory fibers relaying impulses from the ear, and (2) the non-specific or associative fibers connecting the cells in each layer and coördinating their action. Let us suppose that the thresholds of the receptive cells are such that impulses from *both* these sources are required in order to make them discharge, and that when they receive an impulse from the non-specific or associative fibers a simultaneous signal is delivered by these fibers to all the neurons of that layer.   In other words, the firing of a neuron in a mosaic-layer requires both that it receive impulses from the ear and that the whole layer of cells be "alerted." Now let us imagine that the auditory impulses are coming in over the diagonals in the figure, and that the layers of receptive cells are being successively excited by the two sources of excitation mentioned.   Let us say that they are being excited from the bottom layer upward.   As the input along the diagonals moves from the left upward toward the right the receiving cells will become correspondingly excited and their outputs will also move step for step in the direction of the slant.   Impulses will therefore descend in the vertical columns successively from left to right, projecting upon the basal region at all times the *same pattern* that was delivered originally by the stimulus source.   Thus, if the input comprises a musical interval, say, of a fifth, that same interval will be represented in the downward-projected pattern regardless of the specific pitches of the notes that comprise it.   "The output asserts that there were pitches such that there was this or that chord."   There is thus made from one form, as given by the stimulus, the same form, invariant with respect to pitch, in all positions along a basal line.

But what is it that produces the necessary successive alertings of the receptive layers and thus makes such a translation of the chord-interval possible?   This is the scanning mechanism to which we have referred.   Its ascending and descending wave, or sweep, produces pulsations along the non-specific associative fibers that alert the receptive cells of the mosaic-layers successively.   There is believed to be a sweep of this circuit at intervals of about one-tenth of a second, this interval being approximately the limiting time for perceiving chord independently of pitch.   We shall return to this question of a scanning mechanism in a moment.

The deeper parts of the columns in Figure 3 comprise neural elements capable of reverberation and summation over time.   These may serve as computers of the quantities involved in the successive transformations of the group, giving their summation or average during a cycle of scansion to produce an invariant related to the experience of chord irrespective of pitch.   A mathematical paradigm for such computations is provided by the authors.   It is believed that the actual experience of chord regardless of pitch, as based on these computations in the cortex, is mediated by associative efferents leaving the primary auditory region at a lower level and terminating in a secondary region where the processes underlying the "pure chord experience" are believed to take place. This situation, however, is more empirically demonstrable in the visual application of the model to which we shall presently refer.

What mechanism is responsible for the mysterious, but essential, process of scanning in the cortex? Like the scanning beam in television it is believed to coördinate space and time distributions, thus holding intriguing possibilities for explaining perceived relationships. But it is of no use to us unless we can find or identify it in the brain. The attention of cyberneticists has been focused upon the *alpha rhythm* of the brain (brain-waves) as the possible scanning device. Its period is about one-tenth of a second, which is apparently a crucial interval in perceptual processes. Stroud, as a result of certain investigations, has found that a tenth of a second is a sort of minimal quantum of time-experience. The temporal flow of events tends to be perceived in about such units, and *within* that unit discriminations of temporal sequence break down. He has called this interval the "psychological moment in perception."[21] Is this psychological moment determined by the alpha rhythm of the brain? Since incoming and outgoing signals, as well as brain-waves, ascend and descend through the cortex, when the subject attends to some stimulus field the sweep of scansion should be obscured or obliterated by a "twinkle of details," just as the form of the carrier wave in television is obscured by the superimposed signal that modulates it. This inference is in accord with observed facts concerning the alpha rhythm. On the other side, however, is the fact that the frequency of the alpha rhythm can be profoundly altered experimentally in normal individuals without observable modifications either of memory or of perception. Since precise synchronies are demanded both for perception and for the reverberating circuits that underlie memory, this fact would argue against the alpha wave as the scanning mechanism for these processes. On the whole, objections to the alpha-rhythm explanation seem to be increasing. But if the brain-wave mechanism is to be given up as a scanning device, an important link in highly ingenious theories such as that of Pitts and McCulloch will be missing. Their explanatory equipment will not be complete until the gap is filled. (For evidence, however, that there may be some relation of alpha rhythm to rapidity of form perception, see Murphree, 1954.)

In their third problem our authors have applied the conceptual model above described to a similar phenomenon of visual perception. They have asked how it is possible to recognize a certain shape, for

[21] See Von Foerster (ed.), 1950, pp. 27 ff.

example, that of a square or a circle, regardless of the size of the figure concerned. The plan of the model here needs a few minor alterations or extensions. In the first place the transformations involved in change of pitch along a scale occur in only one direction at any one time. If, however, a square or other regular figure whose center is at the fovea is expanded or contracted in size, the dilatations or constrictions will be symmetrical on both sides of the axis of vision. We can adapt Figure 3 to this problem by noting that it represents only a *radial* section, that is, only one side, of the cortical projection-pattern of the figure received from the retina. It needs to be duplicated by repeating the same mechanism, reversed, on the left side of the diagram. If we imagine the diagram thus extended, the ascending diagonals will diverge in two directions, one set (for one half of the stimulus figure and retinal pattern) extending upward to the right, and a corresponding set (for the other half of the figure) extending upward to the left. The diverging diagonals must also be considered as radiating in *all* directions, not just in the plane of the diagram. (This way of stating the case will make the principle evident; actually, the situation is somewhat more complicated.)

Just as in the case of the chord, it will be seen that with a full sweep of scansion the *same shape* of the image will be represented throughout differences in the image size. As the sweep goes upward, successively alerting the layers in divergent directions, *all possible dilatations* of the figure will be produced in the cortex; but the parameters that represent its shape are preserved. If the figure is a square, squareness will still be perceived no matter how much the figure is enlarged. The like will be true upon constriction or diminishing of the figure as the sweep moves downward. Again, at a maximum rate of about ten per second the experience of shape regardless of size will be possible. The patterns of these modifications are again produced seriatim upon efferent cells travelling from the region we are considering to the "parastriate" cortex where functions are made of them and the results added. The immediate basis of the experience of "pure shape" regardless of size then lies in a secondary visual region that receives the information from the primary. The output of excitation from a spot on the primary cortex will turn up in the secondary area as if distributed at random. Hence, from any particular set of spots in the primary area some spot of maximum excitation will appear by chance in the secondary area. Activity here implies activity in some figure of spots in the output of the primary—that is, in this case, shape regardless of size. Electrical stimulation of such a locus in the secondary area in patients whose cortices have been exposed gives rise to an experience of form, such as that of a tree, a house, or a hand. This perceived form, moreover, has no definite position, nor any particular size in the subject's visual field. It does not move when he turns his eyes. It is merely a *shape*, freed from size and position. Since from one of the possible images of the object images of all sizes have been made, the size of the original image does not affect the averages that are computed from the array of dilatations and constrictions. The output is "size-invariant." Such a size-invariant, abstracted from the entire group of dilatations and constrictions, corresponds to the shape of a figure regardless of its size.

Though the problems thus far attacked by the transformation model cover only a few perceived forms or relationships Pitts and McCulloch consider it applicable for the abstraction of a wide range of properties. It gives a highly general procedure for securing, through the action of nerve-networks, invariants corresponding to universals derived from particulars. Such, then, are the present major contributions of cybernetics to perceptual theory. That they will afford a new kind of insight into its problems can scarcely be denied, even though there are some limitations and gaps in their chain of evidence. Only one other group of theorists have made so sophisticated an attempt to correlate the phenomena of perception with happenings in the central nervous system. These are the gestalt psychologists. The cybernetic system, however, presents marked contrasts with that of Köhler. The latter is based upon the dynamics of a field. It is macroscopic and deals with the interplay of field forces in a whole configurational area. Cybernetics is highly specific: its mechanisms have an elementaristic character. Reverberating circuits, feed-backs, group transformations, group scanning, and points in the secondary visual cortex must be envisaged at the microscopic, neuronal level.

The perceptual approach of Pitts and McCulloch does not deal with configurations as such, and there is, in their theory, no hint of isomorphism. The world of phenomenological experience, they believe, may ultimately require a language entirely different than the one we use in the physicalistic study of perceptual mechanisms. McCulloch (1951) asserts that "a nervous net can take any figure in space, requiring an ensemble of a given number of neurons simultaneously, and convert it into a figure of impulses over a single neuron requiring as many relay times as there were neurons in the ensemble, and vice versa." Consequently we "cannot tell what kind of thing we must look for in a brain when it has an idea, except that it must be invariant under all those conditions in which that brain is having that idea."

The cybernetists, then, are not seeking to explain why a square stimulus-figure gives us the particular experience we call square, i.e., why it *looks like* a square. They are explaining only the fact that, given a square stimulus and its cortical pattern of excitation, that pattern can retain a characteristic physiological figure through variations of its size, and in all the canonical presentations of it at the fovea regardless of the retinal region upon which the stimulation first falls.

Nor can it be said that the cybernetists have really dealt with the problem of constancy in the traditional meaning of the term. Constancies in a broader sense they *have* investigated; but their models thus far do not seem to bear upon such central psychological problems as color constancy or the maintenance of a constant perceived size under variations of distance and retinal-image size, or upon the constancy of perceived shape when an object (always considered as in foveal vision) is fixated in different perspectives. It may be that the method of invariants over groups of transformations can be extended to these phenomena; but in attempting to make the application the writer has felt that some essential element was missing. We can see how there can be a size-invariant property of one object that holds constant while size is changing—and that that invariant is shape. But how can there be a "retinal-shape"-invariant that *consists of shape* and that holds constant while "shape," as given by the retinal-stimulation pattern, is changing? It is this latter condition that exemplifies the psychological problem known as constancy. What the cybernetic models do illuminate is the problem of *stable relationships* within an otherwise changing stimulus-pattern, *gestalten* in the sense of formal aspects that persist through translation, transposition, and change of size. Pitts and McCulloch called them "universals." True it is that such relationships have been the subject of much experimenting as well as controversy among psychologists, as in studies of perceptual or discriminatory learning among animals. The problem is indeed important for both animal and human subjects. Cybernetics offers a solution of this problem, at the level of perception, different from the solutions given by either behavioral psychology or gestalt. The old chapters in the story are by no means finished; but new chapters that may prove as significant as the old are beginning.[22]

[22] Another example of this trend is to be found in the treatment of visual perception by the concepts of information theory. See Attneave, 1954. A great deal of visual stimulation from objects is redundant (i.e., more input is provided than is needed to give all the information about the object). Attneave shows where the concentration of information is greatest and how the information yield

A critique of cybernetics must be largely an analysis of its point of view. Since the perceptual part of the theory is inseparable from its general psychological orientation we must take a correspondingly broad view. First, mainly as a matter of interest, there are some striking contrasts between organisms and machines that should be set alongside the similarities earlier described. There are roughly ten billion neurons in the human central nervous system as compared with a maximum of about ten thousand relays in the largest computer. Thus the nervous system is a million times larger in an operational sense, though housed in the remarkably small space of the cranium. If a computer built along modern lines were to have as many relay-units as the human organism we would have difficulty housing it in an ordinary building, and, in McCulloch's dramatic comparison, it would require Niagara Falls to supply the power for running it and the Niagara River to carry away the heat. Vacuum tubes, however, work a thousand times faster than neurons. There is a great saving both in time and errors that can be credited to the machines. There is also an enormous information loss in the organism as information is passed through from the receptors to the effectors. The information-ratio of input to output, according to McCulloch, is about 100 million to one! Passing from nerve to muscle it is about 100 to one. No engineer could afford to build a machine that involves so much "corruption." But, as a penalty, no machine is as likely to go right under conditions so various as those which the organism undergoes. The probability that the information the organism does utilize and relay is due merely to chance is inconceivably small. The "power supply" of organisms is built up from within by metabolism; for the tube or mechanical relay it is provided by potential differences of currents supplied from the outside. Entropic processes go on in both systems, and as open systems, both receive negative entropy from the environment. The organism, however, has special ways of conserving negative entropy. It is not only taken in, but built into the very structure of the system.

---

is related to textures and to gestalt concepts such as contour, gradient, good figure, etc. He also lists the methods by which redundancy might be reduced and the essentials of perceived objects economically gained by an organismic perceptual "computer" operating with such information.

Cybernetics is a fairly parsimonious theory. It is also logically consistent. Because its concepts always have denotable or quaside-notable referents it is a decided improvement over many psychological theories in respect to direct experimental availability. As to agreement with the known facts of physiology and behavior, it is, as we have seen, in good standing on many counts. There are, however, some exceptions, as, for example, in the lack of an organismic analogy for the memory-clearance of the machine and in the question of whether machine-principles permit sufficient equipotentiality.[23] There are also digital-analogue mixtures in the organism that are hard to reconcile with cybernetic models. The notion of the digital nature of neural action becomes strained in view of the fact that there is already some activity in the neuron before its main transmission potential occurs and that after this threshold has been reached further increases in intensity of the stimulus may produce increases in the *frequency* of the impulse. These "frequency" increments ought also to count as information, for they are a part of the transmission and affect the behavioral result. Could they be computed as "bits" in the sense of being made to represent a choice between two alternatives depending on the signal and upon past choices? Some doubts on this score seem to impel us again in the direction of the analogue rather than the digital principle.[24]

It is too early to say whether cybernetics may come to afford a good *general* theory of perception or of psychology as a whole. Though logical deductive thinking and certain aspects of memory are well treated, one wonders how far a concept of information that is so narrowly defined can carry us in dealing with such phenomena as creative thinking, scientific curiosity, or the amazing flexibility of the organism in adapting to new and widely varying conditions. Cybernetic perceptual theory provides some answers, as we have seen, in frame-of-reference phenomena and in the relationship and transposition problems of gestalt. The logarithmic formula for information appears to have some affinity with the Weber-Fechner law; and for dimensionality in general there is some logical provision. Other classes of perceptual phenomena,—true constancy, meaning, set, and many of the configurational effects—so far as the writer knows, have not yet been considered.

One of the most serious limitations of the system lies in the area of perceptual meaning. All meanings that can be expressed quantita-

[23] See in Jeffress (ed.), 1951, pp. 71 ff.
[24] MacKay and McCulloch (1952) attempt to deal with the problem; but it is not certain that they have done full justice to it.

tively, like the invariants of size or position, or the dimensions defining shape, are, of course, inherent in the models. But meanings that are *non*-quantitative, that represent object-character or situation, seem impossible either to code digitally or to transmit analogically. All information that can be handled by computing machines refers to decisions of "this" or "not this," or tells "how much" of this; it never tells what "this" refers to or (how much of) *what* is represented by the numbers employed.[25]   When information is fed to the machine, all that cannot be quantified has been stripped away in advance. Suppose the operator is computing some statistics about chairs. *Quantitative* meanings concerning chairs are fed as numbers into the machine, together with instructions.   The machine itself knows nothing of chairs.   It simply grinds out the calculation and delivers numbers back to the operator.   The operator then "reattaches" the numbers to his concept or meaning of "chair" from which they had previously been separated to accommodate them to the limitations of the machine.   We can never get out of machines any type of meaning other than that which the organism puts into them.   In organisms, on the other hand, meanings of all sorts come into existence and are used as organisms make contact with objects about them.   Organisms can take the cyberneticists' "bits of information" and, by means of something additional that they themselves contribute, develop recognizable "object-character" out of them.

Perhaps there are some who, because they conceive science to be limited to quantities, might ask: What else is there besides quantities that can give the objectivity and precision necessary for scientific work?   Are not the laws of nature *quantitative* laws?   Are not quantities, then, sufficient?   Do we not work non-quantitatively only where it has not yet been possible to develop quantitative methods?

[25] MacKay makes an attempt to reduce content-meanings to quantitative terms by such a device as the following.   Taking the concept of a chair, we note that a chair is characterized by having four legs and a back.   Legs and a back are a part of its meaning.   But a chair does not always have four legs, and sometimes it may not have a back.   What we could do over a long experience with the word "chair" would be to build up a concept of "chairfulness" which could be defined by the proportions of different characters in the ensemble of all chairs experienced.   We could then define meaning in quantitative (vectorial) terms. (See Von Foerster, ed., 1952, pp. 181 ff., especially 190.)   Perhaps so, but would the definition be adequate?   Really to handle the meaning of chair we would need, following MacKay's plan, to go further and define the concepts of "leg" and "back."   Pursuing such a course we would soon find ourselves not with a quantitative theory of the meaning of objects, but in a regressus or in a situation that would leave some elements of content-meaning unaccounted for by any practicable quantification of their components.

Would you have us deal with such subjective things as "qualities"? These questions can be answered clearly if we are willing to lay aside certain rather stereotyped ways of thinking about natural laws and give the matter careful thought. Let us take a simple illustration from everyday life that can as readily be extended to scientific procedures. The hostess who sees that four more chairs are required for her guests does not think in purely quantitative terms. She thinks quantities (the quantity "four") to be sure; but at the same time she thinks "four *chairs*." Her essential meaning here is "*four objects that human beings can make contact with by their buttocks and their backs in a sitting posture, and thereafter, if occasion requires, hold that position though they have broken all contact between their bodies and the floor.*" We note that an essential feature of this definition, or meaning, of chair lies in the fact that it includes references to contacts (events), together with an implication of motions that lie between them. It also disposes these events and movements in a kind of pattern which is describable in more familiar terms as "sitting down" and "raising one's feet." First, let us ask whether such a meaning of "chair" can be unambiguously and completely expressed in terms of quantities, magnitudes, or numbers alone. If the reader will try it, he will see that it cannot be done. Quantities, if used *alone*, will not tell us what events are taking place or even *that* events are occurring (unless we break the rules by assuming them); much less will they tell us the *necessary pattern* of the events (i.e., the pattern of movements and contacts) involved.

In the second place, one might ask whether our statement of "chair-meaning," given in italics above, is objective and precise. What could be more so—when we are dealing continually and exclusively with denotable objects and physicalistic events? Surely the procedure is both as precise and as objective as though we were dealing with numbers; it even goes ahead of mere numbers in its denotive possibilities. It will be noted also that we have said nothing whatever about "quality." We have merely described a natural phenomenon in terms of some of its necessarily non-quantitative specifications.

Third, does our statement afford a sufficient flexibility for transformations and for the development of the abstract meanings or "universals" necessary for science? Here, too, it serves the purpose admirably; for it will be seen to apply (as it stands, or with slight modification) to all types of chairs and to express clearly and adequately the essential character of *any* chair. It is just as "lawful" as any quantitative statement that could be made about chairs.

It will be seen that what we have been talking about in the above italicized definition of chair is a structure of contacts or encounters,—really, a *structure of dynamic ongoings and events*. Structure is not "quality"; and structure, not quality, is the best opposite term for "quantity." It is a lawful and highly general accompaniment of quantity. It plays a part in meanings, or in fact in phenomena generally, that quantity cannot do without.

We are by no means saying that quantities are not *also* applicable and present in connection with the (structured) meaning of chair. They, too, are necessary—let there be no mistake about that. There are sizes, weights, numbers, reflected wave lengths of light, and many other quantities that could be mentioned. Quantities apply also to a person, or persons, and to the number or energic magnitudes of their (defining) acts of sitting in chairs. There are even *some* quantitative implications in the statement of chair-meaning we have given above. Let us go even further and assert the obvious truth that *whatever* exists in some *quantity*. The important point, however, is that, although quantity is always present, there is another side of the picture, and that other side is equally valid. Let us look again at the definition of chair that was given on p. 515. If we did not have clearly in mind, and as objectively demonstrable, some such *non*-quantitative, event-structural statement of "chair" as is contained in this defining statement, *all quantities pertaining to chairs would be pure mathematical abstractions*. They would have no relevance to the work of empirical science. This would be true even if we employed a million quantities, but lacked the above specification of contacts or events and the "structural format" or pattern in which they occur.[26]

A little thought will show that this illustration, though developed with respect to a rather artificial cultural object, can be generalized to practically every isolable or self-delimited phenomenon with which

---

[26] The reader might perhaps imagine that by using a great number of quantities in various directions and of various magnitudes in space and time he could "delineate" a chair quite adequately. But the quantities so used would have to take certain directions and would have to "start" and "stop" at certain points in space or time. What is there in the concept of quantity or dimension, if taken *all by itself*, that could establish these points? What is there in *actual* quantities—but this is a foolish question, because actual quantities or magnitudes, without conceiving event-points to determine them, would have no operational meaning. Perhaps it will now be seen that the reason why we tend so often to think of quantification, measurement, and quantitative laws as the only important business of science is because we evade the very essential question of structures by merely *assuming* them. We think of them as "given," or we wrongly conceive that quantitative laws are the "architects" that make them; and that therefore we do not have to explain them or take them into account in our theories.

a scientist deals. Patterns of events always appear in the phenomenon, or between it and the operations that are necessary to define
it and demonstrate its existence. Non-quantitative, or "structural,"
meanings are both present and necessary in the descriptions of every
field of science. In order to produce a thinking-machine that handles
structure readily and flexibly, that "means" in this full sense of the
term, the inventor would have to be far more supple than he is at
present. He would need to endow his machine with many more
degrees of freedom than any known machine possesses. And he
would also have to go further and give it certain freedoms *that do not
come in degrees at all.* To be like an organism in the full sense a
machine must mean, and in order to mean there must be a setting
which affords an opportunity not merely for the operation of quantitative or covariation laws within a (given) structure, but for the structure itself to come into existence.

CRITIQUE CONTINUED:
BRAINS AS DIGITAL COMPUTING MECHANISMS

As for the explanatory value of cybernetics, we have noted its many
plausible suggestions with respect to abstract ideas, memory, and
perception. There are still, however, some deficiencies in these
topics; and the mechanisms projected for emotion, motivation, and
learning are conjectural. But in order to appraise cybernetic theory
as an explanatory system we need to stand back, as it were, and take
a more comprehensive and detached view. There are matters of
perspective and balance that need to be examined.

Let us go at once to the central idea of organisms, and particularly
of brains, as computing devices. We have seen, for example, the
part this idea has played in cybernetic contributions to perceptual
theory. In this whole notion we find another instance of our old
problem of the *inside* and the *outside.* What is it that computes?
Is it the organism or just the organism's brain? Cybernetic theory
stresses, and quite naturally, the latter. This way, however, lies
"encapsulation" and some very confusing issues. The brain now becomes the "inside" system; and the rest of the body becomes the
"outside," a region under the control of the central cerebral agency.
But does this not give us two levels of operation, the brain and the
organism as a whole? It is bewildering to contemplate that our
brains, in using calculus for solving spatial perceptions, have been employing practically from birth an advanced mathematical strategy
that "*we*" have had to acquire a college education to learn. Our

brains are far better educated than "we" are;—or their education is "inherited" while ours has to be "acquired." Furthermore, it is only by the exercise of the powers of calculus they already possess that our brains can get *us* to understand calculus. Since we assume that the brain operates when we do problems in calculus, and that there must be cortical events that represent the detailed elements of the problem, it would seem important to have some kind of safeguard against getting the two "calculuses," the "end-calculus" and the "means-calculus," mixed up. The action of the brain as a "molar" organ here seems to duplicate its finer constituent operations; the product of the machine is confused with the mechanism that produces it. We are reminded of Stephen Leacock's intriguing bit of nonsense which, in effect, runs somewhat as follows:

> The clock struck ten. Then it struck ten-thirty. Then it struck ten forty-five. Then it struck ten fifty-five. Then it struck striking.

If we are going to "double" ourselves in the matter of mathematical computing and have a calculator within a calculator, we may expect to be in the same predicament as Leacock's clock. This is all very confusing. Assuming that we know what a *brain* is, it is high time that we asked: "Who, or what, are *'we'?*" We can scarcely say we are our brains, nor can we say that we are not. We could not do our calculus without our brain; nor could our brain do its calculus without the rest of us. The engineer's computing machine is practically all brain; so it does not have this problem. But the *engineer* has it when he tries to explain the organism's thinking by mathematical computing-machine analogies. Let us try to get out of the muddle by giving up this dual agency and sticking to one integrated organism. It is the whole organism, therefore, or at least a pretty inclusively structured portion thereof, that learns to perform mathematical operations. The brain helps; that is, it is a part of the entire structural system. Somehow we must get the brain to acting as an integral part of a larger system in a manner much more integrated and interdependent than the way in which the computer is attached to a piece of machinery in order to control its action for the purpose of an operator who is outside the whole mechanical system.

After all, mathematics is a very sophisticated procedure, a part of our long-standing cultural inheritance, acquired through innumerable explicit environmental encounters by the organism, and leading to the acquisition of a set of logical and quantitative meanings. To introject these operations in their fully developed form, and as from birth, into the cerebrum seems a gratuitous enterprise. At the same time, the brain must contribute some intricate equipment and operations that are vital to the problem. We can well agree that the process *looks like* the "brain-solution" of problems by the use of logico-mathematical rules. It *looks as if* the brain is a mathematics-using machine. But perhaps it looks so because, with our particular educational background, this is the way in which *"we"* (as organisms, not brains alone) would operate in bringing about a solution of these problems. This is what we would do if we had to devise a way of using observable brain-mechanisms as tools for arriving at the solutions, just as Wiener did with electronic materials in his computing-machine design. It is one thing, however, to design a brain mathematically and another thing to prove that the design fits the brain of the organism that designed it, or that it puts mathematical disciplines as used by the designer into effect when thinking or perceiving goes on.

The slide rule will move and stop at places on the scale that we can read off as numbers involved in mathematical computations. But it could also simply push some object along that got in the way; and it would push the object along in direct proportion to the magnitude we are reading on the scale. In the latter case the slide-rule-object system could be operating *in agreement with* our arithmetical conceptions, yet not *through* any such conceptions. Our mathematical solutions in the use of a slide-rule would be based upon physical occurrences, but the physical occurrences would not be based upon the mathematical rules.

This purely physicalistic relationship, if we can carry the illustration into the nervous system, might be what constitutes the physiological basis of our sophisticated mathematical reasoning, both in general and about the brain in particular. "Nature," in other words, provides the physical occurrences and their interrelationships, and in order to conceptualize these occurrences we invent and employ a set of mathematical constructs. "We," of course, are a *part* of nature; but it is an open question as to whether "mathematics" occurs in the primordial workings of nature, as in the biological evolution of the brain, or is something that human beings with brains, also operating by natural principles, later work out. Do we not face once more the methodological problem of observer involvement discussed in Chapter 2? Ordinarily we would think that one who works with brains works very objectively, for brains are certainly denotable. But does the observer really work objectively when he reads into their operation the strategies that have become an inalienable part of his equipment as an organism and that he now also sees reflected back from a computing machine into which he himself has built them?

Admittedly, difficult logical and epistemological problems are here involved, and any sort of language used for straightening out our concepts is likely to become tricky.   Pitts and McCulloch have shown a liberal attitude regarding the question, pointing out that there are so many unknowns in the brain, so many possibilities of interchanging space and time distributions in the nervous system, and so many ways of drawing nerve-net diagrams that meet the cortical demands, that we cannot know whether we have the *right* explanation until the brain itself can be more adequately explored. The preceding analysis, of course, does not disprove the possibility that what we know from the machines to be mechanical or electronic calculating processes actually go on in the brain. The present plea is only for greater objectivity and an attempt to unite these problems with the whole field of scientific understanding, a realm in which information is not "just information," but also energy, and the units of energy concerned, although very small and adapted only to meeting threshold requirements that are already almost attained, nevertheless play their role, through structure, in the equilibrizing tendency or in the maintenance, in open systems, of a steady state.

In particular, it seems doubtful that the digitalization of information and its turning of energic quanta into signals of communication is a representative way to look at the operation of neural networks.   We see the continual intrusion of "analogical" principles into organismic circuits, the covariation of the quantitative aspects of structural parts proceeding directly according to physical laws. Cybernetists themselves have emphasized the circular or self-closing character of organismic aggregates. The switching, and its all-or-none basis, could be reconstrued into the role of an energic threshold for the coming into existence, or the raising of the level, of such physiological structures. This interpretation would involve fewer assumptions than making it a link in a mechanism of alternative choices under a set of logical rules.   For in the latter case we would still have to ask who, or what, makes the rules, a question which, though readily answered by the presence of the human designer for the machine, is for the organism unanswerable.

All-or-none action also occurs (phasically) in muscle fibers; and for that matter it probably occurs, in the sense of meeting the requirements of a threshold, in every organ of the body. Here is a widespread phenomenon that we do not fully understand. It seems to operate as the rather sudden rise, to a more macroscopic action-level, of structurings already implicit within the organism. The all-or-none reaction and the "bit of information" that sets the reaction off may represent the last increment of energy needed to raise a slightly sub-threshold, but still structured, manifold to full, self-closing operation (cf. the theory of perceptual set outlined in Chapter 16). In other words, the "bit" of stimulus-input may put into increased action not a single neuron-relay, but an entire dynamic structure of physiological events. Is it not possible that preoccupation with the machine and its switching relays has led to the centering of attention upon thresh-old in the all-or-none action of neurons and to the neglect of that principle in its more general occurrence? If, for example, we have only a linear chain of neuronic relays, where does it lead to? What ultimate entity receives and uses the information? If there is a *closed* chain, involving not only neurons but receptors and effectors, it would be like a last runner in a circuital relay race coming back to the original runner, thus completing a cycle that might continue to carry on in the same manner. In such a self-closed structure of events we would need no final receiving agent; and the notion of the "com-munication" or "relay of information" would itself seem inappropriate. Relays, as *thresholds*, would be seen as built into a structure that would have more meaning. Since the cybernetists do employ self-closing event-series in their models these last statements are not a criticism, but only a plea for a shifting of emphasis.

One interpretation, however, need not exclude the other when it comes to problems at a practical level. If both the energies involved in information and the working parts of the machine that are "in-formed" were reduced to their *elementary* units of energy, the digital and the analogical or physicalistic conceptions would probably merge into one. The "bit" of information would then probably be defined as Planck's constant of action, or as some multiple thereof. At that level the stream of discontinuities would be so fine that the continuous method of the analogue would be the only way of conceptually han-dling it.[27] To say that the brain, like the machine, gives an output similar to that which one would obtain under mathematical rules by computing sums, averages, or invariants, is a stimulating way of putting the matter; but mainly because it makes us very eager, the brain being what it is, to find out what is happening as this result comes about.

[27] For a fuller discussion of the digital versus the analogical properties of the nervous system see Von Foerster (ed.), 1951.

CRITIQUE CONCLUDED: MEANS VERSUS END PURPOSE; GENERALIZ-
ING THE FEED-BACK CONCEPT; VALUE OF THE
CIRCULARITY PRINCIPLE

We come, finally, to the question of teleology. Does the fact that
negative feed-back mechanisms imply the carrying out of purposes
really resolve the philosophical riddle of purpose versus mechanism?
Does it contribute anything fundamental to the explanation of behavior? The examination of this question may open new avenues of
psychological thinking. One of the appealing features of cybernetics, with its strictly denotational concepts, is that it is easy to discern the different features of the machine-system and to distinguish
their roles. It will be seen that there are two main features. If
either of them were taken away, or if they were separated, the feed-
back principle would not have its present meaning. First, there is
what we might call the *"main line production."* This consists of the
essential work the machine is doing and the product it turns out.
Power delivered by a shaft from an engine, the output-flow of products in a chemical plant, the propulsion of a missile in the general
direction of a target—these are characteristic examples. Second, there
is the *negative feed-back mechanism* that connects with the main production part of the system. Such a mechanism keeps the engine not
operating as distinguished from standing still, but operating at a
regular speed if and as it *is* operating. Or it keeps the outflow of
product constant granting that the basic arrangements of the rest of
the system are such that there *is* an outflow. Or again, it directs the
missile more closely to the target providing the missile has been given
the energy to go toward the target at all. There are always these
two subsystems in the total system: the main-line production and the
feed-back. We must not lose sight of this fact nor of the fact that
the two are distinct, even though they are always in some relation of
interdependence in their operations. While the main line production
subsystem *might* operate, though less efficiently, without the feed-
back subsystem, in order to speak of a *feed-back* operation we must
have *both* subsystems. Otherwise there would be nothing for the
feed-back subsystem to "feed back to."

Now the phrase "teleological mechanism" should refer, properly
speaking, only to one of these subsystems, namely, the feed-back
mechanism; for it was through the controlling or steering aspect of
this subsystem that its purposive connotation was established. But
we must remember that the *other* subsystem is also a necessary

feature of the system as a whole. The proprioceptive loop that "guides" the hand in picking up a pencil never operates alone. It must be tangent to a behavioral aggregate or cycle initiated, subjectively speaking, by the need to use a pencil *at all* and "closed" by the performance with the pencil of some adjustive operation. Turning to the machines, much has been said about purpose in connection with the *feed-back* subsystem; but concerning purpose as involved in the main production, even though it is necessary in order for the feed-back to have some ulterior but real purpose to serve, neither the cybernetists nor the philosophers have had much to say.

The reason is not far to seek; it is simply that *that* purpose cannot be found in the feed-back subsystem, and it really cannot be found in any part of the machine. It applies only to the organism that invents or operates the machine. The negative feed-back implies and expresses an *instrumental* purpose, but the operator has an *end* purpose, organismic adjustment, which is the *raison d'être* for the feed-back in the machine. If this were not so, a machine might keep on producing indefinitely regardless of whether a sufficient amount of product had been attained for the moment or not. Or, on the other hand, it might never have been started—nor even invented. There is nothing in either the feed-back subsystem or the main production subsystem of the machine to suggest or express this *end* purposive tendency. It is a property of organisms without analogy in the machine. Even if the machine were so arranged as to stop when a certain supply of the product had been attained, the full description or explanation of this fact would not be found in the machine itself, but would require some reference to an organism that had made such adjustments. For this reason, the concept of teleological mechanisms neither reaches the heart of the philosophical problem nor throws adequate light on the question of what role, if any, purpose plays in the behavior of organisms.

Northrop (*op. cit.*) has tried to provide cybernetic content for motivation and end-purpose by assuming that the "universal ideas" of Pitts and McCulloch, which have their machine-counterpart in reverberating electrical circuits, are their source. This explanation, however, fails when we realize that these universals are never wholly separate from or independent of some environmental source through receptor-input and that they are also affected circularly by the organism's output. They are, in other words, subsystems that play a part in the whole system, that is, in the life-adjustments of organisms. Unless they were thus constituted as substructures in the whole cycle of adjustment they probably would not have come into existence and would probably not maintain themselves. This statement is in accord with what we know of the process of learning. But by making the universals a part of the broader system of organism's behavior, wherein "end-purposes" and "motivations" are to be found, we thereby make them subservient to a process of end-purpose fulfillment already going on. They cannot, therefore, be the origin or explanation of that process. The same is true of feed-backs. In order to have a feed-back mechanism there must be something to feed back to.[28]

Turning to the application of the negative feed-back idea to organisms, we find a tendency to overlook this distinction. Though the omission is probably not intentional, organismic feed-back is discussed not in relation to something to be fed back to, but often as the entire process of adjustment itself. Half the problem is thus thrown away; or rather, it is smuggled in as something that feed-back, or "means-purpose," is capable of taking care of by itself, so that the resulting picture falsely resembles a "purpose within the machine." If, for example, we treat the homeostatic mechanism of heart-rate control merely in terms of feed-back, we overlook the cycle of events in the blood-stream, in the contact of fluid particles with the heart wall, in the automatic contraction of muscle, and so on, that make it possible for the heart to beat at all. The heart has to be "built" as a beating structure, integrated within a larger structure of circulation-events, in order for its *rate* of beating to be controlled. And so it is with the many aggregates that must be present in order that there can be homeostasis in the *amounts of their products* that circulate in the blood-stream. It is these event-structures that afford something for the negative feed-backs of the organism to feed back to; and, in the writer's opinion, they are the source to which the idea of end-purpose peculiar to organisms should be referred. Their pattern is different, however, from the main production line of the machine in that it is closed within the organism itself and does not need to include an outside agent to give them full operational (or purposive) significance. If these "production" subsystems of the aggregate were entirely absent we could perhaps have (though not in the organism) a feed-back loop feeding back just into itself. It would thus become merely a "self-feeder," that is, a reverberatory circuit standing all by

[28] Köhler has made a similar point in distinguishing between "having" a goal and the process by which that goal is achieved. We do not learn what *having* a goal means by the negative feed-back explanation, but only how it is reached. Köhler's discussion contains further criticism of cybernetic theory from the standpoint of gestalt psychology. See Jeffress (ed.), 1951, pp. 65 ff.

iteslf. But this is not the usual cybernetic feed-back idea, and to employ the term in this way would obscure necessary and useful distinctions. It is, moreover, highly doubtful that any organismic mechanism, even a reverberatory circuit, ever operates in so complete an "organismic vacuum."

It is probably unfair to charge cybernetists with any deliberate denial or neglect of these considerations. They would perhaps agree with this analysis of the feed-back principle. The issue concerned may be largely a matter of emphasis. But the reason why we insist on a redistribution of the emphasis may throw the whole matter of feed-back into a different perspective. Merely to illustrate the possibilities, rather than by way of any final or convincing demonstration, we shall take the liberty of launching on a *trend of speculation*. And here the writer will again call tentatively upon his own theory.

We have seen that some of the greatest contributions of cybernetics have arisen from their highly insightful development of the concept of circularity. In explaining further the characteristics of the organism it is now suggested that they could well take a leaf from their own book. The reverberating circuit and negative feed-back have achieved their strategic status because of the fact that they return upon themselves, either directly or through tangency with another subsystem, in a cyclical, self-closing manner. They are *circuital* structures of ongoings and events. The cybernetists could here go further in exploiting the resources of their own tools. We ask why they do not go back to that neglected feature, the main-line production subsystem, and try to conceive that also in the same manner, even though in order to do so they would need to bring the human operator into the cycle. So to conceive it seems at first hard because these production streams appear to be linear, or open-ended, rather than circular. Production systems have an input at one end and an output at the other. And in the organism, also, behavior is often seen as having a "goal" toward which it proceeds in linear fashion. It starts from the stimulus and goes through "intervening variables" to the response, and there it ends. We have seen considerable evidence, however, in our study of perception that there is a definite *circularity* in the arrangement of the perceptual aggregate when set and proprioceptive motor elements are taken into account, or even when perceptual behavior is described in terms of field-theory cycles of disequilibrium and equilibrium, or in the trial-and-check repetitions of the theory of hypothesis-confirmation.

Though the proof will have to wait for later statement, it is the writer's conviction that if we try diligently to describe behavioral systems as aggregates of denotable ongoings and events, rather than teleologically or in terms of functional agency, we shall *always* find that they have a self-delimited, self-closed, and circular character—and that this will apply also to all the *sub*aggregates within the organism. And the writer further believes that this same format of events will also be found, at a higher or more inclusive level, to characterize all collective or societal aggregates in which organisms operate, including the economic, political, and other systems in which men or machines play their parts. Furthermore, all these circularly operating structures may be conceived as interrelated *with one another* by exactly the same set of principles that enter into their individual construction and operation. This, in general, is the idea that we have tried inadequately to express by the phrase "dynamic structure of events" and to bring to bear, in one way or another, in the analysis of perceptual theories.

Consider for a moment the conceptual operation of such an "ongoing-event geometry." Instead of picturing the main-production part of the system as a straight line from input to output or from stimulus to response, and regulated by a circuital feed-back subsystem, we now have *two circles* (i.e., self-closed event-structures, not geometric circles, of course). The main production course of the system is not an open-ended series but a *repeating circuit* that goes from the energic upset or "need" in a manager or ultimate consumer for certain goods, extends through the operations of workers and the production line of the machine, and comes back eventually to manager or consumer where it reduces, through goods provided, the energic state (or need) with which it started. Instead of considering the negative feed-back as a loop that leaves a linear production axis at one point and returns to it at another, we now have *two* cycles, the main-production subsystem and the feed-back, that are "tangent" to each other at two or more points or regions. In cybernetics, these are the points at which the sensings and the interchanges or amplifications of energy as between the feed-back and the main line take place.[29] The picture roughly resembles two rings (but rings each of which is composed of a series of ongoings and intervening events)

---

[29] This, of course, is not the usual geometric meaning of tangency. We mean merely that the two cycles of events are "touching," so that events in one can produce or affect events in the other. It should also be noted that the production cycle of the machine is not closed in the machine itself, but extends to and includes the operator and even the events of marketing, consumption, and· industrial rewards.

that are placed in planes at an angle to each other and touching each other at common points in their circumferences. We can now see what *inter*dependence means more clearly than we could with the older feed-back model in which there was only one circuit attached to a linear production chain. Full interdependence requires *two self-closed structures* in double contact, not one structure in multiple contact with an open-ended line. Each of the structures can thus serve in some cases to augment the energies of the other, or, in other cases, to diminish them, according to the way in which they are arranged.

Suppose now that we generalize and also detail this schematization. Let us *mentally* rearrange the whole industrial plant both internally and in its outside societal relations, as well as the entire aggregate of the inner workings of the organism and the environmental aggregates which it contacts or of which it forms a part, in terms of these same self-closing and tangent structural principles. A great self-closing, dynamic system, enormously complex in detail, but equally simple in principle, now begins to appear. What we previously have called "feed-backs" and "main-line" are now seen in a new light; for everything that is in or related to the entire system is seen as cyclical or self-closing, or as larger and more inclusive cycles of such self-closed structures. All are seen in interstructurance relationships, and all therefore as interdependent and covarying lawfully in their quantities of action. The process is nowhere linear, but always cyclical. The former feed-back that seemed so unique is now only a detail in a more general picture of the same sort. "Feed-back" seems no longer an appropriate term, for there is no one definite linear agent or recipient to feed back *to*. Nor is such a linear recipient needed. All feed ultimately to all in a mutual energic interchange, or by a relationship of the inhibition of one cycle by another. The term "feed" is itself too specialized and figurative. Denotational and energic events of contact, encounter, or mutual negation, take its place. Linear agency and functionalism lose their significance as attempted explanations. The terms molar and molecular, as meaning levels of "bodies," seem no longer appropriate. A newly conceived type of law, a non-teleological and denotational paradigm of dynamic structure, comes into view. Quantities seem of necessity lawfully related, in a positive or a negative way, being viewed as the numerical aspects of the elements of related cyclical structures. Events of tangencies now take the place of information. The interoperation of tangent structures replaces the notion of regulation and control. Energic indices of interstructurance replace communications. All structures—not just those of central, universal ideas or memories—are capable of reverberation and become, to that extent, independent of time. The whole factory operation and the series of events from consumer "need" to consumer satisfaction are no less cyclical and no less truly repetitive than the operation of the feed-back in the machine or the reverberative loops in the nervous systems of the workers. Organization, both as to ends and means, appears to be inherent in the very nature of those quasiautonomous but connected structural manifolds. Function and structure are one and the same thing. "Means-purpose" and "end-purpose" are both accommodated; but the term purpose is no longer necessary unless someone might wish to use it as a synonym for all we have been saying.

And yet there is absolutely nothing that would commit us to concepts of the "mechanical" or "predetermined" in such a view. We have not been hypothesizing a machine but a "broad principle" that might underlie organisms, societies, and machines alike. It will be noted that we have implicitly rejected quantitative laws as the *cause* of the structuring process. They are, if anything, secondary to it. Concepts of "structural probability" will encompass causality. The picture we have presented above for the specific instance is not a fixed or permanent one. Specific structures are always coming into or going out of existence; there is always some flexibility and flux, and much randomness as well. It is only the "*laws* of structurization," delimiting and containing a persistent residue of negative entropy in an otherwise entropic universe, that might be regarded as remaining the same. These are the laws which, in the writer's opinion, we should now discover and try to formulate.[30]

The trail of circularity in the exploration of natural phenomena is an old one. It has emerged repeatedly and can be followed here and there in the thinking of philosophers, physiologists, psychologists, and social-scientists through many decades. The philosopher Hegel recognized the identity of cause and effect in a closed cycle. Bell, as early as 1826, asserted the circular nature of reflex activity, extending from the part stimulated through the nervous system and back to the same part. Lotze's local signs were based on a circuital pattern of activity. John Dewey, in his remarkably prescient article (1896) showed the importance of the principle for psychology, and Holt (1931) employed it in his notions of circular-reflex and reflex circle.

[30] The last few paragraphs, which will probably impress the reader as highly speculative to say the least, are here offered without further defense or elaboration merely as a preview of the writer's theory of event-structure and as a trend of thought toward which cybernetic theory constitutes a suggestive but incomplete approach.

We have met it a number of times in the modern theories of perception; and the contributions of modern neurology to this concept are, as we have seen, impressive.   The theme, however, has been temporarily obscured by the linear models of the associationistic behaviorists.[31]   The vigor with which open-ended chains from stimulus to response, with their intervening variable linkages, have been elaborated into mathematical models of covarying quantities and equations has all but eclipsed the view of behavior as a *circuit of events*.   But now the trail is seen again, and with conviction, in the concepts of cybernetics.   If it is the machines which have given this insight, so much better for the machines.

There is, however, a practical, ad hoc orientation in the designing of control-machines that tends to make means-teleology and functionalism, rather than disinterested study, a matter of primary consideration.   Such an orientation is both proper and indispensable for the work of the engineer; it spells material progress.   But there is a certain danger, if one is too closely committed to it, that it may also mislead us.   It may deprive us of what might be discovered if we take the attitude, also defensible, that the laws of nature, in the last analysis, may be such that they exhibit no concern for the particular schemes of mice and men.   The ignoring of this possibility has perhaps occurred with respect to feed-backs and reverberating loops.   The haste to make something useful out of them and the tendency to interpret them mainly in their functional aspects may have kept us from conceiving them as evidences, brought incidentally to our notice by machine-design, of what might turn out to be a more far-reaching and scientifically important principle.   In the writer's judgment the future contributions of cybernetists to behavioral and perceptual theory will be measured by the success they achieve in attaining whatever insights the machines may give them without losing, at the same time, their touch with the more general and disinterested aims of science.   Would it be out of order to suggest that they may need a negative feed-back to steer them on this narrow and difficult course?

SIGNIFICANCE OF THE CYBERNETIC CONTRIBUTION

We return from these flights of speculation to the sober workaday world of science, to the labors of those who are trying to piece together the fragments of the puzzle by the careful accumulation and sifting of facts.   Theories may be proposed by leaps and bounds, but

[31] Including the present writer in 1924.

their testing and their ultimate acceptance or rejection must proceed by slow and often painful steps. That the scientists of the cybernetic group have been working both with imagination and with care for detail should be evident even from this inadequate review. As must be expected, and as they themselves would be the first to admit, their models of the organism are as yet neither complete nor fully explanatory. Nevertheless they have made contributions to theory which are very significant. They have peered fearlessly into a region that has been closed to molar psychology, and with fresh resources and in new ways. They have given a fresh content to the system-viewpoint and a deeper meaning to the work of open systems in complex aggregates. By their work our store of clues as to how the nervous system may operate has been enhanced. Stimulating conceptualizations of psychological phenomena, including some of the aspects of perception, have been offered; and important principles of structuring, even if not fully developed, have been brought to light. Those who study perception will do well to take stock of these ideas and of the physiological hypotheses they offer. For it is conceivable that they may help to bring about a new day in the understanding of these long neglected foundations of perceptual theory.

As for the machines, cybernetists, generally speaking, are not over-enamoured of them. Their curiosities, like those of all students of the life-sciences, lie deeper. They acknowledge that really to know the organism we must study the organism. But automata also are creatures of nature, even if they are only "second-hand" creatures; and they too may be able to tell us something about the probable constitution of the natural world. In fact they have already done so. The development of mechanisms involving communication and control has been an indispensable aid to our great progress in the techniques by which knowledge is obtained. We should not allow sentiment to divert us from whatever more direct scientific lessons the machines may have to offer. Who knows but that some day they may be able to make in this direction a contribution even more significant than that strange mixture of blessings, complexities, and perils they have thus far brought to the human race.

19

The Unsolved Problem of Meaning
Perception of Object Character
and Situation
Critique of Gestalt Organization
Theories of Meaning

Our survey of representative theories of perception is now completed. Before we proceed with our summary, however, there remains one important task. We have shown that each of the theories took its origin in one or a few of the aspects of perception and developed its major concepts largely within that area. There is one basic feature of perception, however, which, though it has often been touched upon, has neither been fully explained nor considered in sufficient detail by any of the theories. It is the process by which one perceives the concrete character of objects and situations—the *meaning* that one experiences with respect to one's world. It is important to understand the bearing of perceptual theory upon this vital but neglected aspect.

To introduce the subject let us recall a fact familiar to every student of elementary psychology. That which is afforded directly by the sensory processes accounts only for a part of the way the world appears. We have tactual and visual experiences from a stone, combined with kinaesthetic strain sensations as the object resists our pressure. The total experience, however, includes "hardness," and this perceived character is a part of the meaning to us, though only a part, of the object we call a stone. Air waves emanating from vibrating strings can be registered upon the cochlea; but it is only when we "hear the sequence" that the experience we call musical meaning or "melody" comes into existence. If it is a melody we recognize, still further characteristics are added to the experience. And so it is with the perceiving of objects, persons, and situations in general. Percepts almost always contain an awareness of the identity and characteristics of what we are perceiving, a component of *meaning* that accompanies the bare sensory experience. They frequently suggest a continuity with our own past, giving us a sense of familiarity. Our house as we turn into it from the street, the desk at which we write, the objects upon the desk, the sight of a relative or friend, the sound of spoken words, the expression upon the face of an acquaintance, sitting in a familiar classroom, realizing that we are entering our place of business—all these and countless other experiences bear witness to the fact that purely sensory or abstract features such as shapes, intensities, and dimensions are continually being supplemented by a more concrete awareness of what the object *is* that we are perceiving.

These meanings, which we have thus far characterized only phenomenologically, must consist, in the objective or denotational sense, of a pattern of physiological and neurological happenings in the body, and largely, no doubt, in the brain. The capacity for such experiences is what is lost in the disorder known as agnosia, in which familiar objects are not recognized or the patient no longer knows what to do with them. In these cases there may be no paralysis; general motor and sensory functions may be quite intact. Probably there still remain experiences of extensity and segregation, primitive unity of objects, awareness of contours, and the like; but the concrete meaning of objects, and of situations in which the objects might be employed, is gone. The patient does not recognize an "apple," nor would he understand a picture showing a man buying an apple from a vendor's cart. To such a person the world must appear quite different from its appearance to the normal individual. From a genetic standpoint we would say that this aspect of perception is that which is first acquired by the infant through an endless scrutiny, mouthing, and manipulation of objects, and is later continually extended by increasingly complex reactions to the broader physical and social environment. The concrete object and situational character of percepts was one of the phenomena that classical theory had left for future theories of perception to explain. It has come down to us as the unsolved problem of meaning.

REASONS FOR THE NEGLECT OF MEANING BY PSYCHOLOGISTS

Perhaps the fact that perceptions practically always mean something predisposes one to overlook the problem. Meaning might be naïvely taken to be something like the air we breathe. It is perceived in reference to objects around us as we perceive their omnipresent aspects of size, shape, and hue. Meanings are sometimes thought to be immanent in objects and situations themselves; we do not originate them but only acquire them through "intuition" or "empathy." Anything so universal and inherent in the natural and social order does not seem to require a special explanation. Or to put it in another way, some psychologists have believed that meaning is something that lies not in the perceiving process but in the "object" perceived.[1] In some interpretations meaning takes the form of a metaphysical postulate, as in the universal dialectic of Hegel. Since meaning has thus seemed a term for philosophers to conjure with it may have been assumed that psychologists who aspire to be scientific should avoid it. Woodworth, however, recognized object and situational meaning as a basic feature of the psychology of perception when he wrote: "In ordinary life we see not forms but things, and our effort in sense perception is to know the objective situation. The set for perceiving objective facts dominates the receptive process as a whole."[2] A further tendency to avoid troubling ourselves about the matter might have arisen from the fact that nearly every concrete object or situation is "particular" and is, in some way, different from every other; whereas science is supposed to be concerned only with the general. Though it is true that science is concerned with the general, to apply the fact in this way is a misconception. We have general, or class, meanings as well as individualized meanings. But aside from that, even if every concrete meaning involved in every percept were totally different from every other, *some* meaning would always be present. The fact of the universality of concrete meaning is, in itself, highly general.

[1] Philosophical phenomenology, as represented, for example, in the work of Husserl contains the doctrine that experience is self-validating as to the reality of what is experienced (cf. Chapter 4). If the experience brings with it the earmarks of reality, then what is experienced is real. (See Helson, 1951, p. 364.) As applied to meaning this theory would encourage the tendency to give to meaning-content an existence in the object perceived "out there." An example is found in the gestalt concept of "physiognomic characters." The direct, or phenomenological, approach to experience gives us the meaning of an expression on the face of an acquaintance as something directly perceived. We do not need to "project" it from ourselves or derive its meaning by first trying to analyze the probable inner states of the acquaintance. Similarly dark clouds are perceived directly as "threatening," landscapes as "serene," and so on. It is to be noted, however, that gestalt psychologists themselves were not satisfied with this as the full explanation of meaning. They developed another definition to which we shall later refer.

[2] 1938, p. 624.

Still another reason why the problem has been slighted is its great subtlety and complexity. We know so little about the cortical process involved that speculation seems futile and even hazardous. How can we explain anything so evanescent and incorporeal as meaning? We know also that meanings may be unconscious, a fact that offers no help. In perceptual systems the term meaning has been used, but it has not been so defined as to cover the aspect we are here considering. It has been made equivalent, rather, to the particular interest or dynamic principle of the theory concerned. The problem was thus side-stepped, perhaps unconsciously, as psychologists turned to phenomena they were better equipped to handle. Configuration, frame of reference, constancy, dimensional attributes, and the effects of motivation seemed to offer better operational possibilities. So much labor and thought have been expended on these aspects that they have almost come to be regarded as the entire problem of perception. To follow an obscure trail that leads beyond these well-marked boundaries would seem like following a will-of-the-wisp.

Those who are committed to theories of perception without due cognizance of this aspect might be inclined to separate it by *fiat* from the more autochthonous features and to say that it belongs not in perception, but in some other psychological category such as inference, interpretation, cognition, or understanding. But is this distinction sound? A "desk," a "house," a "melody," "the class room," the "sad expression" on the face of a friend—these are certainly experienced directly in their characteristic meaning. The full experience includes, to be sure, their sensory figure and their dimensions; but it includes much more. Admittedly these objects all evoke past experience, associations, interpretations, cognitions, understandings. But they are also the way the world appears to us. Unless we use some prearranged technique or special set we do not segregate the *characters* of objects from the more autochthonous aspect of their sizes, shapes, or brightnesses, or from their continuation, closedness, or goodness of figure. The view that object and situational meanings are not a part of perception but belong exclusively to some other "higher" process can hardly be sustained.

Meaning, though it is found in perception, is far broader than the latter. Running through nearly all the psychological processes, it gives them a common aspect and a kind of unity. When there are no perceived objects before us we can still have meanings, as when we recall past experiences or picture present episodes outside our sensory range. Imagery is usually meaningful, so are dreams. We have abstract meanings as well as concrete. We communicate, write, and think in terms of signs or symbols whose very existence is dependent on meaning. Meanings are of the essence in all thought processes, as well as in all learning problems where some degree of insight is possible. Emotions (except possibly those of very young infants) cannot be named or defined without implying meaningful situations. Personality consists largely of the meanings that are characteristic of a particular individual. Aside from purely automatic habits and reflexes there is scarcely any part of the whole field of behavior into which meaning does not enter.

HISTORY OF THE PROBLEM AND THE SLIGHTING OF OBJECT-MEANING BY PERCEPTUAL THEORIES

Let us begin our re-examination of the problem in perception by going back to its treatment in the Wundt-Titchener school. First, we shall suppose that an observer, A, is describing his own awareness during an activity of perception or thought. We were told that A must be very careful to keep "meaning" out of his report in the sense in which we use the term when we speak, for example, of the meaning of a sentence. The subject must not interpret what he observes. He must not give a verbal recitation of his thought stream or the logical reasons for solutions he has reached. He must not tell what he perceives the object to be. Instead, he must describe the meaning he experiences without telling it. And in describing he must take only what the introspective act gives him as "existential" parts or elements of his consciousness, not some logical meaning he is conscious *of*. All this was simply a carrying over into introspective method of a strict rule of all scientific observation, namely, that the meanings of the observer *about* the datum observed must be carefully separated from the *description of* the datum. According to this method, then, it was implied that meaning might itself be described so long as we do it in terms other than those of what *the* meaning is. When A has a meaning he has something, theoretically at least, that can be described by him, as a conscious process, as factually and disinterestedly as he might report a taste sensation or the course of an afterimage.

The outcome of this program, however, in the hands of the introspectionists was disillusioning. When A tried to observe his meaning he found only the usual elements of consciousness—sensations, images, or feeling. There was no conscious content that corresponded specifically to meaning. Meaning was therefore said to be only a *relationship between* conscious elements, a "context" which one elementary experience (sensation or image) provides for another (Chapter 4). Since, however, a vast amount of meaning occurs in daily life whether we have any consciousness of it or not, the assumption had to be made that it rests upon some automatic action of the brain based upon previously acquired habits and directly evoked in response to stimulation from the environment. Meaning therefore was said to be "carried by" neurophysiological processes.

In defining meaning psychologically as mere context, and in failing to stress the importance of *investigating* the "brain-action" involved, the introspectionists seemed to reduce it to a subject of little importance. Since we believe that it is very far from being unimportant can we not find some approach that will be more rewarding? Such a possibility lies in the fact that introspection is not the only method of study that can be employed. We should not forget the viewpoint of the outsider, the one who does not introspect but observes the behavior and, if need be, the internal arrangements of another person. It is possible in principle, though admittedly difficult in practice, for an "outside" observer, B, to consider A's meaning as something for him (B) to observe and describe. Here again, B must steer clear of logical import and of any ideas that might form the rational content of A's experience. B's own introjected or empathic meanings must also be eliminated from the record. In such an *objective* approach to meaning, if one could make it, the method would be for B to try to observe the actual processes going on in A when A's meaning, as aroused in and reported by A, is occurring. Phenomenological or introspective data would not appear in B's description. Terms such as sensation and image would not be used, but only data that could be physicalistically observed and recorded.

It will be noted that this shift of attack is, in principle, fully consistent with Titchener's position that meaning can be carried in physiological terms. For Titchener, however, this statement signified that the subject had no further interest for the psychologist since a psychologist is concerned only with the descriptive analysis of conscious states. When, therefore, meaning was described merely as sensory or imaginal context, it was considered that the task of psychologists was finished. The tradition thus established, conveying the impression that we are here dealing with a logical abstraction rather than a psychological entity, has probably been largely responsible for the lack of progress in the study of the subject. Yet, as we have seen, the problem of meaning obtrudes itself in nearly every area of psychology, and Titchener himself was compelled to refer to it repeatedly only to explain it away as context or to relegate it to the physiologists in their study of brain action.[3]

Our present position, as stated above, removes the Titchenerian barrier between psychology and physiology. We know that a great deal goes on in the central nervous system that is not correlated with introspective observations. We would not, however, consider that the failure to find meaning as such in existential consciousness is a convincing argument that it should be treated merely as contextual relationship, or that we should regard it as of purely physiological rather than psychological concern. Meaning may well be, in fact, from a theoretical standpoint it must be, some aggregate of relationships and happenings within the organism. Our task now is to find out what this pattern of happenings is by the aid of such experimental ingenuity as we can muster. And in this effort we would naturally look to some plausible theory as a guide.

As psychology became more objective one would have supposed that experimenters would have become more concerned with this approach and that intensive experimental and theoretical efforts would have been forthcoming. This, however, has not been the case. In the field of perception, meaning in its important role as perceived object and situational character seems to have been consistently slighted, though almost every other aspect of perception seems to have been well considered. Psychophysicists studied thresholds and the relations of sensory dimensionality to the dimensions of the stimulus. Gestaltists explored field-like properties, configuration, and grouping; their theory was too formal to deal with concrete meanings. Cell-assembly and phase-sequence theory was limited, in explaining object-perception, to the aspect of figural identity. Adaptation level, sensory-tonic field theory, and probabilistic functionalism were concerned with scalable properties that fell short of describing what the object was perceived to be. Directive-state theory, though it worked with more concretely meaningful materials, was addressed not to the problem of explaining what is involved when one perceives a marginal stimulus to mean an object of this character rather than that, but of showing how values or avertive states affect the dimensions or duration-threshold of the meaningful object, or of predicting which of several possible meanings would be raised above threshold

---

[3] Compare Boring's salty comment (1938, p. 93): "By reducing conscious meaning to relations of conscious contents, he [Titchener] could assert that he had got rid of meaning by having a theory of it." This paradoxical situation, still prevalent, and the need of exploration of the problem in an objective manner comprise the theme of an able article by Higginson (1937).

level. The theory of motor adjustments, and perhaps behavior-theory, came a little closer to the problem, but other interests dominated; and cybernetics has had to omit it because of the machine-postulates of that system. The theories of perception tell why objects appear to be the *size* they do, or why they have their perceived *shape, brightness, slant,* and so on. There are explanations of *how quickly* and *how veridically* objects are perceived, and of the *constancies* of their various properties. But nowhere do we find a truly satisfactory explanation of why they appear like *what* they do. To return to our original example, one might say that the theories give some elaborate way of accounting for almost everything about the perception of an apple except the fact that it is perceived as an *apple*.

A TEST-PROBLEM IN OBJECT AND SITUATIONAL MEANING: CALLING THE ROLL OF THE THEORIES

Can the charge of an omission so serious as this be true? Perceptual theory has always operated against a backdrop of meaning from past experience without which it could never have been clarified even in the most elementary of classroom presentations. Do we not find that at least some of the theories, indirectly if not directly, have provided an adequate basis for the perception of object and situational character in their rationale? In order to explore this possibility let us consider an imaginary but plausible episode involving such meanings, in connection with which the theories can be tested.

The scene of our episode is laid in a two-story house with the owner living on the ground floor and another man living as tenant on the floor above. Four men appear in the driveway. Two of them stand looking at the front entrance of the house, while two place themselves near the back door. The tenant on the second floor, in his shirt-sleeves, is peering from behind window curtains at the men, going from the front to the rear windows of the apartment. Suddenly he turns, quickly puts on his coat and hat, runs to a window at the opposite side of the apartment, throws it open, lowers himself from the sash, drops into a soft bed of shrubbery, runs crouching behind a hedge surrounding the yard, and makes off rapidly down the street. Meanwhile the landlord on the first floor, thinking that the men are from a real-estate firm negotiating to buy his property, goes to the front door and invites them in.

If we use the term appears in a broad sense, we would certainly say that things appear differently to the tenant and the landlord. This difference, together with what is happening inside the two men when it occurs, is summed up in the one word *meaning*. We grant that the episode illustrates the perception of a situation more clearly than it does that of a single concrete object; but perception in the latter sense is also involved. Let us see how this phenomenon fares at the hands of the various theories. What explanation can we find in them for the clearly different meanings that characterized the perceptions of these two men?

It will probably be agreed that psychophysics has little or no bearing upon the case. Shall we say then that the tenant had certain "core data" of a sensory type (sight of the men outside), and so did the landlord, and that these two "cores" were largely the same but were supplemented by contexts of sensations or images that were different in the two cases? This account is hardly sufficient. In addition to sensations and images we would have to introduce "ideas" or "background knowledge" as part of the context. But to introduce such elements would be already to bring in meaning, which we are seeking to explain. (See also the discussion of context-theory in Chapter 4.)

Turning to adaptation-level, we note that the situation seems too closely bound to definite objects and their physical consequences to permit control of quantitative judgments through a shifting frame of reference. Of course, if the tenant had made a recent practice of dropping from windows within a range of different heights, he might say to himself that *this* drop is "not too long," or that it is "short," or "about medium." Though such a reaction might constitute a part of the total meaning, it would not have anything to do with the meanings involved in such crucial questions as "Why take this window to *drop* from?" or "Why drop from a window instead of going out of the door?" For a similar reason Brunswik's probabilistic theory will not greatly help us. It is true that the men outside the window do not seem materially smaller than they would if they were in the same room with the tenant. If they did, our subject might take retinal size as a clue to distance and judge them to be far away. In this case he might make his exit more leisurely through the door below. But whether he would make his exit at all would depend primarily not on a "size" or "distance" meaning with respect to the men, but upon evidences from their behavior that they were coming after him, that they were perhaps "detectives," and also the meaning that they might have some reason to come after him. Such meanings cannot be conveyed by dimensional constancies unless the dimensions can be translated into a degree of probability of some meanings already given. The case is similar with respect to transactional functionalism. *What* the object is, is a consideration that is employed in perceiving its size, shape, or location. But the "what" itself is more than any of these properties, and is left without explanation.

Sensory-tonic field theory might be invoked to show that incipient reaction tendencies, with corresponding changes of tonus in different muscle groups, were entering into the perceptual aggregate, and that these helped to determine how the world appeared to the two men. Here we seem to be getting on the track of something. The tenant is "set" for escaping and obtaining security, and the landlord is "set" to consummate a desirable sale of his property. One would have to be more explicit, however, than we can be at present in order to show *how* such tonic elements of the respective aggregates could make the men outside "look" like detectives to the tenant and like agents to the landlord. The difficulty here takes the following form. It can be generalized and will indicate why purely quantitatively established theories cannot solve such a problem as this. In the experiments upon which sensory-tonic field theory was based the dependent variable (change in the percept) was dimensional. The influence of tonic factors on the perceptual process was exhibited by such data as "how many degrees" the rod is tilted when the subject considers it to be vertical. Spatial considerations of side of the body were also involved. The independent variable also was treated only from an energic, spatial, or dimensional standpoint. No special character or meaning was experimentally assigned to the tone, the shock, the body tilt, or the acceleration. The question was only how stimulus conditions having a certain intensity, laterality, angle, or direction of acceleration affect the percept in dimensional and directional ways.

Our present problem, however, is not a dimensional one. We do not want to know how a tonus distribution (set to escape) can effect some spatial or quantitative attribute, but how it can operate with respect to the *perceived character* of the object. Though it is true that there are also dimensional considerations here, the character of the window as something that can be gotten out of so that one can get away without being seen is definitely something more than a point on a scaled dimension; otherwise a window-sized panel in the wall would do as well. We must provide a basis for the experience that a window when raised provides an opening instead of a glass pane, that between the window and the men outside there is an intervening house, and that outside the window lies the possibility of an escape. The window, the hedge, the house, the man's hat and coat,—all these carry with them bases of choice from which they enter the situation in a "yes or no," "all or none," fashion. They meet threshold requirements for certain meaning-aggregates or they fail to meet them; they play a part in this aggregate or that, or this part in one aggregate and that part in another.   It would be an error to suppose that these essentially non-quantitative features of perceptual meaning can be built up merely by combining quantities or dimensional indices, either phenomenologically or in terms of the neurophysiological processes involved.   Until a sensory-tonic theory can be devised that includes and accounts for empirical data of this sort it cannot be extended to phenomena of the kind we are now trying to explain.

Can directive-state theory help solve our problem? This view, also resting its proof largely on quantification, is similarly restricted. Even though we should agree that the men outside might be perceived *more quickly* or that the window might be perceived as *larger* by the tenant because of the relevance of these objects to his motivational state, we would be merely using object-meanings already familiar to the subject as materials upon which to substantiate a different hypothesis; we would not be stating a theory to explain those meanings or their mode of acquisition.   The subjective accentuation of an object is not its perceived character, but only a change in one or more of its dimensional attributes. Having the tenant manipulate diaphragms, if we could interrupt his precipitate exit for that purpose, would not tell us what we want to know.   Or again, to say that a certain object will satisfy a need is not to say what happens in the organism when such a need is experienced or when the suitability of a particular object for fulfilling it is realized.   The hypothesis-theory of Postman and Bruner tells us very little more; for this too already assumes meanings.   It does not explain the process by which hypotheses or objects *mean*.   Does the autistic branch of directive-state theory help?   It may be true that an organic condition, such as anxiety or fear, may predispose an individual to get one meaning out of a marginal stimulus rather than another.   But that a condition of this sort may not *necessarily* have anything to do with the case can be shown by imagining that the landlord, though he is in no way involved in the tenant's delinquencies, nevertheless knows about his recent past and has "tipped off" the police as a routine matter of doing his duty.   In that case these two individuals, having a background of the same meanings of prior events, but being quite unequal as to emotional or motivational state, might have identical perceptions of the meaning of the situation. This fact would show that the tenant's experience does not *need* to be based upon "autistic" involvement.   But even waiving this argument, an autistically determined choice between meanings would not explain the processes involved in meanings themselves.

Hebb's cell-assembly and phase-sequence theory, in providing an explanation of figural identity, comes closer than some of the others to concrete object meaning; for the contour and bounding points of an object are often closely associated with its meaning.   But it is open to question whether his analysis of the neurological possibilities underlying the perception and generalization of a triangle can serve as a model for the great range and complexity of the meanings perceived in common experience, or that associationistic principles will fully explain them.   In our problem of landlord and tenant we find situations involving some very complex human relationships.   What, for example, would be the figural representation of the meaning "detectives"?   How does the tenant carry around with him the meaning "They're after me"?   How shall we handle such items as "I must take my coat and hat so that I won't be conspicuous," or "By keeping that hedge between me and the men I can get away without being seen"?   Let us suppose, for example, that the tenant had forged a check.   The gap between the perception of a triangular figure and a meaning so complex as "the legal consequences of writing the name of another person on a check and of obtaining money for it at a bank by creating the impression that the signature is genuine" *might* be spanned by the concepts of cell-assembly and phase-sequence, but Hebb's demonstrations have not yet been carried to the point where the explanation is evident.

Hebb has presented his own account of insight and the "meaning of meaning" (1949, pp. 126–134).   The mechanism for the sudden perception of new relationships is explained, *via* context theory, by conceptual systems that have a "fringe of meaning" in contact with other elements.   These latter elements are also in contact with the fringes of still other conceptual systems.   Hence persistent activity in processes A and B, for example, may bring intervening process C above the threshold by facilitation, "and the sudden activation of an effective link between two concepts or percepts, at first unrelated, is a simple case of 'insight.'"   This account, however, seems more like a case of simple abstraction.   In situational insight of the type presented in our problem do we not have the necessity of showing how a *number* of such abstract principles can be integrated into a total aggregate?   This cannot be done by further abstraction, reaching a superordinate concept, for the component abstractions in a meaning are different and complementary, like a structure; they are not hierarchical.   And so Hebb's explanation does not seem to cover the problem.

Freeman's motor adjustment theory came still closer to the problem with its proprioceptive backlash from reactions to the object and its residuals from past learned reactions. The phrase "meaning structure" was also used by this author. Still, the definition of meaning given was more like that of generalized meaning than of the unique object and situational character which we need to explain the reactions of the tenant in perceiving his danger. "Ways of regarding" objects, also, is an explanation that is not specific enough to meet our needs. In behavior-theory Berlyne contributed something toward explaining perception by the use of the fractional anticipatory goal response. But here the stress was upon the reduction of the overt reaction, which, though it had a definite reference to the object reacted to (i.e., was a way of treating that object), failed to do justice to the sensory patterning involved. It is also conceivable that the escaping tenant could have had his perceptual meaning of the men and the situation of escape without having had the degree of overt training in that situation, or in a sufficiently similar one, which would be implied by behavior-theory. Tolman's sign-gestalt expectancy might be taken as a general theory of situational meaning. Cathexis was a term that he used to indicate the linking of field-expectancies with concrete objects as satisfiers of drives, or in cognitive interrelationships. While object-meaning was here involved, the denotational basis of the theory was weak. The theory also seems to have been limited (except for situational "cognitive maps") to "outside" meanings of the object (cf. the discussion of core-context theory in Chapter 4.) The tenant in using the window as a means of escape from the men was operating in a field of means-end expectancies. This circumstance gave meaning without doubt; but does it cover the concrete, "inner" meaning of window and man? Regarding cybernetics little needs to be said. In the preceding chapter we have discussed at length its failure to explain object-character in perception. The universals of Pitts and McCulloch are also too formal to meet the needs of our problem.

GESTALT THEORY OF MEANING AS ORGANIZATION: CRITICISM OF THE FIELD CONCEPT AS AN EXPLANATION OF THE PERCEIVED CHARACTER OF PARTS

Though all the theories thus far canvassed in trying to explain the meanings of the landlord and tenant have proved somewhat disappointing, we have kept our trump card until the end. Surely it would seem that *gestalt theory* must hold the answers. Was it not in just this sort of instance, where a sudden insight is gained into a total situation, that gestalt psychology made one of its most famous contributions?　Consider the case of Köhler's ape, Sultan.　Let us say that an imbalance, corresponding to hunger-need, had produced a tension in the animal's field.　There was fruit outside the cage; and the demand-character of this food, or the animal's desire to obtain it, also contributed to the tension of the field.　There were at hand two sticks that could be readily joined so that they would reach the fruit and enable the animal to pull it into the cage.　After some aimless fumbling in which the sticks happened to get joined together Sultan had a burst of insight and quickly used the new tool to drag in the fruit, which he promptly ate, thus bringing the field to equilibrium and removing the tensions.　Similarly, our tenant had a need to escape (emotional upset of fear).　There were the men outside, the window at the side of the house, the garden plot, the hedge, and the street.　He organized these features meaningfully (just as Sultan organized the stick, the bars of the cage, and the food) and got himself quickly out of the situation so that his tensions were relieved and his field brought back to equilibrium.　Except for the speed with which the organization was accomplished in the latter instance and the fact that reaching equilibrium involved a reaction of withdrawal, the manner in which the second case illustrated the gestalt principles was the same as that of the first.　A similar explanation applies to the landlord.　His desire to make a favorable sale of his property represented the upset in the field, and his going to the door and inviting the man in to discuss the matter comprised the parts of the field as it became organized. The gestalt model thus seems to fit the perception of the meaning of a total situation very well.　Meaning is equivalent to organization.　It is the relationship between the whole and its parts.　The term meaning has been further extended to apply to the experience of *insight* into one's behavior; for behavior with insight is an evidence of the existence of some manifest ego-field organization.　(Koffka, 1935, pp. 175–176, 382.)

Though this account of situational meaning has been regarded as very useful we shall find that it, too, involves some difficulties.　To understand these difficulties, however, we must launch upon a long and rather exacting analysis.　Let us first state the field formulation in more detail.　In the terms used by Köhler (1938) there is a "vector of requiredness," the phenomenological counterpart of a force, extending from the tenant and pointing to a position away from the house where he would be free from arrest.　A *negative* requiredness-vector extends between him and the men outside.　In Koffka's system, also, the notion of a phenomenological field was used.　Koffka called it the "behavioral environment." The "Ego," which Koffka treats as a sub-system within the phenomenological field, and the men outside, whom we shall call for convenience the "object," are parts of the field. The tenent sees both himself (Ego) and the object as in the field, and he experiences a tension (danger) acting as a repulsive force between the two. How can this felt repulsive tension upon the Ego be reduced? Obviously this can be done only in one way. It will be reduced and the field brought to equilibrium when there has taken place an actual, physical, separation between the individual (tenant) and the object (men outside). In other words, the tenant as a physical organism (not merely as an experienced "Ego") must leave the physical scene and must do so without being detected. To accomplish this there must occur suitable behaviors in relation to certain objects in the "geographical" environment (window, hedge, etc.). These behaviors will entail efferent neural impulses and coördinated muscular movements; and Koffka used the term "Executive" to cover whatever processes are here involved. The entire set of physiological reactions that constitutes the escape of the tenant are thus lumped together as the "work of the Executive." "Motoric" is another term used by gestaltists to cover this phase. When the Executive, or the motoric, has performed its function the phenomenological Ego will be effectively separated from the phenomenological object; the repulsive forces will have acted and will now be balanced by other forces so that the field of the tenant will return to a state of equilibrium. Or to express the matter more simply, when he is physically quite away from the scene the tenant will no longer perceive himself as threatened by the men outside.

As thus stated, however, the gestalt paradigm does not distinguish between the percept and the overt act. Our problem here concerns only the initial process or instant of perception of the situation. The tenant "sizes up" the whole situation in advance, including both the danger and the way in which escape can be effected; and this *initial process of perceiving the situation meaningfully* is what we have to explain. We might suppose that the work of the Executive in this initial phase comprises a smaller number of efferent impulses with only slight changes in muscle tonus, "tendencies toward" the appropriate movements rather than full, environmentally effective, movements. The arousal of these reaction-tendencies, then, with reference to the environment will bring the phenomenological field not to complete equilibrium, but *more nearly toward* equilibrium. The tenant "sees" the danger and how he can escape. We shall interpret this incipient equilibrizing tendency as being equivalent to meaning.

We have here then a conception of a phenomenological field enlisting in its service, in order to bring it to equilibrium, a series of physiological and physical events. In the rendering of this service we have an effect produced by those latter events upon the phenomenological field of such a sort as to balance its forces and bring it to equilibrium. This condition of affairs, in incipient or reduced form, we have regarded as the *meaning* of the situation. We must remember, however, that until some acceptable brain isomorph of the percept has been discovered the field must be conceived in terms that are wholly removed from those of the physical world: it must remain purely phenomenological. We would have then, under the limitations of our present knowledge and if the gestalt concept of the Executive were accepted, an interaction of mind with body, a two-way violation of the law of conservation of mass-energy. This is not permissible in any theory. It is clear then that if motor processes are to be invoked in the explaining of situational or object meaning, and it is hard to see how they can be omitted, gestalt theory is not yet equipped with the explanatory concepts necessary for dealing with the problem.

But granting that a suitable physiological isomorph for the percept can be found—the explanation would still be far from complete. We would have to translate the "Executive" into a more realistic account of the efferent, motor, and environmental happenings involved. It would need to be shown also how this phase is integrated with the physiological accompaniment of the objects as perceived. The patterning of efferent impulses, the series of coördinations or tonic changes, and their interplay with the environmental changes produced in the objects by the organism, to say nothing of the ever-changing retinal stimulations and their projections upon the visual cortex, must be very complex. It is not to be expected that any theory of perception could do justice to them in the light of our present knowledge. But the attempt to formulate them all under such a single oversimplified metaphor as "the work of the Executive" or the "motoric" falls short of being acceptable even in the light of our present knowledge.[4]

But there is a further difficulty in trying to explain the meaning of a

[4] Koffka (1935, pp. 625–626) and Köhler (1938, p. 358) both recognize the incompleteness of gestalt theory at this point. Hochberg and Gleitman are a little less diffident about the process, though still not dogmatic. They have developed the motoric theory as a system in which all motivation and goal-directed behavior are swallowed up, in true gestalt fashion, in the service of perception, that is, in bringing the perceptual field to equilibrium. Their article is well worth reading though certain problems are left unsolved. See Bruner and Krech, 1950, pp. 180–191.

situation by the use of the field concept. We must not forget that the cortical, neurophysiological basis of the percept must contain not only forces, but a representation of the objects that enter into the situation. The latter include, in our example, the isomorphs of the perceptions of the tenant, the men outside, the tenant's hat and coat, the window, and all the other objects involved. The situational percept that embraces all these taken together, including the organism's activities with respect to them, is what gestalt psychologists would call the *whole*. The experience of them taken individually would be called the experience of the *parts*. Situational meaning, which is said to represent the relations of the parts to the whole, would then be the work of the field forces that operate upon and between the parts (that is, upon the objects) to bring the whole to equilibrium. In other words, it is the work of the forces that organize the field. (We are, of course, referring here only to the field of brain processes that provide the forces between the brain-representations of the objects.) Not much has been said about the parts, or objects, as represented in the cortex, except to imply that they are what the forces act between or upon. Field forces, proceeding from the brain-isomorph of one object, or from that of the Ego, and acting upon the isomorphs of other objects, are made to carry the entire burden of organization and the meaning of the situation.

But now we are in difficulty. For when we check back from our theoretical model to the empirical situation we find that something was overlooked whose explanation is essential to the entire episode. We have neglected, in our brain-theory, to make any special provision for the *character* of the objects upon which the field forces act. It was simply assumed that the objects were represented in *some* way in the brain processes so that they could be acted upon by the forces of the field. No attempt was made to differentiate the characters of the objects (parts) or to relate the action of the forces to their specific characters. But it is not enough to provide merely for the meaning of the total situation (i.e., the whole). We must give a basis also for the meanings of the parts.[5] If this is not done, the tenant's activity of escape, and his perception as he sizes up the situation, cannot be predicted to occur. No whole will be organized and nr field forces will act.

If anyone requires any proof of this statement, let him imagine that

---

[5] It may be objected that the whole *determines* these part meanings or object characters, and so we do not need to consider them as crucial in the problem. The writer believes that this explanation is unsound. We shall return to the question later.

in place of the men outside there were statues, or that the "window" was really a solid panel in the wall. The entire situation would now be changed. In the first instance no tension or disequilibrium would be set up, and in the second the tension could not be brought to equilibrium. The solid panel in the wall will not do; the field forces, in order to act, require a *window*, or at least something having the object-character of an "aperture." Even if we suppose that the tenant actually tries to act as in the episode as originally related, we would be at a loss to understand his action unless we assumed that he perceived the statues as something other than statues, and the panel in the wall an an aperture. And this requirement would at once presuppose some cortical activities corresponding to these meanings that were related to the field-process as a whole. To account for the *actual* episode we have to assume that the men outside were perceived not only as men but as detectives. The garden below must be perceived as something upon which one can fall without injury. The window must have the character of something that can be climbed through, the hedge something that can be crouched behind, the street something that extends far away. Everywhere the perception of concrete object-character or "part-meanings" is necessary. Unless gestalt theory can show, in terms of the organism, what these part-meanings *are* and how they are connected into the total field of the episode, it will fail in the explanation of perception as related both to objects and to situations.

What then are we to do? We have used our field forces to explain how the tenant behaved (or perceived himself as behaving) *with respect to* the objects, how the objects changed their positions, and so on, as the total field was brought to equilibrium. Can we now use the same field forces to penetrate *into* the isomorphs of objects and account for their individual characters and meanings? If so, they are versatile forces indeed. Having started with organization of the whole as the explanation of meaning and having found that this organization *depends on* meaning (that is, the meaning of the parts), can we now turn about and account for this latter meaning by organization? Could the whole, that is, the entire field of forces acting upon or between the objects, as some gestaltists claim, have *given* these parts (or objects) their meanings? If so, how did they do it? Or do we have separate smaller, internal, sets of forces for the objects—fields operating within fields? How, in this case, would all the forces, inner and outer, interact to produce the total effect? The reader will here recognize again our familiar problem of the *inside* versus the *outside*.

It might be argued that there is really only one field. The "inter-object" and "intraobject" forces, determined externally by the relationships within the environment, combine vectorially in the cortex to produce an equilibrium of the entire field. The "field within the object," in this view, would represent only a special density within the total field. This interpretation seems in accordance with Köhler's brain-field theory. As the whole "unified" field comes to equilibrium the subject would *ipso facto* be attaining the perceptual meanings both of the total situation and of the objects entering into the situation as parts. There are, however, strong objections to this view. The process of equilibrizing the total field cannot be the means by which perceptual meaning comes into existence for the parts because the parts already have some meaning before the total situation becomes organized. This fact is implied by our earlier recognition that the meaning of the parts is necessary for the meaning of the whole; and it will be later pointed out that these meanings, even those which are necessary to the organization of the whole, have existed *prior* to the organization of the latter, that is, they have been experienced in earlier times and at other places. The object therefore must have a separate field that can come to equilibrium by itself and is not dependent upon its relation to the larger whole. We are thus led back to the untenable assumption of a separate smaller field acting within the space and time preempted by a larger one, yet having the action of its forces at least partly isolated from, and independent of, those of the surrounding field. We have here an analogy to the problem that Einstein (1950) has been trying to solve, the problem of bringing the field *within* a particle into the surrounding or total field. Einstein's solution, however, should give pause to the psychologist who attempts the description of behavior *via* field-theory logic. For what has happened in his solution is that the particle itself loses its fundamental significance and becomes only a region of greater field density. By analogy, the unification of the psychological field might mean that we would have to sacrifice the distinctness or identity of the objects within that field. Brunswik has wanted to write a psychology primarily in terms of objects; now we must contemplate a psychology without *any* objects.

Thus far we have considered only the present, or spatial, distribution of the perceptual aggregate. It is equally important to consider its temporal aspect. In order to deal with the episode it is necessary to include in our account some past events. This cannot be done literally, of course, since these events occurred at an earlier time. Some of their effects, however, must be assumed to remain in the organism. Their "meanings," acquired at the earlier time, must have carried over. Such past occurrences, for example, might have included the forging and cashing of a check the day before by the tenant. This earlier situation also breaks into objects or into smaller situations. There were the check, the pen, the signing, the cashier, the conditions of deception, and so on. We can readily conceive that a field of forces was also in operation here, and that an organization of this earlier whole occurred. But again, those forces and their organizing action could not have occurred were it not for the concrete characters or meanings of the objects involved. Now that they *have* occurred we find that the perceived concrete character of this earlier situation persists in the tenant and constitutes one of the items, or parts, that must now be taken into account in predicting the present meaningful whole.

In gestalt theory such past happenings are considered to be represented through neural "traces" that continue as the present field and add their forces, as vector components, to that field. So far, so good. But we need to know what they are traces *of*, and more particularly how the fact that they are traces of one specific past experience and not of another now enables them to contribute to one specific field-configuration and not to another. The blanket notion of vector components is not enough. The landlord also has his traces. Perhaps he has acquired a stock of meanings through a call at the real-estate broker's office the day before. We see that in the temporal as well as the spatial aspect the concrete-object and situational character must be considered. It is their particular aggregate—that is, *what* meanings go into the assemblage for the *landlord* and *what* meanings for the *tenant*—that constitutes a difference in the way the world appears to these two men. It is not enough, therefore, to say that meaning is given by the organization of the whole, unless we surreptitiously bring into the organization of the whole the suborganization of the parts. And we have seen that if we do this, problems are raised with which field theory at present can scarcely deal. In order to achieve organization we must have things to organize, and these things, which are the parts and not the whole, must *already* have some meaning. Meaningless things (if there are any) cannot be organized. It is not enough to say that the meaning of the whole is different from the meaning of parts. We must find some procedure that will enable us to say, in terms of the organism, what the specific meaning of whole *is* and *what* the specific meaning of the parts *are*, and to link the two together in some unified system.

It is the peculiar limitation of field theory that it cannot help us in this task. Its forces must act upon points, or at least upon characterially undifferentiated elements; they cannot be made subject to forces from within the elements they act upon without confusion or loss of the object as a definitive entity. The stipulations of field theory are presented in terms of brain forces acting between brain-representations of objects or parts of objects; they are not given in terms of the character of objects or their parts. Forces are uniform in nature; and they are all either attractive or repulsive. They can differ from one another only in magnitude and vector angle. Objects that are to be integrated by those forces are unique. They can differ from one another in innumerable ways; and their differences can never be entirely expressed in terms of scalar or vector magnitudes. An insoluble problem therefore arises as to how these non-quantitative features of concrete object-character can have their characters represented in a field of purely quantitative and spatially directed forces and brought to bear upon other object-characters in such a way as to produce a meaningful and characteristic whole.[6]

GESTALT THEORY OF MEANING CONCLUDED: ANALYSIS OF THE WHOLE-PART DOCTRINE; ORGANIZATION IN DEPTH

The preceding discussion has centered about the field-theory aspect of gestalt psychology. It will be remembered, however, that gestalt theory has also much to say about wholes and the determinative action of the whole upon its parts. Leaving for the present the terminology of the field, let us canvass the possibility of accounting for the meaning of concrete objects by the gestalt theory of wholeness and the organizing influences that are said to be exerted by the whole. This doctrine has been, at least in the past, a central one in gestalt theory. If the concept of determinative wholes can be made to account fully

[6] It might be maintained that Köhler has solved the problem. In his electrical fields in chemical media in the cortex there are no forces between objects that do not emanate from (or form a part of the field of) the brain-representations of the objects themselves. The fields of percepts in the brain have the non-quantitative feature of a geometric shape corresponding to the environmental objects from whose stimulus-energies they arise. Hence such a characteristic, for example, as the shape of a perceived figure can act at a distance (through its field) upon the shape of another figure. Aside, however, from the fact that this theory still needs support, the difference between the formal effects it contemplates and object and situational character as we have here defined it is obvious. Furthermore, these effects have not been provided with a clearly understandable connection with the motor system of the body, a provision that might be important in explaining the perceived character of objects. Cf. Chapters 5, 9, and 16.

for the perceived character or meaning of the objects which are the parts, gestalt theory can then be considered as providing a satisfactory solution of our problem. .

A corollary to the preceding discussion should first be noted.   If, as we have previously maintained, object-character, or meaning of the *parts*, is necessary in predicting situational character or meaning of the *whole*, it should follow that the former must not be wholly dependent on the latter.   It might be expected to exist apart from the present situational whole, in its own right, at other times or places. We might expect the object-meanings to have been in existence *prior* to this whole, that is, as a result of earlier experience.   And that, in all probability, is what we would find.   Of course, each of the objects has a number of possible meanings.   The window is something that can be decorated, or can let in light or air, as well as something that can be climbed through.   Men have many object-characters beside the possibility of being detectives; and similarly for all the objects in the episode.   But in each case the tenant could have acquired, and probably did acquire, the ability to perceive these object-characters, including meanings that were employed in the present situation, at previous times and in other places.   They had for him an existence independent of the whole we are now considering.

Suppose, then, it be granted that the meanings or object-characters of the parts do enter into the picture and that in the work of organization they must be taken into account.   Let it also be granted that these meanings were not originally given by, or dependent upon, the whole we are considering.   These concessions, so it might be argued, still do not prove that it is necessary to introduce any principle other than the organization of wholes in order to account for part-meanings.   For if the tenant did not learn the meaning of the window as an aperture that could be climbed through in *this* situation, or whole, he undoubtedly acquired it as a part of some other, previously experienced, whole. And so for all the other part-meanings concerned.   In each case there was, at some time and place, a total situation or field that was brought to equilibrium; and in connection with its coming to equilibrium the percept or meaning in question was attained.   Organization of a whole will always be found to have been present when the meaning of a part appears; and so, after all, organization of the whole is the one and only basic principle to be considered.

The writer agrees that organization is universal in experience.   The establishing of that fact is one of the great contributions of gestalt theory.   But he does not accept the conclusion drawn from this premise.   It is admitted that organization is always present when meaning occurs.   But it may be organization of (or within) the parts, as well as organization of the whole. If one accepts our claim that the meaning of the part (object), a meaning now employed in the organization of a particular whole, does not ever need to be dependent for its acquisition or existence upon the organization of *this particular whole*, it would follow that *no specific* whole-organization can be considered as the necessary and sole condition of the meanings of its parts, including the part-meanings that are relevant to that organization. If we trace a part-meaning back to its prior appearance in some earlier occurring whole-organization, we are not obliged to infer that it was "given" or "caused" by that earlier organization.   We might continue to pursue the part-meaning indefinitely from whole-organization to whole-organization without ever being able to anchor it to any one necessary whole.   We only know that whole-meaning and part-meaning, in a general though not a specific sense, are always found together; we have no evidence for concluding that one is logically or causally *prior* to the other.   By tracing the part-meaning backward genetically we could not show that some *original* whole had been its "cause," even if we could find the whole in which it first appeared.   Since parts and wholes always occur together, it would be just as logical to say that there is something about part-meanings which leads to the production of a whole, that is, the parts have an organizing tendency; though in reality neither of these interpretations would be justified.   We thus reach the following conclusion: The argument from a general principle of organization, that is, from the universality of organization in all experience and from the fact that meaning is never present without it, even though such a principle is valid, cannot be successfully invoked to prove that the organization of any whole constitutes the cause and the entire explanation of the meaning of the parts of that or any other whole.   Hence the attempt to prove that the wholeness concept gives a complete accounting of the perceived character of objects within a larger situation fails.

But instead of pursuing the part-meaning from one organized complex to another, the proponent of meaning-determination by wholes might take another course. He could take the same whole with which we started, but break it up into its parts, treating the parts as new wholes.   This is the so-called reductionist method.   In the case of the escaping tenant we have as parts of the total situation a number of objects: the hat and coat that were seized, the window that was thrown open and climbed out of, the garden, and so on.   Each of these parts, in combination with the "part-reactions" toward them, has some meaning of its own.   Let us then consider these parts in complete separation from the whole.   It may now be contended that in conceiving them in this fashion we can no longer regard them as parts; they are now wholes in their own right.   With respect to the present total situation they constitute "subwholes."   Each of them in turn would have its smaller parts.   Thus a man's face is perceived to have eyes, nose, and mouth; a window has frame, sash, and pane, and so on.   It is the work of organization acting upon these smaller parts at the level of this new and less inclusive whole that gives meaning to the object that constitutes this new whole.   And this meaning is carried over when that whole becomes a "part" in the larger whole. Hence again, organization confers meaning and can be claimed as the sole and sufficient principle behind the meaning of both object and situation; though this time it operates at a lower level in the whole-part hierarchy as well as at the higher.

This argument appears sound.   That it will not do, however, as a support for the position of determinative wholes is immediately seen when we realize that each of the parts of the *subwhole* (e.g., the eyes, nose, and mouth that make up the " face") will again have *some* meaning that can readily be experienced when they are taken in isolation from the *sub*whole, even though it is not the meaning they have as features of the face.   We shall thus have to regard these new parts as sub-subwholes and proceed all over again.   We can continue the process as long as any perceivable subwhole remains.   No matter how small it is, it will still have *some* meaning, and by hypothesis that meaning must be explained as the organization of its still lesser components.   But by this regressus we can never arrive at a position where we have one original or ultimate whole that is the sole source of meaning.   The failure of reductionism to establish an utlimate determinative whole was early recognized by the gestaltists.   Koffka himself counselled against the use of the subwhole concept.

Because of this relativity of part and whole to the level at which the observer is perceiving, the gestalt doctrine of whole-part relations is on treacherous ground.   It is true that in perception a certain wholeness-level, for example, a face or a figure-drawing, usually commends itself to us as something to be perceived more than would one of the parts, such as nose or mouth.   We tend to perceive in terms of the most inclusive but clearly delineated wholes.   This fact, however, does not prove that the parts (for example, the separate features of the face) are not continually entering the percept to provide elements necessary for its total meaning.   That they do so enter is apparent. An alteration of the parts, and not merely the change of the relations between them, may produce a decided change in the meaning of the whole; and if the alteration is great enough, it may result in a complete disruption of the organization. Unless the features are seen as having the topographical aspects peculiar to eyes, nose, and mouth, the total configuration is scarcely recognizable as a face. Unless the nose is perceived as having holes (nostrils) and a septum, it might not be recognized as a nose except by the habit of position among other features that are identifiable; and hence it could not contribute to the meaning of face. Similarly, into the perception of eyes there enters the awareness of lids, iris, and so on. All of these characters, including details of the features as well as the features in their entirety, must be present in giving us our normal perception of a face. *More than one wholeness-level is required.*

To pursue the argument further would seem an injustice to the reader. Yet to be fair to those who might wish to take a more extreme position regarding wholes, we must give them a chance to be heard. To them, in spite of what has been said, it would probably seem that the organization of the whole, and that alone, can confer meaning upon whatever is organized; and they would look to *the whole that is organized at the given moment* as the source of the relevant meanings of the parts. They would not look to any other whole, either elsewhere or earlier in the subject's life. Contrary to our former supposition, they would say that the forces of organization do not build upon previously established or "isolationist" characters of the parts. In every case the organization of the whole produces such meanings as properly belonging to that whole *de novo* and "from the ground up." And we must not look to "subwholes" for an explanation of meaning within the whole: at every level the whole creates its own part-meanings uniquely and expresses itself through them. There is an emergent succession of unique wholes. It may be even said that the whole is *prior* to its parts! Such is the doctrine of determinative wholes in its most radical philosophical form. We shall call it the "*extreme* gestalt" position. The crucial propositions we must test in evaluating this theory are these: When we consider the meanings that the parts have as participating in the organization of the whole we shall see that none of these meanings is built upon, or selected from, the meanings the parts possess when experienced separately. And conversely, no meaning possessed by the part when it is observed separately is employed by, or necessary for, the whole in its work of organization. This forthright position seems to be the last stand of those who maintain that concrete object and situational meaning can be fully explained by the organization of the whole. If its claims can be sustained, the character of the parts as well as the role they play within the whole can still be explained by the principle of whole-organization.

Let us consider first the example with which our discussion started. In the case of the chimpanzee, Sultan, an earlier acquired meaning of sticks to be used as reaching objects, or at least as things that extend "from here to there," may be presupposed, also the prior meanings of "fruit to be eaten" and "bars of a cage that can be reached through." The branch of a tree broken off by a human being or an animal to use in reaching food does not, of course, illustrate the common perception which the organism probably has of a limb. It is required that the branch be perceived in a special way in order to have meaning as a part that is relevant to the whole. But this meaning (linear extension) was probably learned for other objects having some of the characteristics of the limb prior to the organization in which it now plays a part. Contrary to the extreme gestalt position we must contend that there probably existed some prior meanings of the parts outside these present wholes, meanings that were employed by, and necessary to, the organization of these wholes. What we notice is that these meanings seem to become more *intense* or *vivid* to the animal through their relevance to the present situation. They are "selected" from a number of alternative meanings of the objects representing their possible uses for other purposes. To say, however, that they are produced *de novo* by the work of organization of the particular whole in which they appear would be false. In the case of the escaping tenant it has already been noted that the object-meanings relevant to the situation could have made their appearance in other, previous, episodes. The perceived properties of a window that could be "climbed through" and of a hedge that could be "hidden behind," though they were rather unusual and though their recognition was called into play by the requirements of the present organization, were not dependent upon that organization for their existence. Though it is again true that "special" meanings were selected and rendered more vivid by the work of organization of the particular whole, that work of organization was not the cause (that, is the sole and necessary condition) of those special meanings; nor did it produce them *de novo*. The most we can say is that it "employed" them. Would it not be the same with insight into almost any problem-situation?

The strongest evidence in support of meaning-determination by wholes, however, seems to lie not in these instances of insightful, manifest organization, but in the "silent" organization familiar to us in figure-drawings, illusions, and similar demonstrations. In these con-

figurational phenomena we perceive continuation, separation, grouping, distortion of line, angle, or area, contouring of figure, relief, shifts
of perspective, illusory motion, rhythm, and many other subjective
effects.   These are often so striking that we are inclined to attribute
almost unlimited powers to the action of the whole, through its forces
of organization, upon the parts.   But even in these cases it can be
readily shown that the parts have characters or meanings of their own
that persist in the whole and are, in fact, necessary for the whole.   A
single line, all by itself, has the meanings of extension and continuation.   It is also "finite"; no line extends indefinitely at either end.
The meaning of "terminal position" is therefore conveyed to us by a
single line.   Dots, discs, and areas that sometimes form parts of
wholes are likewise perceived as "space-bounded."   Lines have also
the meaning of a dimension of length.   They may also have "zero
curvature" (i.e., be straight) or possess a degree of curvature greater
than zero.   Slant is also a property of every line and will be perceived
regardless of whether the line is part of a figure or not.   Then too,
every perceived stimulus element has some "duration"; it also has
some "quality," and one degree or another of "intensity."   It is clear
that all of these perceived properties, or meanings, can exist in these
elements prior to the joining of the elements into some larger configuration; they also exist after the whole is dismembered.   Hence
they are not produced by, or dependent upon, the whole.   So much
for the first step in our demonstration.   The parts which are used
in typical configurational experiments do have independent characteristics and meanings.

We must now ask whether any of these part-characters or meanings
persist as relevant parts when the whole is formed, and whether the
organization of the whole, in achieving its striking whole-effects, in
any way employs or builds upon these part-meanings—that is, we
must inquire whether the part-characters are *necessary* to the whole.
In order to prove the contention of the extreme whole-determinist
these questions must be answered in the negative.   From the standpoint of the facts they are answered in the affirmative.   The part-
characters are certainly relevant to the whole, since what the forces
of whole-organization do in producing their effects is to bring about
some alteration in these characters; and one cannot produce an alteration unless one has something to alter.   Thus the forces of whole-
organization may *expand* or *shrink* the "extension" of the line, changing its perceived dimensional character of "length."   They may
increase its "curvature."   They may *accentuate* or *suppress* its "continuation."   "Line-slant" and "area" are also used through the process

of altering or distorting them in many gestalt figure-drawings. "Extension" is a basic property underlying the effect of figures involving perspective. The forces of organization everywhere exploit the fact that lines, dots, and surfaces are "finite" or space-bounded. This characteristic, together with those of "termini," "quality," and "intensity," are used in the production of the phi-phenomenon. "Boundary-lines" are made to appear as *contours* in figure and ground perception. "Qualities," "intensities," and "finiteness" are put to work under the influence of suppression or accentuation in rhythm; and where the rhythm is auditory, "duration" is also employed. Contrast effects would not be possible without "intensities" or "qualities" to contrast.

In every instance the forces of organization of the whole employ and build their effects upon the characteristic properties or meanings that are already in existence in the parts. In no case do they create or produce these part-characteristics *de novo*. It is also clear that unless these part-characters were present for the forces of the whole to work upon, the effects of the whole could not be produced. *There would, in fact, be no whole.* It is no answer to say that the subject is not directly conscious of these part-meanings and does not separate them from the total effect which includes the modifications superimposed upon them. We know by this time that it is not necessary to be conscious of meanings in order to have them; and the gestaltists themselves have shown that analytical or piecemeal introspection, used in order to bring some particular element or aspect into consciousness, is not a method that should be forced upon the subject. Though he may not be "aware" that the part-meanings are playing an essential role in his perception of the whole-character, the negative-causation test (pp. 76–77) would show that this is true.

It is far from our intention to minimize the important effects that are produced when parts of the whole are brought into relationship *as* a whole (that is, when the forces of organization of the whole are said to act), or to detract from the brilliant work of gestalt psychologists in demonstrating these effects. No one can deny that through whole-organization experiences that are unique and striking appear. The contributions of gestalt theory on this important point will probably stand for all time. All we are saying is that the contention of the extreme whole-determinist that the whole produces or creates *de novo* the characters of the relevant parts, and that none of the previously existing characters of the parts in isolation are employed in the formation of the whole or are requisite to its meaning, is contradicted by the facts.

By approaching the "extreme" gestalt position from still another angle we can be brought to see some of its consequences; and this will lead us to something that is more important, namely, a view of an entire dimension of organization that has been overlooked. We have agreed that organization and meaning go hand in hand. We also accept the universality of organized aggregates (*gestalten*) throughout perception and in nature generally.[7] What we are endeavoring to show is that organization and the meaning that accompanies it must be considered as operating in the part as well as the whole and must be pursued not at one wholeness-level alone, but in every whole-part relationship, or level, that enters into the situation with which we are dealing. In contrast with this view, we have been examining the position we have attributed, perhaps without justification, to the "extreme" gestaltist. It does not greatly matter at this point whether such a person exists or not, or how many would espouse the doctrine we have been criticizing. The theoretical position itself is useful in providing an *entree* to some broader considerations. Let us then try to develop further the view, opposite in character to the one just given, that *might* be held by an advocate of that position.

To be consistent such an advocate would have to assert that when we take a given whole we must *keep* that as the whole. The wholeness-level must be constant and single in every act of perception that we are engaged at the time in explaining. We must not have any traffic with subwholes or shift our ground from one whole to a lesser, *included* whole; for that procedure would be equivalent to conferring the powers of wholes upon what are really parts. It would undermine the basic doctrine that the whole produces the relevant meaning of its parts, for it would break down the distinction upon which that doctrine depends. Any given aggregate must be either a part or a whole, it cannot be both. And we must not admit whole-organization, or *any* organization that is relevant to the operation of the whole, into the separate parts as their own possession. This position must be rigidly maintained or the doctrine of complete whole-determination will be rendered meaningless. Wholeness and whole-organization are thus accepted at one level but rejected at any other.

If the patience of the reader will permit us to take one more look at our tenant who is peering out of the window and seeing the faces of the men outside, we can come directly to the point. Let us say that the tenant perceives on these faces a sinister, threatening look. This part-meaning, the extreme whole-determinist might say, is rele-

---

[7] Later in this book the concept of organization and "forms" will be replaced by a more explicit theory of structure, and the universality of the latter and its relation to meaning will be discussed.

vant to the total situation (whole) and it is produced entirely by that whole through its work of organization (in field terms, through the coming of the total field to equilibrium). The whole determines the character of its relevant parts. An important point, however, has been overlooked. Each of the faces, all by itself and apart from the sinister expression, has, to the tenant, a certain object-character or meaning. It is a "face." Furthermore, it has a wholeness and unity of its own quite apart from its role in the whole that constitutes the collective situation. (At the wholeness level of the face, the eyes, nose, mouth, etc., become the parts.)   Now it was only by the device of leaving completely out of account this wholeness level of the face with its own characteristic meaning, and by clinging to the situation of the entire episode (escape-situation of the tenant) as the one "true" whole, that the extreme gestaltists could assert that the latter whole, through its organizing forces, is the sole determiner of the relevant meaning of its parts, that is, in this case, of the sinister expression. For obviously, as soon as we look more carefully we see that this part-meaning of sinister expression on a face was determined not only by the total episode, but by the perception of a face upon which a sinister expression could be seen. This perception of a face, as a face, certainly did not depend upon the perception of the total situation by the tenant. (The landlord also saw what the tenant was looking at as a face.) It constituted therefore a whole in its own right in the same way that any parts that can exist independently of some larger assembly are themselves wholes.

In terms of gestalt theory the perception of a whole is produced by the forces of organization that constitute, or are proper to, the field of that whole. Hence the forces of organization upon which the perception of the face depended were the forces *not* of the total situation (extreme whole-determinist's whole), but of a quite different wholeness-level, that of the face itself. We have, then, not a whole and a part, but *two dynamic wholes:* the first is a lesser, included, whole whose own forces of organization give it a definite meaning, and the second is a greater, including, whole whose meaning is a composite derived from the forces at its own level of organization combined with those of the lesser, included, whole. Both are necessary in order to account for the meaning represented by the term "sinister expression." Here we see our familiar "inside-outside" problem, phenomenologically, in its true light.

At this point the distinction between parts and wholes begins to be undermined. The role played by the part is the same sort of role as that played by the whole; and this is natural because the part itself *is* a whole. Wholes do not really determine parts; for there are no parts that are not also, in a different but closely connected and quite indispensable relation, wholes. If one shifts one's ground and now admits that the parts are "*sub*wholes," one could not even say that the whole is the sole determiner of the character of its subwholes; for we have found continual evidence that some influence in the opposite direction occurs: some of the properties of the subwhole make contributions that are necessary to the whole. Thus the entire logic of a complete determination exerted by wholes over parts, or exerted by wholes over whatever is within the whole, breaks down. Wholeness itself is a purely relative concept and must give way to a clearer statement of the relationships involved. A concept of structure is indicated, but not a structure of wholes and parts.[8]

But to return to our illustration, let us see how the extreme whole-determinist would deal with the matter of the face, now that it is forced upon his attention. To be consistent again he would have to say that the perception of the face as a face (that is, as something whole in itself) constitutes a new problem. It is an entirely different act of perception. The face is now the wholeness-level we are considering, and it is the only wholeness-level we should accept. As such, it now confers upon its parts, the eyes, nose, and mouth, all

---

[8] What that concept of structure is, or at least the writer's view of it, can be seen by turning back to pages 106–108 in Chapter 4. The problem of the relation of the parts to what we call the whole, a problem that wholeness-theory, laws of whole-organization, configuration, and field have failed to solve, can be elucidated by the concept of *orders of dynamic structuring*. There is no pervasive and separate "whole-meaning" that exercises domination over the parts. There is, instead, a (dual) inside and outside meaning that is yielded in the last analysis by the parts themselves as they operate together. The "inside" meaning gives the internal object-character of the part (object) concerned—the "face" (anatomically) in our last example. The "outside" meaning refers to the manner in which the structure that represents the part or object is "structured in" with other parts (structures) to make up a *more inclusive* order of structuring —the entire situation of escape in our example. The "outside" structuring of the part (face) into this more inclusive order of structuring, and the tenant's awareness of the more inclusive structure, are what determine or facilitate his perception on the face as being "sinister." There is no need for a theory of wholeness-determination or supersummation when the orders of structuring are correctly envisaged. *Both* the inside and the outside meanings (or contexts) of the parts are necessary to make up the *full* meaning: that is, as shown both here and in Chapter 4, *both* are necessary to give the meaning of the "whole." And when these two orders of structuring, one including the other, *are seen together*, the story of the whole and the parts, and their respective and simultaneous meanings, is fully told. The same explanation could be extended to the configurational effects that are observed in figure-drawings.

their relevant meanings and does not employ any meanings that are present in those parts when they are taken in isolation. But again, such an interpretation could not be made unless we *overlook* the role played by certain meanings of those parts that are derived not from the wholeness level of the face but from that of its features. These are the characteristics that are contributed by the eye*lids*, the eye*ball*, the nostrils, the lips, and so on. These latter elements, while they depend anatomically on the existence of an organism with a "face," would still exist for us as perceivable elements having *some* characteristics or meanings even if one feature were shown in isolation from all the others. And these characters are as necessary to the meaning both of feature and of face as are the forces of wholeness-organization at the wholeness levels of feature or face. Try, for example, to perceive a nose without that "mass of tissue" and "openings" we call bridge and nostrils, or a mouth without the "red bands" that we call lips. So again, the concept of a whole that is not required to build upon the characters of its parts, but is believed to *determine* all the relevant part-characters, must be given up.

If we overlook (for the purpose of the argument) its disagreement with the facts and accept the extreme wholeness-determination version at face value, we then find ourselves in the following situation. Either we must say that when we perceive a whole man we do not perceive a whole face and a whole nose, etc., or that if we do perceive these several wholenesses (a fact which can hardly be denied), we have to jump quickly from one wholeness-level to another, reorganizing at each jump our field of forces as well as our identification of whole and parts. At each of the jumps a new whole, which means a new perceptual field, and really a new act of perception, will be required. Introspective evidence for such a shifting about in our ordinary perceptions would be hard to find. If we are driven to such a theory as this, we must conclude that a complete act of perception, one that ought to include simultaneously all the parts (i.e., subwholes) down to the last level of fineness at which they are ordinarily perceived, is now broken up into a series of overlapping wholes. One whole, though it rightfully includes another, is conceived as distinct from the latter, and the latter comes into existence only when the former is relinquished. We have no truly comprehensive whole, no whole of wholes, but only a bundle of tentative wholes into which the act of perception has been analyzed. There can be no way of achieving throughout the perceptual aggregate a unity or organization in "depth" as well as in "breadth." Common experience, however, tells us that both these types of unity exist.

When we see a man we are not only aware of his members, trunk, neck, and head, and the interrelations among them as they make up the total aggregate (view of breadth), but in taking any one of these as an aggregate, we are aware of the still lesser aggregates that are successively included within it (view of depth). Thus we have the meaning of a whole face that is included within the whole head, a whole nose that is included within the whole face, and even of whole nasal details that are included within the whole nose.[9]

The possibility of accounting for this important dimension of includingness and includedness is lost in any theory of organization which prescribes that one perceived whole is the sole determining agency that gives character or meaning to its relevant parts, or in any theory that fails to recognize the pervasiveness of organization throughout the various perceivable wholeness levels. By such a theory the unity of the perceptual act is destroyed. Seen in this perspective the "extreme" gestalt position tends to undo the great lesson gestalt psychology has taught us. For it has the earmarks of an isolationist or *piecemeal* doctrine.

Should we not then, give up the notion of wholes conceived only in breadth, the emphasis upon wholes as something distinct from the interacting parts, and in fact the entire idea of the whole as an explanatory concept? We need to revamp our ideas of organization and to work toward a theory of structure that will deal with the organization of includedness as well as of breadth, that will explain not only organization but the *organization of organizations,* that will apply both within and between the levels,—a theory, moreover, that will hold not only for perception but for all behavior. Macroscopic viewpoints, molar restrictions, and other conventions by which both gestaltists and behaviorists have escaped this difficult problem should eventually give way. Organization has come to be a key word in psychology. But to forget that nature, both in perceptual experience and in the physiological and behavioral realms, is organized not only in breadth but in depth and ascends progressively from the smallest aggregates into the more inclusive orders is to find little or no place in our systems for the work of the other sciences and to neglect the possibility of understanding nature through the search for a fundamental unity within it. Theories of organization that fail to provide a place for such a principle will remain inadequate.

---

[9] We are not saying that all these details are represented by sensory processes arising directly from the proximal stimulus pattern. Much of the perception, as we have already noted, is made up of processes that lie entirely within the perceiver.

To return to the more immediate problem, we can summarize by saying that if meaning is seen at the level of organization we call the whole, so also are meanings seen at the level of organization we call the parts, and both of these must be considered together. We can say that meaning and organization always go hand in hand only if we are willing to extend organization progressively downward through all the aggregates and subaggregates that are represented in the perceptual act. Organization must be seen as *pervasive* or it will lose its value as an explanatory concept. And there is no point at which a whole can be considered as providing the entire relevant meaning of its parts, or that the organization of a whole can be considered as the sole determining principle of the part-meanings that are included within it.[10]

But granting all we have said, it might still be objected that in centering attention upon specific objects and part-meanings, as we have throughout the preceding discussion, we are forgetting that the proper task of science is to provide us with *general* formulations; and the field-model of gestalt is surely general. Why should it make any difference what the particular meanings of the landlord and tenant are, or, for that matter, what the total situation is? These facts will depend on a lot of things which, from the standpoint of science, are fortuitous and therefore irrelevant. So long as the laws of field-organization are borne out in every case that is all we have a right to ask. Though this argument was discussed near the beginning of the chapter the answer needs further development. In the first place, though the instances of meaning we have treated in our discussion are subject to the charge of being specific, we must not forget that all meanings, as processes, are specific.[11] They are also unique wherever the situations in which they occur differ in any essential respect. Life is full of unique, specific meanings; they occur at almost every waking moment and enter into almost every type of psychological process at some stage. The fact that meanings always particularize themselves in objects and situations is itself one of the most general facts in all psychology. A theory of perceptual meaning, therefore, that does not accommodate itself to this broad fact, that fails to give some

[10] A brief criticism of the gestalt theory of organization in general agreement with the foregoing can be found in Skaggs, 1940.

[11] It should scarcely be necessary to point out that we must distinguish between the meaning as a psychological or physiological phenomenon and the content that the meaning is *about* (Titchener's old problem). Thus a meaning whose referent-content is as general as the law of gravitation is still a definite and particular meaning.

understanding of the "universality of particular meaning," can be neither very general nor very helpful.

Our second answer to the objection is that gestalt theory is in need of something that will enable it to bridge the gap, isomorphically, between phenomenology and the physical or physiological realm. This latter realm, as we study it empirically, is always found to consist of specific things. Its elements are explicit and denotable, just as the objects used by Sultan or by the escaping tenant were denotable. It does not itself consist of some general principle, even though the general laws of science are derived from it. If then we need to bridge the gap by trying to find a set of neurophysiological happenings that will be isomorphic with the percept, what better way is there of proceeding, in the problem of meaning, than by dealing with the subject as specificially and concretely as possible? This is especially true since, as we have seen, the attempt to conceive meaningful organization concretely in terms of wholeness doctrine and the abstract and formal properties of configuration has failed. It will be remembered that in the first chapter the work of explanation was defined as being based on two requirements. First, it is necessary to assert some general laws for the phenomenon concerned. Second, it is necessary to show that the instance of the phenomenon under consideration exemplifies the law. And to do the latter one has to show definitely, by the arrangements of happenings in the specific instance, how the relationship stated by the law is given concrete expression. This can be done with respect to meaning only by dealing with particular meanings.

One might protest that if the requirement, as stated above, holds true for meaning, it must also hold for all of psychology and for every other field of science. We may have laws regarding digestion applying to all animals, but stomachs, though they may be "typed" for convenience of study, are always particular things. Every learning situation is specific, though the laws of learning are general. With this the writer is in full agreement. But must we then include in our theory some provision whereby the specific arrangements and happenings involved in a stomach or in the physiological aggregate of a particular learning problem can be tied in with the operation of the general law? Current molar theories say no. In modern behavior-study the intervening variable has been invented with the result that we are spared this obligation and trouble. The position here taken is different. In the writer's opinion we *must* discover such a connection between the general law and the specific instance or our understanding of the phenomenon will be incomplete.

Whether this opinion may come to be generally accepted or not, one thing is clear. If we want to understand meaning in perception, we cannot escape the task of approaching it through the perceived character of objects and situations that have meaning to us. Though there are other phases of meaning (and these were brought out in the theories discussed), that phase which gives us the uniqueness of objects and situations is one of the most central in the whole perceptual process. Using our test case of the contrasting perceptions of the landlord and tenant we have called the roll of the theories to see what each could contribute to the problem. We have found some indications that they had taken cognizance of it, some considerably more than others; but as far as basic understanding is concerned we are still at a loss. Each of the theories has had its shortcomings for our problem; none of them has helped a great deal. One can almost hear the shade of Titchener chuckling as it surveys the scene: "I told them that meaning was nothing but context. And after all these years that is all they have been able to make of it." And so the classical theory of meaning in perception is still unfinished. The problem it forcefully raised and then abandoned remains unsolved.

GENERAL THEORIES OF MEANING

Meaning, as previously noted, has a scope that is wider than the perceived character of objects. It enters also into other processes besides perception. As one writer puts it, "meaning is the very appropriateness which explains perceiving, remembering, thinking, and acting. . . . When we perceive, remember, think, or will, we also mean. . . . By discussing meaning we can coördinate many related aspects of psychology and formulate a clear and more unified picture."[12] Bartlett states the case by saying that every human cognitive reaction can be regarded as "an effort after meaning" (1932, p. 44). Since the future of meaning in perceptual theory may depend somewhat upon the general state of meaning-theory let us digress from the topic of perception long enough to examine the work of psychologists who have approached the problem more broadly.

Looking at meaning, first, objectively, that is, as an aspect of behavior, one recalls the unsuccessful, but provocative, effort of Watson to identify thinking with small, incipient movements of the vocal organs (1919). Supporting evidence for the behavioral view came

[12] Pickford, 1950, pp. 251 ff. This article presents a valuable summary of a number of theories of meaning. The writer is indebted to it for some of the brief accounts that follow.

later from the investigations of Max (1935) who showed the presence of action potentials in the finger muscles of deaf-mutes while dreaming. Jacobson (1930–1931, 1932) made the significant discovery that action potentials arise in muscles simultaneously with the meaning processes with which the activity of the muscle, if overtly carried out, would correspond. For example, if one thinks of a tall object, the effect is shown in the action-current of the muscles that would be involved in looking up. Somewhat more elaborated is Head's notion of neuromuscular schemata (1926), an idea that has been used by some theorists as a basis of meaning. In starting to perform an action, though we do not consciously take account of the position and posture of the bodily member in relation to the object and to our body, such a position is automatically registered in the nervous system and brought into relation with the action. Through perpetual alterations in posture we are constantly building up a "model of ourselves" which is changing continually as each new group of afferent impulses, evoked by further changes of position, arrives at the cortex. An evidence of something like Head's schemata can be seen in the homing activities of animals and in the delayed response. For Pickford (*op. cit.*) meaning is the synthesis of the appropriate subjective or physiological processes and objective conditions that makes adaptive response possible. Where meaning is lacking, an appropriate reaction cannot be made. A number of theories, as indicated in the earlier part of the chapter, have attempted to explain meaning as the tendency to respond in characteristic ways to objects and situations. The motor theory of meaning is indeed plausible; but it has not yet been developed in sufficient clarity of detail.

On the introspective side the investigation of percepts and ideas has led to the description of meaning in terms of imagery, context, and relationship. Discussing word meanings, James (1890) spoke of the fringes of their feelings of fitness or unfitness with respect to the sentence context. A somewhat philosophical view represented meaning as due to an idea or mental act that mediates between a symbol and the object for which the symbol stands. The name of the object brings up the idea of the object, and from this we can pass to the object itself. Through this mental linkage the sign comes to "mean" the object.[13] Moore (1915) found that meaning came before the name of an object and had a longer reaction time than imagery. McDonough (1919) concluded that the image is not the meaning, but the meaning is as truly a "structure" as the image. Concept formation has provided another area for theorizing. Heid-

[13] Cf. Ogden and Richards, 1923.

breder (1946) found that pictures of concrete objects provide a readier basis for the attainment of concepts than do quantitative or figural representations. Two contrasting abilities or sets for dealing meaningfully with objects have been discovered by Goldstein in work with brain-injured patients. He distinguishes these as the "abstract" and the "concrete" attitudes.[14] In Drever's "interest" theory (1921) meaning is a relation of the situation to the self, or between the parts and the whole in terms of which the situation is interpreted. Bartlett (1932, p. 44) makes the significant point that meaning comprises an effort to connect what is given with something else. The immediately present "stands for" something that is not present.

Still another field for exploring meaning is that of remembering and recall. Bartlett (1932), in elaborating the notion of schemata, considered them as built up in temporal sequence in the organism. They continually grow and change, and those that are most recently developed affect action most strongly. Groups of schemata are the basis of memory below the conscious level. In human behavior the schemata are less rigid and circumscribed than among the lower animals. Schematization in human beings breaks down, and remembering represents an active reconstruction of the past in which details are separated out, with their accompanying related schemata, and regrouped. Remembering is thus a meaningful form of response to a situation leading forward to the solution of a problem. Schemata in which there is no consciousness, as illustrated (presumably) in the behavior of primitive forms of life, are referred to as examples of "reactive significance." Experiments on the transmission of rumors provide forceful demonstrations of the "effort after meaning" and of changes produced in recalled material by meaning-seeking activities.[15] In the formulation of these results the concepts of sharpening, levelling, and assimilation to the past context of expectancies in the hearer, ideas developed in earlier experiments on memory, have been employed.

When one thinks of meaning one is also likely to think of signs, symbols, and language. And here an extensive field for experimenting and theorizing has been found. Taking a cue from conditioned-response theory it has been assumed that the stimulus-pattern which is to become the sign, after being presented consistently in connection with an object, comes to act as a substitute stimulus evoking the same response as the object. Morris (1946) held that the stimulus-pattern becomes a sign if it arouses merely a "disposition" to make the same

[14] Goldstein and Scheerer, 1941.
[15] Cf. Allport, G. W., and Postman, 1947.

responses as those evoked by the object.   He distinguished between sign and symbol and stressed the latter as a more highly evolved function by which human beings produce signs that influence their own behavior.

Osgood (1952), believing the substitution theory too broad to differentiate conditioned responses of sign-meanings, describes the process as follows.   The stimulus-pattern that is to constitute the sign comes, by conditioning in the presence of the object, to evoke a "mediating" response consisting of only a fractional part of the total reaction to the object.   The response is reduced to the minimum energic level and omits any features that are antagonistic to goal-attainment.   When this reduced reaction to the sign occurs it produces self-stimulation in the organism, e.g., *via* proprioceptive impulses.   Such stimulation, in turn, by conditioning in the presence of the object, comes to evoke the usual instrumental or adaptive reactions to the latter.   For example, when we see a spider we have, first, a complex reaction including both perception and an autonomic response of fear.   Portions of this total behavior are conditioned to the word "spider" when that word is spoken in connection with our seeing of the animal.   This fractional response produces in us a pattern of self-stimulation which, in turn, elicits the same overt behaviors as the object, such, for example, as emotional expressions, withdrawing, and the like.   The sign thus operates not as a direct substitute stimulus, but by an intervening conditioned response-stimulus sequence through which we "stimulate ourselves" by this partial "meaning" component of the usual overt response.   The result is that upon hearing the word spider we can then react in overt fashion as we would to the object itself.   Seward (1948) also attempts an account of signs and symbols in the framework of behavior theory, employing for the purpose an intervening constuct which he calls the "surrogate response."   The view of G. W. Allport (1947) stresses intentions, values, forward looking meanings, and symbols (in contrast with "signs," to which the lower animals also respond) as concepts appropriate for a theoretical model of human behavior.

The experimental basis of sign-theory provides an interesting chapter in the theory of meaning.   Seward's paper reviews the evidence of sign behavior as revealed in experiments upon animals.   Turning to the human scene we can note an interesting experiment in which measurements were made of salivary reactions evoked by hearing the word "saliva" when that word was spoken in several languages with which the subject was familiar in varying degrees.   The amount of salivation was found to vary directly as the meaningfulness of the word-sign to the subject (Razran, 1935–1936). The psychogalvanic skin response has been used to investigate the emotional effects of words. It has also been employed to study the autonomic accompaniments of the discovery or loss of meaning and of the "meaningfulness" and "importance" of verbal stimuli. The conditioning of responses or inhibitions to verbal signs and the transfer of such effects from one word sign to another (semantic generalization) have been experimentally demonstrated. Verbal stimuli of similar meaning have been found to show a generalization of excitatory tendency, while those of opposed meaning inhibit each other. Experiments of this sort are reviewed in some detail in Osgood's valuable article on "The Nature and Measurement of Meaning" (1952). There is also presented an account of his ingenious method for scaling adjectives on various meaning-dimensions. This is done by judging how much of certain other meanings the adjective seems to connote. For example, the word polite is associated with a high degree of smoothness on a "rough-smooth" scale, with a somewhat lesser degree of strength on a "weak-strong" scale, with a high degree of goodness on the "good-bad" scale, and with a slightly active point on an "active-passive" scale. By this process it is possible to chart the "semantic differential" of a stimulus-word and to determine its position in "semantic space." Attributive sign-meaning-aggregates, then, are like perceptual aggregates in that they possess a dimensional aspect.

But we must note again, as in the case of perception, that dimensionality can refer only to some *attribute* of objects. The meaning-aggregate for an object cannot be *fully* described without using some method that is partly non-quantitative. Thus a "hammer" may be scaled with reference to the meaning (attributive) of "degree of heaviness" or of an attributive function such as "nail-driving capacity"; but the meaning involved in the judgment that the object is (or is not) a hammer is dichotomous and cannot be scaled. That is probably why Osgood turned naturally to adjectives rather than to nouns for his stimulus-words. The statement just made with reference to the dichotomous character of the meaning of the object we call a hammer will be likely to be challenged at first. It may seem that there are all gradations of "hammerness" in the objects we use for driving nails. But a little reflection will show that these are not really degrees of "hammerness" but degrees of clarity or certainty with which our description or our use of them tallies with our meaning of hammer. A more correct statement would be that we use these miscellaneous objects, with varying degrees of success, *as* a hammer; and this statement itself suggests the indivisibility, unity, and non-scalability of our hammer-concept. There are different *kinds* of hammers, of course. But the different kinds do not form a true continuum. Each kind is represented by a specific meaning-aggregate. It has a specialized and *non*-scalable meaning which is in addition to the meaning of its attributes that *can* be scaled.

One of the unfortunate results of the otherwise valuable modern movement of semantics is that we have been led by it to acquire a distrust of dichotomies so strong that when a true dichotomy appears we are likely to reject it. The emphasis upon an ends-use of dimensionality and measurement, as though these were the sole content and guarantee of scientific procedure instead of being merely one of its important tools, has also contributed to this tendency. It has made us neglectful of the other aspect of behavior, and indeed of nature generally, without a consideration of which the task of theories cannot be completed. If it were not for the vast array of dichotomizing, non-dimensionalized, meanings of the objects and situations with which we deal, life would scarcely be possible. (Institutional practices, such as those of government and courts of law, would have to be abandoned—to mention but one of the fatal consequences.) It is in this problem of describing the nature of the aggregates of perception and meaning, in showing what is aggregated with what, and how, that techniques of quantification and measurement, however necessary in other connections, will always be found wanting. An aggregate itself is either this or that, it cannot be *merely* a matter of degree. Precisely because it is a self-contained phenomenon its meaning as an aggregate is discontinuous from that of other aggregates. What Osgood is doing in his ingenious method of "measuring" meaning is to find the degree and direction in which one verbal meaning-aggregate is positively or negatively related to, that is, interacts upon an intensity dimension with, another. What these aggregates *are* that so interact is the basic problem of meaning-theory.[16]

But let us return from dimensionality to the matter of signs and symbols. Engrossing and valuable as all these studies of word-signs

---

[16] Noble (1952) defines meaning as identical with Hull's habit-strength, thus regarding it as a conditioned-response connection. He attempts to measure the *amount* of meaning possessed by a word by the number of words which, on the average, a population of subjects can associate with it in a standard period of time—that is, the number of verbal responses to which a stimulus-word gives rise. Since this method of treating the meaning of a word would seem to depend upon the meaning of the associated words which are "contextual" to it, the criticism given in Chapter 4 of Titchener's context theory would here apply.

In connection with dichotomy in meaning it might be well to review the discussion of meaning in relation to cybernetics (pp. 514–517).

may be, they fail to get to the heart of the meaning problem. Two facts, likely to be overlooked, show that meaning cannot be adequately covered by investigating signs and their functioning. First, an object or situation may have a meaning without having any sign associated with it. If this were not so, we could not explain the obvious manifestations of meanings in animals. When an animal has solved a problem-box we cannot regard the levers or buttons as signs of objects; they are the objects themselves that are to be manipulated. Can we, then, call the stimulations received from tonus changes in the animal's body signs? To do so would involve the absurdity of saying that the total animal is guided in his behavior by parts of himself: a part of the animal provides a sign to the rest of the animal! Second, a stimulus pattern that is called (or is associated with) a sign when considered from the standpoint of communication may have some meaning entirely apart from its sign-significate, or communicative, relationship. The word "ouch," spoken by an individual *when alone,* expresses meaning. An aborigine coming to a modern city and seeing a "policeman" directing traffic would have the meaning that the policeman was a man, though he might have no understanding of his meaning as connoted by his badge and gestures. Such meanings as we are here implying cannot be originally given by signs of objects. They are not "mediated," but are derived directly from dealing with the objects themselves. And without having them in the background sign-meanings would have no anchorage.

It might be argued that Osgood's theory provides for such meanings through the fractional part of the total response that is made originally to the object. This part response (1) provides the meaning of the object and (2) serves through its conditioning to the sign to establish the semantic, or word-sign, meaning. Though this interpretation can be accepted in principle, a great deal is overlooked by passing over the first-named phase so briefly, using it merely as a link in the chain for explaining the semantic process. To return to Osgood's spider, before we begin to have any signs at all we find, in the author's own words, a "visual pattern of a hairy-legged insect body often encountered in a threat context . . . ," and a "complex pattern of behavior . . . " including "autonomic 'fear' activity." Here there is surely the basis for a wealth of object and situational meaning. Can we describe or account for this meaning merely by calling it part of the total reaction to the spider? Clearly we need to distinguish the reduced pattern of meaning involved in this complex from the full overt behavior which might include crushing the spider or running from it. Osgood has pointed out some of the differences, but not all. The meaning pattern occurs more quickly than the overt, it involves far less energy, and what is most significant, it is *covert*. Unlike the overt behavior it does not of itself constitute or produce any change with reference to the object. If the meaning-aggregate, as we may now call it, is a fractional part of the total reaction, we need to explain how this fraction is selected and how the fractioning is carried out. Then too, we note that exteroceptive elements (the visual pattern) are combined in the whole phenomenon with incipient motor-activities, including autonomic reactions. How does this combining take place? It will be remembered that we sought in vain for an answer to this question in our review of the sensory-tonic and motor adjustment theories. But there is still more in the meaning-aggregate that must be accounted for. The spider is perceived as a "living thing" and an "animal." If we had no word signs for these concepts at all, we would still probably have *some* meanings corresponding to these phenomena. How can these be described? In all this listing of unknowns we are brought to the realization that the fundamental questions about meaning are still unanswered.

It is, then, to the basic problem of the spider's meaning, rather than to the word-sign that "means" the spider, that we should address ourselves if we wish to discover the true nature of meaning. This problem has nothing to do with signs. Word-signs, of course, involve meaning too; but they constitute a separate meaning problem. *Their* meaning is to be found in the interaction by which they enable the original and independently established meaning of the spider to recur in the spider's absence and to be integrated within broader aggregates of communication or thinking. They are therefore wholly contingent upon this earlier and separately formed meaning. In the prelinguistic period of the human race a spider-meaning of some sort probably existed before there was any word-sign for spider. A young child, also, probably acquires many meanings before he learns to associate names with the objects concerned. Much confusion has arisen because of the tendency to identify meaning *in toto* with language and to think that when we have covered the semantic aspect we have solved the problem. We cannot understand meaning so long as we restrict it to the meaning of language signs; it must be studied independently of language. The linguistic process itself cannot be adequately described until we come to understand the more basic process of object and situational meaning. Not only in the theories of perception, but in studies devoted directly to the problem, the true nature of meaning still curiously eludes us.

Our review, though far from complete, has brought to light many shrewd observations and suggestive findings. It has revealed some important generalizations. But out of it all there has not yet come a theory that promises to be fully explanatory and general. The work of Max and Jacobson and the observations of Head hold possible clues, but they stand almost alone as landmarks on an uncharted course. Behavior-theory and the motor-adjustments concept have added something. Most modern behaviorists, however, seem to spurn the problem as being "too metaphysical." Too few outwardly observable indicators, operationally defined and capable of being rendered into equations, have as yet appeared. Preoccupation with language symbols, elements that can be overtly produced, observed, and quantified, has diverted attention from the major problem. Not many theorists are prepared to assume the arduous responsibility for an explanation of meaning that will be truly objective, though the need for such a theory is becoming increasingly apparent. Even Pickford, after presenting his able review and his own ideas on many of the manifest phenomena, concludes by saying that the idea of meaning is a psychological abstraction.

If meaning is so essential for psychology, and if the progress made in its understanding has been so meager, the question arises as to how it has been possible for psychological theories to have developed so extensively. Perhaps the question can be answered in the following way. It has been assumed that we understood meaning, or else that it presented no new or significant issues. To meet the inescapable necessity of dealing with it substitute-concepts have been formulated, constructs of meaning in disguise. In this way the theories were able to go forward, though some of the concepts on which they depended were little more than words. It would be interesting, though disconcerting, to imagine what would happen if there could be put into effect a rule that no psychologist who did not have a competent theory of meaning would be allowed to use any of these substitutes, or any terms that implied meaning, in his system. We have seen that gestalt theorists must assume some meaning-phenomena they cannot fully explain. Directive-state theorists, if such a rule were enforced, could find little or nothing they could say about their results. We would note that Tolman's sign-gestalt theory, resting upon the perceived or remembered relation of means to ends, would, under such a rule, immediately collapse. With it would go the expectancy theory of learning, Krech's "hypotheses," and vicarious trial and error. Theories of cognition would be no more. Personality theories, depending now upon meaningful traits and themas, would be so limited that they would cease to be useful; while projective techniques would become empty rituals. Psychoanalysis and other psychotherapies would have to close up shop within twenty-four hours or else move entirely away from the theoretical community. No one could attempt to explain delayed response or the orientation of animals in a maze without feeling that he was walking on eggs. Hull's behavior theory might struggle along in its tough-minded way; but with its afferent neural interaction, its fractional anticipatory goal response, and its patterning of stimulus compounds under continual suspicion it might eventually have to succumb. Only Skinner would be left. But even he would have to be careful to reject meaning-processes in certain performances of his rats, behaviors which, if we saw them performed by human beings, would clearly suggest that such processes were going on.

Meaning, a concept born under the malediction of introspectionists, bandied about by philosophers, overformalized by configurationists, disguised by behaviorists who could not afford to disown it, has long been a neglected stepchild in psychology. Or perhaps it is like Cinderella, a ragged waif compelled by those who are ignorant of its identity to carry the burden of their theories without recognition until such time as it can be touched by an understanding that will reveal its true nature and illuminate the systems it has been compelled to serve.

20

Summary and Conclusions
Eight Major Generalizations
of the Theories
Perception as a Dynamic Structure
of Events

The main part of our task is now finished. Thirteen major theories of perception, as well as a number of related viewpoints, have been examined.[1] Many answers, all of them interesting, have been given to Koffka's question of why things appear as they do; and the problem of perception itself has been redefined in a variety of ways. There remains now the work of drawing the threads together, of making comparisons and appraisals, and of showing such convergences, divergences, and lines of development as may appear. We shall then try to list the outstanding contributions of the theories to our knowledge of perception and the major problems that now stand in need of solution. Throughout the preceding analyses of theories many foreshadowing references to structure have been introduced as a background theme. In the final chapter we shall carry these observations further in the attempt to reach some broader and more basic conclusion about the nature of perception.

---

[1] Some of these were probably not intended as complete statements having a universal coverage. In a way this may be true of most of them; though they are all "broad" theories in the sense that they are attempts to formulate basic processes, mechanisms, or laws of perception. We shall include them all in the following appraisal since our objective is to see where perceptual theory as a whole now stands. The writer's contribution on set and set-interaction (Chapter 16), which might be considered a fourteenth theory, is a part of a more general viewpoint to be discussed later.

SUMMARY OF VIEWS CONCERNING THE PERCEPTUAL AGGREGATE

Instead of giving a résumé of each theory by itself, a more useful procedure will be to compare their content with respect to a series of significant questions. This interrogatory may well center about the nature and operation of the perceptual aggregate, a concept we have found to be very useful. The following list of nine questions is proposed for eliciting answers from the various theories:

1. Of what elements is the perceptual aggregate composed from the standpoint of phenomenology?

2. Of what elements is it composed from the physiological or physical standpoint?

3. How is the aggregate formed? By what relationships are the elements held together, and how does it "operate"?

4. What relationship is conceived between the physiological and phenomenological data of perception?

5. What are the temporal aspects of the aggregate's formation and operation, including its relation to learning?

6. What are its spatial aspects?

7. What are the relationships between the aggregate and other aggregates, or between the various subaggregates of which it is composed?

8. What sorts of perceptual meanings are present in the aggregate, and how is meaning explained?

9. What is dimensionality in perception? What is the basis of quantification in the various theories? What explanation is provided for showing the connection between dimensional properties and other aspects of perception?

1. Since the starting point of most of the theories is the way the world appears to the individual the phenomenological aggregate is a good place to begin. What items compose it? Here there is a considerable range in number and complexity. At the simpler end of the scale we have theories that are concerned with the mere awareness of the object or with stimulus attributes such as qualities and dimensions. Core-context theory with its sensory core and contextual items, psychophysics, adaptation-level, and the functionalistic theories of Brunswik and the Ames group represent this class. Next come Hebb's figural identities and "non-sensory figures," the position and motion experiences of sensory-tonic field theory and motor adjustments, and

the configurational and topological field-theories with their directly perceived, segregated, and articulated wholes and form-qualities, and their experienced tensions, requirednesses, and physiognomic and demand characters. Cybernetics belongs here with its invariants under successive transformations. In a slightly different class belongs the awareness-manifold of directive-state theory with its meaningful autistic percepts, its affect and emotions, its misperceptions, and its alleged accentuations of valued or significant objects, phenomena that are shared to some extent with hypothesis-theory. Every theory has its phenomenology except behaviorism.

2. We now consider the aggregate as conceived in its physicalistic or physiological character. What gets aggregated with what as perception takes place? The development here parallels, in general, that of phenomenological description. All theories must assume a stimulus object, receptors and their proximal patterns of stimulation, afferent neural impulses, and some kind of cortical process. In some theories the list ends with these. In probabilistic theory emphasis is upon the distal object and proximal stimulus pattern together with the "cues" involved. Köhler, after surveying the topography of neurons and ganglion layers in the cortex, posits chemical solutions between nerve-endings as a medium for a field. These are added to the apparatus of stimulation and afferent impulses. Helson, in adaptation-level theory, postulates a central physiological calculating mechanism. Hebb utilizes cell-assemblies of pathways in the cortex and end-knobs at synapses. Efferent neurons and muscular contractions are also parts of his aggregate. Motor elements and proprioceptors with their afferents are suggested in core-context theory and are strongly featured as partners with the exteroceptive stimulus and its afferents in the sensory-tonic apparatus and in Freeman's tension-patterns and backlash. In directive-state theory and in hypothesis-theory autonomic factors (emotions) and the physiological bases of motives are added to the exteroceptive sensory and cortical components; and for hypothesis-theory a reference to physiological set is basic. Cybernetics employs proprioceptors, reverberating circuits, synaptic relays, and scanning elements. Topological field-theory ignores the whole question, as does behavior theory except for the obvious stimulus and response mechanisms and certain postulates about afferent neural interaction, fractionated responses, drives, and the like.

3. The next question relates to the coming into existence of the aggregate and its mode of operation. How does it "work"? Here we have the central explanatory problem which the theories must solve.

Since phenomenology is either silent or metaphorical on such matters we can consider the question only from the physiological standpoint. Here the slate is largely blank for topological field theory, and the writing in some of the other theories is sketchy. Core-context theory delegates the matter to physiology without further comment. Adaptation-level employs, for the pooling by which the aggregate is quantified, some process resembling the cerebrally computed coördinates, invariants of translation, and negative feed-back of the Pitts-McCulloch model. In sensory-tonic field theory various stimulating conditions are equivalent for producing summative changes in tonic energy distribution, thus affecting the perception. Motor adjustments theory has backlash effects, from reactions, that affect the cortical process; also "homeostatic" tension-sets, "induction," and "surrogation." Directive-state theorists have hierarchies of thresholds and responses that get "tripped off." Hypothesis-theory has no stipulated mechanism other than its general reference to set, but speaks in such terms as trial and check, stimulus-information and transformation, selection, and shift. In gestalt theory there are brain fields of electrical energy set up by sensory stimulation in the chemical medium, and these involve changes of ion-concentrations. These fields get disturbed by changes of electrostatic potential and then attain a steady state. The resulting stationary state of the process is the isomorphic basis of the percept. The aggregate is held together or articulated by the self-distribution of electric currents that "portray" the stimulus object in the cortex. Persisting "traces" of the field are also involved. The central terminations of afferent fibers from receptors act as "constraints of the field"; they are the topographical limits imposed upon perception by anatomy and the world outside. For cell-assembly theory Hebb uses associationistic postulates—the operation of assemblies and phase sequences organized and rendered permanent through lowered synaptic resistance due to growth with use at the end-knobs. He also employs reverberating circuits, interfacilitation, timing-coördination, "cement-like" action of eye-movements between parts of the figure, and recruitment. In behavior-theory little attempt is made at explicitly describing the formation and operation of the aggregate; though there is mention of fractionated goal responses, afferent neural interaction, stimulus compounding, drive-components in the blood, associative spreading, and the usual "intervening variables." Cybernetics has a rich equipment of action-processes with its relaying of information-units digital-fashion by synapses, its "brain-coding," its feed-backs keeping a steady state, its reverberating circuits for memory and recognition, its sampling and scanning devices, and its mechanisms for extracting invariants or universals under transformations.   The aggregate is thus conceived by the different theories as forming and working in quite different ways.

4. What relationship between the physiological and the phenomenological aggregates is postulated by the theories?   It is one of isomorphic dualism for gestalt, with topological representation of the stimulus field in the brain.   In most of the other theories it is left unspecified but is presumably a relation of psychophysical parallelism, with danger of confusion of the two aspects, or of animistic interaction, in topological field-theory and directive-state.   In core-context theory meaning is "carried by" kinaesthesis and imagery, or, unconsciously, by physiological processes.   Cell-assembly theory might be called isomorphic, though it is an isomorphism with the minuter elements of the percept rather than with its macroscopic properties.   In cybernetics phenomenology is not an isomorph of the brain state but a "different language."   Behavior-theory, being unilateral, needs no parallelistic postulate.

5. The temporal aspects of the aggregate are a topic of considerable controversy.   Though there is agreement upon the very brief time-span required for familiar objects to be perceived, there is a sharp difference of opinion as to whether perceiving is based originally on previous experience, that is, as to whether *at the beginning* a perception is a learned habit and therefore requires time and repetitions to establish.   Psychophysics is traditionally nativistic: time and experience neither produce nor change the dimensionality of the percept.   Gestalt theory is either nativistic or insistent that the organized whole is given immediately in every act, and hence is not susceptible to increments of growth through time; though it is expected to change through time by its own laws of organization.   In Lewin's field-theory field-organization occurs only in a momentary cross-section of time.   Past or future count only as they are represented in an "irreality plane" of the phenomenological present.   In all the remaining theories the role of past experience and learning is either stressed or implied; and it becomes the central feature of behavior-theory.   Temporal duration of the aggregate is provided by continuing field-forces in gestalt brain-field theory and by the regenerative or reverberating loops and permanent storage devices of cybernetics.   Koffka's theory translates the temporal dimension of the brain field into a spatial differential.

6. Under spatial aspects we can consider the locality of the physiological aggregate as well as its localized or diffused character and the

morphological fineness of its composition.   The notion of a one-to-one correspondence of points in the receptor pattern with features of the cortical process was anathema to the gestaltists.   The cortical space of the gestalt aggregate is macroscopic.   It is given by a self-distribution of field-forces corresponding to the extendedness of figures, to the adjacencies of their boundaries, to segregation, and to symmetry and closure.   Field-forces of the figure can act at a distance from the figure itself.   For cell-assembly theory the elements of the aggregate, being brain cells, are microscopic.   The units of the figure are not diffused but sharply localized, though "alternates" are provided.   Cell assemblies comprise a three-dimensional lattice in the cortex with a probable duplication in various areas to take care of equipotentiality. Freeman's motor adjustments theory is related to focal tension patterns, with wider marginal spreads of tonicity.   Adaptation-level and cybernetics contemplate microscopic arrangements within sensory and association areas of the cortex as in the models earlier described. Other theories are largely silent regarding spatial distribution except for Lewin's field theory which is concerned not with physical space but with phenomenological "life space" and the topological and hodological spaces of mathematics.   It should be noted that in all cases the spatial distribution of elements is broader than indicated above, since it includes not only cortical features but peripheral elements such as receptors and in some cases the somatic, and even the visceral, musculature.

7. What are the relationships between perceptual aggregates, between subaggregates within a unified system, and between perceptual aggregates and other systems of the organism?   This problem-area may be taken for convenience to include generalization, equivalence, and equipotentiality, as well as the relationships of facilitation and opposition.   Transposition effects and form-qualities are explained in gestalt theory through field gradients and in cybernetics through computed invariants of transformation groups.   Gestalt theorists have recognized subsystems acting upon each other laterally, though they have rejected subwholes and have slighted the depth aspect of organization. Lewin's theory has differentiated subregions, with their interrelations, within the person.   These, however, are not integrated with the outer life space in which the concept of locomotion in a field is used, nor with the subregions of that space.   The relation of an aggregate within a larger aggregate to which it belongs as a subsystem is, of course, the "inside-outside" problem that arose in connection with core-context theory (Chapter 4).   We now see that it has reappeared

as the besetting difficulty of topological field-theory and of functionalism from Helmholtz through Brunswik, the transactionists, and directive-state. It occurs in the question of what to "encapsulate" or to leave outside in the perceptual act. It appears also in "molar-molecular" alternatives, in the confused zone of individual and collective relations in "perceptual defense," in gestalt field difficulties of object-meaning and of wholes and parts, and in the "internal calculator" of cybernetics. Cell-assembly theory provides for substitution within or among cortical assemblages and phase-sequences, as well as for generalization through the wholeness concept, "t." Werner and Wapner show, in their sensory-tonic theory, that different tonus-producing conditions act in equivalent mutually supporting or inhibiting ways, while Brunswik's probabilistic theory exploits the functional equivalence of cues. Translations of a dimensional scale *in toto* can be achieved through a shift of an adaptation-level or frame of reference.

Turning to the question of facilitation versus opposition, we see that field-forces, according to gestalt theory, are active in opposition along the contours of figures and in support or opposition in the "unum" or "duo" relationships of complex patterns. Gestalt organization, if translated into the terminology of aggregates, becomes a matter of mutual facilitation among subaggregates. Opposition of phenomenologically conceived forces, with resultant vectors, occurs in topological field-theory. Phase-sequences in cell-assembly theory can be disrupted by such systems as emotion, hunger, and pain, thus leading to new organizations. Contrast effects of aggregates that seem to be "pulling apart" occur in psychophysics and are mentioned in connection with Helson's adaptation-level. The so-called vicarious experiences of the sensory-tonic field theory, veridical as contrasted with illusory, may be regarded as aggregates that negate each other. Opposed assumptions reduce the surety of the percept in transactionism. Antagonism of sets and perceptual shifts are recognized in Freeman's motor adjustments, and a similar provision is made in cybernetics. The feed-back arrangements of cybernetics are either "positive" or "negative" to the main-line subsystem. Such hypotheses as "perceptual defense" and "value resonance" in directive-state theory, though they were not successful, imply the notions of contrarelevance, opposition, or facilitation among perceptual aggregates. The point is covered in the Postman-Bruner theory by "hypothesis-combining," "competing hypotheses" and "monopoly." Interaggregate phenomena in perception, involving mutual support or mutual antagonism, are so prevalent and striking that nearly every theory has taken note of them.

The distribution of such phenomena is, of course, broader than the field of perception. Facilitating and inhibiting effects are well known throughout the entire field of psychology, giving us again an intimation of the pervasiveness of the allied and opposed dynamics of structures and a sign of the basic unity of psychological problems.

8. How is meaning related to the aggregate, and what sort of meaning is it? Though it should be remembered that none of the theories has given a good account of concrete object and situational meaning and that there is no satisfactory general meaning-theory, some use of meaning is present either directly or by implication in nearly every case. In core-context theory concrete meaning, though itself "non-existential" and purely logical, is determined by the context which elements provided for one another. For the dimensionally oriented theories, such as adaptation-level, some meaning lies in the ordering of quantitative judgments such as "light" or "heavy," or "loud," "medium," or "faint." In psychophysics, meanings other than sensory magnitude, intensity, and the like are carefully excluded. For the probabilistic theory perceptual meaning might be the degree of some scalable attribute perceived in the object attained; or it might lie in the (unconscious) weighing and combining of cue-probabilities that lead to such awareness, as in the "significances" of transactional functionalism. Gestalt theorists consider meaning to be organization, attainment of equilibrium, and insight into whole-part relationships (manifest organization). For topological field-theory, meaning is given by the organization of the field. Meaning for cell-assembly theory starts with the recognition of the identity of a figure and includes its generalization. It arises also in the association of two concepts (phase-cycles) through the activation of a common link. In the sensory-tonic system meaning is illustrated in the way in which static position and motion are interpreted in relation to each other ("vicariousness"). Meaning in Freeman's motor theory has the character of abstraction through common ways of looking at objects. There are also surrogation effects for the transfer of meanings of qualities from one sensory process to another. Directive-state theorists do not explain meaning, but they employ it instrumentally as the significance of the object to the organism for satisfying its needs or values. Hypothesis theorists might consider it to be present in the hypothesis and in the checking against stimulus information by which the hypothesis is tested. Behavior theorists can refer to fractional anticipatory goal responses. Cybernetists alone are deprived of a mechanism that "means." Thus

nearly every theory treats of meaning in its own terms, though none of them inquires sufficiently into its nature; and the ways in which it is handled are as diverse as the aggregates and operations concerned.

9. We come finally to the much debated topic of dimensionality. Let us here digress a little in order to develop some of the issues of the earlier discussions.   In terms of the aggregate-concept a logical way to look at dimensions would be as follows.   Let it first be noted that there *is* a perceptual aggregate of some sort, both phenomenologically and physiologically.   In our review of the preceding problem-areas, as well as in the earlier discussions of theories, we have seen that its full description requires some terms other than those of a purely quantitative or numerical sort.   At the same time, quantitative or dimensional features are *always present*.   Every percept of an object or situation contains some dimensionality.   Things are always seen in sizes or brightnesses, weights are felt as heavy or light, tones are perceived with loudness or pitch, and so on.   Would it not seem, then, that the quantitative aspects represent *the amounts or degrees in which the aggregate occurs?*   Given the same aggregate with respect to its type of elements, its reciprocal patterns of arrangements, and its temporal and spatial distribution, are there not differences with respect to the *number* of elements involved and their *energic properties,* in short, in the levels of intensity or energy with which the given aggregate is capable of operating?   If so, these varying numbers or energies would constitute the dimensional aspect of the aggregate.

We should not confuse the amount in which the aggregate occurs with the probability of its occurrence.   Though at threshold points there is an obvious relationship, the two concepts should be differentiated.   In an automobile, for example, the structure of the aggregate determines whether or not it will "occur," that is, whether the machine will operate.   Ordinarily high and constant in probability of occurrence, its probability falls in some sudden, stepwise interval toward zero when one of the running parts is damaged or removed.   It is, however, possible to change *continuously* the frequency in time of the events involved in its operation (occurrence) when it *does* operate; that is, we can change the *amount* of its running in unit time.   This is done by feeding in a larger or smaller supply of gasoline.   Such a procedure and its consequences, however, must be regarded (at superthreshold levels) as something that is added to, and not to be confused with, the *fact* of occurrence or non-occurrence of the aggregate, a fact which is structurally determined in an all or none rather than a dimensional way.   Events may occur in differing numbers of times or repetitions, but there cannot be dimensionality within a single event. An event cannot "partly" occur; it either happens or it does not. The same would be true of a pattern of events if the pattern taken is an integrated whole.

If, as seems evident, an automobile's action, or aggregate, comprises a *pattern* of all-or-none events (as well as quantities) and if the events must occur in proper time and space interrelationships to insure probability of the aggregate's occurrence, then there is clearly *a certain necessary aspect* of the aggregate's occurrence that does not depend upon numbers of events or their energic increments *alone*. Numbers or quantities are always present. But these alone are not enough. There might, for example, be an enormous volume of events in the cylinder explosions; but if the connecting rods were broken, the operation of the automobile as a vehicle would be nil. There may be a change of probability that the automobile will run under different circumstances, according to the nature and extent of the damage to an essential part. For example, a spark plug may be fouled, resulting in the "missing" of a cylinder-explosion. The word missing itself indicates the all or none character of the event (event-region) of explosion in that cylinder. Since there are a number of cylinders the motor may still run; though its probability of operation, under the normal range of conditions, will be less. It is to be noted, also, that if one cylinder after another goes out of action, we have a decrease in the probability of operation that is stepwise and not a true continuum or dimension. The same would be true in case of the breaking, one by one, of connecting rods that relate the pistons to the crankshaft. If there is a loose mainline electrical connection, so that the probability of contact through time is abruptly altered under conditions of vibration, we have another instance of variation in probability, this time of the occurrence of the motor's action *in toto*. In all such cases the "probability" of which we are speaking involves the likelihood not of continuous changes upon a quantitative dimension, *but of a cluster of related events all occurring, and all occurring in an all or none fashion*. It is a *structural* probability; that is, it is both the individual and the combined probability of a whole pattern or "format" of events occurring, all within certain interdependent relationships as to position, sequence, and the ongoing of the elements involved. This is the concept of *dynamic structure;* and it is something that must be conceived as quite distinct from (though not unrelated to) variable quantities and dimensional increases or decreases that may appear within the aggregate.

In terms of the organism the distinction we are making can be illustrated by the act of eating. The occurrence of the aggregate, that is, the *fact* that some food is taken into the mouth and also swallowed, is, as a pattern of events we call eating, an all-or-none matter; though of course there may be varying numbers of such occurrences of the aggregate in a given time as well as variations in the amount taken at each aggregate (mouthful). And, of course, food can be taken into the mouth without being swallowed (eating-aggregate not completed). But in practically every case it can be said either that the organism eats or that it does not eat. This dichotomy is always present regardless of how much, or how rapidly, it eats. There are also different *probabilities* that it will eat under different circumstances, just as in the case of the running of the automobile. Once it *is* eating, however, (that is, granting that the energic threshold of the eating-aggregate is exceeded), the bare, all-or-none fact that the aggregate *occurs* becomes, within limits, quite independent of the amount eaten in unit time. And within the limits of satiation it is also independent of the cumulative amount eaten. It might be objected that the amount already eaten and the probability of eating-occurrence are related. That is true, as shown, for example, by satiation curves. Still, the probability of eating depends also on something else, namely, the "intactness" of the dynamic structure that comprises the eating act. Just as in the case of the automobile, if we were to interfere with the ongoings of that structure, as, for example, by narcotizing the neurons involved in the act of eating, we would find that probability of occurence would fall abruptly to zero. This will take place, moreover, at any point on the dimension of rate of eating or amount eaten at which the interference is introduced. Clearly then, a distinction, though one accompanied by a relationship, must be maintained between the probability of the aggregate's occurrence and the amount in which it occurs.

Applying the same reasoning to perception, could we not say that there is always a non-quantitative aspect, or "format," of the aggregate which provides a kind of framework within which energies representing the quantities or dimensions of the object as perceived are released? Or better, we can conceive that a particular structure, through the multiplication of elements and events in its "event-roles," has at any given time a definite amount of energy that constitutes the basis of the perceived dimensionality of the object. The physiological basis of the dimension-experience could thus be the quantity in which a structure of events, which in its basic pattern or format is non-quantitative, operates.

How perceived dimensionality can be explained in detail by this or any other conception is a question that none of the theories is fully prepared to answer. We have seen the difficulties that arise merely in defining a dimension when different operations are employed for evoking the judgments of the subjects. This difficulty is paralleled on the theoretical side by the plurality of answers given to the question by the various theories. In psychophysics sensory dimension is bound up to some obscure relationship with sensory physiological processes. Core-context theory has little to say about it except in the contextual reinterpretations of Boring. Cell-assembly theory is somewhat vague in this respect. For gestalt and topological field-theory dimension would probably depend on field-strength and vector components. Sensory-tonic theory would explain it by the amount of tonic excitation and the effect of tonus changes that participate in the physiological aggregate, as, for example, in different rotation speeds or degrees of body-tilt. Motor-adjustments theory might bring in the strength of tension-patterns or the "amount of displacement" of the organism. Adaptation-level would order perceived dimension to a weighted mean intensity or magnitude in the aggregate, resulting from the range of intensities of the stimulus-series. In the functional theories the explanation would lie in the resultant of all the cue-weightings and combinings or the assumptions connected therewith. Directive-state and hypothesis theorists, who conceive a motivationally increased dimensionality under the term accentuation, would propose that the energies of some organic need or value combine their strength with the external stimulus energies, or that increased dimensionality results from the strength and combination of the subject's hypotheses.

There is also the matter of duration threshold for object-recognition. This phenomenon would represent the amount of time necessary for sufficient stimulus-energies to accumulate in the aggregate to permit the object to be perceived. Here we are dealing with the quantitative aspect in a different form. In work on recognition-threshold, hypothesis-strength is considered measurable by the amount of stimulus-input needed for confirmation or infirmation. The stimulus exposures here required are translated in behavior-theory into measures of reaction-potential *via* "latency." In cybernetics perceived spatial or frequency dimensions could be given in terms of intervals upon receptor surfaces and their brain projections, with cerebral mechanisms serving as computing devices. This theory employs quantification in terms of "bits of information." There are thus almost as many explanations of dimensionality as there are theories.

Meanwhile there has been pretty general neglect of the point discussed above, namely, that the structural conditions underlying the probability that the aggregate will occur *at all,* though they are not unrelated to the dimension of its operation, must be studied independently of the latter; and that, because of the dependence of dimensionality upon them, an understanding of these structural conditions is necessary in order to understand perceived dimension itself. The writer would venture to say that if we do not have a structure that has some essential *non*-quantitative aspect, we shall have no dimensional quantities; and this principle probably holds not only for behavior but for every phenomenon that endures and is distinct enough to have been given a name.[2]

CONCLUDING APPRAISALS OF THE THEORIES

We turn now from the content-summary of the theories to a final effort at appraisal. Throughout the preceding chapters an attempt has been made to test the theories of perception according to certain criteria. These estimates will now be summarized. Again the reader is asked to bear in mind the limitations of the writer and the possibility of his bias owing to his own theoretical viewpoint. Another caution to be borne in mind is the hazard of attempting an appraisal in such a state of flux as that represented by contemporary psychological theory. This caution is particularly necessary with respect to the theories discussed in the last seven chapters.

Let us first say a word about the criteria themselves. It might seem somewhat artificial or academic to have set up these six standards when the one great question about theories is, after all, their *truth.* But here we are limited, because in the inductive procedures of science we never know fully what the truth may turn out to be. We must find truth, moreover, that we, with our limited human intelligence, can grasp: it must have a place for us in the rationale of our thinking. The standards we have chosen are merely ways of "assessing the likelihood" that the theory under consideration *is* true and of determining whether it is intelligible. Here, in the interests of intelligibility and the search for knowledge that will give predictions, we have to invoke the "faith of the scientist." This faith holds that nature is not inconsistent, that its basic principles are not infinite in

---

[2] Many illustrations of this principle could be cited. Where, for example, were all the covariation laws of physiology before living systems evolved upon the earth? Where would be the economists' quantitative laws of token price or money in a culture of isolated family groups or in an object-barter system? Some knowledge of the structures involved in these cases, even though it be only an imperfect knowledge, is essential for the biologist and economist.

number but limited, or at least in some way unified, and that there is
an order that is manifested by broad natural laws.   These postulates
might not be true; but if science is to have a point we must gamble on
the assumption that they are.   Such assumptions then give us our
criteria of logical consistency, parsimony, and generality.   As to agreement with observed facts, experimental availability, and explanatory
value, it would seem likely that a theory that is both articulate and
true will eventually be found to qualify by all these tests.   And, conversely, if a theory does so qualify, we might assume that it is more
likely than it would otherwise be to be true.   Though all the criteria
are meaningful, the most crucial immediate test is, of course, agreement with the facts.   If we bear in mind these considerations, the task
of appraisal by the six criteria may seem less arbitrary and more worth
while.

   Core-context theory was considered by the writer to be parsimonious and in agreement with the somewhat limited range of facts called
upon to support it.   Though it centered upon object meaning it had a
potentiality for generalization to a few other aspects of perception.
It was found weak, however, in logical consistency, direct availability
of its concepts, and explanatory value.   Its chief merit is that it recognized, though it did not greatly illuminate, the part played in perception by object and situational meaning.

   Gestalt theory is believed to be basically consistent, with some reservation as to the treatment of wholes and parts; and it is parsimonious
through its unity if not through the range of principles which it
adopts.   It subsumes a large number of phenomenological, configurational, and frame-of-reference findings in a broad field paradigm that
is brilliantly conceived and elaborated.   It rests upon a large number
of experiments that support its phenomenological generalizations.
Though it has become directly and experimentally available through
brain-field theory, it runs into difficulties with the facts of brain physiology on the basis both of general knowledge and experiment.   It is
at odds, also, with some genetic and clinical observations.   Without
better physiological support it will fail to achieve a satisfactory explanation of the perceptual process.   It is, moreover, incomplete, in
that configurational principles are themselves probably too limited.
They do not generalize convincingly to sensory dimension, to certain
aspects of constancy, to concrete meaning, or to the prevailing state or
set of the perceiver.

   Topological field-theory is in agreement with many facts that could
be interpreted under its concepts.   Predictions deduced from it have
also been confirmed by experiments, provided one takes a very liberal

view of "field-forces" and related concepts. Lewin's original field idea was fairly unified and parsimonious; but later developments by various theorists, including Lewin, have departed from this ideal. The direct experimental availability of the theory's concepts, and their explanatory value in the absence of physiological supports, are, in the writer's opinion, practically nil. Logical consistency suffers because of the failure to discriminate between physicalistic and phenomenological data or between the inside of the organism and its outside relationships or environment. In its coverage the theory depends on gestalt for configuration, constancy, and the like. It is lacking where gestalt theory is lacking, including the limitation of field theory in general for explaining object-character, but with the important exception that it considers more adequately than gestalt, and indeed than most of the other theories, the motivational state of the perceiver. Topological field-theory is probably better than it looks from the standpoint of the criteria. It affords a way of describing perception (and behavior generally) that gives room for its self-delimited yet highly flexible and changing character; and it presents a useful practical model for depicting the relationships involved. Because it intermingles physicalistic conceptions with phenomenology it is not so useful for explaining the perceptual process.

Cell-assembly theory seems to be fairly logical and parsimonious. It is built directly upon certain facts of neurophysiology, genetic development, and brain pathology; and it provides some plausible and perhaps significant explanatory principles as well as an experimental availability for its concepts. Certain limitations of gestalt field-theory are avoided, though its phenomenological sampling is very limited. "Explanatory trouble" arises with respect to equipotentiality, and the theory fails to be convincing in its treatment of wholes. As for completeness, it is not adept at handling such aspects as dimension, constancy, and frame of reference; and its figural-identity generalization does not fully cover concrete object meaning or configuration. It makes a good place for motor aspects and learning, but slights the prevailing state of the perceiver.

Sensory-tonic field theory, though it is well supported by experimental findings and productive of some important and perhaps far-reaching generalizations, fails to explain the interrelation of sensory and tonic factors in a clear and logical manner. The experimental availability of its concepts is weakened through such notions as prior whole, total dynamic process, sensory-tonic events, sensory-tonic energy, and a not too explicit use of the field-concept. There seems also to be some confusion with respect to equivalence, interaction, and vicariousness, and a failure to treat sensory and tonic events in a sufficiently denotational manner.   On the other hand, its explanatory concepts of summation of tonic effects, organismic and equilibrial state, minimal disturbance, and the like have shown a steady and promising development; and, though terms have multiplied, there is parsimony in their unity.   As for generalization, the prevailing state of the organism is covered in terms of its background tonic characteristics; sensory dimension is of course involved; and the theory has been extended, in principle at least, to such configurational phenomena as figure and ground, demand-character, and certain aspects of motivation and personality.   Perhaps the theory could also provide some limited application to frame of reference and constancy.   Such suggestions arise, however, only in a tentative way; and there is a deficiency in integrating the motor components (which are its important contribution) with the meaning of the object as visually perceived.

Motor adjustments theory is logical, unified, and based, directly or indirectly, upon experimental findings.   It is in general working agreement with motor physiology.   Its concepts, for the most part, are direct and denotational in principle.   Some useful tools for explanation are provided in backlash effects, ways of regarding objects, peripheral motor adjustments in sensory accommodation, muscular tension patterns, homeostasis, and the "five principles."   These concepts, however, are not employed with sufficient attention to detail for explanatory purposes, as in the case of object-meaning and quality surrogation.   Again there is a failure fully to unite exteroceptive sensory and motor elements in the perceptual process.   Generalization extends to prevailing state, meaning, and, by a reference only, to configuration.   Otherwise it seems not to have been attempted.

Adaptation-level theory is logical and supported by experimental facts.   It has proved surprisingly supple in generalizing a range of observations.   If taken on the basis of its experimental formulation alone, it has an admirable parsimony.   In addition to its clear application to frame of reference and dimensions, it has something to say about constancy and may be regarded as a way of looking at prevailing state or set.   It does not seem readily applicable, however, to the phenomena of configuration.   Like other dimensionally oriented theories it falls short in interpreting the non-quantitative aspects of perceptual aggregates, including object and situational meaning.   Its method of handling stimulus and reaction data quantitatively, however, is valuable.   Though the theory achieves something rare and desirable in system-building, a set of mathematical equations by which it can be tested in experiments, its full experimental availability and explanatory value must wait upon further confirmation of the cybernetic model. The concepts of weighting and pooling seem very significant; and the theory as a whole has done much to clarify the phenomenon of frame of reference.

Probabilistic functionalism is parsimonious and in agreement with the facts thus far available. Its working concept of cues, insofar as cues are stated in molar and "object" terms, have referents that are readily available. The notion of weighting by probability is a novel and suggestive contribution to perceptual explanations. The strictly molar outlook, however, which neglects the study of intraorganismic aspects, limits its experimental availability of concepts and its explanatory value, a limitation that is increased by a predilection for functionalism and a concentration upon the distal object. The attainment of objects is defined in such a way as to refer only to scaled attributive properties and to exclude much that is important under frame of reference, configurational aspects, prevailing state, and concrete meaning. In spite of its provocative method of conceiving dimensionality, constancy, and the world of objects to which organisms must adjust, the scope of the theory therefore remains somewhat limited. A strictly molar position in perception, moreover, is likely to involve an inconsistency in the use of organismic cues.

Transactional functionalism gives a brilliant demonstration of the perceiver's (non-veridical) assumptions and greatly extends the functionalistic basis in experimental facts. Otherwise its virtues and defects are similar to those of probabilistic theory, except for the area of generality, in which it is superior. Its main principles could probably be subsumed under theories that deal with set.

Directive state theory, though it opens a new field of dynamic possibilities, rests upon a series of hypotheses not yet securely in agreement with the facts. If its general hypothesis should be confirmed, this system, dealing as it does with the non-veridical, would need for completeness to be developed within a theoretical framework that treats perceptual distortions as limiting cases of broader principles. Efforts toward explanatory concepts in the form of functional devices or mechanisms have not been wanting in this theory; but they are unorganized, unparsimonious, and in some cases lacking in direct availability to experiment. Particularly difficult has been the problem of explaining an experimental result that might turn out to be a "pseudofinding," the indication, namely, of a process of "perceptual defense." The reason for the difficulty lies in the fact that the *prima facie* results of some of the experiments seemed to imply a logical inconsistency. Final judgment must wait upon further experimental evidence.   There is also a conflict between the theory's functionalistic position and the generally accepted notion of biological function. The explanatory work of the theory has frequently been impeded by uncertainties as to how the present results should be interpreted. Directive-state investigations have largely neglected such aspects of perception as cannot be subsumed under dimensionalism and the prevailing state or individuality of the perceiver.   Nevertheless the movement has brought to light a field of hitherto uninvestigated phenomena and has shown that individual or atypical cases should be taken into account.   It has indicated that earlier views of perception need to be reconsidered.

Hypothesis-theory is in accord with experimental findings though the output is as yet not large.   It does, however, succeed in drawing together and harmonizing many of the more discordant results of directive-state experiments.   As a restatement of that theory it is greatly improved in logical consistency and coverage.   Its one central postulate of hypothesis, based on the concept of set, together with two covariation-theorems and a few propositions concerning hypothesis-strength, mark an advance in parsimony and unity.   Failing, however, to follow through with a theory of set, its concepts lack direct experimental availability, despite the fact that the theory focuses upon a good experimental program.   For the same reason it is deficient, as it now stands, in explanatory principles for hypothesis checking, stimulus-transformation, monopoly, and similar processes.   Its generality continues to be limited by the confining of interest largely to non-veridical areas of perception.   Except for certain brief references to constancy and configuration the theory extends only to dimensions and the prevailing state of the perceiver.   But apart from the standard aspects of perception great gains in generality have been made. Learning and motivation are accommodated, the cognitive processes are synthesized, and the way is opened through the set-concept for incorporating veridical as well as non-veridical perceptions, thus closing a previous rift and moving in the direction of a unified theory.

The *behavior theory* of perception, though still in a formative stage, has made considerable progress in supporting by facts its central contention that word-perceptions are learned responses.   In establishing learning as an integral feature of the aggregate's formation (though thus far only in verbal perceptions) it has rendered an important service.   Its logic seems sound.   The Hullian system in general has been charged with a lack of parsimony; but this condition does not seem too evident, thus far, in the approach to perception.   Some neural mechanisms and fractionated responses are mentioned that are denotable in principle; but the intervening-variable and molar-quantitative viewpoints lessen the experimental availability of these concepts. Explanation proceeds in the usual manner of increments of habit strength or reaction potential through a succession of reinforced trials, or in terms of stimulus-generalization and the like. "Perceptual" concepts and operations can be rather successfully translated into behavior-theory terms; but explanation, in the more definite sense of what goes on in the organism, is limited. The theory has some bearing upon object-meaning, and set can be stated, though not denotively explained, by its intervening variables. There is still some question as to whether behavior-theory can be generalized to cover fully the phenomena of sensory dimension, constancy, frame of reference, and configuration. Its descriptions must, of course, be given without reference to the phenomenology of such aspects.

The *cybernetic theory* of the organism and of perception calls upon a large number of facts for its support, and some direct experiments have been conducted. In certain matters, especially those interpreted by feed-back and oscillation, and in some phenomena of perception and imagery, the correspondence seems good. Neural anatomy and physiology are also in agreement in some respects. There are doubts, however, in other directions, as, for example, in the question of digitalization of information in the nervous system, time limitations placed upon the reverberating circuit, and the difficulty of establishing a satisfactory scanning device. The logic of the theory seems adequate, though a confusion inherent in the inside-outside problem may arise in considering the brain as a computing organ. The theory's parsimony might be questioned. There are, however, unifying features in the broad concepts of invariants of transformations, feed-back circularity, and the general notion of control and regulation. Through its constant use of a denotive method cybernetic concepts probably excel those of any other theory with respect to the availability of their referents. The same can perhaps be said for their explanatory value, both in their range and their explicitness. Detailed brain-models have been developed for certain problems. Reverberatory circuits have been well utilized to deal with memorial aspects associated with perception; and there is a convergence with adaptation-level theory. Transformation and group theory have provided invariants for constants of perception. A few gaps, however, occur in the treatment of perception; and certain other areas of behavior, such as learning and emotion, are not well elucidated as to arrangements within the organism. As for generality for the classes of perceptual phenomena, the coverage of cybernetics is thus far distinctly limited. Attention has been devoted chiefly to what have been called "universals" of perception—phenomena that belong to the configurational class of von Ehrenfels' form-qualities, or perhaps to frame of reference. Other areas of perception do not seem to have been included. The cybernetic notion of "teleological mechanisms" leaves something to be desired as a basic concept in the explanation of behavior; and the theory has a peculiar limitation with respect to meaning. On the whole, however, cybernetics has contributed some valuable structural ideas and has made important suggestions for the theory of open systems and neurophysiology.

LINES OF DEVELOPMENT AND PROGRESS; DIVERGENCES

Returning now to the summary by way of questions about the aggregate (pp. 577–588) it will be seen that we have acquired some insights that only a synoptic view of the theories could give. There have been important covergences, not so much in the theories themselves as in their recognition of certain important facts or principles. Such instances are seen in the notion of a cycle of equilibrium-disturbance and restoration, in the principle of "pooling," in the significance of motor factors, and in the role of familiarity and learning. More will be said about these convergences later. In many cases, also, definite progress can be observed toward conceptions that are more firm and explicit. This improvement has occurred in the sequence from directive-state through hypothesis-theory to set, in the transition from attitudes and determining tendencies to tension-sets, in the culmination of von Ehrenfels' earlier problem in the modern transformations and invariants of perception, in the advancement from idea and image through trace to the regenerative circuits of cybernetics, and in the shift from "higher phenomenological objects," "creative resultants," and "mental chemistry" to the brain-field hypothesis of gestalt. Improvement is also shown in the progress from the classical motor theories to sensory-tonic field-theory, from the earlier views of norm and frame of reference to adaptation-level, from local-sign circuits to negative proprioceptive feed-back, from Hume's "gentle forces of attraction" through core-context associationism to the behavior-theory of perception, and from Mach's configurational equilibrium to the steady state of open systems and negative entropy. There has thus been considerable agreement as to basic phenomena; and growth and maturing have occurred in the several strands of theorizing as the years have gone by. Problems are more clearly seen even if their full solution is not yet at hand.

But taking the theories as they stand, and apart from the historical continuities implied above, our summary has served all too clearly another purpose. There are, of course, other views on perception beside those we have examined. But if our selection has been a fair sample of the more cogent and systematic, we cannot fail to see how specialized, divergent, and often discordant the present theories are. We must accept this condition along with their deeper insights and significant contributions. No one theory covers all the aspects of perception. On the other hand, there are instances where several descend incontinently upon the same aspect with different explanations. Size-constancy is explained in four different ways by classical theory of the Helmholtz variety, gestalt doctrine, probabilistic functionalism, and Pratt's use of combined cues and the psychophysical law. No less than six types of influence are brought to bear by as many theories in accounting for dimensionality. Figure and ground in directive-state theory, and also in sensory-tonic field theory, are said to depend upon determinants quite alien to those of gestaltists who staked the claim. Form-qualities or relationships are treated in different ways by gestalt theory, behavior-theory, and cybernetics.

Conflicting emphases upon different components or operations occur frequently. These are reflected in such contrasts as autochthonous versus behavioral determinants, pure perception versus judgment and inference, sensory versus cognitive, familiarity versus motivational direction, continuity versus discontinuity, perception as learning versus learning as perception, veridical versus non-veridical, distal or proximal stimulation versus central organization. Some use dimensionality as an end; others use it only as a means. Clashes of basic working postulates are also numerous. We have strict isomorphism versus a looser parallelism, nativism versus empiricism, phenomenology versus observable behavior, brain-fields versus phenomenological fields, whole-determination versus part-assemblies, field-theory versus associationism, macroscopic versus microscopic, equipotentiality versus specificity, molar versus molecular, linearity versus circularity. Starting from different aspects of perception, influenced by varying philosophical backgrounds, employing differing aggregates and methodologies, the theories have gone their several ways. We can sum the matter up by quoting from Brunswik's picturesque conclusion in an article following the anxious forecast of Bruner and Postman (pp. 343, 404).[3] "This leaves us," says Brunswik, "with a total of six distinct kinds of perception psychology. . . . Bruner and Postman

---

[3] See Bruner and Krech, eds., 1950, pp. 30 and 64.

thus have hit it on the dot in their nightmarish prophecy of a multifarious tower of Babel. . . . ”

Though the author of this quotation did not divide the psychologies of perception according to our listing of the theories, and though he did not believe their differences to be as drastic as might at first appear, our survey has shown them to be divergent indeed.   Notwithstanding the progress made in many directions and the recognition of common basic factors, the outlines of a single broad theory, factually supported, logically consistent, and possessing a power for explaining and generalizing the many ways in which the world appears, are not yet visible upon the horizon.   “So many theories!” our Martian visitor might well exclaim. “How can they all be right?”

THE MAJOR COMMON GENERALIZATIONS OF THE THEORIES

But whether they can all be right or not, our study of the contemporary theories of perception has given much ground for encouragement.   In the opening chapter we spoke of theory-building as the mulling over, outside the experimental situation, of the findings of research, in an effort to arrive at new and significant generalizations. One then goes back into the laboratory to acquire further facts and to test specific hypotheses generated by such reflections.   After that, the theorist retreats and studies the matter again; and so on.   Practically all theories that are worthwhile have come into existence in this manner.   Out of the “mullings over” of the experimental facts of perception some truly great generalizations have arisen.   We feel fairly confident of their soundness and vitality because a number of observers have made them.   The various investigators did not know, in many cases, that they were looking at the same phenomenon; and since they worked apart from one another and with different backgrounds they dressed their findings in different terminology and elaborated systems which, as we have seen, could not well be harmonized.   The basic facts or principles, however, were there for all to see.   As we now stand back and survey the scene from our synoptic viewpoint, the broad outlines of these great generalizations begin to emerge.   We shall try to state them under the following eight headings.   Each of them clearly deals in some way with the plurum of parts or elements we have called the perceptual aggregate.   For the most part our interest in explanation will lead us to state them and to think of them, if possible, in a physicalistic and denotational manner. Generally speaking, however, each may also be considered as having some phenomenological counterpart in the percept.   In view of the extensive agreements among the present theories upon these principles we would probably be justified in regarding them as features that must be included and logically integrated in any complete theory of perception.

I.   *Interrelatedness, compounding, includingness.* The parts or elements that make up the aggregate of perception are interrelated and interdependent.   This fact was seen even in the earlier days of "mental chemistry," "*vorstellungen,*" and "creative synthesis." It is expressed in topological field-theory and in the gestalt principles of organization and articulation.   The very term configuration implies interrelatedness.   The same notion has appeared in core-context theory, in the theory of open systems, in cell-assemblies, and in the determination of adaptation-level.   It has, in fact, been a feature of every theory.   Everywhere it is recognized that the aggregate is made up of elements or parts whose existences or actions affect one another in lawful ways.   One important phase of relatedness is the fact that aggregates themselves can be joined or interconnected.   This phenomenon occurs either in a "side-by-side" relationship of aggregates of a single order that do not represent inclusion of one within the other, or in a relationship in which a larger aggregate is made up of smaller ones of a lower order—the relation of "includingness."   Compounding of aggregates, without includingness, is seen in the subsystems of gestalt theory, in the subregions of Lewin's model, in the "globality" of Freeman's motor adjustments, in Bruner's combining of hypotheses, in Hull's stimulus compounds and their effects, and in the interrelation of subsystems in cybernetics.   The includingness aspect was present earlier in Meinong's higher orders of "superiora," and it appears in physiological terms in Hebbs' cell-assemblies and phase-sequences, and again in the habit-hierarchies of learning theory.   We may refer also to our analysis of core-context theory (Chapter 4) and to the question of contexts within contexts that was there raised.   Under a slightly different meaning of compounding we might mention the frequently noted interaction between exteroceptive sensory processes, on the one hand, and motor activities, motivation, memory processes, and cognition, on the other.   The aggregate may indeed become very broad in the parts or operations assembled.   But whether the aggregation is large or small the interdependence and interrelatedness of parts is clearly a primary postulate upon which the ultimate unified theory of perception must build.

II.   *Self-closedness and circularity.*   Perceptual aggregates appear as definitely defined, even if complex, units.   Whether they extend themselves with reference to space, to time, or to both, they are never undetermined in their limits. This generalization is, in effect, a geometric one, though in a topological rather than a Euclidean sense. We might call it a "geometry of dynamic self-closedness." It is really a necessary condition or a consequence of the first generalization, the interrelatedness of parts. Complete interrelation cannot be achieved in an open-ended system. No part can be left hanging without connections with elements of the aggregate that come on one side and on the other, or that come either before or after. The perceptual aggregate must "close itself" in both space and time. And this is true even though some connection with elements lying *outside* the aggregate must still be afforded. Examples of the self-closing principles are found in the topological boundary of life-space used by Lewin, gestalt closure, boundaries of figures and fields, figures contouring themselves upon grounds, Hebb's cell-assemblies, symmetrization, and the set-format or "hypothesis" that is "completed" by stimulus-information. Some of these cases represent self-delimitedness or closure in space. We must think of the principle as applying also to time and motion. Of great importance, for example, is the cybernetic generalization of circularity in systems. Lotze's local retinal signs, backlash from movement or tonic change, as well as negative feed-back, oscillation, and reverberatory circuit in cybernetics—all these represent cycles that are self-closing through time as well as in space. We can speak of this feature as a space-and-time, or "*kinematic*," circularity in distinction from another type of cycle (energic) that will be presently described. However we may conceive the self-closing phenomenon, it must stand as one of the principles of which an adequate theory of perception should take account.

III. *Space and time building.* Quite apart from the "here" and "now" of the operation of self-closing aggregates, we must think also of space and time as dimensions through which they are *assembled* or "built up." Here there are involved past exposures to stimulus-elements, past trials, past learnings. Though the empiricist aspect and genetic growth of aggregates are not recognized by gestalt-theory, other theorists have found time and space assembly through past experience too evident to be denied. Hebb points out that perceptions are sometimes built by irregular (spatial) shifts of eye-movement from one detail of an object to another. Adaptation-level is reached by assembling and pooling through *time*. Behavior-theory and hypothesis-theory require reinforced repetitions or repeated confirmations in a temporal succession of trials. The reverberatory circuits of cybernetics, involving always the same pathways, endure through time and can add their elements to the aggregate, as required, in a temporal series.

A remarkable circumstance to which we should become accustomed is the *equivalence* or *interchangeability* of space and time in the assembling or persistence of the aggregate. Distribution of events in the aggregate must be thought of as comprising a space and time *volume* of happenings which appears on one occasion as spatial and upon another as temporal. Presumably the "learning" of aggregates involves both these dimensions as well as their "volumic" combination. Lashley's theory of cortical order postulates a mechanism to translate cerebral space-order into time-order in the reaction. Koffka's system translates environmental time into a spatial field of forces. Cybernetics deals with the interchanging of space and time through scanning circuits and neural conduction patterns. We remember also that spatial and temporal summation are equivalent at the synapses of the central nervous system. The way in which an aggregate becomes predictable through the accumulation, through space and its past history, of the events or their recurrences that compose it is perhaps the very basis of the process of learning, not only in the building of perceptions but also generally. The ultimate theory we are seeking can hardly succeed unless it incorporates this genetic aspect of perception along with the others.

IV. *Flexibility*. Looking at the aggregate from the phenomenological standpoint the theories show us a characteristic of deformability or flexibility. Perceived spaces, times, movements, angles, and directions, features that constitute continuances between sharp dichotomous boundary-events, are often subject to distortion; and such distortions sometimes seem, in fact, to constitute the very essence of the interrelationships. The deformation, however, does not usually extend to the complete disruption of the aggregate. There is still unity, or else division into a plurality of unified aggregates. A "topological" invariance is said to persist as the constant feature that withstands the flexing principle. We enter here the whole field of non-veridical perceptions; and much of configurationism comes under this head. Illusion-figures illustrate the characteristic; figure and ground reversals also suggest it. Phi-movement, the distortion of judged durations, and subjective rhythm give the phenomenon in time. Requiredness and prägnanz are gestalt generalizations that are relevant to flexibility. Gestalt brain-fields are supposed to handle the matter; while in Lewin's "disembodied" topology we have the flexible Jordan curve that encloses the life-space. We encounter the generalization again in directive-state and hypothesis-theory where explanations using such terms as autism, perceptual accentuation, and stimulus-transformation have been developed. Set-theory includes non-veridical sets with stimulus-deformations related to them. In Chapter 2 it was suggested that these effects are the work of brain processes which "fill in" the "continuities" between the energic events in the cortex that arise from patterns of receptor stimulation. Flexibility, however, exists along with order and stability. Limits are recognized by all the theories, "anchorage points" that keep the deformation within certain bounds. In this sense the constancies also belong under this generalization, since their percepts, though controlled toward the veridical, depict the physical object only *approximately* (Brunswik's "between-objects"). The transactionists' demonstrations, however, show that the bounds within which flexible deformation can occur are very broad. The property of flexibility clearly distinguishes perception from machine-like action. A complete understanding of perception will require some provision for it among the laws of the aggregate's operation.

V. *Establishment and persistence of constant relationships.* Another broad generalization about perceiving states that perceived quantitative or dimensional intervals, or even shapes, can be retained through time in spite of shifts of the absolute magnitudes of their components. Here we have a stabilizing principle that compensates for flexibility. From von Ehrenfels' form-qualities and Meinong's "higher objects" the problem has come down through gestalt-theory (where it was dealt with by fields and gradients) to the transformations, invariants, and universals of cybernetics. An important chapter in this topic is provided by frame of reference theory, Helson's adaptation-level, and Sherif's stimulating work in perceptual social psychology. The estimation of a magnitude or dimension with reference to a norm (average) is surely a perception of a relationship; and if the norm changes, as it frequently does, the judgments of quantities, degrees, appropriateness, and so on, relative to that norm are preserved as invariants regardless of the absolute magnitudes of the stimuli concerned. In sensory-tonic field theory the same principle appears in the reference of estimated tilt to an equilibrial axis of the subject. Behavior-theorists do not deny reactions to stimuli in pattern relationships; but they try to handle them by such constructs as afferent neural interaction, stimulus-generalization, summation, and the patterning of stimulus compounds. In perceptually oriented theories of learning, perceptions of constant relationships are accepted in their own right.

In a broad sense the constancies of perception belong under this fifth generalization. To perceive a table top, from a foreshortened, distorted retinal image, as "rectangular," or a man as "about so tall" at varying distances and retinal sizes, is to be aware of certain constant relationships among the parts of a stimulus-pattern. These cases, however, differ somewhat from form-quality constants in that they have a more direct bearing upon veridicality with respect to the environment and seem to involve more definite meanings with regard to physicalistic space and time.   In this they are unlike the more abstract universals of Pitts and McCulloch.   Their explanation eludes the perceptual theorists, though Brunswik's theory probably comes the closest to them.   The ability to perceive invariant relationships amid a flux of stimulations, a process that is probably subject to phylogenetic development, is of great importance in biological adaptation.   To be complete our overall theory of perception must include it.

VI.   *Energic cycle or level-maintenance.*   The preceding generalizations have been concerned largely, though not exclusively, with what might be called the geometric or kinematic features of the aggregate. Though some quantitative interpretations have been introduced, relatedness, self-closing or circularity, space and time assembly, flexibility, and constant relationships seem to have more to do with the "format" or form of assembly of the aggregate than with its dimensional or energic features.   We now come to a very significant generalization that deals again with a cycle, though of a kind that is different from kinematic self-closedness.   It is, rather, a cycle of energy-change, of energic concentration and diffusion.   The aggregate is here seen as undergoing the following cycle of changes.   Beginning with a state of equilibrium in the field or system, there occurs some disturbance of that equilibrium from outside influences.   The change is followed by a return to a balance of forces or to the energic distribution that constituted the original equilibrium-state.   The return to equilibrium is believed to be the physiological process that underlies the percept or the overt behavior, as the case may be.

This principle has come to our attention forcefully in gestalt theory, topological field-theory, motor-adjustments, and the sensory-tonic system.   In the last named the "equilibrizing" principle is considered as basic to the determination of certain spatial positions and magnitudes (dimensionalism).   In motor-adjustments it is called homeostasis; and the reaction of the subject to "displacement" describes a segment of the "homeostatic curve." In the system viewpoint (cybernetics), and in Köhler's writings, the energic phenomenon is a sustained, but active, "steady-state." It is cyclical in the sense that a disturbance of the state will be followed by a return to it; but emphasis in explaining perceptual phenomena is placed upon the maintenance of the state rather than upon the cycle of disturbance and restoration. In either case the principle is linked, though differently, with the entropy concept. Complete equilibrium would mean the maximum entropy of which the system is capable, a state as near to the absence of organized ongoings as it can attain. In an open system maintaining a steady state there is a holding to a maximum attainable level of negative entropy. "*Levels* of attained equilibrium" that can vary in energic density, a concept favored by some writers, seems to combine both views.

Though it is not stated energically the general idea of a return to equilibrium appears in hypothesis-theory as expressed in its "stabilization" of the percept through repeated "trial and check." Behavior-theory adumbrates the equilibrial principle in still another way under the notion of reinforcement through the reduction of a need state. The idea is also implied in the widely used formulation that behavior begins with the occurrence of a need-state (or drive) that disturbs quiescence and terminates with the reduction of the need and the return to quiescence. Here, perhaps, through the intervening movements of the behavioral act, we have a combination of the energic cycle with circularity in the kinetic and spatio-temporal, or *kinematic*, sense. But since behavior, overt or covert, is always involved, perhaps the energic cycle is to be thought of as concurrent with the kinematic in *all* the theories. In the concept of the energic-equilibrium or maintenance cycle the identity of perceptual behavior with the behavioral acts or adjustments of organisms in general is seen with special clarity. The ultimate and adequate theory of perception, since it will be a theory about organisms as open systems, must do justice to this important principle.

VII. *Energic weighting and pooling.* This next great generalization also deals with energies. The second part of the principle states that the energies of events in the aggregate sum themselves algebraically or else yield an average of their values. Perceptions involve the composite density of a large number of specific energic occurrences or magnitudes. The first part of the idea, as stated above, is that in such combining the various contributing inputs may not always be equal, but may be weighted according to certain conditions. (It should be noted here that not all of the theorists thought of these pooled or summated increments as energy-units. This more general interpretation is the writer's. It is of much interest that in practically all the examples now to be given the weighting-and-pooling concept was assigned as the explanation of the dimensional or intensive aspect of perception.

Let us recall, first, Helson's adaptation level of intensity or magnitude judgments, whose weighting and pooling procedures were described in Chapter 10. In sensory-tonic field theory weighting for the "extraneous" stimuli is established (in principle) by the *amount* of the stimulus (degree of body-tilt and the like); and pooling occurs by algebraic summation for the various stimuli that are operating. In the functionalistic theories weighting is given by probability of veridical reference of the cue or cue-pattern, and pooling is accomplished by combining these probabilities. In hypothesis theory, where a prediction is made (as in accentuation) from a combination of hypotheses, weighting is by the strength of hypotheses and pooling is by their (weighted) summation. In our own interpretation of the accentuation phenomenon (pp. 354–361) weighting could represent the degree of relevance of the (cognitive) means-value aggregate or structure to the end-value (motivational) structure; and the summation might include the energies of the means-value aggregate together with the weighted energy-index of whatever end-value aggregates were "constructurant" with it. In the set-theory outlined in Chapter 16 we could speculate that the energies of a set-perception aggregate could best be summed with its stimulus-input *after weighting* the input by the degree of its relevance to the set. In cybernetics weights or values are assigned in the process of controlling outcomes or of summing or computing averages to secure universals. Even in behavior-theory, where phenomenological dimension does not enter, there is a weighting of habit-strength increments by drive in determining a complex reaction-potential; and summation of increments of habit or reaction strength is a highly characteristic feature of the system.

Surely pooling, or pooling combined with weighting, a principle that has received such widespread theoretical recognition, must have far-reaching consequences for a complete theory of perception and probably with particular reference to the dimensional or quantitative aspect. Though this aspect has taken many different forms (intensities, pitches, spatial magnitudes, positions, angles, temporal thresholds, probability of veridicality, and probability of evocation) a common denominator for all of them might be thought of as the amount of energies present within the format of the aggregate during its operation (pp. 584–586).[4]

VIII. *Interfacilitation and opposition of aggregates.* As a last significant generalization we find that separate aggregates stand to one another in the role either of facilitators or inhibitors. In a way such a principle derives from the universal facts of self-closedness and close interconnectedness within the aggregate. Such features would scarcely be possible unless there were a considerable amount of mutual support among the aggregates forming a higher-order system and a negation of the tendency to support outside, or alien, systems. Two unrelated systems, if brought close together in space and time, can thus be expected to produce interference or inhibitory effects upon one another. Without repeating the summary of this topic given earlier we can say that nearly all the theories of perception take cognizance, either directly or by implication, of both allied and antagonistic aggregate-relationships. Looking at organisms and at nature generally we have here again a very broad principle, one that we can expect a truly general theory of perception to include.

Thus, although the terminology, models, and *modus operandi* of the theories differ widely, many if not most of them have arrived, in one form or another, at these eight basic generalizations. There has been substantial agreement in depicting the perceptual act or process as having the characteristics of internal relatedness, self-closedness or circularity, space and time building, flexibility, constancy of relationships, energic cycle or maintenance, energic or dimensional weighting and pooling, and interaggregate facilitation or opposition. These broad conceptions are the main fruit of our study of the theories. They represent, in the writer's opinion, the true greatness of their achievement. All the theories, in one way or another, have contributed to their discovery and formulation. Since they are true convergences upon common principles we may perhaps accept them as our most substantial present insights into the nature of the perceptual act, the best explanations, thus far available, of why things appear to the perceiver as they do. They also indicate lines of inquiry along which perceptual theory can be expected profitably to develop.[5]

[4] See also the citation from the work of Lawrence (1949) given on page 102 and following in Blake and Ramsey, eds., 1951.

[5] We must guard, however, against the conclusion that they cover the entire field of possibilities. It is apparent that among the six aspects of perception listed in Chapter 3 they omit specific formulations covering set and concrete

What then are the present issues in perceptual theory?   What problems remain to be solved?   It seems evident, first of all, that we need to discover some clue to the relationships among these eight principles. They need to be brought together into one consistent theory.   If such parsimony and unity could be achieved, we might then, perhaps, be coming near to a full and adequate understanding of perception. This task would be likely to involve a still deeper study of the principles and the raising of more questions about them.   As they stand, with few exceptions, it is not clear at the moment why they are necessary for one another.   But in addition to questions bearing upon these broad generalizations many other issues and perplexities have arisen in the preceding chapters, questions whose relation to the major generalizations is not yet clear but may be important.   Perhaps these queries could be re-assembled at this point in the attempt to outline a broad theoretical program.   The following list of problems is suggested, the first eight comprising detailed questions about the major generalizations themselves.   The questions should all be considered as calling for a search for the pertinent objectively determinable facts as well as for a theoretical ordering of the knowledge gained.

i. *Relatedness, etc:* How can the interrelations or interconnections of the parts of aggregates be more definitely and physicalistically described?   How can we depict the interconnections of aggregates?

ii. *Self-closedness and circularity:* What does self-closedness, or quasi-self-closedness, mean in terms of actual events?   What is the full story of backlash, feed-back, oscillation, and reverberatory circuits? Can all acts of behavior, both overt and perceptual, be accurately described as cycles of ongoings and events?

iii. *Space and time building:* How can we explain in explicit terms the equivalence and interchangeability of events or element-distributions in space and time?   How can perceptual aggregates be "built up" and then persist and retain their autonomy?   Under what conditions are they broken down?

---

meaning.   Meaning was implicit in nearly all the theories, but attained no common statement in the form of a definite generalization.   The same was true of set, a concept that received systematic recognition only in the motor and hypothesis theories; and even in these it was not adequately developed.   It is also possible that in the future some entirely new generalizations of the perceptual aggregate may attain the status of a common acceptance.

iv. *Flexibility:* How can deformations and other aspects of configuration be explained? Does the explanation that may be offered comport with the phenomenological findings of gestalt? What is stimulus-transformation? What is "accentuation"? How can the flexibility of the aggregate be reconciled with the invariance of perceived relationships?

v. *Persistence of invariant relationships:* Which of the several interpretations of this phenomenon is true—or must a still different explanation be found? What about "scanning" and "computing"? Can transposition, form-qualities, universals, norm and frame of reference, and perception of relations in general be brought under one hypothesis having a place in a unified perceptual theory?

vi. *Energic cycle or level-maintenance:* How can *energic* cycles be pictured in detail? How are they related to the kinetic, spatiotemporal circularity of aggregate? What are the connections between the concepts of equilibrium, steady state, entropy, and the organism-environment relationship?

vii. *Energic weighting and pooling:* How are these operations accomplished? What, in terms of events, is the adaptation-level of Helson? What are the organismic facts of probability weighting and combining (Brunswik) and of tonic-effect summation (Werner and Wapner)? How do these processes underwrite perceptual dimensionality?

viii. *Interfacilitation and opposition:* Can we devise a general theory to explain how these effects take place, thus providing for set-compatibility and antagonism, and for whatever basis there might be for such notions as "resultants of forces" (field-theory), "vicariousness" (Werner and Wapner), "perceptual defense," "value-resonance," and "selection" (directive-state), and "combination, competition, and monopoly of hypotheses" (Bruner and Postman)?

ix. *Quantitative versus non-quantitative:* How can the distinction between the quantitative and non-quantitative aspects of perception be clarified by a model of what is believed to happen in the organism? How can the relationship between the two be hypothesized in such a way as to show the place of dimensions and of quantitative, covariational, laws?

x. *Fields:* Are field explanations of behavior possible from a physiological standpoint? Could a field-theory be devised that would integrate the macroscopic character of the field with the more specific details of sensory and motor process?

xi. *Gestalt concepts:* If field explanations fail, how can we account for such reported phenomenological features as organization, prägnanz, articulation, requiredness, and whole-character? Can the alleged phenomenon of supersummation be given an explicit meaning?

xii. *Equipotentiality:* How can equipotentiality and mass-action be explained and reconciled with the specific character of perceptual acts?

xiii. *Dimensionality:* What is sensory or perceptual dimension in terms of the physiology of the organism, both peripherally and centrally? How is it related to energy and to weighting and pooling? What common denominator, if any, exists among different dimensionalities? Can the different operations by which the same class of dimensional judgments are elicited be brought together?

xiv. *Motor aspects:* How can motor (proprioceptive-sensory) elements be integrated with exteroceptive sensory elements in the perception of objects or situations? (Werner and Wapner, Freeman.)

xv. *Sensory-tonic conceptions:* How are sensory and tonic (motor) events specifically related in the aggregate? Between what processes or elements do equivalence, interaction, and summation lie? How should interaction be defined? (Werner and Wapner.)

xvi. *Set and hypothesis:* What is set and what is its precise relation to the perceptual act, including preparatory and sustaining sets and the question of central versus peripheral sets? (Freeman.) Can further light be thrown upon the difference between tonic and phasic contractions and their sustaining effects? How can the "hypothesis" concept, hypothesis-strength, stimulus-information, and hypothesis-testing be related to the physiological facts of set? (Bruner and Postman.)

xvii. *Frame of reference:* Does frame-of-reference theory really have a frame? If so, how can it be denotively formulated, and what is its explicit relation to the "norm"? What is the best explanation of the dynamics of "perceptual" or "social" norms? (Sherif.) What does conformity mean?

xviii. *Constancy:* Can a satisfactory explanation of constancy (both in the broader and the narrower sense) be achieved?

xix. *Threshold:* What is a threshold in terms of definite happenings in the organism? What is its relation to energies, dimensions, and set? What are *sub*threshold aggregates or phenomena, if they exist? Can such formulations be rendered into one consistent theory that will handle the various *kinds* of thresholds (brightness, weight, duration of exposure, and the like)? What, if anything, could be meant, physiologically, by such expressions as "raising or lowering the threshold," "hierarchy of thresholds," "subception," "autism," "reinforcement of a perception" and the like? (Directive-state.)

xx. *Psychophysics:* What is the psychophysical law (Weber and Fechner) in terms of the perceptual aggregate and its operation?

xxi. *Motivation and value:* Can the effects of motivational processes be conceived to play a part in the perceptual aggregate? If so, how? What is motivation, and what is its relation to cognition? How does "value" relate to these two concepts as bearing on perception?

xxii. *Cognition and memory:* Is cognition, where it occurs in perception, an inalienable part of the perceptual act? By what physiological schema, if any, can we make a continuous transition between object-perceptions in the narrower, or purely sensory, sense and object-perceptions which are highly cognitive? What is the basis in the organism of "memory processes," and how does it relate to the physiological aggregate of perception?

xxiii. *Veridical and non-veridical:* How can perceptual theory unify veridical and non-veridical perceptions and their sets in one explanatory system?

xxiv. *Learning:* What happens in the organism in learning? How can the apparently close affiliation between learning and perception be explained? (Solomon, Howes, Postman.) Can learning concepts, *via* behavior-theory, explain configuration and the perception of relationships? Are learning and perception two different processes, or are they different phases of the same process? What is a "fully formed," immediately veridical, perception, as contrasted with one in the process of "forming" through past experience? Can the answers to these questions throw light on the issue between continuity and discontinuity theories of learning? Can they lead to a solution or reformulation of the nativist-empiricist issue?

xxv. *Cybernetics:* Can perceptual problems be formulated successfully and generally in terms of such concepts as information, digitalization, brain coding and computing, and communication and control?

xxvi. *Functionalism, etc.:* To what extent are functionalistic concepts useful in dealing with perception? Do they have limitations? If so, what? Can the various "brands" of functionalism now represented in perceptual theories be harmonized? Can the teleological-mechanism notion of cybernetics be usefully extended? What is the value (if any) of the molar-molecular distinction in perception? In psychology generally? (Brunswik, behavior-theory.) How can "agency" be supplanted in perceptual theory—or is it a *necessary* concept?

xxvii. *Inside-outside relationships:* How can the problem of the continuity between the "inside" operations of the aggregate and its "outside" relationships be solved? How can "encapsulation" or "excapsulation," at any level, be avoided? (Core-context, gestalt theory, topological field-theory, functionalism, directive-state, cybernetics, et. al.) How could the collective or social surroundings be explicitly related to the perceptual act if we were to assume there is some connection between them?

xxviii. *Meaning:* What is the nature and source of meaning in perception, both generally and with respect to concrete-objects and situations? Can it be explained in terms of physiological aggregates or processes? If so, how? Could its correct explanation illuminate other aspects or problems of perceptual activity? Can concrete and abstract meaning be denotively differentiated? What is the relation between linguistic and other occurrences of meaning?

xxix. *Phenomenology:* Can further light be thrown on the nature of the "conscious percept"? Can methodological improvements be made in this area? Why is the percept non-denotable and non-objective? What are sensory quality and modality? Can we find a better concept to replace specific energies? Is the physiological basis of the percept isomorphic to the percept? If not, can we make some reasonable assumption as to what, physicalistically, corresponds with the phenomenology of the perceptual act? Should phenomenology be given up? If not, what is its true role or use?

xxx. *Conscious elements:* To say that the percept as well as the physicalistic aspect of perception represents an "aggregate" is to imply the existence of phenomenological elements of some sort. Their existence is also implied in the perception of relationships, in the constancies, in set and hypothesis-theory, in space and time building, in probabilistic functionalism, in the content of meanings, and perhaps also in the motor theories. Is the case for introspective elements really closed? If it is, then what shall we call the "parts" of the perceived aggregate (the subject surely perceives these parts)? If the case for elements is not closed, what new elements might be proposed? That is to say, what universal part-aspects could be said to make up the percept, which, in their integrated relationships, can be seen to produce its "whole-character" more clearly and logically than could the mental elements of the earlier introspection? Could isomorphs for such elements be found? Could a compromise with gestalt psychology be made to the effect that although the elements are never seen as dissociated from one another, they are still true *elements* of the percept and participate in the whole-character determination?

Might such a reformulated elementarism take over the gestalt task of accounting for the phenomena of configuration and succeed where determination by wholes and macroscopic brain-fields have thus far failed?

These, then, are the questions that perceptual theory of the future must answer. They are not, of course, problems of theory alone. Behind them, everywhere, lie questions of empirical fact; and theorists must work at all times in the closest touch with experimentation, checking their conceptions against findings and obtaining new findings to test the hypotheses to which their theories have given rise. The above list of problems seems very formidable. It might appear at first glance that little progress had been made. Such an impression, however, would be quite misleading. We do, indeed, know a great deal about perception. The first eight sets of questions are merely the carrying forward of the same quest that has already yielded the basic generalizations with which they deal. Every one of the long list of items reflects some past experience, either of failures, of quandaries, or of brilliant successes, that has attended the careful efforts of workers in the field. The questions themselves are pitched at an abstruse level; and few of them could now be even asked unless there lay behind them a long background of substantial achievement. The list as a whole summarizes by implication the progress that has been made in many directions. It also indicates the present theoretical needs.

CAN THERE BE A SYNTHESIS? THE INDICATIONS OF STRUCTURE IN THE PERCEPTUAL ACT

What strategy for the future can be proposed? Probably no one would maintain that the present situation, in which we have thirteen theories of perception, all aiming in some degree to be general, yet nearly all different, is a happy one. One answer might be to attempt a synthesis of the theories. Each of them provides some important insight as well as some empirical support. This course, however, would meet with difficulties. Their postulates and systems of thought are too diverse to permit their integration into a single theory. Though perhaps not a "Tower of Babel" they are multifarious and speak in a great variety of theoretical idioms. Instead of attempting to synthesize the theories could we not take a more direct course? Could we not try to synthesize *their major contributions*, the significant generalizations that have emerged from them in whatever language?   We might thus launch a new and more general effort based upon the combined insights of the old.   It might, of course, turn out to be only "another" theory and not a *general* theory; but at least it could start from a broader base than has been readily available in the past, and it could have a wider range of data for its testing.   Let us then try to reach some synthesis that will provide a broader theoretical conception.

What clues can be found for a theory of this sort?   We have said that the eight major principles stated by the theories seem at first glance to be somewhat heterogeneous and unrelated.   But let us look more closely and see whether, by restating and recombining them, a clearer portrait of the perceptual process can be made to emerge.   To link the generalizations in a more connected fashion, we could say that the perceptual aggregate, according to fairly general consensus, is to be conceived as composed of interrelated and interdependent parts, that it is assembled in space and through time, and that it is self-delimited and self-closed in its ongoings or operations.   In its action, like all systems that have a give and take of energies with the outside, it either departs from and returns to energic equilibrium or it maintains a steady state; and in so doing it manifests an operant energy-ratio or weighting among its parts, a summing or averaging of their energies, a flexibility, and yet a stability of certain inner relationships or proportions.   And in all this it endures, in one state or another, through time, possessing an autonomy which dictates that in its relation to other adjacent aggregates it will either be joined as a unit into a larger system or else oppose and tend to nullify the others.   Stated in this manner the picture begins to take on more unity and form. What does it signify?

It is conceded that the writer's interpretation of the theories and his selection of their major contributions might be biased by his own views; and the reader should therefore make all due allowance for such a possible slanting.   But when he has done this, will he not still see in the above description what the writer sees—namely, the clear evidence that a perceptual act is really a dynamically operating *structure,* that it presents the very picture of a self-delimited and self-contained structuring of ongoings and events?   It appears as a structure that is closely knit, yet not isolated from surrounding happenings, that is built up of the events of ongoing and interacting elements—events that have assembled, as it were, through space and time, a structure that can endure, that is flexible and yet ordered and resistant to disruption, that has both a non-quantitative and a quantitative aspect, that pools or averages its energies, that "gears in" with some adjacent structures and opposes or reduces others, and that operates as self-closing or self-renewing cycles.   In other words, a perceptual act can be thought of as a structure that exhibits a kind of "geometry of dynamic self-closedness"; and through this geometric or "kinematic" aspect, together with the energies there accumulated and expended, it gives rise both to the many formal non-quantitative phenomena observed in perceptual studies and to the dimensional or variable properties for which it constitutes a necessary "format" as they covary according to quantitative laws.   Here then, as the writer sees it, might be our clue.   If we could discover a way of conceptualizing such a dynamic structure in clear denotational terms, we might find ourselves in possession of a concept that would bring the great generalizations of perceptual theory together and a key that would unlock many doors.   In the very midst of their differences the theories of perception seem, almost univocally, to call for such a solution.

21

Outline of a General Theory of Event-Structure A Tentative Statement with Applications to the Problems of Perception

The theme of structure presented at the close of the preceding chapter stands out from the positive contributions of the theories. Can we not say that their negative aspects, the features in which they are limited, also bear witness to the need and value of such a concept? Our study has indicated that the places where the theories themselves were confused or lacking were often the places where an added structural interpretation has aided in their clarification. Many such supplementary analyses have been provided along the way; and these analyses are also related to the eight major generalizations reviewed in the preceding chapter. We shall now bring these interpretations together and develop them further in the hope that we may, in this final chapter, gain a clearer notion of the *kind* of structure the theories seem to be implying. As a conclusion we shall present a tentative outline of a general structural theory and endeavor to show its relationship to the current problems and the theories we have been reviewing.

ELEMENTS OF A GEOMETRY OF STRUCTURE IN THE ORGANISM

We started, in Chapter 2, with the notion of an aggregate of element-processes and physiological occurrences, accompanied by the phenomenological percept. This aggregate was said to be an arrangement of events that corresponded approximately to the object perceived and also comprised, or underlay, its meaning. Let us now try to make this conception more explicit, so that it can serve as a starting point for a structural theory. Two kinds of elements are here represented. The *ongoing processes*, such as receptor activities, neural impulses, muscular contractions, and the like, constitute one type. They involve, at an elementary or minute level, some form of motion, an ongoing through space and during time. We shall not be concerned here with the specific electrical or chemical changes that take place, but only with the fact of continuous ongoings as one of the elements for building a format of dynamic structure. The other type of element, or aspect, of structure consists of *events*. These are the "junction points" of the format. They are the points of "contact" or "encounter" between the ongoing processes just mentioned. Events, defined in this way, are *not* extended or continuous either in space or time. They are "dichotomies" that link an ongoing process on one side with an ongoing process on the other; and they are also time-points that separate what went before from what comes after. There is, between each two adjacent ongoings, an event or "event-point"; and successive events are connected by ongoings. We thus have a "structure" of ongoings and events; and the possibility of postulating a geometry for such a structure arises.

Though the model thus far is quite abstract and its justification at the minute physiological and electrochemical levels would require further inquiry, it is clear enough, *as an hypothesis*, for our present purposes. It can be readily illustrated in a realm with which we are already familiar. For example, "events" of stimulation occur as energies (or particles) from an ongoing stimulus-process strike a receptor. There is also an "ongoing process" in the receptor. An event now follows at the point where an excitation begins in an afferent neuron. The ongoing process which then exists in this neuron leads to an event at a "synapse" in the brain as a succeeding central neuron is fired. The ongoing process which follows in the latter may lead to a succession of other synaptic events and ongoings, involving other neurons in the cortex or lower brain parts. There is frequently, no doubt, a whole network of ongoings and their inter-connecting "event-points" in the cortex. To these we must add further elements representing internal bodily changes that may provide synaptic event connections with the cerebral pattern; and especially we must consider the synaptic events and the ongoings of efferent neural excitation and conduction, and the setting off, at neural end-plate events, of (ongoing) contractions in muscle fibers of the body. We also recall that ongoings of muscle-fiber movements (contractions) are linked, through events of proprioceptive stimulation of receptors in the muscle, with the ongoings of afferent neural backlash. These latter return to provide other event-points with the neural ongoings that are already existing in the brain. It will be seen that events are thus *not* to be thought of as "acts" of "agents" (of nerves, muscles, etc.) which perform them. A traveling neural impulse or a muscle fiber undergoing contraction is not, in the present terms, an "event." It is an "ongoing." The event, when pictured most clearly, represents a point in space and time at which such ongoing processes contact or "encounter" each other.

Events are thus given a distinct status in the model. The events, fully as much as the ongoing processes which they connect and which connect them, are elements that are necessary to the concept of a structure. We are not dealing with a structure composed of anatomical units or bodies, that is, of receptors, neurons, and muscles. That would be a purely morphological and static conception. Instead, we are dealing with dynamic elements, with ongoing processes and events. Events are given a relatedness, as a structure, by the ongoings that connect them—and so we have a "structure of events." Ongoings are also connected by the events; the structure is really one of ongoings *and* events. Ongoings and events are the elements that make up the geometry of dynamic structure. It is important to keep this more explicit picture, which we have drawn from known physiological facts, before us in our further discussions. We shall thus have a definite referent for our thinking whenever the term structure is mentioned. It can be applied quite generally, in principle, not only to neurophysiological aggregates and organisms but to dynamic structures of every sort, including even those of a mechanical type.

It was conjectured in Chapter 2 that since not all the denotable points of the stimulus-object enter into the composition of the perceptual aggregate, there is a "filling-in of the gaps" by further ongoings and events in the organism (probably in the cortex). Such a filling-in was thought to give the pattern its connected character. The "reasonable resemblance" of this filled-in "organismic" structure to the stimulus manifold was pointed out. The aggregate or structure is conceived to have both spatial and temporal aspects and to be built up through the assembling of its various ongoings at their intervening events. The above attempt to describe the aggregate through a concept of a structure of ongoings and events is, of course, merely a carrying on of a basic problem of the classical theories as outlined in Chapter 4; and the effort of the present writer has been, by this device, to conceive its elements in denotational and objective terms.

ATTEMPTS OF THE THEORIES TO SOLVE THE PROBLEM OF PERCEPTUAL STRUCTURING

But having defined the elements of the structured aggregate, there now arises a further fundamental question, also bequeathed to us from the classical theories—the problem of how the structuring or aggregating process takes place. In what terms can we conceive the synthesis or integration of the perceptual act? What gives it unity and self-delimitedness? These questions will lead us eventually to the heart of the structural problem. A number of answers to them have been examined. Each has contributed something of value; but each has certain limitations. In core-context theory the problem was seen as related to meaning, and meaning was said to be the context provided by surrounding sensory items to a sensory "core.". Further examination, however, cast doubt upon such an explanation. The core seemed to evaporate, and we found two levels or orders of meaning of the object, one "inside" and the other "outside" the object concerned. Context itself was a purely "logical" idea which became better clarified when it was translated into the concepts of structure and successively inclusive orders of structuring. Gestalt theory postulated, as the aggregating principle, the determinative whole, supersummation, and the laws of organization of the whole. This idea was found to be equally vague in that no "whole" could be explicitly identified that was not, at the same time, one or more of the operating "parts." It was seen that part-characters or part-meanings exist in their own right and even contribute to the meaning of the whole. If structure is to be conceived as organization, then organization has to be pervasive throughout all the parts or "subwholes" of the aggregate. Again it would seem that structuring, involving including and included structures, is a better conception than wholeness-determination. In considering the "building-block" theory of the elder Mill, though his notion of compounding sensory elements was crude and overlooked the fact that the whole has a character different from the character of the *separate* parts, we still found, by the test of "negative-causation," that some fairly veridical representation of the *parts* in a stimulus-manifold was necessary to the perception of the whole. And so again, there arose the inference of a perceptual structure composed of interconnected elements. Hebb, though clearly recognizing this principle, sought to base an independent wholeness concept upon a special added aggregate, which he called "t." This attempt, however, did not seem entirely satisfactory. In all these cases we have come back to the notion of a structure of some sort; though the exact form of that structure and how its integrating action takes place are not yet clear.

Another answer given to the question of what produces perceptual integration is the concept of the field. The effort of gestalt theorists to explain object or situational meaning by the organization of forces and the tendency of the field to come to equilibrium was canvassed in detail. It was found to be difficult, if not impossible, to provide a field paradigm that would simultaneously account for both the meaning of the object in its outer relationships and the meaning of the object in itself. The inside-outside problem that arose in core-context theory again presents an impasse in field-theory in dealing with the question of wholes versus parts. And once more the suggestion of a dynamic structuring in which lesser structures are joined to make up a more inclusive order of structure seems to provide a clearer answer. Field forces, moreover, in their quantitative and vectorial character lack certain elements that are necessary in order to explain the uniqueness of patterns of object-meaning; and Köhler's effort to "portray" the object by field-distributions of currents in the cortex is thus far lacking in empirical confirmation. In topological field theory a questionable strategy for solving the inside-outside problem was found to be employed in the device of "everting" the contents of the "inside" field, thus avoiding the essential structuring problem and producing a model that lacked consistency. In spite of its apparent agreement with the phenomena of flexibility and configuration, field-theory does not seem to be the answer. As a continuum for the propagation of forces that can vary by all gradations of intensity and direction, it fails to provide for the patterns of all-or-none particularities that appear in the perceived situation and the unique meanings ascribable thereto. It fails also to incorporate motor elements within the aggregate in any clear fashion. Yet because of these very limitations, we become the more clearly aware of the kind of aggregating or structuring principle that is needed.

A more naïve attempt to describe the aggregating process is seen in the concept of molar agency, a notion which appears in the more functionalistic theories beginning with Helmholtz's unconscious inference. The implications of this way of thinking, and its tendency toward anthropomorphic and preperceiver solutions, have been traced. If one is looking for the principle of aggregating, one must look closely enough to see the elements that are aggregated. A reasonably fine grain of denotation must be used. But when one does this one finds only elements in relationship; the agent disappears. Nevertheless this attempt at a solution, though futile, helps us again by suggesting that structure cannot be seen from the molar viewpoint, that the search for it must proceed along more explicit lines, and that a concept of *dynamic* structure, if it could be achieved at whatever level of denotation may be necessary, might make reliance upon functional explanations unnecessary.

Still another way of trying to conceive the aggregating principle, or perhaps to escape from the necessity of conceiving it, is to subsume it under a concept of order that is purely quantitative and dimensional. Constancy is treated as an attributive or dimensional problem by Brunswik, and non-veridical percepts of position have been investigated quantitatively, and as the basis of a theory, by Werner and Wapner. Helson finds order in the subject's organismic level of (dimensional) adaptation, though he did seek an underlying mechanism for explaining it. The behavior-theory of perception deals essentially with the quantitative variables of frequency of stimulus-presentation and molar response-evocation, substituting intervening-variables for the search for structure. And here the need for explaining the aggregating process becomes the more apparent because the problem is so largely neglected. It is perhaps assumed in many such theories that aggregation, and the facts to which we have referred as indicating the non-quantitative format or structure of the aggregate, could be explained by the operation of quantitative laws, or at least that they are secondary to such laws. The need for discovering the actual process of integrating becomes overshadowed by an interest in the dimensional aspects of whatever is integrated, and by the belief that "order in nature" means only quantitative order. If we know in what amounts things happen and can state the lawful relationships of these amounts, we do not need to know *what* is happening.

We have repeatedly tried to show the limitedness of this viewpoint. At the outset it was pointed out that it is not measurement, quantity, or number that gives the true criterion of objectivity, but denotation, and that an identifying encounter of denotation, per se, is not quantifiable, but is an all or none, yes or no, experience. And so it is with the role of events in theory-construction. An event, *defined as an encounter*, cannot be fractionated; it simply "occurs." There cannot be "degrees" of an event. Therefore it cannot be quantified or measured. And the same is true of the *patterning* of events which we have called a "structural format." Perceptions are characterized by formats of events as well as by quantities on dimensionally graded continua; and the former are needed as a kind of framework for the latter. Thus in discussing core-context theory doubt was raised as to whether the attributive aspects of sensations could provide a context adequate for the full perceptual meaning of objects. Dimensional theories were found wanting, also, in explaining the meanings involved in the problem of the landlord and tenant. Though cybernetic theory, in so far as it operates through computations based on "bits of information," can handle all relationships that can be quantitatively expressed, it is lacking in other features no less essential for the physiology of the perceptual act. Thus meaning, as illustrated, for example, in the ongoing-event pattern that defines the percept "chair," is impossible to explain through the unaided assumption that the organism operates as a computing mechanism. *Structure* is necessary in order to provide object or situational meaning. The suggestion was also offered by the writer that "bits of information" may not be items through which the organism digitally calculates a resulting quantity, but energic increments that serve to raise the energies in an essentially non-quantitative format to the threshold point of reliably predictive operation. In reference to theories dealing with methods of "measuring" meaning the same objection was raised. Meaning-aggregates, as patternings of events, are unique. They involve dichotomous features and have something about them that cannot be quantified. The only way in which one can convince one's self that the laws of perception are always "quantitative" laws is to *assume* the structure within whose format the quantities appear without trying to explain it.

It should be evident that laws stated in terms of variable quantities and their functional relationships, however true and useful they may be, cannot satisfy the need for an aggregating or integrating principle in the perceptual act. Mathematical or numerical order and the order that comes through structuring, though unquestionably related, are really different things. No question is here raised of the validity or significance of dimensions, quantifications, and quantitative laws. They are both omnipresent and important in scientific experiment and theory. Structurization must somehow be united or interlaid with quantification in any complete model of the perceptual act. But structurization *also* must be there. Both by what they include and by what they omit, the theories are again pointing the way toward the character of the ultimate solution. The question of the quantitative, however, and its relation to the non-quantitative in theory-construction, is so important in all fields of science, as well as for our present search for the aggregating principle, that we must now pause to examine it in some detail.

INABILITY OF QUANTITATIVE LAWS TO ACCOUNT FOR STRUCTURE; TWO KINDS OF LAWS IN NATURE

Throughout the preceding chapters we have, by implication, taken a position regarding quantification that may seem somewhat unfamiliar in traditional methodology.   We can now bring the matter to a head by the following statement.   The laws of nature have commonly been regarded as homogeneous—that is, all of one type.   It is usually, or at least frequently, thought that the more precise expression of all natural laws is one that is based upon quantities or measurements, and that any seeming differences in *kinds* of laws or propositions about nature have come from the fact that we have not yet been able to state some of them in precise, quantitative form.   When all statements about nature that could possibly be made have been made, *and when all of them have been formulated in quantitative terms,* it is thought that the work of science will be finished.   With these assumptions the present writer disagrees; and he would be so bold as to suggest that, in spite of the great progress that has been possible mainly through quantitative methods, a somewhat broader program for scientific inquiry might now be more rewarding.   He proposes the view that the phenomena of nature point invariably to the need of two kinds of statement in formulating natural laws.   Perhaps we could even say that there is not one type of natural law, but *two.*   By this we do not mean that there is any duality in nature.   The two kinds of law to which we are referring, though they must be separately studied to be understood, are not separate in their operation.   Every phenomenon involves an invariable and completely lawful interrelationship of the two.   They are merely two aspects of one total picture.   The *one* type of law, universally known or investigated, relates to quantities or dimensions and their relationship in the phenomenon concerned; the *other* type, which we have scarcely begun to understand or study, deals with its structural aspect.   Though quantities are always associated with this aspect, this latter type of law requires some terms *other than* those of quantity or dimension for its statement.   It will probably be found to be expressible, ultimately, by some kind of kinematic or geometric paradigm.   The elementary principles of such a model will not be equations relating measured variables of conditions, forces, or outcomes, but type-patternings of ongoings and events.   The full story of science will thus be told not in terms of quantitative laws alone, but only when these *two* types of laws have been discovered and their relationship clearly understood. These two types of laws, though always related, are distinct; one must not be confused with the other or substituted for it.

Evidences of form and structure in phenomena are, of course, very familiar in almost every field of science. Aside from the efforts of the configurationists, however, relatively slight attention has been paid to them except in such rather static disciplines as morphology, or in methodologies in which the elements of the hypothesized structures are themselves stated largely in quantitative terms. Though physicists have produced some important models the emphasis is usually centered upon mathematical formulations describing how the structure operates with respect to its *dimensional variations*, rather than upon what the structure is, in and for itself. Consequently, since the covariational laws of the myriads of phenomena seem to be almost innumerable and fail to show clearly any underlying unity in nature, it has been assumed that the classes of aggregates to which these laws refer must likewise be uncoördinated and diverse. The notion that *all* structures in nature, at every level, may have some "family resemblance" and may obey some *uniform* law or related set of laws that are as definite and general as those upon which quantitative relationships depend, has not been widely and seriously considered. It has been assumed either that structures are fortuitous, endlessly varied, and inexplicable, or else that the quantitative laws and equations will always suffice, in principle, to explain them whenever they need explaining. This latter belief is held in spite of the fact that no one seems to have been able to supply the details of such an explanation— and certainly not in the field of organismic phenomena and behavior.

The exact opposite of this view, namely, the proposition that structures are neither random, endlessly varied, inexplicable, nor amenable only to quantitative laws, but that there is such a thing as unique *structural* law *sui generis*, is the thesis which the writer here proposes to defend. Structures, in other words, are as lawful as quantitative relationships; but they are lawful in a different way—in a way that quantitative formulations are quite unable to state. The writer believes that such a structural type of law may exist, and that, in order to understand it, the possibility of its existence must be studied, or at least conceived, in the first instance, in complete independence of all quantitative considerations. He further believes that such a way of conceiving laws of this type is both possible and suggested by empirical evidence. The facts and theories of perception, as a special instance, seem not only to point to them but to suggest their actual character.

This thesis of lawfulness in structure is, of course, not completely new.   It has been adumbrated at various times, though usually in special fields and in a rather indecisive manner.   What is new here is the general and thoroughgoing way in which it has been stated.   We are, in effect, postulating a second type of law, the law of structure, as being completely general in nature.   And we have said that such a law must be at first conceived in terms that do not depend in any way upon measurements or laws of quantities.   Can such assumptions be defended?

For the sake of argument let us consider an example from the field of mechanics where, if anywhere, quantitative laws might be espoused as the sole and sufficient conditions of structure.   The analogy was given earlier of the carpenter who is placing a beam in a house under construction.   Both types of law, or at least both aspects, the quantitative and the structural, are here illustrated.   First, we observe that the beam gives spatial extension and strength—these are dimensional or quantitative considerations.   It must be noted that these can vary, in amounts or degrees, with varying conditions.   The ability to vary along graded continua of infinitesimal (or smallest practicable) steps is a prerequisite to their very definition and understanding.   There are no breaks, salient points, or beginnings or endings that could yield "all or none" or "yes or no" statements.   All possible lengths or strengths are capable of being represented on the continuum.   If this were not true, measurement itself would be impossible.   Our contention now is that laws dealing with such aspects, however valid and useful they may be, cannot cover the entire situation we are considering.   When the carpenter places the beam in its proper position, that is, in such a manner that its ends join other beams, something takes place which these continuous quantitative laws can never completely describe; nor can quantitatively expressed "forces" account for it unless we read into the equations more than is actually there.   This "something" is the "event" or "contact," that is, the encounter, that takes place between the new beam and an adjacent timber.   This event is a fact of "structure."

Now let us be clear about one point.   It is perfectly true that laws and quantities of mechanics, such as vectors of force (laws that express something about the way in which the beam butts against those with which it is brought in contact), *are always assignable to the event.*   There are *always* quantities or dimensions that are *associated with* the event as it takes place.   But two other facts are equally true and important.   First, the quantitative laws of mechanics *cannot describe the event itself;* they can only assume it.   It is a condition upon which their equations are based. The laws, as we have seen, cover only continuously varying quantities and their relationship. There is no sharp dividing point, no break or dichotomy, with respect to the equations by which they are stated. Their functions are always "continuous." An event, however, defined as an encounter has a character of exactly the opposite sort. It is discontinuous rather than continuous; it is not a "variable" but an "all or none," "yes or no," fact. It represents a dichotomy or point in space and time that clearly separates the ongoing process on one side of it from that on the other and divides what comes before it in time from what comes after. It is obviously, therefore, something different from a mere degree along a continuum. Something *besides* a quantity of an abstracted variable is necessary in order to describe it; and in fact, the act of quantification itself could not take place without it. An event, in this sense, though certainly a part of nature and capable of objective observation, therefore does not really belong in the realm of variable or dimensional considerations.

It is true, of course, that the *number* of events can be counted (quantitative aspect); but *an* event, in the sense here used, cannot be quantified or measured; it simply occurs or it does not occur. It cannot occur "partially" or in degrees. Two bodies can come by degrees closer to each other and then by degrees away from each other; but the point, or instant, just before which they are observed to be approaching each other and just after which they are observed to be receding from each other cannot be subject to degrees. And yet that there *is* such a point, and that it is present in all collisions of bodies, is an incontestable fact of the physically observed world.[1]

The second point to note is that, although the equations involving mass, velocity, forces, and conservation always hold true when the beam is put into place, that is, as the beam is moved and as it strikes

---

[1] The foregoing statements can also be shown to be true, phenomenally, under the supposition of general relativity theory in which objects never completely collide but only come, by the curvature of space-time, to "near points" and then recede from each other. Though bodies may "curve" toward one another and then "curve" away, an observer on either of the bodies will see the straight-line distance between them in his frame of reference grow smaller through time and then begin to grow greater. Though the motion of each body separately is continuous, between these two relative states (approach and recession) the observer will see, at the "turning point," no continuity in space, time, or motion, but only a "near point" of the bodies, a dichotomy that separates the fact of approach from the fact of recession. Furthermore, though Einstein's field is a true continuum of points in space-time, in order to have a phenomenally experienceable event some physical, denotational encounter must occur at some point within it.

against the adjacent beams, it is also just as true that such equations could never be assigned to such manifolds *unless events occur.* The carpenter's hands must "encounter" the beam in order for force to be applied to it; the first beam must "encounter" the second in order for quantitative determinations with respect to the encounter to be made. If anyone is inclined to stress the forces or quantitative laws as the basis of the event, let him remember that the event, a happening outside the realm of quantifiability, is also just as necessary as a condition of the quantitative laws.   Without it we would have no evidence that a quantitative law *exists.*   If there were no events, there would be no operationally testable resultants of forces and no operational equations for the conservation of momentum.   Events are necessary as a kind of "framework" within which dimensional or quantitative laws appear.   Perhaps one might object by saying that the event is "presupposed" by the quantitative law itself; the laws of direction, force, momentum, and so on, *include* the events.   But if this is true, we have a statement of variable quantities combined into a "law" with items that are *not* quantitatively variable.   There would be a distinction *within* the law itself that would still prove our point.

The above consideration should also give pause to anyone who invokes "causality" and tries to set up quantitative laws as the "causes" of structure.   For a "cause" means only a necessary and sufficient condition.   When one elects to assign the quantitative or covariation law as the "cause" of events occurring he merely follows a convention adopted for convenience in the work-ways of science in which quantitative procedures are usually given precedence.   If we regard events merely as dichotomies that divide but also connect ongoings, it would be just as logical to regard *them* as the cause of the *quantitative laws;* for they are necessary conditions of those laws.   However, the notion of causality as applied *either* to quantitative law *or* to the event represents a naïve and somewhat primitive type of thinking and will not help to clarify the problem.   It is better to say merely that both the quantitative law and the events are valid, but different, parts of the description of the total phenomenon.   Even if we say that we could *predict* the event, at a certain time and place, by the vectors of force involved in the motions of beams, this statement, also, would not be enough to cover the character of the event itself or to establish for it a definite causation.   The particular vector field might be a "sufficient" condition of the event, but it is not a "necessary" condition and therefore not a "cause"; for resultants of an indefinite number of other combinations of directions and amounts of forces could also enable us to predict an event at that point of space and time.   Causation by an infinite number of alternative possible combinations is really not causation by anything. And though the statement that we could "predict" the event by the mechanical laws if all conditions are known is true, it still leaves untouched that troublesome feature of the "discontinuous" character of the event.

Let us note, moreover, that the mechanical model, in order to be completely general, must be fully applicable to organisms. Now one of the striking features about behavior is the marked variation in time and place in which events can occur and still leave the *pattern* of the events, in the sense of a certain definite and recognizable process or act, quite integrated and intact. Such indeed is the rule in all acts of adjustive behavior that are sufficiently predictable and stable to be given a name. The mechanical laws, in order to predict a specific event, must be able to predict it at some definite time and place within a given frame of reference. How can the mechanical laws account for this *pattern* type of prediction in which event-points in space and time do not stay put in successive repetitions of the same act, and variability is a part of the act itself? The very emphasis upon quantitative precision which is indispensable to the measuring process militates against its usefulness in dealing with this organismic aspect of the natural world. It is true that we have not proved quantitative laws to be unworkable in predicting the events of a physical system such as the construction of a house. Nevertheless when applied to behavior they leave something important unaccounted for. There still *might* be a general law of "structuring," not statable in quantitative terms, that *might* account for both the organismic activity and the mechanical phenomenon, treating the latter, perhaps, as a special or limiting case.

But there is a further reason why mechanical and quantitative laws will not serve as a universal method of accounting for structure, and why, therefore, the possibility and need of some more general ways of accounting for it are still open. Looking again for some solution that will be general, let us descend to the lowest orders of nature, to the ultramicroscopic particles that are in continual motion. In order to apply mechanical laws here for the prediction of the events (encounters) of these particles we would have to be able to determine, as in the case of the house, both the present positions and the velocities of these particles, as well as their directions. This, according to the physical "principle of uncertainty," cannot be done. For the problem of putting beams together these determinations are quite practicable, but they are not so at the level of very minute particles traveling at high speeds. In the latter realm, if we know accurately the *position* of the particle, there will be an error in our determination of its *velocity*, and vice versa.   At this level the very concepts of position and velocity, *if taken together*, have no operational meaning.   And yet events, and so, presumably, the ongoing-event structure of aggregates of particles at this ultramicroscopic order, seem to be realities.   It thus appears that when we view the matter of structure in terms of the possibility of a completely general law (a possibility which we have not yet, of course, proved to be an actuality) it will be necessary if we are ever to discover such a law, to employ some working concepts *other than* the quantitative variables of the mechanical laws.

One of the principal reasons why one clings to the belief that quantitative laws produce the structure is that one tends to regard them as agencies.   One forgets that the concepts of force and momentum, of elasticity, strain, cohesion, and the like, are only formal expressions that combine the descriptive measurements of such variables as mass, velocity, and acceleration.   One is inclined to think of a "force" not merely as a mathematical equation, derived from mass and kinetic measurements, but as something that is "forceful," that has a "potency" for separating things or bringing them together, that is, in short, a "dynamic cause" of aggregation.   If we are willing to lay aside these somewhat anthropomorphic ideas, as Einstein, for example, has done, and look at the forces more objectively, we can see these quantitative laws of nature in a new and more liberal setting. They can be regarded, from one standpoint, as due to properties of the curving continuum of space-time.   Geometric conceptions thus supplement covariation laws and serve as a better interpretation of those laws than the dynamic properties previously assigned to them. For our present problem it will be suggested that quantities can be conceived as properties incident to self-delimited and cyclical patterns of ongoings and events.   And it will be our task to try to describe these patterns.   With the notion of such a geometry of ongoings and events before us we have at once the possibility of a theory of kinetic structure and a possible access to the phenomena of life and behavior for the understanding of which such a theory is needed.   The dynamics of the situation would then be hypothesized as lying in the geometry of this basic structure, rather than in its accompanying quantitative features which are presented for the observer's measurement.   Energy itself, clear down to the ultimate units implied by Planck's constant of action, might be seen as having, or depending upon, a "structure." Such a view, if properly elaborated, though it might require an unusual detachment from familiar ways of thinking, could satisfy all the demands of the foregoing analysis and yet leave the lawful and predictive status of the quantitative laws inviolate. Nothing important would be lost of the old, but substantial gains might be made of something that is new.

What then, to return to our example, is a house that is under construction? What is the process of its building? Since the building of a house is more like an organismic activity than is the completed product, let us concentrate upon the latter question. If one were to ignore the whole preceding discussion, one might say that the construction of a house is a process by which masses of material are brought and held together through (or in accordance with) mechanical laws. But this answer as we have seen, is dubious, or at best only partial. The construction of the house, whatever else it may be, is a *patterning or structuring of contacts or events.* It has the geometric format of continuances (ongoings) connected by dichotomies (events). Quantitative formulations, such as those of forces, are not enough, by themselves, to describe this pattern of events since they are not enough for the complete description of a single event. Nor do such forces act as "agencies" for the structuring of a house. These criticisms hold in spite of the fact that the quantitative laws *always operate,* and with great exactness, whenever structurings of events occur. Quantitative laws are omnipresent and invariable in nature. They are highly important theoretically as well as for practical purposes. *But so are events and the structuring of events.* Quantitative laws cannot logically be called the "architects" or "causes" of event-structuring. Speaking generally, they do not account for some of its most significant aspects. If the latter are to be fully understood, their explanation must be sought in another quarter. We suggest that one should search for a structural type of law.

But here some vigorous objections might be forthcoming. What could such a type of law possibly be? Let it be granted that the laws of quantity fail to account for *everything;* that fact has long been conceded. But is there anything lawful about "just structure"? Are not all laws of nature, by necessity, quantitative laws? What other type of law could there be that could be stated with precision? Everything that happens, happens in some amount; *ergo,* should we not expect that all laws will be quantitative? Do we not always merely have to *assume* structures in nature and let it go at that? In raising this problem of structure are we not posing a question which science (if it cannot answer it quantitatively) finds unanswerable, and probably always will? Whether the structure that appears along with the quantitative laws be that of an atom, a molecule, a house, a machine, an organism, a pathological syndrome, an act of behavior, or a social institution, if we cannot explain the structure by quantitative laws, are we then not obliged to accept it as something for which there is no law, something that is either fortuitous or else an "emergent," the work of some unfathomable holistic or vitalistic principle in nature? Affirmative answers to most of these questions probably represent the implicit attitude of many workers in the field of science.

Though it is deeply entrenched in our thinking, the writer believes that this attitude really reflects only a sterotyped way of looking at the matter, a way adopted not by logical necessity or through a careful analysis of the situation, but in order to ease the discomfort of our present ignorance in the face of a very difficult, but not necessarily insoluble, problem. To take this negative attitude about structure permits us to forget the issue and to get on more rapidly with the important business of finding quantitative laws. Yet such an attitude cannot be justified by the commonest facts of daily observation. Take, for example, a developing embyro, a physiological process, an act of learned overt behavior, or the perception of an object. All these phenomena imply structure. Are they not lawful and predictable? Are they merely fortuitous? Is there not *some* predicability even in an economic system or in the workings of a legislature or a court of law? Do not collective or societal structurings of considerable stability and regularity arise on every hand, either as institutions or otherwise, to meet the variety of human needs? Must we assume that all these structures must either be explained in quantitative terms or else remain forever inexplicable so far as the laws of nature are concerned? To do this would seem like giving up half of the problem of science without even attempting its solution. Are we not, then, *obliged* to think of structuring as a primary fact of nature and of the possibility, therefore, of its following some lawful principle? Can we be any longer justified in trying to explain it by purely metaphysical constructs? Admittedly it is difficult to think precisely in terms of laws other than those of quantity; but do not the very circumstances of our experience compel us to make the attempt?

The problem of the two types of law does not trouble us in practical matters such as building a house. This is true, however, only because we do not have to "discover" the structure. It is present, prospectively, on the blueprint before us; hence we can safely "assume" it. This blueprint came from an architect's behavior—his brain probably had a good deal to do with it; and presumably some kind of structuring, analogous to that of the house, must have gone on in his cortex. But since that is over and done, and since it is beside the point, anyway, for the immediate work of the builder, why worry about it?

The quantitative laws of physics are quite enough to enable us to build the house—once we have the blueprint in hand. To be sure we have to have some blueprint or plan; but why make so much ado about it? Why not call it simply a "human invention"? The architect himself had to work according to the quantitative laws of *neurophysiology* in order to produce it. Besides, the particular house is not a *universal* phenomenon; and natural laws are concerned only with universals. We do not need, therefore, to invoke any special principle of aggregation. The quantitative laws are quite enough. If they are not enough, we can readily invoke some "agent" who assembles the structure "according to" natural (i.e., quantitative) laws.

The superficiality of such thinking becomes apparent as soon as we apply it to something whose structural plan is not already given, such, for example, as a perceptual act, or for that matter, any act of behavior. Surely, some kind of event-structuring goes on in the organism, or in the cortex, when an act of perception takes place. This structuring, moreover, is not a human artifact, but a part of the very constitution of the organism, and, as such, is not particularistic, but *highly lawful and general*. If this were not true, our perceptions could not have the stability and regularity which they obviously possess. No architect or agent can be found who designed this structure. There is no one who can give us nature's blueprint for the pattern that occurs in an act of perception. It is not something that can be invented, but something that must be discovered. And its discovery is as essential to a successful theory of perception as having the architect's blueprint is necessary for building the house. We might also add that all the quantitative or dimensional laws discovered in perceptual experiments will, by themselves, be unable to give us that blueprint. Perhaps one might think that we already know from physiology and anatomy the structure of events in perception. But this would be a very hasty assumption. We have still to find that structure. As for invention, when human beings invent something, they are themselves operating as structures in structurally ordering the materials in their environment. What we need to discover are the more universal principles of structuring that lie behind *both* the artefact and its human inventor, and the connection between these principles and the quantitative laws which are also manifested in both.

If one requires still further evidence that quantitative procedures are not enough to explain the phenomena of aggregation, one might ask one's self why intensities or dimensionalities, though energies above zero are present, are powerless to bring about macroscopic phenomena at *subthreshold* quantitative levels. Why is it that at a *certain* energic level of sensory, neural, or motor activity the phenomenon of behavior *suddenly* appears? If the structure of the phenomenon depended upon quantities, or upon laws of quantitative variation alone, it ought to appear gradually as we increase the energic level from zero. There would be no macroscopic "threshold." Threshold, however, is a pervasive phenomenon in all the life sciences, if not in the physical world as well. Or again, why is it that energy itself does not approach zero as a lower (quantitative) limit, but occurs only as multiples of a certain minimum amount, discontinuously present in all phenomena? A continuous dimensional function, such as that involved in our familiar covariation laws, has within it no property that can provide a key for such riddles of discontinuity as these. There must be something else. Could we not infer, as a working hypothesis, that this "something else" is a *structural* law, or set of laws, that always works *along with* quantitative laws and yet is, in itself, distinct from them? If we could discover, for example, some principle by which the elements of the perceptual aggregate suddenly "come together" in a characteristic structure, without entangling our explanation in dimensions and quantities, we would then be achieving a solution of our problem. Vagueness, however, will not help. We must find a structural paradigm which is not only lawful, but can be stated in terms as definite and objective as any of the quantitative formulations. And the final statement must also provide a place for the quantitative aspects that are likewise always present. We must try to discover *two* types of laws of nature, not merely one; and we must find their interrelationship within the total scheme.

PROLEGOMENA TO A STRUCTURAL THEORY; STRUCTURAL PROBABILITY

May it not be conceded, then, that the possibility of a structural principle in nature, playing a part in perception, is sufficiently plausible to encourage us to go ahead, using this idea as a working hypothesis to see where it will lead? If this much can be granted, we can return directly to the problems of perception, combining our search for a principle of perceptual aggregation with this new hypothesis of a general integrating law. This effort might lead us, finally, to a conceptualization of the way in which quantitative laws find their place within the structural setting. First, merely as a suggestion of how the two principles seem to work together in perception, let us recall some of the comments made earlier in connection with the theories.

It was proposed, for example, that Helson's pooling and weighting theory required some kind of "judgmental" structure in order to give the dimensional law of adaptation-level its full significance. The same was said to be true of the frames of reference with which the quantitative law of the social norm was associated in Sherif's theory. We saw that a frame was needed for frame of reference theory. Following our broad definition of structure as a pattern of ongoings and events, the "frame" could be considered to be a collective structure in which the "perceiving" or "overtly acting" structure of the individual is a part or substructure. Such a concept would be more explicit than the commonly employed notion of an individual acting as a member of a "reference group." The application appeared again in so-called perceptual defense. Here the possibility arose of a relationship between collective and individual orders of structuring that might, in turn, be related to the lengths of exposure-time required to perceive socially tabooed words. The sign and degree of "relevance" of a perceptual (i.e., individual) structure to the collective structure of which the former is a part, and in which the individual is "potently involved," might conceivably affect the amount of energies of the perceptual structure. Such statements are of course made in a purely hypothetical way, pending the clarification of the experimental situation. In the theory of set-dynamics (Chapter 16) we found it illuminating to distinguish between the *format*, or structural aspect, of the set, which was given its completion by the presentation of the expected stimulus-object, on the one hand, and the *energies* of the events of stimulus-input, on the other, energies that raised the set-perception aggregate to the threshold level of activity. Here again, the picture was seen in both its non-quantitative and quantitative aspects. The hypothesis of the two types of law was usefully employed.

These illustrations are, of course, merely suggestive. We have as yet given no substantial clue as to what the structural format of the set or perception is like, or of the integrating principle that must be latent in structural law if the latter is to have explanatory significance. But let us recall some further points in our earlier commentary. In the preceding chapter some attempt was made to bring the quantitative and structural aspects together in a single scheme. It will be remembered that the automobile and the act of eating were used as illustrations. It was suggested that perceived dimensionality and other quantitative aspects of perception could be considered to be the *degree* or *amount* in which a structure operates, though this structure, *as a pattern*, is non-quantitative in its description. That is, they can represent the energies that are involved within a structure which is *not limited* to these energic considerations, but has a kinematic, or geometric, aspect as well. In contrast with this "amount" in which a structure occurs there was postulated, as a separate, but in part related, principle, the *probability* that the structure would occur *at all*. The latter principle did not, in itself, admit of continuous or dimensional variation, but was based upon the combined occurrence of a constellation of elementary, all-or-none, events. To this notion we gave the name *"structural probability."* We have further contended that, while every aggregate occurs or operates *in some amount* and while quantitative and covariation laws always hold good in the process, it is just as true that without the "probability" of the structure's occurrence as a constellation of events there would be no quantitative law pertaining to the structure at all. Structural probability, then, which is postulated as being a probability of structuring that is greater than randomness or chance, can be a part of our answer to the problem of the aggregating principle. It also gives us a partial content for our assertion that there is, in nature, a type of universal law that is not embraced under the usual quantitative or dimensional formulas. Such a law could be, in part, a law of probabilities that events will occur at certain regions of space through time.

But obviously structural probability is not the whole answer. It is the structural aspect itself, not merely the probabilities of its occurrence, that must now engage our attention. Probability of events, though it gives us something besides measured quantities to work with, still leaves us rather vague about the "format" of the structured aggregate. In order to have a prediction of the latter we must find some principle that "biases" probability away from pure chance and in favor of the structure's occurrence. If the perceptual theories have failed to find the key to perceptual aggregation in such ideas as contexts, configurations, determinative wholes, molar agencies, and fields, and if the dimensional laws cannot supply this key but themselves depend upon it, what then *is* the secret of this principle? When we speak of the probability of the structure's occurrence as a connected pattern of events, what is it, in general terms, that occurs? What is the pattern like? By what means does it possess a format that is self-delimited and autonomous through time, and that serves as a basis for the characteristics which the eight major generalizations of the theories have attributed to it? Has it, perhaps, some kind of spatiotemporal "layout" some "kinematic geometry," that is characteristic? If so, perhaps this fact will lead us to the principle of aggregation and help to provide the theoretical foundations we need. In finding such a solution we would also be answering the puzzling question as to what kind of law *other than* quantitative could be conceived as existing in nature.

A THEORY OF THE STRUCTURING OF EVENTS: STRUCTURAL KINEMATICS AND DYNAMICS; THE MODEL

Let us recall for a moment the elements of which the aggregate is composed. There are stimulus-events at receptor surfaces. These are both exteroceptive (eye, ear, etc.) and proprioceptive (events at kinaesthetic end-organs from sensory-accommodation responses or changes of tonus). There are events at the neural end-plates adjacent to muscle fibers. There are innumerable (synaptic) events in the lower brain regions and especially in the cortex. There are probably events in internal bodily changes that might be included in the aggregate. And everywhere there are ongoing processes (conducted neural impulses, muscle-fiber contractions, and the like) which have the aforementioned events as their junction points. Has this ongoing-event pattern any characteristic form? If so, what is it? Instead of regarding its form in the traditionally familiar manner, as an open-ended, linear chain from receptor to cortex or from stimulus to response, we shall now take a different course. Let us follow the lead of certain theories which make use of *the principle of circularity.* Let us think of the series as *always coming back upon itself and completing a cycle.* The cycle of ongoings and events can be terminated at the region from which it starts, or it can be conceived as continuing, *repeating itself indefinitely in circular fashion.*

In order to visualize the situation let us think of a *thin wire hoop,* capable of being bent in any direction or shape, but always remaining a *hoop,* upon which are placed, at intervals, a number of cross-marks (x's). Think of the cross-marks as actually cutting the hoop into segments. The model is, of course, kinetic, not static. The segments of wire into which the hoop is broken by the cross-marks represent *ongoing processes;* the cross-marks are the *events* between these ongoings. It is clearer, perhaps, to call the cross-marks "event-*points.*" A succession of ongoings and events thus occurs around the hoop, and the succession can repeat itself indefinitely. Much evidence for this sort of ongoing-event geometry has already been cited. Proprioceptive backlash with repeated circuits of motor adjustment, self-maintaining cycles of sensory accommodation, and other reflex postural tensions are familiar to us in the motor theories. Cybernetists have exploited circular feed-back systems and reverberatory circuits to great advantage. The latter structures have given a basis for the "universals" of perception, for ideation, and for memory. We shall employ this circuital idea as a hypothetical basis on which to build a theory of "structural kinematics."

Self-closedness and self-delimitation are essential to any concept of structure, a fact which applies both to the whole and to its constituent parts. No part can be "left hanging" without interrelations with other parts. The concept of a circularity of the ongoing and event series seems the best possible means of securing such self-closedness and interdependence of parts. In a *cycle* of ongoings and events each ongoing element is related to others. It is connected to others by events both on one side and on the other in space, and with events both before and after it in time. No element is left out or unconnected; and the "negative causation" test (p. 76) would show that every element is necessary. With this circular paradigm as the basis of a structural theory we can now achieve, by its various possible elaborations and logical extensions, some interesting results.

Starting, then, with the "hoop-model," the writer will continue in the direction of his own theory, which he has called a *"theory of event-structure."* It consists, essentially, of a kinetic geometry or kinematics of the self-closedness of ongoing-event series and a probability concept of the energies (i.e., events) involved in such self-closed structures and their interrelationships. The model and its elaborations are to be conceived from the beginning in abstract terms so that the theory can be applied, broadly, to phenomena at any level. Though our preceding "hoop-construction" of a cycle of ongoings and events was illustrated concretely in the physiology of the behavioral act, it could have been exemplified in many other realms. *The first step of the theory is the conceptualization of a complete and potentially repetitive cycle of ongoings and events.* The construction has already been typified by the "hoop" that was broken into a succession of ongoing processes with event-points between them. This aspect can be called the *"c"* lay of structure (*c* is for circuital or circular). *It is the elementary form upon which the geometry of self-closedness is built,* though the way in which it is here stated will later be seen to need some modification.

We are now ready for a further aspect. Picture now *two* segmentalized hoops like that of our original model, placed in planes at right angles to each other, and fitted together in such a way that their circumferences are touching at two points (that is, two "event-points"). By bending the hoops into irregular forms and permitting any angle between them they might also be made to touch each other at more than two points. Or again, one might be made to run parallel with the other through a part of its ongoing-event series, and then depart from the other to return later—making a kind of loop. We thus have "tangencies" of cycles through which events can be "contributed" by one cycle to another ("positive interstructurance"), or through which one cycle might "*prevent*" or "*inhibit*" events in the other ("negative interstructurance"). Both these effects might be present in one double-tangency system, as in the principle of the "negative feed-back" if the main line production is also considered as a cycle. It is possible, of course, that such systems may be made up not merely of two, but of a considerable number of such tangent cycles. This construction we shall call an "event-*system*," as distinguished from the single event-*cycle*. This development of the model will carry circularity further, in that it can provide for facilitating and inhibiting relationships within a self-closed system. (But let us imagine also that two event-cycles might have a facilitating or an inhibiting relationship if they were not a true system but, like two hoops laid side by side, possessed only a single point of tangency, a situation that might be called "out-structural" tangency.)

We now proceed to a further step. The closed chain of ongoings and events, since it is neither open-ended nor indefinitely extended in space, but a real (cyclical) structural entity, can be used as a unit of a structure of a larger or "compounded" type. Thus we can imagine that we have a considerable number of segmentalized hoops like the first one; and we put them together into a larger *circle of hoops*. Each hoop touches two others at event-points (one on the one side and one on the other). Since we must remember that ongoings are involved, the two contacts of each hoop will also represent a succession in time. A larger self-closed structure is now formed that is composed entirely of the single hoop structures as parts. The total structure is the "including" structure; the single hoop structures are the "included." In other words, we can build a "higher order" of structure made up of a *cycle of cycles* of ongoings and events. Still higher orders can be structured as cycles of these larger cycles, and so on. This development of the model will be called the property of "*order*." It should now be noted that the principle of ordering is not limited to event-cycles; it can apply also to event-*systems*.

A three-dimensional or spherical model would be required to show such a situation, but the reader can no doubt visualize it.

It is obvious that these possibilities (and there are others we cannot take time to mention) arise because of the one basic stipulation that the ongoing-event series is self-closing. Without this assumption it is hard to see how any sort of kinematics of structure could be developed. Of course, a network of single straight lines could be drawn, and one might attempt to call that a structure. But it should be remembered that we are dealing with ongoings (motions). Can an ongoing start from "rest" at a junction with a given line and then proceed to another "rest point" as it touches another line? Aside from the fact that relativity-theory shows us that there *is no* absolute rest, we have to make our model fit the microcosm as well as the macrocosm; and we have firm reason to believe that the minute particles of nature are *always* ongoing. If, then, we do not bring the ongoing around to self-completion, as a cycle, we have to imagine that it is infinitely extended. But structures, if they are anything at all, must be finite. Moreover, they cannot close one another, as lines butting against one another enclose empty spaces; they must be *self*-closed; that is, they must have a cyclical, or circuital, format; and this must be true down to the smallest units of which a structure is composed. One cannot build a true structure out of linear, open-ended, or infinitely extended materials.

This thought immediately makes us doubt the method of our first construction, the "c" lay of the hoop. For here the segments were simply lines that extended between the cross-marks or events. Let us now correct that construction and think of these *line-segments also* as (smaller) *self-closed cycles.* So again we have a relationship of order: a cycle composed of smaller cycles. There is now, if we apply this correction to all the preceding models, *no unit* in our whole set of constructions that is not completely cyclical or self-closing; and the same is true of every construction as a whole. We have now extended the property of order (cycles of cycles) "downward" as well as "upward"; we have a complete and pervasive structuring "in depth." For practical purposes we shall proceed in some of the later constructions, for the sake of clarity, as though our hoop segments were still linear rather than self-closed. The reader, however, should always try to conceive the situation in the terms of self-closingness of *every structural unit.* Every structure except the smallest or "lowest" is now imagined as made up, in its *c* lay, of parts which are themselves self-closing structures of ongoings and events; and the self-closing of the parts makes the self-closing of the whole possible. The "lowest," or elementary, structures are, of course, cycles merely of on-going. We are never, then, without a self-delimitation and unity of the aggregate, from the simplest to the most elaborate systems or the highest orders. The kinematic resources of this model for depicting the closely knit and unified character of the aggregate are indeed great.

There is a likelihood, at this point, that the reader may become confused, or that he may raise an objection by asking "What has all this to do with the organism?" Even at the very start of our model-building with the hoop it may have seemed inappropriate to say that ongoings are "*connected*" by events. Is it not rather a case of one ongoing *starting* a succeeding ongoing, as in the "event" of the activation of the receptor by the stimulus, or the firing of one neuron by another (or others) at the synaptic junctions? The first ongoing process releases some energy that is "stored" in the second. It serves as an excitant that "triggers" the response of the second. And so it is also with the relation of neuron to muscle fiber. This linear, agent-like concept of ongoings and events, however, is quite foreign to the structural concept and must be avoided in order to understand the theory we are here presenting. Events are the facts (or points) of contact and nothing more; they are not acts or processes. But can we *justify* our present concept of the connecting of two ongoings (as if both were already in process) by what we are here calling an event (really an event-*point*)? And are we permitted to go even further and say, as we have just said, that two ongoings that come to event-point are really continuing cycles in themselves, so that whatever elements "go on" (for example, two minute particles) move in cycles that converge toward each other, come to "event-point," and then go away from each other again? The reader may object that neural conduction across synapses is a one-way affair, from axone to dendrite, not a two-way affair at the synapse as we seem to be making it.

Yet the idea as we have stated it is exactly what the writer wishes to defend. We must think, however, in terms smaller than the whole neuron or muscle fiber in defining our ongoings. In the first place, as to whether there could be ongoing in the neuron without having a preceding neuron "fire" it, we must reply affirmatively. There is probably some continual activity (self-firing) in cortical neurons. As for one-way conduction, this exists only at synapses, not in the body of the neuron itself; in the latter, conduction can take place in *either* direction. At the synapse the one-way transmission is probably due only to the fact that dendrites of the succeeding neuron are closer together than axone terminations and can therefore provide a larger (i.e., threshold) spatial summation as they are "fed into" by the terminations of preceding axones. The spike potential by which the main neural impulse travels axonewards, moreover, seems to fade out near the end of the neuron, or at least the local potential is relatively enhanced, so that the state of affairs there, as a "one-way conduction," is not clear.

But when we look at the picture conceptually from an ultramicroscopic viewpoint something still more revealing is seen. The travelling impulse really consists of a wave of temporary depolarization of the membrane, followed, in its wake, by a return of the membrane to polarization. What does this wave consist of if not of a succession of *minute cycles* of positive ions passing from the outside through the neuron's membrane to the inside where electrical neutralization is produced by association with other (negative) ions, and from there passing back again to the outside (repolarization)? The so called "wave," then, is "propagated" by successive events· (or dichotomies) between the cyclical ongoings of molecular or atomic structures. The writer does not pretend that this picture is accurate or specific in detail, but it does show that we have at least some ground for our claim that ongoings in neurons really *are* cyclical affairs, if we take them at an elementary level, and that the "particles" involved can be conceived as converging to event-points and then diverging from each other. And so it could be, also, at the synapse, where "interneuronal transmission" is said to take place. Though when viewed more grossly interneuronal transmission across synapses seems to be a one-way affair, it is not unreasonable to conceive that this effect, in finer detail, represents minute cycles of ongoings which are connected by event-points. The same sort of situation may well be true in the muscle fiber. Tonus contraction of a muscle seems to suggest a series of continual cyclical ongoings at the molecular level. Phasic muscular action is a more macroscopic phenomenon, but still cyclical, in terms of contraction and relaxation. We do, therefore, have some basis for our model in which events, as we have defined them, occur between cyclical ongoings at the minute or elementary levels. It is true, of course, that a large part of the energies of neural and muscular activity come from the neuron or muscle fiber itself. Though we cannot here go into this matter, it is the writer's opinion that such energic supply could also be interpreted through similar structural kinematic principles at a lower level. Perhaps these considerations will satisfy the reader, at least tentatively, so that he will be willing to proceed.

Another important feature must now be added to the model. In an earlier paragraph we spoke of the "probability" of the structure's occurrence as an aspect of the integrating or aggregating principle. The model, thus far, seems to omit provision for this aspect, since with our hoops it seems a *certainty*, not merely a probability, that events will occur between the segments (cycles) of ongoing. Furthermore we have made no provision for the varying quantities or amounts in which the structure may operate. We have laid no basis for quantitative laws or dimensions. These deficiencies, however, can soon be remedied. In the remedy we shall offer, the model can still be regarded as general, adapting itself to phenomena in all the different realms or levels. For concreteness, however, let us take an example from the field of behavior.

Whenever an act of perception or any other form of behavior occurs we do not have a series consisting of a succession of a single receptor-cell, single neuron, and single muscle fiber, but a succession consisting of a large number of each of these elements. At each segment (sub-cycle) of the cyclical succession there is a whole "sheaf" of elements, operating, as it were, "in parallel." That is to say, there is not a single ongoing constituting an ongoing segment, but an ongoing "role" in which many element-processes proceed together. Many receptor cells are active side by side, many afferent neurons convey their impulses together, many muscle fibers "in parallel" contract as we complete the cycle in a single perceptual or overt-behavioral act. And similarly, we must conclude that the series of events that lie between the ongoings does not comprise a circular pattern of single events but a circular series of clusters of multiplicities of events. Instead of thinking of single events between the segments (or subcycles) of the hoop, we can now think of "event-*regions*," or separate and successive volumes of space through time, within which the events in the respective "event-roles" occur. The situation can be conceived by taking up a large number (or bundle) of hoops in our hand, their ongoing-event series all running along side by side, and so arranged that the cross-marks (events) come together in clusters (i.e., each cluster within its own "region"). We now have a hoop-"format," or cyclical arrangement composed of many hoops side by side. We have thus added a further "lay" to the kinematics of structure. Let us call it the "n" lay (n signifies number, though we are referring here only to the format aspect, rather than to quantities).

This property when used in a quantitative sense, will help us to account for intensities and other dimensions in the perceptual (or behavioral) act. In the energic sense, summations or averages at event-regions are here appropriate; and it can be conceived that perceived spatial magnitudes as well as intensities may result from such summations. It is important to remember that, in applying all the earlier constructions (systems and orders), whenever we do anything with our hoop or structure of hoops, *the structure is always to be conceived in this "n lay" fashion.* Every cycle, or cycle of cycles, of ongoings and events has its n lay as well as its c lay. In every system the several cycles are to be conceived in the same manner.

As for the matter of the "probability" of the structure's occurrence, this can now be readily conceived by a further slight change in the hoop-model. Now that we have a *bundle* of ongoings in each of the segments of the c lay, let us suppose that there is not a hard and fast, one-to-one, connection of ongoings by intervening events as shown at the x-marks on the hoops, but only a *probability* (depending on a number of conditions) that events will occur between them. Some of the small cyclical ongoings in one ongoing role *may not* come to event-point with an ongoing in the succeeding role. There is always a degree of randomness at minute levels in nature that must not be overlooked. It is for this reason that we have employed the concept of "event-region." There is a weighted probability, but not a certainty, that events will occur in what we have called the event-regions. How many there will be depends in part upon the probabilities of encounter of a single ongoing with another in the space and time theoretically chosen for the region concerned, and in part upon the number of ongoings that enter the region. Statistical considerations and the notion of "probable density" of events are here brought into play. The probability will, of course, depend in part upon the number of ongoing elements present in the n lay of the structure at or near the region in question.

But this aspect is only a spatial one. We must remember also that the subcycles making up a larger cycle can *repeat* themselves, with definite *time periods* of completion, so that the probable density of event-points will also depend upon another feature or lay of structure. *This feature we can call the "repetitive" or "r" lay.*[2] Cycles of very short period (high frequency) that feed into a "region" will afford the possibility of more event-points *through time* in that region than will cycles of a longer period. In other words, probability in a region represents the summation of events in the region in both space and

---

[2] The r lay must now be added to the c and n lays as a universal property of all structures. It occurs not only in single cycles but in cycles at the higher orders.

time.   Probability of the *structure's* occurrence means a density of events in the several event regions, resulting from the *two* lays (*n* and *r*) of each of the two converging sets of ongoings, that will exceed the "macroscopic" threshold.   To predict the structure's occurrence as a whole we must, of course, think of this occurrence as the *combined* probability for *all* the event-regions of the structure.   Threshold, in terms of the theory, is a small scalar range within which a very rapid rise in the ascending curve of such combined event-probability takes place.   It is based, in part, upon the consideration that, when two approximately equal clusters of ongoings (as of particles) come into a common region, and the particles move randomly *within* the region, the probable number of collisions will increase as the *square* of the number of particles in a cluster.[3]   As the number of such ongoings becomes very large, therefore, the density of encounters is so great that an effect is macroscopically observable, and this effect appears rather suddenly.   We say, at that moment, that the "threshold has been crossed."   It is to be remembered that the event-region has a *time* dimension (due to *r* lay of structure) as well as the three spatial dimensions.   There can be temporal as well as spatial summation to attain the threshold density.   Beyond threshold density further increases of density will provide variations in perceptual or overt-behavorial *quantities, energies,* or *dimensions*—in short, in the *amounts* in which the structure is seen to operate.   Since probability of an encounter has a limit of 1.0, a condition represented by the complete filling of the space and time of the regions by ongoings (as of particles), there will also be an upper limit to the density of events in the structures (upper threshold, asymptote of learning curve, etc.).

And so we have finally provided a place for the *quantitative and covariational laws;* and we have done so within a cyclical format of events which, *as a format,* is essentially kinematic and non-quantitative.   The *n* lay, or the *r* lay, of the cycle could be anything, *quantitatively,* from one to an immense number; but the cyclical *character* of the structure, which cannot in itself (that is, apart from any specific diameter) be described quantitatively, remains as a kinematic constant.[4]

[3] The occurrence of a state of affairs in which there is non-randomness of a cluster as a whole, but randomness *within* the cluster, is illustrated by the movement of the minute droplets in a fog that is contained in a glass vessel.   Their *zigzag* course (under Brownian motion) combined with the fact that they have an average tendency to *descend* (gravitation) shows both randomness and non-randomness (Schroedinger, 1946).

[4] In order to have a clear understanding of what follows it is recommended that the reader reread the section just concluded, visualizing the constructions and

Such in briefest outline are some of the principal concepts on which the writer's theory of event-structure is based. Only the main aspects have been sketched, and many features essential to a clear understanding have had to be omitted. A few of these, however, will be referred to later. Such a model, of course, takes us beyond what the theories of perception have envisaged; and it is not limited to perception, or even to psychology, but is stated in terms that can be completely general for organismic phenomena. Though it was formulated by the writer prior to, and independently of, his study of the theories of perception, it will be interesting in what follows to observe that, with the help of a few added postulates, it would also seem to develop naturally from the major generalizations of theories themselves. At least it seems in good accord, as we shall try to show, with what these theories have taught us. The writer believes that such a structural kinematics and dynamics, elaborated from the simple concept of a self-closing cycle of ongoings and events, might take us far along toward a solution of our present problem. It might provide us with a glimpse of a possible type of natural law that is *other than quantitative,* yet at the same time making a definite place for quantitative law and bringing about a unification of the two aspects. And it might, in so doing, give us a key to the riddle of perceptual integration and a means of realizing the full potentialities of the perceptual theories through discovering the essential unity of their contributions.

FACTS OF ORGANISMIC BEHAVIOR THAT SUPPORT THE MODEL

It is evident that the usefulness of event-structure theory will depend upon how closely the paradigm of structure outlined above can be shown to accord with physiological facts and the happenings involved in the behavior of organisms. In other words, can circularity be proved as the true kinematic format of all acts of perception, and beyond that, for all instances of behavior? Though our habits of thinking of behavior in linear terms and in terms of agent-like, functional, or molar actions are deeply embedded, so that a *circularity* of the ongoing-event series may seem difficult to envisage as a general principle, the writer believes that it can be established in accordance with known facts. We shall here give only a brief outline of this demonstration.

---

familiarizing himself as fully as possible with the terms and relationships employed.

We have already canvassed the matter to some extent in the smaller order of cyclical ongoings at the molecular or atomic levels. Are the ongoing-event series of higher (more inclusive) orders that are made up of these structural units also cyclical? Here we consider acts of behavior as such. Since the question is one of circularity, what we have to show is that such acts comprise ongoing-event chains (of subcycles) that come back, kinematically, to the event-region from which they started. In coming back they can either result in a lowering of the energies (event-points) of that initial region so that the cycle tends to stop there (mere completion, $r = 1$), or they can lead, if the energy level is kept up, to a repetition of the cycle ($r > 1$). The essential point is that they *come back to the starting region*.

It will be evident, on reflection, that this condition does hold for all the so-called primary or "biological" acts of behavior. The "thirst quenching" behavior-cycle can be said to start with a drying of the mucous membrane of the mouth and throat. The ensuing subcycles of ongoings and events (receptoral, neural afferent-central-efferent, muscular, water-glass contacting and tipping, water-flowing, etc.) lead around to an event in which water contacts the mucous membrane of the throat and dryness is lessened. The r lay of the cycle, or of a loop of it, will probably be apparent as more than one swallow is taken, and so on, until the energic density in the initial "throat" region is brought to equilibrium with the rest of the cycle. Our point here is simply that there is a true kinematic cycle *returning to the initial event-region* (mucous membrane of the throat). "Hunger" behavior will be seen to follow a similar pattern; and so will the mating act (from events involved in "tumescence" in event regions within the genitals around back to "detumescence" in those same regions). An $r > 1$ lay is involved in the kinematics of the act of copulation. In the righting of body-tilting the cycle begins with an increase of density of events in the area of the semicircular canals and returns through the ongoings and events in subcycles of the total "righting behavior" cycle to a restoration of the initial or usual density in that same region. Avoiding-behavior cycles (where the r lay is often 1), as in the removing of the hand from a hot object, again begin at an event-density region (at the skin surface) and complete themselves by subcycles of ongoings and events that return to the same region (region of contact of hand with hot object), with event-point density at that region abruptly lowered (by withdrawal) toward zero. In perceptual behavior, sensory-accommodation, and reflex adjustments of all sorts, we have ongoings and events of circular proprioceptive backlash cycles ($r > 1$). Here the c lay is relatively low (i.e., number of event-regions in the cycle is less) as compared with more complex acts of behavior that involve numerous environmental contacts and a greater number of synaptic event-regions. This fact may account for their readier meeting of the combined regional probability-density requirement of structurization and therefore for the early and apparently spontaneous appearance of these structures (theory of nativism). We shall not attempt here to demonstrate kinematic circularity in the so-called derived or "higher" behaviors of thinking, functional autonomies, and the like; but they are believed to follow the same principle. In our later discussion of interstructurance and meaning the cyclical kinematic possibilities for these acts will more clearly emerge.

The evidence, then, so far as we have reviewed it, seems to point to the soundness of the event-structure paradigm for behavior. The model does seem to fit the organism. We shall therefore hypothesize, for present purposes, that every act of behavior—not just proprioceptive feed-backs, backlash, circular reflexes, or cortical circuits (cycles already recognized in the theories), but *every* behavioral phenomenon—follows a structural law or paradigm of the type suggested by our model. Every perceptual or overt-behavioral activity will be hypothetically regarded as a self-closing series of ongoings and events with the various "lays" above described, a structure not only comprising a circuital series of events, but presenting also the possibilities of interstructuring, through event-tangencies, into self-closed *systems,* or into larger cycles or systems of more inclusive orders.

FURTHER ASPECTS OF THE THEORY; ITS BEARING UPON CONFIGURATION, EXPLANATION OF LEARNING, UNIFICATION OF LEARNING AND PERCEPTION, AND EQUIPOTENTIALITY

We need, now, to give attention to a few other features of the model that follow as corollaries from its basic statement. Most of these, also, are quite in harmony with the theories of perception and are, in fact, called for by them; and all are consistent with the postulates thus far employed. Through these additions we can pass directly to a structural interpretation of the major generalizations of the theories and an attack upon some of the perceptual problems earlier listed.

First, let us note that since the purely kinematic or geometric aspects of the model are describable in complete independence of specific quantities and covariation laws, we do not need to be concerned here either with size or direction, or with any fixed temporal limits of the structure. Our interest in the cycles, as structural format, is not a metric one. Ongoing-event geometry is a geometry of self-closedness, of the cyclical tendency or completion of ongoing-event series and their tangencies, and of that alone. The structures can be of any time-period or duration (r-lay), or of any type of spatial deformation or distortion, so long as their fundamental property of self-closedness remains. They can be of any radius of curvature, from the radius of the universe down to the vibrations of the "elementary physical particle"; or they can be of changing radius. In this way we can provide for flexibility, configuration, and the non-veridical as well as the veridical transformations that are found in the perceptual aggregate.

Second, as previously suggested, the events or encounters in the cycle or between cycles can be regarded not only as geometric features, having a role of format-connection, but as units or increments of energy. For events, as happenings in the physical world, always involve energies. The ongoings of the cycles provide the "formats" in which these units of energy occur. A concept of *"structural-dynamics"* is thus interlaid within the "structural-kinematic" framework. Energy, even in its smallest units, always implies structure.

Third, we should not regard a cycle or system-structure as closed in the sense that it is completely isolated from surrounding aggregates (i.e., other structures). On what corresponds to both the "receptor" and "effector" sides of the organism or the act of behavior there are tangent relations with outside "environmental" structures. Such relationships also hold at lower orders of structuring within the organism. Events thus occur between the "organism" and its "environment" both as "stimulations" and as environmental changes produced by "effector movements;" and these events add energies (capacity for event-points) to the mean, or "proper," energy-level of the structure, or, on the other hand, reduce its energic level. We thus identify our self-closing structure as an open-system, having, in terms of system theory, its energic "input" and "output." In the receipt and passing on by the structure of energies from and to the outside the "steady state" characteristic of open-system aggregates is maintained; or, by progressive displacement of energy within the structure, it can be said that the structure itself "comes to its own equilibrium." In so doing, however, *it retains, in either case, its cyclical character.* These relationships of a structure to other (outside) structures are called "out-structural tangencies."

Fourth, since self-repeating cycles (r lay) are "independent of time," different parts of a total structure, themselves structures, can be "readied" or in operation continually or at different times and later brought together in the self-closing order of succession of the total format. There is also a possibility of "storage" of cycles or subcycles at various orders of elaboration (cf. the cybernetic theory of memory and universals). A hypothetical illustration of the former principle can be seen in our theorem of set, where the set-structure is not complete and lacks certain elements, i.e., subcycles, yet to be brought into the structure ("hypothesis is yet to be confirmed"). The possibility, also, of "scanning-cycles" has a meaning here, as does the frequently observed interchangeability of the spatial and temporal distribution of energic elements (c and r lays of structure).

Fifth, and finally, all structures of ongoings and events can be thought of as occurring by the principle of *structural probability* earlier described. Whether the structure will operate or not is a matter not of variational quantitative law (though such laws are associated with its operation), but of the joint, or combined, densities of the probability of occurrence of events in all the event-regions necessary to the structure. The curving or self-closing character of the elementary ongoings, which, as will be seen, is suggestive of the general theory of relativity and which, in accordance with that theory, is *more* curving in regions of "matter" or "greater density of the field," is a feature that is believed to bias the probability toward a density of event-occurrences in the event-regions that is greater than that which would be produced by randomness or chance. And this condition is equivalent to the "negative entropy" of the structure. From a dynamic point of view the probable densities within the event-regions are the "energies" of the structure.

These considerations throw light upon the temporal or genetic development of an act of behavior. The degree of predictability of a particular perception or overt act through time and "trials," or at various durations of exposure of the stimulus, may be simply a matter of the distribution through time and/or trials of the structure's (complete) occurrence. The probability densities in the event-regions increase cumulatively through successive trials or through lengthened exposures (r lay or n lay). Suppose we plot a curve, the abscissa indicating the successive time intervals and repeated trials or presentations of the stimulus object or situation, and the ordinate showing the *probability*, from 0 to 1.0, of the structure's complete occurrence as empirically determined through blocks of trials. We now have a curve of learning, that is, a curve of the distribution of probability through successive periods of time and successive blocks of trials that the act will be "correctly" performed. The curve rises asymptotically toward an ultimate limiting probability of 1.0. But we also have here a curve that could show equally well the cumulative densities in the acquisition, through successive trials, of a perception.   The only difference between the two is the steepness with which the curve rises to its asymptote level, a condition that depends on various "probability biasing" conditions arising from the particular experimental task (maze turns, starting point, food in goal box, point of stimulus presentation, verbal-structuring requirement for "report" in a perceptual experiment, and so on).   The structural-dynamic conditions would give us a probability curve of great steepness (threshold) for the perception of an already familiar ("meaning-structured") object in a situation in which stimulus exposures (shown on the abscissa) are gradually lengthened from a hundredth of a second up to the threshold point.   The percept-*acquisition* curve, for simple percepts, probably rises suddenly early in life and stays at a high probability-level thereafter.   The curve of so-called "continuity" learning is *gradual* in the increase of its ordinate values of probability of structural occurrence, a fact which is due to the meager (or "ambiguous") nature of the kinematic biasing conditions employed in such (trial and error) experiments.   Such learning requires a greater number of presentations of the biasing situation than do cases of discontinuity or perceptual learning where biasing by the kinematic features of the situation and the act called for is greater and the probability curve therefore rises more steeply.   Another factor, of course, may be the difference in the c lay of the structures (complexity of the cognitive or overt problem).   In "latent learning," probability densities of a structure already in process of structurization can be conceived as stepped up suddenly by the introduction of events connected with a "relevant" or kinematically appropriate "reward."   We now see that event-structure theory might be able not only to embrace perception and learning in a single theoretical system but to go further and reconcile the issue over continuity and discontinuity learning.   Self-closing dynamic structure, with changing probability of occurrence, appears as a unifying concept not only for perceptual aggregates, but for behavior as a whole.

Since it is conceivable that structural probability could occur at its maximum at the very start (i.e., at the very first perception of an object) there might, in some cases, be an absence of any curve of "acquisition."   The probability density of the structure would, in these instances, be at its asymptote level from the beginning.   This consideration might explain cases of perception that have been claimed as "nativistic."   The nativism-empiricism controversy would thus be seen to resolve itself into a mere question of the character of the curve of probability of a structure's occurrence as plotted against the time-span of the individual's life with birth as the zero point.

The somewhat obscure phenomena of equipotentiality and mass action (p. 165f.) can also be elucidated by event-structure postulates. The findings of Lashley demonstrated that with certain qualifications one part of the cortex is as good as another for mediating learned acts involving perception and overt behavior. The notion of the specificity of any set of neural or synaptic elements with respect to a particular percept or habit must be rejected. Now in our model of structure we have been careful to deny any certainty that any two *specific* ongoing elements would come to an event-point, that is, that an event would take place between any two specific ongoings. Prediction of structurization was based only upon the *probable number* of encounters, their density in event-regions.

Consider for a moment the situation that leads to a structure's occurrence. There are vast numbers of "possible" receptor-loci at which, as event regions, clusters of events from a vast number of minute energy-providing elements scattered in the environmental manifold can occur. There are a multitude of objects, or points *in* objects, that can be contacted by effectors. These are dispersed, near and far, and in different densities, in the environment. There are large numbers of possibilities that muscle fibers can be activated at the efferent neural terminations at end-plates. There are innumerable morphological synaptic arrangements in the brain affording any number and distribution of possible event-regions. The problem before us is *not* how specific stimulated receptor elements, specific afferent and central neurons, specific synapses, and specific efferent neurons and muscle fibers get linked together to build up an enduring habitual response. This would be too gross, linear, and macroscopic a view. The problem is, rather, how, from the vast matrix of event-possibilities above-mentioned, and considering the matter as the ongoings of minute cycles, concerning the exact position, direction, or velocity of whose particles there is always an uncertainty, a particular self-closed structure of events (as a cycle of these minute cycles) gets built up to the "performance level" of density and thereafter maintains that level whenever the proper stimulus manifold or other characteristic conditions, external and internal, are presented. We do not start with specific pieces and try to put them together. We start with the entire manifold and ask how it knits together, how it "jells," as it were, into a particular structure. And the answer, here, is probability. There is no predictability as to what specific element-ongoing will come to event-point with what other, or exactly where or when this event will take place; but we *can* predict that within given space and time regions (event-regions) certain overall event-densities, or average numbers of encounters, will occur.

We assume a general self-closing tendency in cycles at every order. But we can also assume certain *"bounding"* or *"biasing"* conditions in predicting our structure. These are implied in what is called the general behavioral or learning situation. It seems obvious that the structure which will be most likely to occur in a given situation will be the one for some of whose event-regions opportunities are afforded by the environment (or by the ongoings of tangent internal structural manifolds already existing) *in the greatest event or energic density.* For example, an "eating"-structure will be more likely to occur when an apple is at hand and when we are "hungry" than in situations in which either or both of these conditions are absent. Hunger contractions (ongoings) in the stomach and events of contact of effectors with the apple are parts of the eating structure itself. Hence the general situation in which the individual acts or learns is already affording biasing conditions for the appearance of a certain structure, because it is already supplying a part of the (potential) format of that structure.

Our thesis now is that, given, first, the universal tendency of ongoings towards self-closing and, second, the biasing conditions present in the behavioral situation from environmental or internal already-existing structures, we can count on probability of encounters in the now restricted space and time volumes brought about by these circumstances to do the rest. We are here employing the fact of the universal randomness or indeterminacy now known to exist at the most elementary and minute levels of nature; but we are considering it not as a *complete* indeterminacy, but as biased, in a general way by the kinematic principle of circularity, and in a particular way by the *bounding conditions,* toward structurization. The randomness, in other words, is "partial" and "controlled." It is randomness *within* a condition of general ongoing that follows a definite law. In making our predictions that a structure will occur, or of what the structure will be (perceiving a certain object, eating, drinking, mating, or whatever other act), we do not need to care at all about any specific receptor or neural or motor element, nor about any specific synaptic connection or chain of specific connections. Probability densities at event-regions, under the influence of the conditions stated, will suffice.

But to return to Lashley's problem, we must now ask what must appear in the cortical part of the structure when probability densities in the structure as a whole are increasing or are high, as in a learned perception or habit. The answer, obviously, is an increase in n and/

or *r* lays of the structure, since the number and frequency in these lays are what determine the structure's event-capacity. More cycles "running parallel," like our bundle of hoops, in the structural format, or cycles of greater frequency of completion, are conceived to be present, with resulting increases of structural density (i.e., probability). But our notion of "parallel" is here somewhat crude and figurative. There is no reason to suppose that the *n* lay ongoings are really spatially parallel, or that they are confined to narrow bundles or bands. They are parallel only in the sense that they continue to be in their proper ongoing roles, so that the successive event-regions proper to the structure are maintained. Spatially they will, of course, be subject to the curvatures of the cortex, but they may lie spread out over it *We can conceive them as lying fairly uniformly distributed in large regions of the cortical substance.* If some of them are "longer" than others, we still have their frequencies (*r* lay) that can provide the necessary density of events in the proper regions.

If these suppositions are true, it will be seen that if we cut away a part of the cortex of an animal which has "learned a given habit," the amount of loss of the habit, as shown on relearning, will be about as great for removal in one portion of the cortex as it will for an equal amount removed in another portion. The probability density of event-points will not be affected because the amount of *n* lay removed will be about equal in the two cases, and the remaining *n* lay of the structure will therefore be the same. Hence we have the law of "equipotentiality": one part of the cortex (within limits) will be as efficient as another in "mediating a habit." What we *would* predict is that when a *large* portion, anywhere, is removed, the habit loss will be greater than when a smaller portion, anywhere, is removed; for there would be, in the former case, a greater reduction of cycles in the *n* lay and a corresponding loss of event-capacity at the structure's event-regions. This outcome, the positive correlation of habit loss with the *amount* of tissue removed, is just what Lashley found in his experiment. It was formulated as the "law of mass action" of the cortex.

FURTHER DEVELOPMENT OF STRUCTURAL DYNAMICS (ENERGICS): KINEMATIC AND ENERGIC CLOSURE; PRIMARY EVENT-REGION; EXPLANATION OF EQUILIBRIUM, STEADY STATE, SET, AND MOTIVATION

Using the intimate combination of structural kinematics (the non-quantitative aspect) with structural energies or dynamics (quantitative aspect), a new approach can be made to the major generalizations of the perceptual theories and to the phenomena and problems of behavior generally. Let us consider, for example, the familiar generalizations regarding equilibrium and steady state. The cycle of ongoings and events has, as we have seen, two forms of self-closing. One is a "kinematic closure," or completing of the format, with a possibility of repetitions of the cycle (r lay). The other is an "energic closure" which represents the coming of the cycle to equilibrium at a certain energic level or the return to, and maintenance of, a steady-state. The two are closely related. It is hypothesized that the self-closed, or closing, format of the structure, at least for "learned acts," "memories," "meanings," and so on, is maintained steadily through time (r lay) at a mean energic level (probability density) greater than chance, but less than the higher probability of which it might be capable if reinforced by a greater than usual number of events from tangent or environmental structures. This phase is the "autonomous" or "proper" level of the structure. In the energic balance of the organism's structural manifold it can be said to represent the "homeostatic" level of the structure. When some further stimulus (energic density) occurs that is adjacent to this structure (tangency), the density of event-point availability (capacity for energies) of the ongoing elements of the structure thus contacted is increased. The locus of this change as it first occurs within the structure is called the *"primary event-region."* The result is a displacement of energy, starting with the primary event-region, being communicated through the structure, and tending to raise its total energic state above the autonomous level. This effect will continue as long as the input from the adjacent structure lasts. We may assume, however, at least in typical cases of overt behavior, that there are also out-structural tangencies on the "effector" side of the organismic cycle, where energies are "given off" through event-points to environmental structures. By the law of entropy there is a continual tendency for these three structural manifolds (the organismic and the two environmental structures) to come to equilibrium with one another. The tendency, however, is not completely carried out, since the organismic structure is kinematically "quasiclosed" with respect to the outside and hence retains at least its autonomous level, and perhaps, for a time, an even higher level, according to the amount and persistence of the energies provided by an outside source to its primary event-region. As the organismic structure comes to its kinematic closure or completion it may be that the stimulus-energy source is cut off through some negative-interstructurance tangency. In that case the organismic structure quickly comes to its own equilibrium (energic closure). An instance of this sort would be found in a man's turning up his coat collar against a cold wind. In other cases the energic closure may be more gradual. For example, when strong "hunger-stimuli" persist in the body (resulting in a persisting primary event-region of an "eating" structure) and when the amount of food taken at one cycle-completion (mouthful) is small, the cycle of the eating act may go on, kinematically repeating itself, until some negative interstructurance with the "nutrient-carrying" blood-stream cycle reduces the primary events of the behavioral eating cycle to a level at which equilibrium can be attained.

Not only is there an energy-balancing tendency of the organismic cycle with respect to "out-structures" on one side and the other, but there is also a tendency for it to come to equilibrium *within itself;* for we must remember that it has a certain amount of "closedness" from its surroundings. This condition would mean an equalization of energies (probable density of event-points) among all the structure's event-regions, the effect of the primary event-region's enhancement becoming equally distributed within it. However, there would not necessarily be a cessation of the kinematics or ongoings of the structure. The cycle of ongoings and events could continue (r lay) even though the densities of the regions were equalized. Such a situation would be realized when, in the order of a cycle of cycles, each subcycle is passing on to the next subcycle, all around the total *repeating* cycle, exactly as much capacity for event-points (energies) as it is receiving from the preceding subcycle. This state of affairs represents the maximum entropy *for the structure.* But it also may represent a certain amount of *negative*-entropy of the organismic structure as a whole *if taken in connection with the adjacent outstructural manifolds.* In other words, it represents a "steady state" (cf. the discussion of open systems and Köhler's illustration of the candle-flame in Chapter 18). This steady state, however, is maintained above the autonomous level only so long as the total energic distribution is in favor of the density on the receiving, or input, side.

A steady state of this sort could be present in the lasting action of a sustaining *set.* It would, in such a case, be a continually "higher than usual" condition of the energic density of the structure, requiring a "less than usual" stimulus-input to bring it up to the threshold-probability level. This general situation accords with the facts of set (cf. also the covariation theorems of hypothesis theory and Chapter 16). The term *kinematic* closure means the serial completion of the self-closing chain of ongoings and events—for example, the overt act kinetically "performed" or the perception "attained." As we have seen, it may sometimes occur as one completion of the r lay, and at other times it may involve continued repetitions of the cycle. *Energic* closure means the "equilibrizing" process or the steady state within the structure, which not only proceeds by itself, but is also complicated, as we have seen, by the kinematic relationships of the structure to adjacent and tangent structural manifolds. Both types of closure must be considered in order to understand behavior. The non-quantitative aspect of structural format must, as we have seen so often, be present in order to give the quantitative law its full meaning. Even at subthreshold levels and subset levels of energy there are assumed to be energic densities in the event-regions of a structure that indicate some kinematic structurance above chance. These structural conditions are those of the "learned" or "retained" state of the act or the perceptual meaning. They represent the "autonomous" levels of structurance, the "retention of our habits through time."

Structural dynamics and the primary-event region enable us to incorporate another important and very general psychological concept within the theory, namely, motivation. For motivation of any sort (stimulation, drive, need-state, energizing effect of an emotion, etc.) can be regarded simply as a local increase or imbalance of probability density of event-points in a structure. That is to say, *motivation represents the energies of a primary event-region.* The primary-event region may be *anywhere in the cycle,* and there may be *more than one* such region. We should not, however, exclude the possibility that such a primary event-density may also be contributed by tangency with another cycle within an event-system. Some cycles of a system may reinforce ("motivate") others. An emotion, for example, probably represents a cycle of this sort, involving, in part, "autonomic" and "visceral" ongoings and events. It may also be kinematically *anti*structurant, rather than positively reinforcing, to a tangent cycle. It is necessary to keep the *kinematics* of structure always before us in order to understand the lay of the energies within the behavioral act.

EVENT-STRUCTURE THEORY IN RELATION TO THE PROBLEMS AND THEORIES OF PERCEPTION: DIMENSIONS, MEANING, PERSONALITY ASPECTS, CONSTANCY, FORM-QUALITY, FACILITATION AND INHIBITION; THEOREM OF INTERSTRUCTURANCE AND WEIGHTING

But let us continue with other problems more directly related to perception. Returning to perceived dimensions, we recall that we can here link up the structural aspect with quantitative law. Having provided a place within the non-quantitatively described format for energies as events, we can consider perceptual quantities or dimensions as the densities of events at the event-regions of (or between) the structures. These regions, of course, are variable as to their possible densities, depending upon the extent or intensities of stimulations, and perhaps upon the energic density of organismic structures that are tangent to the "perceiving" structure itself (hypothesis of directive-state theory). Dimensions or perceptual quantities are thus the "amounts" in which the structure operates. The events of the structure "pool" their energies, with a corresponding effect within the percept. An "average level" of them through a space and time volume may be automatically established, as is so often the case in manifolds comprised of myriads of minute elements or happenings. Perceptual threshold, as we have seen, is the lower limit of such densities for full perceptual performance.

The troublesome problem of perceptual meaning can now be handled. We can regard meaning both as an energically reduced state of structure and also as a kinematic modification of some originally *full and overt act,* such, for example, as the act of "handling" or otherwise "reacting to" an object. The meanings of objects originally come, in other words, from actual dealings with the environment. In this modification of the act-structure the event-cycle or system concerned has been abridged so that its operation is now largely "covert." A decreased n lay is probably also involved. Meanings require little energy—probably relatively few structural elements "in parallel" (n lay) are included. To say that the cycle is now abridged and covert is to imply that it is reduced in spatial extent by a shrinkage in its number of event-regions (c lay). For the events of actual environmental contact that originally occurred in the overt behavior are eliminated in "meanings about" the environment, or at least they are greatly reduced. The events and ongoings of the cycle in its "motor" regions may comprise merely those of tonic excitation and proprioceptive backlash. In some cases all peripheral regions may be left out, and the cycle may be limited *to the cortex alone. It is still, however, like every other instance of behavior, a self-closed structure.* It is a "meaning *cycle*" or cyclical system; and, though some events of contact with the environment are lost from its format, the meaning-cycle still follows, in an abridged way, the pattern of the full overt act which was its genetic basis. In other words, a meaning is simply an energically diminished and kinematically abridged behavioral act (act-structure). Such an interpretation is supported by the reduced, but still "appropriate," motor phenomena observed to be present in meaning situations (Jacobson, et. al.). We note from the theory, however, that the loss of elements of the c lay may be compensated for by an increase in the r lay. Meanings persist structurally through time, whereas the full energies of the structure of an overt act are present in the structure only for a short time.

An *abstract* meaning may be one in which the c lay is still further reduced until it comprises only the *"minimum essentials"* of event-regions common to the meaning-cycles for members of a class. *Linguistic* meaning consists of "language"-cycles, involving ongoings and event-points in the auditory receptors, the cortex, and the speech-organs, but capable also of similar abridgment, to covert meaning-cycle status. Such "language"-cycles, or linguistic meaning-cycles, are tangent, in a system relation, to the meaning-cycle for the object to which the "language" refers. (Recall again the two "hoop" event-cycles placed at an angle and touching each other at two or more event-regions.) Linguistic meaning is thus *dependent upon* other, earlier acquired, object-meanings (cf. pp. 571–573). It should be borne in mind that meaning-structures, also, occur by the probability-principle earlier described. Meaning-cycles, as well as overt-behavioral cycles, have their kinematic and energic closures and their thresholds. The threshold for such structures is lower (probability greater) than for overt acts because of the reduction of the number of event-regions (c lay).

The meaning-cycle concept throws light on the problem of personality, which, as we have seen, is related, through themas, projective techniques, and the like, to perception. A characteristic of personality in an individual is a meaning-cycle or system which, compared with other meanings, is strongly energic, and is also *characteristic in the individual's behavior-structure manifold*. It was previously called, in this book, a *"trend."* It represents, in familiar terms, what the individual is "characteristically trying to do," that is, what meaning he is always trying to achieve (closure of trend meaning-cycle). Trend meaning-cycles are tangent, in system-relation, to as many overt-behavioral act-cycles as the kinematic conditions of the individual's environmental manifold will permit (generalization or consistency of personality); and it might perhaps be interstructured with some of the perceptual cycles of the individual. Trend structures are conceived as interstructured into larger systems (unity of personality). A *"trait,"* on the other hand, is a meaning-cycle *in another individual*, or individuals, "concerning" the individual in question. Through the operation of this structure in an acquaintance the subject in question is "judged," in "adjective" terms, on an *inter*individual or societal continuum, on the basis of the number of events which his behavior-systems "give off" in collective structures as a result of the operation of his trend meaning structures.   There is a definite and discoverable (but not a one to one) relation between the individual's "traits" and "trends."   (Cf. the discussion of personality in connection with the inside-outside problem: pp. 100, footnote, and 107, footnote.)

With meanings provided for we might be able to pass with clearer understanding to the problem of the *constancies*, for these probably involve meanings of a highly universal and generalized sort.   Perhaps we could find a basis for Brunswik's probabilistic weighting of cues in the density of the perceptual meaning-cycles for surrounding conditions, together with density of interstructurance (in system relation) of these cycles with that for the object itself, the "unaided" dimensionality of the latter being determined by the perceptual structure in which retinal-stimulation events of the object, per se, play a role. When the aggregate is structurally conceived it is also easier to understand the *invariants of perception* (preserved relationships, form-qualities, and the like); for the very nature of the model provides for enduring relationships that can persist through variations of (energic) quantities or dimensions.   Once we have event-cycles, for example, that underlie the perception of tones, we can interpret a constant interval between two tones (chord) as a "ratio of the interstructurance" of their event-cycles.   This *ratio* will hold constant while the tones themselves are changed in pitch (frequency, or *r* lay).

Finally, we can envisage more clearly the basis of interaggregate facilitation and opposition.   Adjacent structures (cycles), whether in a system or otherwise, may be tangent to one another either in a positive and energically reinforcing or a negative and inhibiting way. Their kinematic arrangements could be such that one would either contribute, at a common event-region, to the other's probability of event-points (i.e., energies) or else detract from that probability. The significance is here seen of the energic summations of extraneous stimuli in producing a dislocation of perceived verticality in the sensory-tonic field theory.   "Vicariousness," competition and monopoly of hypotheses, and similar conditions alluded to by the theories can also be explained on the *negative* side, together with the mutually opposing action of sets for neutral and tabooed words as hypothesized in our set-theory bearing upon so-called perceptual defense (Chapter 16).   We could go even further and postulate that there are *degrees* of positive or negative interstructurance of structures with one another, providing a specific energic *rate* or *ratio*, in each case, for their interaction. Thus energic increases in cycle A might increase the energies of a tangent cycle B by a large ratio to its own increase of energies, while the ratio of increase which it gives tangent cycle C might be smaller or even negligible. And the same would be true for the ratio of *decreases* produced by cycle A in various other cycles in negative interstructurance. These ratios, in our earlier, less exact, terminology, were called the degrees of "relevance" of one structure to another. Such ratios, or "indices of interstructurance," might serve as a basis of "weighting" in the weighting and pooling effects that have appeared in certain theories. Tangencies of "motivational" or "end-value" structures with "cognitive" or "means-value" structures (see latter part of Chapter 13) might exploit such a weighting index and help us to explain the memorial accentuation of valued objects or their perceptual accentuation if such is found to occur. In such cases the prediction of the amount of accentuation would be based upon the summated energies of the immediate perceptual structure (or system) and of whatever end-value structures were involved, the latter, however, being weighted by their respective indices of interstructurance with the *means*-value meaning-cycle of the object, which is itself a part of the immediate perceptual system. The importance of the concept of meaning-structures in this whole theoretical procedure is clear.[5]

[5] Structurance (S) and interstructurance (I) are more general terms that now replace the agent-like and subjective expressions "potency of involvement" and "relevance," respectively, that were used near the end of Chapter 13. The hypothesized *structural-dynamic equation* for the total amount of energy in any structure (cycle or system) can be stated as follows:

$$(1) \qquad E_1 \sim S_1 + S_2 I_{21} + S_3 I_{31} \cdots + S_n I_{n1}$$

where the subscripts indicate the structures involved; E_1 is the *total* energy of the structure (1) whose energy is being measured; S_1 is the autonomous or "proper" energy of that structure; $S_2 S_3$, etc., are the proper energies of all the structures, up to the nth or final one, that are interstructurant with structure 1; I_{21}, I_{31}, etc., are the indices of interstructurance of these structures with the structure concerned (1); and $\sim$ means "varies directly with." The summation to the right of S_1 is called the "manifold energy" (or manifold energic increments) accruing to structure 1 by reason of its interstructurance with other structures. It is to be noted that in some cases the sign of I may be negative (*vide infra*); hence the summation is *algebraic*. In briefer form the equation can be written

$$(2) \qquad E_1 \sim S_1 + \sum_2^n S_i I_{i1}$$

where i represents each of the structures of the manifold in the summation. *This equation is believed to be general for structures at all orders of phenomena.*

Interorder relationships of individual perceptual structures within collective structures, represented however at the *meaning-level* within

As applied to the problem of accentuation, E_1 would represent, through the diaphragm adjustment made by the subject, the total energies in re the remembered (or perhaps perceived) phenomenological size of the coin. E_1 is the experimental dependent variable. Structure 1 is an event-system (structure) involving the *proper "unaided" size of the coin* as given by the strictly optical part of the structure, together with meaning-cycles representing the general meaning of "money" and the recognition of the coin's denomination. S_1 is the "proper" energy of this system. It may be taken here to mean the energy which structure 1 would have if the perception of the coin's size were veridical. The total energy of structure 1 is, however, increased up to E_1 by the addition (equation 1) of increments at the right side of the equation. S_2, S_3, etc., are the energic values (structurance energy) of the related "end-value" meaning-structures (2, 3, etc.)—"need for food," "need for clothes," etc. (manifold). I_{21}, I_{31}, etc., which should here be written I_{12}, I_{13}, are the ratios of the proportionate increases of energic closure that would be made possible in structures 2, 3, etc., by increases in the amount of money-value to increases of money-value as represented on a scale of increasing denominational value of coins. I is always limited to 1.0; and in general it may be either positive or negative. Thus the amount of energy that would be added to S_1 to give the total energy of the "memory," or perhaps the "percept," (E_1) will be a (summational) function both of the strength of the "end-values" (needs) and the ratios in which the object perceived would be instrumental, respectively, in satisfying those needs. Individuals of differing economic status may differ with respect both to S and to I (see discussion in latter part of Chapter 13). The energy of brightness accentuation can be hypothesized as following the same principle. The structural-dynamic equation has been demonstrated by operational and correlational procedures as holding true in a number of experiments dealing with other areas of behavior. (See Allport, F. H., 1954, and Allport, Reimer, and Valentine, 1954.) Its use, as above, for perceptual problems has yet to be rendered operational and empirically tested.

In order to understand the true meaning of this equation it is necessary that its structural basis be kept clearly in mind. It could not have been developed without the structural kinematics presented earlier in this chapter. For its symbols and subscripts cannot refer meaningfully to the "molar" organism, nor to percepts, values, needs, or cognitions in the usual senses of these terms. The equation's symbols refer, rather, to the energies of actual self-closing structures, and their interstructurances, into which the foregoing non-denotive concepts have been reinterpreted by the postulates and theorems earlier presented. (For example, they could refer to the energies of meaning-structures of clothes-procuring and of eating, to a coin-denominational meaning's inter-structurance with these cycles, to the coin-size matching structure, and so on.) Only within such a structural conception can prediction through the relationships expressed in the formula acquire a rational basis, and become amenable, as energy-summation, to mathematical treatment. Through this logic, also, the structural-dynamic equation becomes highly general. It can apply, theoretically, to the prediction of the intensity of any act of behavior (overt or covert), as E_1, and can extend to organismic phenomena outside the field of psychology.

the individual, might be similarly used in accounting for the "social" frame of reference and for the lower energic status that might characterize the structures of socially tabooed perceptions or overt acts. In the latter (tabooed) case the interstructurance index would be negative. Energic increases in the tabooed word-perceiving or word-speaking structure would be regarded (meaning-structure) as *diminishing* the energies ("successful operation") of the (polite) collective structure, and vice versa. It is unnecessary, here, to imagine a "shift" in threshold for the tabooed word or acts. How a threshold could be "raised" or "lowered" would indeed be a mystery. Depending as it does on probability, we would expect that it would remain constant. What *is* raised is the amount of stimulus input of the tabooed word, as given by varying exposure-lengths in the experimental situation. The energies ordinarily available in the tabooed word or act structure, since they are reduced by their negative interstructurance with the collective structure (which is itself probably fairly high in energy), simply fail to meet the threshold unless a relatively long stimulus-exposure (large amount of input-energy) is provided. We do not, need, here, to prejudge the experimental issue. It will be seen that the above explanation can hold whether we consider the energically diminished structure to be only the speaking of the tabooed word or its actual perception. Through these applications of the event-structure model a possible *modus operandi* for the various features of perceptual dynamics hypothesized by the theories now begins to appear.

THE THEOREM OF ORDER: STRUCTURAL-KINEMATIC TREATMENT
OF PARTS AND WHOLES; SOLUTION OF THE INSIDE-OUTSIDE
PROBLEM; STRUCTURE OF COLLECTIVITIES OR "GROUPS"

The topic last discussed, involving a consideration of two orders of structuring, leads us to a final theorem of event-structure—to one which, though pertinent to perception, has many broader implications. The question bears, on the one hand, upon our old problem of part versus whole and upon the problem of the "inside" versus the "outside" in the perception of an object's meaning. The need for a solution of this problem was keenly felt, for example, in core-context theory, in field-theory, in probabilistic and transactional functionalism, in directive-state, and in the gestalt concept of organization. On the other hand, the topic was also reflected in the major generalizations of the theories, as in the notion of the compounding of aggregates or assemblies. For dealing with this problem event-structure theory offers the structural property of *order*.   The concept was illustrated (pp. 636–638) by the arrangement in which our hoops, that were already cycles or systems of ongoings and events, were joined into a larger cycle or system.   The "higher" order consists merely of the structuring of structures of the "lower" order into a more inclusive structure (a hoop of hoops of hoops, and so on).   The latter structure, however, repeats, *at its own order*, the same type of kinematic geometry that was present in the component structures.   That is, it, too, has its own c, n, and r lays, and the same type of system-possibilities, closures, and general structural dynamics.

What is it that brings the higher order into existence?   The answer has already been given in the concepts of probable density of event-points and threshold.   Whenever event-density in all the tangency-regions between the lower-order cycles becomes sufficiently great the higher or more "macroscopic" structure becomes suddenly "probable" (i.e., appears).   When a higher order is thus attained, the lower-order "parts" (substructures), which previously had only their own "inside" meaning, now acquire also an "outside" meaning through their role within the larger, more inclusive, structure.

This principle of ordering can be seen within the organism's general behavior manifold.   It occurs, for example, when a number of "inside" meaning-cycles are aggregated into a higher-order structure by the principle just described.   One could readily illustrate the situation by the "inside" and "outside" perceived meanings of a "plant," as analyzed in Chapter 4, or in the difference in the perception of the visitors on the part of landlord and tenant in Chapter 19.   For variety, however, let us take the problem of linguistic meaning in a sentence.   In order to do this we should recall what was earlier said in describing meaning-cycles of a linguistic character.   In our present problem, then, we have the joining of "*word*"-cycles (semantics) into a "*sentence*"-cycle (syntax).   The inside (word) meanings represent the lower-order event-structures; the outside (sentence) meaning is a larger or higher-order cycle composed, and composed entirely, of these individual "word-structures."   We do not here have a "piecemeal" *summation* of words, a conception of which Wertheimer complained.   Since we are talking in terms of kinematics rather than quantities, the term summation is inappropriate.   Nor do we have a "supersummative whole."   What we do have in the sentence is a higher-order self-closed structure composed of smaller self-closed structures of ongoings and events. In this structure a new meaning occurs at its own proper order.   Such a meaning, however, always includes, and can never do without, some meanings that can also occur independently at the lower, word-cycle, order, that is, the "inside" meaning of the words. Such *additional* word-meanings, however, as occur as the *sentence* is spoken and that occur also *by virtue of* the sentence-format, are what we refer to when we speak of the "outside" meanings of the words (cf. p. 109). The structuring of higher orders out of lower orders thus gives a rational solution of the inside-outside problem in language. The principle of order, and the solution it gives for the whole-part and inside-outside problems, are not, however, limited to linguistics or even to meaning. They might be found in a structural-kinematic analysis of any complex behavioral aggregate.

But the ordering principle can be extended still further. It can describe not only the rise of the more complex meanings, perceptions, or overt behaviors of the individual, but the aggregation of individuals themselves (that is, of their behavior-structures) into more inclusive collective or "social" aggregates. That is to say, there can be structures composed of the behavior-structures of individuals. So-called "groups," "institutions," "societies," and "nations" can be conceived as representing such higher orders of structuring. These collective cycles or self-closing systems start, energically, with the imbalance of individuals' behavior structures, specifically in primary event-regions of the latter; and they come around to completion at that same region (in each individual) through the mediation of the event-connected behavior-cycles of other individuals. The closures of the component individuals' cycles are thus attained through cycle-completion at the order of the collective structure.

This structure, however, repeats the same lays and properties that are manifested at the lower (individual) order. That is, a social structure has its own c, n, and r dimensionalities and may be organized as a system of component tangent cycles. The same paradigm of structure thus holds throughout the orders. Again, we conceive the collective event-regions, which by occurring *between* individuals' structures define the collective-structure, not as specific space and time locations at which a certainty of encounters between specific individuals exists, but as space and time *regions* within which there is an above-chance *probability* of such collective-structuring encounters of individuals and therefore an above-chance incidence of such events. The collective-structure event-*format* (so-called "reality of the group") is thus preserved, though the particular contacts of individuals may vary in space, time, and number. It is also worth noting that the collective structure itself is often represented, usually in a schematic or abridged format, *in the meaning-cycles of the individuals involved,* on the basis of their contacts with other individuals in the regular and repetitive course of the structure's operation. (Cf. Sherif's interiorization of social norms, socialization of the individual, etc.)   A single "individual," as an organism that may form a part of collective aggregates, is considered as a "matrix-system" that includes, along with physiological orders and personality meaning-structures or "trends," the regions of tangency of an indefinite number of collective structures which he is said to be "in" by reason of his own included behavior-structures.   Within a collective structure the behavior of the individual has not merely an "inside" aspect.   As in the case of words in a sentence it acquires an outside ("social") aspect as well.[6]   And finally, the representation of the collective-structures, with the individual in them, in the meaning-cycles *within* the individual now gives us an explicit structural basis for perceptual-social "frames of reference" and for the (interstructurant) meanings of "social norms," "social customs or tabus," "collective attitudes," and all that is implied when we speak of "conformity to a reference group."[7]

EVENT- STRUCTURE THEORY AS A METHODOLOGICAL REORIENTATION

To apply the reasoning above outlined will, of course, demand some modification of our present habits of thinking.   In the preceding

[6] The concept of "personality-trait," as defined on page 656f., is an example of such an "outside" aspect of the individual's behavioral structure.

[7] To state the matter more explicitly, when we consider the behavior structures (including meanings) of the individual as part of and covertly representing the more inclusive collective structure, we can make the following theoretical deductions.   The amount of inhibition (perceptual or linguistic) in "perceptual defense," the stress on a norm in a social frame of reference, the intensity of an attitude or of institutional ideologies and behaviors, the degree of conformity to customs and mores found by the anthropologist, the strength of public opinion on an issue, the "force" or "pressure" toward communication in groups or toward conformity, member-acceptance, and favor for a related attitude-object (group dynamics)—all these and many other features of collective action can be quantitatively predicted as algebraic summations or means from the appropriate structurance and interstructurance values, for the population concerned, as given by the generalized equation on p. 658.   That is to say, the energies "intrinsic" to these special behavioral structures plus the interstructurance increments (or decrements) accruing to them, respectively, through all the *other* structures which are "in the individual" (personality) or which the "individual is in" (collective order) will equal the total energy which we may expect the individual to expend in the special structures concerned.   (Where the computed E_1 for any of the structures to be predicted turns out negative, it is expected that the energy in question will be expended in structures that are antistructurant to them.)   The above deductions have already gained some support in investigations in the fields of attitude determination and other behaviors (results to be published later).   The development of these and other implications of the system for social theory will be undertaken by the writer in a later volume.

account the terms "individual" and "group" do not refer to agents, or even to "entities." We do not chart "individuals" as such, or their associations as "groups," in the cartography of event-structure. These terms become merely rough "signposts" which help us to locate and chart the precise structurings concerned. The same interpretation would hold for terms referring, at lower levels, to cellular, molecular, atomic, or subatomic "bodies." "Bodies" or "things," as such, disappear in event-structure theory; we think, instead, with kinematic concepts that are abstract and geometric, but always denotably testable in principle.

What is it, then, that really composes the "material world"? What is it that actually "goes on"? Since our cyclical structure is conceived as pervasive and interconnected through all orders, no events being conceived as occurring in the higher orders that do not also occur either in or between the cycles of the lower (cf. the model of the hoops), we must answer the question of what actually goes on by positing the minutest ongoing element (or particle?) that can be conceived as existing in a physicalistic sense. The "heads" of the cyclical ongoings might thus be of a finite order of magnitude very slightly above zero. These minute "kinematic constructs" represent the "elements" whose encounters theoretically constitute our events and whose cyclical (i.e., structural) ongoings manifest, through event-points, the elementary units of energy. Only in this way can structure meet the requirement of being universal through all the orders. If it does *not* meet this requirement, some "miracle," quite inaccessible to the evidence of denotation, would be needed to bring it into existence at the level where it is first observed. In order to have a structure come into existence there must be *at the start* something other than randomness to work with. Some already existing structure must be present. Structure per se must be a law of nature at the lowest order and from the beginning. The only alternative would be to postulate some agency as a special "higher-level" creator of structure, whose existence and ways of working could not be submitted to any objective test. The quest of understanding structure in nature would then be handed over from science to metaphysics and theology.

It might seem, at first, that we are here guilty of the most rank and extreme reductionism, that by rejecting all determinative wholes, supersummations, and emergents, and by taking such restricted and minimal theoretical particles as the basis of all things, we have lost the reality of the group, the organism or person, the cell, the molecule, the atom, and perhaps, even, of the proton and electron. But this statement is really the opposite of the truth. We have now *regained* all these in a clearer fashion than would otherwise have been possible.

For the "elementary particles," as defined, are *not* taken by us as the basis of all things, or of anything. Through our kinematic geometry the distinctive reality of phenomenal aggregates is now seen to lie *not* in these ultimate and uniform particle-elements, but in their *cyclical ongoings* and in *the diverse cycles, systems, and orders to* which, by their events of encounter, they give rise. It is these relatively enduring and myriad structures of ongoings and events, rather than the compounding or aggregation of "particles," that provide the phenomena of nature in all their uniqueness and variety.

If we seek to describe the world of our experience physicalistically rather than phenomenologically, and if we are careful to look at all its levels or orders, we may find that it is essentially a world of such cyclical ongoings or motions, and of the self-closing structurings of ongoing made possible by their events or contacting points. We may find that it is not, in the last analysis, a world of "bodies" or "things." Nor is the world as we know it "material"; unless we include absolute, cyclical ongoing as a part of the very definition of matter. This view, therefore, is not a reductionism to a sea of component material particles; nor is it a reduction of macroscopic variety to dead microscopic uniformity. On the contrary, it is the building of a theoretical model for describing the fundamental character, in all its richness, of the phenomena which we actually perceive. The world of objects, behaving organisms, and societies is therefore not lost but gained. If we are willing to lay aside our attempts at linear and molar-agency explanation and take this less familiar road in our thinking, we shall, as the writer sees it, be able to eliminate a large number of the difficulties that now beset us in the construction not only of perceptual theories but also of theories in general. Since we are hypothesizing a single universal paradigm of structure we might also be on the way toward a possible ultimate understanding of the unity that may exist in nature.[8]

CONCLUSION

Such then, in the writer's opinion, is the kind of structural conception for which the present theories of perception seem to call.

[8] In the light of the interpretations given in this chapter the reader might wish to go back and reread some of the critical discussions in earlier chapters. Their import for a theory of structure should now be more clearly seen. (See Index.)

A condensed, formal, statement of event-structure theory, with diagrams, will be found in Allport, F. H., 1954. This article, if read in connection with the present chapter, may help the reader toward a clearer visualization of the structural postulates involved.

Through both their positive contributions and the character of their limitations they seem to suggest its need and possibility. They contain an inkling of some such solution; and their major generalizations are consistent with it.

As we close this tentative account of the theory of event-structure perhaps the reader will agree that we have, at least in a measure, fulfilled our earlier promise. The demonstrations have, of course, been limited; but the model has been defined in terms that are capable of being widely generalized. We have shown that it is possible to conceive the laws of nature under two distinct, though related, headings. A formal principle of nature *other than* quantitative has been postulated and has been given some empirical exemplification of a sort that argues for its general and lawful character. It has also been stated in terms that are quite as objective as those of enumeration, measured quantities, and laws of covariation. At the same time, the model has been shown to *incorporate* the quantitative aspects of phenomena. If the theory is true, nature is not a machine, nor are organisms "controlled by" quantitative or mechanical laws—even though such laws are manifested in their operations. Machine and organism are conceived as exhibiting a more basic principle which underlies both of them and their quantitative aspects as well. Social relationships, which are also a part of nature, may be conceived as exhibiting the same principle. It is believed that the proposed paradigm or hypothesis of structure, when taken together with the quantitative laws for which it must always provide a place, might be found to constitute a rewarding area for exploring the phenomena of life and behavior. Since perceptions, too, are natural phenomena it is believed that this dual area and the methods that may be devised for its study might contribute significantly to the development of perceptual theory.

The writer's theory of event-structure is here presented as a suggestive rather than a definitive or final solution. It is advanced merely as one way of looking at the problem of structure, one attempt to fathom the mystery of the form and unity of nature which have thus far been left largely untouched by science. Much remains to be done before the theory can be regarded as sufficiently clarified. Much experimental work must provide findings that will test it. How can a structural theory of the sort outlined in this brief fashion be worked out in more complete detail? What kind of physical postulates will be required? How can the ongoing-event-like format and the circuital character of behavior and collective action be more firmly established in consistency with what is known about the physics, biochemistry, neurophysiology, environmental contacts, and societal arrangements of the organism? What basis for the probability concept do the microscopical anatomy and physiology of the organism afford?   What symbols of denotational reference can be devised for diagramming or charting such a self-closed ongoing-event geometry with its various properties and orders?   Can we ever discover for a certainty what it is that "biases" the kinematic situation toward structure, so that that which, if left to randomness or chance, would be highly improbable, now becomes a probability?   How, specifically, do dimensionalities arise from the energies at event-regions within structural manifolds?   By what further equations can the amount of energy of a ·ucture be predicted, so that a quantitative aspect of the theory can ᵗequately developed?   How can such equations be experimentally ᴵᴵ these questions, and many others, must find an answer of the theory's postulates and methods.   Though the ᵇᵃt he believes to be an answer to some of these be able to answer them more fully.   He ole to develop the theory of the structuring ᵗh the aim of testing its relationship to our order and its further bearing upon the or, and collective action.

ort toward structural understanding the ᵗorkers in the field of perception have ey have not only provided many signific ᴵ areas, but have also helped to lay an nt the experimental work that has yet ᵗd unmistakably to an increasingly gation in which the true synthesis of be found; and they seem to beckon ᵗbtedness to these many devoted and for the patient and thorough ᴵ-while theory could exist, is there- them we do so with appreciation ome, through devious bypaths as es, to the end of our story.   Like ᵗved to be only a new beginning.

The writer hopes that the reader has enjoyed this journey through the theories of perception.   If he has gained some benefit from their insights and has, perhaps, in addition, experienced a growing interest in the possibilities of structural theory, the effort will have been well spent.   For theories are the stage upon which our experiments are conducted—the ground for hope that our labors will yield us a clearer knowledge of ourselves and the world in which we live.

BIBLIOGRAPHY

Aborn, M., and H. Rubenstein. 1952. Information theory and immediate recall. *J. Exp. Psychol., 44,* 260–266.

Adams, J., and D. R. Brown. 1953. Values, word frequencies, and perception. *Psychol. Rev., 60,* 50–54.

Allport, F. H. 1924. *Social psychology.* Boston: Houghton Mifflin.

Allport, F. H. 1954. The structuring of events: outline of a general theory with applications to psychology. *Psychol. Rev., 61,* 281–303.

Allport, F. H., E. W. Reimer, and J. A. Valentine. 1954. The structural energies of learning: a study of the effect of personality-trend and collective structures on reading-rate improvement. Mimeographed release of the Office of Naval Research.

Allport, G. W. 1937. *Personality: a psychological interpretation.* New York: Holt.

Allport, G. W. 1947. Scientific models and human morals. *Psychol. Rev., 54,* 182–192.

Allport, G. W., and L. Postman. 1947. *The psychology of rumor.* New York: Holt.

Ames, A., Jr. 1951. Visual perception and the rotating trapezoidal window. *Psychol. Monogr. 65,* No. 7. Whole No. 324.

Ames, A., Jr. 1953. Chapter on "Reconsideration of the origin and nature of perception," in Ratner, S. (ed.). *Vision and action.* New Brunswick: Rutgers Univ. Press.

Ansbacher, H. 1937. Perception of number as affected by the monetary value of the objects. *Arch. Psychol.,* No. 215, 5–25.

Asch, S. E. 1952. *Social psychology.* New York: Prentice-Hall.

Ashby, W. R. 1952. *Design for a brain.* New York: Wiley.

Ashley, W. R., R. S. Harper, and D. L. Runyon. 1951. The perceived size of coins in normal and hypnotically induced economic states. *Amer. J. Psychol., LXIV,* 564–572.

Attneave, F. 1954. Some informational aspects of visual perception. *Psychol. Rev., 61,* 183–193.

Barrett, E. 1950. Cybernetics as applied to a study of normal and abnormal adjustment mechanisms. *J. Psychol., 30,* first half, 11–31.

Barrett, E., and G. Post. 1950. Introduction to some principles of applied cybernetics. *J. Psychol., 30,* first half, 3–10.

Bartlett, F. C. 1932. *Remembering.* Cambridge: Cambridge Univ. Press.

Beams, H. L., and G. G. Thompson. 1952. Affectivity as a factor in the perception of the magnitude of food objects. *Amer. Psychol., 7,* 323. (Abstract.)

Berlyne, D. E. 1951. Attention, perception and behavior theory. *Psychol. Rev., 58,* 137–146.

Bertalanffy, von, L. 1950. The theory of open systems in physics and biology. *Science, 111,* 23–29.

Bertalanffy, von, L. 1951. Theoretical models in biology and psychology. *J. Personal., 20,* 24–38.

Birch, H. G., and M. E. Bitterman. 1949. Reinforcement and learning: the process of sensory integration. *Psychol. Rev., 56,* 292–308.

Birch, H. G., and M. E. Bitterman. 1951. Sensory integration and cognitive theory. *Psychol. Rev.*, 58, 355–361.

Blake, R. R., and G. V. Ramsey (eds.). 1951. *Perception—an approach to personality.* New York: Ronald.

Blake, R. R., and J. M. Vanderplas. 1950–1951. The effect of prerecognition hypotheses on veridical recognition thresholds in auditory perception. *J. Personal.*, 19, 95–115.

Boring, E. G. 1937. A psychological function is the relation of successive differentiations of events in the organism. *Psychol. Rev.*, 44, 445–461.

Boring, E. G. 1938. Titchener on meaning. *Psychol. Rev.*, 45, 92–95.

Boring, E. G. 1942. *Sensation and perception in the history of experimental psychology.* New York: Appleton-Century-Crofts.

Boring, E. G. 1946. The perception of objects. *Amer. J. Phys.*, 14, 99–107.

Boring, E. G. 1953. A history of introspection. *Psychol. Bull.*, 50, 169–189.

Bricker, P. D., and A. Chapanis. 1953. Do incorrectly perceived tachistoscopic stimuli convey some information? *Psychol. Rev.*, 60, 181–188.

Bridgman, P. W. 1949. *The logic of modern physics.* New York: Macmillan.

Brillouin, L. 1949. Life, thermodynamics, and cybernetics. *Amer. Sci.*, 37, 554–568.

Brogden, W. J. 1939. Sensory pre-conditioning. *J. Exp. Psychol.*, 25, 323–332.

Brown, J. F. 1936. *Psychology and the social order.* New York: McGraw-Hill.

Brozek, J., H. Guetzkow, and M. V. Baldwin. 1950–1951. A quantitative study of perception and association in experimental semistarvation. *J. Personal.*, 19, 245–264.

Bruner, J. S. 1951. One kind of perception: a reply to Professor Luchins. *Psychol. Rev.*, 58, 306–312.

Bruner, J. S., and C. D. Goodman. 1947. Value and need as organizing factors in perception. *J. Abnorm. Soc. Psychol.*, 42, 33–44.

Bruner, J. S., and D. Krech. 1950. *Perception and personality: a symposium.* Durham: Duke Univ. Press.

Bruner, J. S., and L. Postman. 1947. Tension and tension-release as organizing factors in perception. *J. Personal.*, 15, 300–308.

Bruner, J. S., and L. Postman. 1948. Symbolic value as an organizing factor in perception. *J. Soc. Psychol.*, 27, 203–208.

Bruner, J. S., and J. S. Rodrigues. 1953. Some determinants of apparent size. *J. Abnorm. Soc. Psychol.*, 48, 17–24.

Brunswik, E. 1933. Die Zugänglichkeit von Gegenständen für die Wahrnehmung. *Arch. ges. Psychol.*, 88, 377–418.

Brunswik, E. 1936. Psychology in terms of objects. *Proc. 25th Anniv. Celebr. Inaug. Grad. Stud.* Los Angeles: Univ. Southern Calif. Press.

Brunswik, E. 1939a. The conceptual focus of some psychological systems. *J. Unif. Sci.*, 8, 36–49.

Brunswik, E. 1939b. Probability as a determiner of rat behavior. *J. Exp. Psychol.*, 25, 175–197.

Brunswik, E. 1943. Organismic achievement and environmental probability. *Psychol. Rev.*, 50, 255–272.

Brunswik, E. 1944. Distal focusing of perception: size-constancy in a representative sample of situations. *Psychol. Monogr.*, 56, No. 1, Whole No. 254.

Brunswik, E. 1949. *Systematic and representative design of psychological experiments.* Berkeley: Univ. Calif. Press.

Brunswik, E. 1950. The conceptual framework of psychology. *Int. Encycl. Unif. Sci.*, Vol. I, No. 10. Chicago: Univ. of Chicago Press.

Caldwell, W. E. 1953. The mathematical formulation of a unified field theory. *Psychol. Rev.*, *60*, 64–72.

Cantril, H. 1947. *Understanding man's social behavior: preliminary notes.* Princeton: Office of Public Opinion Research.

Cantril, H. 1948. The nature of social perception. *Trans. N.Y. Acad. Sci.*, *10*, 142–153.

Cantril, H. 1950*a*. *The "why" of man's experience.* New York: Macmillan.

Cantril, H. 1950*b*. An inquiry concerning the characteristics of man. *J. Abnorm. Soc. Psychol.*, *45*, 490–503.

Cantril, H., A. Ames, Jr., A. H. Hastorf, and W. H. Ittelson. 1949. Psychology and scientific research. *Science, 110*, 461–464, 491–497, 517–522.

Carter, L. F., and K. Schooler. 1949. Value, need, and other factors in perception. *Psychol. Rev.*, *56*, 200–207.

Cartwright, D., and A. Zander. 1953. *Group dynamics.* Evanston: Row, Peterson & Co.

Cattell, R. B., and P. W. Wenig. 1952. Dynamic and cognitive factors controlling misperception. *J. Abnorm. Soc. Psychol.*, *47*, 797–809.

Chein, I., R. Lane, G. Murphy, H. Proshansky, and R. Schafer. 1951. Need as a determinant of perception: a reply to Pastore. *J. Psychol.*, *31* (first half), 129–136.

Cowen, E. L., and E. G. Beier. 1950–1951. The influence of "threat-expectancy" on perception. *J. Personal.*, *19*, 85–94.

Cowen, E. L., and E. G. Beier. 1952. A further study of the "threat-expectancy" variable in perception. *Amer. Psychol.*, *7*, 320–321. (Abstract.)

Cowen, E. L., and E. G. Beier. 1954. Threat-expectancy, word frequencies, and perceptual prerecognition hypotheses. *J. Abnorm. and Soc. Psychol.*, *49*, 178–182.

Dallenbach, K. M. 1953. The place of theory in science. *Psychol. Rev.*, *60*, 33–39.

Dashiell, J. F. 1940. A neglected fourth dimension to psychological research. *Psychol. Rev.*, *47*, 289–305.

Dashiell, J. F. 1949. *Fundamentals of general psychology.* Boston: Houghton Mifflin.

Dennis, W. (ed.). 1948. *Current trends in social psychology.* Pittsburgh: Univ. of Pittsburgh Press.

Dennis, W. (ed.). 1951. *Current trends in psychological theory.* Pittsburgh: Univ. of Pittsburgh Press.

Dewey, J. 1896. The reflex arc concept in psychology. *Psychol. Rev.*, *3*, 357–370.

Dewey, J., and A. F. Bentley. 1949. *Knowing and the known.* Boston: Beacon Press.

Drever, J. 1921. *Instinct in man.* Cambridge: Cambridge Univ. Press.

Duncker, E. 1939. The influence of past experience upon perceptual properties. *Amer. J. Psychol.*, *52*, 255–265.

Einstein, A. 1950. On the generalized theory of gravitation. *Sci. Amer., 182*, No. 4. 13–17.

Einstein, A., and L. Infeld. 1942. *The evolution of physics.* New York: Simon & Schuster.

Ellis, W. D. (ed.). 1938. *A source book of gestalt psychology.* New York: Harcourt.

Eriksen, C. W. 1950. Perceptual defense as a function of unacceptable needs. *Amer. Psychol., 5,* 306. (Abstract.)

Eriksen, C. W. 1950–1951. Some implications for TAT interpretation arising from need and perception experiments. *J. Personal., 19,* 282–288.

Eriksen, C. W. 1954. The case for perceptual defense. *Psychol. Rev., 61,* 175–182.

Ewert, P. H. 1930. A study of the effect of inverted retinal stimulation upon spatially coordinated behavior. *Genet. Psychol. Monogr., 7,* Nos. 3 and 4.

Freeman, G. L. 1929. An experimental study of the perception of objects. *J. Exp. Psychol., 12,* 341–358.

Freeman, G. L. 1939. The problem of set. *Amer. J. Psychol., 52,* 16–30.

Freeman, G. L. 1940a. Concerning the 'field' in 'field' psychology. *Psychol. Rev., 47,* 416–424.

Freeman, G. L. 1940b. Discussion: 'central' vs. 'peripheral' locus of set; a critique of the Mowrer, Rayman and Bliss 'demonstration.' *J. Exp. Psychol., 26,* 622–628.

Freeman, G. L. 1948a. *Physiological psychology.* New York: Van Nostrand.

Freeman, G. L. 1948b. *The energetics of human behavior.* Ithaca: Cornell Univ. Press.

George, F. H. 1952. Errors of visual recognition. *J. Exp. Psychol., 43,* 202–206.

Gibson, J. J. 1941. A critical review of the concept of set in contemporary experimental psychology. *Psychol. Bull., 38,* 781–817.

Gibson, J. J. 1950. *The perception of the visual world.* Boston: Houghton Mifflin.

Gibson, J. J. 1951. What is a form? *Psychol. Rev., 58,* 403–412.

Gibson, J. J., and L. E. Crooks. 1938. A theoretical field-analysis of automobile-driving. *Amer. J. Psychol. LI,* 453–471.

Gilchrist, J. C., and L. S. Nesberg. 1952. Need and perceptual change in need-related objects. *J. Exp. Psychol., 44,* 369–376.

Goldstein, K., and M. Scheerer. 1941. Abstract and concrete behavior: an experimental study with special tests. *Psychol. Monogr. 53.*

Graham, C. H. 1950. Behavior, perception and the psychophysical methods. *Psychol. Rev., 57,* 108–120.

Haire, M., and W. F. Grunes. 1950. Perceptual defenses: processes protecting an organized perception of another personality. *Human Relations, 3,* 403–412.

Hartmann, G. W. 1935. *Gestalt psychology.* New York: Ronald Press.

Hastorf, A. H. 1950. The influence of suggestion on the relationship between stimulus size and perceived distance. *J. Psychol., 29* (first half), 195–217.

Hastorf, A. H., and H. Cantril. 1954. They saw a game: a case study. *J. Abnorm. Soc. Psychol., 49,* 129–134.

Hastorf, A. H., and A. L. Knutson. 1949. Motivation, perception and attitude change. *Psychol. Rev., 56,* 88–97.

Head, H. 1926. *Aphasia and kindred disorders of speech.* Cambridge: Cambridge Univ. Press.

Hebb, D. O. 1949. *The organization of behavior.* New York: Wiley.

Hebb, D. O. 1951. The role of neurological ideas in psychology. *J. Personal., 20,* 39–55.

Heidbreder, E. 1933. *Seven psychologies.* New York: Appleton-Century.

Heidbreder, E. 1946. The attainment of concepts: I. *J. Gen. Psychol., 35,* 173–189.

Helmholtz, S. von. 1866. *Physiological optics.* Ed. by J. P. S. Southall. Optical Society of America, 1925. Vol. III.

Helson, H. 1930. The nature and problem of perception. Reading XX in Wheeler, R. H. (ed.). *Readings in Psychology.* New York: Crowell.

Helson, H. 1933. The fundamental propositions of gestalt psychology. *Psychol. Rev., 40,* 13–32.

Helson, H. 1947. Adaptation-level as frame of reference for prediction of psychophysical data. *Amer. J. Psychol., LX,* 1–29.

Helson, H. 1948. Adaptation-level as a basis for a quantitative theory of frames of reference. *Psychol. Rev., 55,* 297–313.

Helson, H. 1951. Perception. Chapter 8 in Helson, H. (ed.). *Theoretical foundations of psychology.* New York: Van Nostrand.

Helson, H. (ed.). 1951. *Theoretical foundations of psychology.* New York: Van Nostrand.

Henle, M. 1942. An experimental investigation of past experience as a determinant of visual form perception. *J. Exp. Psychol., 30,* 1–21.

Higginson, G. D. 1937. The place of meaning in psychology. *Psychol. Rev., 44,* 491–504.

Hilgard, E. R. 1948. *Theories of learning.* New York: Appleton-Century-Crofts.

Hoagland, H. 1949. Rhythmic behavior of the nervous system. *Science, 109,* 157–164.

Holt, E. B. 1931. *Animal drive and the learning process.* New York: Holt.

Holway, A. H., and E. G. Boring. 1941. Determinants of apparent visual size with distance variant. *Amer. J. Psychol., 54,* 21–37.

Householder, A. S. 1947. Neural structure in perception and response. *Psychol. Rev., 54,* 169–176.

Howes, D. 1954a. A statistical theory of the phenomenon of subception. *Psychol. Rev., 61,* 98–110.

Howes, D. 1954b. On the interpretation of word frequency as a variable affecting speed of recognition. *J. Exp. Psychol., 48,* 106–112.

Howes, D. H., and R. L. Solomon. 1950. A note on McGinnies' "Emotionality and perceptual defense." *Psychol. Rev., 57,* 229–234.

Howes, D. H., and R. L. Solomon. 1951. Visual duration threshold as a function of word probability. *J. Exp. Psychol., 41,* 401–410.

Howie, D. 1952. Perceptual defense. *Psychol. Rev., 59,* 308–315.

Hull, C. L. 1943a. The problem of intervening variables in molar behavior theory. *Psychol. Rev., 50,* 273–291.

Hull, C. L. 1943b. *Principles of behavior: an introduction to behavior theory.* New York: Appleton-Century-Crofts.

Hull, C. L. 1951. *Essentials of behavior.* New Haven: Yale Univ. Press.

Hull, C. L. 1952. *A behavior system: an introduction to behavior theory concerning the individual organism.* New Haven: Yale Univ. Press.

Humphrey, G. 1933. *The nature of learning in its relation to the living system.* London: Kegan Paul, Trench, Trubner and Co.

Ittelson, W. H. 1951. The constancies in perceptual theory. *Psychol. Rev., 58,* 285–294.

Ittelson, W. H. 1952. *The Ames demonstrations in perception.* Princeton: Princeton Univ. Press.

Ittelson, W. H., and H. Cantril. 1954. *Perception: a transactional approach.* Garden City: Doubleday.

Ittelson, W. H., and F. P. Kilpatrick. 1951. Experiments in perception. *Sci. Amer., 185,* No. 2. 50–55.

Jacobson, E. 1930–1931. Electrical measurements of neuromuscular states during mental activities. *Amer. J. Physiol.,* 1930, *91,* 567–608; *94,* 22–34; *95,* 694–712; *95,* 703–712; 1931, *96,* 115–121; *96,* 122–125; *97,* 200–209.

Jacobson, E. 1932. Electrophysiology of mental activities. *Amer. J. Psychol., 44,* 677–694.

James, H. 1953. An application of Helson's theory of adaptation level to the problem of transposition. *Psychol. Rev., 60,* 345–352.

James, W. 1890. *Principles of psychology.* London: Macmillan.

Jeffress, L. A. (ed.). 1951. *Cerebral mechanisms in behavior* (The Hixon symposium). New York: Wiley.

Kilpatrick, F. P. (ed.). 1952. *Human behavior from the transactional point of view.* Princeton: Institute for Associated Research.

Kilpatrick, F. P. 1954. Two processes in perceptual learning. *J. Exp. Psychol., 47,* 362–370.

King, G. W. 1952. Information. *Sci. Amer., 187,* 132–148.

Klein, G. S., and D. Krech. 1951. The problem of personality and its theory. *J. Personal., 20,* 2–23.

Klein, G. S., H. J. Schlesinger, and D. E. Meister. 1951. The effect of personal values on perception: an experimental critique. *Psychol. Rev., 58,* 96–112.

Koch, S. 1951. Theoretical psychology, 1950: an overview. *Psychol. Rev., 58,* 295–301.

Koffka, K. 1935. *Principles of gestalt psychology.* New York: Harcourt.

Köhler, W. 1929. *Gestalt psychology.* New York: Liveright.

Köhler, W. 1938. *The place of value in a world of facts.* New York: Liveright.

Köhler, W. 1940. *Dynamics in psychology.* New York: Liveright.

Köhler, W. 1951. Relational determination in perception. In Jeffress, L. A. (ed.). *Cerebral mechanisms in behavior,* pp. 200–230. New York: Wiley.

Köhler, W., and R. Held. 1949. The cortical correlate of pattern vision. *Science, 110,* 414–419.

Köhler, W., and H. Wallach. 1944. Figural after-effects: an investigation of visual processes. *Proc. Amer. Phil. Soc., 88,* 269–357.

Korte, A. 1915. Kinematoskopische Untersuchungen. *Z. Psychol., 72,* 193–206; 271–296.

Krech, D. 1949. Notes toward a psychological theory. *J. Personal., 18,* 66–87.

Krech, D. 1950a. Dynamic systems, psychological fields, and hypothetical constructs. *Psychol. Rev., 57,* 283–290.

Krech, D. 1950b. Dynamic systems as open neurological systems. *Psychol. Rev., 57,* 345–361.

Krech, D., and A. Calvin. 1953. Levels of perceptual organization and cognition. *J. Abnorm. Soc. Psychol., 48,* 394–400.

Krech, D., and R. S. Crutchfield. 1948. *Theory and problems of social psychology.* New York: McGraw-Hill.

Lambert, W. W., R. L. Solomon, and P. D. Watson. 1949. Reinforcement and extinction as factors in size estimation. *J. Exp. Psychol., 39,* 637–641.

Lashley, K. S. 1929. *Brain mechanisms and intelligence.* Chicago: Univ. Chicago Press.

Lashley, K. S. 1942*a.* The problem of cerebral organization in vision. In H. Klüver (ed.). *Biological symposia,* Vol. VII. Lancaster, Pa.: Jaques Cattell Press.

Lashley, K. S. 1942*b.* An examination of the "continuity theory" as applied to discriminative learning. *J. Gen. Psychol.,* 26, 241–265.

Lashley, K. S., K. L. Chow, and J. Semmes. 1951. An examination of the electrical field theory of cerebral integration. *Psychol. Rev.,* 58, 123–136.

Lashley, K. S., and M. Wade. 1946. The Pavlovian theory of generalization. *Psychol. Rev.,* 53, 72–87.

Lawrence, M. 1949*a.* *Studies in human behavior.* Princeton: Princeton Univ. Press.

Lawrence, M. 1949*b.* *An inquiry into the nature of perception.* Princeton: Institute for Associated Research.

Lazarus, R. S., C. W. Eriksen, and C. P. Fonda. 1950–1951. Personality dynamics and auditory perceptual recognition. *J. Personal.,* 19, 471–482.

Leeper, R. 1943. *Lewin's topological and vector psychology, a digest and a critique.* Eugene, Oregon: Univ. Oregon Press.

Leeper, R. 1950. The organization of behavior: a. neuropsychological theory (review). *J. Abnorm. Soc. Psychol.,* 45, 768–775.

Levine, R., I. Chein, I. and G. Murphy. 1942. The relation of the intensity of a need to the amount of perceptual distortion. *J. Psychol.,* 13, 283–293.

Lewin, K. 1935. *A dynamic theory of personality.* New York: McGraw-Hill.

Lewin, K. 1936. *Principles of topological psychology.* New York: McGraw-Hill.

Lewin, K. 1938. The conceptual representation and measurement of psychological forces. *Contr. Psychol. Theor., I,* No. 4.

Lewin, K. 1946. Behavior and development as a function of the total situation. In L. Carmichael (ed.). *Manual of child psychology.* New York: Wiley.

Lewin, K. 1951. *Field theory in social science.* (Papers posthumously edited by D. Cartwright.) New York: Harper.

Littman, R. A., and E. Rosen. 1950. Molar and molecular. *Psychol. Rev.,* 57, 58–65.

Lorente de Nó, R. 1938. Analysis of the activity of the chains of internuncial neurons. *J. Neurophysiol.,* 1, 207–244.

Luchins, A. S. 1950–1951. On an approach to social perception. *J. Personal.,* 19, 64–84.

Luchins, A. S. 1951. An evaluation of some current criticisms of gestalt psychological work on perception. *Psychol. Rev.,* 58, 69–95.

Luchins, A. S., and E. H. Luchins. 1953. The satiation theory of figural aftereffects and the principle of prägnanz. *J. Gen. Psychol.,* 49, 185–199.

Lysak, W. 1954. The effects of punishment upon syllable recognition thresholds. *J. Exp. Psychol.,* 47, 343–350.

McClelland, D., and J. Atkinson. 1948. The projective expression of needs: I. The effect of different intensities of the hunger drive on perception. *J. Psychol.,* 25, 205–222.

McCulloch, W. S. 1946. Finality and form. Fifteenth James Arthus Lecture, New York Academy of Science.

McCulloch, W. S. 1951. Why the mind is in the head. In Jeffress, L. A.

(ed.). *Cerebral mechanisms in behavior* (The Hixon symposium), pp. 42–57. New York: Wiley.

McCulloch, W. S., and J. Pfeiffer. 1949. Of digital computers called brains. *Sci. Mon., 69*, 368–376.

McCulloch, W. S., and W. Pitts. 1948. The statistical organization of nervous activity. *J. Amer. Statist. Ass., 4*, 91–99.

McDonough, A R. 1919. The development of meaning. *Psychol. Monogr., 27.*

McGinnies, E. 1949. Emotionality and perceptual defense. *Psychol. Rev., 56,* 244–251.

McGinnies, E. 1950. Discussion of Howes' and Solomon's note on "Emotionality and perceptual defense." *Psychol. Rev., 57,* 235–240.

MacCorquodale, K., and P. E. Meehl. 1948. On a distinction between hypothetical constructs and intervening variables. *Psychol. Rev., 55,* 95–107.

MacKay, D. M., and W. S. McCulloch. 1952. The limiting informational capacity of a neuronal link. *Bull. Math. Biophys., 14,* 127–135.

MacLeod, R. B. 1947. The phenomenological approach to social psychology. *Psychol. Rev. 54,* 193–210.

MacLeod, R. B. 1951. The place of phenomenological analysis in social psychological theory. In J. H. Rohrer and M. Sherif, eds. *Social psychology at the crossroads.* New York: Harper.

Marx, M. H. 1951. *Psychological theory: contemporary readings.* New York: Macmillan.

Max, L. W. 1935. An experimental study of the motor theory of consciousness: III. *J. Comp. Psychol., 19,* 469–486.

Miller, G. A. 1953. What is information measurement? *Amer. Psychol., 8,* 3–11.

Minturn, A. L., and J. S. Bruner. 1951. Cognitive hypotheses and perceptual closure. *Amer. Psychol., 6,* 256. (Abstract.)

Moore, T. V. 1915. The temporal relations of meaning and imagery. *Psychol. Rev., 22,* 177–215.

Morgan, C. T., and E. Stellar. 1950. *Physiological psychology.* New York: McGraw-Hill.

Morris, C. 1946. *Signs, language and behavior.* New York: Prentice-Hall.

Mowrer, O. H., N. N. Rayman, and E. L. Bliss. 1940. Preparatory set (expectancy)—an experimental demonstration of its 'central' locus. *J. Exp. Psychol., 26,* 357–372.

Murphree, O. D. 1954. Maximum rates of form perception and the alpha rhythm: an investigation and test of current nerve net theory. *J. Exp. Psychol., 48,* 57–61.

Murphy, G. 1929. *An historical introduction to modern psychology.* New York: Harcourt.

Murphy, G. 1947. *Personality: a biosocial approach to origins and structure.* New York: Harper.

Murphy, G., and J. Hochberg. 1951. Perceptual development: some tentative hypotheses. *Psychol. Rev., 58,* 332–349.

Noble, C. E. 1952. An analysis of meaning. *Psychol. Rev., 59,* 421–430.

Northrop, F. S. C. 1948. The neurological and behavioristic psychological basis of the ordering of society by means of ideas. *Science, 107,* 411–417.

Ogden, C. K., and I. A. Richards. 1923. *The meaning of meaning.* London: Kegan Paul.

Osgood, C. E. 1952. The nature and measurement of meaning. *Psychol. Bull.*, *49*, 197–237.

Osgood, C. E., and A. W. Heyer, Jr. 1952. A new interpretation of figural after-effects. *Psychol. Rev.*, *59*, 98–118.

Pastore, N. 1949. Need as a determinant of perception. *J. Psychol.*, *28* (second half), 457–475.

Pickford, R. W. 1950. Aspects of the psychology of meaning. *J. Genet. Psychol.*, *77*, 231–255.

Pitts, W., and W. S. McCulloch. 1947. How we know universals: the perception of auditory and visual forms. *Bull. Math. Biophys.*, *9*, 127–147.

Postman, L. 1953. On the problem of perceptual defense. *Psychol. Rev.*, *60*, 298–306.

Postman, L., J. S. Bruner, and E. McGinnies. 1948. Personal values as selective factors in perception. *J. Abnorm. Soc. Psychol.*, *43*, 142–154.

Postman, L., J. S. Bruner, and R. D. Walk. 1951. The perception of error. *Brit. J. Psychol.*, *42*, 1–10.

Postman, L., and G. Leytham. 1950–1951. Perceptual selectivity and ambivalence of stimuli. *J. Personal.*, *19*, 390–405.

Postman, L., and G. A. Miller. 1945. Anchoring of temporal judgments. *Amer. J. Psychol.*, *LVIII*, 43–53.

Postman, L., and B. H. Schneider. 1951. Personal values, visual recognition, and recall. *Psychol. Rev.*, *58*, 271–284.

Postman, L., and R. L. Solomon. 1950. Perceptual sensitivity to completed and uncompleted tasks. *J. Personal.*, *18*, 347–357.

Pratt, C. C. 1939. *The logic of modern psychology.* New York: Macmillan.

Pratt, C. C. 1950. The role of past experience in visual perception. *J. Psychol.*, *30* (first half), 85–107.

Proshansky, H. M., and G. Murphy. 1942. The effects of reward and punishment on perception. *J. Psychol.*, *13*, 295–305.

Ratner, S. (ed.). *Vision and action.* 1953. New Brunswick: Rutgers Univ. Press.

Razran, G. 1935–1936. Salivating and thinking in different languages. *J. Psychol.*, *1*, 145–151.

Razran, G. 1949. Stimulus generalization of conditioned responses. *Psychol. Bull.*, *46*, 337–365.

Reece, M. M. 1954. The effect of shock on recognition thresholds. *J. Abnorm. Soc. Psychol.*, *49*, 165–172.

Reichenbach, H. 1938. *Experience and prediction.* Chicago: Univ. of Chicago Press.

Ridenour, L. N. 1952. The role of the computer. *Sci. Amer. 187*, 116–130.

Rigby, M. K., and W. K. Rigby. 1952. Perceptual thresholds as a function of reinforcement and frequency. *Amer. Psychol.*, *7*, 321. (Abstract.)

Rock, I., and F. S. Fleck. 1950. A re-examination of the effect of monetary reward and punishment on figure-ground perception. *J. Exp. Psychol.*, *40*, 766–776.

Rohrer, J. H., and M. Sherif. (eds.). 1951. *Social psychology at the crossroads.* New York: Harper.

Rosenblueth, A., N. Wiener, and J. Bigelow. 1943. Behavior, purpose, and teleology. *Phil. Science, 10*, 18–24.

Rosenthal, B. G. 1951. Attitude toward money, need, and methods of presentation as determinants of perception of coins from six to ten years of age. *Amer. Psychol.*, *6*, 317. (Abstract.)

Schafer, R., and G. Murphy. 1943. The role of autism in visual figure-ground relationship. *J. Exp. Psychol.*, *32*, 335–343.

Schrödinger, E. 1946. *What is life?* New York: Macmillan.

Seward, J. P. 1948. The sign of a symbol: a reply to Professor Allport. *Psychol. Rev.*, *55*, 277–296.

Sherif, M. 1936. *The psychology of social norms.* New York: Harper.

Sherif, M. 1948. *An outline of social psychology.* New York: Harper.

Sherif, M., and H. Cantril. 1945. The psychology of attitudes. *Psychol. Rev.*, *52*, 295–319.

Sherif, M., and H. Cantril. 1947. *The psychology of ego-involvements.* New York: Wiley.

Skaggs, E. B. 1940. Atomism versus gestaltism in perception. *Psychol. Rev.*, *47*, 347–354.

Skinner, B. F. 1950. Are theories of learning necessary? *Psychol. Rev.*, *57*, 193–216.

Smith, D. E., and J. E. Hochberg. 1952. The autistic effect of punishment on figure-ground perception. *Amer. Psychol.*, *7*, 243–244. (Abstract.)

Smith, D. E., and J. E. Hochberg. 1954. The effect of "punishment" (electric shock) on figure-ground perception. *J. Psychol.*, *38* (first half), 83–87.

Smith, K. R., G. B. Parker, and G. A. Robinson. 1950. An exploratory investigation of autistic perception. *Amer. Psychol.*, *5*, 313–314. (Abstract.)

Solomon, R. L., and D. H. Howes. 1951. Word frequency, personal values, and visual duration thresholds. *Psychol. Rev.*, *58*, 256–270.

Solomon, R. L., and L. Postman. 1952. Frequency of usage as a determinant of recognition thresholds for words. *J. Exp. Psychol.*, *43*, 195–201.

Spence, K. W. 1944. The nature of theory construction in contemporary psychology. *Psychol. Rev.*, *51*, 47–68.

Spence, K. W. 1948. The methods and postulates of "behaviorism." *Psychol. Rev.*, *55*, 67–78.

Spence, K. W. 1951. Theoretical interpretations of learning. Chapter 8 in *Comparative psychology*, Stone, C. P. (ed.). Third edition. New York: Prentice-Hall.

Sperry, R. W. 1952. Neurology and the mind-brain problem. *Amer. Sci.*, *40*, 291–312.

Stevens, S. S. 1935a. The operational basis of psychology. *Amer. J. Psychol.*, *47*, 323–330.

Stevens, S. S. 1935b. The operational definition of psychological concepts. *Psychol. Rev.*, *42*, 517–525.

Stratton, G. M. 1897. Vision without inversion of the retinal image. *Psychol. Rev.*, *4*, 341–360; 463–481.

Thouless, R. H. 1931. Phenomenal regression to the real object. *Brit. J. Psychol.*, *21*, 339–359; *22*, 1–30.

Thurstone, L. L. 1944. *A factorial study of perception.* Chicago: Univ. of Chicago Press.

Titchener, E. B. 1909. *Experimental psychology of the thought processes.* New York: Macmillan.

Titchener, E. B. 1914. *A textbook of psychology.* New York: Macmillan.

Titchener, E. B. 1915. *A beginner's psychology.* New York: Macmillan.

Tolman, E. C. 1932. *Purposive behavior in animals and men.* New York: Century.

Tolman, E. C. 1936. Operational behaviorism and current trends in psychology. *Proc. 25th Anniv. Celebr. Inaug. Grad. Stud.* Los Angeles: Univ. Southern Calif. Press.

Tolman, E. C. 1938. The determiners of behavior at a choice point. *Psychol. Rev., 45,* 1–41.

Tolman, E. C. 1948. Cognitive maps in rats and men. *Psychol. Rev., 55,* 189–208.

Tolman, E. C. 1949. The psychology of social learning. *J. Soc. Issues, V, Suppl. No. 3.*

Tolman, E. C. 1952. A cognition motivation model. *Psychol. Rev., 59,* 389–400.

Tolman, E. C., and E. Brunswik. 1935. The organism and the causal texture of the environment. *Psychol. Rev., 42,* 43–77.

Trimmer, J. D. 1950. *Response of physical systems.* New York: Wiley.

Tustin, A. 1952. Feedback. *Sci. Amer., 187,* 48–55.

Von Foerster, H. (ed.). 1950. *Cybernetics* (Transactions of the sixth conference, March 24–25, 1949). New York: Josiah Macy, Jr. Foundation.

Von Foerster, H. (ed.). 1951. *Cybernetics* (Transactions of the seventh conference, March 23–24, 1950). New York: Josiah Macy, Jr. Foundation.

Von Foerster, H. (ed.). 1952. *Cybernetics* (Transactions of the eighth conference, March 15–16, 1951). New York: Josiah Macy, Jr. Foundation.

Wapner, S., and H. Werner. 1952. Experiments on sensory-tonic field theory of perception: V. Effect of body status on the kinaesthetic perception of verticality. *J. Exp. Psychol., 44,* 126–131.

Wapner, S., H. Werner, and K. A. Chandler. 1951. Experiments on sensory-tonic field theory of perception: I. Effect of extraneous stimulation on the visual perception of verticality. *J. Exp. Psychol., 42,* 341–345.

Wapner, S., H. Werner, and R. B. Morant. 1951. Experiments on sensory-tonic field theory of perception: III. Effect of body rotation on the visual perception of verticality. *J. Exp. Psychol., 42,* 351–357.

Watson, J. B. 1919. *Psychology from the standpoint of a behaviorist.* Philadelphia: Lippincott.

Werner, H. 1945. Motion and motion perception: a study on vicarious functioning. *J. Psychol., 19,* 317–327.

Werner, H., and S. Wapner. 1952. Toward a general theory of perception. *Psychol. Rev., 59,* 324–338.

Werner, H., and S. Wapner. 1954. Studies in physiognomic perception: I. Effect of configurational dynamics and meaning-induced sets on the position of the apparent median plane. *J. Psychol., 38,* first half, 51–65.

Werner, H., S. Wapner, and K. A. Chandler. 1951. Experiments on sensory-tonic field theory of perception: II. Effect of supported and unsupported tilt of the body on the visual perception of verticality. *J. Exp. Psychol., 42,* 346–350.

Wertheimer, M. 1912. Experimentelle Studien über das Sehen von Bewegung. *Z. Psychol., 61,* 161–265.

Wherry, R. J., and D. Rethlingshafer. 1954. An experimental verification of the structural nature of set. *J. Gen. Psychol., 51,* first half, 161–172.

Wiener, N. 1948. *Cybernetics.* New York: Wiley.

Wispé, L. G., and N. C. Drambarean. 1953. Physiological need, word frequency, and visual duration thresholds. *J. Exp. Psychol.*, *46*, 25–31.

Woodworth, R. S. 1938. *Experimental psychology.* New York: Holt.

Woodworth, R. S. 1947. Reënforcement of perception. *Amer. J. Psychol.*, *LX*, 119–124.

Woodworth, R. S. 1948. *Contemporary schools of psychology.* New York: Ronald Press.

Index of Names

The more important references are given in italics. These include the mention or description of theoretical and experimental contributions and citation of the author's relevant publications. References to the editorship of books, or to tests or scales bearing the names of their authors, are not italicized.

Index of Subjects

The following abbreviations are used:

adapt. l.	adaptation-level
beh.	behavior (S-R theory)
c. assem.	cell assembly and phase sequence
cor. con.	core-context
cyb.	cybernetic, cybernetics
dir. stat.	directive-state
e. s.	event-structure
gest.	gestalt
hyp.	hypothesis
mot. adj.	motor adjustments
prob. funct.	probabilistic functionalism
set dyn.	set-dynamic, set-dynamics
set int.	set-interaction
s. t. f.	sensory-tonic field
top. f.	topological field
trans. funct.	transactional functionalism
expl.	explained, explanation

In references in which the page number is followed by an "f." the page cited, *in some cases,* contains merely introductory statements, the essentials of the topic under consideration being discussed on the following page.

Abstraction, in c. assem. theory, 174, 542

Accentuation: experiments of Bruner and Goodman et al., 312–315; of Carter and Schooler et al., 328 f.; critique of, 329 f., 345–349, 355–361; expl. by e.s. theory, 658 f., by hyp. theory, 400 f., by set. dyn. theory, 414; in relation to object meaning, 541. *See also* motivation, need, *and* value, *etc., under* Motivation

Accommodation, *see* Fixation, etc.

Action, in relation to assumptions and percept (trans. funct.), 277–279

Adaptation-level: components of the "pool" in, 246; deductions from experiments tested, 249; definition and description of, 244 f.; generalization of, 249–251; Helson's equations of, 248 f.; limitations of, 251 f.; mechanism of, 250, 502; pooling and weighting, 245,; relation of to dir. stat. findings, 323; relation of to psychophysical law, 248 f.; thing-constancy approach as contrasted with, 292–294

Afferent neural interaction, 444; as expl. of perceptual phenomena, 465; in relation to gest. "wholeness," 449

Aftereffects, *see* Figural aftereffects

Purpose: in relation to cyb. theory, 84; end-purpose in relation to universals and reverberating circuits; 523 f.; means-purpose and end-purpose as coalescing in e.s. theory, 528; means-purpose versus end-purpose in organisms and cyb. models, 522–524; perceptual defense, inconsistency of teleological view in, 321 f.; purpose in trans. funct., 280 (critique, 283). *See also* Teleological mechanisms

Qualities, role of in perceptual theories, 45, 59–61, 68, 73, 139, 184, 193, 235, 237, 387 f., 465, 577

Quantification and quantitative aspects: as an attempt to account for structure, 619–631; continuous nature of, 623 f.; critique of, in perception, 295; cyb. quantitative theory of meaning, 514; as dependent on non-quantitative aspects, 586, 588; limitations of in expressing object-meaning, 514–516; macroscopic quant. laws as inappropriate in microcosm, 626 f.; not to be taken as causes of events, 625; as a problem in perception, 607; quantities associated with non-quantitative meanings, 516; quantitative laws as dependent on events and structure, 625, 633, as failing to account for structure, 628–630, as failing to account for threshold, 631, as non-relevant to patterning, 626; quantitative meanings as characteristic of cyb., 514; summary of for the theories, 584–587. *See also* Measurement; Dimensions, *etc.* For quantitative aspects of e.s. theory, *see* Structure

Quantum-theory, statistical laws of, 473 f.

r lay (e.s. theory), 641 f., 644 f., 646 f., 647, 650 f., 652–654, 655 f.; at higher orders, 661 f.

Randomness, as limited by bounding conditions, 650; *see also* Entropy

Rhythm, perception of, 78, 115

Reaction-potential, 440, 449

Reaction-time, sensory and motor, 216

Recency, as a factor in perception, 396–398

Recognition, 79, 108 f., 122–124, 167–169, 531 f.

Recognition threshold, *see* Threshold

Recruitment, 171

Reduction screen, 94

Redundancy, *see* Information, *etc.*

Reference-group phenomena, e.s. interpretation of, 663

Reinforcement: criticism of perceptual experiments on, 326, 329 f.; experiments of Lambert, Solomon, and Watson, 314, of Murphy, Schafer, Proshansky, and the Rigbys, 310 f., of Reece, 459 f.; reinforcement of a habit, 440; of a perception, 300, 447, 450 f.; secondary reinforcement, 440

Relationships, perception of: as expl. by cyb., 511; examples of, 62; expl. by gest. theory, 120–122; Hebb's theory of, 542; as insight in gest. theory, 544 f.; Lashley's view of, 446; synopsis of for the theories, 601 f. *See also* Form-quality, Transformation, Transposition

Relativity, theory of, in relation to e.s. theory, 624, 647

Relay, *see* Computing machines (digital)

Relevance, in accentuation experiments, 356; kind and degree of, 353; of stimulus input, to set, in set dyn. theory, 421 f., 424 f., 426 f., 428. *See also* Interstructurance; Set-interaction equations, *and related discussion*

Requiredness 91, 117, 387, 544